CONTRACT LAW

AUSTRALIA
Law Book Co.
Sydney

CANADA and **USA**
Carswell
Toronto

HONG KONG
Sweet & Maxwell
Asia

NEW ZEALAND
Brookers
Wellington

SINGAPORE and **MALAYSIA**
Sweet & Maxwell Asia
Singapore and Kuala Lumpur

CONTRACT LAW

Sweet & Maxwell's Textbook Series

By George Applebey

LONDON
SWEET & MAXWELL
2001

Published in 2001 by
Sweet & Maxwell Limited of
100 Avenue Road, Swiss Cottage, London NW3 3PF
(http://www.sweetandmaxwell.co.uk)
Typeset by J&L Composition Ltd, Filey, North Yorkshire
Printed in England by
MPG Books, Bodmin, Cornwall

No natural forests were destroyed to make this product;
only farmed timber was used and replanted

A C.I.P. catalogue record for this book is available from the British Library

ISBN 0-421-571 209

To my mother, Christine

PREFACE

The pace of change in the field of contract law has quickened over the last two or three years. What was once a slowly changing subject is now face to face with a number of unprecedented forces with which the common law is rapidly having to come to terms. The expansion of activity by the European Union, the rise of e-commerce and the internet as a means of trading goods and services and changing conceptions of the basics of contract law are transforming the subject as never before. Changes which have been afoot for years, such as the use of standard form contracts, fairness in consumer contract law and elsewhere and the appreciation of contracts as relationships of a lasting nature rather than "one off" transactions, continue to develop new rules and principles. This area of law is at an interesting stage in its long history.

Contract law occupies a central place in all law degrees, and with good reason. There are different views as to what contract law is about and, therefore, alternative ways of teaching and learning the subject. Broadly speaking, these can be broken down into the traditional, lawyer oriented rule-based approach, the theoretical, the socio-legal, the practical, and more recently, the economic analysis of contract law, and critical legal studies. Some of those approaches should be combined for a sensible discussion of the subject even though some are at odds with one another, *e.g.* the black letter law based method and the critical method. Modern students tend to be good at adjusting to the various styles and preferences of their teachers.

There are many ways of talking about contract law. This book takes a largely rule-based approach and combines this, where appropriate, with the main underlying theories, as well as discussing how the law might change in certain key areas, taking account of other common law jurisdictions such as Australia, New Zealand, Canada and the United States. In other words, the objective is to give students a grasp of principle along with a reasonably comprehensive survey of the main rules including, where relevant, both an historical and future perspective. It is also designed to be readable, accessible and interesting to the present generation of law student. Flowcharts and examples involving recognisable persons are meant to assist as aids to the learning process in what can at first appear to be a daunting subject. Contract is, after all, one of the great cathedrals of the common law.

In writing this book I have attempted to heed the warning given by the Court of Appeal on April 11, 2000 in *Hamblin v. Field* that "excessive citation of authorities was to be deplored". A view, no doubt, with which most law students would heartily agree. Regrettably I may not have altogether managed to avoid this tendency in places. I have adopted the new terminology, following Lord Woolf's reforms in April 1999, in using "claimant" rather than "plaintiff" for the person bringing proceedings. For cases prior to that date, I have maintained the old name to avoid confusion. Also, the descriptions "pursuer" and "defender" are used in relation to cases from Scots law. It should be obvious that these refer to claimant and defendant.

I should like to express my thanks to several people for their help in producing this book. First to my publishers, Sweet and Maxwell, for enduring an enormously long haul from the start of this work to its ultimate publication. In particular, to Nick O'Dell, Sarah Harrison, Richard Crouch and latterly Michelle Gallagher who have all been superb in their patience, understanding and support for this project, and finally to Rebecca Atkins for diligently editing my manuscript. Within the School of Law, two excellent people who typed and re-typed the manuscript have my deepest gratitude. To Pamela Kimmins, now retired, who laboured skilfully with the text and showed wonderful support throughout, and to Nadene Bryan who deciphered and put up with my handwriting and showed stoical patience in doing so. My thanks also to the staff of the Harding Law Library, particularly Sheila McDougal and Margaret Vaughan, for all their help, and to our librarian until December 2000, Laurence Bebbington, for his skills with information technology and then in the same role, to Lindsey Withecombe. Finally, my greatest thanks go to my mother, whose determination and love reassured and inspired me to see the book through its darker days to a conclusion. I am very grateful to all of them.

George Applebey
School of Law
Edgbaston
September, 2001.

TABLE OF CONTENTS

	Para
Preface	*vii*
Table of Cases	*xiii*
Table of Statutes	*li*
Table of Statutory Instruments	*liv*

1 INTRODUCTION **1.1**
The nature and scope of contract law *1.1*

2 THE ROAD TO AGREEMENT **2.1**
Contract as a legally recognised agreement *2.2*
Objectivity and subjectivity in contract law *2.8*

3 THE OFFER **3.1**
The offer *3.1*
Terminating the offer *3.10*

4 ACCEPTANCE **4.1**
The fact of acceptance *4.1*
Communication of acceptance *4.7*
When communication of acceptance is not necessary *4.21*
*The revocation of a previously posted acceptance by
    the offeree* *4.26*

5 PROBLEMATIC AGREEMENTS **5.1**
Difficult cases *5.1*
Taking a more relaxed view of offer and acceptance *5.4*
"The battle of the forms" *5.7*
Certainty as a formation requirement *5.11*
Incompleteness *5.15*
The effect of failure to agree or lack of finality *5.18*

6 MISTAKE IN RELATION TO AGREEMENT **6.1**
Agreement mistake *6.2*
The categories of agreement mistake *6.7*
Mistaken identity *6.11*

7 BASIC DOCTRINES OF CONSIDERATION **7.1**
Promise and consideration *7.1*
What is consideration? *7.5*
The basic rules in relation to contractual formation *7.9*

8 VARYING THE CONTRACTUAL NEXUS **8.1**
Giving extra *8.1*
Taking a lesser sum *8.14*
Contractual variations *8.20*
Reforming consideration *8.25*

9 EQUITABLE ESTOPPEL 9.1
  The background to promissory estoppel 9.2
  The basic rules of promissory estoppel 9.6
  Promissory estoppel as a cause of action in other
    common law jurisdictions 9.13
  The varieties of equitable estoppel 9.15
  A single doctrine of equitable estoppel 9.19
10 THIRD PARTIES 10.1
  The background of the privity of contract rule 10.2
  Reforming the privity rule 10.5
  The Contracts (Rights of Third Parties) Act 1999 ....10.9
  The surviving common law 10.24
11 INTENTION CAPACITY AND FORM 11.1
  Intention to create legal relations 11.1
  Capacity to contract 11.6
  Form 11.8
12 THE PARAMETERS OF THE CONTRACT 12.1
  Determining the contents of a contract 12.1
  The admissibility of evidence 12.2
  The parol evidence rule 12.4
  The rules of interpretation and construction 12.12
  Implied terms and gapfilling 12.14
13 THE CLASSIFICATION OF TERMS 13.1
  Terms and representations 13.1
  Contractual obligations 13.4
  Promissory terms 13.8
  The modern approaches to the classification of
    promissory terms 13.9
  Time in contract law: how vital is punctuality? 13.19
  Efficient breach, good faith and restitution 13.24
14 CONCEPTS OF FAIRNESS IN CONTRACT LAW 14.1
  Law and equity 14.1
  Fairness at common law 14.6
  Fairness in equity 14.14
  Good faith: a new overarching principle of contract law? 14.21
  The choice of fairness concepts 14.31
15 ASPECTS OF FAIRNESS: DISCLOSURE AND CONSUMER CONTRACTS 15.1
  The absence of a general duty of disclosure 15.1
  When disclosure is required or non disclosure is
    actionable 15.7
  The Unfair Terms in Consumer Contracts
    Regulations 1999 ....15.15
  Should consumer contracts and commercial contracts
    be regarded as different subjects? 15.31
16 EXEMPTION CLAUSES AT COMMON LAW 16.1
  The incorporation of exemption clauses at common law 16.5
  The construction of exemption clauses "contra
    proferentem" 16.19
  The doctrine of fundamental breach 16.24
  Exemption clauses and third parties 6.29
  A common law test of reasonableness for terms falling
    outside the Unfair Contract Terms Act 16.30
17 THE UNFAIR CONTRACT TERMS ACT 1977 ....17.1
  The background to the legislation 17.1
  The scope of the Act 17.5
  The key provisions of the Act 17.8
  Interpreting the Act 17.11

18 MISREPRESENTATION **18.1**
    Flawed agreements *18.1*
    Misrepresentation *18.3*
    The four types of misrepresentation *18.11*
    Remedies for misrepresentation *18.16*
    Misrepresentation or non-disclosure by an agent or
        employee *18.24*
    Excluding liability for non-fraudulent misrepresentation *18.25*
19 ILLEGITIMATE PRESSURE **19.1**
    Duress at common law *19.1*
    Undue influence in equity *19.8*
    Undue influence by third parties *19.18*
    Rebutting the presumption of undue influence *19.25*
    Remedies for undue influence *19.28*
20 ILLEGALITY AND PUBLIC POLICY **20.1**
    The role of public policy *20.1*
    Illegality by statute *20.3*
    Contracts contrary to public policy at common law *20.8*
    The differing effects of illegality of contracts *20.13*
    Reforming the law on illegality *20.21*
    Contracts in restraint of trade at common law *20.23*
    Particular remedies for dealing with restraint of trade *20.29*
21 COMMON MISTAKE AND REMEDIES FOR MISTAKE AT COMMON LAW AND IN
    EQUITY **21.1**
    Common mistake at common law *21.4*
    Common mistake in equity *21.12*
    Non est factum: documents signed by mistake *21.16*
    The effect of mistake *21.19*
    The reform of mistake in contract law *21.24*
22 FRUSTRATION OF CONTRACT **22.1**
    The common law background to frustration *22.3*
    The development of frustration *22.6*
    When frustration will not apply *22.18*
    The test of frustration *22.22*
    The effect of frustration *22.24*
23 DISCHARGE BY BREACH AND PERFORMANCE **23.1**
    Breach of contract *23.1*
    The doctrine of anticipatory breach of contract *23.5*
    Repudiation of the contract *23.11*
    Discharge by performance *23.18*
24 THE GOVERNING PRINCIPLES OF DAMAGES FOR BREACH OF
    CONTRACT **24.1**
    Introduction *24.1*
    The choice between the expectation and reliance
        principles *24.10*
    Applying the tests for compensation for breach of
        contract *24.22*
25 THE BOUNDARIES OF COMPENSATION **25.1**
    Remoteness *25.2*
    Damages for mental distress *25.9*
    Causation *25.22*
    Mitigation of loss *25.24*
    Contributory negligence by the plaintiff *25.27*
    Liquidated damages and penalty clauses *25.29*
    Putting damages into practice *25.36*

26 EQUITABLE REMEDIES AND RESTITUTION IN THE FIELD OF CONTRACT LAW 26.1
Self help remedies 26.1
Equitable remedies in the context of contract law 26.2
Restitution in the field on contract law 26.19

Index 487

TABLE OF CASES

A Roberts & Co. v. Leicestershire CC; *sub nom.* A Roberts and Co. Ltd v. Leicestershire
County Council [1961] Ch. 555; [1961] 2 W.L.R. 1000, Ch D 21.21, 21.22
A Roberts and Co. Ltd v. Leicestershire County Council. *See* A Roberts & Co v.
Leicestershire CC
A/B Karlshamns Oljefabriker v. Monarch Steamship Co. Ltd. *See* Monarch Steamship
Co. Ltd v. A/B Karlshamns Oljefabriker
Abrahams v. Abrahams Trustee in Bankruptcy. *See* Abrahams v. Trustee in Bankruptcy of
Abrahams
Abrahams v. Trustee in Bankruptcy of Abrahams; *sub nom.* Abrahams v. Abrahams
Trustee in Bankruptcy [1999] B.P.I.R. 637; (2000) 1 W.T.L.R. 593, Ch D 20.11
Adam v. Newbigging (1888) L.R. 13 App. Cas. 308 .... 18.20
Adamastos Shipping Co. Ltd v. Anglo Saxon Petroleum Co. Ltd; *sub nom.* Anglo Saxon
Petroleum Co. Ltd v. Adamastos Shipping Co. Ltd [1959] A.C. 133; [1958] 2 W.L.R.
688, HL 12.1
Adams v. Lindsell (1818) 1 B and Ald 681; 106 E.R. 250 ....1.10, 3.11, 4.12–4.14
Addis v. Gramophone Co. Ltd [1909] A.C. 488, HL.............25.10, 25.11–25.13, 25.15, 25.20
Adler v. Dickson (No.1) [1955] 1 Q.B. 158; [1954] 3 W.L.R. 696, CA 10.11, 16.29
AEG (UK) Ltd v. Logic Resource Ltd [1996] C.L.C. 265, CA; [1995] CCH Commercial
Law Reports 266 ....2.4, 14.12, 16.15, 17.33
Aello, The. *See* Sociedad Financiera de Bienes Raices SA v. Agrimpex Hungarian Trading
Co. for Agricultural Products (The Aello)
Afovos Shipping Co. SA v. R Pagnan & Fratelli (The Afovos) [1983] 1 W.L.R. 195; [1983]
1 All E.R. 449; [1983] 1 Lloyd's Rep. 335, HL; [1980] 2 Lloyd's Rep. 469, QBD (Comm
Ct) 4.9
Ailsa Craig Fishing Co. Ltd v. Malvern Fishing Co. Ltd. *See* Ailsa Craig Fishing Co. v.
Malvern Fishing Co. and Securicor (Scotland)
Ailsa Craig Fishing Co. v. Malvern Fishing Co. and Securicor (Scotland); *sub nom.*
Malvern Fishing Co. Ltd v. Ailsa Craig Fishing Co. Ltd and Securicor (Scotland) Ltd
[1983] 1 W.L.R. 964; [1983] 1 All E.R. 101, HL... 16.22
Ajayi v. Briscoe. *See* Ajayi (t/a Colony Carrier Co.) v. RT Briscoe (Nigeria) Ltd ....
Ajayi (t/a Colony Carrier Co.) v. RT Briscoe (Nigeria) Ltd; *sub nom.* Emmanuel Ajayi v.
R.T. Briscoe (Nigeria) Ltd [1964] 1 W.L.R. 1326; [1964] 3 All E.R. 556, PC 9.3, 9.8, 9.11,
9.12
Albazero, The. *See* Owners of Cargo Laden on Board the Albacruz v. Owners of the
Albazero (The Albacruz and The Albazero)
Albert v. Motor Insurers Bureau [1972] A.C. 301; [1971] 3 W.L.R. 291; [1971] 2 All E.R.
1345, HL 11.4
Alder v. Moore [1961] 2 Q.B. 57; [1961] 2 W.L.R. 426, CA.. 25.34
Alderslade v. Hendon Laundry Ltd [1945] K.B. 189; [1945] 1 All E.R. 244, CA 6.20
Alec Lobb Garages Ltd v. Total Oil Great Britain Ltd [1985] 1 W.L.R. 173; [1985] 1 All
E.R. 303, CA; [1983] 1 W.L.R. 87, Ch. D 14.16, 14.17

Alexander v. Rayson [1936] 1 K.B. 169; 114 A.L.R. 357, CA..20.6, 20.14
Alfred C Toepfer v. Peter Cremer GmbH & Co.; *sub nom.* Toepfer v Cremer; Toepfer v.
 Peter Cremer [1975] 2 Lloyd's Rep. 118; (1975) 119 S.J. 506, CA 9.18
Alfred C Toepfer International GmbH v. Itex Itagrani Export SA; *sub nom.* Toepfer
 International GmbH v. Itex Itagrani Export SA [1993] 1 Lloyd's Rep. 360, QBD
 (Comm Ct) 23.15
Alfred McAlpine Construction Ltd v. Panatown Ltd (No.1); *sub nom.* Panatown Ltd v
 Alfred McAlpine Construction Ltd; Panatown Ltd v. Alfred McAlpine [2000] 3
 W.L.R. 946; [2000] 4 All E.R. 97, HL 10.1, 10.29, 10.30, 24.6, 25.16, 25.19
Alghussein Establishment v. Eton College [1988] 1 W.L.R. 587; [1991] 1 All E.R. 267, HL   23.4
Allcard v. Skinner (1887) L.R. 36 Ch. D. 145, CA 19.8, 19.9, 19.14–19.16, 19.28
Allen v. Rescous (1677) 2 Lev. 174; 83 E.R. 505 ....   20.8
Alliance & Leicester Building Society v. Edgestop Ltd; Alliance & Leicester Building
 Society v. Dhanoa; Alliance & Leicester Building Society v. Samra [1999] Lloyd's Rep.
 P.N. 868, Ch. D 18.8, 25.28
Allied Maples Group Ltd v. Simmons & Simmons [1995] 1 W.L.R. 1602; [1995] 4 All E.R.
 907, CA 24.17
Allied Marine Transport v. Vale do Rio Doce Navegacao SA (The Leonidas D); Vale do
 Rio Doce Navegacao SA v. Ocean Freighters Corp. [1985] 1 W.L.R. 925; [1985] 2 All
 E.R. 796, CA 2.7
Amalgamated Investment & Property Co. v. John Walker & Sons; *sub nom.* Amalgamated
 Investment and Property Co. Ltd v. John Walker and Sons [1977] 1 W.L.R. 164; [1976]
 3 All E.R. 509, CA 22.13
Amalgamated Investment and Property Co. Ltd v. John Walker and Sons. *See*
 Amalgamated Investment & Property Co. v. John Walker & Sons
Amalgamated Investment & Property Co. Ltd (In Liquidation) v. Texas Commerce
 International Bank Ltd [1982] Q.B. 84; [1981] 3 W.L.R. 565, CA 9.1, 9.9, 9.15, 9.17, 9.19,
                                                                                         9.20, 9.21
Amar Singh v. Kulubya [1964] A.C. 142; [1963] 3 W.L.R. 513, PC 20.18
American Cyanamid Co. v Ethicon Ltd [1975] A.C. 396; [1975] 2 W.L.R. 316, HL 26.7
Anangel Atlas Compania Naviera SA v. Ishikawajima-Harima Heavy Industries Co.
 (No.2) [1990] 2 Lloyd's Rep. 526, QBD (Comm Ct) 8.13
Anderton v. Rowland. *See* Anderton & Rowland v. Rowland
Anderton & Rowland v. Rowland; *sub nom.* Anderton v. Rowland *The Times*, November
 5, 1999, QBD (Merc Ct) 5.2
André et Cie SA v. Etablissements Michel Blanc et Fils; *sub nom.* André et Cie SA v. Ets
 Michel Blanc and Fils [1979] 2 Lloyd's Rep. 427, CA; [1977] 2 Lloyd's Rep. 166, QBD
 (Comm Ct) 18.6
André et Cie SA v. Ets Michel Blanc and Fils. *See* André et Cie SA v. Etablissements
 Michel Blanc et Fils
Andre et Cie SA v. Marine Transocean Ltd (The Splendid Sun) [1981] Q.B. 694; [1981] 3
 W.L.R. 43, CA 2.7
Andrew Brothers (Bournemouth) Ltd v. Singer and Co. Ltd [1934] 1 K.B. 17 ....   16.19
Andrews v. Hopkinson [1957] 1 Q.B. 229; [1956] 3 W.L.R. 732, Assizes (Leeds)................   12.7
Anemone, The. *See* Clipper Maritime Ltd v. Shirlstar Container Transport Ltd (The
 Anemone)
Anglia Television Ltd v. Reed [1972] 1 Q.B. 60; [1971] 3 W.L.R. 528, CA 24.5, 24.10, 24.18
Anglo Saxon Petroleum Co. Ltd v. Adamastos Shipping Co. Ltd. *See* Adamastos Shipping
 Co. Ltd v. Anglo Saxon Petroleum Co. Ltd
Appleby v. Dods (1807) 8 East 300; 103 E.R. 356..............................23.20, 23.21, 23.31
Appleby v. Myers (1867) L.R. 2 C.P. 651..23.23, 23.24
Appleson v. Littlewoods Ltd [1939] 1 All E.R. 464...   11.2
Appleton v. Campbell (1826) 2 C & P 347; 172 E.R. 157
Arbitration Between Mahmoud and Ispahani, Re. *See* Mahmoud and Ispahani, Re
Arbitration Between Moore & Co. Ltd and Landauer & Co. Re. *See* FW Moore & Co. Ltd
 v. Landauer & Co.

Archbolds (Freightage) Ltd v. S Spanglett Ltd [1961] 1 Q.B. 374; [1961] 2 W.L.R. 170, CA   20.6

Arcos Ltd v. EA Ronaasen & Son; *sub nom.* Ronaasen & Son v. Arcos Ltd, [1933] A.C. 470; (1933) 45 Ll. L. Rep. 33, HL 13.11

Armhouse Lee Ltd v. Chappell *The Times,* August 7, 1996; *The Independent,* July 26, 1996, CA 20.9, 20.10

Arrale v. Costain Civil Engineer; *sub nom.* Arrale v. Costain Civil Engineering Ltd [1976] 1 Lloyd's Rep. 98; (1975) 119 S.J. 527, CA 7.11

Arrale v. Costain Civil Engineering Ltd. *See* Arrale v Costain Civil Engineer

Ashbury Railway Carriage and Iron Co. v. Richie; *sub nom.* Riche v. Ashbury Railway Carriage & Iron Co. Ltd (1875) L.R. 7 H.L. 653, HL; (1873–74) L.R. 9 Ex. 224, Ex Ct 11.7

Ashmore v. Corp. of Lloyd's (No.2) [1992] 2 Lloyd's Rep. 620; *The Times,* July 17, 1992, QBD (Comm Ct) 12.29, 14.24

Associated Japanese Bank (International) Ltd v. Credit du Nord SA [1989] 1 W.L.R. 255; [1988] 3 All E.R. 902, QBD 1.6, 15.13, 21.3, 21.6, 21.8, 21.13, 21.14

Astley v. Reynolds (1731) 2 Str. 915; 93 E.R. 939 ....   19.3

Atkinson v. JCL Marine. *See* Rasbora v. JCL Marine

Atkinson v. Ritchie [1809 10 East 530; 103 E.R. 877 ....   22.15

Atlantic Lines & Navigation Co. Inc. v. Hallam Ltd (The Lucy); *sub nom.* Atlantic Lines Ltd v. Hallam Ltd, The Lucy [1983] 1 Lloyd's Rep. 188, QBD (Comm Ct) 18.9

Atlantic Lines Ltd v. Hallam Ltd, The Lucy. *See* Atlantic Lines & Navigation Co. Inc. v. Hallam Ltd (The Lucy

Atlas Express Ltd v. Kafco (Importers and Distributors) Ltd [1989] Q.B. 833; [1989] 3 W.L.R. 389; [1989] 1 All E.R. 641, QBD 19.5

Attica Sea Carriers Corp. v. Ferrostaal Poseidon Bulk Reederei GmbH (The Puerto Buitrago) [1976] 1 Lloyd's Rep. 250; *The Times,* November 25, 1975, CA 23.9, 23.10

Attorney General Europe v. International Insurance, *The Times,* June 23, 2001 ....   12.2

Attorney General v. Blake [2001] 1 A.C. 268; [2000] 3 W.L.R. 625, HL; [1998] 1 All E.R. 833, CA 24.8, 26.16, 26.17, 26.36, 26.39, 26.41

Attwood v. Lamont [1920] 3 K.B. 571, CA;[1920] 2 K.B. 146, KBD 20.28, 20.30

Attwood v. Small. *See* Small v. Attwood

Australia v. Amann Aviation Pty Ltd. *See* Commonwealth of Australia v. Amann Aviation Pty

Australia v. Verwayen; *sub nom.* Commonwealth v. Verwayen (1990) 95 A.L.R. 321 ....9.20, 9.21, 14.18

Australian Securities Commission v. Marlborough Gold Mines Ltd (1993) 177 C.L.R. 506   9.20

Avery v. Bowden (1855) 5 E and B 714 ....23.5, 23.6

Avon Finance Co. v. Bridger [1985] 2 All E.R. 281; 123 S.J. 705, CA 14.9, 19.16

Avon Insurance v. Swire Fraser. *See* Avon Insurance Plc v. Swire Fraser Ltd

Avon Insurance Plc v. Swire Fraser Ltd; *sub nom.* Avon Insurance v. Swire Fraser [2000] 1 All E.R. (Comm) 573; [2000] C.L.C. 665, QBD (Comm Ct) 18.4, 18.7, 18.10, 18.15, 18.18

Awilco of Oslo A/S v. Fulvia SpA di Navigazione of Cagliari (The Chikuma) [1981] 1 W.L.R. 314; [1981] 1 All E.R. 652, HL 13.19, 13.20, 13.24, 14.3

Awwad v. Geraghty & Co.; *sub nom.* Geraghty & Co. v. Awwad [2000] 3 W.L.R. 1041; [2000] 1 All E.R. 608, CA 20.12

Geraghty & Co. v. Awwad. *See* Awwad v. Geraghty & Co.

Aylesbury Football Club (1997) Ltd v. Watford Association Football Club Ltd, unreported, June 12, 2000 ....   11.6

B v. B. *See* Backhouse v. Backhouse

BCCI v. Aboody. *See* Bank of Credit and Commerce International SA v. Aboody

BCCI v. Ali. *See* Bank of Credit and Commerce International SA v. Ali (Assessment of Costs)

BCCI v. Ali (Assessment of Costs). *See* Bank of Credit and Commerce International SA v. Ali (Assessment of Costs)

BCCI SA, Re. *See* Malik v. Bank of Credit and Commerce International SA (In Liquidation) B & S Contracts and Design v. Victor Green Publications [1984] I.C.R. 419; (1984) 81 L.S.G. 893, CA 19.5

BHP Petroleum Ltd v. British Steel Plc [2000] 2 All E.R. (Comm) 133; [2000] 2 Lloyd's Rep. 277, CA; [1999] 2 All E.R. (Comm) 544, QBD.. 16.22

BP v. Hunt. *See* BP Exploration Co. (Libya) Ltd v. Hunt (No.2)

BP v. Hunt (No.2). *See* BP Exploration Co. (Libya) Ltd v. Hunt (No.2)

BP Exploration v. Hunt. *See* BP Exploration Co. (Libya) Ltd v. Hunt (No.2)

BP Exploration Co. (Libya) Ltd v. Hunt (No.2); *sub nom.* BP Exploration v. Hunt; BP v. Hunt; BP v. Hunt (No.2) [1983] 2 A.C. 352; [1982] 2 W.L.R. 253, HL; [1979] 1 W.L.R. 783, QBD...9.18, 22.25–22.28

BP Refinery (Westernpoint) Pty Ltd v. Shire of Hastings; *sub nom.* BP (Westernport) Pty Ltd v. The President, Councillors and Ratepayers of Hastings (1977) 180 C.L.R. 266; (1978) 52 A.L.J.R. 20 ....12.29, 12.30

BP (Westernport) Pty Ltd v. The President, Councillors and Ratepayers of Hastings. *See* BP Refinery (Westernpoint) Pty Ltd v. Shire of Hastings BTP Tioxide Ltd v Pioneer Shipping Ltd. *See* Pioneer Shipping Ltd v. BTP Tioxide Ltd (The Nema) (No.2)

Backhouse v. Backhouse; *sub nom.* B v B [1978] 1 W.L.R. 243; [1978] 1 All E.R. 1158, Fam. Div. 14.9, 14.15

Bailey v. Bullock [1950] 2 All E.R. 1167; 66 T.L.R. (Pt. 2) 791, KBD 25.18

Bainbridge v. Browne (1891) 18 Ch. 188 .... 19.14

Balfour v. Balfour [1919] 2 K.B. 571, CA...11.1, 11.3

Balfour Beatty Civil Engineering Ltd v. Docklands Light Railway Ltd [1996] C.L.C. 1435; 78 B.L.R. 42; 49 Con. L.R. 1; (1996) 12 Const. L.J. 259, CA 14.25

Balfour Beatty Construction (Scotland) v. Scottish Power plc. *See* Balfour Beatty Construction (Scotland) Ltd v. Scottish Power

Balfour Beatty Construction (Scotland) Ltd v. Scottish Power; *sub nom.* Balfour Beatty Construction (Scotland) v. Scottish Power plc 1994 S.L.T. 807, HL; 1993 S.C. 350, 2 Div... 25.7

Ball (1983) 99 L.Q.R. 572 .... 5.5

Baltic Shipping Co. v. Dillon (1993) 176 C.L.R. 344.. 26.25

Banco de Portugal v. Waterlow & Sons Ltd; Waterlow & Sons Ltd v. Banco de Portugal [1932] A.C. 452; [1932] All E.R. Rep. 181, HL..25.7, 25.24

Banco Exterior Internacional v. Mann [1995] 1 All E.R. 936; [1995] 1 F.L.R. 602, CA 19.22

Banco Exterior Internacional SA v. Thomas [1997] 1 W.L.R. 221; [1997] 1 All E.R. 46, CA   19.25

Bangladesh Export Import Co. Ltd v. Sucden Kerry SA [1995] 2 Lloyd's Rep. 1, CA 22.15

Bank Line v. Arthur Capel. *See* Bank Line Ltd v. Arthur Capel & Co.

Bank Line Ltd v. Arthur Capel & Co.; *sub nom.* Bank Line v. Arthur Capel [1919] A.C. 435, HL 22.6

Bank of Credit and Commerce International SA v. Aboody; *sub nom.* BCCI v. Aboody [1990] 1 Q.B. 923; [1989] 2 W.L.R. 759. CA 19.10, 19.11–19.13

Bank of Credit and Commerce International SA v. Ali (Assessment of Costs); *sub nom.* BCCI v. Ali (Assessment of Costs); BCCI v. Ali [2000] 2 Costs L.R. 243; [2001] 2 W.L.R. 735; *The Times,* May 10, 2000, HC 7.12, 14.16, 15.4, 15.5, 25.21

Bank of Credit and Commerce International SA (In Liquidation) v. Ali (No. 1); *sub nom.* BCCI v. Ali (No. 1) [2000] 3 All E.R. 51; [2000] I.C.R. 1410...................................... 14.16

Bank of Cyprus (London) Ltd v. Markou [1999] 2 All E.R. 707; [1999] 2 F.L.R. 17, Ch D

Bank of India v. Trans Continental Commodity Merchants Ltd. *See* Bank of India v. Trans Continental Commodity Merchants Ltd (No.2)

Bank of India v. Trans Continental Commodity Merchants Ltd (No.2); *sub nom.* Bank of India v. Trans Continental Commodity Merchants Ltd [1983] 2 Lloyd's Rep. 298, CA; [1982] 1 Lloyd's Rep. 506, QBD.. 20.2

Bank of Montreal v. Stuart [1911] A.C. 120, PC...19.10, 19.12

Bank of Nova Scotia v. Hellenic Mutual War Risk Association (Bermuda) Ltd (The Good Luck) (No.2) [1992] 1 A.C. 233; [1991] 2 W.L.R. 1279, HL 22.14

Bank of Scotland v Dunedin Property Investment Co Ltd (No.1) 1998 S.C. 657; 1999 S.L.T. 470, 1 Div.. 12.3

Banque Bruxelles v. Eagle Star Insurance Co. Ltd. *See* Banque Bruxelles Lambert SA v. Eagle Star Insurance Co. Ltd

Banque Bruxelles Lambert SA v. Eagle Star Insurance Co. Ltd; United Bank of Kuwait Plc v. Prudential Property Services Ltd; Nykredit Mortgage Bank Plc v. Edward Erdman Group Ltd; BNP Mortgages Ltd v. Key Surveyors Nationwide Ltd; BNP Mortgages Ltd v. Goadsby & Harding Ltd; Mortgage Express Ltd v. Bowerman & Partners (No.2); *sub nom.* Banque Bruxelles v. Eagle Star Insurance Co. Ltd [1997] A.C. 191; [1995] Q.B. 375; [1995] 2 W.L.R. 607, CA 18.17

Banque Financière de la Cite v. Westgate Insurance Co. Ltd. *See* Banque Financière de la Cite SA (formerly Banque Keyser Ullmann SA) v. Westgate Insurance Co. (formerly Hodge General & Mercantile Co. Ltd)

Banque Financière de la Cite SA (formerly Banque Keyser Ullmann SA) v. Westgate Insurance Co. (formerly Hodge General & Mercantile Co. Ltd); *sub nom.* Banque Financière de la Cite v. Westgate Insurance Co. Ltd; Banque Keyser Ullmann SA v. Skandia (UK) Insurance Co; Skandia (UK) Insurance Co. v. Chemical Bank; Skandia (UK) Insurance Co. v. Credit Lyonnais Bank Nederland NV [1991] 2 A.C. 249; [1990] 3 W.L.R. 364; [1989] 2 All E.R. 952, CA 15.9

Banque Keyser Ullmann SA v. Skandia (UK) Insurance Co. *See* Banque Financière de la Cite SA (formerly Banque Keyser Ullmann SA) v. Westgate Insurance Co. (formerly Hodge General & Mercantile Co Ltd) Barber v. NWS Bank Plc [1996] 1 W.L.R. 641; [1996] 1 All E.R. 906, CA 13.14

Barber v. RJB Mining (UK) Ltd [1999] 2 C.M.L.R. 833; [1999] I.C.R. 679; *The Times*, March 8, 1999, QBD 5.2

Barclays Bank v. Coleman. *See* Barclays Bank Plc v. Coleman

Barclays Bank Plc v. Boulter [1999] 1 W.L.R. 1919; [1999] 4 All E.R. 513, HL 19.20

Barclays Bank Plc v. Coleman; *sub nom.* Barclays Bank v. Coleman [2001] Q.B. 20; [2000] 3 W.L.R. 405; [2000] 1 All E.R. 385, CA 19.12, 19.23

Barclays Bank Plc v. Fairclough Building Ltd. *See* Barclays Bank Plc v. Fairclough Building Ltd (No.1)

Barclays Bank Plc v. Fairclough Building Ltd (No.1); *sub nom.* Barclays Bank Plc v. Fairclough Building Ltd [1995] Q.B. 214; [1994] 3 W.L.R. 1057; [1995] 1 All E.R. 289, CA 25.27

Barclays Bank Plc v. O'Brien [1994] 1 A.C. 180; [1993] 3 W.L.R. 786, HL 19.14, 19.15, 19.19, 19.22, 19.27

Barrett McKenzie and Co. Ltd v. Escada (UK) Ltd *The Times*, May 15, 2001 .... 24.29

Barry v. Davies (t/a Heathcote Ball & Co.); *sub nom.* Heathcote Ball & Co. (Commercial Auctions) Ltd v. Barry; Barry v. Heathcote Ball & Co. (Commercial Auctions) Ltd [2000] 1 W.L.R. 1962; [2001] 1 All E.R. 944, CA 3.7, 24.21

Barry v. Heathcote Ball & Co. (Commercial Auctions) Ltd. *See* Barry v. Davies (t/a Heathcote Ball & Co.)

Barton v. County Natwest Ltd; *sub nom.* County Natwest Ltd v Barton [1999] Lloyd's Rep. Bank. 408; [1999] E.G.C.S. 103; *The Times*, July 29, 1999, CA 18.7, 18.9

Barton (Alexander) v. Armstrong (Alexander Ewan); *sub nom.* Barton v. Armstrong [1976] A.C. 104; [1975] 2 W.L.R. 1050, PC 19.2, 19.7

Basham (Deceased), Re [1986] 1 W.L.R. 1498; [1987] 1 All E.R. 405, Ch. D 9.15

Bayer AG v. Commission of the European Communities [2001] All E.R. (EC) 1; [2001] 4 C.M.L.R. 4; *The Times*, February 9, 2001, CFI (5th Chamber) 2.11

Bell v. Lever Bros Ltd; *sub nom.* Lever Bros Ltd v Bell [1932] A.C. 161, HL; [1931] 1 K.B. 557, CA 15.4, 15.5, 15.9, 21.6–21.11, 21.13, 21.14

Belvoir Finance Co. Ltd v. Stapleton [1971] 1 Q.B. 210; [1970] 3 W.L.R. 530, CA 20.17

Bem Dis A Turk Ticaret S/A TR v. International Agri Trade Co. Ltd (The Selda) [1999] 1 All E.R. (Comm.) 619; [1999] 1 Lloyd's Rep. 729, CA; [1998] 1 Lloyd's Rep. 416 .... 24.10, 25.32

Bence Graphics International Ltd v. Fasson UK Ltd [1998] Q.B. 87; [1997] 3 W.L.R. 205, CA 24.22

Bennett v. Bennett [1952] 1 K.B. 249; [1952] 1 All E.R. 413, CA 20.19

Benyon v. Nettlefold (1850) 3 Mas and G 94; 42 E.R. 196 .... 20.9

Beoco v. Alfa Laval Co. [1995] Q.B. 137; [1994] 3 W.L.R. 1179, CA 25.22

Beresford v. Royal Insurance Co. Ltd [1938] A.C. 586, HL; [1937] 2 K.B. 197, CA 20.8

Beswick v. Beswick [1968] A.C. 58; [1967] 3 W.L.R. 932, HL 10.4, 10.8, 10.11, 10.28, 26.4

Bettini v. Gye (1875–76) L.R. 1 Q.B.D. 183, QBD... 13.10

Bigg v. Boyd Gibbins [1971] 1 W.L.R. 913; [1971] 2 All E.R. 183, CA.............................. 3.5

Biggin & Co. Ltd v. Permanite Ltd [1951] 2 K.B. 314; [1951] 2 All E.R. 191, CA; [1951] 1
    K.B. 422, KBD 24.14

Biggin Hill Airport Ltd v. Bromley LBC (2001) 98(3) L.S.G. 42; [2000] N.P.C. 130; *The
    Times*, January 9, 2001, Ch D... 1.15

Bigos v. Bousted [1951] 1 All E.R. 92, KBD.. 20.8

Birkett v. Acorn Business Machines Ltd [1999] 2 All E.R. (Comm) 429; (1999) 96(31)
    L.S.G. 35, CA.. 20.2

Birmingham and District Land Co. v. London & NW Railway (1888) 40 Ch. 268 .... 9.3, 9.4

Bisset v. Wilkinson [1927] A.C. 177, PC... 18.5

Blackburn Bobbin Co. Ltd v. Allen (TW) and Sons Ltd. *See* Blackburn Bobbin Co. Ltd
    v. TW Allen & Sons Ltd

Blackburn Bobbin Co. Ltd v. T W Allen & Sons Ltd; *sub nom.* Blackburn Bobbin Co. Ltd
    v. Allen (TW) and Sons Ltd [1918] 2 K.B. 467; 3 A.L.R. 11, CA 22.19

Blackpool Aero Club v. Blackpool Borough Council. *See* Blackpool and Fylde Aero Club
    v. Blackpool BC

Blackpool and Fylde Aero Club v. Blackpool BC [1990] 1 W.L.R. 1195; [1990] 3 All E.R.
    25, CA 3.9, 5.6, 14.27, 24.16

Bland v. Sparks (1871) LR Ex. 7.. 13.7

Bliss v. South East Thames Regional Health Authority. *See* Bliss v. South East Thames
    R H A

Bliss v. South East Thames RHA; *sub nom.* Bliss v. South East Thames Regional Health
    Authority [1987] I.C.R. 700; [1985] I.R.L.R. 308, CA; [1985] I.C.R. 308.............25.10, 25.14

Bob Guiness Ltd v. Salomonsen. *See* Guiness (Bob) v. Salomonsen

Bolton v. Mahadeva [1972] 1 W.L.R. 1009; [1972] 2 All E.R. 1322, CA 23.19, 23.30

Bomze v. Bomze. *See* Lloyds Bank Ltd, Re

Boone v. Eyre (1779) 126 E.R. 160 .... 23.29

Bouchard Servais v. Princes Hall Restaurant; *sub nom.* Servais Bouchard v. Princes Hall
    Restaurant (1904) 20 T.L.R. 574.. 20.25

Boulton v. Jones (1857) 2 H and N; 157 E.R. 232.. 6.9

Boustany v. Piggott (1995) 69 P. & C.R. 298; [1993] E.G.C.S. 85, PC............................14.9, 14.18

Bovis Construction (Scotland) Ltd v. Whatlings Construction Ltd 1995 S.C. (H.L.) 19;
    1995 S.L.T. 1339, HL... 16.22

Bowerman v. ABTA. *See* Bowerman v. Association of British Travel Agents Ltd

Bowerman v. Association of British Travel Agents Ltd [1996] C.L.C. 451; (1995) 145 N.L.J.
    1815, CA 2.6, 3.6, 11.2, 12.16, 16.14

Bowes v. Shand (1876–77) L.R. 2 App. Cas. 455, HL; (1876–77) L.R. 2 Q.B.D. 112, QBD... 13.14

Bowmakers Ltd v. Barnet Instruments Ltd [1945] K.B. 65, CA; [1944] 2 All E.R. 579..........20.14,
                                                                                                           20.18, 20.19

Boyd v. Hind (1857) 1 H and N 938; 156 E.R. 1481 .... 8.18

Boyd & Forrest v. Glasgow & South Western Railway Co. 1915 S.C. (H.L) 20.................... 18.22

Boyle v. Walker. *See* Walker v. Boyle

Brace v. Calder [1895] 2 Q.B. 253, CA 25.24

Branca v. Cobarro [1947] K.B. 854; [1947] 2 All E.R. 101, CA...................................... 4.2

Bremer Handels GmbH v. Vanden-Avenne Izegem PVBA; *sub nom.* Bremer
    Handelsgesellschaft mbH v. Vanden Avenne-Izegem PVBA [1978] 2 Lloyd's Rep. 109,
    HL; [1977] 2 Lloyd's Rep. 329, CA 9.7, 13.16

Bremer Handelsgesellschaft mbH v Vanden Avenne- Izegem PVBA. *See* Bremer Handels
    GmbH v. Vanden-Avenne Izegem PVBA

Bridge v. Campbell Discount Co. Ltd; *sub nom.* Campbell Discount Co. Ltd v. Bridge
    [1962] A.C. 600; [1962] 2 W.L.R. 439, HL; [1963] 1 Q.B. 887.................................23.2, 25.34

Brigden v. American Express Bank Ltd [2000] I.R.L.R. 94, QBD....................................... 7.7

Brinkibon v. Stahag Stahl und Stahlwarenhandels GmbH; *sub nom.* Brinkibon Ltd v.
    Stahag Stahl und Stahlwarenhandelsgesellschaft mbH [1983] 2 A.C. 34; [1982] 2

W.L.R. 264, HL 4.10
Brinkibon Ltd v. Stahag Stahl und Stahlwarenhandelsgesellschaft mbH *See* Brinkibon v
    Stahag Stahl und Stahlwarenhandels GmbH
Bristol and West Building Society v. Northern [1996] 4 All E.R. 699 .... 15.11
British and American Telegraph v. Colsons L.R. 6 Exch. 108 (1871)....................... 4.15
British & Commonwealth Holdings Plc v. Quadrex Holdings Inc. (No.1) [1989] Q.B. 842;
    [1989] 3 W.L.R. 723; [1989] 3 All E.R. 492, CA... 13.23
British Crane Hire Corp. Ltd v. Ipswich Plant Hire Ltd [1975] Q.B. 303; [1974] 2 W.L.R.
    856, CA 16.18
British Road Services Ltd v. Arthur V Crutchley & Co. Ltd (No.1); *sub nom.* British Road
    Services Ltd v. Arthur V Crutchley & Co. (Factory Guards Ltd) [1968] 1 All E.R. 811;
    [1968] 1 Lloyd's Rep. 271, CA... 5.8
British Russian Gazette & Trade Outlook Ltd v. Associated Newspapers Ltd; Talbot v
    Associated Newspapers Ltd [1933] 2 K.B. 616, CA 8.20
British Steel Corp. v. Cleveland Bridge & Engineering Co. Ltd [1984] 1 All E.R. 504; [1982]
    Com. L.R. 54, QBD 5.5, 5.18
British Westinghouse Electric & Manufacturing Co. Ltd v. Underground Electric Railways
    Co. of London Ltd (No.2); *sub nom.* British Westinghouse Electric and
    Manufacturing Co. Ltd v. Underground Electric Rlys Co. of London Ltd [1912] A.C.
    673, HL; [1912] 3 K.B. 128, CA 24.1, 25.26
British Westinghouse Electric and Manufacturing Co. Ltd v. Underground Electric Rlys
    Co. of London Ltd. *See* British Westinghouse Electric & Manufacturing Co. Ltd v.
    Underground Electric Railways Co. of London Ltd (No.2)
Broadwater Manor School v. Davis; [1999] 5 C.L. 208; unreported, January 8, 1999, CC .. 15.23
Brogden v. American Express Bank Ltd [2000] 1 R.L.R. 94 .... 17.13
Brogden v. Metropolitan Railway Co. (1877) L.R. 2 App. Cas. 666, HL 4.4
Brown v. Manchester Sheffield and Lincolnshire Railway Co. *See* Manchester, Sheffield
    and Lincolnshire Railway Co. v. Brown
Brown v. Sheen and Richmond Car Sales Ltd [1950] 1 All E.R. 1102; [1950] W.N. 316,
    KBD.. 10.27
Bruner v. Moore [1904] 1 Ch. 305, Ch D 4.11, 4.14
Budgett & Co. v. Binnington & Co. [1891] 1 Q.B. 35, CA; (1890) L.R. 25 Q.B.D. 320,
    QBD.. 22.4
Bullock v. Lloyds Bank Ltd [1955] Ch. 317; [1955] 2 W.L.R. 1, Ch D 19.14
Bunge Corp. v. Tradax Export SA [1981] 1 W.L.R. 711; [1981] 2 All E.R. 540, HL 13.18, 13.21
Butler Machine Tool Co. v. Ex-cell-o Corp. (England) [1979] 1 W.L.R. 401; [1979] 1 All
    E.R. 965, CA 5.7, 5.8
Byrne & Co v. Leon Van Tien Hoven & Co. (1879–80) L.R. 5 C.P.D. 344, CPD 3.12, 4.14, 4.15

C (A Debtor), Re [1996] B.P.I.R. 535, CA...8.11, 8.16
C & P Haulage v. Middleton [1983] 1 W.L.R. 1461; [1983] 3 All E.R. 94, CA 24.11
C Czarnikow Ltd v. Centrala Handlu Zagranicznego Rolimpex (CHZ); *sub nom.*
    Czarnikow Ltd v. Centrala Handlu Zagranicznego "Rolimpex" [1979] A.C. 351;
    [1978] 3 W.L.R. 274, HL... 22.21
C Czarnikow Ltd v. Koufos (The Heron II). *See* C Czarnikow Ltd v. Koufos (The
    Heron II)
CCC Films (London) v. Impact Quadrant Films [1985] Q.B. 16; [1984] 3 W.L.R. 245, QBD
    ....4.14, 24.11
Callisher v. Bischoffsheim (1869) L.R. 5 Q.B. 449, QB 7.12
CIBC Mortgages Plc v. Pitt; *sub nom.* CIBC Mortgages v. Pitt [1994] 1 A.C. 200; [1993] 3
    W.L.R. 802; [1993] 4 All E.R. 433, HL..19.11, 19.12, 19.22
CIBC Mortgages v. Pitt. *See* CIBC Mortgages Plc v. Pitt
CTN Cash and Carry Ltd v. Gallaher Ltd [1994] 4 All E.R. 714, CA 19.6
Camden LBC v. McBride [1999] 1 C.L. 284... 15.23
Campbell Discount Co. Ltd. *See* Bridge v. Campbell Discount Co. Ltd
Canada Steamship Lines Ltd v. King, The [1952] A.C. 192; [1952] 1 All E.R. 305, HL 6.20

Caparo Industries plc v. Dickman [1990] 2 A.C. 605; [1990] 2 W.L.R. 358; [1990] 1 All
 E.R. 568 .... 18.13
Capital Quality Homes Ltd v. Colwyn Construction Ltd (1975) 61 D.L.R. 385 (Ontario
 Court of Appeal)
Car and Universal Finance Co. Ltd v. Caldwell [1965] 1 Q.B. 525; [1964] 2 W.L.R. 600,
 CA 18.21
Carlill v. Carbolic Smoke Ball Co [1893] 1 Q.B. 256, CA; [1892] 2 Q.B. 484, QBD......2.5, 3.4, 3.6,
                                                                        4.21, 7.17, 11.1, 11.2, 16.14, 18.6
Carmichael v. Carmichael's Executrix (1920) S.C. (HL) 195 .... 10.1
Carter v. Boehm (1766) 3 Burr 1905, ER 15.10
Case of an Hostler (1605) Yelv. 66; 80 E.R. 47 .... 23.26
Cehave NV v. Bremer Handels GmbH (The Hansa Nord) *sub nom.* Cehave NV v. Bremer
 Handelgesellschaft mbH (The Hansa Nord).[1976] Q.B. 44; [1975] 3 W.L.R. 447, CA
 ....1.4, 13.17
Cellulose Acetate Silk Co. Ltd v. Widnes Foundry (1925) Ltd; *sub nom.* Widnes Foundry
 (1925) Ltd v. Cellulose Acetate Silk Co. Ltd [1933] A.C. 20, HL; [1931] 2 K.B. 393,
 CA 25.33
Central London Property Trust v. High Trees House [1947] K.B. 130; [1956] 1 All E.R. 256
 (Note), KBD 8.22, 9.1, 9.4, 9.5
Central Newbury Car Auctions v. Unity Finance [1957] 1 Q.B. 371; [1956] 3 W.L.R. 1068,
 CA 9.17
Chandler v. Webster [1904] 1 K.B. 493, CA 22.12
Chanel Home Centers Division of Grace Retail Corporation v. Grossman, 795 F.2d.291
 (1986)... 5.16
Chanter v. Hopkins (1838) 4 M and W 399; 150 E.R. 1484 ....16.24, 16.25
Chapelton v. Barry Urban DC [1940] 1 K.B. 532, CA 16.13
Chaplin v. Hicks [1911] 2 K.B. 786, CA 24.15
Chapman v. Aberdeen Construction Group Plc 1993 S.L.T. 1205; [1991] I.R.L.R. 505,
 2 Div. 17.13
Chappell & Co. Ltd v. Nestlé Co. Ltd [1960] A.C. 87; [1959] 3 W.L.R. 168, HL.............. 7.10
Chaproniere v. Mason (1905) 21 T.L.R. 633 .... 12.22
Charles Rickards Ltd v. Oppenheim; *sub nom.* Rickards (Charles) v. Oppenhaim [1950] 1
 K.B. 616; [1950] 1 All E.R. 420, CA 9.4, 13.22
Charter v. Sullivan [1957] 2 Q.B. 117; [1957] 2 W.L.R. 528, CA...................................... 24.27
Cheese v. Thomas [1994] 1 W.L.R. 129; [1994] 1 All E.R. 35, CA.................................... 19.15
Chester Grosvenor Hotel Co. v. Alfred McAlpine Management 56 B.L.R. 115................... 17.16
Chesterfield v. Janssen; *sub nom.* Earl of Chesterfield v. Janssen [1750] 1 Atk. 301; (1750)
 2 Ves. Sen 125; 28 E.R. 82 .... 14.14
Chikuma, The. *See* Awilco of Oslo A/S v. Fulvia SpA di Navigazione of Cagliari (The
 Chikuma)
Christofi v. Barclays Bank Plc [2000] 1 W.L.R. 937; [1999] 4 All E.R. 437; *The Times,* July
 1, 1999, CA.. 15.5
Circle Freight International Ltd v. Medeast Gulf Exports Ltd [1988] 2 Lloyd's Rep. 427,
 CA 16.15
Citibank NA v. Brown Shipley & Co. Ltd; Midland Bank Plc v. Brown Shipley & Co. Ltd
 [1991] 2 All E.R. 690; [1991] 1 Lloyd's Rep. 576, QBD 6.9, 6.11, 6.16
City and Westminster Properties (1934) Ltd v. Mudd [1959] Ch. 129; [1958] 3 W.L.R. 312,
 Ch. D.. 12.7
City of New Orleans v. Firemans Charitable Association 9 So. 486 (1891)....................... 26.39
Clansmen Sporting Club Ltd v. Robinson *The Times,* May 22, 1995, QBD 5.2
Clarion Ltd v. National Provident Institution [2000] 1 W.L.R. 1888; [2000] 2 All E.R. 265,
 Ch D...21.2, 21.15
Clark v. Lindsay (1903) 19 T.L.R. 202 .... 22.13
Clark v. University of Lincolnshire and Humberside [2000] 1 W.L.R. 1988; [2000] 3 All
 E.R. 752; *The Times,* May 2, 2000, CA 5.2
Clark v. Urquhart; Stracey v. Urquhart; *sub nom.* Urquhart v. Clark; Urquhart v. Stracey
 [1930] A.C. 28; (1929) 34 Ll. L. Rep. 359, HL (NI) 18.16

Clarke v. Earl of Dunraven (The Satanita) [1897] A.C. 59, HL; [1895] P. 248, CA 5.1, 5.2

Clarke v. West Ham Corp. [1909] 2 K.B. 858, CA... 14.7

Clark Boyce v. Mouat [1994] 1 A.C. 428 .... 19.21

Clay v. Yates (1856) 1 H and N 73 .... 20.8

Clea Shipping Corp. v. Bulk Oil International (The Alaskan Trader) (No.2); *sub nom.* Clea
Shipping Corporation v. Bulk Oil International Ltd "The Alaskan Trader" [1984] 1
All E.R. 129; [1983] 2 Lloyd's Rep. 645, QBD (Comm Ct) 23.8

Clea Shipping Corporation v. Bulk Oil International Ltd "The Alaskan Trader". *See* Clea
Shipping Corp. v. Bulk Oil International (The Alaskan Trader) (No.2)

Cleeves Western Valleys Anthracite Collieries Ltd v. Owners of The Penelope [1928] P. 180;
(1928) 31 Ll. L. Rep. 96, PDAD 22.17

Clef Aquitaine Sarl v. Laporte Materials (Barrow) Ltd; *sub nom.* Clef Aquitaine Sarl v.
Sovereign Chemical Industries Ltd [2001] Q.B. 488; [2000] 3 W.L.R. 1760; [2000] 3 All
E.R. 493, CA 18.17, 24.5

Clef Aquitaine Sarl v. Sovereign Chemical Industries Ltd. *See* Clef Aquitaine Sarl v.
Laporte Materials (Barrow) Ltd

Clifton v. Palumbo [1944] 2 All E.R. 497, CA 3.5

Clipper Maritime Ltd v. Shirlstar Container Transport Ltd (The Anemone) [1987] 1
Lloyd's Rep. 546, QBD (Comm Ct)... 12.1

Clydebank Engineering & Shipbuilding Co. Ltd v. Don José Ramos Yzquierdo y
Castaneda [1905] A.C. 6, HL; (1903) 5 F. (Ct. of Sess.) 1016, 2 Div...................... 25.30

Cohen v. Nessdale Ltd [1982] 2 All E.R. 97, CA; [1981] 3 All E.R. 118; (1982) 263 E.G.
437, QBD 5.15

Coker v. Diocese of Southwark. *See* Diocese of Southwark v. Coker

Collins v. Godefroy (1831) 1 Ad 950; 109 E.R. 1040... 8.1

Collins v. Jones *The Times*, February 3, 2000 Ch D 21.22, 21.23

Colonia v. Amoco. *See* Colonia Versicherung AG v. Amoco Oil Co (The Wind Star)

Colonia Versicherung AG v. Amoco Oil Co (The Wind Star); *sub nom.* Colonia v. Amoco
[1997] 1 Lloyd's Rep. 261; [1997] C.L.C. 454 , CA; [1995] 1 Lloyd's Rep. 570, QBD
(Comm Ct) 7.17

Combe v. Combe; *sub nom.* Coombe v Coombe [1951] 2 K.B. 215; [1951] 1 All E.R. 767,
CA 7.13, 9.1, 9.4, 9.9

Commercial Bank of Australia v. Amadio (1983) 46 A.L.R. 402; [1983] 151 C.L.R. 447
.... 14.18

Commission for the New Towns v. Cooper (GB) Ltd. *See* Commission for the New Towns
v. Cooper (Great Britain) Ltd (formerly Coopind UK)

Commission for the New Towns v. Cooper (Great Britain) Ltd (formerly Coopind UK);
sub nom. Milton Keynes Development Corp v. Cooper (Great Britain); Commission
for the New Towns v. Cooper (GB) Ltd [1995] Ch. 259; [1995] 2 W.L.R. 677; [1995] 2
All E.R. 929, CA 21.22

Commissioner of Public Works v. Hills; *sub nom.* Public Works Commissioners v. Hills
[1906] A.C. 368, PC 25.30

Commonwealth of Australia v. Amann Aviation Pty; *sub nom.* Australia v. Amann
Aviation Pty Ltd [1991] 174 C.L.R. 64; (1991) 66 A.L.J.R. 123 ....24.10, 24.14, 24.18, 25.4

Commonwealth v. Verwayen. *See* Australia v Verwayen

Concord Petroleum Corp. v Gosford Marine Panama SA. *See* Owners of Cargo Laden on
Board the Albacruz v. Owners of the Albazero (The Albacruz and The Albazero)

Condor v. The Barron Knights Ltd [1966] 1 W.L.R. 87; 110 S.J. 71................................. 22.9

Cook v. Wright (1861) 1 B & S 559, 121 E.R. 822 .... 7.12

Cooke v. Oxley (1790) 3 T.R 653, 100 E.R. 785..1.10, 3.11, 4.13

Coombe v. Coombe. *See* Combe v. Combe

Cooper v. Phibbs (1867) L.R. 2 H.L. 149 ....21.10, 21.11

Cooperative Insurance Society Ltd v. Argyll Stores (Holdings) Ltd [1998] A.C. 1; [1997] 2
W.L.R. 898, HL...26.4–26.6

Couchman v. Hill [1947] K.B. 554; [1947] 1 All E.R. 103, CA 12.6, 13.1

Couldery v. Bartrum (1881–82) L.R. 19 Ch. D. 394, CA 8.14

Coulls v. Bagot's Executor and Trustee Co. (1967) 40 A.L.J.R. 471 .... 10.27

Countess of Dunmore v. Alexander 1830 9 S.C. 190 .... 4.27
County Natwest Ltd v. Barton. *See* Barton v. County Natwest Ltd
Courage Ltd v. Crehan *The Daily Telegraph*, September 25, 2001 .... 20.28
Court v. Ambergate Railway Co. (1851) 17 Q.B. 127 .... 23.6
Court Line Ltd v. Dant & Russell Inc. (1939) 64 Ll. L. Rep. 212, KBD; [1939] 3 All E.R.
    314 .... 22.16
Courtney & Fairburn v. Tolaini Bros (Hotels). *See* Courtney & Fairbairn Ltd v. Tolaini
    Brothers (Hotels) Ltd Courtney & Fairbairn Ltd v. Tolaini Brothers (Hotels) Ltd ; *sub
    nom.* Courtney & Fairburn v. Tolaini Bros (Hotels) [1975] 1 W.L.R. 297; [1975] 1 All
    E.R. 716, CA 5.15
Couturier v. Hastie; *sub nom.* Gustavus Couturier v. Hastie (1856) 5 H.L. Cas. 673; 10 E.R.
    1065 .... 21.4, 21.5
Coward v. Motor Insurers Bureau [1963] 1 Q.B. 259; [1962] 2 W.L.R. 663, CA 11.4
Cox v. Philips. *See* Cox v. Phillips Industries Ltd
Cox v. Phillips Industries Ltd; *sub nom.* Cox v. Philips [1976] 1 W.L.R. 638; [1976] 3 All
    E.R. 161, QBD 25.10
Crabb v. Arun DC (No.1); *sub nom.* Crabb v. Arun District Council [1976] Ch. 179; [1975]
    3 W.L.R. 847, CA 9.12, 9.15, 9.19
Crabb v. Arun District Council. *See* Crabb v. Arun DC (No.1)
Craig, Re. *See* Craig (Deceased), Re
Craig (Deceased), Re; *sub nom.* Meneces v. Middleton; Craig, Re; Re Craig (Dec'd) [1971]
    Ch. 95; [1970] 2 W.L.R. 1219; [1970] 2 All E.R. 390, Ch D 19.14
Credit Lyonnais Bank Nederland NV v. Burch [1997] 1 All E.R. 144; [1996] 5 Bank. L.R.
    233, CA 19.15, 19.22, 19.24, 19.24
Cremdean Properties v. Nash (1977) 244 E.G. 547, CA; (1977) 241 E.G. 837 .... 18.5
Cresswell v. Potter [1978] 1 W.L.R. 255, Ch. D 11.7, 14.15
Cumming v. Ince (1847) 11 Q.B. 112; 116 E.R. 418 .... 19.2
Cundy v. Lindsay; *sub nom.* Lindsay v. Cundy (1878) L.R. 3 App. Cas. 459; [1874–80] All
    E.R. Rep. 1149, HL 6.11, 6.12, 21.20
Cunliffe-Owen v. Teather & Greenwood; Cunliffe Owen v. Schaverien Habermann, Simon
    & Co; Cunliffe Owen v. LA Seligmann & Co. [1967] 1 W.L.R. 1421; [1967] 3 All E.R.
    561, Ch. D 12.18
Currie v. Misa (1874–75) L.R. 10 Ex. 153, Ex Chamber 7.5
Curtis v. Chemical Cleaning & Dyeing Co. [1951] 1 K.B. 805; [1951] 1 All E.R. 631, CA
    .... 16.10
Cutter v. Powell (1795) 6 Term Rep. 320; 101 E.R. 573 ....23.20, 23.21, 23.23, 23.31
Czarnikow Ltd v. Centrala Handlu Zagranicznego "Rolimpex". *See* C Czarnikow Ltd v.
    Centrala Handlu Zagranicznego Rolimpex (CHZ)

D & C Builders Ltd v. Rees [1966] 2 Q.B. 617; [1966] 2 W.L.R. 288, CA 8.11, 8.16, 9.10
DO Ferguson Associates v. M Sohl. *See* DO Ferguson Associates v. Sohl
DO Ferguson Associates v. Sohl; *sub nom.* DO Ferguson Associates v. M Sohl 62 B.L.R.
    95; *The Times*, December 24, 1992, CA .26.26, 26.34Da Costa v. Jones (1778) Comp.
    729; 98 E.R. 133 ....20.9, 20.11
Daines v. Taylor [1974] A.C. 207 .... 24.17
Dakin v. Lee. *See* H Dakin & Co. v. Lee
Dakin & Co. v. Lee. *See* H Dakin & Co. v. Lee
Dakin (H) and Co. Ltd v. Lee. *See* H Dakin & Co. v. Lee
Dampskibsselskabet AF 1912 v. Motis Exports Ltd. *See* Motis Exports Ltd v.
    Dampskibsselskabet AF1912 A/S (No.1)
Daniels v. R White and Tarbard. *See* Daniels v. White & Sons Ltd
Daniels v. White & Sons Ltd; *sub nom.* Daniels v. R White and Tarbard [1938] 4 All E.R.
    258, KBD 10.25, 12.22, 23.18
Danka Rentals Ltd v. Xi Software Ltd (1998) 17 Tr. L.R. 74, QBD 17.28
Darlington BC v. Wiltshier Northern Ltd; *sub nom.* Darlington Borough Council [1995] 1
    W.L.R. 68; [1995] 3 All E.R. 895, CA 10.5, 10.7, 10.30, 24.7

Darlington Borough Council. *See* Darlington BC v. Wiltshier Northern Ltd

Dataliner Ltd v. Vehicle Builders and Repairers Association *The Independent*, August 30, 1995, CA 24.11

Daulia Ltd v. Four Millbank Nominees Ltd [1978] Ch. 231; [1978] 2 W.L.R. 621 ....   3.13

David Securities Pty v. Commonwealth Bank of Australia (1992) 175 C.L.R. 353, HC (Aus)   26.24

Davies v. Collins [1945] 1 All E.R. 247, CA 10.28

Davies v. Directloans Ltd ; *sub nom.* Davies and Hedley-Cheney v. Directloans Ltd [1986] 1 W.L.R. 823; [1986] 2 All E.R. 783, Ch D 14.19

Davies v. London and Provincial Marine Insurance Co. (1878) L.R. 8 Ch. D. 469; (1878) 26 W.R. 794, Ch D 15.8

Davies v. Sumner; *sub nom.* Sumner v. Davies [1984] 1 W.L.R. 405, QBD; [1984] 1 W.L.R. 1301; [1984] 3 All E.R. 831, HL 17.13

Davis v. Fareham UDC. *See* Davis Contractors v. Fareham Urban DC

Davis v. Richardson (1790) 1 Bay 105 ....   24.3

Davies and Hedley-Cheney v. Directloans Ltd. *See* Davies v. Directloans Ltd

Davis Contractors v. Fareham Urban DC; *sub nom.* Davis v. Fareham UDC [1956] A.C. 696; [1956] 3 W.L.R. 37, HL 22.8, 22.14, 22.22, 22.23

De Bernardy v. Harding (1853) 8 Ex. 822; 155 E.R. 1586 .... 26.33

Decro-Wall International SA v. Practitioners in Marketing [1971] 1 W.L.R. 361; [1971] 2 All E.R. 216, CA 23.10

Deepak Fertilisers & Petrochemical Corp. v. Davy McKee (London) Ltd; *sub nom.* Deepak Fertilisers & Petrochemicals Corp. v. ICI Chemicals and Polymers Ltd [1999] 1 All E.R. (Comm.) 69; [1999] 1 Lloyd's Rep. 387; [1999] B.L.R. 41, CA 12.9, 16.21

Deepak Fertilisers & Petrochemicals Corp. v. ICI Chemicals and Polymers Ltd. *See* Deepak Fertilisers & Petrochemical Corp. v. Davy McKee (London) Ltd

Denny v. Hancock (1870) LR 6 Ch. App 1 .... 21.19

Denny Mott & Dickson v. James B Fraser & Co.; *sub nom.* James B Fraser & Co. Ltd v Denny Mott & Dickson Ltd; Denny Mott & Dickson Ltd v. James B Fraser [1944] A.C. 265; 1945 S.L.T. 2, HL 22.6, 22.15, 22.16

Denny Mott & Dickson Ltd v. James B Fraser. *See* Denny Mott & Dickson v. James B Fraser & Co.

Derry v. Peek; *sub nom.* Peek v Derry .(1889) L.R. 14 App. Cas. 337; (1889) 5 T.L.R. 625, HL 18.11, 18.18

Dick Bentley Productions Ltd v. Harold Smith (Motors) Ltd [1965] 1 W.L.R. 623; [1965] 2 All E.R. 65, CA 13.1

Dickinson v. Dodds (1875–76) L.R. 2 Ch. D. 463, CA 3.10, 3.12

Diesen v. Samson 1971 S.L.T. (Sh. Ct.) 49, Sh Ct 25.15

Dimmock v. Hallett (1866–67) L.R. 2 Ch. App. 21; (1866) 12 Jur. N.S. 953, CA in Chancery 15.7, 18.6

Diocese of Southwark v. Coker; *sub nom.* Coker v Diocese of Southwark [1998] I.C.R. 140; (1997) 94(29) L.S.G. 29, CA 11.5

Director General of Fair Trading v. First National Bank Plc [2000] Q.B. 672; [2000] 2 W.L.R. 1353; [2000] 2 All E.R. 759, CA 14.23, 15.13, 15.22, 15.23, 15.29, 17.21

Donoghue v. Stevenson; *sub nom.* McAlister v. Stevenson [1932] A.C. 562; 1932 S.C. (H.L.) 31, HL 10.2, 10.25, 26.28

Dorimex v. Visage Imports Ltd, unreported, May 18, 1999, CA 7.4

Doughboy Industries Inc., Matter of, 233 N.Y.S. 2d 488 (1962) 5.10

Dowling & Rutter v. Abacus Frozen Foods Ltd. *See* Dowling & Rutter v. Abacus Frozen Foods Ltd (No.1)

Dowling & Rutter v. Abacus Frozen Foods Ltd (No.1); *sub nom.* Dowling & Rutter v. Abacus Frozen Foods Ltd 2000 G.W.D. 12–412; *The Times*, April 26, 2000, OH 20.6

Downs v. Chappell; Downs v Stephenson Smart [1997] 1 W.L.R. 426; [1996] 3 All E.R. 344; [1996] C.L.C. 1492, CA 18.10, 18.12, 18.17

Doyle v. Olby (Ironmongers) Ltd [1969] 2 Q.B. 158; [1969] 2 W.L.R. 673, CA 18.16

Doyle v. White City Stadium Ltd [1935] 1 K.B. 110, CA 11.6

Drennan v. Star Paving Co., 51 Cal 2d 409, 33 P. 2d 757 (1958) 3.14

Drive Yourself Hire Co. (London) Ltd v. Strutt [1954] 1 Q.B. 250; [1953] 3 W.L.R. 1111,
    CA... 10.2
Duffen v. FRA BO SpA. *See* Duffen v. FRA BO SpA (No.1)
Duffen v. FRA BO SpA (No.1); *sub nom.* Duffen v. FRA BO SpA [1999] E.C.C. 58; *The
    Times*, June 15, 1998, CA 25.31
Dunbar Bank Plc v. Nadeem [1998] 3 All E.R. 876; [1998] 2 F.L.R. 457, CA....19.11, 19.12, 19.19
Dunlop v. Lambert (1839) 6 Cl. & F. 600 ....10.29, 10.30
Dunlop Pneumatic Tyre Co. Ltd v. New Garage & Motor Co. Ltd [1915] A.C. 79,
    HL 25.30, 25.31
Dunlop Pneumatic Tyre Co. Ltd v. Selfridge & Co. Ltd [1915] A.C. 847, HL; [1914] W.N.
    59, CA 7.7, 10.2
Dunn v. Disc Jockey Unlimited Co. (1978) 87 D.L.R. (3d) 408, District Ct (Ont) 25.16
Durham Fancy Goods Ltd v. Michael Jackson (Fancy Goods) Ltd [1968] 2 Q.B. 839;
    [1968] 3 W.L.R. 225, QBD 9.4, 9.11

E A Ajayi v. R T Briscoe (Nigeria) Ltd. *See* Ajayi (t/a Colony Carrier Co.) v. RT Briscoe
    (Nigeria) Ltd
EE Caledonia Ltd (formerly Occidental Petroleum (Caledonia)) v. Orbit Valve Co. Europe
    Plc; *sub nom.* Elf Enterprise Caledonia Ltd (Formerly Occidental Petroleum
    (Caledonia)) v.Orbit Valve Co Europe Plc; EE Caledonia v. Orbit Valve plc [1994] 1
    W.L.R. 1515; [1995] 1 All E.R. 174, CA 16.21, 16.22
EE Caledonia v. Orbit Valve plc. *See* EE Caledonia Ltd (formerly Occidental Petroleum
    (Caledonia)) v. Orbit Valve Co. Europe Plc
Earl of Aylesford v. Morris (1873) L.R. 8 Ch. App. 484, CA 14.14
Earl of Chesterfield v. Janssen. *See* Chesterfield v. Janssen
East v. Maurer [1991] 1 W.L.R. 461; [1991] 2 All E.R. 733, CA.. 18.16
East Ham Corp. v. Bernard Sunley & Sons [1966] A.C. 406; [1965] 3 W.L.R. 1096, HL..... 24.24
Eastbourne Borough Council v. Foster *The Times*, August 17, 2001 .... 23.16
Eastham v. Newcastle United Football Club [1964] Ch. 413; [1963] 3 W.L.R. 574, Ch 26.18
Easton v. Hitchcock [1912] 1 K.B. 535, KBD 12.26
Eastwood v. Kenyon (1840) 11 A and E 438; 113 E.R. 482 ....7.2, 7.14, 7.18
Economides v. Commercial Union Assurance Co. Plc [1998] Q.B. 587; [1997] 3 W.L.R.
    1066, CA 18.5
Edgington v Fitzmaurice (1885) L.R. 29 Ch. D. 459, CA 18.6
Edmund Murray v. BSP International Foundations 33 Con. L.R. 1, CA 16.27
Edmunds v. Merchants' Despatch Transportation Co. (1883) 135 Mass. 283..................... 6.14
Edwards v. Skyways [1964] 1 W.L.R. 349; [1964] 1 All E.R. 494, QBD............................. 11.2
Egg Stores (Stamford Hill), The v. Leibovici (L); *sub nom.* The Egg Stores (Stamford Hill)
    Ltd v. Leibovici [1976] I.R.L.R. 376, EAT 22.9
Elbe, The. *See* Oom v. Bruce
Eleanor Thomas v. Benjamin Thomas (1842) 2 Q.B.851; 114 E.R. 330 ....7.5, 7.16
Electricity Supply Nominees Ltd v. IAF Group Ltd [1993] 1 W.L.R. 1059; [1993] 3 All E.R.
    372, QBD 17.6
Elf Enterprise Caledonia Ltd (Formerly Occidental Petroleum (Caledonia)) v. Orbit Valve
    Co. Europe Plc. *See* EE Caledonia Ltd (formerly Occidental Petroleum (Caledonia))
    v. Orbit Valve Co. Europe Plc
Emmanuel Ajayi v. R.T. Briscoe (Nigeria) Ltd. *See* Ajayi (t/a Colony Carrier Co.) v. RT
    Briscoe (Nigeria) Ltd
Enderby Town FC v. The Football Association. *See* Enderby Town Football Club v.
    Football Association
Enderby Town Football Club v. Football Association; *sub nom.* Enderby Town FC v. The
    Football Association [1971] Ch. 591; [1970] 3 W.L.R. 1021, CA 20.1
Entores Ltd v. Miles Far East Corp.; *sub nom.* Newcomb v. De Roos [1955] 2 Q.B. 327;
    [1955] 3 W.L.R. 48, CA... 4.8
Epaphus, The. *See* Eurico SpA v. Philipp Bros (The Epaphus)
Errington v. Errington and Woods [1952] 1 K.B. 290; [1952] 1 All E.R. 149, CA............... 3.13

Ertel Berber v. Rio Tinto. *See* Ertel Berber & Co. v. Rio Tinto Co. Ltd

Ertel Berber & Co. v. Rio Tinto Co. Ltd; Dynamit AG (Vormals Alfred Nobel Co.) v. Rio
 Tinto Co. Ltd; Vereingte Koenigs v. Rio Tinto Co. Ltd ; *sub nom.* Ertel Berber v. Rio
 Tinto [1918] A.C. 260, HL.. 22.21

Esso Petroleum Co. Ltd. v. Customs and Excise Commissioners [1976] 1 W.L.R. 1; [1976]
 1 All E.R. 117, HL   7.10

Esso Petroleum Co. Ltd v. Harper's Garage (Stourpourt) Ltd [1968] A.C. 269; [1967]
 2 W.L.R. 871; [1967] 1 All E.R. 699 .... 20.25

Esso Petroleum Co. Ltd v. Mardon [1976] Q.B. 801; [1976] 2 W.L.R. 583,CA 18.5, 18.17

Esso Petroleum Co. Ltd v. Milton [1997] 1 W.L.R. 938; [1997] 2 All E.R. 593, CA 8.17

Eurico SpA v. Philipp Bros (The Epaphus) [1987] 2 Lloyd's Rep. 215; [1987] 2 F.T.L.R. 213,
 CA 22.5

Euro-Diam v. Bathurst. *See* Euro-Diam Ltd v. Bathurst

Euro-Diam Ltd v. Bathurst; *sub nom.* Euro-Diam v. Bathurst [1990] 1 Q.B. 1; [1988] 2
 W.L.R. 517 [1990] 1 Q.B. 1; [1988] 2 W.L.R. 517, CA.............................. 20.20

Eurymedon, The. *See* New Zealand Shipping Co. Ltd v. AM Satterthwaite & Co. Ltd (The
 Eurymedon)

Evenden v.Guildford City Association AFC. *See* Evenden v. Guildford City Association
 Football Club

Evenden v. Guildford City Association Football Club; *sub nom.* Guildford City AFC
 [1975] Q.B. 917; [1975] 3 W.L.R. 251, CA.. 9.11

Eves v. Eves [1996] C.L. 638... 9.15

Export Credits Guarantee Department v. Universal Oil Products Co. *See* Export Credits
 Guarantee Department v. Universal Oil Products Co. & Procon Inc. and Procon
 (Great Britain) Ltd

Export Credits Guarantee Department v. Universal Oil Products Co. & Procon Inc.
 and Procon (Great Britain) Ltd; *sub nom.* Export Credits Guarantee
 Department v. Universal Oil Products Co. [1983] 1 W.L.R. 399; [1983] 2 All E.R. 205.
 HL... 25.34

Extrudakerb (Maltby Engineering) Ltd v. White Mountain Quarries Ltd [1996] N.I. 567;
 [1996] C.L.C. 1747; *The Times,* July 10, 1996, QBD (NI) 12.1

FA Tamplin Steamship Co. Ltd v. Anglo Mexican Petroleum Products Co. Ltd; *sub nom.*
 Tamplin SS Ltd v. Anglo Mexican Petroleum Products Co. [1916] 2 A.C. 397, HL;
 [1916] 1 K.B. 485, CA 12.30, 22.23

FW Moore & Co. Ltd v. Landauer & Co.; *sub nom.* Arbitration Between Moore & Co. Ltd
 and Landauer & Co Re; Moore and Landauer and Co., Re [1921] 2 K.B. 519; (1921)
 6 Ll. L. Rep. 384, CA 13.11

Fairclough Building Ltd v. Port Talbot BC (1993)62 B.L.R. 82; 33 Con. L.R. 24, CA 3.9, 14.27

Falck v. Williams [1900] A.C. 176, PC 6.8

Farley v. Skinner. *See* Farley v. Skinner (No.2)

Farley v. Skinner (No.2); *sub nom.* Farley v. Skinner [2001] UKHL 49; *The Times,*
 October 15, 2001 .... 24.27

Farley v. Skinner (No.2); *sub nom.* Farley v. Skinner 73 Con. L.R. 70; [2000] Lloyd's Rep.
 P.N. 516; *The Times*, April 14, 2000, CA....................................25.18, 25.19

Fawcett v. Saint Merat. *See* Fawcett v Star Car Sales

Fawcett v. Star Car Sales; *sub nom.* Fawcett v Saint Merat [1960] N.Z.L.R. 406, CA; [1959]
 N.Z.L.R. 952 .... 6.17

Federal Commerce & Navigation Co. Ltd v. Molena Alpha Inc. (The Nanfri); Federal
 Commerce & Navigation Co. Ltd v. Molena Beta Inc. (The Benfri); Federal
 Commerce & Navigation Co. Ltd v. Molena Gamma Inc. (The Lorfri) [1979] A.C.
 757; [1978] 3 W.L.R. 991, HL; [1976] 1 Lloyd's Rep. 201....................23.12– 23.14

Felthouse v. Bindley (1862) 6 L.T. 157; 11 C.B.(N.S.) 869, 142 E.R. 1037 ....2.10, 4.22, 4.24

Fenton v. Victoria Seats Agency (1903) 19 T.L.R. 16....................................... 22.13

Fercometal Sarl v. Mediterranean Shipping. *See* Fercometal Sarl v. MSC Mediterranean
 Shipping Co. SA (The Simona)

Fercometal Sarl v. MSC Mediterranean Shipping Co. SA (The Simona); *sub nom.*

Fercometal Sarl v. Mediterranean Shipping [1989] A.C. 788; [1988] 3 W.L.R. 200; [1988] 2 All E.R. 742, HL 23.5, 23.6

Fibrosa Societé Anonyme v. Fairbairn Lawson Combe Barbour Ltd. *See* Fibrosa Spolka Akcyjna v. Fairbairn Lawson Combe Barbour Ltd

Fibrosa Spolka Akcyjna v. Fairbairn Lawson. *See* Fibrosa Spolka Akcyjna v. Fairbairn Lawson Combe Barbour Ltd

Fibrosa Spolka Akcyjna v. Fairbairn Lawson Combe Barbour Ltd; *sub nom.* Fibrosa Societé Anonyme v. Fairbairn Lawson Combe Barbour Ltd; Fibrosa Spolka Akcyjna v. Fairbairn Lawson [1943] A.C. 32; [1942] 2 All E.R. 122, HL 22.11, 22.23, 26.30

Financings v. Stimson [1962] 1 W.L.R. 1184; [1962] 3 All E.R. 386, CA 3.14

Financings Ltd v. Baldock [1963] 2 Q.B. 104; [1963] 2 W.L.R. 359, CA; [1962] A.C. 600 ... 25.34

Finland Steamship Co. Ltd v. Felixstowe Dock & Railway Co. 1980] 2 Lloyd's Rep. 287, QBD (Comm Ct) 8.6

First Energy (UK) v. Hungarian International Bank [1993] 2 Lloyd's Rep. 194; [1993] B.C.L.C. 1409, CA 1.6

First National Bank Plc v. Thompson [1996] Ch. 231; [1996] 2 W.L.R. 293; [1996] 1 All E.R. 140, CA 9.19

First Sport Ltd v. Barclays Bank Plc [1993] 1 W.L.R. 1229; [1993] 3 All E.R. 789, CA 4.21

Firstpost Homes Ltd v. Johnson [1995] 1 W.L.R. 1567; [1995] 4 All E.R. 355, CA 11.9

Fisher v Bell [1961] 1 Q.B. 394; [1960] 3 W.L.R. 919, DC 3.4

Fitch v. Snedaker, 38 N.Y. 248 (1868).. 4.6

Flamar Interocean v. Denmac (The Flamar Pride and The Flamar Progress); *sub nom.* Flamar Interocean Ltd v. Denmac Ltd The Flamar Pride [1990] 1 Lloyd's Rep. 434; *Lloyd's List*, January 5, 1990, QBD (Comm Ct) 17.15, 17.31

Flamar Interocean Ltd v. Denmac Ltd The Flamar Pride. *See* Flamar Interocean v. Denmac (The Flamar Pride and The Flamar Progress)

Flavell, Re; *sub nom.* Murray v Flavell (1884) L.R. 25 Ch. D. 89, CA 10.26

Foakes v. Beer (1884) L.R. 9 App. Cas. 605, HL 8.10, 8.11, 8.14–8.17, 8.23, 8.24, 9.3, 9.5

Foley v. Classique Coaches Ltd [1934] 2 K.B. 1, CA.. 5.13

Food Corp of India v. Antclizo Shipping Corp (The Antclizo) [1988] 1 W.L.R. 603; [1988] 2 All E.R. 513, HL; [1987] 2 Lloyd's Rep. 130, CA.. 2.7

Ford Motor Company v. Armstrong (1915) 31 T.L.R. 267 .... 15.32

Forman & Co. Proprietary Ltd v. Liddesdale, The; *sub nom.* Forman & Co. Proprietary Ltd v. The Ship Liddesdale [1900] A.C. 190, PC 23.22, 23.24

Forman & Co. Proprietary Ltd v. The Ship Liddesdale. *See* Forman & Co. Proprietary Ltd v. Liddesdale, The

Forsikringsaktieselskapet Vesta v. Butcher [1989] A.C. 852; [1989] 2 W.L.R. 290, HL; [1988] 2 All E.R. 43..25.27, 25.28

Forster v. Silvermere Golf and Equestrian Centre 125 S.J. 397 .... 10.5

Frances & Jane, The v. Luna, The. *See* Luna, The

Frederick E Rose (London) Ltd v. William H Pim Junior & Co. Ltd [1953] 2 Q.B. 450; [1953] 3 W.L.R. 497; [1953] 2 All E.R. 739, CA.. 21.12

Freeguard v. Rogers (No.1); *sub nom.* Margo Freeguard v. Ingrid Rogers[1999] 1 W.L.R. 375; [1998] E.G.C.S. 145; *The Times*, October 22, 1998, CA...................................... 12.7

Freeth v. Burr (1873–74) L.R. 9 C.P. 208, CCP 23.11

Fry v. Lane; *sub nom.* Whittet v Bush; Fry, Re (1889) L.R. 40 Ch. D. 312, Ch. D 14.14, 14.15, 14.17, 17.27

Furness Withy (Australia) Ltd v. Metal Distributors (UK) Ltd (The Amazonia) [1990] 1 Lloyd's Rep. 236[1989] 1 Lloyd's Rep. 403, QBD (Comm Ct)................................... 2.10

Fyffes Group Ltd v. Reefer Express Lines Pty Ltd [1996] 2 Lloyd's Rep. 171, QBD (Comm Ct) 25.5

G. Percy Trentham Ltd v. Archital Luxfer Ltd [1993] 1 Lloyd's Rep. 25; 63 B.L.R. 44, CA 5.5

G. Scammell and Nephew Ltd v. H.C. & J.G. Ouston [1941] A.C. 251, HL.....................5.11, 5.12

Gafford v. Graham (1999) 77 P. & C.R. 73; [1999] 3 E.G.L.R. 75; (1998) 95(21) L.S.G. 36, CA.. 26.16

Gallie v. Lee. *See* Saunders (Executrix of the Estate of Rose Maud Gallie) v. Anglia Building Society (formerly Northampton Town and County Building Society)

Galoo Ltd v. Bright Grahame Murray [1994] 1 W.L.R. 1360; [1994] 1 All E.R. 16, CA 25.22

Gamerco SA v. ICM/Fair Warning (Agency) Ltd [1995] 1 W.L.R. 1126; [1995] E.M.L.R. 263, QBD 5.17, 22.26, 22.28, 22.29

Gator Shipping Corp. v. Trans-Asiatic Oil SA and Occidental Shipping Etablissement SA (The Odenfeld); *sub nom.* The Gator Shipping Corp. v. Trans-Asiatic Oil SA The Odenfeld [1978] 2 Lloyd's Rep. 357, QBD (Comm Ct) 23.10

Gatty v. Maclaine. *See* Maclaine v. Gatty

Gebr Van Weelde Scheepvaart Kantoor BV v. Compania Naviera Sea Orient SA (The Agrabele) (No.2) [1987] 2 Lloyd's Rep. 223, CA; [1985] 2 Lloyd's Rep. 496, QBD (Comm Ct) 2.7

George Mitchell (Chesterhall) Ltd v. Finney Lock Seeds Ltd [1983] 2 A.C. 803; [1983] 3 W.L.R. 163, HL; [1983] 1 All E.R. 108, CA 13.4, 16.19, 16.24, 16.25, 17.26, 17.28, 17.32

George Smith v. William Kay (1859) 7 H.L.C. 750; 11 E.R. 299 .... 19.15

Gibbons v. Proctor (1891) 64 L.T. 594 .... 4.6

Gibson v. Manchester City Council [1979] 1 W.L.R. 294; [1979] 1 All E.R. 972, HL; [1978] 2 All E.R. 583, CA 5.4

Gilbert Ash v. Modern Engineering. *See* Gilbert Ash (Northern) Ltd v. Modern Engineering (Bristol) Ltd

Gilbert Ash (Northern) Ltd v. Modern Engineering (Bristol) Ltd; *sub nom.* Modern Engineering (Bristol) Ltd v. Gilbert Ash (Northern) Ltd; Gilbert Ash v. Modern Engineering [1974] A.C. 689; [1973] 3 W.L.R. 421, HL 25.35

Gillespie v. Cheney Egar & Co. *See* Gillespie Bros & Co. v. Cheney Eggar & Co.

Gillespie Bros & Co. v Cheney Eggar & Co.; *sub nom.* Gillespie v. Cheney Egar & Co. [1896] 2 Q.B. 59, QBD 12.6, 12.10

Gillett v. Holt [2001] Ch. 210; [2000] 3 W.L.R. 815; [2000] 2 All E.R. 289, CA 9.15, 9.16

Giumelli v. Giumelli [1999] H.C.A. 10 ....9.21, 24.21

Glamorgan CC v. Glasbrook Bros Ltd. *See* Glasbrook Bros Ltd v. Glamorgan CC

Glasbrook Brothers v. Glamorgan County Council. *See* Glasbrook Bros Ltd v. Glamorgan CC Glasbrook Bros Ltd v. Glamorgan CC; *sub nom.* Glamorgan CC v. Glasbrook Bros Ltd; Glasbrook Brothers v. Glamorgan County Council [1925] A.C. 270, HL; [1924] 1 K.B. 879, CA 8.1

Glencore Grain Rotterdam BV v. Lebanese Organisation for International Commerce (The Lorico); *sub nom.* Glencore Grain Rotterdam BV v. LORICO [1997] 4 All E.R. 514; [1997] 2 Lloyd's Rep. 386, CA 9.18

Glencore Grain Rotterdam BV v. LORICO. *See* Glencore Grain Rotterdam BV v. Lebanese Organisation for International Commerce (The Lorico)

Global Tankers Inc. v. Amercoat Europe [1975] 1 Lloyd's Rep. 666, QBD 4.2

Goddard v. O'Brien (1882) L.R. 9 Q.B.D. 37, QBD 8.16

Godley v. Perry [1960] 1 W.L.R. 9; [1960] 1 All E.R. 36, QBD 12.21

Gogay v. Hertfordshire CC [2000] I.R.L.R. 703; [2001] 1 F.L.R. 280, CA 25.13

Goldsmith v. Rodger [1962] 2 Lloyd's Rep. 249, CA 18.4

Goldsworthy v. Brickell [1987] Ch. 378; [1987] 2 W.L.R. 133, CA 9.8, 19.15, 19.16

Good v. Cheeseman (1831) 2 B and Ad 328; 172 E.R. 805 .... 8.18

Good Luck, The. *See* Bank of Nova Scotia v. Hellenic Mutual War Risk Association (Bermuda) Ltd (The Good Luck) (No.2)

Gordon v. Selico Co. (1986) 18 H.L.R. 219; [1986] 1 E.G.L.R. 71; (1986) 278 E.G. 53, CA 15.7, 18.4

Gore v. Gibson (1843) 13 M and W, 623; 153 E.R. 260 ....11.5, 11.7

Gosling v. Anderson (1972) 223 E.G. 1743; *The Times,* February 8, 1972, CA 18.24

Goss v. Chilcott [1996] A.C. 788; [1996] 3 W.L.R. 180, PC 26.24

Goulden v. Wilson Barca. *See* Goulden v. Wilson Barca (A Firm)

Goulden v. Wilson Barca (A Firm); *sub nom.* Goulden v. Wilson Barca [2000] 1 W.L.R. 167; (1999) 96(31) L.S.G. 35; *The Times*, August 20, 1999, CA... 8.1

Grainger & Son v. Gough (Surveyor of Taxes) [1896] A.C. 325, HL; [1895] 1 Q.B. 71, CA 3.6

Gran Gelato Ltd v. Richcliff (Group) Ltd [1992] Ch. 560; [1992] 2 W.L.R. 867; [1992] 1 All
    E.R. 865, Ch D 25.28
Greasley v. Cooke [1980] 1 W.L.R. 1306; [1980] 3 All E.R. 710, CA 9.15
Great Northern Railway Company v. Witham (1873) LR 9 CP 16 .... 3.12
Greater London Council v. Connolly [1970] 2 Q.B. 100; [1970] 2 W.L.R. 658, CA 5.11
Greaves & Co. (Contractors) Ltd v. Baynham Meikle & Partners [1975] 1 W.L.R. 1095;
    [1975] 3 All E.R. 99, CA 12.26
Griffiths v. Brymer (1903) 19 T.L.R. 434 ....21.6, 22.13
Grist v. Bailey [1967] Ch. 532; [1966] 3 W.L.R. 618, Ch D 21.12, 21.19
Grogan v. Robin Meredith Plant Hire [1996] C.L.C. 1127; 53 Con. L.R. 87, CA 16.9
Guildford v. Lockyer [1975] Crim. L.R. 235; (1975) 119 S.J. 353, DC 3.3
Guimelli v. Guimelli (1999) 161 A.L.R. 473 ....9.21, 24.20
Guiness (Bob) v. Salomonsen: *sub nom.* Bob Guiness Ltd v. Salomonsen [1948] 2 K.B. 42;
    64 T.L.R. 306, KBD 7.4, 7.16, 8.18
Gustavus Couturier v. Hastie. *See* Couturier v. Hastie

H Dakin & Co. v. Lee; *sub nom.* Dakin & Co. v. Lee; Dakin v. Lee; Dakin (H) and Co. Ltd
    v. Lee [1916] 1 K.B. 566, CA 23.30
H Parsons v. Uttley Ingham and Co. Ltd. *See* Parsons (Livestock) Ltd v. Uttley Ingham &
    Co. Ltd
H.M. 24 Hour Vehicle Recovery v. Hall, unreported, July 5, 1996, CC; (1996) C.L.Y.1128   9.2
HSBC Plc v. Mutual Insurance (UK) Ltd *The Times*, June 11, 2001 .... 12.12
Hadley v. Baxendale (1854) 9 Ex. 341, Ex Ct; 156 E.R. 145 ....24.13, 25.3–25.5, 25.6, 25.8
Halifax Financial Services Ltd v. Intuitive Systems Ltd [1999] 1 All E.R. (Comm) 303;
    (2000) 2 T.C.L.R. 35, QBD 5.16, 13.6, 14.29
Hall v. Woolston Hall Leisure Ltd [2001] 1 W.L.R. 225; [2000] 4 All E.R. 787, CA 20.6
Hamer v. Sidway 27 NE 256 (1891)...7.11, 7.12
Hamlyn & Co. v. Wood & Co. [1891] 2 Q.B. 488, CA 12.24
Hanjin Shipping Co. Ltd v. Zenith Chartering Corp. (The Mercedes Envoy) [1995] 2
    Lloyd's Rep. 559, QBD (Comm Ct) 5.16, 11.2
Harbutts Plasticine v. Wayne Tank & Pump Co. Ltd. *See* Harbutt's Plasticine Ltd v. Wayne
    Tank & Pump Co. Ltd
Harbutt's Plasticine v. Wayne Tank & Pump Co. Ltd; *sub nom.* Harbutts Plasticine v.
    Wayne Tank & Pump Co. Ltd [1970] 1 Q.B. 447; [1970] 2 W.L.R. 198, CA 16.25, 23.3
Hardwick Game Farm v. Suffolk Agricultural and Poultry Producers Association Ltd. *See*
    Henry Kendall & Sons v. William Lillico & Sons Ltd
Hare v. Murphy Bros [1974] 3 All E.R. 940; [1974] I.C.R. 603, CA 22.9
Harris v. Great Western Railway Co. (1875–76) L.R. 1 Q.B.D. 515, QBD 16.8
Harris v. Nickerson (1873) L.R. 8 Q.B. 286 .... 3.7
Harris v. Sheffield United Football Club; *sub nom.* Sheffield United Football Club v. South
    Yorkshire Police Authority [1988] Q.B. 77; [1987] 3 W.L.R. 305; [1987] 2 All E.R. 838   8.1
Harris v. Watson (1791) Peake 102; 170 E.R. 94 ....8.2, 8.8
Harris v. Wyre Forest DC [1990] A.C.831; [1988] Q.B. 835; [1988] 2 W.L.R. 1173, CA
    ....17.10, 17.17
Harrods Ltd v. Schwartz-Sackin & Co Ltd [1991] F.S.R. 209, CA; [1986] F.S.R. 490,
    Ch. D.. 12.2
Hart v. O'Connor [1985] A.C. 1000; [1985] 3 W.L.R. 214, PC 11.7, 14.3
Hartley v. Hymans [1920] 3 K.B. 475, KBD 13.23
Hartley v. Ponsonby (1857) 7 E and B 872.. 8.3
Hartog v. Colin and Shields [1939] 3 All E.R. 566 .... 6.3
Harvela Investments Ltd v Royal Trust Co. of Canada (CI) Ltd [1986] A.C. 207; [1985] 3
    W.L.R. 276, HL... 3.8
Harvey v. Ventilatoren-Fabrik Oelde GmbH (1989) 8 Tr. L.R. 138; *The Financial Times*,
    November 11, 1988, CA 16.6
Hawkes v. Saunders (1782) 1 Cowp 289; 98 E.R. 1091 .... 7.2
Hayes v. Dodd. *See* Hayes v. James & Charles Dodd (A Firm)

Hayes v. James & Charles Dodd (A Firm); *sub nom.* Hayes v. Dodd [1990] 2 All E.R. 815;
    (1988) 138 N.L.J. 259, CA 24.19, 25.9
Hayes v. Securities and Facilities Division. *See* Hayes v. Security Facilities Division
Hayes v. Security Facilities Division; *sub nom.* Hayes v. Securities and Facilities Division
    The Times, April 26, 2000, CA 8.21
Heathcote Ball & Co. (Commercial Auctions) Ltd v. Barry. *See* Barry v. Davies (t/a
    Heathcote Ball & Co.)
Hedley Byrne v. Joseph Heller and Partners. *See* Hedley Byrne & Co Ltd v. Heller &
    Partners Ltd
Hedley Byrne & Co. Ltd v. Heller & Partners Ltd; *sub nom.* Hedley Byrne v. Joseph Heller
    and Partners [1964] A.C. 465; [1963] 3 W.L.R. 101, HL..18.11, 18.13
Heilbut Symons & Co. v. Buckleton [1913] A.C. 30, HL 11.1
Henderson v. Merrett Syndicates Ltd; Hallam-Eames v. Merrett Syndicates Ltd; Hughes
    v. Merrett Syndicates Ltd; Arbuthnott v. Fagan and Feltrim Underwriting Agencies;
    Deeny v. Gooda Walker Ltd[1995] 2 A.C. 145; [1994] 3 W.L.R. 761; [1994] 3 All E.R.
    506, HL 1.5
Henderson v. Stevenson (1875) L.R. 2 Sc. 470; (1875) 2 R. (H.L.) 71, HL 16.12
Henkel v. Pape 6 Ex. 7 (1870) 4.16
Henry Kendall & Sons v. William Lillico & Sons Ltd : *sub nom.* Hardwick Game Farm v.
    Suffolk Agricultural and Poultry Producers Association Ltd; Holland Colombo
    Trading Society Ltd v. Grimsdale & Sons Ltd; Grimsdale & Sons Ltd v. Suffolk
    Agricultural Poultry Producers Association [1969] 2 A.C. 31; [1968] 3 W.L.R. 110,
    HL 5.9, 16.17
Henry Pigot's case. *See* Pigots's Case.
Henthorn v. Fraser [1892] 2 Ch. 27, CA 3.12, 4.15, 4.17
Hermann v. Charlesworth [1905] 2 K.B. 123, CA; [1905] 1 K.B. 24, KBD 20.12
Herne Bay Steam Boat Co. v. Hutton [1903] 2 K.B. 683, CA 22.10, 22.11
Heron Garage Properties Ltd v. Moss [1974] 1 W.L.R. 148; [1974] 1 All E.R. 421;
    (1974) 28 P. & C.R. 54 .... 13.6
Heyman v. Darwins Ltd [1942] A.C. 356; [1942] 1 All E.R. 337, HL................................ 23.3
Heywood v. Wellers. *See* Heywood v. Wellers (A Firm)
Heywood v. Wellers (A Firm); *sub nom.* Heywood v. Wellers [1976] Q.B. 446; [1976] 2
    W.L.R. 101, CA 25.17
Hichens v. General Guarantee Corp Ltd. *See* Hitchens v. General Guarantee Corp Ltd
Highland and Universal Properties Ltd v. Safeway Properties Ltd. *See* Highland and
    Universal Properties Ltd v. Safeway Properties Ltd (No.2)
Highland and Universal Properties Ltd v. Safeway Properties Ltd (No.2); *sub nom.*
    Highland and Universal Properties Ltd v. Safeway Properties Ltd 2000 S.C. 297; 2000
    S.L.T. 414, 1 Div. 26.6
Hill v. CA Parsons & Co.; *sub nom.* Hill v. Parsons and Co. [1972] Ch. 305; [1971] 3 W.L.R.
    995, CA 26.8
Hill v. Parsons and Co. *See* Hill v. CA Parsons & Co.
Hillas & Co. v. Arcos (1932) 147 L.T. 503.. 5.12
Hirachand Punamchand v. Temple [1911] 2 K.B. 330, CA 8.17
Hirji Mulji v. Cheong Yue SS Co. Ltd. *See* Hirji Mulji v. Cheong Yue Steamship Co. Ltd
Hirji Mulji v. Cheong Yue Steamship Co. Ltd; *sub nom.* Hirji Mulji v. Cheong Yue SS Co.
    Ltd [1926] A.C. 497; [1926] W.N. 89, PC 22.22, 22.24
Hispanica de Petroles SA v. Vencedora Oceanica Navegacion SA (The Kapetan Markos
    NL) (No.2) [1987] 2 Lloyd's Rep. 321, CA; [1986] 1 Lloyd's Rep. 238 (Note), QBD
    (Comm Ct) 5.6
Hitchens v. General Guarantee Corp Ltd; *sub nom.* Hichens v General Guarantee Corp
    Ltd [2001] EWCA Civ 359; *The Times*, March 13, 2001, CA 4.1
Hobbs v. London & South Western Railway, Co.; *sub nom.* Hobbs v. London and S.W.
    Railway Co. (1875) L.R. 10 Q.B. 111, QB 25.18
Hobbs v. London and S.W. Railway Co. *See* Hobbs v. London & South Western Railway,
    Co.

Hobson v. Pattenden (1903) 19 T.L.R. 186 .... 22.12
Hochster v. De La Tour (1853) 2 El. & Bl. 678 ....23.5, 23.6
Hoenig v. Isaacs [1952] 2 All E.R. 176; [1952] 1 T.L.R. 1360, CA 23.30, 23.31
Hoffman v. Red Owl Stores 133 N.W. 2d 267 ....9.9, 9.14
Hollier v. Rambler Motors (AMC) Ltd. *See* Hollier v. Rambler Motors
Hollier v. Rambler Motors; *sub nom.* Hollier v. Rambler Motors (AMC) Ltd [1972] 2 Q.B.
    71; [1972] 2 W.L.R. 401; [1972] 1 All E.R. 399, CA 16.18
Holman v. Johnson (1775) 1 Cowp. 341; 98 E.R. 1120...20.15, 20.20
Holwell Securities Ltd v. Hughes [1974] 1 W.L.R. 155; [1974] 1 All E.R. 161, CA............ 4.15
Hone v. Going Places Leisure Travel *The Times*, August 6, 2001 .... 13.3
Hong Kong Fir Shipping Co. Ltd v. Kawasaki Kisen Kaisha Ltd (The Hongkong Fir)
    [1962] 2 Q.B. 26; [1962] 2 W.L.R. 474, CA 13.15, 13.16, 13.18, 13.21
Horne v. Midland Railway Co. (1872–73) L.R. 8 C.P. 131, Ex Chamber........................... 25.5
Horsfall v. Thomas (1862) 1 H and C 90; 158 E.R. 813.. 18.8
Hostler, Case of an. *See* Case of an Hostler
Hotson v. East Berkshire HA; *sub nom.* Hotson v. Fitzgerald; Hotson v. East Berkshire
    Health Authority [1987] A.C. 750; [1987] 3 W.L.R. 232, HL 24.17
Hotson v. East Berkshire Health Authority. *See* Hotson v. East Berkshire H A
Hotson v. Fitzgerald. *See* Hotson v. East Berkshire H A
Hounslow LBC v. Twickenham Garden Developments Ltd [1971] Ch. 233; [1970] 3 W.L.R.
    538, Ch D.. 23.8
Household Fire & Carriage Accident Insurance Co. Ltd v. Grant (1878–79) L.R. 4 Ex. D.
    216, CA 4.14
Howard Marine & Dredging Co. Ltd v. A Ogden & Sons (Excavations) Ltd [1978] Q.B.
    574; [1978] 2 W.L.R. 515, CA...18.14, 18.25
Howard v. Pickford Tool Co. [1951] 1 K.B. 417; 95 S.J. 44, CA 23.3
Howard v. Shirlstar Container Transport [1990] 1 W.L.R. 1292; [1990] 3 All E.R. 366,
    CA.. 20.20
Howatson v. Webb [1908] 1 Ch. 1..21.18, 21.19
Hughes v. Asset Managers Plc [1995] 3 All E.R. 669; *The Independent*, June 13, 1994 (C.S.),
    CA.. 20.3
Hughes v. Clewley (The Siben) (No.2); *sub nom.* Hughes v. Vail Blyth Clewley (The Siben)
    [1996] 1 Lloyd's Rep. 35, QBD (Adm Ct) 18.12, 18.23, 20.10, 20.20
Hughes v. Greenwich LBC [1994] 1 A.C. 170; [1993] 3 W.L.R. 821, HL............................ 12.30
Hughes v. Metropolitan Railway Co. (1877) L.R. 2 App. Cas. 439, HL.............8.22–8.24, 9.3, 9.4,
    9.10–9.12
Hughes v. Vail Blyth Clewley (The Siben). *See* Hughes v. Clewley (The Siben) (No.2)
Hutton v. Warren (1836) M and W 466; 150 E.R. 517... 12.18
Hyde v. Wrench (1840) 3 Beav. 334, 49 E.R.132... 4.2

Imperial Group Pension Trust Ltd v. Imperial Tobacco Ltd [1991] 1 W.L.R. 589; [1991] 2
    All E.R. 597, Ch D... 14.25
Industrial Properties Ltd v. Associated Electrical Industries Ltd. *See* Industrial Properties
    (Barton Hill) Ltd v. Associated Electrical Industries Ltd Industrial Properties (Barton
    Hill) Ltd v. Associated Electrical Industries Ltd; *sub nom.* Industrial Properties Ltd v.
    Associated Electrical Industries Ltd [1977] Q.B. 580; [1977] 2 W.L.R. 726, CA.......... 18.10
Ingmar GB v. Eaton Leonard Technologies. *See* Ingmar GB Ltd v. Eaton Leonard
    Technologies Inc.
Ingmar GB Ltd v. Eaton Leonard Technologies Inc.; *sub nom.* Ingmar GB v. Eaton
    Leonard Technologies [2001] All E.R. (EC) 57; [2001] 1 All E.R. (Comm) 329; *The
    Times*, November 16, 2000, ECJ (5th Chamber) 24.28
Ingram v Little; *sub nom.* Little v. Ingram [1961] 1 Q.B. 31; [1960] 3 W.L.R. 504, CA......2.2, 6.15,
    6.17, 18.1, 21.19, 21.25
Inntrepreneur Pub Co. (GL) v. East Crown Ltd. *See* Inntrepreneur Pub Co. Ltd v. East
    Crown Ltd
Inntrepreneur Pub Co. Ltd v. East Crown Ltd; *sub nom.* Inntrepreneur Pub Co. (GL) v.

East Crown Ltd [2000] 2 Lloyd's Rep. 611; [2000] 3 E.G.L.R. 31; *The Times,*
    September 5, 2000, Ch. D 12.9, 16.10
Interfoto Picture Library Ltd v. Stiletto Visual Programmes Ltd [1989] Q.B. 433; [1988] 2
    W.L.R. 615, CA 14.10, 14.11, 14.12, 14.21, 16.7, 16.8, 16.15
Investors Compensation Scheme Ltd v. West Bromwich Building Society (No.1); Investors
    Compensation Scheme Ltd v. Hopkin & Sons; Alford v. West Bromwich Building
    Society; Armitage v. West Bromwich Building Society [1998] 1 W.L.R. 896; [1998] 1
    All E.R. 98, HL 12.2
Irons v. Partick Thistle Football Club Ltd 1997 S.L.T. 983, OH.......................................   12.6

J Evans & Son (Portsmouth) Ltd v. Andrea Merzario Ltd [1976] 1 W.L.R. 1078; [1976] 2
    All E.R. 930, CA 16.10
J Lauritzen A/S v. Wijsmuller BV (The Super Servant Two) [1990] 1 Lloyd's Rep. 1, CA;
    [1989] 1 Lloyd's Rep. 148, QBD (Comm Ct) 22.18, 22.22
JEB Fasteners Ltd v. Marks Bloom & Co. [1983] 1 All E.R. 583, CA; [1981] 3 All E.R. 289,
    QBD 18.7, 18.9
Jackson v. Horizon Holidays Ltd [1975] 1 W.L.R. 1468; [1975] 3 All E.R. 92, CA 10.8, 10.26,
                                                                                                      10.29, 24.7, 25.16
Jacobs v. Batavia and General Plantations Trust Ltd [1924] 2 Ch. 329, CA; [1924] 1 Ch.
    287, Ch D 12.4
Jaggard v. Sawyer [1995] 1 W.L.R. 269; [1995] 2 All E.R. 189, CA 26.11, 26.12, 26.14–26.17
James B Fraser & Co. Ltd v Denny Mott & Dickson Ltd. *See* Denny Mott & Dickson v.
    James B Fraser & Co.
James Cundy and T. Bevington v. Thomas Lindsay. *See* Cundy v. Lindsay
James Miller & Partners Ltd v. Whitworth Street Estates (Manchester) Ltd. *See* Whitworth
    Street Estates (Manchester) Ltd v. James Miller & Partners Ltd
James Scott & Sons Ltd v. R and N Del Sel (1922) S.C. 592...   22.8
Jarvis v. Swans Tours Ltd [1973] Q.B. 233; [1972] 3 W.L.R. 954, CA 25.15
Jesse v. Roy (1834) 1 CM and R 316; 149 E.R. 1101 ....   23.21
Jobson v. Johnson [1989] 1 W.L.R. 1026; [1989] 1 All E.R. 621, CA..................................   25.33
Joel v. Law Union and Crown Insurance Co. [1908] 2 K.B. 863, CA; [1908] 2 K.B. 431,
    KBD...   15.10
Johnson v. Agnew [1980] A.C. 367; [1979] 2 W.L.R. 487, HL 23.4, 26.12, 26.16
Johnson v. Unisys Ltd [2001] UKHL 13; [2001] 2 W.L.R. 1076; Times, March 23, 2001, HL
    ....1.12, 25.10, 25.11, 25.13
Johnson Matthey Bankers Ltd v. State Trading Corp. of India Ltd [1984] 1 Lloyd's Rep.
    427, QBD (Comm Ct) 5.7
Johnstone v. Bloomsbury Area Health Authority. *See* Johnstone v. Bloomsbury HA
Johnstone v. Bloomsbury HA; *sub nom.* Johnstone v. Bloomsbury Area Health Authority
    [1992] Q.B. 333; [1991] 2 W.L.R. 1362; [1991] 2 All E.R. 293, CA 12.30, 17.19
Jones v. Daniel [1894] 2 Ch. 332, Ch D 4.2
Jones v. Just (1868) LR 3 Q.B. 197..   12.20
Jones v. Padavatton [1969] 1 W.L.R. 328; [1969] 2 All E.R. 616, CA 11.3
Jones v. Schiffman (1971) 124 C.L.R. 303
Jorden v. Money (1854) 5 H.L. Cas 185; 10 E.R. 868 ....9.2, 9.5
Joscelin and Shelton's Case [1557] 3 Leonard 4; 74 E.R. 503
Joscelyne v. Nissen [1970] 2 Q.B. 86; [1970] 2 W.L.R. 509, CA ....'..........   21.21
Joseph Constantine Steamship Line Ltd v. Imperial Smelting. *See* Joseph Constantine
    Steamship Line Ltd v. Imperial Smelting Corp. Ltd
Joseph Constantine Steamship Line Ltd v. Imperial Smelting Corp. Ltd; *sub nom.* Joseph
    Constantine Steamship Line Ltd v. Imperial Smelting [1942] A.C. 154; [1941] 2 All
    E.R. 165, HL 22.18
Joseph Rann v. Isabella Hughes. *See* Rann v. Hughes

Kalsep Ltd v. X-Flow BV *The Times,* May 3, 2001, Ch D 14.17, 21.3
Karsales (Harrow) Ltd v. Wallis [1956] 1 W.L.R. 936; [1956] 2 All E.R. 866, CA...............   16.24

Kaufman v. Gerson [1904] 1 K.B. 591, CA; [1903] 2 K.B. 114, KBD 19.4
Kearley v. Thomson (1890) L.R. 24 Q.B.D. 742, CA 20.16
Kemble v. Farren (1829) 6 Bing. 141; 130 E.R. 1234... 25.29
Kendall Sons v. Lillico and Sons Ltd. *See* Henry Kendall & Sons v. William Lillico & Sons
    Ltd
Kennedy v. Thomassen [1929] 1 Ch. 426, Ch D 4.7
Ketley v. Scott [1981] I.C.R. 241 .... 14.19
King v. T Tunnock Ltd 2000 S.C. 424; 2000 S.L.T. 744; *The Times*, May 12, 2000, Ex. Div.
    ....1.16, 24.28
King's Motors (Oxford) v. Lax; *sub nom.* Kings Motors (Oxford) Ltd v. Lax [1970] 1
    W.L.R. 426; [1969] 3 All E.R. 665, Chancery Ct of Lancaster 5.12
Kings Motors (Oxford) Ltd v. Lax. *See* King's Motors (Oxford) v. Lax
King's Norton Metal Co. v. Edridge Merrett & Co. (1897) 14 T.L.R. 98 .... 6.11, 6.12
Kiriri Cotton Co. Ltd v. Dewani; *sub nom.* Kiriri Cotton Ct v. Dewani [1960] A.C. 192;
    [1960] 2 W.L.R. 127, PC 20.16
Kiriri Cotton Ct v. Dewani. *See* Kiriri Cotton Co. Ltd v. Dewani
Kitchen v. Royal Air Force Association [1958] 1 W.L.R. 563; [1958] 2 All E.R. 241,
    CA... 24.16
Kleinwort Benson Ltd v. Malaysia Mining Corp Bhd [1989] 1 W.L.R. 379; [1989] 1 All
    E.R. 785, CA 11.2
Koufos v. C Czarnikow Ltd. *See* Koufos v. C Czarnikow Ltd (The Heron II)
Koufos v. C Czarnikow Ltd (The Heron II); *sub nom.* Koufos v. C Czarnikow Ltd;
    C Czarnikow Ltd v. Koufos (The Heron II) [1969] 1 A.C. 350; [1967] 3 W.L.R. 1491,
    HL 25.4, 25.5, 25.6
Krell v. Henry [1903] 2 K.B. 740, CA....................................12.7, 22.10–22.12, 22.19, 22.20
Kristina Sheffield v. Pickfords Ltd. *See* Sheffield v. Pickfords Ltd

Lake v. Simmons [1927] A.C. 487; (1927) 27 Ll. L. Rep. 377, HL...................................... 6.16
Lambert v. Cooperative Insurance Society Ltd [1975] 2 Lloyd's Rep. 485, CA 15.10
Lambert (Rae) v. HTV Cymru (Wales) Ltd [1998] E.M.L.R. 629; [1998] F.S.R. 874, CA... 5.17
Lampleigh v. Braithwaite (1615) Hob. 105; 80 E.R. 255 .... 7.15
Lansdown v. Lansdown (1730) Mos. 364; 2 Jac and W 205; 37 E.R. 605........................... 21.10
Laurence v Lexcourt Holdings [1978] 1 W.L.R. 1128; [1978] 2 All E.R. 810, CA 18.6
Lawrence v. Fox 20 N.Y. 268 (1859) 10.1, 10.7
Lazenby Garages v. Wright [1976] 1 W.L.R. 459; [1976] 2 All E.R. 770, CA 24.27
Leaf v. International Galleries [1950] 2 K.B. 86; [1950] 1 All E.R. 693, CA..............6.10, 18.22
Lease Management Services v. Purnell Secretarial Services; *sub nom.* Purrnell Secretarial
    Services v. Lease Management Services[1994] Tr. L.R. 337;[1994] C.C.L.R. 127; *The
    Times,* April 1, 1994, CA..16.27, 17.28
Lee-Parker v. Izzet (No.2) [1972] 1 W.L.R. 775; [1972] 2 All E.R. 800 .... 13.6
Leeds Industrial Cooperative Society Ltd v. Slack. *See* Slack v. Leeds Industrial
    Cooperative Society Ltd (No.1)
Lefkowitz v. Great Minneapolis Surplus Store 86 N.W. 2d 289 (1958).............................. 3.4
Leggatt v. National Westminster Bank Plc. *See* National Westminster Bank Plc v. Leggatt
Legione v. Hateley (1983) 46 A.L.R. 1; (1983) 152 C.L.R. 406 .... 9.20
Leighton v. Michael; Leighton v. Charlambous [1995] I.C.R. 1091; [1996] I.R.L.R. 67,
    EAT 20.6
Leopold Walford (LONDON) Ltd v. Les Affreteurs Reunis SA. *See* Les Affreteurs Reunis
    SA v. Leopold Walford (London) Ltd
Les Affrèteurs Reunis SA v. Leopold Walford (London) Ltd; *sub nom.* Leopold Walford
    (LONDON) Ltd v. Les Affreteurs Reunis SA [1919] A.C. 801, HL; [1918] 2 K.B. 498,
    CA... 10.26
L'Éstrange v. F Graucob Ltd [1934] 2 K.B. 394, KBD......................16.5, 16.6, 16.8, 16.10, 21.16
Lever Bros Ltd v. Bell. *See* Bell v. Lever Bros Ltd
Levison v. Patent Steam Carpet Cleaning Co. [1978] Q.B. 69; [1977] 3 W.L.R. 90, CA....... 16.26
Lewis v. Averay (No.1) [1972] 1 Q.B. 198; [1971] 3 W.L.R. 603, CA 6.14, 6.15, 6.16

Lewis v. Clay (1897) 67 L.J. Q.B. 224 .... 21.16
Licences Insurance Corporation v. Lawson [1896] 12 T.L.R. 502 .... 11.2
Liddesdale, The. *See* Forman & Co. Proprietary Ltd v. Liddesdale, The
Liesbosch Dredger v. SS Edison. *See* Liesbosch, The
Liesbosch, The; *sub nom.* Owner of Dredger Liesbosch v. Owners of SS Edison; Liesbosch
    Dredger v. SS Edison [1933] A.C. 449; [1933] All E.R. Rep. 144, HL 25.1
Linden Gardens v. Lenesta Sludge Disposals. *See* Linden Gardens Trust Ltd v. Lenesta
    Sludge Disposals Ltd Linden Gardens Trust Ltd v. Lenesta Sludge Disposals Ltd; *sub*
    nom. Linden Gardens v. Lenesta Sludge Disposals; St Martins Property Corp. Ltd v.
    Sir Robert McAlpine & Sons [1994] 1 A.C. 85; [1993] 3 W.L.R. 408, HL 10.8, 10.29–10.31
Lindsay v. Cundy. *See* Cundy v. Lindsay
Lipkin Gorman v. Karpnale Ltd [1991] 2 A.C. 548; [1991] 3 W.L.R. 10, HL 26.22
Lister v. Romford Ice and Cold Storage Co. Ltd; *sub nom.* Romford Ice & Cold Storage
    Co. v. Lister [1957] A.C. 555; [1957] 2 W.L.R. 158, HL 12.16, 12.27, 12.30
Little v. Courage Ltd (1995) 70 P. & C.R. 469, CA; (1995) 69 P. & C.R. 447, Ch D
    ....5.17, 12.16, 12.30
Little v. Ingram. *See* Ingram v. Little
Liverpool City Council v. Irwin [1977] A.C. 239; [1976] 2 W.L.R. 562; 1 Q.B. 319, CA ..12.26–12.29
Lloyd v. Grace Smith & Co. [1912] A.C. 716, HL; [1911] 2 K.B. 489, CA 18.24
Lloyd v. Stanbury [1971] 1 W.L.R. 535; [1971] 2 All E.R. 267, Ch D................................ 24.5
Lloyds Bank Ltd, Re; Lederman v. Bomze; *sub nom.* Bomze v. Bomze; Lloyds Bank Ltd,
    Bomze and Lederman v. Bomze; Lloyd's Bank Bomze v. Bomze, Re [1931] 1 Ch. 289,
    Ch D... 19.14
Lloyd's Bank Bomze v. Bomze, Re. *See* Lloyds Bank Ltd, Re
Lloyds Bank Ltd v. Bundy [1975] Q.B. 326; [1974] 3 W.L.R. 501, CA 14.8, 19.3, 19.15, 19.16
Lloyds Bank Ltd, Bomze and Lederman v. Bomze. *See* Lloyds Bank Ltd, Re
Lloyds Bank Plc v. Waterhouse [1993] 2 F.L.R. 97; (1991) 10 Tr. L.R. 161, CA 21.18
Lloyd's of London v. Khan. *See* Society of Lloyd's v. Khan
Lockett v. A and M Charles Ltd. *See* Lockett v. Charles
Lockett v. Charles; *sub nom.* Lockett v. A and M Charles Ltd [1938] 4 All E.R. 170.......5.3, 12.23
Loftus v. Roberts (1902) 18 T.L.R. 532
Lombard North Central Plc v. Butterworth [1987] Q.B. 527; [1987] 2 W.L.R. 7, CA.......... 13.12
Lombard North Central Plc v. Stobart (1990) 9 Tr. L.R. 105; [1990] C.C.L.R. 53, CA 9.17
Lombard Tricity Finance v. Paton [1989] 1 All E.R. 918; (1989) 8 Tr. L.R. 129, CA 5.13, 8.20
London Drugs Ltd v. Kuehne & Nagle International Ltd [1992] 3 S.C.R. 299 .... 16.29
London General Omnibus Co. Ltd v. Holloway [1912] 2 K.B. 72, CA 15.13
Long v. Lloyd [1958] 1 W.L.R. 753; [1958] 2 All E.R. 402, CA 18.23
Longstaff v. Birtles *The Times*, September 18, 2001 .... 15.11
Lord Elphinstone v. Markland Iron & Coal Co. Ltd. *See* Lord Elphinstone v. Monkland
    Iron and Coal Co. Ltd
Lord Elphinstone v. Monkland Iron and Coal Co. Ltd; *sub nom.* Lord Elphinstone v.
    Markland Iron & Coal Co. Ltd (1886) L.R. 11 App. Cas. 332, HL 25.30
Lord Strathcona Steamship Co. Ltd v. Dominion Coal Co. Ltd [1926] A.C. 108; (1925) 23
    Ll. L. Rep. 145
Lotus Cars Ltd v. Southampton Cargo Handling plc. *See* Lotus Cars Ltd v. Southampton
    Cargo Handling Plc (The Rigoletto)
Lotus Cars Ltd v. Southampton Cargo Handling Plc (The Rigoletto); *sub nom.*
    Southampton Cargo Handling Plc v. Lotus Cars Ltd (The Rigoletto); Lotus Cars Ltd
    v. Southampton Cargo Handling plc; Southampton Cargo Handling Plc v. Associated
    British Ports [2000] 2 All E.R. (Comm) 705; [2000] 2 Lloyd's Rep. 532, CA............... 16.29
Low v. Bouverie [1891] 3 Ch. 82, CA 9.17
Lucy v. Zehmer (1954) 196 V.A. 493, 84 S.E.2d 516 ....2.13, 11.2, 11.7
Lumley v. Gye (1853) 2 El. & Bl. 216... 26.8
Lumley v. Wagner (1852) 1 De G.M. & G. 604; 42 E.R. 687 .... 26.8
Luna, The; *sub nom.* Frances & Jane, The v. Luna, The [1920] P. 22; (1919) 1 Ll. L. Rep.
    475, PDAD 16.5, 17.6
Luxor (Eastbourne) Ltd v. Cooper [1941] A.C. 108, HL 2.6

MDIS Ltd (formerly McDonnell Information Systems Ltd) v. Swinbank; *sub nom.*
McDonnell Information Systems Ltd v. Swinbank; MDIS v. Swinbank [1999] 2 All
E.R. (Comm) 722; [1999] C.L.C. 1800, CA; [1999] 1 Lloyd's Rep. I.R. 98, QBD
(Comm Ct) 12.2
MDIS v. Swinbank. *See* MDIS Ltd (formerly McDonnell Information Systems Ltd) v.
Swinbank
Mace v. Rutland House Textiles Ltd (1999) 96(46) L.S.G. 37; (2000) 144 S.J.L.B. 7; *The
Times*, January 11, 2000, Ch D 21.21
McAlister v. Stevenson. *See* Donoghue v. Stevenson
McArdle, Re [1951] Ch. 669; [1951] 1 All E.R. 905, CA 7.15
McArthur v. Seaforth (1810) 2 Taunt 257; 127 E.R. 1076 .... 24.3
McCrone v. Boots Farm Sales Ltd 1981 S.C. 68; 1981 S.L.T. 103, OH 17.16
McCullagh v. Lane Fox and Partners Ltd 49 Con. L.R. 124; [1996] P.N.L.R. 205; *The
Times*, December 22, 1995, CA 17.31
McCutcheon v. David MacBrayne Ltd [1964] 1 W.L.R. 125; [1964] 1 All E.R. 430, H....16.8, 16.18
McDonnell Information Systems Ltd v. Swinbank. *See* MDIS Ltd (formerly McDonnell
Information Systems Ltd) v. Swinbank
Maclaine v. Gatty; *sub nom.* Gatty v Maclaine [1921] 1 A.C. 376; 1921 S.C. (H.L.) 1, HL .. 9.2
McRae v. Commonwealth Disposals Commission (1951) 84 C.L.R. 377 ....6.10, 21.5, 21.13, 24.13
Magee v. Pennine Insurance Co. [1969] 2 Q.B. 507; [1969] 2 W.L.R. 1278, CA 21.12
Mahmoud v. Ispahani, Re; *sub nom.* Arbitration Between Mahmoud and Ispahani, Re;
Mahmoud v Ispahani; [1921] 2 K.B. 716; (1921) 6 Ll. L. Rep. 344, CA 20.2, 20.4
Mahmoud v Ispahani. *See* Mahmoud v Ispahani, Re
Mahmud v. Bank of Credit and Commerce International SA (In Liquidation). *See* Malik
v. Bank of Credit and Commerce International SA (In Liquidation)
Mahoney v. Purnell [1996] 3 All E.R. 61; [1997] 1 F.L.R. 612, QBD 19.28
Malcolm v. Chancellor, Masters and Scholars of the University of Oxford (t/a Oxford
University Press) [1994] E.M.L.R. 17; *The Times*, December 19, 1990, CA 5.14
Malik v. Bank of Credit and Commerce International SA (In Liquidation); *sub nom.*
Mahmud v. Bank of Credit and Commerce International SA (In Liquidation); BCCI
SA, Re [1998] A.C. 20; [1997] 3 W.L.R. 95, HL; [1995] 3 All E.R. 545, CA...........14.24, 15.5,
25.10–25.13, 25.20, 25.21, 25.38
Malvern Fishing Co. Ltd v. Ailsa Craig Fishing Co. Ltd and Securicor (Scotland) Ltd. *See*
Ailsa Craig Fishing Co. v Malvern Fishing Co. and Securicor (Scotland)
Manchester, Sheffield and Lincolnshire Railway Co v. Brown; *sub nom.* Brown v
Manchester Sheffield and Lincolnshire Railway Co. (1882–83) L.R. 8 App. Cas. 703,
HL 17.22
Manubens v. Leon [1919] 1 K.B. 208, KBD 24.16
Marcic v. Thames Water Utilities Ltd [2001] 4 All E.R. 326; [2001] B.L.R. 366; (2001)
151 N.L.J. 1180 .... 26.11
Mardorf Peach & Co. v. Attica Sea Carriers Corp of Liberia (The Laconia) [1977] A.C.
850; [1977] 2 W.L.R. 286, HL 13.14
Maredelanto Compania Naviera SA v. Bergbau-Handel GmbH (The Mihalis Angelos)
[1971] 1 Q.B. 164; [1970] 3 W.L.R. 601, CA 13.13, 22.17
Margo Freeguard v. Ingrid Rogers. *See* Freeguard v. Rogers (No.1)
Maritime National Fish Ltd v. Ocean Trawlers Ltd; *sub nom.* Ocean Trawlers Ltd v
Maritime National Fish Ltd, [1935] A.C. 524; (1935) 51 Ll. L. Rep. 299, PC 22.18
Marles v. Philip Trant & Sons Ltd. *See* Marles v. Philip Trant & Sons Ltd (No.2)
Marles v. Philip Trant & Sons Ltd (No.2); *sub nom.* Marles v. Philip Trant & Sons Ltd
[1954] 1 Q.B. 29; [1953] 2 W.L.R. 564, CA 20.8
Marsh v. Thomson Tour Operators [2000] C.L.Y. 4044 .... 12.30
Marshall v. N M Financial Management Ltd; *sub nom.* N M Financial Management
Ltd v. Marshall [1997] 1 W.L.R. 1527; [1997] I.C.R. 1065, CA; [1995] 4 All E.R.
785 ....20.30, 20.31
Martin-Smith v. Williams [1999] E.M.L.R. 571, CA; [1998] E.M.L.R. 334, Ch D 2.2, 15.11
Maskell v. Horner [1915] 3 K.B. 106, CA...19.3, 19.7

Mason v. Provident Clothing. *See* Provident Clothing & Supply Co. Ltd v. Mason

Mason v. Provident Clothing and Supply Co. Ltd. *See* Provident Clothing & Supply Co. Ltd v. Mason

Massey v. Midland Bank Plc [1995] 1 All E.R. 929; [1994] 2 F.L.R. 342, CA 19.22

Mathieson Gee (Ayrshire) Ltd v. Quigley 1952 S.C. (H.L.) 38; 1952 S.L.T. 239; [1952] W.N. 193; 96 S.J. 295, HL 2.10, 4.1

Matter of Doughboy Industries Inc. *See* Doughboy Industries Inc., Matter of

Maxim Nordenfelt Guns & Ammunition Co. v. Nordenfelt. *See* Nordenfelt v. Maxim Nordenfelt Guns & Ammunition Co. Ltd

May & Butcher Ltd v. King, The; *sub nom.* May & Butcher Ltd v. R [1934] 2 K.B. 17; [1929] All E.R. Rep. 679, HL 5.13

Medforth v. Blake [2000] Ch. 86; [1999] 3 W.L.R. 922, CA 14.25

Melachrino v. Nicholl and Knight. *See* Melachrino v. Nickoll

Melachrino v. Nickoll; *sub nom.* Melachrino v. Nicholl and Knight [1920] 1 K.B. 693; (1919) 1 Ll. L. Rep. 595, KBD (Comm Ct) 25.4

Meneces v. Middleton. *See* Craig (Deceased), Re

Merritt v. Babb [2001] EWCA Civ 214; [2001] 3 W.L.R. 1; [2001] Lloyd's Rep. P.N. 468 ... 18.24

Merritt v. Merritt [1970] 1 W.L.R. 1211; [1970] 2 All E.R. 760, CA 11.3

Metal Scrap Trade Corp. Ltd v Kate Shipping Co. Ltd (The Gladys) (No.2)[1994] 2 Lloyd's Rep. 402, QBD (Comm Ct)...2.10, 4.2, 5.9

Metall Rohstoff v. Donaldson Lufkin. *See* Metall und Rohstoff AG v. Donaldson Lufkin & Jenrette Inc. ....

Metall und Rohstoff AG v. Donaldson Lufkin & Jenrette Inc.; *sub nom.* Metall Rohstoff AG v. Donaldson Lufkin [1990] 1 Q.B. 391; [1989] 3 W.L.R. 563; [1989] 3 All E.R. 14, CA 19.4

Metropolitan Water Board v. Dick Kerr & Co. Ltd [1918] A.C. 119, HL; [1917] 2 K.B. 1, CA 22.14

Micklefield v. SAC Technology Ltd [1990] 1 W.L.R. 1002; [1991] 1 All E.R. 275; [1990] I.R.L.R. 218, Ch.D 17.13

Midland Silicones Ltd v. Scruttons Ltd. *See* Scruttons Ltd v. Midland Silicones Ltd

Miles v. Wakefield MDC; *sub nom.* Miles v. Wakefield Metropolitan District Council [1987] A.C. 539; [1987] 2 W.L.R. 795, CA 26.34

Miles v. Wakefield Metropolitan District Council. *See* Miles v. Wakefield MDC

Milton Keynes Development Corp. v. Cooper (Great Britain). *See* Commission for the New Towns v. Cooper (Great Britain) Ltd (formerly Coopind UK)

Minories Finance v. Afribank Nigeria Ltd [1995] 1 Lloyd's Rep. 134, QBD (Comm Ct).... 4.23

Mitchell v. Homfray (1881) 8 Q.B.D. 587.. 19.14

Modern Engineering (Bristol) Ltd v. Gilbert Ash (Northern) Ltd. *See* Gilbert Ash (Northern) Ltd v. Modern Engineering (Bristol) Ltd

Mohamed v. Alaga. *See* Mohamed v. Alaga & Co.

Mohamed v. Alaga & Co.; *sub nom.* Mohamed v. Alaga; Mohammed v. Alaga & Co. [2000] 1 W.L.R. 1815; [1999] 3 All E.R. 699, CA 20.12, 20.16, 26.30

Molander v. Evans *The Times*, June 25, 2001 .... 18.11

Monarch Steamship Co. Ltd v. A/B Karlshamns Oljefabriker; *sub nom.* A/B Karlshamns Oljefabriker v. Monarch Steamship Co. Ltd [1949] A.C. 196; [1949] 1 All E.R. 1, HL 25.5, 25.7, 25.23

Monvia Motorship Corp. v. Keppel Shipyard (Private) Ltd (The Master Stelios) [1983] 1 Lloyd's Rep. 356, PC.. 4.3

Moorcock, The (1889) L.R. 14 P.D. 64; [1886–90] All E.R. Rep. 530, CA......................... 12.25

Moore v. Piretta PTA Ltd [1999] 1 All E.R. 174; [1998] C.L.C. 992, QBD 1.16, 24.28

Moran v. University College Salford (No.2) *The Times*, November 23, 1993; *The Independent*, November 26, 1993, CA.. 4.16

Morgan v. Manser [1948] 1 K.B. 184; [1947] 2 All E.R. 666, KBD 22.9

Morrison v. Thoelke 155 So. 2d 889 (1963)... 4.26

Moses v. Macferlan (1760) 2 Burr. 1005; 97 E.R. 676 .... 26.21

Motis Exports Ltd v. Dampskibsselskabet AF1912 A/S (No.1); *sub nom.*

Dampskibsselskabet AF 1912 v Motis Exports Ltd [2000] 1 All E.R. (Comm) 91;
    [2000] 1 Lloyd's Rep. 211, CA 16.23, 16.28
Mountford v. Scott [1975] Ch. 258; [1975] 2 W.L.R. 114, CA 7.9
Multiservice Bookbinding Ltd v. Marden [1979] Ch. 84; [1978] 2 W.L.R. 535; [1978] 2 All
    E.R. 489, Ch D 14.18
Munroe v. Butt (1858) 8 El and Bl 738; 120 E.R. 275................................23.23, 23.32
Murphy v. Wexford CC; sub nom. Murphy v. Wexford County Council [1921] 2 I.R. 230 .. 26.35
Murphy v. Wexford County Council. See Murphy v. Wexford CC
Murray v. Flavell. See Flavell, Re
Museprime Properties Ltd v. Adhill Properties Ltd (1991) 61 P. & C.R. 111; [1990] 36 E.G.
    114, Ch.D 18.7

N M Financial Management Ltd v. Marshall. See Marshall v. N M Financial
    Management Ltd
Naidoo v. Naidu The Times, November 1, 2000, Ch D 19.24, 19.25
Nash v. Inman [1908] 2 K.B. 1, CA 11.6
National Bank of Greece SA v. Pinios Shipping Co. (No.1); sub nom. Pinios Shipping Co.
    v. National Bank of Greece SA; National Bank of Greece SA v. Pinios Shipping Co.
    "The Maira" [1990] 1 A.C. 637; [1989] 3 W.L.R. 1330; [1990] 1 All E.R. 78, HL
Pinios Shipping Co. v. National Bank of Greece SA. See National Bank of Greece SA v.
    Pinios Shipping Co. (No.1)
National Bank of Greece SA v. Pinios Shipping Co. "The Maira". See National Bank of
    Greece SA v. Pinios Shipping Co. (No.1)
National Carriers Ltd v. Panalpina (Northern) Ltd [1981] A.C. 675; [1981] 2 W.L.R. 45,
    HL 22.3, 22.17
National Westminster Bank Plc v. Leggatt; sub nom. Leggatt v. National Westminster Bank
    Plc [2001] 1 F.L.R. 563; [2001] 1 F.C.R. 523, CA; [2000] All E.R. 1458 ......19.12, 19.22, 19.26
National Westminster Bank Plc v. Morgan [1985] A.C. 686; [1985] 2 W.L.R. 588, HL 14.9,
                                                                              19.10, 19.11, 19.12
New Zealand Shipping Co. Ltd v. AM Satterthwaite & Co. Ltd (The Eurymedon); sub
    nom. AM Satterthwaite & Co. Ltd v. New Zealand Shipping Co. Ltd [1975] A.C. 154;
    [1974] 2 W.L.R. 865, PC...............................2.6, 5.4, 10.8, 10.21, 10.26, 16.29, 17.6
Newbold v. Leicester City Council [1999] I.C.R. 1182; (2000) 2 L.G.L.R. 303; The Times,
    August 20, 1999, CA..   7.10
Newcomb v. De Roos. See Entores Ltd v. Miles Far East Corp.
Newman v. A. and S. Gatti (1907) 24 T.L.R. 18 ....   12.5
Nicholson and Venn v. Smith-Marriott (1947) 177 L.T. 189 ....   21.9
Nicolene Ltd v. Simmonds [1953] 1 Q.B. 543; [1953] 2 W.L.R. 717; [1953] 1 All E.R. 822,
    CA...   5.12
Nordenfelt v. Maxim Nordenfelt Guns & Ammunition Co. Ltd; sub nom. Maxim
    Nordenfelt Guns & Ammunition Co. v. Nordenfelt [1894] A.C. 535, HL; [1893] 1 Ch.
    630, CA..20.27, 20.28
North Ocean Shipping Co. v. Hyundai Construction Co. (The Atlantic Baron) [1979] Q.B.
    705; [1979] 3 W.L.R. 419, QBD (Comm Ct) 19.5
Northrop Corp. v. Litronic Industries, 29 F.3rd 1173 (1994)............................   5.10
Norwegian American Cruises v. Paul Mundy, "The Vistafiord" [1988] 2 Lloyd's Rep. 343......   9.17
Norwich City Council v. Harvey. See Norwich City Council v. Harvey (Paul Clarke)
Norwich City Council v. Harvey (Paul Clarke); sub nom. Norwich City Council v. Harvey
    [1989] 1 W.L.R. 828; [1989] 1 All E.R. 1180, CA......................................   16.29
Norwich Union Fire Insurance Society Ltd v. Price. See Norwich Union Fire Insurance
    Society Ltd v. WMH Price Ltd
Norwich Union Fire Insurance Society Ltd v. William Price Ltd. See Norwich Union Fire
    Insurance Society Ltd v. WMH Price Ltd
Norwich Union Fire Insurance Society Ltd v. WMH Price Ltd; sub nom. Norwich Union
    Fire Insurance Society Ltd v. Price; Norwich Union Fire Insurance Society Ltd v.
    William Price Ltd [1934] A.C. 455; (1934) 49 Ll. L. Rep. 55, PC................................   21.11

Notcutt v. Universal Equipment Co. (London) [1986] 1 W.L.R. 641; [1986] 3 All E.R. 582, CA 22.22
Nottingham Building Society v. Eurodynamics Systems Plc [1995] F.S.R. 605, CA; [1993] F.S.R. 468, Ch D 23.13
Nottingham University v. Fishel [2000] I.C.R. 1462; *The Times,* January 19, 2000 .... 15.12
Nutbrown v. Thornton (1804) 10 Ves. Jun 160; 32 E.R. 805 .... 26.4
Nutt v. Read (2000) 32 H.L.R. 761; (1999) 96(42) L.S.G. 44; *The Times*, December 3, 1999, CA 21.7, 21.13, 21.14

OTM v. Hydranautics [1981] 2 Lloyd's Rep. 211, QBD (Comm Ct) 5.10
Obagi v. Stanborough (Developments) Ltd (1995) 69 P. & C.R. 573; [1993] E.G.C.S. 205, Ch D 5.17
O'Brien v. MGN Ltd *The Times,* August 8, 2001 .... 14.11
O'Callaghan v. Coral Racing Ltd *The Times,* November 26, 1998; *The Independent,* November 26, 1998, CA 20.11
Occidental Worldwide Investment Corp. v. Skibs A/S Avanti (The Siboen and The Sibotre) [1976] 1 Lloyd's Rep. 293, QBD (Comm Ct) 19.3, 26.35
Ocean Tramp Tankers Corp. v. V/O Sovfracht (The Eugenia) [1964] 2 Q.B. 226; [1964] 2 W.L.R. 114, CA 22.20
Ocean Trawlers Ltd v Maritime National Fish Ltd. *See* Maritime National Fish Ltd v. Ocean Trawlers Ltd
Ogdens Ltd v. Nelson; Ogdens Ltd v. Telford [1905] A.C. 109, HL 23.2
Olley v. Marlborough Court Ltd [1949] 1 K.B. 532; [1949] 1 All E.R. 127, CA 16.13
Omnium d'Enterprises v. Sutherland [1919] 1 K.B. 618, CA 23.2
Oom v. Bruce (1810) 12 Egst 225; 104 E.R. 87 .... 20.17
Orion Insurance Co. Plc v. Sphere Drake Insurance Plc [1992] 1 Lloyd's Rep. 239, CA; [1990] 1 Lloyd's Rep. 465, QBD (Comm Ct) 11.2
Oscar Chess v. Williams [1957] 1 W.L.R. 370; [1957] 1 All E.R. 325; 101 S.J. 186, CA 13.1
O'Sullivan v. Management Agency and Music Ltd; *sub nom.* C [1985] Q.B. 428; [1984] 3 W.L.R. 448, CA 19.15, 19.17, 19.28
O'Sullivan v. Management Agency. *See* O'Sullivan v. Management Agency and Music Ltd
Overbrooke Estates Ltd v. Glencombe Properties Ltd [1974] 1 W.L.R. 1335; [1974] 3 All E.R. 511, Ch.D 18.25
Overland Shoes Ltd v. Schenkers Ltd; Overland Shoes Ltd v. Schenkers International Deutschland GmbH [1998] 1 Lloyd's Rep. 498; (1998) 95(11) L.S.G. 36, CA 17.19
Overseas Medical Supplies Ltd v. Orient Transport Services Ltd [1999] 1 All E.R. (Comm) 981; [1999] 2 Lloyd's Rep. 273, CA 17.24
Overseas Tankship (UK) Ltd v. Miller Steamship Co. Pty Ltd "The Wagon Mound" (No.2) [1967] 1 A.C. 617; [1966] 3 W.L.R. 498; [1966] 2 All E.R. 709 .... 25.1
Owner of Dredger Liesbosch v. Owners of SS Edison. *See* Liesbosch, The
Owners of Cargo Laden on Board the Albacruz v. Owners of the Albazero (The Albacruz and The Albazero); *sub nom.* Concord Petroleum Corp. v. Gosford Marine Panama SA [1977] A.C. 774; [1976] 3 W.L.R. 419, HL 10.29, 10.30
Owners of the SS Istros v. FW Dahlstroem & Co. 1931] 1 K.B. 247; (1930) 38 Ll. L. Rep. 84, KBD 17.17

P J Van der Zijden Wildhandel NV v. Tucker & Cross Ltd (No.1) [1975] 2 Lloyd's Rep. 240, QBD (Comm Ct) 22.21
Paal Wilson & Co. A/S v Partenreederei Hannah Blumenthal (The Hannah Blumenthal) [1983] 1 A.C. 854; [1982] 3 W.L.R. 1149, HL 2.7
Page One Records Ltd v. Britton [1968] 1 W.L.R. 157; [1967] 3 All E.R. 822, Ch D- 26.9
Pagnan SpA v. Feed Products Ltd [1987] 2 Lloyd's Rep. 601, CA 2.10, 3.1, 4.3, 5.3, 5.9
Pan Atlantic Insurance Co. Ltd v. Pine Top Insurance Co. Ltd [1995] 1 A.C. 501; [1994] 3 W.L.R. 677; [1994] 3 All E.R. 581, HL 15.10
Panatown Ltd v. Alfred McAlpine. *See* Alfred McAlpine Construction Ltd v. Panatown

Ltd (No.1) Panatown Ltd v. Alfred McAlpine Construction Ltd. *See* Alfred McAlpine Construction Ltd v. Panatown Ltd (No.1)

Panayiotou v. Sony Music Entertainment. *See* Panayiotou v. Sony Music Entertainment (UK) Ltd

Panayiotou v. Sony Music Entertainment (UK) Ltd; *Sub nom.* Panayiotou v. Sony Music Entertainment [1994] E.M.L.R., CA 20.23

Panchaud Freres SA v. Etablissements General Grain Co.; *sub nom.* Panchaud Freres SA v. Ets General Grain Co [1970] 1 Lloyd's Rep. 53, CA; [1969] 2 Lloyd's Rep. 109, QBD (Comm Ct)...9.17, 9.18, 9.20

Panchaud Freres SA v. Ets General Grain Co. *See* Panchaud Freres SA v Etablissements General Grain Co.

Pao On v. Lau Yiu Long [1980] A.C. 614; [1979] 3 W.L.R. 435, PC 7.15, 8.5

Paola Faccini Dori v. Recreb Srl. (C-91/91) [1994]... 4.17

Pappadakis v. Pappadakis (2000) 1 W.T.L.R. 719; *The Times*, January 19, 2000, Ch D...... 21.23

Paradine v. Jane [1647] Aleyn 26; 82 E.R. 897...22.3, 22.17

Parker v. Clark [1960] 1 W.L.R. 286; [1960] 1 All E.R. 93; 104 S.J. 251, Assizes (Exeter) ... 11.4

Parker v. S.E. Railway Co. (1877) 2 C.P.D. 416 ....16.11, 16.12, 17.34

Parkinson v. College of Ambulance Ltd; *sub nom.* Parkinson v. College of Ambulance Ltd & Harrison [1925] 2 K.B. 1, KBD..20.8, 20.15

Parkinson v. College of Ambulance Ltd & Harrison. *See* Parkinson v. College of Ambulance Ltd

Parsons (Livestock) Ltd v. Uttley Ingham & Co. Ltd; *sub nom.* H Parsons v. Uttley Ingham and Co. Ltd [1978] Q.B. 791; [1977] 3 W.L.R. 990; [1978] 1 All E.R. 525, CA............ 25.8

Partridge v. Crittenden [1968] 1 W.L.R. 1204; [1968] 2 All E.R. 421, DC 3.6

Patel v. Ali [1984] Ch. 283; [1984] 2 W.L.R. 960, Ch D 26.4

Patricia Thompson v. Sheffield Fertility Clinic. *See* Thompson v. Sheffield Fertility Clinic

Paula Lee Ltd v. Zehil & Co. Ltd [1983] 2 All E.R. 390, QBD 12.15

Payne v. Cave (1789) 3 Term Rep 148 .... 3.7

Payzu Ltd v. Saunders [1919] 2 K.B. 581, CA 25.2425.25

Pearce v. Brooks (1865–66) L.R. 1 Ex. 213, Ex Ct.. 20.9

Pearce v. Merriman [1904] 1 K.B. 80, KBD 11.3

Pearl Carriers Inc. v. Japan Line Ltd (The Chemical Venture) [1993] 1 Lloyd's Rep. 508, QBD (Comm Ct)... 7.16

Peck v. North Staffordshire Railway Co. (1862–3) 10 H.L.C.473; 11 E.R. 1109 .... 17.22

Peek v. Derry. *See* Derry v. Peek

Pegase, The. *See* Satef-Huttenes Alberns SpA v. Paloma Tercera Shipping Co. SA (The Pegase)

Penarth Dock Engineering Co. v. Pounds [1963] 1 Lloyd's Rep. 359, QBD 26.37

Penelope, The. *See* Cleeves Western Valleys Anthracite Collieries Ltd v. Owners of The Penelope

Pennsylvania Shipping Co. v. Compagnie Nationale de Navigation (1936) 55 Ll. L. Rep. 271, KBD; [1936] 2 All E.R. 1167 .... 13.2

Perry v. Sidney Phillips & Son [1982] 1 W.L.R. 1297; [1982] 3 All E.R. 705, CA 25.18

Peter Pan Manufacturing Corp. v. Corsets Silhouette Ltd [1964] 1 W.L.R. 96; [1963] 3 All E.R. 402, Ch D... 26.37

Peter Symmons and Co. v. Cook (1981) 131 N.L.J 758...................................... 17.12

Peyman v. Lanjani [1985] Ch. 457; [1985] 2 W.L.R. 154, CA 18.23

Pharmaceutical Society of Great Britain v. Boots Cash Chemists (Southern) Ltd [1953] 1 Q.B. 401; [1953] 2 W.L.R. 427, CA 3.4

Philips Electronique v. Bsky Broadcasting. *See* Philips Electronique Grand Public SA v. British Sky Broadcasting Ltd

Philips Electronique Grand Public SA v. British Sky Broadcasting Ltd; *sub nom.* Philips Electronique v. BSky Broadcasting [1995] E.M.L.R. 472; *The Independent,* October 31, 1994 (C.S.), CA 12.29, 14.25

Philips Products v. Hyland [1987] 2 All E.R. 620 ....17.18, 17.20

Phillips v. Brooks Ltd [1919] 2 K.B. 243...6.14, 6.15, 6.17

Phoenix General Insurance Co. of Greece SA v. Administratia Asigurarilor de Stat;
    Phoenix General Insurance Co. of Greece SA v. Halvanon Insurance [1988] Q.B. 216;
    [1987] 2 W.L.R. 512; [1987] 2 All E.R. 152, CA.. 20.5
Photo Production Ltd v. Securicor Transport Ltd [1980] A.C. 827; [1980] 2 W.L.R. 283,
    HL 13.4, 16.20, 16.21, 16.25, 17.6, 17.17, 17.18, 23.3
Pickering v. Ilfracombe Railway Co. (1867–68) L.R. 3 C.P. 235, CCP 20.30
Pigots's Case; *sub nom.* Henry Pigot's case (1614) 11 Co. Rep. 266; 77 E.R. 1177..........8.21, 20.30
Pillans v. Van Mierop; *sub nom.* Pillans and Rose v. Van Mierop and Hopkins (1765) 3
    Burr. 1663, 97 E.R. 1035 .... 7.2
Pillans and Rose v. Van Mierop and Hopkins. *See* Pillans v. Van Mierop
Pinnell's Case (1602) 5 Co. Rep. 117a; 77 E.R. 237 ....8.14, 8.15, 8.27
Pinner v. Mayor of Wellington (1884) 9 App. Cas 699... 9.16
Pioneer Shipping Ltd v. BTP Tioxide Ltd "The Nema". *See* Pioneer Shipping Ltd v. BTP
    Tioxide Ltd (The Nema) (No.2)
Pioneer Shipping Ltd v. BTP Tioxide Ltd (The Nema) (No.2);BTP Tioxide Ltd v.
    Armada Marine SA *sub nom.* BTP Tioxide Ltd v Pioneer Shipping Ltd; Pioneer
    Shipping Ltd v. BTP Tioxide Ltd "The Nema" [1982] A.C. 724; [1981] 3 W.L.R. 292,
    HL 22.6, 22.17
Pitt v. PHH Asset Management Ltd [1994] 1 W.L.R. 327; [1993] 4 All E.R. 961, CA 5.15
Planché v. Colbourn (1831) 8 Bing. 14; 172 E.R. 876..23.27, 26.32
Poosathurai v. Kannappa Chettiar (1919) L.R. 47 Ind. App. 1 .... 19.10
Port Line v. Ben Line Steamers; *sub nom.* Port Line Ltd v Ben Line Steamers Ltd [1958] 2
    Q.B. 146; [1958] 2 W.L.R. 551, QBD 10.24
Port Line Ltd v. Ben Line Steamers Ltd. *See* Port Line v. Ben Line Steamers
Posner v. Scott-Lewis [1987] Ch. 25; [1986] 3 W.L.R. 531, Ch D 26.4
Post Chaser, The. *See* Societe Italo-Belge Pour le Commerce et L'Industrié SA (Antwerp)
    v. Palm and Vegetable Oils (Malaysia) Sdn Bhd (The Post Chaser)
Poussard v. Spiers & Pond (1875–76) L.R. 1 Q.B.D. 410, QBD 13.9
Powell v. Brent LBC; *sub nom.* Powell v. London Borough of Brent [1988] I.C.R. 176;
    [1987] I.R.L.R. 446, CA 26.8
Powell v. London Borough of Brent. *See* Powell v. Brent LBC
Prenn v. Simmonds [1971] 1 W.L.R. 1381; [1971] 3 All E.R. 237, HL................................ 12.2
Price v. Eastor (1833) 4 B and Ad. 433; 110 E.R. 518.. 10.2
Proctor & Gamble Phillippine Manufacturing Co. v. Peter Cremer "The Manila"
Procter & Gamble Phillippine Manufacturing Corp. v. Peter Cremer GmbH & Co. (The
    Manila) (No.2); *sub nom.* Proctor & Gamble Phillippine Manufacturing Co. v. Peter
    Cremer "The Manila" [1988] 3 All E.R. 843; *Independent,* April 15, 1988.................. 9.18
Prosper Homes Ltd v. Hambros Bank Executor and Trustee Co. Ltd (1980) 39 P. & C.R.
    395, Ch. D 9.4
Provident Clothing & Supply Co. Ltd v. Mason; *sub nom.* Mason v. Provident Clothing
    and Supply Co. Ltd; Mason v. Provident Clothing [1913] A.C. 724, HL; [1913] 1 K.B.
    65, CA 20.28
Provident Financial Group and Whitegates Estate Agency v. Hayward; *sub nom.* Provident
    Fund group plc v. Hayward [1989] 3 All E.R. 298; [1989] I.C.R. 160, CA................... 26.10
Provident Fund group plc v. Hayward. *See* Provident Financial Group and Whitegates
    Estate Agency v. Hayward
Public Works Commissioners v. Hills. *See* Commissioner of Public Works v. Hills
Puerto Buitrage, The. *See* Attica Sea Carriers Corp. v. Ferrostaal Poseidon Bulk Reederei
    GmbH (The Puerto Buitrago)
Purnell Secretarial Services v. Lease Management Services. *See* Lease Management
    Services v. Purnell Secretarial Services
Pym v. Campbell (1866) 6 El and Bl 370; 119 E.R. 903...12.6, 13.5

Quadrant Visual Communications v. Hutchison Telephone (UK) [1993] B.C.L.C. 442;
    (1992) 89(3) L.S.G. 31, CA 26.3
Quinn v. Burch Bros (Builders) Ltd[19662] 2 Q.B. 370; [1966] 2 W.L.R. 1017, CA 25.22

R v. Clarke (1927) 40 C.L.R. 227 .... 4.5, 4.6
R & B Customs Brokers Co. Ltd v. United Dominions Trust Ltd [1988] 1 W.L.R. 321;
    [1988] 1 All E.R. 847, CA 17.13
R W Green Ltd v. Cade Bros Farms [1978] 1 Lloyd's Rep. 602, QBD 17.32
Radford v. De Froberville [1977] 1 W.L.R. 1262; [1978] 1 All E.R. 33, Ch D ..10.30, 24.6, 24.24, 24.26
Raffles v. Wichelhaus; *sub nom.* Raffles v. Wichelhaus and Busch (1864) 2 Hurl. & C. 906,
    159 E.R. 375 .... 6.7
Raffles v. Wichelhaus and Busch. *See* Raffles v. Wichelhaus
Rafsanjan Pistachio Producers Cooperative v. Kaufmanns Ltd Independent, January 12,
    1998 (C.S.), QBD (Comm Ct) 5.14
Raiffeisen Zentralbank Osterreich AG v Cross Seas Shipping. *See* Raiffeisen Zentralbank
    Osterreich AG v Crossseas Shipping Ltd
Raiffeisen Zentralbank Osterreich AG v. Crossseas Shipping Ltd; *sub nom.* Raiffeisen
    Zentralbank Osterreich AG v Cross Seas Shipping [2000] 1 W.L.R. 1135; [2000] 3 All
    E.R. 274 .... 8.21
Ramsgate Victoria Hotel Co. v. Montefiore (1866) L.R. 1 Ex. 109 .... 3.14
Rann v. Hughes; *sub nom.* Joseph Rann v. Isabella Hughes (1778) 7 Term Rep. 350 (Note);
    2 E.R. 18 .... 7.2
Rasbora v. JCL Marine; *sub nom.* Atkinson v. JCL Marine [1977] 1 Lloyd's Rep. 645, QBD
    .... 8.22, 17.13
Rayfield v. Hands [1960] Ch. 1; [1958] 2 W.L.R. 851, Ch D 5.1
Ready Mixed Concrete (South East) Ltd v. Minister of Pensions and National Insurance;
    Minister for Social Security v. Greenham Ready Mixed Concrete Ltd; Minister for
    Social Security v. Ready Mixed Concrete (South East) Ltd [968] 2 Q.B. 497; [1968] 2
    W.L.R. 775, QBD 11.5
Reardon Smith Line Ltd v. Hansen-Tangen (The Diana Prosperity); Hansen-Tangen v
    Sanko Steamship Co Ltd [1976] 1 W.L.R. 989; [1976] 3 All E.R. 570, HL 12.2, 13.17
Redgrave v. Hurd (1881–82) L.R. 20 Ch. D. 1, CA 18.7, 18.8
Redrow Homes v. Bett Brothers. *See* Redrow Homes Ltd v. Bett Brothers Plc
Redrow Homes Ltd v. Bett Brothers Plc; *sub nom.* Redrow Homes v. Bett Brothers [1999]
    1 A.C. 197; [1998] 2 W.L.R. 198, HL 26.37
Reese River Silver Mining Co. v. Smith (1869) L.R. 4 H.L. 64 .... 18.21
Regalian Properties Plc v. London Docklands Development Corp. [1995] 1 W.L.R. 212;
    [1995] 1 All E.R. 1005, Ch D 5.18
Reichhold Norway ASA v. Goldman Sachs International [2000] 1 W.L.R. 173; [2000] 2 All
    E.R. 679; *The Times,* July 20, 1999, CA 13.6
Reigate v. Union Manufacturing Co. *See* Reigate v. Union Manufacturing Co.
    (Ramsbottom) Ltd
Reigate v. Union Manufacturing Co. (Ramsbottom) Ltd; *sub nom.* Reigate v. Union
    Manufacturing Co.[1918] 1 K.B. 592, CA 12.25
Resolute Maritime Inc. v. Nippon Kaiji Kyokai (The Skopas) [1983] 1 W.L.R. 857; [1983]
    2 All E.R. 1, QBD 18.24
Rialto, The [1891] P. 175, PDAD 19.6
Rice v. Great Yarmouth Borough Council. *See* Rice (t/a Garden Guardian) v. Great
    Yarmouth BC
Rice (t/a Garden Guardian) v. Great Yarmouth BC; *sub nom.* Rice v. Great Yarmouth
    Borough Council (2001) 3 L.G.L.R. 4; *The Times,* Times, July 26, 2000, CA 13.16
Richardson v. Mellish (1824) 2 Bing 229; 130 E.E. 294 .... 20.1
Rickards (Charles) v. Openhaim. *See* Charles Rickards Ltd v. Oppenheim
Ridge v. Crawley (1959) 173 E.G. 959, CA;(1958) 172 E.G. 637 .... 18.4
Riverlate Properties Ltd v. Paul [1975] Ch. 133; [1974] 3 W.L.R. 564, CA 21.21, 21.22
Robertson v. Minister of Pensions [1949] 1 K.B. 227; [1948] 2 All E.R. 767, KBD 9.6
Robinson v. Customs and Excise Commissioners *The Times,* April 28, 2000, QBD 11.1
Robinson v. Harman (1848) 1 Exch. 850; 154 E.R. 363; 154 E.R. 363 ....24.1, 24.4, 24.18, 24.19
Robinson v. Mollett (1875) L.R. 7 H.L. 802 .... 12.19
Roche v. Sherrington [1982] 1 W.L.R. 599; [1982] 2 All E.R. 426, Ch D 19.16

Roe v. R A Naylor Ltd; *sub nom.* Roe v Naylor [1917] 1 K.B. 712; [1918] 87 L.J. K.B. 958,
KBD 16.6
Roe v. Naylor. *See* Roe v. RA Naylor Ltd
Roebuck v. Mungovin [1994] 2 A.C. 224; [1994] 2 W.L.R. 290, HL 9.12
Romford Ice & Cold Storage Co. v. Lister. *See* Lister v. Romford Ice and Cold Storage Co.
Ltd
Ronaasen & Son v. Arcos Ltd. *See* Arcos Ltd v. EA Ronaasen & Son
Rooke v. Dawson [1895] 1 Ch. 480, Ch D 3.6
Roscorla v. Thomas (1842) 3 Q.B. 235; 114 E.R. 496 .... 7.14
Rose & Frank & Co. v. Crompton & Bros Ltd & Brittains Ltd. *See* Rose & Frank Co. v. J
R Crompton & Bros Ltd
Rose & Frank Co. v. J R Crompton & Bros Ltd; *sub nom.* Rose & Frank & Co. v.
Crompton & Bros Ltd & Brittains Ltd; Rose & Frank Co. v. Brittains Ltd [1925] A.C.
445; (1924) 20 Ll. L. Rep. 249, HL 11.2
Routledge v. McKay [1954] 1 W.L.R. 615; [1954] 1 All E.R. 855 .... 13.1
Rover International Ltd v. Cannon Film Ltd. *See* Rover International Ltd v. Cannon Film
Sales Ltd (No.3)
Rover International Ltd v. Cannon Film Sales Ltd (No.3); *sub nom.* Rover
International Ltd v. Cannon Film Ltd [1989] 1 W.L.R. 912; [1989] 3 All E.R. 423,
CA 26.24, 26.29
Rowland v. Divall [1923] 2 K.B. 500, CA 26.23
Royal Bank v. Etridge (No.2). *See* Royal Bank of Scotland Plc v. Etridge (No.2)
Royal Bank of Scotland Plc v. Etridge. *See* Royal Bank of Scotland Plc v. Etridge
(No.1)
Royal Bank of Scotland Plc v. Etridge (No.1); *sub nom.* Royal Bank of Scotland Plc v.
Etridge [1997] 3 All E.R. 628; [1997] 2 F.L.R. 847, CA 19.23
Royal Bank of Scotland Plc v. Etridge (No.2); *sub nom.* Royal Bank v. Etridge (No.2)
[1998] 4 All E.R. 705; [1998] 2 F.L.R. 843, CA 19.10, 19.12, 19.13, 19.21–19.23, 19.27
Royal Bank of Scotland v. Etridge (No.2) *The Times*, October 17, 2001 ....19.12, 19.22
Royscott Trust v. Maidenhead Honda Centre. *See* Royscott Trust v. Rogerson
Royscott Trust v. Rogerson; *sub nom.* Royscott Trust v. Maidenhead Honda Centre [1991]
2 Q.B. 297; [1991] 3 W.L.R. 57; [1991] 3 All E.R. 294, CA 18.18, 25.8
Russell v. Fulling *The Times*, June 23, 1999, Ch D 20.11
Rust v. Abbey Life Insurance Co. Ltd [1979] 2 Lloyd's Rep. 334, CA; [1978] 2 Lloyd's Rep.
386, QBD 4.22
Ruxley Electronics v. Forsyth. *See* Ruxley Electronics and Construction Ltd v. Forsyth
Ruxley Electronics and Construction Ltd v. Forsyth; Laddingford Enclosures Ltd v.
Forsyth; *sub nom.* Ruxley Electronics v. Forsyth [1996] 1 A.C. 344; [1995] 3 W.L.R.
118, HL 24.7, 24.25, 24.26, 25.19
Ryan v. Mutual Tontine Westminster Chambers Association [1893] 1 Ch. 116, CA; [1892]
1 Ch. 427, Ch D 26.3

S Pearson & Son Ltd v. Dublin Corp. [1907] A.C. 351, HL (UK-Irl); [1907] 2 I.R. 27, CA
(UK-Irl) 18.8, 18.25
Sadler v. Imperial Life Assurance Co. of Canada Ltd [1988] I.R.L.R. 388; *The Times*,
January 8, 1988, QBD 20.31
St Albans City and District Council v. ICL. *See* St Albans City and District Council v.
International Computers Ltd
St Albans City and District Council v. International Computers Ltd; *sub nom.* St Alban's
City and District Council v. ICL [1997–98] Info. T.L.R. 25, QBD; [1996] 4 All E.R.
481; [1997–98] Info. T.L.R. 58; [1995] F.S.R. 686, CA 12.23, 17.11, 17.15, 17.27
St John Shipping Corp. v. Joseph Rank Ltd [1957] 1 Q.B. 267; [1956] 3 W.L.R. 870,
QBD 20.5, 20.6, 20.14
St Martins Property Corp. Ltd v. Sir Robert McAlpine & Sons; *sub nom.* St Martins
Property Corporation v. Sir Robert McAlpine Ltd; Linden Gardens Trust Ltd v.
Lenesta Sludge Disposals Ltd [1994] 1 A.C. 85; [1993] 3 W.L.R. 408, HL 10.30

St Martins Property Corporation v. Sir Robert McAlpine Ltd. *See* St Martins Property
    Corp. Ltd v. Sir Robert McAlpine & Sons
St Marylebone Property Co. Ltd v. Payne [1994] 45 E.G. 156, CC 18.4
Sally Wertheim v. Chicoutimi Pulp Co. *See* Wertheim v. Chicoutimi Pulp Co.
Salvage Association v. CAP Financial Services Ltd; *sub nom.* Salvage Association v. CAP
    [1995] F.S.R. 654, QBD 17.6, 17.15, 17.23
Salvage Association v. CAP. *See* Salvage Association v. CAP Financial Services Ltd
Sapwell v. Bass [1910] 2 K.B. 486, KBD 24.13
Sargant v. Cit (England) (t/a Citalia) [1994] C.L.Y.566; unreported, June 6, 1994, CC
    (Croydon) 17.34
Satanita, The. *See* Clarke v. Earl of Dunraven (The Satanita)
Satef-Huttenes v. Paloma Tercera Shipping Co., The Pegase. *See* Satef-Huttenes Alberns
    SpA v. Paloma Tercera Shipping Co. SA (The Pegase)
Satef-Huttenes Alberns SpA v. Paloma Tercera Shipping Co. SA (The Pegase); *sub nom.*
    Satef-Huttenes v. Paloma Tercera Shipping Co., The Pegase [1981] 1 Lloyd's Rep. 175;
    [1980] Com. L.R. 9, QBD (Comm Ct) 25.6
Saunders v. Anglia Building Society. *See* Saunders (Executrix of the Estate of Rose Maud
    Gallie) v. Anglia Building Society (formerly Northampton Town and County
    Building Society)
Saunders v. Edwards [1987] 1 W.L.R. 1116; [1987] 2 All E.R. 651, CA 20.14, 20.19, 20.20
Saunders (Executrix of the Estate of Rose Maud Gallie) v. Anglia Building Society
    (formerly Northampton Town and County Building Society); *sub nom* Saunders v.
    Anglia Building Society; Gallie v Lee [1971] A.C. 1004; [1970] 3 W.L.R. 1078, HL 21.17
Scammell v. Dicker [2000] All E.R. (D) 2438 .... 3.10
Scandinavian Trading Tanker Co. AB v. Flota Petrolera Ecuatoriana (The Scaptrade)
    [1983] 2 A.C. 694; [1983] 3 W.L.R. 203, HL 9.7, 9.10, 13.23
Schebsman (Deceased) Ex p. Official Receiver, Re; *sub nom.* Trustee v Cargo
    Superintendents (London) Ltd; Schebsman, Official Receiver, Re v. Cargo
    Superintendents (London) Ltd and Schebsman [1944] Ch. 83; [1943] 2 All E.R. 768,
    CA... 10.26
Schelde Delta Shipping BV v. Astarte Shipping BV (The Pamela) [1995] 2 Lloyd's Rep.
    249, QBD (Comm Ct) 4.10
Schuler AG v. Wickman Machine Tool Sales Ltd; *sub nom.* Wickman Machine Tool Sales
    Ltd v. L Schuler AG [1974] A.C. 235; [1973] 2 W.L.R. 683; [1973] 2 All E.R. 39,
    HL 12.2, 13.12
Scotson v. Pegg (1861) 6 H and N 295; 158 E.R. 121.. 8.3
Scott v. Avery (1856) 5 H.L. Cas. 811, HL 13.6, 20.11
Scottish Power Plc v. Britoil (Exploration) Ltd (1997) 94(47) L.S.G. 30; (1997) 141 S.J.L.B.
    246; *The Times,* December 2, 1997, CA 12.3
Scrutton v. Midlands Silicones Ltd. *See* Scruttons Ltd v. Midland Silicones Ltd
Scruttons Ltd v. Midland Silicones Ltd; *sub nom.* Midland Silicones Ltd v. Scruttons Ltd;
    Scrutton v. Midlands Silicones Ltd [1962] A.C. 446; [1962] 2 W.L.R. 186, HL........10.2, 10.3,
    16.29
Scully v. Southern Health and Social Services Board [1992] 1 A.C. 294; [1990] 4 All
    E.R.563... 15.2
Selectmove, Re [1995] 1 W.L.R. 474; [1995] 2 All E.R. 531, CA 4.24, 8.10, 8.23, 8.24, 9.10
Servais Bouchard v. Princes Hall Restaurant. *See* Bouchard Servais v. Princes Hall Restaurant
Shadwell v. Shadwell
Shadwell v. Shadwell (1860) 9 C.B.N.S. 159; 142 E.R. 627... 7.11
Shanklin Pier Ltd v. Detel Products Ltd [1951] 2 K.B. 854; [1951] 2 All E.R. 471, KBD
    ....10.27, 12.7
Shanning International Ltd v. Lloyd's TSB Bank *The Times,* July 2, 2001 .... 22.24
Sharington v. Strotton (1565) 1 Plowd 300; 75 E.R. 454 .... 7.3
Sheffield v. Pickfords Ltd; *sub nom.* Kristina Sheffield v. Pickfords Ltd [1997] C.L.C. 648;
    (1997) 16 Tr. L.R. 337, CA 17.22
Sheffield United Football Club v. South Yorkshire Police Authority. *See* Harris v. Sheffield
    United Football Club

Sheikh Bros v. Ochsner. *See* Sheikh Bros v. Ochsner (Arnold Julius)

Sheikh Bros v. Ochsner (Arnold Julius); *sub nom.* Sheikh Bros v. Ochsner [1957] A.C. 136; [1957] 2 W.L.R. 254, PC 21.6

Shelfer v. City of London Electric Lighting Co. *See* Shelfer v. City of London Electric Lighting Co. (No.1)

Shelfer v. City of London Electric Lighting Co. (No.1); Meux's Brewery Co. v. City of London Electric Lighting Co.); *sub nom.* Shelfer v. City of London Electric Lighting Co. [1895] 1 Ch. 287, CA 26.11

Shell v. Lostock Garages. *See* Shell (UK) Ltd v. Lostock Garage Ltd

Shell (UK) Ltd v. Lostock Garage Ltd; *sub nom.* Shell v. Lostock Garages [1976] 1 W.L.R. 1187; [1977] 1 All E.R. 481, CA 12.28

Shepherd v. Johnson (1802) 2 East 211; 102 E.R. 349 .... 24.3

Shepp v. U.S. 444 U.S. 507 (1980) 26.39

Shiloh Spinners Ltd v. Harding. *See* Shiloh Spinners Ltd v. Harding (No.1)

Shiloh Spinners Ltd v. Harding (No.1); *sub nom.* Shiloh Spinners Ltd v. Harding [1973] A.C. 691; [1973] 2 W.L.R. 28, HL 26.3

Shirlaw v. Southern Foundries. *See* Southern Foundries (1926) Ltd v. Shirlaw

Shogun Finance Ltd v. Hudson [2000] All E.R. (D) 306 .... 6.12, 18.22

Shuey v. US, 92 U.S. 73 (1875) 3.13

Siboen, The. *See* Occidental Worldwide Investment Corp. v. Skibs A/S Avanti (The Siboen and The Sibotre)

Sibotre, The. *See* Occidental Worldwide Investment Corp. v. Skibs A/S Avanti (The Siboen and The Sibotre)

Simmons v. United States, 308 F.2d, 160 (1962) 4.4

Simon Container Machinery Ltd v. Emba Machinery AB [1998] 2 Lloyd's Rep. 429, QBD (Comm Ct) 8.12

Simpkins v. Pays [1955] 1 W.L.R. 975; [1955] 3 All E.R. 10, Assizes (Chester) 11.4

Sinclair v. Bowles (1829) 9 B and C 92; 109 E.R.35 .... 23.23

Singh v. Ali [1960] A.C. 167; [1960] 2 W.L.R. 180, PC 20.17

Sir Anthony Sturlyn v. Albany (1587) Cro. Eliz; 78 E.R. 327 .... 7.6

Skandia (UK) Insurance Co. v. Chemical Bank. *See* Banque Financièere de la Cite SA (formerly Banque Keyser Ullmann SA) v. Westgate Insurance Co. (formerly Hodge General & Mercantile Co. Ltd)

Skandia (UK) Insurance Co. v. Credit Lyonnais Bank Nederland NV. *See* Banque Financière de la Cite SA (formerly Banque Keyser Ullmann SA) v. Westgate Insurance Co. (formerly Hodge General & Mercantile Co. Ltd)

Skeate v. Beale (1841) 11 Ad and E 983; 113 E.R. 688 .... 19.3

Slack v. Leeds Industrial Cooperative Society Ltd. *See* Slack v. Leeds Industrial Cooperative Society Ltd (No.1)

Slack v. Leeds Industrial Cooperative Society Ltd (No.1); *sub nom.* Leeds Industrial Cooperative Society Ltd v. Slack; Slack v. Leeds Industrial Cooperative Society Ltd [1924] A.C. 851; [1924] All E.R. Rep. 264, HL 26.11

Slade's Case [1602] 4 Co. Rep. 91a; 76 E.R. 1072 .... 7.2

Small v. Attwood; *sub nom.* Attwood v. Small (1838) 3 Y. & C. Ex. 150 .... 18.8

Smith v. Chadwick (1883–84) L.R. 9 App. Cas. 187, HL; (1881–82) L.R. 20 Ch. D. 27, CA ...18.7, 18.8

Smith v. Eric S Bush; Harris v. Wyre Forest DC; *sub nom.* Smith v. Eric Bush [1990] 1 A.C. 831; [1989] 2 W.L.R. 790; [1989] 2 All E.R. 514, HL 17.19

Smith v. Hughes (1871) LR. 6 Q.B. 597 ....2.8, 6.3, 6.4, 6.6, 21.20

Smith v. Land & House Property Corp. (1885) L.R. 28 Ch. D. 7, CA 18.5

Smith v. River Douglas Catchment Board; *sub nom.* Smith and Snipes Hall Farm Ltd v. River Douglas Catchment Board [1949] 2 K.B. 500; [1949] 2 All E.R. 179, CA 10.2

Smith v. Wilson (1832) 3 B and Ad 738 E.R. ....1.11, 12.18 ?? A or Ad

Smith and Snipes Hall Farm Ltd v. River Douglas Catchment Board. *See* Smith v. River Douglas Catchment Board

Smith New Court Securities Ltd v. Citibank NA; Smith New Court Securities Ltd v. Scrimgeour Vickers (Asset Management) Ltd [1997] A.C. 254; [1996] 3 W.L.R. 1051, HL 18.16, 18.18

Snelling v. John G Snelling Ltd [1973] Q.B. 87; [1972] 2 W.L.R. 588 .... 10.28

Sociedad Financiera de Bienes Raices SA v. Agrimpex Hungarian Trading Co. for
Agricultural Products (The Aello); *sub nom.* Agrimpex Hungarian Trading Co. for
Agricultural Products v. Sociedad Financiera de Bienes Raices SA, [1961] A.C. 135;
[1960] 3 W.L.R. 145, HL.. 22.18

Societé Italo-Belge Pour le Commerce et L'Industrié SA (Antwerp) v. Palm and Vegetable
Oils (Malaysia) Sdn Bhd (The Post Chaser); *sub nom.* The Post Chaser [1982] 1 All
E.R. 19; [1981] 2 Lloyd's Rep. 695, QBD...9.4, 9.8, 9.10, 13.21

Society of Lloyd's v. Khan; *sub nom.* Lloyd's of London v. Khan [1999] 1 F.L.R. 246;
[1998] 3 F.C.R. 93, QBC (Comm Ct).. 19.12

Society of Lloyd's v. Twinn (Geoffrey George); Society of Lloyd's v. Twinn (Gail Sally)
(2000) 97(15) L.S.G. 40; *The Times*, April 4, 2000, CA.. 4.3

Solle v. Butcher [1950] 1 K.B. 671; [1949] 2 All E.R. 1107, CA.....2.10, 6.7, 6.16, 21.6, 21.9, 21.11,
21.12–21.14, 21.20

Sonicare International Ltd v. East Anglia Freight Terminal Ltd; Sonicare International
Ltd v. Neptune Orient Lines Ltd [1997] 2 Lloyd's Rep. 48, CC (Central London) 17.30

Sotiros Shipping Inc. v. Shmeiet Solholt (The Solholt) [1983] 1 Lloyd's Rep. 605; [1983]
Com. L.R. 114, Ca 25.26

Southampton Cargo Handling Plc v. Lotus Cars Ltd (The Rigoletto). *See* Lotus Cars Ltd
v. Southampton Cargo Handling Plc (The Rigoletto)

Southampton Container Terminals Ltd v. Hansa Schiffahrts GmbH. *See* Southampton
Container Terminals Ltd v. Hansa Schiffahrts GmbH (The Maersk Colombo)

Southampton Container Terminals Ltd v. Hansa Schiffahrts GmbH (The Maersk
Colombo); *sub nom.* Southampton Container Terminals Ltd v. Schiffahrisgesellsch
"Hansa Australia" MGH & Co.; Southampton Container Terminals Ltd v. Hansa
Schiffahrtsgesellschaft mbH; Southampton Container Terminals Ltd v. Hansa
Schiffahrts GmbH [2001] EWCA Civ 717; (2001) 98(24) L.S.G. 43; *The Times*, June
13, 2001, CA.. 24.26

Southampton Container Terminals Ltd v. Hansa Schiffahrtsgesellschaft mbH. *See*
Southampton Container Terminals Ltd v. Hansa Schiffahrts GmbH (The Maersk
Colombo)

Southampton Container Terminals Ltd v. Schiffahrisgesellsch "Hansa Australia" MGH &
Co. *See* Southampton Container Terminals Ltd v. Hansa Schiffahrts GmbH (The
Maersk Colombo)

Southern Foundries (1926) Ltd v Shirlaw; *sub nom.* Shirlaw v. Southern Foundries [1940]
A.C. 701, HL; [1939] 2 K.B. 206, CA...12.25, 12.30

Southern Water Authority v. Carey [1985] 2 All E.R. 1077, QBD 16.29

Sovereign Finance Ltd v. Silver Crest Furniture Ltd (1997) 16 Tr. L.R. 370; [1997]
C.C.L.R. 76, QBD... 16.27

Sowler v. Potter [1940] 1 K.B. 271, KBD 6.16

Spector v. Ageda [1973] Ch. 30; [1971] 3 W.L.R. 498, Ch D 20.19

Spencer v. Harding (1870) L.R. 5 C.P. 561 .... 3.3

Spice Girls Ltd v. Aprilia World Service BV; *sub nom.* Spice Girls Ltd v Aprilla World
Service BV [2000] E.M.L.R. 478; *The Times,* April 5, 2000, Ch. D........................15.8, 18.4, 18.14

Spice Girls Ltd v. Aprilla World Service BV. *See* Spice Girls Ltd v. Aprilia World
Service BV

Spurling Ltd v. Bradshaw [1956] 1 W.L.R. 461; [1956] 2 All E.R. 121, CA 16.15, 16.17

Stag Line Ltd v. Tyne Ship Repair Group Ltd (The Zinnia) [1984] 2 Lloyd's Rep. 211;
(1985) 4 Tr. L. 33, QBD (Comm. Ct).. 17.31

Starling v. Lloyds TSB Bank Plc [2000] Lloyd's Rep. Bank. 8; [2000] 1 E.G.L.R. 101; *The
Times,* October 29, 1999, CA... 14.25

Startup v. Macdonald (1843) 6 Man. & G. 593; 134 E.R. 1029 .... 21.34

State Trading Corp. of India Ltd v. M Golodetz & Co. Inc. Ltd; *sub nom.* State Trading
Corporation of India Ltd v. M Golodetz Inc. Ltd [1989] 2 Lloyd's Rep. 277, CA;
[1988] 2 Lloyd's Rep. 182, QBD (Comm Ct).. 23.16

State Trading Corporation of India Ltd v. M Golodetz Inc. Ltd. *See* State Trading Corp.
of India Ltd v. M Golodetz & Co. Inc. Ltd

Steinberg v. Scala (Leeds) Ltd [1923] 2 Ch. 452, CA.. 11.6
Stephens v. Avery [1988] Ch. 449; [1988] 2 W.L.R. 128, Ch D 20.10
Stevenson v. Rogers [1999] Q.B. 1028; [1999] 2 W.L.R. 1064; [1999] 1 All E.R. 61,
    CA...17.11, 17.13, 17.14
Stevenson Jacques and Co. v. McLean (1880) 5 Q.B.D. 346...................................... 4.2
Stewart Gill Ltd v. Horatio Myer & Co. Ltd [1992] Q.B. 600; [1992] 2 W.L.R. 721; [1992]
    2 All E.R. 257, CA...17.19, 17.32
Stilk v. Myrick (1809) 2 Camp. 317; 170 E.R. 1168; 6 Esp 129; 170 E.R. 851 ....8.2, 8.5, 8.6,
                                                                                       8.8, 8.13
Stocznia Gdanska SA v. Latreefers Inc. *See* Stocznia Gdanska SA v. Latvian Shipping Co.
Stocznia Gdanska SA v. Latvian Shipping Co.; *sub nom.* Stocznia Gdanska SA v.
    Latreefers Inc. [1998] 1 W.L.R. 574; [1998] 1 All E.R. 883, HL.................................. 26.23
Strickland v. Sarah Turner (1852) 7 Exch. 208; 155 E.R. 919 .... 21.7
Strongman (1945) v. Sincock [1955] 2 Q.B. 525; [1955] 3 W.L.R. 360, CA 20.19
Stuart v. Wilkins (1778) 1 Doug 18; 99 E.R. 15...7.10
Sudbrook Trading Estate Ltd v. Eggleton [1983] 1 A.C. 444; [1982] 3 W.L.R. 315, HL...... 5.12
Suisse Atlantique Société d'Armement SA v. NV Rotterdamsche Kolen Centrale [1967] 1
    A.C. 361; [1966] 2 W.L.R. 944, HL 16.25
Sumner v. Davies. *See* Davies v. Sumner
Sumpter v. Hedges [1898] 1 Q.B. 673, CA 23.25, 23.28
Surrey CC and Mole DC v. Bredero Homes Ltd; *sub nom.* Surrey County Council v.
    Bredero Homes [1993] 1 W.L.R. 1361; [1993] 3 All E.R. 705, CA 24.8, 26.15, 26.17,
                                                                                       26.36, 26.37
Surrey County Council v. Bredero Homes. *See* Surrey CC and Mole DC v. Bredero Homes
    Ltd
Swain v. Law Society [1983] 1 A.C. 598; [1982] 3 W.L.R. 261 .... 10.5
Syros Shipping Co. SA v. Elaghill Trading Co. (The Proodos C) [1981] 3 All E.R. 189;
    [1980] 2 Lloyd's Rep. 390, QBD...9.1, 9.9, 9.11, 9.18

T C Industrial Plants Pty Ltd v. Robert's Queensland Pty Ltd [1963] 37 A.L.J.R. 289 .... 24.19
T W Thomas & Co. Ltd v. Portsea Steamship Co. Ltd (The Portsmouth) [1912] A.C. 1,
    HL; [1911] P. 54, CA.. 12.2
Tai Hing Cotton Mill Ltd v. Liu Chong Hing Bank Ltd (No.1)[1986] A.C. 80; [1985] 3
    W.L.R. 317, PC.. 1.5
Tamplin SS Ltd v. Anglo Mexican Petroleum Products Co. *See* FA Tamplin Steamship Co.
    Ltd v. Anglo Mexican Petroleum Products Co. Ltd
Tanner v. Tanner (No.1) [1975] 1 W.L.R. 1346; [1975] 3 All E.R. 776, CA 7.6
Tate v. Williamson (1866) L.R. 2 Ch. App. 55, CA in Chancery; (1865–66) L.R. 1 Eq. 528,
    Ct of Chancery.. 19.15
Tatem Ltd v. Gamboa. *See* W J Tatem Ltd v. Gamboa
Taylor Fashions Ltd v. Liverpool Victoria Trustees Co. Ltd; *sub nom.* Taylor's Fashions v.
    Liverpool Trustees; Old & Campbell Ltd v. Liverpool Victoria Friendly Society [1982]
    Q.B. 133; [1981] 2 W.L.R. 576, Ch D 9.16, 9.20, 9.21
Taylor v. Allon [1966] 1 Q.B. 304; [1965] 2 W.L.R. 598, DC 4.6
Taylor v. Bowers (1875–76) L.R. 1 Q.B.D. 291, CA 20.16
Taylor v. Caldwell (1863) 32 L.J. Q.B. 164; (1863) 3 B & S 826; 122 E.R. 309...............22.8, 22.22
Taylor v. Dickens [1998] 1 F.L.R. 806; [1998] 3 F.C.R. 455, Ch D 9.16
Taylor v. Johnson [1983] 45 A.L.R. 265, HC (Aus); [1982–83] 151 C.L.R. 422 .... 21.24
Taylor's Fashions v. Liverpool Trustees. *See* Taylor Fashions Ltd v. Liverpool Victoria
    Trustees Co. Ltd
Teacher v. Calder [1899] A.C. 451; (1899) 7 S.L.T.153, HL; SC 1 (HL) 39......................... 24.9
Tenax Steamship Co. v. Owners of the Motor Vessel Brimnes (The Brimnes); *sub nom.*
    Tenax Steamship Co. v. Reinante Transoceanica Navegacion SA (The Brimnes) [1975]
    Q.B. 929; [1974] 3 W.L.R. 613, CA 4.9
Tenax Steamship Co. v. Reinante Transoceanica Navegacion SA (The Brimnes). *See* Tenax
    Steamship Co. v. Owners of the Motor Vessel Brimnes (The Brimnes)
Thackwell v. Barclays Bank Plc [1986] 1 All E.R. 676; *The Times*, December 5, 1984, QBD... 20.20

Thai Trading v. Taylor. *See* Thai Trading Co. v. Taylor

Thai Trading Co. v. Taylor; *sub nom.* Thai Trading v. Taylor [1998] Q.B. 781; [1998] 2
 W.L.R. 893; [1998] 3 All E.R. 65, CA 20.12

The Egg Stores (Stamford Hill) Ltd v. Leibovici. *See* Egg Stores (Stamford Hill), The v.
 Leibovici (L)

The Gator Shipping Corp. v. Trans-Asiatic Oil SA The Odenfeld. *See* Gator Shipping
 Corp. v. Trans-Asiatic Oil SA and Occidental Shipping Etablissement SA (The
 Odenfeld) The Rialto. *See* Rialto, The

Thomas v. Thomas. *See* Eleanor Thomas v. Benjamin Thomas

Thomas Bates v. Wyndham's (Lingerie) Ltd. *See* Thomas Bates & Son Ltd v. Wyndham's
 (Lingerie) Ltd

Thomas Bates & Son Ltd v. Wyndham's (Lingerie) Ltd; *sub nom.* Thomas Bates v.
 Wyndham's (Lingerie) Ltd [1981] 1 W.L.R. 505; [1981] 1 All E.R. 1077, CA 21.21, 21.22

Thomas Witter Ltd v. TBP Industries Ltd [1996] 2 All E.R. 573, Ch. D; [1994] T.L.R.
 145 ....12.9, 18.19

Thompson v. Sheffield Fertility Clinic; *sub nom.* Patricia Thompson, unreported,
 November 24, 2000, QBD 11.4

Thompson v. T Lohan (Plant Hire) and Hurdiss (JW); *sub nom.* Thompson v. T Lohan
 (Plant Hire) Ltd [1987] 1 W.L.R. 649; [1987] 2 All E.R. 631, CA 17.20

Thompson v. T Lohan (Plant Hire) Ltd. *See* Thompson v. T Lohan (Plant Hire) and
 Hurdiss (JW)

Thompson (WL) Ltd v. Robinson (Gunmakers) Ltd. *See* W L Thompson Ltd v. R
 Robinson (Gunmakers) Ltd

Thomson v. LMS Railway [1931 1 K.B. 41 ....   16.12

Thorensen Car Ferries v. Weymouth Portland BC [1977] 2 Lloyd's Rep. 614, QBD (Comm
 Ct) 5.1

Thornton v. Abbey National *The Times*, March 4, 1993, CA 23.4

Thornton v. Shoe Lane Parking [1971] 2 Q.B. 163; [1971] 2 W.L.R. 585, CA 2.4, 5.1, 16.12, 16.15
 Thoroughgood's Case (1582) 2 Co. Rep. 9a; 76 E.R. 408 ....   21.16

Tilden Rent-a-Car v. Clendenning (1978) 83 D.L.R. (3d) 400, CA (Ont) 16.7, 16.15

Timeload Ltd v. British Telecommunications Plc [1995] E.M.L.R. 459, CA 14.11, 16.30

Tinn v. Hoffman (1873) 29 L.T. 271 ....   5.1,

Tinsley v. Milligan [1994] 1 A.C. 340; [1993] 3 W.L.R. 126, HL 20.6, 20.18–20.20

Tito v. Waddell (No.2); Tito v. Attorney General [1977] Ch. 106; [1977] 3 W.L.R. 972,
 Ch D 24.24, 26.4, 26.35

Toepfer International GmbH v. Itex Itagrani Export SA. *See* Alfred C Toepfer
 International GmbH v. Itex Itagrani Export SA

Toepfer v. Cremer. *See* Alfred C Toepfer v. Peter Cremer GmbH & Co.

Toepfer v. Peter Cremer. *See* Alfred C Toepfer v. Peter Cremer GmbH & Co.

Toker v. Westerman (1969) 274 A. 2d 78 ....   14.19

Tolhurst v Smith (No.1) [1994] E.M.L.R. 508, Ch D 19.17

Tool Metal Manufacture Co. Ltd v. Tungsten Electric Co. Ltd. *See* Tool Metal
 Manufacture Co. Ltd v. Tungsten Electric Co. Ltd

Toomey v. Eagle Star Insurance. *See* Toomey v. Eagle Star Insurance Co Ltd (No.2)

Toomey v. Eagle Star Insurance Co. Ltd (No.2); *sub nom.* Toomey v. Eagle Star Insurance
 [1995] 2 Lloyd's Rep. 88, QBD (Comm Ct) 18.25

Torrance v. Bolton (1872) L.R. 8 Ch. App. 118, CA in Chancery 21.20

Torvald Klaveness A/S v. Arni Maritime Corp (The Gregos) [1994] 1 W.L.R. 1465; [1994]
 4 All E.R. 998, HL 13.22

Total Liban SAL v. Vitol Energy SA [2000] 3 W.L.R. 1142; [2000] 1 All E.R. 267, QBD ...   10.32

Tradax Export v. Goldschmidt SA [1977] 2 Lloyd's Rep. 604 ....   13.18

Tribe v. Tribe [1996] Ch. 107; [1995] 3 W.L.R. 913; [1995] 4 All E.R. 236, CA 20.19

Trollope & Colls Ltd v. Atomic Power Constructions Ltd; *sub nom.* Trollope & Colls Ltd
 and Holland & Hannen and Cubitts Ltd (t/a Nuclear Civil Constructions) v. Atomic
 Power Constructions Ltd [1963] 1 W.L.R. 333; [1962] 3 All E.R. 1035, QBD 3.8, 5.5

Trollope and Colls Ltd t/a Nuclear Civil Contractors v. Atomic Power Construction Ltd.
 See Trollope & Colls Ltd v. Atomic Power Constructions Ltd

Trustee v. Cargo Superintendents (London) Ltd. *See* Schebsman (Deceased) Ex p. Official
Receiver, Re
Tsakiroglou & Co. Ltd v. Noblee Thorl GmbH; Albert D Gaon & Co. v. Societe
Interprofessionelle des Oleagineux Fluides Alimentaires [1962] A.C. 93; [1961] 2
W.L.R. 633, HL.. 22.14
Tudor Grange Holdings Ltd v. Citibank NA [1992] Ch. 53; [1991] 3 W.L.R. 750; [1991] 4
All E.R. 1, Ch. D.. 17.10
Tufton v. Sperni [1952] 2 T.L.R. 516; [1952] W.N. 439, CA............................... 19.15
Tulk v. Moxhay (1848) 2 Ph. 774; (1848) 18 L.J. Ch. 83................................... 10.24
Tungsten Electric Co. Ltd v. Tool Metal Manufacturing Co. Ltd (No.3); *sub nom.* Tool
Metal Manufacture Co. Ltd v. Tungsten Electric Co. Ltd [1955] 1 W.L.R. 761; [1955]
2 All E.R. 657, HL..9.7, 9.8, 9.12
Turner v. Green [1895] 2 Ch. 205 Ch D...14.22, 15.2
Turner v. Owen (1862) 3 Fed F 176; 176 E.R. 79 .... 8.3
Tweddle v. Atkinson (1861) 1 B. & S. 393; 121 E.R. 762 ....10.2, 10.5, 10.8

UCB Bank Plc v. Hepherd Winstanley & Pugh [1999] Lloyd's Rep. P.N. 963; (1999) 96(34)
L.S.G. 34; *The Times*, August 25, 1999, CA 25.28
Union Eagle Ltd v. Golden Achievement Ltd [1997] A.C. 514; [1997] 2 W.L.R. 341, PC ... 13.23
Unique Mariner, The (No.2) [1979] 1 Lloyd's Rep. 37, QBD (Adm Ct).......................... 23.2
United Dominions Trust (Commercial) v. Eagle Aircraft Services; *sub nom.* United
Dominions Trust (Commercial) v. Eagle Aviation [1968] 1 W.L.R. 74; [1968] 1 All
E.R. 104, CA 4.21, 13.18
United Dominions Trust (Commercial) v. Eagle Aviation. *See* United Dominions Trust
(Commercial) v. Eagle Aircraft Services
Universal Cargo Carriers Corp. v. Citati (No.1); *sub nom.* Universal Cargo Carriers v.
Citati [1957] 1 W.L.R. 979; [1957] 3 All E.R. 234, CA; [1957] 2 Q.B. 401,
QBD 22.19, 23.5
Universal Cargo Carriers v. Citati. *See* Universal Cargo Carriers Corp. v. Citati (No.1)
Universe Sentinel, The. *See* Universe Tankships Inc. of Monrovia v. International
Transport Workers Federation (The Universe Sentinel)
Universe Tankships Inc. of Monrovia v. International Transport Workers Federation (The
Universe Sentinel); *sub nom.* Universe Tankships v. ITF [1983] 1 A.C. 366; [1982] 2
W.L.R. 803, HL 19.1, 19.4, 9.7
Universe Tankships v. ITF. *See* Universe Tankships Inc. of Monrovia v. International
Transport Workers Federation (The Universe Sentinel)
University of Nottingham v. Eyett (No.1) [1999] 2 All E.R. 437; [1999] I.C.R. 721, Ch. D... 15.2
Upton-on-Severn Rural DC v. Powell [1942] 1 All E.R. 220, CA 5.3
Urquhart v. Clark. *See* Clark v. Urquhart
Urquhart v. Stracey. *See* Clark v. Urquhart

Vacwell Engineering Co. Ltd v. BDH Chemicals Ltd; *sub nom.* Vacwell Engineering Co. v.
British Drug House Chemicals [1971] 1 Q.B. 88; [1969] 3 W.L.R. 927, QBD 25.7
Vacwell Engineering Co. v. British Drug House Chemicals. *See* Vacwell Engineering Co.
Ltd v. BDH Chemicals Ltd
Vadusz v. Pioneer Concrete (SA) Pty Ltd (1895) 130 A.L.R. 570 .... 18.22
Vanbergen v. St Edmunds Properties Ltd [1933] 2 K.B. 223, CA; [1933] 1 K.B. 345, KBD... 8.16
Vandepitte v. Preferred Accident Insurance Co. of New York. *See* Vandepitte v. Preferred
Accident Insurance Corp. of New York
Vandepitte v. Preferred Accident Insurance Corp. of New York; *sub nom.* Vandepitte v.
Preferred Accident Insurance Co. of New York [1933] A.C. 70; (1932) 44 Ll. L. Rep.
41, PC.. 10.26
Vaswani v. Italian Motors (Sales and Services) Ltd [1996] 1 W.L.R. 270; [1996] R.T.R. 115,
PC..14.27, 23.11
Victoria Laundry (Windsor) v. Newman Industries [1949] 2 K.B. 528; [1949] 1 All E.R.
997, CA..25.4, 25.5, 25.6
Victoria Seats Agency v. Paget (1903) 19 T.L.R. 16 .... 22.13

Vine v. Waltham Forest LBC [2000] 1 W.L.R. 2383; [2000] 4 All E.R. 169, CA 16.1, 16.14
Vita Food Products Inc. v. Unus Shipping Co. Ltd (In Liquidation); *sub nom.* Vita Food
   Products Inc v. Unus Shipping Co. Ltd .....[1939] A.C. 277; (1939) 63 Ll. L. Rep. 21,
   PC 20.5
Vita Food Products Inc v. Unus Shipping Co. Ltd. *See* Vita Food Products Inc. v. Unus
   Shipping Co. Ltd (In Liquidation)
Vitol SA v. Norelf Ltd (The Santa Clara) [1996] A.C. 800; [1996] 3 W.L.R. 105, HL 4.23, 23.16
Von Hatzfeldt Wildenburg v. Alexander [1912] 1 Ch. 284, Ch D 5.15

W v. Commissioner of Police of the Metropolis; *sub nom.* Waters v. Commissioner of
   Police of the Metropolis [2000] 1 W.L.R. 1607; [2000] 4 All E.R. 934; [2000] I.C.R.
   1064; [2000] I.R.L.R. 720, HL..   25.14
W.F. Trustees Ltd v. Expo Safety Systems Ltd *The Times,* May 24, 1993, Ch D...............   12.11
W J Alan & Co. Ltd v. El Nasr Export & Import Co. [1972] 2 Q.B. 189; [1972] 2 W.L.R.
   800, CA 9.8, 9.12, 10.17
W J Tatem Ltd v. Gamboa; *sub nom.* Tatem Ltd v. Gamboa [1939] 1 K.B. 132; (1938) 61
   Ll. L. Rep. 149
W L Thompson Ltd v. R Robinson (Gunmakers) Ltd; *sub nom.* Thompson (WL) Ltd v.
   Robinson (Gunmakers) Ltd [1955] Ch. 177; [1955] 2 W.L.R. 185, Ch D 24.27
Wales v. Wadham [1977] 1 W.L.R. 199; [1977] 1 All E.R. 125, Fam. Div. 15.3
Walford v. Miles [1992] 2 A.C. 128; [1992] 2 W.L.R. 174, HL...............................5.16, 13.6, 14.29
Walker v. Boyle; *sub nom.* Boyle v Walker [1982] 1 W.L.R. 495; [1982] 1 All E.R. 634,
   Ch. D..   18.25
Walker v. Northumberland CC [1995] 1 All E.R. 737; [1995] I.C.R. 702, QBD 25.13
Walker, Re [1905] 1 Ch. 160, CA..   11.7
Wall v. Rederi ABet Luggude [1915] 3 K.B. 66, KBD..   25.33
Wallis Son & Wells v. Pratt & Haynes [1911] A.C. 394, HL; [1910] 2 K.B. 1003, CA 13.8
Walton Harvey Ltd v. Walker & Homfrays Ltd [1931] 1 Ch. 274, CA; [1931] 1 Ch. 145,
   Ch D..   22.15
Waltons Stores (Interstate) Ltd v. Maher (1988)164 C.L.R 387.............................9.9, 9.13, 24.20
Ward v. Byham [1956] 1 W.L.R. 496; [1956] 2 All E.R. 318, CA.....................................7.3, 8.5
Warlow v. Harrison (1859) E1 & E1 309; 120 E.R. 920 ....   3.7
Warner Bros Pictures Inc. v. Nelson; *sub nom.* Warner Brothers Pictures Inc. v. Nelson
   [1937] 1 K.B. 209, KBD..   26.9
Warner Brothers Pictures Inc. v. Nelson. *See* Warner Bros Pictures Inc. v. Nelson
Warren v. Mendy [1989] 1 W.L.R. 853; [1989] 3 All E.R. 103, CA......................................   26.9
Waters v. Commissioner of Police of the Metropolis. *See* W v. Commissioner of Police of
   the Metropolis
Watford Electronics Ltd v. Sanderson CFL Ltd [2001] EWCA Civ 317; [2001] 1 All E.R.
   (Comm) 696; [2000] 2 All E.R. (Comm) 984; *The Times,* March 9, 2001....16.10, 16.22, 17.30
Watson v. Prager [1991] 1 W.L.R. 726; [1991] 3 All E.R. 487; [1993] E.M.L.R. 275, Ch D....   20.26
Watts v. Morrow [1991] 1 W.L.R. 1421; [1991] 4 All E.R. 937, CA....................................   24.23
Wayling v. Jones [1995] 2 F.L.R. 1029; [1996] 2 F.C.R. 41; (1995) 69 P. & C.R. 170, CA 9.15
Weatherby v. Banhan (1832) C and P 228; 172 E.R. 950 ....   4.23
Webster v. Bosanquet [1912] A.C. 394, PC...   25.30
Wenkheim v. Arendt (NZ) 1 JR 73 (1973) 4.26
Wennall v. Adney (1802) 3 B and P 249; 127 E.R. 137 ....1.10, 7.2, 7.19
Wertheim v. Chicoutimi Pulp Co.; *sub nom.* Sally Wertheim v. Chicoutimi Pulp Co. [1911]
   A.C. 301, PC..   24.22
West London Commercial Bank Ltd v. Kitson; West London Commercial Bank Ltd v.
   Porter; West London Commercial Bank Ltd v. Woodward (1883–84) L.R. 13 Q.B.D.
   360, CA; (1883–84) L.R. 12 Q.B.D. 157, QBD 18.6
Westacre Investments Inc. v. Jugoimport SPDR Holding Co. Ltd; *sub nom.* Westacre
   Investments Inc. v. Jugoimport [2000] Q.B. 288; [1999] 3 W.L.R. 811; [1999] 3 All E.R.
   864, CA 20.8
Westacre Investments Inc. v. Jugoimport. *See* Westacre Investments Inc. v. Jugoimport
   SPDR Holding Co. Ltd

Westdeutsche Landesbank Girozentrale v. Islington Borough Council. *See* Westdeutsche
    Landesbank Girozentrale v. Islington LBC
Westdeutsche Landesbank Girozentrale v. Islington LBC; Kleinwort Benson Ltd v.
    Sandwell BC; *sub nom.* Westdeutsche Landesbank Girozentrale v. Islington Borough
    Council [1996] A.C. 669; [1996] 2 W.L.R. 802; [1996] 2 All E.R. 961, HL 26.22
Wettern Electric Ltd v. Welsh Development Agency [1983] Q.B. 796; [1983] 2 W.L.R. 897,
    QBD 4.4
Whelpdale's case (1604) 5 Co. Rep 119; 77 E.R. 239 .... 19.1
White & Carter (Councils) Ltd v. McGregor [1962] A.C. 413; [1962] 2 W.L.R. 17, HL
    .... 23.7, 23.8, 23.9, 23.10, 25.24
White Arrow Express Ltd v. Lamey's Distribution Ltd (1996) 15 Tr. L.R. 69; (1995) 145
    N.L.J. 1504, CA 24.14, 24.23
White v. Bluett (1853) 23 LJ Ex 36 .... 7.11, 7.12
White v. John Warwick & Co. [1953] 1 W.L.R. 1285; [1953] 2 All E.R. 1021, CA 16.20
White v. Jones [1995] 2 A.C. 207; [1995] 2 W.L.R. 187; [1995] 1 All E.R. 691, HL ...8.25, 10.5, 10.12
Whittet v. Bush. *See* Fry v. Lane
Whittington v. Seale-Hayne (1900) 82 L.T. 49 .... 18.20
Whitworth Street Estates (Manchester) Ltd v. James Miller & Partners Ltd; *sub nom.*
    James Miller & Partners Ltd v. Whitworth Street Estates (Manchester) Ltd [1970]
    A.C. 583; [1970] 2 W.L.R. 728, HL 12.2
Wickman Machine Tool Sales Ltd v. L Schuler AG. *See* L Schuler AG v. Wickman
    Machine Tool Sales Ltd
Widnes Foundry (1925) Ltd v. Cellulose Acetate Silk Co. Ltd. *See* Cellulose Acetate Silk
    Co. Ltd v. Widnes Foundry (1925) Ltd
Wigan v. English and Scottish Law Life Assurance Association [1909] 1 Ch. 291, Ch D.... 7.13
Wight v. British Railways Board (1983) C.L.Y. 424; unreported, October 11, 1981, CC.... 17.34
William Cory & Son Ltd v. London Corp. [1951] 2 K.B. 476; [1951] 2 All E.R. 85, CA ..11.7, 23.1
William Sindall Plc v. Cambridgeshire CC [1994] 1 W.L.R. 1016; [1994] 3 All E.R. 932,
    CA 18.16, 18.20, 21.3,
                                                                                                       21.14, 21.15
Williams v. Carwardine (1833) 4 B and Ad 621; 110 E.R. 590 .... 4.6
Williams v. Roffey Brothers & Nicholls (Contractors) Ltd [1991] 1 Q.B. 1; [1990] 2 W.L.R.
    1153, CA...............................7.3, 7.5, 7.8, 7.16, 8.4–8.6, 8.9–8.13, 8.23, 8.24, 8.28, 23.29
Williams v. Roffey. *See* Williams v. Roffey Brothers & Nicholls (Contractors) Ltd
Williams v. Walker Thomas Furniture Co. (1965) 350 F. 2d 445 .... 14.20
Williams v. Williams (Enforceability of Agreement) [1957] 1 W.L.R. 148; [1957] 1 All E.R.
    305, CA 7.3, 8.5
Williamson (J.C.) Ltd v. Lukey and Mulholland (1931) 45 C.L.R. 282 .... 26.5
Wilson v. First County Trust Ltd (No.2); *sub nom.* Wilson v. First County Trust Ltd [2001]
    EWCA Civ 633; (2001) 151 N.L.J. 882, [2001] All E.R. (D) 28; *The Times*, May 16,
    2001, CA...1.15, 4.1, 11.11, 18.2
    Wilson v. First County Trust Ltd. *See* Wilson v. First County Trust Ltd (No.2)
Winterbottom v. Wright (1842) 10 M and W 109; 107 E.R. 171 ....10.2, 10.25
With v. O'Flanagan [1936] Ch. 575, CA 15.8
Woodar Investment Development Ltd v. Wimpey Construction UK Ltd; *sub nom.* Woodar
    Investment v. Wimpy Construction UK [1980] 1 W.L.R. 277; [1980] 1 All E.R. 571,
    HL 10.5, 14.27, 23.11, 23.12, 25.16
Woodar Investment v. Wimpy Construction UK. *See* Woodar Investment Development
    Ltd v. Wimpey Construction UK Ltd
Woodhouse AC Israel Cocoa SA v. Nigerian Produce Marketing Co. Ltd; *sub nom.*
    Woodhouse v. Nigerian Produce Marketing Co. Ltd [1972] A.C. 741; [1972] 2 W.L.R.
    1090, HL 9.7, 9.19
Woodhouse v. Nigerian Produce Marketing Co. Ltd. *See* Woodhouse AC Israel Cocoa SA
    v. Nigerian Produce Marketing Co. Ltd
Woodman v. Photo Trade Processing (1931) New Law Journal 935 .... 17.34
Woolls v. Powling *The Times,* March 9, 1999, CA 12.11
Woolwich Building Society (formerly Woolwich Equitable Building Society) v. Inland

Revenue Commissioners; *sub nom.* Woolwich Building Society v. Inland Revenue
  Commissioners [1993] A.C. 70; [1992] 3 W.L.R. 366, HL 26.22
Woolwich Building Society v. Inland Revenue Commissioners. *See* Woolwich Building
  Society (formerly Woolwich Equitable Building Society) v. Inland Revenue
  Commissioners
Wright v. Carter [1903] 1 Ch. 27, CA.. 19.14
WRM Group Ltd v. Wood [1998] C.L.C. 189, CA 17.19
Wroth v. Tyler [1974] Ch. 30; [1973] 2 W.L.R. 405, Ch D 26.12
Wrotham Park Estate Co. Ltd v. Parkside Homes Ltd ; *sub nom.* Wrotham Park Estate v.
  Parkside Homes [1974] 1 W.L.R. 798; [1974] 2 All E.R. 321, Ch D 26.11–26.13, 26.15, 26.17
Wrotham Park Estate v. Parkside Homes. *See* Wrotham Park Estate Co. Ltd v. Parkside
  Homes Ltd

Xydhias v. Xydhias [1999] 2 All E.R. 386; [1999] 1 F.L.R. 683; *The Times,* January 12,
  1999, CA 11.3

Yaxley v. Gott. *See* Yaxley v. Gotts
Yaxley v. Gotts; *sub nom* Yaxley v Gott [2000] Ch. 162; [1999] 3 W.L.R. 1217; [1999] 2
  F.L.R. 941; *The Times,* July 8, 1999, CA 9.17, 11.9, 18.2
Yetton v. Eastwood Froy Ltd [1967] 1 W.L.R. 104; [1966] 3 All E.R. 353, QBD 25.24
Youell v. Bland Welch & Co. Ltd (No.1) [1992] 2 Lloyd's Rep. 127, CA; [1990] 2 Lloyd's
  Rep. 423, QBD Comm Ct) 12.3
Yukong Line Ltd of Korea v. Rendsburg Investments Corp. of Liberia (The Rialto)
  (Preliminary Issues); *sub nom.* Yukong Line of Korea v. Rendsburg Investments
  Corporation of Liberia [1996] 2 Lloyd's Rep. 604, QBD (Comm Ct) 23.17
Yukong Line of Korea v. Rendsburg Investments Corporation of Liberia. *See* Yukong
  Line Ltd of Korea v. Rendsburg Investments Corp. of Liberia (The Rialto)
  (Preliminary Issues)

Zambia Steel & Building Supplies Ltd v. James Clark & Eaton Ltd [1986] 2 Lloyd's Rep.
  225; Financial Times, August 15, 1986, CA... 5.8
Zanzibar v. British Aerospace (Lancaster House) Ltd [2000] 1 W.L.R. 2333; [2000] C.L.C.
  735; *The Times,* January 26, 2000; *The Times,* March 28, 2000, QBD (Comm Ct) 18.19
Zealander v. Laing Homes Ltd (2000) 2 T.C.L.R. 724, QBD (T&CC)...............15.16, 15.23,15.26
Zoan v. Rouamba [2000] 1 W.L.R. 1509; [2000] 2 All E.R. 620; *The Times,* March 7, 2000,
  CA.. 12.12
Zockoll Group Ltd v. Mercury Communications Ltd (No.1) [1998] F.S.R. 354, CA 14.11
Williams & Glyn's Bank Ltd v. Boland; Williams & Glyn's Bank Ltd v. Brown [1981] A.C.
  487; [1980] 3 W.L.R. 138, HL 19.18
Attorney General of Hong Kong v. Humphreys Estate (Queen's Gardens) Ltd [1987] A.C.
  114; [1987] 2 W.L.R. 343, PC 5.18, 9.13, 9.20
Court: CA.. 26.8
Court: KBD 22.01, 22.20
Court: PC 10.24
Court: QBD (Comm Ct)... 17.31

Table of UK Statutes

1677 Statute of Frauds (29 Car. 2, c.3) 1.15, 7.1, 11.8, 11.9
    s.4 .... 11.9

1845 Gaming Act (8 & 9 Vict., c.109) . 20.11, 26.22

1854 Railway and Canal Traffic Act (17 & 18 Vict., c.31) 14.7, 17.22

1858 Chancery Amendment Act (21 & 22 Vict., c.27) 26.11–26.16, 26.37

1870 Apportionment Act (33 & 34 Vict., c.35)........................... 23.31
    s.2 .... 23.31

1870 Tramways Act (33 & 34 Vict., c.78) 14.7

1873 Supreme Court of Judicature Act (36 & 37 Vict., c.66)...... 26.11

1878 Bills of Sale Act (41 & 42 Vict., c.31) 11.9

1882 Bills of Exchange Act (45 & 46 Vict., c.61) 1.15, 10.21, 10.33
    s3(1)..................................... 11.9

1882 Married Women's Property Act (45 & 46 Vict., c.75) ....
    s.11.. 10.33

1893 Sale of Goods Act (50 & 51 Vict., c.71) 1.15, 10.25, 12.20, 13.8, 17.1, 24.24
    s.61(2).............................13.17

1906 Marine Insurance Act (5 & 6 Edw. 7, c.41) 1.15, 12.16

1908 Companies (Consolidation) Act (7 & 8 Edw. 7, c.69)............

1911 Official Secrets Act (1 & 2 Geo. 5, c.28) 26.39

1925 Law of Property Act (15 & 16 Geo. 5, c.20)........................ 10.33
    s.40.. 11.9

1930 Third Parties (Rights Against Insurers) Act (20 & 21 Geo. 5, c.25) 10.33

1933 Pharmacy and Poisons Act (23 & 24 Geo. 5, c.25) 3.4

1943 Law Reform (Frustrated Contracts) Act (6 & 7 Geo. 6, c.40)................1.18, 22.1, 22.12, 22.24–22.30, 23.31, 23.33, 26.20
    s.1(1) 22.25
    s.1(2) 22.2, 22.26, 22.28, 22.29, 23.21
    s.1(3)................................22.27, 22.28
    s.1(3)(a)................................. 22.27
    s.1(3)(b)................................. 22.27
    s.2(2)..................................... 22.30
    s.2(3)................................22.1, 22.24
    s.2(4)..................................... 22.30
    s.2(5)..................................... 22.30

1945 Law Reform Contributory Negligence Act (9 & 10 Geo. 6, c.28) 25.27, 25.38
    s.1(1)..................................... 25.27

1957 Occupiers Liability Act (5 & 6 Eliz. 2, c.31) 17.5

1961 Carriage by Air Act (9 & 10 Eliz. 2, c.27) 1.17

1964 Hire Purchase Act (c.53) 6.12
    s.27(3) 13.14

1965 Carriage of Goods by Road Act (c.37) 1.17

1967 Misrepresentation Act (c.7)...1.15, 1.18, 17.1, 17.14, 25.28
    s.1 .... 13.2
    s.2(1) 14.6, 18.18, 18.20, 18.24, 18.25, 24.5, 25.8, 25.28
    s.2(2) 18.18–18.20
    s.2(3) 18.20
    s.3 ....17.1, 18.25

1967 Criminal Law Act (c.58)............. 20.12

1968 Trade Descriptions Act (c.29) 3.5, 17.13

1968 Theft Act (c.60)
    s. 16(1) 3.3

1969	Family Law Reform Act (c.46)	
	s.1	11.6
1970	Law Reform (Miscellaneous Provisions) Act (c.33)	
	s.1(1)	11.4
1971	Unsolicited Goods and Services Act (c.30)	4.25
1973	Supply of Goods (Implied Terms) Act (c.13)	15.32, 17.1, 17.13
1973	Fair Trading Act (c.41)	14.19, 17.35
1974	Consumer Credit Act (c.39)	1.15, 4.19, 11.11, 15.32
	s.29	4.1
	s.55	15.13
	s.60	11.10
	s.61	11.10
	s.127(3)	1.15, 11.11
	ss.137–140	14.19
1976	Lotteries and Amusements Act (c.32)	
	s.1	20.11
	s.3	20.11
1977	Unfair Contract Terms Act (c.50)	1.15, 1.18, 2.4, 10.22, 12.20, 14.6, 14.7, 14.11, 14.12, 15.16, 15.21, 15.34, 16.1, 16.4, 16.7, 16.15, 16.16, 16.19, 17.1–17.35
	s.1	17.5
	s.1(3)	17.11
	s.1(4)	17.6
	s.2	17.6, 17.8
	s.2(1)	10.22, 12.30, 16.13, 17.3, 17.6, 17.7, 17.20
	s.2(2)	10.22, 16.28, 17.4, 17.7, 17.20
	s.2(3)	17.9
	ss.2–7	17.5, 17.6
	s.3	13.14, 15.32, 16.4, 16.24, 17.4, 17.7–17.9, 17.15, 17.16, 17.20, 17.27
	s.3(2)	16.29
	s.4	17.9
	s.4(1)	17.4
	s.5	8.26, 15.19, 17.3, 17.8, 17.9
	s.6	12.16, 15.32, 17.3, 17.8–17.10, 17.13, 17.35
	s.6(2)	17.4
	s6(4)	17.5, 17.11, 17.14
	s.7	15.32, 17.3, 17.4, 17.8, 17.9
	s.8	17.1
	s.9	13.14, 16.4, 16.24, 17.9
	s.10	17.10
	s.11	16.26, 17.10, 17.22, 17.23, 17.27
	s.12	17.9, 17.12
	s.12(1)(a)	17.12
	s.12(1)(b)	17.12, 17.14
1977	Unfair Contract Terms Act —cont.	
	s.12(1)(c)	17.12
	s.12(2)	17.12
	s.12(3)	17.12
	s.13	17.9, 17.18, 17.19
	s.13(1)	17.10
	s.13(1)(b)	17.19
	s.13(1)(c)	17.18
	s.13(2)	15.26, 17.10
	s.14	17.5, 17.9, 17.11
	s.15	17.9
	s.26	17.7
	s.27(1)	17.7
	s.27(2)	17.7
	s.27(2)(a)	17.7
	s.27(2)(b)	17.7
	Sched.1	16.4, 17.4, 17.6
	Sched.2	14.22, 15.20, 17.10, 17.22, 17.24, 17.34
	Sched.2, para.(a)	14.9, 17.24
	Sched.2, para.(b)	17.24
	Sched.2, para.(c)	17.24
1979	Sale of Goods Act (c.54)	1.2, 1.6, 1.18, 3.7, 5.13, 10.25, 12.16, 12.20, 12.21, 12.22, 12.23, 13.11, 13.17, 13.18, 17.11, 17.27
	s.3(2)	11.7
	s.3(3)	11.6
	s.6	1.4, 21.4
	s.8(2)	5.13
	s.8(3)	5.13
	s.10	13.23
	s.10(2)	13.23
	s.12	12.20
	s.13	12.20, 13.11
	s.13(1)	21.9
	ss.13–15	23.18
	s.14	13.11
	s.14(2)	12.20, 12.30
	s.14(2A)	12.20
	s.14(2)(2B)	12.20
	s.14(3)	12.30
	s.14(3)(b)	12.20
	s.15	12.21, 13.11
	s.15(2)	13.11
	s.15(2)(a)	12.20
	s.15A	13.11, 15.32
	s.35	23.17
	s.50	24.21
	s.50(3)	24.21
	s.51	24.21
	s.51(2)	24.22
	s.51(3)	24.21
	s.53	24.23
1981	Supreme Court Act (c.54)	26.11
	s.49	26.2

	s.50 ....26.2, 26.11	
1982	Supply of Goods and Services Act (c.29) 1.18, 12.23	
	s.13 ....13.18, 12.23	
	s.14 ....13.18, 12.23	
	s.15...............5.13, 12.23, 13.18, 26.31	
1982	Forfeiture Act (c.34) 20.8	
1983	International Transport Conventions Act (c.14) 1.17	
1983	Mental Health Act (c.20)............ 11.7	
1984	Occupier's Liability Act (c.3)	
	s.2 .... 17.5	
1985	Companies Act (c.6)	
	s.14...........................5.1, 10.21, 10.33	
1986	Insolvency Act (c.45).................. 18.11	
1986	Financial Services Act (c.60)	
	s.5 .... 20.4	
1987	Consumer Protection Act (c.43).. 3.4	
1987	Minor's Contracts Act (c.13)...... 1.18	
1988	Road Traffic Act (c.52) 10.33	
1989	Law of Property (Miscellaneous Provisions) Act (c.34)	
	s.1 .... 11.10	
	s.1(2) 11.10	
	s.1(3) 11.10	
	s.2 .... 9.16	
1990	Courts and Legal Services Act (c.41)	
	s.58 .... 20.12	
1992	Timeshare Act (c.35)..........4.19, 11.10, 15.32	
1992	Carriage of Goods by Sea Act (c.50) 1.17, 1.18, 2.6, 16.29	
1993	National Lottery Act (c.39)	
	s.2(1) 20.11	
1994	Sale and Supply of Goods Act (c.35)...........................1.18, 13.18	
1995	Requirements of Writing (Scotland) Act (c.7)............. 11.12	
	s.1(2)(a)(i) 11.12	
	s.1(2)(a)(ii) 11.12	
1995	Merchant Shipping Act (c.21) 23.21, 23.31	
	s.30.. 23.31	
	s.30(4) 23.31	
	s.35.. 23.31	
	s.38.. 23.31	
1996	Employment Rights Act (c.18)	
	s.43A-L 15.6, 20.7, 25.21	
	s.117(3) 26.8	
1996	Arbitration Act (c.23)........10.22, 15.22,	

		17.10
	ss.67–71................................. 20.11	
1998	Public Interest Disclosure Act (c.23)..........12.26, 15.6, 20.7, 25.21	
1998	Competition Act (c.41) 1.15, 20.27, 20.29	
1998	Human Rights Act (c.42)........1.15, 4.1, 11.11, 24.5, 25.21, 26.11	
	s.4(2) 11.11	
1999	Contracts (Rights of Third Parties) Act (c.31) 1.4, 1.6, 1.15, 1.18, 2.6, 6.18, 8.3, 8.25, 8.27, 10.1, 10.5, 10.9–10.28, 10.30, 10.33, 16.4, 16.28, 17.35	
	s.1 ......10.9, 10.21, 10.25, 10.30, 10.32	
	s.1(a)..................................... 10.11	
	s.1(c) 10.18	
	s.1(1)(a)................................. 10.11	
	s.1(1)(b).........................10.12, 10.13	
	s.1(2)...............................10.12, 10.13	
	s.1(3)....................10.11, 10.23, 16.28	
	s.1(4)...............................10.13, 10.14	
	s.1(5) 10.14	
	s.1(6) 10.11, 10.14, 10.19, 10.20, 10.22, 16.28	
	s.2 .... 10.9	
	s.2(1)(b)................................ 10.17	
	s.2(1)(c) 10.16, 10.17	
	s.2(2) 10.16	
	s.2(2)(a)................................ 10.16	
	s.2(2)(b).........................4.16, 10.16	
	s.2(3) 10.18	
	s.2(4)...............................10.18, 10.19	
	s.2(5) 10.18	
	s.2(6) 10.18	
	s.3(2)(a)................................ 10.19	
	s.3(2)(b)................................ 10.19	
	s.3(6) 10.20	
	s.4 ....10.20, 10.32	
	s.5 ....10.20, 10.32	
	s.6(1) 10.21	
	s.6(2) 10.21	
	s.6(3) 10.21	
	s.6(5) 10.21	
	s.6(5)(b)................................ 10.21	
	s.7(1) 10.24	
	s.7(2) 16.28	
	s.7(4)..................10.12, 10.14, 10.22	
	s.8 .... 10.22	
	s.10.. 10.9	
	Pt 4 .... 10.15	

TABLE OF STATUTORY INSTRUMENTS

1976 Consumer Transactions (Restrictions on Statements) Order (S.I. 1976, No. 1813) 17.35
1987 Consumer Protection (Cancellation of Contracts Concluded away from Business Premises) Regulations (S.I. 1987 No. 2117) 4.17, 4.19, 15.30
1991 Public Supply Contracts Regulations (S.I. 1991 No. 2679) 3.8
1991 Public Works Contracts Regulations (S.I. 1991 No. 2680) 3.8
1992 Package Travel, Package Holidays and Package Tours Regulations (S.I. 1992 No. 3288).........4.19, 10.33, 13.3, 15.30, 15.32, 25.15
    reg.5................................... 4.19
    reg.15................................. 10.33
1993 Commercial Agents (Council Directive) Regulations (S.I. 1993 No. 3053)...........14.24, 14.26, 15.32, 24.28
    reg.17(6)..........................24.28, 25.31
    reg.17(7)............................... 24.28
1994 Unfair Terms in Consumer Contracts Regulations (S.I. 1994 No. 3159)...........14.22, 14.23, 15.20, 15.27, 15.29
    Sched.1 .... 15.27
1995 Conditional Fee Agreements Order (S.I. 1995 No. 1674) .. 20.12
1998 Working Time Regulations (S.I. 1998 No. 1833) 5.2, 12.30
    reg.18..................................... 12.30
    reg.20..................................... 12.30
1999 Unfair Terms in Consumer Contracts Regulations (S.I. 1999 No. 2083)..........4.19, 7.3, 7.9,

    7.10, 14.12, 14.22, 14.26, 15.15–15.30, 15.32, 16.10, 17.2, 17.6, 17.12, 17.13, 7.16, 17.21, 17.34, 20.22, 26.10
    reg.3(1) 14.26
    reg.3(2) 15.18
    reg.3(2)(a) 5.18
    reg.3(2)(b) 15.18
    reg.4(1) 14.26
    reg.5(1) 15.20
    reg.5(2) 15.16
    reg.5(3) 15.16
    reg.5(4) 15.16
    reg.7....................................... 15.19
    reg.7(1) 15.19
    reg.7(2) 6.20
    reg.8....................................... 15.27
    reg.8(1) 15.27
    reg.10..................................... 15.28
    regs 10–15 .... 15.28
    reg.12..............................15.19, 15.28
    reg.12(3)............................... 15.28
    reg.13..................................... 15.28
    reg.14..................................... 15.28
    reg.15..................................... 15.28
    Sched.1 .... 25.32
    Sched.2 .... 15.21
2000 Consumer Protection (Distance Selling) Regulations (S.I. 2000 No. 2334).........4.7, 4.8, 4.18, 4.19, 4.27, 11.11, 14.26, 15.13, 15.30
    reg.7....................................... 4.18
    reg.10..................................... 4.19
    reg.11(2)............................... 4.18
    regs 22–24 .... 4.25
    reg.24(1)............................... 4.25
    reg.24(2)............................... 4.25
    reg.25..................................... 20.7
2001 Stop Now Orders (EC Directive) Regulations (S.I. 2001 No. 1422) 4.19, 15.30, 15.32, 26.10

Chapter 1

INTRODUCTION

THE NATURE AND SCOPE OF CONTRACT LAW

"The whole business of human negotiations"

> "Various and important as are the topics which present themselves to a student of the **1.1**
> law of *England*, there does not appear to me any which opens so wide and extensive a
> field for investigation, as that which is the subject of the following Essay. *Contracts,
> comprehend the whole business of human negotiations.* They are applicable to the cor-
> respondence of nations, as well as to the concerns of domestic life. They include every
> change and relation of private property, and consequently furnish the principal
> subject, on which all legal and equitable jurisdiction is exercised. But however differ-
> ent the objects, the contracts respecting them must uniformly be determined by the
> principles of natural or civil equity."

These words were written by John Joseph Powell, a barrister of the Middle Temple,
author of the first book devoted exclusively to the law of contract in England. Powell's
work *An Essay upon the Law of Contracts and Agreements* (significantly both plural) was
first published in 1790.[1] Other works, most notably Blackstone[2] had previously dealt
with contracts, but Powell's treatise can claim to be forerunner of what is now a
plethora of books dealing with contract law. Two centuries have elapsed since Powell's
words were published and the world has changed considerably during that time. The core
of his introduction remains true, that contracts cover "the whole business of human
negotiations." Contract law is indeed about the full range of economic transactions.
Powell's mention of equity (twice in the opening paragraph) is also interesting. Contract
law is one of the great achievements of the common lawyers. In Powell's day, equity may
still have had a lingering role to play in contract law[3]. Today fairness, reasonableness,
unconscionability and good faith are back in vogue, particularly under the influence of

---

[1] London, J. Johnson and T. Whieldon, 1790. The significance of the singular (*i.e.* law of contract) or plural
lies in whether the subject is to be seen as a set of general principles applicable to all contracts or a series of
rules for different types of contracts. In this book, as in most other modern textbooks, the subject is treated as
a single unified whole (see pp. 3–4).

[2] *Commentaries on the Law of England*, 1765–69. Blackstone's treatment of contracts was fairly cursory by
modern standards. Property rights exercised a much more dominating influence in the eighteenth century.
Freedom of trade and capitalism changed this fundamentally in favour of freedom of contract.

[3] See the "Transformation Debate", Chap. 14.

the European Union. So equitable ideas again resonate in this area and are one of the themes of this book. The age old relationship of law and equity is nowhere better illustrated than in contract law and how that relationship grew and should develop in the future remains one of the great questions of English (and indeed Western) jurisprudence.

Contract law is a set of changing rules and principles for the modern commercial world

1.2 The heart of contract law lies in commercial matters, trade, property transactions, employment relations, construction, consumer contracts, industrial manufacturing and financial services. Even if, in theory, formalities are rarely required, commercial contracts are mostly in writing, often in considerable detail. Negotiating, drafting and litigating over contracts are everyday activities for lawyers. The law of contract is not static, but an evolving and changing system. With the rise of the e-economy, contract law is having to adapt to new information technologies.[4] For example, an air travel ticket is a source of contractual terms and conditions. The passenger should have been given an opportunity, or by course of dealings should have known, the contents of the small print. With an e-ticket, the passenger receives no such written documents. Is the traveller bound by the airline's limitation of liability for personal injury or loss of luggage?[5] The legal system is having to adjust quickly to the expansion of economic activity as a result of the invention of the Internet and e-commerce. An important step in this direction in the United Kingdom is the implementation of the Consumer Protection (Distance Selling) Regulations 2000.[6] The European directive on Electronic Commerce 2000[7] will also have an increasing impact on contract law in years to come.

Contracts have a huge part to play in everything from great engineering and technological projects such as building a high speed rail link to the channel tunnel or putting a tele-communications satellite into orbit, to organising great sporting or cultural events, such as a Rugby World Cup or a Spice Girls Tour. Each of these requires networks or chains of carefully drafted contracts. Such contracts often resemble legislation by the time they are completed.[8] Many contracts also incorporate very detailed standard form contracts.[9] These are pre-drafted and included in the contract by mutual agreement or reference, one of the best examples being a construction contract.[10] Lawyers need to become familiar with the minutiae of these documents. Traditionally the law of contract covers everything from buying a magazine at a news-stand to chartering a supertanker by a multi-national oil company. Modern contract law is, therefore, a very wide ranging and expending subject.

---

[4] Electronic commerce is rapidly doing away with written contractual documents in some areas such as bills of lading, in international carriage of goods by sea (the "Bolero" project). Many other commercial contracts will soon go the same way, with major ramifications for contract law in the future. (See Brownsword and Howells, "When Surfers start to shop: Internet Commerce and Contract Law" (1999) 19 Legal Studies 287).
[5] Discussed in Chaps 16 and 17. The written confirmation of travel literally contains printed conditions.
[6] See Chap. 4.
[7] Directive 2000/31/EC on "certain aspects of information society services, in particular electronic commerce in the internal market", see Chap. 4.
[8] The contract to rebuild Walsgrave Hospital, Coventry ran to 17,000 pages according to a report in *The Times*, June 18, 1996.
[9] See Chap. 16.
[10] The JCT Building Contract, in civil engineering contracts or the ICE Conditions.

Contracts are also everyday events in the lives of all of us, as consumers, employees, homeowners or tenants. Many people make contracts without realising that they are doing so. Unlike commercial contract law where written agreements are almost universal, in the case of consumer contracts no documents are usually involved, formalities are rarely necessary and signature is seldom required. There are however standard written terms lurking in the background,[11] which may only become apparent when disputes arise or questions of rights or duties are asked. The most obvious example of a consumer contract is a bilateral,[12] executed,[13] retail transaction. Jane buys a cup of coffee or a pair of tights at a shop in the concourse of a railway station and pays by cash for her purchases. Both transactions are contracts for the sale of goods and each is over in a matter of seconds. It is only if Jane is dissatisfied with her cappuccino or the quality of her hosiery that the question of implied terms in contracts for the sale of goods will arise.[14] Both transactions are governed by contract law.[15]

The commonplace nature of contract can be quickly grasped if one considers how often in an average day, most of us make a contract of one kind or another. If we use the example of our friend Jane again, she may make many contracts every day. For instance, a newspaper or bottle of milk is delivered to her door in the morning. She catches a train or tube to work, or takes a taxi, and thereby makes a contract for services with her independent contractor taxi driver. During the afternoon Jane calls a service repair man to deal with her broken washing machine and books a holiday in Italy for her summer vacation. Jane later has an interview for a new job and accepts the firm's offer of employment. In the evening she purchases her week's groceries, does some purchasing over the Internet and books a ticket for a concert by telephone using her credit card. She may have used a reward card at the supermarket when she was purchasing the food and drink. This is another contract between store and customer. Contract law forms the basic structure in all of these different transactions. Consumer contracts are the most numerically significant aspect of contract law, and indeed it is now possible to regard these transactions as a separate species of contract law.[16]

Commercial lawyers tend to see contracts as a series of rules for particular contracts. **1.3** The answer to contractual issues is indeed usually to be found in detailed provisions governing special types of contract such as marine insurance, landlord and tenant or carriage of goods by sea, etc. The general law of contract described in this book is occasionally treated with cynicism by practitioners of law. Historically, in England there were remedies for various wrongdoings and contract grew out of this system. Certain types of wrongdoing, such as breach of an undertaking, would result in damages at common law. The situations where this applied were narrow by modern standards however, roughly 200 years ago general principles of contract law began to emerge.[17] Every form of relationship, even marriage, was governed by the law of contract, but this process went into reverse in the twentieth century. Different types of contract developed their own special rules either by judicial interpretation or as a result of statutory intervention. Sale of

---

[11] See Chap. 16.
[12] See Chap. 2.
[13] See Chap. 7.
[14] See Chap. 12.
[15] The Sale of Goods 1979 Act implies terms into the contract of sale, see later Chap. 12.
[16] See Chap. 15.
[17] See Atiyah, *The Rise and Fall of Freedom of Contract* (1979, Clarendon Press, Oxford).

goods and employment being two obvious examples of areas where the law is now mainly statutory. This has led to the view that there are really as many kinds of contract law as there are varieties of contract and that general principles have either disappeared or been superseded. In the United States, the subject is generally known in the plural as the Law of *Contracts*.

1.4   The truth is that the basic rules of contract still form a coherent underpinning for most contracts. Offer and acceptance, breach, misrepresentation rules, etc apply right across the board and, as a subject, contract is as alive now as it has ever been in its history. In spite of the tendency for the subject to break up, enough remains of general principle to regard contract law as intact.[18] There is judicial support for this point of view. In *Cehave NV v. Bremer Handelsgessellschaft, The Hansa Nord*,[19] Lord Justice Roskill stated that: "Sale of goods law is but one branch of the general law of contract. It is desirable that the same legal principles should apply to law of contract as a whole and that different legal principles should not apply to different branches of the law". General concepts in contract law such as intermediate terms,[20] control of exemption clauses[21] and doctrines such as economic duress[22] all tend to cut across subject boundaries and enforce the view of contract as a general set of principles which is still very much alive. *Contract law is that set of general principles governing contracts as a whole.* It forms the basic anatomy on which transactions depend and without a foundation in contract law, you cannot be a commercial lawyer. Unlike criminal law, one is not compelled to adhere to every rule of contract law. The parties are generally free to state that they have no intention to create legal relations and will not be legally bound.[23] Once a contract is formed, within the context of the rules themselves there are two main groups. Mandatory rules are those which apply even if the parties wish otherwise, *e.g.* in a consumer sale, the seller cannot now exclude liability for selling goods of a defective quality.[24] Default rules only apply if the parties do not express a contrary intention. Even Acts of Parliament can have this status in contract law. The Contracts (Rights of Third Parties) Act 1999 does not apply if the parties express an intention that the Act shall not govern their contractual relations.

Contract as part of the law of obligations

1.5   Contract, tort and restitution together make up the law of obligations. Traditionally contractual obligations were voluntarily assumed, whereas those in tort arose by operation of law. Restitution, which was once regarded by contract lawyers as a mere appendage, quasi-contract, is now treated as a subject in its own right existing for the purpose of reversing instances of unjust enrichment.[25] Until recently the unchallenged rule was that the existence of a contractual action barred a restitutionary claim. This is still the general

---

[18] For the opposite view see G. Gilmore, *The Death of Contract* (1974, Ohio State University Press).
[19] [1976] Q.B. 44 (at p. 71).
[20] See Chap. 13.
[21] See Chaps 16 and 17.
[22] See Chap. 19.
[23] See Chap. 12. They may not however exclude contract law nor the jurisdiction of the courts once a contract has been deemed to be formed.
[24] See the Unfair Contract Terms Act 1977 s. 6(2).
[25] See later Chap. 26.

principle. The emerging new relationship between contract law and restitution is one of the key themes of this book. A contract lawyer in the twenty first century must be familiar with restitution law as never before. Contract and tort are, by contrast, sisters. They exist side by side and often overlap. On the same facts, *e.g.* an accident at work, an action may be either in negligence or for breach of an implied term in the contract of employment. This is known as concurrent liability.

There has been much judicial policy-making over the years as to whether liability in tort should be allowed or encouraged where there is an existing contract. In *Tai Hing Cotton Mill v. Liu Chong Hing Bank*[26] there was a clear statement that the existence of a contract should lead courts to be wary of adding an additional remedy in tort. However the judicial pendulum has moved again. Since then, as a result of the House of Lords judgment in *Henderson v. Merrett Syndicates Ltd*[27], the policy seems to have swung in the opposite direction. New tort claims are emerging in the shadows of an existing contract. Where there is an overlap a party can choose whichever is most advantageous to them. There are, however, many differences between contract and tort. For example, pure economic loss is the normal item of recovery in contract, not in tort. The tests for remoteness of damage are different and so are the rules governing the calculation of damages.[28]

THE OBJECTIVES AND FUNCTIONS OF CONTRACT LAW[29]

The fulfilment of reasonable expectations

If a single word or principle delimits contract from other areas of law it is "expectation". **1.6** It can be used in two principal ways: as if an objective *i.e.*, the fulfilment of reasonable expectations, and second, as contract law's defining principle of compensation in the award of damages.[30] In *First Energy (UK) Ltd v. Hungarian International Bank*[31] Steyn L.J. began his judgment with these words: "A theme that runs through our law of contract is that the reasonable expectations of honest men must be protected. It is not a rule or a principle of law. It is the objective which has been and still is the principal moulding force of our law of contract. It affords no licence to a judge to depart from binding precedent. On the other hand, if the prima facie solution to a problem runs counter to the reasonable expectations of honest men, this criterion sometimes requires a rigorous re-examination of the problem to ascertain whether the law does indeed compel demonstrable unfairness."

The key objective for the law is to live up to reasonable expectations, reflecting and keeping pace with certain values of commonsense and understanding. The difficulty with this justifiable aim of contract law lies in relation to the dilemma over intervening in contractual matters or allowing freedom of contract to determine the outcome of contractual disputes, and legal issues. In *Associated Japanese Bank (International)*

---

[26] [1986] A.C. 80.
[27] [1994] 3 All E.R. 506.
[28] See Chap. 25.
[29] For a critique of modern theories of contract law, see Hillman *The Richness of Contract Law* (1998, Kluwer Academic Publishers, Dordrecht).
[30] We discuss this latter meaning in detail later, see Chap. 24.
[31] [1993] 2 Lloyds L.R. 194 (at p. 196).

Ltd v. Credit du Nord[32] Steyn J. stated: "Throughout the law of contract two themes regularly recur – respect for the sanctity of contract and the need to give effect to the reasonable expectations of honest men. Usually these themes work in the same direction. Occasionally they point to opposite solutions".[33] The phrase "reasonable expectations" appears in many disparate areas of contract law, for instance as a means of relaxing offer and acceptance,[33a] as a possible test for the meaning of an exemption clause under the Unfair Contract Terms Act 1977, *i.e.* any term which defeats the "reasonable expectations" of the parties,[34] in the reasonable expectation test in relation to the rights acquired by third parties under the Contracts (Rights of Third Parties) Act 1999[35] and as one of the crucial elements in the meaning of good faith.[35a] Disappointed expectation also has an outlet in modern contract law as a heading of damages in certain kinds of contract to provide entertainment or enjoyment.[36]

The reversal of detrimental reliance

1.7 The word "reliance" appears frequently in contract law, *e.g.* reliance on a misrepresentation,[37] an exemption clause,[38] or a promise giving rise to an estoppel.[39] Such instances of reliance do not yet merge into a single coherent theory in England, though there are many who argue that reliance theory, or the reversal of detrimental reliance, is (or should be) the true basis for liability across the law obligations.[40] The argument over whether contract law should adhere to its present exchange theory which is based on consideration or adopt a reliance theory, has been an important debate for over 70 years. The debate in its classic form took place in the United States in the arguments over the American Law Institute's Restatement of Contracts in the 1930s. There were two principal protagonists in the academic argument at that time. A reliance theory was supported by Professor Arthur Corbin of Yale Law School who won the day at the expense of Professor Samuel Williston of Harvard Law School.

Reliance theory would extend the range of contractual obligations to cater for situations where a party had conferred a detriment without necessarily making a contract by providing consideration. The basis for contract law becomes the reversal of detrimental reliance. The most obvious example of this is in the doctrine of promissory estoppel. A reliance view has already had an impact across a range of contractual doctrines. For instance, on the law of misrepresentation[41] in allowing a more

---

[32] [1989] 1 W.L.R. 255 Steyn J. (at p. 257).
[33] See further Steyn, "Contract Law: Fulfilling the Reasonable Expectations of Honest Men" (1997) 113 L.Q.R. 433.
[33a] See Chap. 5, *Percy Trentham Ltd v. Architital Luxfer* [1993] 1 Lloyd's Rep. 25.
[34] See Chap. 17.
[35] See Chap. 10.
[35a] See Chap. 14.
[36] See Chap. 25.
[37] See Chap. 18.
[38] See Chap. 16.
[39] See Chap. 9.
[40] This was really a debate over the inclusion of s. 90 into the American Law Institute Restatement of Contracts. This allows promissory estoppel as a cause of action, *i.e.* a promise can be enforced, without the need for consideration, on the basis of reliance alone (see Chap. 9).
[41] See Chap. 18. For misrepresentation to be actionable there must be reliance upon a statement of fact.

THE OBJECTIVES AND FUNCTIONS OF CONTRACT LAW

relaxed view of offer and acceptance where one or both parties have performed,[42] in dealing with uncertainty[43] and in limiting the scope of the expectation principle of damages in favour of a reliance measure.[44] Supporters of a reliance theory also tend to downgrade the importance of the doctrine of consideration.[45][46] A wider version of reliance theory, that of "reasonable" reliance, would not insist on detriment to the party concerned.[47] Any reliance by a person on another's words or conduct might be sufficient if regarded as reasonable in the circumstances. This would take into account public policy. The traditional view, and still the current theory, is to reject reliance alone. This is likely to be so into the foreseeable future. Contracts are formally binding because something is given in return. This is shown by providing consideration for a promise. Exchange remains the cornerstone of contract law for the time being. Like its counterpart, expectation, the word reliance is also used with a very different meaning elsewhere, namely as one of the principles underlying the assessment of damages in contract.[48]

The functions of contract making and the role of contract law

A number of key functions have been identified in association with the formation of contracts. First, contracts are to make transactions more secure. If trust is lacking, a system of legal rules is necessary to back up agreements sealed to allocate risks. This decides who will be liable if things go wrong. Parties wish to know in advance and do this by means of contractual provisions, for instance in terms dealing with mistake, exemption clauses and frustration. Third, contract law exists to resolve disputes and provide for sanctions if one party breaks his word, defaults or breaks the rules of contract law. Contract law enforces a person's word, making promises that are seriously given enforceable by law. There is an ethical element, therefore, in the origins of contract law.[49]   **1.8**

At the other end of the scale, the rules of contract law can be used, or even abused on occasion, to a party's advantage in his commercial relationship with his contracting partner. When this relationship deteriorates or breaks down, the parties may use the opportunities afforded by the rules to ensure their own advantage when disputes arise. At worst this can result in a self-interested manipulation of the rules, a phenomenon which contract law is slowly taking steps to prevent. The development of concepts of good faith and unconscionability are attempts to move contract law in this direction.[50] In modern times, contract law is moving towards producing greater fairness in transactions, particularly where there is inequality of bargaining power. Contract law can,

---

[42] See Chap. 5.
[43] See Chap. 6.
[44] See Chap. 24.
[45] See Chap. 7 and 8.
[46] Atiyah, "Contracts, Promises and the Law of Obligations" (1978) 94 L.Q.R. 193 and "Consideration: A Restatement" in *Essays on Contract*, Clarendon Press, Oxford, 1986, "Exchange Contracts, Expectation, Damages and the Economic Analysis of Contract" in the same volume. See also Henderson, "Promissory Estoppel and Traditional Contract Doctrine" (1968) 78 Yale Law Journal 343.
[47] Detriment is not necessary for promissory estoppel, see Chap. 9.
[48] See Chap. 24. A "performance interest" is now recognised by the courts, see *Panatown Ltd v. Alfred McAlpine Construction Ltd* [2000] 4 All E.R. 97, discussed in Chap. 24.
[49] See Fried, *Contract as Promise* (1981, Harvard University Press, Cambridge, Mass).
[50] See Chap. 14.

therefore, become a tool to achieve economic and social justice, although in the past the effect of freedom of contract was often the reverse.

THE SOURCES OF MODERN CONTRACT LAW

A brief historical background

1.9   Contracts go back to the origins of mankind, indeed even before recorded history. When the first pastoral farmer exchanged a sheep for some of his arable farming neighbour's field of grain, he and the other party were making a contract. Both were better off as a result of their exchange. Trade and contracts became the keys to economic development.[51] Laws governing contracts can be traced as far back as the Babylonian Code of Hammurabi (thought to be approximately 1750 BC) and even earlier.[51a] The Roman lawyers developed a sophisticated system of contracts within a classification which still stands, the law of obligations. Roman law was codified by the Byzantine Emperor Justinian in the sixth century and still forms the basis of the European Civilian systems today containing many current ideas such as good faith.[52] The English common law developed after the Norman Conquest particularly in the reign of King Henry II (1154–1189). Medieval contract law was a complex set of rules and actions but very different from the law we know today.[53] The practice of the Court of Common Pleas sitting at a central court in Westminster Hall in four regular law terms emerged in the 1190s, along with royal courts going on circuits or eyres. Much of what we should now call contract law developed outside of the Royal Courts in numerous local courts in market towns, based on the custom and trade practices of merchants, farmers and artisans.

The first glimmerings of what we would recognise today as contract law, the doctrine of consideration, emerged in Elizabethan times. However, the subject of this book is really just over 200 years old. If there is a starting point for modern contract law it is to be found in the last quarter of the eighteenth century, a period of significant economic change following the industrial revolution. Atiyah describes this era in his historical work.[54] Powell's book was well timed. In 1790, offer and acceptance made its appearance in *Cooke v. Oxley*.[55] Offer and acceptance as a settled rule dates from *Adams v. Lindsell*.[56] Consideration was defined in its present form (after a period of uncertainty) in *Wennall v. Adney*.[57] The principle of expectation damages for breach of contract was emerging in *Shepherd v. Johnson*.[58] The association (which is still there) was with individualism and

---

[51]   Some form of exchange existed in most efficient societies as embryonic contracts. For an anthropological account, see Marcel Mauss, *The Gift* (1970, Routledge and Kegan Paul, London).
[51a]   Richardson, *Hammurabis Laws* (2000, Adelaide Press, Sheffield).
[52]   See Chap. 14.
[53]   For a history up to the Statute of Frauds 1677 see A.W.B. Simpson, *A History of the Common Law of Contract* (1975, Oxford, Clarendon Press).
[54]   Atiyah, *The Rise and Fall of Freedom of Contract* (1979, Clarendon Press, Oxford). The author dates the rise from 1770 onwards. Adam Smith's work, *The Wealth of Nations*, a classic account of free market capitalism, was published in 1776.
[55]   (1790) 3 T.R. 653, 100 E.R. 785.
[56]   (1818) 1 B and Ald 681, 106 E.R. 250.
[57]   (1802) 3 B and P 249, 127 E.R. 137.
[58]   (1802) 2 East 211, 102 E.R. 349.

the market economy. Doctrines such as mistake and frustration only developed in the middle of the nineteenth century. Nowadays the State and increasingly the European Union have a large say in contract law. Contract law is increasingly consumerist in orientation. However the subject still remains largely common law and judge made.

The role of the common law judges throughout the world

Contract law is the creation of the common law judges and has spread across the globe   **1.10**
as the basis of the law in many other jurisdictions, notably the United States, Canada, New Zealand, Australia, India and large parts of Africa. This process is also to be observed in reverse nowadays with the law from these common law jurisdictions increasingly cited by English lawyers. In this text we shall mention examples of case law and statute from throughout the common law world.

Customary rules

The common law grew out of the many rules of custom which it superseded by being the   **1.11**
"common" law of the entire kingdom governed by the Royal Courts. Custom is usually distinguished from common law in that it can apply to a limited class of persons or to a particular area. As a modern source of law it is practically extinct but it has provided a fertile source of legal rules in the past.[59]

Commercial business practice: discrete transactions and relational contracts

The trade practices, attitudes and expectations of those working in the commercial world   **1.12**
are constantly being fed into contract law. These range from how the building and construction industry operates, the activities of agents and managers of footballers and rock stars, to the practices of merchant bankers and the carriage of goods by sea in international trade. It is interesting to note that not only English business but also world commerce has influenced contract law, particularly over the last 50 years. The practices of many international trade associations such as the Grain and Feed Traders Association (GAFTA) based in the City of London, drafting their standard form contracts based on English contract law, has led to numerous contract cases, many of which will appear later in this book.

Contracts are influenced by the way people do things in trade and commerce. Many trade practices are incorporated into contracts by means of implied terms.[60] There is surprisingly little research on the realities of contractual relations.[61] A leading work is that of Professor Ian MacNeil, on relational contracts, *i.e.* those involving longer

---

[59] *Smith v. Wilson* (1832) 3 B and A 728, see Chap. 12.
[60] See Chap. 12.
[61] The notable exceptions are (in the United States) S. Macaulay (1977) Law and Society Rev 507 (in the UK) Beale and Dugdale, "Contracts between Businessmen" (1975) 2 Brit J Law and Society 45, and V. Jones [1993] 12 C.J.Q. 337.
[62] MacNeil, *Contracts: Exchange Transactions and Relations* (1978, 2nd ed., Foundation Press, New York). See also *The Relational Theory of Contract: Selected Works of Ian MacNeil* (2001, Campbell, Sweet and Maxwell, London).

terms relations and treating these as a different species from discrete transactions, *i.e.* largely one-off events.[62] Generally speaking, relationships tend to predominate in commercial transactions, such as employment or construction contracts. In order to maintain the relationship parties are more likely to ignore or gloss over what might otherwise affect their legal relations. So a more relaxed view might be taken of breach of contract[63] and formation issues such as offer and acceptance, or even lack of consideration. This can also be linked to reliance theory where the parties have acted on each other's promise. Of course if one party wants out of the relationship, then contract law works very well to allow an excuse for doing so. Whether a party should be allowed to do so is another question.[64] Some relations and transactions are also highly dependent on trust and confidence between the parties and it is here that arguments over good faith are most relevant.[65] It is interesting to note that even in the context of consumer transactions, which are usually discrete transactions, there is a visible effort to turn these into relationships, *e.g.* by supermarkets by offering reward cards, or airlines giving air miles points in an attempt to create customer loyalty and thereby engage in further contracts. This distinction between relations and discrete contracts might well mature into an important distinction within contract law in the future though it has yet to have any substantial impact on the rules themselves. The courts have begun to adopt the relational concept particularly in employment cases. In *Johnson v. Unisys Ltd*,[66] Lord Steyn stated: "it is no longer right to equate a contract of employment with commercial contracts. One possible way of describing a contract of employment in modern times is as a relational contract." We discuss this later.[67]

The use of standard form contracts

1.13 Standard form contracts are those drafted in advance by one side, usually a seller or supplier of goods and services. They are widespread not only in business but also in consumer transactions. They have great advantages to firms in terms of efficiency but they also have a tendency to unfairness since the other party is often unaware of the terms. We discuss this particularly in relation to Exemption Clauses.[68]

The growth of consumerism and consumers' rights

1.14 One of the biggest developments in contract law since the 1960s, has been the development of rules giving greater rights to consumers. These cover many aspects of law but in contract these have resulted in controls on exemption clauses[69] and now also in the requirement of "fairness" in the terms of consumer contracts.[70] The extent of special rules for consumers has led some to agree that there is, or ought to be, two contract laws,

---

[63] See Chap. 23.
[64] See discussion of a "Efficient Breach" Chap. 3.
[65] See Chap. 14.
[66] *The Times*, March 23, 2001.
[67] See Chap. 25.
[68] See Chaps 16 and 17.
[69] See Chap. 17.
[70] See Chap. 15.

one for consumer contracts, the other for commercial contracts. There may be some merit in this idea, particularly if grounded in the concept of inequality of bargaining power.[71]

Statute law

The intervention of Parliament to regulate contracts has been spasmodic. In the early   **1.15**
days there was very limited legislation, although the Statute of Frauds 1677 had a huge impact, not only in England but throughout the common law world where it was re-enacted and still resonates an importance today, long after its decline in England. Then, in the late nineteenth and early twentieth century, there was a fashion for codifying statutes in the area of commercial law, such as the Bills of Exchange Act 1882, the Marine Insurance Act 1906 and, most important of all, the Sale of Goods Act 1893.[72] There have recently been suggestions for a full commercial code.[73] Two major statutes of importance are the Misrepresentation Act 1967[74] and the Unfair Contract Terms Act 1977.[75]

Some areas that were once entirely common law are now largely statutory, *e.g.* restraint of trade is now governed by the Competition Act 1998. The Contracts (Rights of Third Parties) Act 1999 Act transforms what is known as privity of contract. The Human Rights Act 1998 incorporating the European Convention on Human Rights will eventually have an impact on contract law, particularly contracts of employment.[76] Attempts have already been made to include convention rights into contractual relations. In *Biggin Hill Airport Ltd v. Bromley London Borough Council*[77] the court rejected an attempt to join local residents as parties to an action over a lease claiming their rights would be infringed by increased aircraft noise if flights were increased at an airport. The court held that the Act would not be applied retrospectively in such a case. The first declaration of "incompatibility" with the Human Rights Act has now been applied to a statutory provision in contract law.[78]

The European dimension

The European Union did not seek to have an impact on English private law, including   **1.16**
contract law, until the mid-1980s. The Single European Act 1986 and the single market has significantly changed the picture. In recent years there have been directives on self-employed commercial agents, doorstep selling, package tours and holidays, consumer credit and unfair terms in consumer contracts, timeshare property sales and distance selling to consumers which have become part of British contract law. Consumer law in

---

[71] See Chap. 14.
[72] Other examples, include the Marine Insurance Act 1906 and the Bills of Exchange Act 1882.
[73] See Arden, "Time for an English Commercial Code?" (1997) 56 C.L.J. 516–536.
[74] See Chap. 19.
[75] See Chap. 17.
[76] See O'Dempsey *et al.*, *Employment Law and the Human Rights Act* (2001, Jordans, Bristol).
[77] *The Times*, January 9, 2001. The facts relied upon can pre-date the Act, see *Edgar v. Meteorological Office*, *The Times*, August 15, 2001.
[78] The Consumer Credit Act 1974 s. 127(3) in *Wilson v. First County Trust* [2001] 2 W.L.R. 302, see Chap. 11.
[79] See Chap. 4.

particular is now transformed by a range of European Directives enforceable since 2001 by Stop Now Orders in the courts.[79]

On occasion European directives are in conflict with settled English tradition. In such cases the common law must give way. Contract law, once largely judge-made common law, is now increasingly European in influence. The need for British common lawyers to become familiar with European principles is illustrated by the decision of the Scottish Court of Session in *King v. T. Tunnock Ltd.*[80][81] The Court held that in assessing compensation under the Commercial Agents (Council Directive) Regulations 1993, based upon an earlier European Directive,[82] the correct approach was to quantify damages under the principles of French law (upon which the Directive was based) rather than common law rules, which did not apply.[82a] If, on the other hand, a plaintiff claims an indemnity under the regulations, it was held in *Moore v. Piretta*[83] that the principles are based on German law.[84] In this respect, parts of the United Kingdom, Scots and English law can be treated on an equal footing with regard to European Regulations. The European Union has also helped sponsor the Commission on European Contract Law. This is not a law making body but a committee of academic lawyers laying down principles of contract law as a declaration of future intent towards a unified set of guiding principles. These do not yet have any legal status and implementation of such a programme must be many years away, if indeed it ever happens.[85] In July 2001 the European commission launched an initiative towards a general harmonisation of European Contract laws. This long term project would transform contract law if it is successful.[85a]

European influence is hardly new. European medieval law was shaped by the widely used law merchant or *lex mercatoria* used by traders across the whole of the continent. This was an amalgam of Roman law and the common practices of traders. In the formulative period of contract around the end of the eighteenth century an influential work on contract was that of the French jurist Robert Pothier, Professor at the University of Orleans.[86] A recent work claims that many of our contract principles emerged from the natural law thinkers of the late medieval world, based upon St Thomas Aquinas, especially Francisco de Vitoria and those who followed him at the University of Salamanca in Spain.[87] This may well come as a surprise to many English contract lawyers, who have hitherto regarded their subject as entirely the product of centuries of English history.

---

[80]   *The Times*, May 12, 2000.
[81]   See Chap. 24.
[82]   86/653/EEC.
[82a]   However, see *Barrett Mackenzie & Co. v. Escada (UK) Ltd*, *The Times*, May 15, 2001, discussed in Chap. 24.
[83]   [1999] 1 All E.R. 174.
[84]   See Burbidge (2000) N.L.J. 1269–1272.
[85]   The first part of the commission's work is published as "Principles of European Contract Law", Part 1; Performance, Non-Performance and Remedies (eds Lando and Beale, Martinus Nijhoff, 1995).
[85a]   Communication from the Commission to the Council and Parliament, July 11, 2001 (COM 2001) 398 final.
[86]   *Traité des Obligations*, 1761.
[87]   Gordley, *The Philosophical Origins of Modern Contract Doctrine* (1991, Clarendon Press, Oxford), especially Chap. 6 "The Anglo-American Reception". See also Chap. 14.

International uniform laws   1.17

For several decades there have been developments in international law affecting contracts. For instance conventions on carriage of goods by sea, road, rail and air[88] have
been incorporated into the law of the United Kingdom. Otherwise international law
remains a source of inspiration for comparative lawyers but not directly applicable as
rules for English contract lawyers. The best example of such an international set of
rules in contract law is the 1980 Vienna Convention of the United Nations on
Contracts for the International Sale of Goods drafted by UNCITRAL (United
Nations Committee on Trade Law). This has not yet been ratified by the United
Kingdom. The American Law Institute Restatement (Second) of Contracts 1981, a set
of rules written as guidance by distinguished American academics to be of persuasive
authority across the United States, and the Uniform Commercial Code which now
governs sale and other commercial contracts across the United States are of interest to
English contract lawyers as model codes. We make reference to both of these in a
number of places as we proceed.

REFORMING CONTRACT LAW

The Law Commission was set up in 1965 as a successor to the Law Revision Committee.   **1.18**
Among its earliest projects was an attempt to codify the law of contract. This had been
done once before in Victorian times for India and resulted in the Indian Contract Act
1872. The Law Commission proposal to publish a draft Contract Code was abandoned
in 1972. This would have been a major law reforming measure, including the dropping of
the requirement of consideration. Its latest and final version was published in 1993.[89] In
civilian systems of Europe Contract law is codified. The Civil Code is also the source of
contract law in Québec, Louisiana and throughout Latin America.[89a] Law Commission
Reports Consultation and Working Papers have been an interesting source of proposals
on contract law over the years, many of which have led to important pieces of law
reform.[90] Reforming the law is always a matter for debate, rarely heated in contract law
perhaps, but nevertheless lively and intense. There are those who regard altering or tam-
pering with tradition with hostility. They may point out, with some justification, that
many attempts by statute to change the common law have merely made matters worse.
This is exacerbated by poor or opaque draftsmanship. The fate of the Misrepresentation
Act 1967 may, for some, fall into this category.[91] Equally the effect of some acts may be
unpopular. The Law Reform (Frustrated Contracts) Act 1943 is widely written out

---

[88] Implemented in the U.K. by the Carriage of Goods by Sea Act 1992 (originally 1971), Carriage of Goods
by Road Act 1965, International Transport Conventions Act 1983 and the Carriage by Air Act 1961.
[89] See H. McGregor, *Contract Code drawn up on behalf of the English Law Commission* (Giuffrè Sweet &
Maxwell, 1993).
[89a] Codification as a tradition goes back to Roman laws later developed by Napoleon. Argentina, a major football team, bears the name of the draftsman of its Civil Code, Velez Sarsfield.
[90] The Contracts (Rights of Third Parties) Act 1999, Unfair Contract Terms Act 1977, Supply of Goods and
Services Act 1982, Minors' Contracts Act 1987, Sale and Supply of Goods Act 1994 (amending the Sale of
Goods Act 1979) and the Carriage of Goods by Sea 1992.
[91] See Chap. 18.

of contracts and in its entire existence has spawned a mere two reported cases.[92] The established principles of contract law, such as consideration and offer and acceptance, both beset by criticism, still have much to recommend them. They have made the law reasonably certain, particularly in comparison with what might take their place, detrimental or (least certain of all) reasonable reliance. However, only unreconstructed traditionalists could argue that English contract law is perfect.

The reform of contract law in England certainly merits attention and debate. It is probably fair to say that English contract law remains behind other common law jurisdictions. In later chapters, we shall discuss how contract law may change in years to come. Modernisation and rationalisation are probably overdue, without throwing away some of the great values which have traditionally supported the subject. Everyone can and should have their own ideas for reforming contract law, preferably after having gained an understanding of its rules and principles rather than at the outset in an introductory course at University. Every list of potential reforms will be different, but among those considered later will be the following:

(a)   the scope of promissory estoppel, waiver and other variations of contracts;[93]

(b)   should promissory estoppel give a right of action?[94]

(c)   should there be a single merged concept of equitable estoppel?[95]

(d)   reform of the requirement of consideration;

(e)   the meaning of consideration redefined;[96]

(f)   is the reversal of detrimental reliance a preferable theory?[97]

(g)   dealing with uncertainty, the "battle of the forms";[98]

(h)   the doctrine and effect of mistake at common law and equity;[99]

(i)   the meaning and effects of illegality;[1]

(j)   the scope for a restitutionary principle in damages for breach of contract;[2]

(k)   the relationship between contract and restitution law;[3]

(l)   should there be a separate code of contract law for consumers?[4]

(m) should parties be allowed to breach a contract for economic reasons?[5]

---

[92] See Chap. 22.
[93] See Chap. 9.
[94] See Chap. 9.
[95] See Chap. 9.
[96] See Chap. 8.
[97] See Chap. 9.
[98] See Chap. 4.
[99] See Chap. 6 and 21.
[1] See Chap. 18.
[2] See Chap. 26.
[3] See Chap. 26.
[4] See Chap. 15.
[5] See Chap. 23.

(n)   reforming the confused state of the law on minors' contracts;[6]

(o)   should the effects of the entire contracts rule be changed to guarantee a restitutional remedy?[6a]

(p)   how far should contributory negligence have a part to play in breach of contract?[6b]

(q)   does contract law require a new overarching principle such as good faith, unconscionability, or inequality of bargaining power?[6c]

We shall consider each of these along the course of our journey through the life of contracts from birth to ultimate demise and aftermath.

CONTRACT LAW IN OUTLINE

Before we begin, it may be valuable to summarise the structure of the subject matter of contract law which we shall consider.   **1.19**

The subject matter of contract law is divided up into six main areas in this textbook

(i) Formation rules: Agreement, consideration, intention to create legal relations and surrounding issues such as the role of estoppel. We discuss these in Chaps 2–11.

(ii) Terms: The rules governing what is included, or excluded, in the contract. Implied terms and the classification of express terms into conditions, warranties and intermediate terms. These are dealt with in Chaps 12 and 13.

(iii) Rules for setting aside contracts: The situations in which contracts are void or voidable. This includes the three types of mistake (both at common law and in equity), misrepresentation, duress, undue influence and illegality (Chaps 6, and 18–21).

(iv) "Fairness" rules: The rules controlling exemption clauses, and unfair terms, at common law and under statute or regulation. We also consider fairness in relation to various concepts, such as unconscionability, good faith and inequality of bargaining power. This is covered in Chaps 14–17.

(v) Discharge of contract, *i.e.* bringing the contract to an end: Principally, breach of contract and other means of discharging a contract, *i.e.* performance, by agreement or by reason of frustration. This will be discussed in Chaps 22 and 23.

(vi) Remedies: The primary remedy in English law is damages. There are also equitable and restitutionary remedies. Chapters 24–26 cover this subject area. Frequent reference should be made to chapters on remedies even when looking at other topics, as remedies have a part to play at all stages of contract law.

---

[6]   See Chap. 11.
[6a]   See Chap. 23.
[6b]   See Chap. 25.
[6c]   See Chap. 14.

Chapter 2

THE ROAD TO AGREEMENT

Introduction

There are three main requirements for the formation of contracts: **2.1**

- Agreement

- Consideration

- Intention to create legal relations

To this must be added two requirements which are only relevant in the minority of contracts where either may be required or is lacking:

- Formalities

- Capacity to make a contract

The concept of a contract differs between legal systems and even the requirements within a particular jurisdiction can change. Historically, the doctrine of consideration emerged first as the determinant of a contract, and this has been followed throughout the common law world from the United States to Australia. The European civilian notion of contract as a legally recognised agreement developed in England from the earliest years of the nineteenth Century.[1] Agreement between the parties is now the starting point of contract formation.

CONTRACT AS A LEGALLY RECOGNISED AGREEMENT

The mechanism of offer and acceptance

The analysis into offer and acceptance is the basic judicial tool for finding agreement. **2.2** This provides a real and tangible test for the philosophical concept of agreement or "meeting of the minds". Agreement is the vital requirement of contract formation. Offer and acceptance provides an external, practical and meaningful expression to the idea.

---

[1] Simpson, "Innovation in 19th Century Contract Law" (1975) 91 L.Q.R. 247.

Contract lawyers operate in the commercial world, and the rules, therefore, have to be real and workable. In *Martin-Smith v. Williams*[2] an action involving the entertainer Robbie Williams on the issue as to whether or not there had been an extension of his contract with his management, Ferris J. commented, "In my view if, in relation to such a matter, parties reach accord by means of offer and acceptance then they should be treated as contractually bound to each other unless it is shown that either or both of the offer or the acceptance which lead to such accord are subject to a condition which prevents them being legally bound." Devlin J. in *Ingram v. Little*[3] also made that point, stating that "the first thing for a judge to do is to satisfy himself that the alleged contract has been properly formed . . . There must be offer and acceptance. The offer must be addressed to the offeree, either as an individual or as a member of a class of the public. The acceptance must come from the one who is so addressed and must be addressed to the offeror".[4] Later we shall discuss some problems with analysing agreement,[5] but meanwhile we shall proceed on this basis. There must be an offer and acceptance.

(1) Bilateral and unilateral contracts

2.3   There are two kinds of contract. The usual variety is called bilateral (or "synallagmatic", *i.e.* based upon a reciprocal obligation) in which both parties promise to do something for the other, and are bound together from a precise moment in time. This is sometimes referred to as "mutuality of undertaking".[6] The less common species is the unilateral contract, in which only one party promises. The other makes no promise but performs an act in return for the other party's promise. The bilateral situation is the more normal one and is a mutual contractual obligation from the outset. The contract is formed before anything is done, though often only seconds before performance begins. The unilateral contract, on the other hand, is formed only after completion of the act. Performance by one party and his acceptance coincide. In both bilateral and unilateral contracts there is offer and acceptance, but the analysis differs, as we shall see.

(1)   The bilateral contract

2.4   An example of this type of contract is *Thornton v. Shoe Lane Parking*[7] in which a professional musician, Francis Thornton, had a job for the day playing his trumpet for the BBC at Farringdon Hall in central London. The plaintiff decided to leave his car nearby in a recently opened multi-storey car park in Shoe Lane close to Fleet Street. He drove up, pressed a button and received a ticket, at which point the barrier rose up and he and his car entered the car park. A lift took his car to an upper floor. Three hours later the plaintiff returned from his appointment. The car was brought down again on a lift to the place where Thornton was waiting, but as he was loading some items into the boot of his car, an accident occurred. Part of the blame for the accident lay with himself and part

---

[2] [1998] E.M.L.R. 334 (at p. 358).
[3] [1961] 1 Q.B. 31.
[4] At p. 64.
[5] See Chap. 5.
[6] See Treitel, "Mutuality in Contract" (1961) 77 L.Q.R. 83. There is a distinction between mutuality of undertaking and mutuality of obligation. Care must be taken with this latter expression which is also used in relation to enforcing equitable remedies such as specific performance (see Chap. 26).
[7] [1971] 2 Q.B. 163.

with the car park as a result of negligence by one of the attendants. Mr Thornton sued Shoe Lane Parking Ltd for his own personal injuries and damage to his car. The Court of Appeal eventually awarded him £3,637 for his injuries (he had been 50% contributorily negligent), but nothing for the car. It was held that a contract had been formed as soon as he passed the ticket barrier, there being offer and acceptance and, therefore, agreement. The contract formed was bilateral in that the plaintiff had promised to pay in return for the defendants looking after his car. Because this was a bilateral contract, both parties were bound contemporaneously.

The central issue in *Thornton v. Shoe Lane Parking*[8] was whether certain attempts by Shoe Lane Parking to exclude liability for personal injuries and damage to the car had been incorporated into the contract. Altogether, there were three attempts to do so by the defendants: (i) the sign outside the car park as the driver approached the car park, (ii) the ticket which came out of the machine and (iii) a notice inside the car park itself excluding damage to the car.[9] The rule is that only terms brought to the contracting parties' attention at the time of, or before the contract is formed can be incorporated into the contract.[10] Anything said or written after the agreement is made, *i.e.* after the acceptance of the offer, is too late. Offer and acceptance determined the precise moment at which the parties were contractually bound. On this basis the Court of Appeal held, the contract having been formed at the barrier, that the notice outside was included, but the ticket and sign inside were not.

The Court of Appeal were not unanimous on the moment of formation. Lord Denning thought the offer was made by Shoe Lane Parking to customers who drove up to the barrier. Acceptance occurred when the plaintiff arrived at the barrier with an intention to park his car.[11] Therefore, the ticket came after the contract was formed, *i.e.* too late to be incorporated. Lord Denning may have been wrong on this point and the answer is certainly debatable.[12] Megaw L.J. reserved judgment on the offer and acceptance point. The contract was certainly made by the time plaintiff drove through the barrier. Normally the barrier would be regarded as merely an invitation to treat, and the driver would make an offer when he approached the ticket machine. The ticket which emerged containing conditions is not acceptance, but a counter offer which is accepted by the driver keeping the ticket and driving into the car park. Although the precise analysis into offer and acceptance is problematic in *Thornton*, the case illustrates the importance of determining how and when the agreement occurred. It also shows that finding an offer and acceptance is not always a neat process or free from difficulty.[13] [14]

---

[8] [1971] 2 Q.B. 163.

[9] On exemption clauses, see Chaps 16 and 17.

[10] See Chap. 16.

[11] In *Thornton*, Lord Denning described the barrier and ticket machine as "a booking clerk in disguise", *i.e.* equivalent to a real person in a face to face transaction. By a curious twist of irony this view is supported in the Consumer Protection (Distance Selling) Regulations 2001 which exempt automatic vending machines as not being distance contracts (Regulation 5(1)(d)) (See Chap. 4).

[12] The outcome of the action would now be determined under the Unfair Contract Terms Act 1977. Clauses excluding liability for personal injuries are void under s. 2(1) (see Chap. 17).

[13] See Chap. 6.

[14] The longer term authority of *Thornton* lies in the view of Megaw L.J. that a special notice test was appropriate in relation to unusual or onerous terms such as the exclusion clause inside the car park. This was applied in *AEG v. Logic Resources* [1995] C.L.C. 265 (see Chap. 16).

(2) The unilateral contract

2.5 The concept of a unilateral contract is illustrated by reference to a classic contract law case, *Carlill v. Carbolic Smoke Ball Co Ltd.*[15] The defendant, Frederick Roe, the proprietor of a medical preparation called "The Carbolic Smoke Ball", placed an advertisement in "The Pall Mall Gazette" promising to pay £100 to anyone who used the Carbolic Smoke Ball for two weeks and who, for a limited period thereafter, contracted influenza. Mrs Louise Carlill did both and sued to recover her £100, as promised. In the High Court, the defences of the Smoke Ball Company, indeed most of the arguments, appear to have been about the facts rather than the law. In commercial contract practice and litigation, or arbitration over disputes, the facts are indeed often more complicated and relevant to the final outcome than the law in question. In *Carlill* some of the factual arguments were that the advertisement was not accurately reported, the plaintiff had not relied on it in any case, had not used it properly, had never actually caught influenza and, if she did, never reported it to the defendant. The court found for the plaintiff.[16]

In the Court of Appeal, the Carbolic Smoke Ball Co as appellants raised a number of legal points relevant to contract law: (i) The advertisement was not an offer, but an invitation to treat. In the old fashioned language of the day "a mere puff". In other words, there was no intention of making an offer; (ii) The advertisement was too vague to be an offer; (iii) An offer could not be made to the whole world; (iv) There was no consideration for the promise (this raised the question of whether the plaintiff herself had actually bought the Smoke Ball);[17] (v) Where was the acceptance of the offer? In a bilateral contract the acceptance is normally communicated, and that was not done here; (vi) the advertisement was a bet or wagering contract, in which case it would be void as contrary to public policy.

The Court of Appeal rejected most of these arguments and held that there was a contract. The advertisement was held to be a promise which was an offer to the whole world, and was capable of amounting to an offer of a unilateral contract. Communication of acceptance is not necessary in the case of a unilateral contract.[18] Consideration and acceptance could be found in Mrs Carlill taking and using the Smoke Ball for the full two weeks. It was only at the end of this time that the promise became legally binding. The Smoke Ball Company's offer could be revoked at any time until she had completed performance.[19] The Court of Appeal also dealt with the consideration point. Catching influenza was not the consideration but a "condition" (sometimes called an "if" clause). (I will pay you if a certain event happens, which you do not promise to bring about or which is outside of your control).[20] Consideration was found in Mrs Carlill using the Smoke Ball. The Court of Appeal also found that there was an intention by the parties to treat the arrangement as contractual. The deposit of money was an important indicator of contractual intention. *Carlill* was the first case to explicitly state a requirement of intention to create legal relations.[21] The advertisement was more than a "mere puff".

---

[15] [1893] 1 Q.B. 256. On the contextual background, see Simpson, "Quackery and Contract Law" in *Leading Cases in the Common Law* Clarendon, Oxford 1995.
[16] Reported at first instance in [1892] 2 Q.B. 484, Hawkins J.
[17] In fact she purchased it from a retailer in London.
[18] See further Chap. 4.
[19] See Chap. 3.
[20] See Goodhart, "Unilateral Contracts and Consideration" (1953) 69 L.Q.R. 99.
[21] See Chap. 11.

It was intended to be taken seriously. On an objective test, a reasonable person in Mrs Carlill's position would take the advertisement to be an offer. This was furthered strengthened by the statement that £1000 had been deposited in the Alliance Bank, to deal with any liabilities "showing our sincerity in the matter". Lindley L.J. called this "a promise, as plain as words can make it".[22]

Unilateral contracts are less common than their bilateral counterparts. A ubiquitous example is to be found in automatic vending machines. In *Luxor (Eastbourne) Ltd v. Cooper*[23] it was suggested that when a house is put in the hands of an estate agent to sell, this is a unilateral contract. The estate agent is not under a duty to act, but can recover her commission if she does sell the house. Credit card transactions are also probably best analysed as a unilateral contract between the credit card company and retailer.[24] In the case of *Bowerman v. ABTA*[25], a notice in the offices of a travel agent had a direct contractual effect in forming a contract with a customer.[26] Offer and acceptance can become a very elastic concept when faced with more complex commercial realities.

2.6

An example of a seed sown by a unilateral promise ripening into a contract is to be found in *New Zealand Shipping Co Ltd v. A. M. Satterthwaite and Co. Ltd "The Eurymedon".*[27] The case arose in the context of international carriage of goods by sea and the attempt of those who performed services such as loading or unloading ships and damaged them in the process to limit their liability to a particular sum of money. A drilling machine sent from Liverpool was damaged while being unloaded at Wellington in New Zealand. The company who sent the goods ("the consignors") and those receiving the goods ("the consignees") did not appear to have a contract with the stevedores unloading the *Eurymedon*. The question for the Privy Council was whether a contract could be found tying all of the parties together and, if so, where was the offer and acceptance? By the rules of international trade, such limitations were required by law[28] but difficult to accommodate within the framework of the English rules on privity.[29] The Privy Council held that one of the contractual documents, the bill of lading, brought a contract into existence. There was a promise initially unilateral, but capable of becoming mutual, between the shipper and the stevedore made through the carrier as agent which became a full contract when the stevedores performed services by unloading the goods. The unilateral offer was accepted by the stevedores when they undertook the work in question.

Lord Wilberforce pointed out the difficulties of fitting the facts into the traditional analysis of offer and acceptance and consideration[30]: "The performance of these services for the benefit of the shipper was the consideration for the agreement by the shipper that the appellant should have the benefit of the exemptions and limitations contained in the bill of lading". The conception of a "unilateral" contract of this kind . . . is well established". The consignee was entitled to the benefit of, and bound by, the stipulations in

---

[22] Advertisements are usually treated as merely invitations to treat, not offers. (See Chap. 3.)
[23] [1941] A.C. 108.
[24] On credit cards and retailers, see Chap. 4.
[25] [1995] 145 N.L.J.R. 1815.
[26] Discussed in Chap. 16.
[27] [1975] A.C. 154.
[28] The Hague/Visby Rules
[29] See Chap. 10.
[30] At p. 168.

the bill of lading by his acceptance of it and by his request for delivery of the goods under the bill. Thankfully, the need for such complexity, in this area at least, is now reduced by a combination of the Carriage of Goods by Sea Act 1992 and the Contracts (Rights of Third Parties) Act 1999.[31] It remains an example of how legal principles may often need to be adapted with commercial practices in order to meet one of the overriding objectives of contract law, that of fulfilling the reasonable expectations of the parties.

(1) An extreme case: offer and acceptance by silence

2.7   This sounds curious, even a contradiction in terms. Not only the acceptance but also the offer are made without spoken or written words. Normally even acceptance is not possible by silence alone.[32] All the reported cases concern the abandonment of arbitration clauses in commercial contracts in which neither party does anything about proceeding with the arbitration. In such rare circumstances it is possible to construe both offer and acceptance from silence even though Goff L.J. in *The Leonidas D*[33] stated that it was "difficult to imagine how silence and inaction can be anything but equivocal". Bingham L.J. in Food Corporation of *India v. Antclizo Shipping Corporation "The Antclizo"*[34] was less hesitant and asked the question of whether the parties had manifested their "mutual assent" abandonment. He stated that "where the parties conduct consisted of silence and inaction the evidence had to be scrutinized with care, but having made such scrutiny it was for the Court to draw whatever influence was proper in the circumstances". In other words, both offer and acceptance were possible from silence.[35]

In *Gebr. Van Weelde Schapvaartkantor BV v. Compania Naviera Sea Orient SA "The Agrabele"*[36], Evans J. held that arbitration had been abandoned by offer and acceptance without either party expressly saying or doing anything. Evans J. stated in the Commercial Court that the plaintiffs were entitled to succeed on the basis that the agreement to abandon the reference which they alleged had been proved. The Court of Appeal reversed this judgment holding that the charterers had adopted an entirely passive role. They had taken "no initiatives and made no preparations" . . . no inference could be drawn that the charterers by their conduct accepted the owners' offer to agree that the reference should be abandoned or that any such acceptance was communicated to the owners".[37] Lord Justice Neill applied the reasoning of an earlier case[38] that it was possible to construct an implied contract of abandonment from a prolonged period of silence and inactivity but it had to be shown that the requirements were met. These were: "(a) some conduct by one party (O) which, objectively considered, constitutes an offer to abandon. (b) the belief by the other party (A) that the conduct of (O) represents his actual intention to make an offer to abandon. (c) some conduct by (A) which, objectively considered, constitutes the acceptance of (O)'s offer. It may be that it is also necessary to prove the belief by (O) that (A) had accepted his offer. This further element would be consistent with the general principle that the acceptance of an offer must be

---

[31] See Chap. 10.
[32] See Chap. 4.
[33] [1985] 2 All E.R. 796.
[34] [1987] 2 Lloyds Law Reports 130 (at p. 141).
[35] As we shall discuss in Chap. 4 the normal rule is that acceptance is not to be construed from silence.
[36] [1987] 2 Lloyds Law Reports 223.
[37] At p. 234.
[38] *The Splendid Sun* [1981] 1 Q.B. 694.

communicated to the offeror".[39] Neill L.J. thought this would be consistent with Lord Diplock's judgment in *The Hannah Blumenthal*[40] where the test was the inference that a reasonable man would draw from the prolonged failure of the claimant to submit to arbitration. There were three stages to consider. First, it had to be shown that the claimant was willing to consent to abandonment. Secondly, the other party drew this conclusion and thereafter by his own inaction indicated his own acceptance of abandonment. Finally, this assent was understood by the claimant. Only after this could the arbitration agreement be said to be abandoned by a process of offer and acceptance. The key to understanding the complexity of this situation lies in the concepts of objectivity and subjectivity in contract law to which we will now turn our attention.

OBJECTIVITY AND SUBJECTIVITY IN CONTRACT LAW[41]

The concepts of objectivity and subjectivity are two of the keys to an understanding of contract law. Generally speaking the law of contract takes an objective rather than a subjective view of the parties intentions. As we shall discuss later subjectivity also plays a part.[42] There are three possible meanings of objectivity in contract law.

(1) Promisor objectivity

This version of objectivity is based on an objective view of what the promisor really meant by their words. The subjective understanding of the promisor is relevant if he or she really knows that the other party will not grasp the true meaning of their words, *i.e.* what they actually intend. It is a difficult concept to grasp. A rather grim example of this is used by Howarth.[43] It is drawn from classical antiquity. In ancient history, the General Temures promised the people of the city of Sebastia (in modern day Israel), which he was in the process of besieging, that if they surrendered no drop of the inhabitants' blood would be shed. The people surrendered, no doubt grateful for his mercy. The ruthless general then proceeded to bury them alive. On a promisor's objectivity basis he never intended to spare them and this was the true meaning to be given to his statement. In *Smith v. Hughes*,[44] Hennen J. took the view that it was the state of the promisor's mind that was important.[45] This theory is closest to subjectivity, and draws the least support among the judges and academic commentators.

2.8

(2) Promisee objectivity

This version of objectivity is the most widely favoured. The promise should be looked at as it would be by a reasonable observer placed in the position of the promisee, *i.e.* in the other person's shoes. The words are to be understood as they would appear to a reasonable person in the position of the person to whom they were addressed. Note it is *not* the

2.9

---

[39] At p. 235.
[40] [1983] 1 A.C. 854 (at p. 916).
[41] The literature on objectivity is extensive: see Howarth (1984) 100 L.Q.R. 265; (1987) L.Q.R. 527; Spencer (1973) C.L.J. 104; and Vorster (1987) L.Q.R. 274.
[42] See p. 25 and Chap. 6.
[43] Quoting Paley, *Principles of Moral and Political Philosophy* (1824).
[44] (1871) L.R. 6 Q.B. 597.
[45] We discuss the question of subjectivitiy in relation to mistake later in Chap. 6.

subjective understanding of the promisee, *i.e.* in his own mind, but a reasonable person in the place of the promisee.

(3) Detached objectivity

2.10   This involves the judge taking on the role of a detached third party, or a hypothetical "fly on the wall". Lord Denning was a proponent of this approach. In *Solle v. Butcher*[46] he stated,[47] "once a contract has been made, that is to say, once the parties, whatever their innermost states of mind, have to all outward appearances agreed with sufficient certainty in the same terms on the same subject-matter, then the contract is good. Neither party can rely on his own mistake to say it was a nullity from the beginning, no matter that it was a mistake which to his mind was fundamental, and no matter that the other party knew that he was under a mistake."

On balance, this view may be regarded as going too far. The judge is placed in the position of making or unmaking agreements where both parties might believe the opposite. This is generally regarded as too interventionist and goes beyond freedom of contract. This argument can be pursued in relation to the question of who decides if there is a contract? Is it up to the parties themselves or the court to decide if there is a contract? If the parties believe there is a contract, can the courts say there is not? Similarly vice versa, if the parties do not believe a contract exists, can the courts determine differently?

The answer goes back to objectivity displacing the subjective views of the parties. Normally the objective test will correspond with at least one of the parties' own subjective view. However, the courts are the final arbiters of agreement. Their judgment must also take account of the rules of contract law. If, on an objective test, there is no contract then there will be none even if one or both parties subjectively believed there was. For instance, in *Felthouse v. Bindley*[48] both parties acted as if a contract had been formed, but the rule that silence is not to be taken as acceptance[49] prevailed over the parties' own understanding and there never was a contract. Willes J. stated that, "The uncle seems to have thought that he had on that occasion bought the horse for £30, the nephew that he had sold it for 30 guineas: but there was clearly no complete bargain at that time . . ."[50] Even though the nephew, subjectively, intended his uncle to have the horse he had not communicated his intention to the uncle so there was no contract.[51] An uncommunicated subjective intention to accept is not enough to create a contract.

In *Mathieson Gee (Ayrshire) Ltd v. Quigley*,[52] a Scottish case appealed to the House of Lords, there was a dispute over the existence of a contract for the removal of silt from a pond at a house in the town of Rutherglen, near Glasgow. The action arose out of the interpretation of two letters: the "offer" of the building contractors and the reply by the appellant, Dr Quigley. Both parties believed there was a contract. The House of Lords held that there was no contract. Lord Reid stated,[53] "In my opinion, it must be open to a court so to decide . . . if it clearly appears to the court that the true construction of the

---

[46] [1950] 1 K.B. 671.
[47] At p. 691.
[48] (1862) 11 C.B.(N.S.) 869, 142 E.R. 1037.
[49] See Chap. 4.
[50] At p. 1039.
[51] But see Miller "Felthouse v. Bindley Re-visited" (1972) 35 M.L.R. 489.
[52] 1952 S.C. (HL) 38.
[53] At p. 43.

document is such as to show there was no agreement, then it is plainly an impossible task for the court to find the terms of an agreement which never existed". The Court's "objective" view of the correspondence prevailed over the parties own subjective opinion. Lord Normand stated,[54] "I have no doubt that, when the parties to a litigation put forward what they say is a concluded contract and ask the court to construe it, it is competent for the court to find that there was no contract and nothing to be construed".

Equally there are dicta in support of holding that there is a contract even if neither party thought so at the time. In *Furness Withy (Australia) Pty Ltd v. Metal Distributors (UK) Ltd "The Amazonia"*[55], Staughton L.J. stated: "the test for establishing a contract is, or may be, objective. If the parties correspondence and conduct shows such an intention it will not, or may not, matter that neither privately intended to make a contract". Traditionalists would argue that this goes too far.[56] The courts task is not to insert their own views. As Bingham J. stated in *Pagnan, SpA v. Feed Products*[57]: "The parties are to be regarded as masters of their contractual fate. It is their intentions which matter and to which the court must strive to give effect". In *Metal Scrap Trade Corporation v. Kate Shipping Co. Ltd (The Gladys) (No 2)*,[58] Potter J. approved the view of Bingham J. in *Pagnan*,[59] "The Court's task is to review what the parties said and did and from that material to infer whether the parties' objective intentions as expressed to each other were to enter into a mutually binding contract. The Court is not of course concerned with what the parties may subjectively have intended".

There is also a role for subjectivity in contract law[60]

The subjective views of the parties are clearly relevant to the question of evidence as to what each believed they were agreeing. In two areas in particular, subjectivity has a part to play, namely (a) implied terms[61] and (b) mistaken agreement.[62]

2.11

Historically, subjectivity had a large role to play in contract law. Agreement was defined as *consensus* and *idem*, or a meeting of the minds, and the subjective intentions of the parties were uppermost in this concept. The law of contract rested upon a will theory in which the intention of the parties was central. Gradually this theory fell out of favour and is now largely discarded. The objectively manifested external aspect of agreement is the decisive element. In European civilian systems, subjectively ascertained agreement is still the norm. This also applies generally to European law. In *Bayer AG v. Commission of the European Communities*[63] the European Court of Justice held that the central element in the meaning of agreement in article 81(1) of the EU Treaty, which renders unlawful certain anti-competitive agreements between undertakings, was the

---

[54] At p. 43.
[55] [1990] 1 Lloyd's Rep. 236 (at p. 243).
[56] See Treitel, *The Law of Contract* 10th ed, Sweet and Maxwell, London, 1999.
[57] [1987] 2 Lloyd's Rep. 601 (at p. 611).
[58] [1994] 2 Lloyd's Rep. 402.
[59] At p. 610.
[60] For a comparison of objectivity and subjectivity in agreement in English and French law, see Anne de Moor (1986) 6 O.J.L.S. 275.
[61] See Chap. 12.
[62] See Chap. 6.
[63] *The Times*, February 9, 2001.

concurrence of wills between two parties. The subjective element dominates this question, and the form in which the agreement was manifested was unimportant so long as it represented the true expression of the parties' intention.

The common law reverses these rules. The external manifestation of agreement on an objective basis is the preferred approach. Given the increasing Europeanisation of contract law and the historic role of subjectivity, this is likely to remain an important debate.

Objectivity and subjectivity: theory into practice, hopefully.

2.12 Let us take a simple example. Oliver sends Andrew a letter from his business address "offering" to sell him a car for £5,000. Should this be taken seriously as an offer to sell the car or merely an invitation to treat, *i.e.* an attempt to solicit an offer.[64] The subjective approach would be to ask Oliver if he really intended the letter to be an offer. Oliver may say yes or no, depending on the state of his mind at the time. This would be a subjective test. Oliver might well tell the truth as he saw it but he might also tell you what best suited his purposes now, rather than what he believed at the time. For instance he might not want to be liable in damages for not selling the vehicle so he might say he had no contractual intention. No one could prove this false if the only question was what he was thinking at the time. It would be a charter for dishonesty and it would be impractical.

The objective test asks what effect the letter would have on a reasonable person in Andrew's position. It gives the courts a workable tool. It is also flexible to the facts of the case. It can be based on common sense. It is also based on outward manifestations rather than internal reasoning. Contract law could scarcely exist without it. There are a number questions to ask about Oliver's letter. How would the letter appear to a reasonable, neutral observer? What is Oliver's business? If Oliver is in the business of selling cars and the letter looks as if it might have been sent to many other people, it is advertising, not an offer – a reasonable person would conclude it was merely an invitation to treat. On the other hand, if Oliver's business is not selling cars, and Andrew and he are friends, a reasonable person in Andrew's position may be entitled to conclude that the letter is a promise to sell at a definite price. The letter would appear to be intended to be taken seriously. A reasonable conclusion would be that this was an offer. It is for the court ultimately to decide. Andrew's views on the letter may be relevant but only subjective. It is an objective view of a reasonable person in Andrew's position that counts. The concept of objectivity is a very useful instrument for contractual interpretation. It is one of the core keys to understanding contract law.

Objectivity applied: does humour have a part to play in contract law?

2.13 The role of objectivity in the formation of contract law is illustrated in the question of whether a party may raise a defence to an action for breach of contract that he was only joking, or that he is incapable of making a contract because he has indulged in too much alcohol. This was the issue in the American case of *Lucy v. Zehmer*[65] where two friends

---

[64] See Chap. 3.
[65] (1954) 196 V.A. 493, 84 S.E. 2d 516.

met in a restaurant in the small town of McKinney, near Richmond in Virginia. After they had a large amount to drink, a drunken offer to sell a farm for $50,000 US dollars was treated seriously by the other party and a scrap of paper signed to this effect. In an action for specific performance of the agreement, the defendant claimed: (a) that he was drunk, (b) that it was intended as a joke and that the plaintiff knew this when he offered to sell him the farm and (c) it was all a bluff since he believed the plaintiff did not have $50,000 in cash. The outcome depended upon an objective view of the parties state of mind.

The Supreme Court of Virginia held that there was a contract. The parties were not too drunk to know what they were doing, and that the offer was more of a bluff than a joke. Crucially, even if Zehmer never intended to contract, and the entire transaction was not serious in his own mind, the plaintiff never got the point. A reasonable person in Lucy's shoes would have taken the defendant's remarks seriously. Zehmer's own subjective view was not sufficient to prevent a contract being formed. However, if both parties were so drunk that they would not form the requisite contractual intention nor take an objective view of the other's contractual intention both would be lacking in contractual capacity and no contract would exist.[66]

---

[66] On capacity and intention to contract, see Chap. 11.

Chapter 3

OFFER

THE OFFER

The Law Commission's Draft Contract Code (which never came to fruition) defined an **3.1** offer as "a statement of terms which the offeror proposes to the offeree as the basis of an agreement, coupled with a promise, express or implied, to adhere to those terms if the offer is accepted".[1] The essence is a promise, as objectively understood by the offeree. Offer is the cornerstone upon which a contract is built. However, although contract teachers often like to begin with the idea of an offer as the basis for the making of a contract, in commercial matters the offer is frequently not the starting point of formation, but rather the final lap in reaching agreement. There may have been a great deal of correspondence, discussions, negotiations, even arguments, faxes, telephone calls and numerous e-mails before the final contract is made. Conversely, in many simple transactions such as the straight forward bilateral, executed contract between two parties who are face to face (such as buying a newspaper), offer and acceptance are both obvious, and immediate. The contract is made and performed in a matter of seconds. The different circumstances vary enormously. In *Pagnan v. Food Products*[2] Bingham J. pointed out the practices in contract formation and the court's task in construing offer and acceptance of terms:

> "the proper inference to draw may differ widely according to the facts of the particular case. One case may concern a protracted negotiation, perhaps conducted in writing through lawyers, between parties who have had no dealings of any kind before. Another may concern a series of quick-fire exchanges between professionals, both of them practitioners of the same trade, both having had many previous dealings, and with a wide measure of common experience, knowledge, language and understanding between them. One could not sensibly approach these cases in the same way. Inferences which it would be appropriate to draw in one case might be quite inappropriate in the other. But the Court's task remains essentially the same: to discern and give effect to the objective intentions of the parties."

Offer is a vital element on the road to agreement. It must be distinguished from all **3.2** other statements made in the process of negotiating. Only an offer is capable of being

---

[1] Harvey MacGregor, *Contract Code: Drawn Up On Behalf of the English Law Commission* (1993, Sweet and Maxwell, and Guifrè Editore, Milan).
[2] [1987] 2 Lloyd's Rep. 601 (at p. 611).

accepted and, therefore, making a contract. The party seeking to show that there is a contract must prove the existence of an offer. As we have defined it, an offer is a promise to be bound which is capable of acceptance. It must be clear and unambiguous and intended to be legal binding. It is distinguished from:(a) commercial advertising or sales talk; (b)"invitations to treat"; (c) representations or inducements to enter into a contract[3] and (d) pre-contractual negotiations.[4] The precise concurrence of offer and acceptance is important in order to ascertain whether a valid contract has been formed and when the contract is made. This may be important, *e.g.* in selling shares, where prices fluctuate. The acceptance can also determine where the contract is made. This may be vital if the parties are contracting between different jurisdictions by fax, telex, e-mail or on the Internet or other forms of instantaneous communications. The place of formation of the contract may also become important if a dispute arises and the rules of conflicts of laws have to be applied to decide the question of which law governs. Generally speaking this will be the legal system where the contract was made, unless the parties provide otherwise by a "choice of law" clause. In determining the existence of an offer the courts consider (in descending order):

(a)   the intentions of the parties (analysed objectively);

(b)   rules of law (if these are mandatory they may supersede the above);

(c)   the facts of individual cases;

(d)   custom or trade practices;

(e)   surrounding circumstances;

(f)   course of dealings between the parties; and finally

(g)   common sense. (The latter can be a very inaccurate test of correctness in legal matters.)

Offers and invitations to treat

3.3   Invitations to treat are a collection of disparate instances of situations which can trigger an offer. Essentially their purpose is to solicit an offer or to initiate negotiations. There is no intention to contract immediately but instead to seek an offer from the other party. In many cases, the status of an offer is determined by pre-ordained rules, as we shall discuss, but mainly this depends upon the intention of the parties. Invitations to treat are preliminaries on the road to agreement. An offer, on the other hand, is a promise to be bound. It is capable of acceptance and clear enough to be acted on. The issue can some-times be difficult to decide. In *Guildford v. Lockyer*,[5] a criminal case, there was a point of interest for contract lawyers. The defendant was one of a group of five persons who went to a Chinese restaurant. He ordered but did not receive the correct dish. Instead he ate some of another dish sent to his table. Having tried the food but not liking it, he left the

---

[3] See Chap. 18.
[4] See Chap. 12.
[5] [1975] Crim. L.R. 235.

restaurant without paying. He was convicted of contravening the Theft Act 1968 s. 16(1). This was quashed by the Divisional Court on the basis that there had been no contract formed to buy the meal in question. The defendant had not received what he had ordered, *i.e.* "offered" to purchase. The menu was merely an invitation to treat (as well as an invitation to eat, of course).

Merely using the word "offer" does not mean it has that effect legally. It is the legal meaning or construction placed upon it that is important. There is a legal maxim that the law looks at "substance rather than the form". This means that it is the real nature of the phrase, rather than merely the language used, which counts. So, for example in *Spencer v. Harding*,[6] the words "offer . . . for sale by tender" were held to be merely an invitation to treat. So even if a shop advertises "a special offer", this is in fact usually no more than an invitation to treat. However, as we shall discuss shortly, if the word offer was intended to be taken seriously by the public, it may have this effect.[7] We shall now turn to some examples of the process of differentiating offers from other things.

(1) Goods on display in shops or supermarkets

Goods on display in a shop window or on a supermarket shelf are an invitation to treat, not an offer. In *Fisher v. Bell*[8] a flick knife (which was an illegal weapon) was displayed in a shop window for sale. An offence would be committed if the shopkeeper was offering it for sale. It was held that no offering for sale had taken place, as the goods in the window were only an invitation to treat and no offence had been committed. In supermarkets where goods are arranged in shelves the situation appears more complex. No obvious rule seems to compel itself although a rule is required to clarify the moment at which the contract is made. Is the offer made when: (i) the goods are on display; (ii) they are picked up by the customer; (iii) taken to the check out; (iv) accepted by the person at the till by putting them through the bar code reader or (v) paid for? The answer is (iv). The goods on display are an invitation to treat. These are picked up and offered by the customer to the person at the check out to put through her machine to read the bar code and record the sale. This is an acceptance by the store's employee. There is a contract from this point and ownership passes with it. If the goods are broken or damaged before this, the customer would be legally liable as they still belong to the shop. If they break as the customer is taking them out to the carpark, the risk is on the buyer as they are now the owner. If the items on the shelf were on the offer, then the act of putting them into the trolley would amount to acceptance and the customer would be bound to pay even if she changed her mind.

The rule on the point of offer and acceptance goes back to *Pharmaceutical Society of Great Britain v. Boots Cash Chemists Southern Ltd*[9] in which the Divisional Court held that the self service system did not amount to an offer by the defendants to sell medicines and drugs, but was merely an invitation to the customer to offer to buy. The offer had been accepted at the cashier's desk under the supervision of a registered pharmacist. There had been no offence committed of selling medicines without the correct supervision of a qualified pharmacist. The prosecution had been brought over the sale of

3.4

---

[6] (1870) L.R. 5 CP 561.
[7] See p. 32.
[8] [1961] 1 Q.B. 394.
[9] [1953] 1 Q.B. 401.

medicines at a chemists shop in Edgware contrary to the Pharmacy and Poisons Act 1933. By holding that the contract was concluded at the cash-desk, the defendants were not guilty of the offence. The customer took the items to the shop assistant and made an offence. This could be accepted or rejected by the retailer. Somervell L.J.[10] stated: "I can see no reason for implying from this self-service arrangement any implication other than that . . . it is a convenient method of enabling customers to see what there is and choose, and possibly put back and substitute, articles which they wish to have, and then go up to the cashier and offer to buy what they have so far chosen." The rule is based largely on practical convenience, business practice and common sense, rather than logic and this is as it should be.

The shopping situation requires a clear cut answer. Here the legal rule will normally prevail over the parties' intentions. In other words, if you see something in the window of a shop, you cannot insist on buying it at the price shown.[11] However, exceptionally this might not be true. Take for instance an "offer" by a department store to sell a new digital television worth £1,000 to the first person into the shop on Monday morning (other than employees of course) for a knock down price of £50. Sarah goes along on the strength of this statement with her sleeping bag and sits out all night in order to be the first there. Can the shop turn around and say this is only an advertising gimmick or an invitation to treat? The obvious answer is that this was merely an invitation to treat and that they do not have to sell the television to Sarah. However, Sarah may also have an argument. First the act of sitting out and being first in the queue was a unilateral contract in return for the store's promise. The store's statement was an offer because it was expressed in such a way and was meant to be taken seriously by anyone reading it. They would, therefore, be bound to sell the television set to Sarah.

There is authority in support of Sarah's view in the United States. In *Lefkowitz v. Great Minneapolis Surplus Store*[12] the plaintiff relied on a newspaper advertisement that several ladies' fur coats and scarves worth 100 dollars each would be sold on the basis of "first come, first served" for one dollar each. The plaintiff was the first to present himself but because the offer applied to womens' clothing, and he was a man, the store refused to sell the items to him. He succeeded in his action for breach of contract. The advertisement which (as in *Carlill* was capable of being an offer to the public at large), was an offer, not an invitation to treat, so long as "some performance was promised in positive terms in return for something requested". According to Justice Murphy when the offer is "clear, definite and explicit and leaves nothing open for negotiation, it constitutes an offer, acceptance of which will complete the contract".

(2) Statements of price

3.5   A statement of price is usually an attempt to "set the ball rolling", which is as good a definition as there is for an invitation to treat. It is therefore not an offer. In *Clifton v. Palumbo*[13] the plaintiff wrote, "I am prepared to offer you . . . my . . . estate for £600,000 . . .". The defendant later tried to accept this "offer". The Court of Appeal held that it

---

[10] At p. 406.
[11] If the price is wrong or misleading it will be in breach of the Consumer Protection Act 1987 s. 20 which creates a criminal or regulatory offence rather than a civil liability.
[12] (1958) 86 N.W. 2d 289.
[13] [1944] 2 All E.R. 497.

was in fact merely a preliminary statement of the asking price in order to start negotiations. The defendant's "acceptance" was itself an offer to buy. On the other hand, in *Bigg v. Boyd Gibbins Ltd*[14] during negotiations for the sale of Shortgrove Hall, a property in Essex, the plaintiffs wrote to the defendants, "For a quick sale I would accept £26,000". The defendants replied "I accept your offer". The plaintiffs wrote back again later saying they were placing the matter with their solicitors and that they were pleased that "you are purchasing the property". The Court of Appeal held that there was a contract. The price statement was this time construed as an offer. The correspondence constituted a binding contract for the sale and purchase of the property. The plaintiffs were entitled to an order of specific performance. Requests for information, such as to price or whether a property is for sale, are generally not to be treated as an offer to buy.

(3) Catalogues and Advertisements

These are traditionally not regarded as offers but rather are designed to attract business **3.6** and so are only invitations to treat. In *Grainger & Son v. Gough*[15] a catalogue from a wine merchant in Fenchurch Street was held to be merely an intention to treat. The supplier could, however, protect himself here by merely stating that the offer was open only while stocks last, or that they were on offer on a "first come, first served" basis. In *Partridge v. Crittenden*,[16] an item in the classified advertisements of a magazine for the sale of bramble finches (selling such birds was illegal) was held to be merely an invitation to treat and not an offer. The offence of "offering for sale" had therefore not been committed. Similarly, in *Rooke v. Dawson*[17] an advertisement of a scholarship to University College, London was held to be only an invitation to treat and not an offer. The scholarship was to be given after examination of pupils at Mill Hill School. The action was for a declaration that the plaintiff was entitled to the prize.[18] Advertisements of unilateral contracts can amount to offers.[19] The Consumer Protection (Distance Selling) Regulations 2000 may also treat statements and letters as offers when trading online or even by post. This would be a radical departure for English law.[19a]

(4) Auction Sales

In the discretely hushed atmosphere of the auction room, offer and acceptance is at its **3.7** most apparent. As long ago as in *Payne v. Cave*[20] it was held that an auctioneer's request for bids is an invitation to treat. The potential buyer makes an offer when she bids. The Sale of Goods Act 1979 s. 57, provides that a sale is completed by acceptance with the fall of the auctioneer's hammer. A higher bid knocks out all earlier ones. Lots can be withdrawn at any time until acceptance. Advertising an auction is not an offer to hold it, nor does it bind the auctioneer to sell the goods. In *Harris v. Nickerson*,[21] the plaintiff could not recover the money wasted on travelling to attend an auction which was

---

[14] [1971] 1 W.L.R. 913.
[15] [1896] A.C. 325.
[16] [1968] 2 All E.R. 421.
[17] [1895] 1 Ch. 480.
[18] On this remedy see Chap. 26.
[19] See *Carlill v. Carbolic Smoke Ball Co. Ltd* [1893] 1 Q.B. 256; *Bowerman v. ABTA* [1995] 145 N.L.J.R. 1815.
[19a] See Chap. 4.
[20] (1789) 3 Term Rep 148.
[21] (1873) L.R. 8 Q.B. 286.

cancelled. The advertisement was merely an invitation to treat. Normally auctions take place with a reserve price. If the highest bid does not reach this price then the lot is withdrawn. However, if the auction is advertised as being without a reserve price, the highest bidder has the right to acquire the goods. In an early case, *Warlow v. Harrison,*[22] it was suggested, *obiter dicta,* that there might be a contract between the highest bidder and the auctioneer (not the seller) based upon a collateral warranty between the two parties. The request for bids would then be an offer by the auctioneer that he would accept the highest bid.[23] If the auctioneer refused to sell the item to the highest bidder, this could be a breach of contract. This view is now confirmed by the Court of Appeal's judgment in *Barry v. Davies.*[24] The facts of this case appear unusual. The claimant bid £200 each for two new engine analysers at a sale without reserve. The claimant was the only bidder for the items. The auctioneer defendant withdrew the two engines believing the bid to be unreasonable (their price as new was £14,000 each). The Court of Appeal held that the auctioneer was obliged to sell the machines to the claimant as a result of a collateral agreement between the auctioneer and bidder and was in breach of contract in failing to do so. By not putting a reserve price on the goods, the auctioneer had taken the risk and left himself liable to the person making the highest (or in this case, only) bid.[25]

(5) Tenders

3.8   Tendering for contracts is an everyday part of commercial life, and an important process in contract formation. In many industries, such as construction and civil engineering, tendering is widely used, and in some areas, particularly contracts procured by public bodies, even compulsory.[26] The request for tenders is an invitation to treat. The tender is an offer, so there is normally no obligation to accept a particular bid, or even the highest (or lowest depending on the circumstances). A good example of a tendering at work is *Trollope and Colls Ltd t/a Nuclear Civil Contractors v. Atomic Power Construction Ltd.*[27] The plaintiffs submitted a tender to carry out civil engineering work on a nuclear power station at Trawsfynydd in the old county of Merioneth in mid-Wales. The tender was for a lump sum price, but allowed the defendants to make variations in the "form, quality and quantity of the work" which would be taken into account in adjusting the contract price later for costs of labour and materials. Both parties intended from the outset that a legally binding contract should be made between them, and in June 1959, the plaintiffs, at the request of the defendants, began work on the project. The contract was only agreed and signed later on April 11, 1960.

The question for the Queen's Bench Division was, "whether there was a contract between the plaintiffs and the defendants governing their rights as to the work done since June 1959". It was held by Megaw J. that there was a contract. The parties had acted on the understanding and in anticipation that when a contract was made it would govern what was done meanwhile. The tender was an offer which contemplated variations, and

[22] (1859) E1 & E1 309, 120 E.R. 925.
[23] See Harvey and Meisel, *Auctions Law and Practice* (1995, 2nd ed. OUP) esp. pp. 29–33.
[24] [2000] 1 W.L.R. 1962, see also Meisel "What price auctions without reserve?" (2000) 64 M.L.R. 468.
[25] On the calculation of damages in this case, see Chap. 24.
[26] See the Public Works Contracts Regulations 1991 (S.I. 1991 No. 2680) and the Public Supply Contracts Regulations 1991 (S.I. 1991 No. 2679) implementing the EU Directives 93/36, 93/37, and 93/38 EEC O.J.L. 199/1, 54, 84.
[27] [1963] 1 W.L.R. 333.

this had been accepted by the defendants. The contract which came into existence on April 11 "could rightly be supported as governing the rights of the parties as to prior work". There was also a term to be implied into the contract of April 1960, retrospectively to give business efficacy to the transaction. The Court held that: "The tender for the works constituted an offer that contemplated variation of the work and the ultimate acceptance of that offer was in the circumstances, an acceptance of the offer as applied to and embracing the changes requested and agreed in anticipation of the ultimate acceptance".[28] This case is a good example of the courts taking account of reliance. Both parties had started performance even if the paperwork had not been completed. The law takes account of this by allowing a retrospective offer and acceptance, though only in narrow circumstances.[29] Referential bids are a different type of offer made in reference to others, *e.g.* £100 higher than the highest bid received. This is treated as a kind of tender and such bids are valid in principle.[30]

(6) Overlooked tenders

When a tender is unsuccessful there is normally very little that can be done about it, **3.9** because the tender is merely an offer. The tenderer will normally have done some work in preparation and may have been put to considerable expense, so there is concern if a tender has been improperly overlooked.[31] A tender was overlooked in *Blackpool and Fylde Aero Club v. Blackpool Borough Council*[32] in which the plaintiffs, among others, had been invited to tender by the defendants for the right to operate pleasure flights from the airport at Blackpool. The tenders had to be submitted by mid-day on a particular date. The plaintiffs' tender was submitted at 11 a.m. but the letter box at the Town Hall, which was where the tender had to be placed, was not emptied by council staff until later. Believing that the plaintiffs' tender had not arrived, the defendants awarded the contract to a third party. The Court of Appeal held that there was an implied unilateral contract that all tenders meeting the requirements laid down would be considered. According to Bingham L.J.: "the council's invitation to tender was, to this limited extent, an offer, and the club's submission of a timely and conforming tender an acceptance."[33] In *Blackpool Aero Club* the contractual obligation was only to consider the bid. The Council was not obliged to award them the contract.[34]

A duty to consider tenders was also discussed in *Fairclough Building Ltd v. Port Talbot Borough Council*[35] in which the defendant council in South Wales had a short listing procedure which could exclude a bid if there were "reasonable grounds" for doing so. The plaintiff contractors had tendered to build a new civic centre in Port Talbot. One of the members of the committee considering the applications was Mrs Peggy George, who was

---

[28] The case also illustrates that in the real commercial world/signing the contract lagged some way behind actually starting the work (in this case by 9 months), and that offer and acceptance may not be taken quite as seriously by business people as it is by many contract law teachers.

[29] See Chap. 5.

[30] See *Harvela Investments Ltd v. Royal Trust of Canada Ltd* [1986] A.C. 207.

[31] He may however have a remedy in restitution law, see later Chap. 26.

[32] [1990] 3 All E.R. 25.

[33] At p. 31.

[34] See Adams and Brownsword "More in Expectation than Hope: The Blackpool Airport Case" (1991) 54 M.L.R. pp. 281–287; and Phang "Tenders Implied Terms and Fairness in the Law of Contract (1998) 13 J.C.L. pp. 126–142.

[35] (1993) 62 Build. L.R. 82, 33 Con. L.R. 24.

the wife of a director of the plaintiffs. When this became known, Mrs George was first removed from the committee and the plaintiffs were excluded from the tender list for the project. The Court of Appeal upheld the Judge's decision to dismiss the action for breach of contract. Although there was an implied contract formed by conduct that the defendants would consider the tender, in the circumstances the council had only two alternatives, either to remove Mrs George or to remove the plaintiffs from the list. By deciding to do the latter, the Council had acted reasonably. They were under no duty to permit the company to stay on the list throughout the whole tendering process. The Court of Appeal distinguished the *Blackpool Aero Club* case, Parker L.J. taking the view that there was no conflict between the two judgments on the ground that in this case the council had a duty to act in a manner in which was reasonable. By removing Fairclough from the list, they had acted reasonably and were not in breach of contract.[36] They acted in a way which the Council considered to be reasonable and which the Judge held to be reasonable. Nolan L.J. agreed that the two cases were consistent:

"A tenderer is always at risk of having his tender rejected, either on its intrinsic merits or on the ground of some disqualifying factor personal to the tenderer. Provided that the ground of rejection does not conflict with some binding undertaking or representation previously given by the customer to the tenderer, the latter cannot complain. It is not sufficient for him to say, however understandably, that he regards the ground of rejection as unreasonable."[37]

TERMINATING THE OFFER

An offer may be brought to an end on a number of different grounds. If this is effectively achieved before acceptance occurs then there is no contract.

Revocation

3.10   An offer may be revoked at any time until it has been accepted or brought to an end by other means. This is an aspect of the doctrine for consideration since without consideration to support it, the promise of the offer is not binding. In *Dickinson v. Dodds*[38] the defendant told the plaintiff that the offer was to be left over till 9 a.m. on Friday. It was held that he could nevertheless withdraw before Friday, since there was nothing given in return for the promise. An offer can be held open for a period of time. A "firm offer" is one in which something, even a nominal sum, is provided in return.[39] In *Routledge v. Grant*[40] the defendant promised to keep an offer open for six weeks. After only three weeks he purported to revoke the offer. After this, but before the six week period had elapsed, the plaintiff then "accepted" it. It was held the offer was revoked as there was

---

[36] The duty to act in good faith was also considered, see Chap. 14.
[37] At p. 36.
[38] (1876) 2 Ch. 463.
[39] See "Firm offers". Law Commission Working Paper No. 60.
[40] (1828) 4 Bing. 653; 130 E.R. 920.

nothing given in return for keeping the promise open. In *Scammell v. Dicker*,[41] Aldous L.J. held that an offer to settle a legal action under Part 26 of the Civil Procedure Rules could be withdrawn at any time prior to acceptance. An offer which had been withdrawn within a time period of 21 days for acceptance, was therefore no longer capable of acceptance.

(1) The case of the hogsheads of tobacco

The rule on revocation goes back to the dawn of modern contract law. Indeed the fol- **3.11** lowing case could be said to have heralded in the start of the classical era. In *Cooke v. Oxley*[42] the parties had a discussion about a contract to buy 266 hogsheads of tobacco. The defendant proposed to sell the tobacco to the plaintiff, who asked the defendant to give him time to think about the proposal until 4 p.m. that day. The defendant agreed to this, but then went back on his word and sold the tobacco to a third party, in spite of the fact that although the plaintiff had told him that he wished to buy the tobacco after all. Kenyon C.J. stated,[43] "Nothing can be clearer than that at the time of entering into this contract the engagement was all on one side; the other party was not bound. It was there-fore *nudum pactum*", *i.e.* a bare promise. According to Buller J.[44]: "In order to sustain a promise, there must be either a damage to the plaintiff, or an advantage to the defendant; but here was neither when the contract was first made." *Cooke v. Oxley* has several important points for modern law:[45] (i) An undertaking to keep an offer open is not binding because of lack of consideration; (ii) It is probably the earliest authority on offer and acceptance (it was one of only two cases cited in *Adams v. Lindsell*); and (iii) the case is also an early example of a subjective approach in contract law taking precedence over an objective test. The subjective view of revocation by merely changing one's mind was later rejected under the weight of objective theory.[46]

(2) Communicating a revocation in a bilateral contract.

The postal rule does not apply to revocation even if postal services are used to make the **3.12** offer and acceptance. The classic case is *Byrne & Co. v. Leon Van Tienhoven & Co*[47] in which it was held that a contract had been formed on October 11 when the acceptance was telegraphed, not on October 8 when the letter revoking the offer was sent. In fact, the offer could have been accepted at any time until October 20 when the revocation arrived with the offeree. The revocation does not have to be communicated to the offeree in person. It is enough that he was aware of the revocation before they attempted to accept.[48] If the offeree fails to read the revocation or has moved address without telling the offeror, then the revocation will be effective. Finally, if the attempted revocation and the acceptance cross in the post then, applying the rules, a contract will be formed if the acceptance is posted before the revocation arrives.[49]

---

[41] [2001] 1 W.L.R. 631. See also *Pitchmastic plc v. Birse Construction Ltd, The Times*, June 21, 2000.
[42] (1790) 3 T.R. 653, 100 E.R. 785.
[43] At p. 786.
[44] At p. 786.
[45] In the same year, John Joseph Powell wrote the first text exclusively on contract law in England (see Chap. 1, p. 1). The year 1790 can therefore claim to be an auspicious year for the subject.
[46] See E. Allan Farnsworth, *Contracts* (1990, 2nd Ed, Little Brown and Co, Boston).
[47] (1880) 5 C.P.D. 344.
[48] See *Dickinson v. Dodds* (1876) 2 Ch. 463.
[49] See *Henthorn v. Fraser* [1892] 2 Ch. 27.

(3) Communicating Revocation of a Unilateral Contract: The famous "walk to York" situation.[50]

3.13   The issue is whether an offer of a unilateral contract can be withdrawn at any time before complete acceptance, or does the offeror lose this right after the offeree begins his performance? On traditional principles the answer must be the former. The promisor is entitled to revoke at any time until performance is completed. Acceptance occurs only on complete performance of the act requested, and until that time the offer remains capable of revocation. This does not seem entirely justifiable. There have been suggestions going back to the last century[51] that once performance has started it may be too late to revoke the offer. A second promise should be implied not to revoke once performance has begun.[52] In the United States this idea has taken root preventing the revocation of an offer. The United States Restatement (Second) of Contracts restricts the right of the offeror to revoke once performance is started.[52a] The obligation on the offeror to pay is conditional on completing performance.

This point has not yet been established in English law but there are indications that such an approach might be preferred if the point was to arise today. Two Court of Appeal judgments contain *obiter dicta* that a promise not to revoke should be implied into contracts. In *Errington v. Errington and Woods*,[53] a father bought a house in Newcastle for his son and daughter-in-law. The father promised to let them have the house if they paid the mortgage instalments on a £250 loan in the meantime. When he died, he left the property to his widow, Mary, the plaintiff. It was held that there was an implied term that the offer would not be revoked so long as the son and his wife continued to pay the instalments. According to Denning L.J. the promise could not be revoked once the payments were being made, stating that[54] the father's promise was: "a unilateral contract – a promise of the house in return for their act of paying the instalments. It could not be revoked by him once the couple entered on performance of the act, but it would cease to bind him if they left it incomplete and unperformed, which they have not done". Lord Denning's view in *Errington* is supported by *obiter dicta* in *Daulia Ltd v. Four Mill Bank Nominees Ltd.*[55] According to Goff L.J. there was scope for arguing that the offer was not revocable.[56] Goff L.J. stated that, "there must be an implied obligation on the part of the offeror not to prevent the condition becoming satisfied, which obligation it seems to me must raise as soon as the offeree starts to perform. Until then the offeror can revoke the whole thing, but once the offeree has embarked upon performance it is too late for the offeror to revoke his offer." Normally it may be relatively straight forward to revoke an offer to a single individual but there may be considerable practical difficulties revoking an offer in a unilateral contract if it has been made to a large number of people. The offeror is

---

[50]   This is the classical example used by Brett J. in *Great Northern Railway Company v. Witham* (1873) LR 9 CP 16, at p. 19): I offer you £100 if you will walk to York, I can revoke my offer at any time before you reach York. It is known in the United States as the "Brooklyn Bridge hypothetical", *i.e.* I will pay you 10 dollars if you will cross the bridge to Manhattan Island.
[51]   For example, Pollock *Principles of Contracts*, 1876.
[52]   See McGovney (1914) 27 Harvard Law Review 644.
[52a]   Section 45.
[53]   [1952] 1 K.B. 290.
[54]   At p. 295.
[55]   [1978] 1 Ch. 231.
[56]   At p. 239.

only required to use reasonable steps to revoke the offer. A revocation to the whole world would be impossible. It will be sufficient if the offeror publishes the revocation by similar means to that used for making the offer. In the American case of *Shuey v. US*,[57] William Shuey, the plaintiff, was the executor of a man named Henry Saint-Marie who claimed to be entitled to a reward of $25,000 offered by the American government for the "discovery and apprehension" of John Surratt who was being sought in connection with the assassination of President Abraham Lincoln. Henry Saint-Marie had given information to the American Minister in Rome, where he pointed out Surratt who had fled there after the murder. The United States Court of Claims held that to be entitled to the reward Saint-Marie would have had to have apprehended the fugitive in the person: "The terms of such an offer are rightly prescribed by the person offering it, and must be strictly complied with by him who claims the reward". In fact, however, the offer had been revoked by the time of Saint-Marie's information. The Court of Claims held that the offer could be revoked by similar means to those for making the offer in the first place, *i.e.* by newspaper or other public statement. The plaintiff did not know of the revocation of the offer of the reward, but this did not matter, and his. The plaintiff's action did not succeed.

(4) The Possible Extension of Promissory Estoppel to Deal with Revocation of Offers

The doctrine of promissory estoppel,[58] designed to prevent a person going back on his word, has been used in this context to turn an offer without consideration, which can be revoked, into an enforceable promise in American law. In *Drennan v. Star Paving Co.*[59] the Supreme Court of California held that an offer to do some building work, which included a "subsidiary promise" not to withdraw until the "plaintiff should have at least an opportunity to accept the offer", could not be revoked. The offeree had spent money and time in reliance on the offer. The offeror's intention was to induce the offeree to rely on the offer and to incur a detriment on the basis of such reliance. The American Restatement (Second) of Contracts s. 90[60] was the basis for turning the offer into a binding promise. In *Drennan*, the defendant knew that the plaintiff would rely on the offer if its bid for the paving work in question was the lowest received. Justice Traynor stated that the plaintiff should have been given a reasonable chance to accept the offer. **3.14**

(2) Other means of terminating an offer

(1) The offer is Subject to Express Or Implied Condition

An offer may be made subject to a condition. If the condition is not satisfied, the offer cannot be accepted.[61]

---

[57] (1875) 92 U.S. 73.
[58] Promissory estoppel is discussed in Chap. 10.
[59] 51 Cal 2d 409, 33 P. 2d 757 (1958).
[60] S.90 Restatement 2d. provides that "a promise which the promissor should reasonably expect to induce action or for bearance on the part of the promisee" and which does so, is binding, so long as injustice can be avoided only by enforcement of the promise.
[61] *Financings Ltd. v. Stimson* [1962] 3 All E.R. 386.

(2) Lapse of Time

If the offeror gives a time limit then that is effective to terminate the offer when it lapses. Where there is no express time limit, an offer is usually deemed to remain open for a reasonable time. What constitutes "reasonable" will depend on the circumstances.[62]

(3) Death of one of the parties

3.15 The effect of the death of the offeror depends upon the nature of the offer. If it is personal to the offeror, then the offer cannot be accepted once news of the death has been communicated. If the offer does not depend on personal performance and may be satisfied out of his estate, death may not prevent acceptance of the offer. The death of the offeree normally has a similar effect.

(4) Rejection

A rejection terminates the offer. An offer that is rejected cannot later be accepted in theory, neither can an offer be resurrected after anything which is construed as a counter offer. We shall now turn to the position where the offer survives to meet its match, acceptance, on the way to form a contract.

---

[62] *Ramsgate Victoria Hotel Co Ltd v. Montefiore* (1866) L.R. 1 Ex 109.

Flowchart A: The Offer

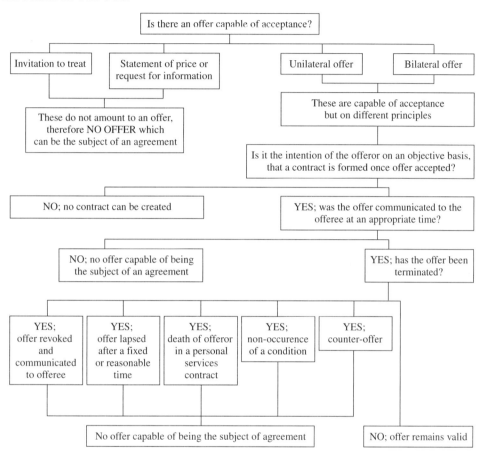

Chapter 4

ACCEPTANCE

Acceptance comes in two stages:

(1) The fact of acceptance,
(2) Communication of the acceptance.

THE FACT OF ACCEPTANCE

The fact of acceptance must be proved by a party seeking to do so on the balance of **4.1** probabilities. In *Hitchens v. General Guarantee Corporation*[1] the Court of Appeal held that it was proper to apply the normal burden of proof in civil matters to infer that a hire purchase agreement between an individual and a finance company had been accepted by the company by telephone. The Judge having found that there had been an oral acceptance, held this created a valid contract. The subsequent signature by the offeree simply ratified an earlier acceptance.[2]

Acceptance by words

(1) Acceptance must correspond exactly with the offer

The acceptance should reflect the offer precisely in order to result in agreement. This is what used to be called *"consensus ad idem"* or "meeting of the minds". Agreement was a nineteenth century innovation in contract law.[3] This required a clear subjective understanding between the parties which was often, in reality, hard to prove. The rule of acceptance echoes this by requiring the acceptance to match the offer exactly. A good example of the application of the so called "mirror image" test is *Mathieson Gee (Ayrshire) Ltd v. Quigley*[4] the main issue of which was the interpretation of two letters, as to whether an offer had been accepted by another letter on the following day. The first letter appeared to

---

[1] *The Times*, March 13, 2001.
[2] Under the Consumer Credit Act 1974 s. 29, such agreements must be signed to be properly executed. An improperly executed agreement is not entirely invalid, and can be enforced by order of a court. On the impact of the Human Rights Act 1998 on an unenforceable consumer credit agreement, see *Wilson v. First County Trust Ltd* [2001] 2 W.L.R. 302, discussed later in Chap. 11.
[3] See Simpson (1975) L.Q.R. 247.
[4] 1952 SC (HL) 38.

Lord Normand to be "free from all ambiguity. It is an offer to supply the necessary mechanical plant, with an undertaking that the plant would consist initially of specified machines." The letter of March 3 was "a purported acceptance of a contract to remove the silt, [in an expression derived from Roman law] *a locatio operis*", *i.e.* contract for work and materials. This was a "different kind of contract from that in the offer and with different incidents . . . no contract existed between the parties. The respondents offered one kind of contract and the appellant accepted another kind of contract".[5] The reply therefore failed the "mirror image" rule and no contract was formed.

(2) The reply is a counter offer

4.2 The question is whether a reasonable person would regard the statement as being a counter offer or as introducing a new term rather than acceptance.[6] A statement will be regarded as a counter offer if the reply: (a) introduces new terms; (b) varies the offer; (c) imposes new conditions; (d) is only a limited or qualified agreement; or (e) is merely an agreement to agree a future contract.[7] However; it will not be a counter offer if the offeree is: (a) seeking clarification; (b) seeking further information about the offer; or it is merely (c) a "provisional" agreement, pending the making of a more formal document. In *Hyde v. Wrench*[8] the defendant made an offer to sell his farm at Luddenham for £1000. The defendant initially responded that he would buy the property for £950, then changed his mind and purported to accept the original asking price of £1000. The court applied a strict logic to the correspondence and held that the potential purchaser response to buy at £950 was a refusal of the offer at £1000, followed by a counter offer at £950. The plaintiff's action for specific performance of the contract therefore failed. A request for clarification is not a counter offer. If the offeree is merely seeking further information before deciding whether to accept an offer, this will not be regarded as a counter-offer, and therefore the original offer is still capable of acceptance. In *Stevenson Jacques and Co. v. McLean*[9] the defendant wrote to the plaintiffs in Middlesborough regarding the purchase of a quantity of iron. The plaintiffs sent a telegraph "please write whether you would accept forty for delivery over two months, or if not, longest limit you could give". Lush J. held that this was not to be construed as a rejection of the defendant's offer but merely an inquiry "which should have been answered and not treated as a rejection of the offer".[10]

In *Jones v. Daniel*[11] the offeree purported to "accept" the offer but sent a document to be signed which contained terms not included in the offer. This conditional acceptance was really a counter offer. If there is a conditional acceptance, or merely "conditional" agreement, then there is no contract. However, a "provisional" agreement can be a contract if it appears that the parties have agreed on the essentials, and the provisional agreement is intended to be binding. In *Branca v. Cobarro*[12], the vendor agreed to sell the lease and goodwill of a mushroom farm for £5,000. The agreement con-

---

[5] At p. 42.
[6] See *Global Tankers Inc. v. Amercoat Europa MV* [1975] 1 Lloyd's Rep. 666.
[7] See Chap. 5.
[8] (1840) 3 Beav 334, 49 E.R. 132.
[9] (1880) 5 Q.B.D. 346.
[10] At p. 350.
[11] [1894] 2 Ch. 332.
[12] [1947] 2 All E.R. 101.

cluded that "This is a provisional agreement until a fully legalised agreement drawn up by a solicitor and embodying the conditions herewith stated is signed." The provisional agreement was made in July 1946. Branca paid a deposit of £500, with the balance due in December 1946. The Court of Appeal held that the word "until" implied that the agreement was intended to be immediately fully binding and to remain so unless and until superseded by a subsequent agreement of the "same tenor but expressed in a more precise and formal language". Asquith L.J. stated:[13] "The word `until' seems to me plainly to imply that the agreement is to be immediately fully binding unless and until superseded by a subsequent agreement of the same tenor, but expressed in more precise and formal language". The appeal against the judgment of Denning J. was allowed. He had held that this arrangement was merely tentative and therefore not binding. In general, if points are left outstanding there will be no agreement. This will be inferred from the parties' words or actions that there will be no contract until the matters have been clarified.[14]

It is possible to have an acceptance which is given with the *caveat* that the person   **4.3** accepting had some doubt over his or her ability to perform the contract. This is not a conditional acceptance so long as it clear that the party is accepting the offer otherwise unconditionally. In *Society of Lloyds v. Twinn*,[15] Geoffrey and Gail Thinn had a bankruptcy order against them as Lloyds names, set aside. They had agreed to a "reconstruction and renewal settlement order" but expressed doubts about being able to perform the agreement and asked Lloyds for an indulgence. The Court of Appeal held that an expression of doubt in such cases could be regarded as a collateral counter offer which if accepted meant that the main contract was accepted in terms of the original offer. An acceptance subject to such an indulgence could be valid. Sir Richard Scott V.C. stated that:

> "An offeree who purports to accept an offer must accept unconditionally. An acceptance which adds a new term to the contract is not an unconditional acceptance. But there is, conceptually at least, no reason why an offeree should not accept an offer unconditionally and, at the same time, make a collateral offer to the original offeror. The original offeror may or may not accept the collateral offer but, whether he does or does not do so, the unconditional acceptance will stand as having concluded the contract on the terms of the original offer".

An "acceptance" which introduces new terms is ineffective and will normally be treated as a counter-offer. However, in *Monvia Motorship Corporation v. Keppel Shipyard (Private) Ltd "The Master Stelios"*[16] in an exceptional case the Privy Council held that the exchange of telexes could be treated as an acceptance of a contract for drydocking and a screwschaft survey. This was coupled with an offer to enter into a further agreement to do repairs if necessary. New terms cannot be added after acceptance. The acceptance brings the negotiating stage of the contract to an end. Once the contract has

---

[13] At p. 104.
[14] See *Metal Scrap Trade Corporation v. Kate Shipping Co Ltd "The Gladys"* (No.2) [1994] 2 Lloyd's Rep. 402.
[15] *The Times*, April 4, 2000.
[16] [1983] 1 Lloyd's Rep. 356.

been formed by offer and acceptance it is too late to add to or vary the terms agreed. Bingham J. in *Pagnan v. Feed Products*[17] stated that:

> "once a definite offer has been made, and it has been accepted without qualification, and it appears that the letters of offer and acceptance contained all the terms agreed on between the parties, the complete contract thus arrived at cannot be affected by subsequent negotiation. When once it is shown that there is a complete contract, further negotiations between the parties cannot, without the consent of both, get rid of the contract already arrived at."

Acceptance by conduct

4.4   Acceptance may be brought about by conduct alone, without the need for words. The classic authority is *Brogden v. Metropolitan Railway Co.,*[18] in which colliery owners who had delivered coal to a railway company for many years without a contract (a not uncommon practice in some industries). However, when they eventually did decide to make a contract, the offer contained a blank space for the insertion of the name of an arbitrator in the event of disputes between them. This space was filled in and the document returned. The document was by now a counter offer since a new term had been inserted, so the new agreement was never formally accepted. The parties continued to supply and receive the coal. When a dispute arose, Brogden claimed there was no contract. The House of Lords held a contract had been formed by the conduct of ordering the coal on the new terms or in supplying it.[19]

Normally the act constituting acceptance must have been performed with the intention of accepting the offer. The offeree must have some knowledge of the offer but it need not be the only reason for acting. If there are other reasons for doing this does not necessarily prevent the conduct amounting to acceptance. This is illustrated by cases involving rewards and prizes as unilateral contracts. In the American case of *Simmons v. United States*[20] it was held that so long as an offer of a prize is known, a person may accept an offer of a unilateral contract by doing the thing in question, even if he does so primarily for reasons unrelated to the offer. The case concerned a rock fish swimming in Cheseapeake Bay on the Eastern Coast of America. This particular fish had an identification tag placed on it and was given a name, "Diamond Jim 3rd". The fish was placed in the Bay by organisers of an event called the Third Annual American Beer Fishing Derby. Anyone who caught Diamond Jim 3rd and produced the identification tag and an affidavit that it had been caught by hook and line would win a cash prize of $25,000. A fisherman named William Simmons caught Diamond Jim 3rd one morning while going about his normal fishing activities. He knew about the prize but he did not set out to catch the fish in question as he intended to fish anyway. According to the facts as stated by Sobeloff, Chief Judge of the United States 4th Circuit Court of Appeals "after Simmons and his fishing companions appropriately marked the happy event, he hastened to claim his prize . . . Simmons knew about the contest, but as an experienced fisherman,

---

[17] [1987] 2 Lloyd's Rep. 601 (at p. 611).
[18] (1877) 2 App. Cas 666.
[19] See also *Wettern Electric Ltd v. Welsh Development Agency* [1983] Q.B. 796.
[20] (1962) 308 F.2d. 160.

he knew that his chances of catching that fish were minimal, and he did not have Diamond Jim 3rd in mind when he set out that morning". The case arose because the US Internal Revenue saw him receive the prize on television and claimed tax on the sum. Was it a pure lottery or had William Simmons entered into a contract so that the organisers had to pay the money to him? The Court held that there was a contract. He had done the requested act, albeit for other motives, so this could be acceptance.

> "Under accepted principles of contract law . . . the company was legally obligated to award the prize once Simmons had caught the fish and complied with the remaining conditions precedent. The offer of a prize or reward for doing a specified act, like catching a criminal, is an offer for a unilateral contract. For the offer to be accepted and the contract to become binding, the desired act must be performed with knowledge of the offer. The evidence is clear that Simmons knew about the Fishing Derby the morning he caught Diamond Jim III. It is not fatal to his claim for refund that he did not go fishing for the express purpose of catching one of the prize fish. So long as the outstanding offer was known to him, a person may accept an offer for a unilateral contract, by rendering performance, even if he does so primarily for reasons unrelated to the offer".[21]

By contrast, in *R v. Clarke*[22], an Australian case, £1,000 was offered to anyone for evidence concerning the killing of two police men. Evan Clarke gave evidence, and though involved in the murder, and was released. He claimed the £1,000 but the High Court of Australia held that he could not recover. His motive was entirely to save his own skin, not to claim the reward. Starke J. stated that[23]: "unless a person performs the conditions of the offer, acting upon its faith and in reliance upon it, he does not accept the offer and the offer is not bound to him". On the other hand, "as a matter of proof, any person knowing of the offer who performs its conditions establishes *prima facie* an acceptance of that offer". The case is often seen as being based on public policy considerations. But ignorance is not bliss, in this instance at least. There cannot be acceptance in ignorance of the offer. If the plaintiff does the act without knowledge of the offer, then there is no contract. In *Clarke* the motive was such as to have put the reward out of the plaintiff's mind. Although the plaintiff had seen the offer, according to Higgin J.[24] "it was not present to his mind – he had forgotten it, and gave no consideration to it, in his intense excitement as to his own danger. There cannot be assent without knowledge of the offer; and ignorance of the offer is the same thing whether it is due to never hearing of it or [to forgetting] it after hearing".   **4.5**

There is some English authority for being able to claim a reward in ignorance. In *Gibbons v. Proctor*[25] the Divisional Court upheld the payment of a reward printed in a handbill, though the person giving it did not know of the handbill until afterwards.[26] An American case *Fitch v. Snedaker*[27] is usually cited as giving the contrary and also   **4.6**

---

[21] At p. 164.
[22] (1927) 40 C.L.R. 227.
[23] At p. 244.
[24] At p. 241.
[25] (1891) 64 L.T. 594.
[26] See Hudson "Gibbons v. Proctor Revisited" (1968) 84 L.Q.R. 503.
[27] (1868) 38 N.Y. 248.

"correct" view that an acceptance cannot be made in ignorance of the offer (though not much attention is given to the case in the leading American texts).[28] In *Clarke,* Higgin J. commented on *Gibbons v. Proctor and Fitch v. Snedaker.* The former was to be regarded as "wrong" and the latter "faultless" and "correct in principle". The court held that the motive inducing consent may be immaterial but was consent and vital without it there was no contract. If the person acts for a motive entirely other than claiming the reward then there will be no contract. In *Williams v. Carwardine,*[29] the plaintiff responded to an offer of a reward for information leading to the conviction of the murderer of a man found dead in the river Wye, who had been last seen in a public house in Hereford. Mrs Anne Williams had been badly beaten by her husband and gave evidence to the authorities which led to his conviction. The Court found that she had done so believing that her life expectancy was short as a result of the assault and she wished to ease her conscience and save her soul. The Court held that she was not entitled to the reward.

COMMUNICATION OF ACCEPTANCE

4.7   The fact of agreement by itself does not make a contract, there must also be communication of the acceptance to the offeror. This requires some external evidence of acceptance. This would not be provided by a person merely making up her mind to accept. The risk of failing to communicate falls largely on the offeree. It is up to her to make the necessary effort to accept. The offeror meanwhile can make his own requirements for the acceptance, for instance a letter of acceptance must be delivered "to my home by mid-day on Friday". The offeror can also prescribe the means of acceptance, *e.g.* by telephone or e-mail. The offeror is in charge of the process of communication. An uncommunicated acceptance is ineffective. If a person writes down an acceptance on a piece of paper which he does not send to the other, there is no acceptance.[30] However, the offeror may have the acceptance brought to her attention from other sources. This does not have to be by the offeree telling her directly, it could be by an agent, third party or friend. On the other hand, mere rumour of acceptance is not enough. By a combination of precedents there are historically two rules, rather than one which would not only be neater, but also more satisfactory. The two rules sitting side by side create far more difficulties than they are worth and turn this into a more complex area of contract law than is necessary. To this may be added a third new category. Special rules now also apply to consumer contracts concluded through distance communications under the Consumer Protection (Distance Selling) Regulations 2000. We shall consider each of these in turn.

The general rule: instantaneous communications

4.8   The general rule applies to so called "instantaneous" communications. This ranges from the human voice when parties are face to face or on the telephone, to telex, fax machines,

---

[28] The case receives no mention at all in Farnsworth, *Contracts 2nd ed,* Little Brown or Farnsworth and Young *Cases and Materials on Contracts,* Foundation Press, or Murphy and Speidel *Studies in Contract Law,* Foundation.
[29] (1833) 4 B and Ad 621, 110 E.R. 590.
[30] See *Kennedy v. Thomassen* [1929] 1 Ch. 426.

the Internet and e-mails.[31] The rule here is that it is for the offeree to communicate the acceptance. This must be "received" by the offeror. If communication fails, the risk lies on the offeree, *i.e.* there is no contract. So, if the telephone line goes dead at the vital moment, the dog starts barking so you cannot hear, or a police helicopter hovering overhead drowns out your conversation, there will be no contract. The offeree has to start again, or risk losing the contract. The communication must be received by the offeror. Questions may arise over whether this means at the instant the message arrives in the offeror's office, is read by a colleague or secretary, or is actually communicated to the offeror. For instance, is there acceptance if messages arrive out of hours, when a person is away from work, letters are unread, mistakenly thrown in the waste paper basket, or in garbled form or simply unintelligible?[32] In *Entores v. Miles Far Eastern Corporation*[33] a telex machine was treated as instantaneous communication. The Court of Appeal held a telex was to be equated with the telephone as instantaneous and that it was communicated when it was received by the offeror. The rule would therefore also apply to other forms of communication such as e-mail. If a message arrives at a person's business during normal working hours it is communicated. In *Entores* Lord Denning introduced the concept of fault into his judgment.[34] If there was fault on the part of the offeror, acceptance of the message could be said to be received without actual communication. On the other hand, if there was no fault on the offeror's part, even if the offeree reasonably believed it to have been received, then there would be no contract. As the case law has developed it now depends on whether the acceptance arrived (a) within or (b) outside of, normal working hours.

(1) "Normal" office hours

If an acceptance arrives within normal office hours then it will usually be treated as communicated to the offeree. If a fax or e-mail arrives and is read by a secretary or personal assistant it may be deemed to be received, even if not seen by the person to whom it is addressed. In *Tenax Steamship Co Ltd v. The Brimnes (Owners) "The Brimnes"*[35] a telex of revocation of an offer arrived between 5.30 and 6 o'clock in the afternoon local time but was not read until the following day. It was held that this was within normal working hours and so was to be regarded as communicated even though no one had seen it. This is not an absolute rule, however, and the courts will look at the particular circumstances of the case. In *Afovos Shipping Co SA v. R Pagnan and Fratelli (The Afovos)*, at first instance,[36] Lloyd J. stated that communication occurs[37] "when the telex is received and tested by the receiving bank"; so that if the owners were to make an inquiry at the bank they would be told "Yes the money has arrived for your account". This was affirmed by the House of Lords.[38] Lord Roskill stated that: "the correct answer ... is likely to depend, at least in most cases, upon proof of the

4.9

---

[31] Under the Consumer Protection (Distance Selling) Regulations 2000 e-mails are regarded as hard copy for the purpose of confirming the necessary information under the regulations.

[32] On garbled communications, see p. 54.

[33] [1955] 2 Q.B. 327.

[34] At p. 333.

[35] [1975] Q.B. 929.

[36] [1980] 2 Lloyd's Rep. 469.

[37] At p. 473.

[38] [1983] 1 Lloyd's Rep. 335.

practice of bankers current when the question arises rather than upon any determina-tion of it as a matter of law."[39] This is closer to the position when the communication is sent out of hours. "Normal" business hours is an uncertain concept these days. There may be quite a difference depending on whether you are dealing with a solicitor in a big city firm, a round the clock factory working flexi-hour shifts, a large retail store open at weekends or the availability of your university lecturer or personal tutor. In international trade huge differences in time zone may also apply. So "normal" is diffi-cult to judge in this context, particularly in the modern global economy.

(2) Outside of normal office hours

4.10   In *Brinkibon Ltd v. Stahag Stahl und Stahlwarenhandels GmbH*[40] the House of Lords had to consider the situation in which, even by telex, communication was not in fact instan-taneous, *i.e.* where a telex was sent at night or outside office hours. Lord Wilberforce stated[41] that in relation to such circumstances many variations may occur. No universal rule covers every situation. The court however should take into account three factors. First, the intentions of the parties, second, "sound business practice" and thirdly, in some cases, where the risk should lie. This is where the allocation risk rule is particularly important. In the case of instantaneous communications the risk is on the offeree to communicate. If communication is not effected correctly it is on the offeree to repeat acceptance or they will lose the contract. The issue arose in *Schelde Delta Shipping BV v. Astarte Shipping Ltd "The Pamela"*[42] in which a telex notifying of withdrawal of a vessel for non payment of hire arrived on the charterer's telex at 23.41 while the office was closed for the weekend. It was held that the message was not communicated until the office opened again on Monday morning. Gatehouse J. stated that: "the tribunal were right to find that the notice was not received by the charterers until the opening of busi-ness on Dec. 5th".[43] The court applied Lord Wilberforce's words in *Brinkibon* and deter-mined this issue by reference to the particular circumstances.[44]

The postal rule[45]

4.11   This is sometimes treated as an exception to the general rule. It is really an alternative rule which applies when a different means of communication is used, most obviously the postal service but also means of delivery which can be said to the analogous to it. There are not many examples of this nowadays. The rule used to apply to telegrams transmit-ted by the Post Office but these are now extinct,[46] and it may be that the rule also applies to fast mail or courier services but this is not clear.[47] The postal rule means that commu-nication occurs as soon as the letter is posted, not when it arrives or is delivered to the offeror. When the letter or document is put in the box or is otherwise out of the hands

---

[39]   At p. 342.
[40]   [1983] 2 A.C. 34.
[41]   At p. 42.
[42]   [1995] 2 Lloyd's Rep. 249.
[43]   At p. 252.
[44]   At p. 252.
[45]   See Gardner, "Trashing with Trollope: A Deconstruction of the Postal Rule" (1992) 12 O.J.L.S. 170.
[46]   See *Bruner v. Moore* [1904] 1 Ch. 305.
[47]   See later p. 54.

of the offeree, the contract is complete. This is so even if the letter is delayed, or never arrives. The offeree must prove posting, however, and often this can be difficult. Recorded and registered delivery of important documents are useful in this regard. The onus is on the party alleging there is a contract to prove it. The risk when the post is used is the reverse of that for the "general rule" described above. It is on the offeror, who chose to use the post in the first place. If they wish to avoid the postal rule they may do so. If no letter turns up then there can still be agreement if it was proved to be posted. The rule also means that during the time it takes for the letter to be delivered, only one party knows for certain that he is bound. Both parties are however bound at the same moment, *i.e.* on posting, but the offeror is unaware. This may explain why the postal rule is not especially popular. Having described the postal rule as an "exception" to the general rule, it is ironic that the postal rule probably arrived first (in the following case).

(1) The wool deal that got held up in the post

Adams v. Lindsell[48] is one of the classic cases of contract law. It is an example of the strange **4.12** process by which cases, which may appear trivial at the time, can develop and leave an indelible mark on the common law. This case heard originally at an Assize Court in Worcester was an instance of "first impression", a novel point of law which had to be determined ostensibly, without any clear guiding rule to compel any given result. The case may also be taken as the original authority laying down the requirement of offer and acceptance in the formation of contracts in English law. In *Adams v. Lindsell* the defendants were wool dealers at St. Ives in Huntingdonshire. On Tuesday September 2 1817 they sent a letter to the plaintiffs, who were woollen manufacturers at Bromsgrove in Worcestershire, as follows: "We now offer you eight hundred tods of whether fleeces, of a sound fair quality of our country wool, at 36s. 6d. per tod, to be delivered at Leicester, and to be paid for . . . in two months. . . receiving your answer in course of post". This letter was wrongly addressed to a Bromsgrove in Leicestershire. It finally arrived at the plaintiffs' premises in Bromsgrove, Worcestershire at 7.00 p.m. on Friday September 5. The plaintiffs immediately sent off a reply accepting the defendants offer of the wood on the terms proposed. The reply was received at the defendants in St. Ives on Tuesday September 9 (*i.e.* a week after the original letter of offer had been sent). On the Monday September 6, having received no reply from the plaintiffs (as they thought), the defendants sold the wool in question to a third party. The plaintiffs claimed the wood was theirs as they had accepted the defendants' offer. The defendants denied that there ever was a contractual relationship. When was the contract formed? (i) when the letter of acceptance was put in the post? (ii) when it was delivered to the offeror's address? or (iii) when actually brought to the offeror's attention?

At first instance, Burroughs J. held that the delay having been caused by the defen- **4.13** dants misaddressing their offer, they must take the blame. There was, in other words, a contract. On appeal in the Court of King's Bench[49] the judgment was upheld. There was a contract made on the Friday night when the acceptance was sent, not when it was received on the following Tuesday. The Court adopted option (a) above and thereby established "the postal rule". The Court held that the offer was accepted as soon as the letter of acceptance was posted. The contract was made before the sale of the wood to

---

[48] (1818) 1 B and Ald 681, 106 E.R. 205.
[49] Actually on the ancient *nisi prius* procedure of rehearing on a point of law.

the third party even though the letter of acceptance had not been received by the defendants. The defendants were liable for breach of contract in selling the wool in the meantime. There are a number of possible reasons for the judgment which was to all intents and purposes an "unprovided case" in which no definitive answer was compelled by precedent. First, practical convenience played a part. The plaintiff was successful because "if the defendants were not bound by their offer when accepted by the plaintiffs till the answer was received, then the plaintiffs ought not to be bound till after they had received the notification that the defendants had received their answer and assented to it. And so it might go on ad infinitum".[50] Secondly, the dispute was due to the defendants' fault: "As to the delay . . . that arises entirely from the mistake of the defendants and it therefore must be taken as against them".[51] Thirdly, the precedent of *Cooke v. Oxley*[52] was cited as authority in which counsel argued[53] that before "the answer was actually received there could be no binding contract between the parties and before then, the defendants had retracted their offer, by selling the wool to other persons". In other words the sale to the third party was a revocation of the offer. The Court in *Adams v. Lindsell* rejected this: "if that were so, no contract could ever be completed by the post".

(2) Applying the postal rule

4.14   The postal rule has been limited to communications in a permanent form, mostly letters. It was applied to telegrams sent through the Post Office in printed form but communicated by instantaneous means in *Bruner v. Moore*.[54] Replaced by telemessages, these also died out by the 1980s.[55] A postal reply will finalise a contract if it is sent before a revocation of the original offer. In *Byrne and Co. v. Leon van Tiehoven and Co.*[56] it was held that for a revocation of an offer to be effective it must actually be communicated to the offeree before the acceptance is posted. The postal rule was applied in *Household Fire and Carriage Accident Insurance Co v. Grant*[57]. In this case a contract was formed on posting even when it never arrived. The post office was treated as the agent of both parties. Thesiger J., stated[58]:

> "as soon as the letter of acceptance is delivered to the post office, the contract is made as complete and final and absolutely binding as if the acceptor had put his letter in the hands of a messenger sent by the offeror himself as his agent to deliver and offer and receive the acceptance. What other principle can be adopted short of holding that the contract is not complete by acceptance until and except from the time that the letter containing the acceptance is delivered to the offeror a principle that has been distinctly negatives".[59]

---

[50] At p. 251.
[51] At p. 251.
[52] (1790) 3 T.R. 653, 100 E.R. 785.
[53] At p. 251.
[54] [1904] 1 Ch. 304.
[55] It is interesting to note that under the Consumer Protection (Distance Selling) Regulations e-mails along with faxes are treated as durable or written, along with the post, for the purpose of communication, see p. 55.
[56] (1880) 5 C.P.D. 344.
[57] (1879) 4 Ex.D. 216.
[58] At p. 221.
[59] At p. 221.

In *CCC Firms (London) Ltd v. Impact Quadrant Films Ltd*[60] three film tapes which were supposed to be sent by recorded delivery were sent by unrecorded mail without insurance. The tapes never arrived, however Hutchison J,[61] though he had doubts about the evidence was "not prepared to hold that he did not in fact post them"[62]. The question is one of evidence and the burden of proof is on the party alleging there is a contract. Merely asserting that a person posted an unrecorded document would not be sufficient. An improperly addressed offer led in *Adams v. Lindsell* to the defendant being held liable. There does not appear to be clear authority on the point but on the basis of practical convenience it would seem unlikely that a court would hold the offeror liable when the offeree misdirected his acceptance.

(3) Limitations on the postal rule

The postal rule is kept within strict confines. It only applies to postal services when the post **4.15** is the proper method of communication.[63] It does not apply to the revocation of offers which must be actually received.[64] As we have discussed, if the reply is not properly addressed or lacks a stamp then the acceptance is unlikely to be completed. It must also be reasonable to use the post. *Henthorn v. Fraser*[65] involved a contract between parties in Liverpool and Birkenhead and, Lord Herschell stated the rule of when it is reasonable to use the post as follows: "the circumstances are such that it must have been within the contemplation of the parties that, according to the ordinary usages of mankind, the post might be used as a means of communicating the acceptance of the offer, that acceptance is complete as soon as it is posted'." The contract in this case was duly completed on posting. In *Holwell Securities v. Hughes*[66] there was a dispute over whether a notice exercising an option to purchase premises at High Road, Wembley, had been communicated. Lawton L.J. held that the postal rule did not apply when the offer expressly stated that the acceptance must reach the offeror. An offeror could exclude the postal rule in the offer if he or she wished. This transfers the risk of the acceptance going astray from offeror to the offeree. There were two paths to an answer in this case, a short path and a "roundabout path". The postal rule provided the latter. Lawton L.J. held that the parties did not intend that posting the letter should be sufficient. The offeror clearly wished to be notified directly. Lawton L.J. also noted the two other factors, namely manifest inconvenience and absurdity.[67] In his judgment: "[these factors] were but illustrations of a wider principle namely, that the rule does not apply, if having regard to all the circumstances, including the nature of the subject matter under consideration, the negotiating parties cannot have intended that there should be a binding agreement until the party accepting an offer or exercising an option had in fact communicated the acceptance to the other".[68]

The postal rule is commonly written out of offers, *e.g.* in relation to football pool **4.16** coupons, which must be returned to the organiser before they are received and accepted.

---

[60] [1985] Q.B. 16.
[61] At p. 271.
[62] For the collection of damages awarded in this case, see Chap. 24.
[63] [1974] 1 W.L.R. 155.
[64] See *Byrne v. Leon van Tienhoven* (1880) 5 C.P.P. 344.
[65] [1892] 2 Ch. 27.
[66] [1974] 1 W.L.R. 155.
[67] See also Lord Bramwell, in *British and American Telegraph v. Colsons* (1871) L.R. 6 Exch. 108.
[68] At p. 161.

Claiming that it was posted but never received is not sufficient, for obvious reasons. The promoter of the pools exclude the postal rule for their own convenience and also to limit fraud.[69] The Contracts (Rights of Third Parties) Act 1999 s. 2(2)(b) excludes the postal rule as far as acceptance by a third party of his or her rights under the Act are concerned. The subsection provides: "if sent to the promisor by post or other means, shall not be regarded as communicated to the promisor until received by him". The 1999 Act in fact provides three means of acceptance: communication, reliance or reasonable reliance.[70]

Difficulties can also arise in relation to garbled messages or words which get confused or mixed up in their communication which could be by letter, fax or e-mail. The effect of garbled messages depends on whether this concerns the offer or acceptance and the means of communication used. In *Henkel v. Pape*[71] the plaintiff sent a telegram asking if the defendant was interested in offering to buy 50 rifles. The defendant replied "send three rifles" (this being the number he wished to purchase). The telegram was wrongly transcribed and read "send the rifles". The plaintiff sent 50 rifles to the defendant but the court held that he need only accept three. The courts may also apply the notion of objectivity, to the parties' intention to offer or accept[72] and the doctrine of mistake may be relevant and applied to any agreement.[73] Thus a statement may be construed as an offer if a reasonable offeree would take it to be one, even if subjectively, no offer was intended. In *Moran v. University College Salford (No. 2)*[74] a University was held bound by an unconditional offer to a student which should not have been made.

Communication by distant means and information technology

(1) Privatised mail services

4.17   The growth of courier services, and the break up of the Royal Mail's monopoly along with other competition for postal services by commercial firms, means that the issue of when contracts are formed remains a live one. Is this when documents are handed over or picked up by the courier, or when they arrive (at the precise minute as promised)? If, following the dictum in *Henthorn v. Fraser*, the use of this method of communication is within the reasonable contemplation of the parties, the postal rule could apply rather than the general rule. So far there is no case on the point. In the Vienna Convention on contracts for the International Sale of Goods (a document not yet ratified by the United Kingdom) under article 18(2) acceptance only becomes effective when it reaches the offeror. In other words, the postal rule does not apply. However, if the acceptance is delayed in transmission it is still effective unless the offeror informs the offeree that the offer has lapsed.[75] The postal rule is rapidly appearing to be antiquated in the modern world. Until recently, the majority of commercial contracts are still in written form and posted in the traditional way but the practice is obviously and quickly changing.

---

[69] Such competitions are not in any case legally binding agreements, see Chap. 11.
[70] See Chap. 10.
[71] (1870) 6 Ex. 7.
[72] See Chap. 2.
[73] See Chap. 6.
[74] *The Times*, November 23, 1993.
[75] Art. 21(2).

(2) The Consumer Protection (Cancellation of Contracts Concluded away from Business Premises) Regulations 1987

The Consumer Protection (Cancellation of Contracts Concluded away from Business Premises) Regulations 1987 implement the European Union "Doorstep Selling" directive.[76] As this name suggests, the 1987 regulations apply to unsolicited visits by a trader to a persons home, or place of work for the purpose of soliciting sales of consumer goods and services.[77] If a contract of sale or other agreement results then the consumer is given a right to cancel within 7 days of making the contract.[78] The customer must serve a notice of cancellation in writing.

(3) The Consumer Protection (Distance Selling) Regulations 2000.[79]

A significant set of regulations applying to consumers using the Internet and e-commerce, purchasing by telephone, catalogue or even by post are the Consumer Protection (Distance Selling) Regulations 2000.[80] The regulations apply widely to all contracts between sellers and suppliers and consumers made exclusively by means of distance communication, *i.e.* without the simultaneous physical presence of the seller and buyer. This means any situation other than face to face contact. The consumer must be given a list of key relevant information before they are legally bound. This includes the name of the supplier, the price and how it should be paid for, the description of goods sold, the means of delivery and also the customer's right to cancel. The supplier must confirm these details in a written or durable form, such as letter or fax. The information must be made available and accessible by the consumer. The written details after the sale has been made must include the rules as to how the contract may be cancelled, the address of the supplier for complaints and details of after sales services and any guarantees. Under regulation 7, the relevant information must be provided in a "clear and comprehensible matter" with regard in particular to the principles of "good faith" in commercial transactions and the protection of those unable to give their consent, *e.g.* minors. The key remedy is the consumer's right to cancel any contract. In the case of sale of goods, the customer is given seven working days from the day after delivery of the goods.[81] For services, the seven working day period starts the day after the contract was formed. If the supplier complies with the information requirements set out, the cooling off period ends with the expiry of seven working days starting with the day after the consumer receives the goods.[82] If the supplier has not given all the information required by the regulations, the cancellation period is extended to three months. The regulations do not apply to non-consumer contracts, commercial and other sales of property or financial services[82a], auctions, payphones or automatic vending machines. The rights of

4.18

---

[76]   85/577/EEC. on the effect of an un-implemented Directive on the rights of an individual consumer. See *Paola Faccini Dori v. Recreb Srl. (Case C-91/91)* [1994], in which this Directive was applied to a contract made at High Central Railway Station for an English language course.

[77]   Reg. 3.

[78]   Reg. 4.

[79]   SI 2000/2334, which cane into force on October, 31 2000. The regulations are based upon directive 97/71/EC.

[80]   See Brownsword and Howells, "When surfers start to shop: Internet Commerce and Contract Law" (1999) 19 Legal Studies p. 287–315; Arden, "Electronic Commerce" (1999) New Law Journal 1685.

[81]   Reg. 11.

[82]   Reg. 11(2).

[82a]   A proposed directive on distance selling of financial services was still under discussion in the autumn of 2001.

cancellation are also excluded from contracts which are subject to fluctuations on the market, goods which perish quickly, "time sensitive" goods *i.e.* which get rapidly out of date and various other categories including the regular delivery of food and drink to homes, *i.e.* local milk roundsmen.

4.19   The Distance Selling Regulations impose a stringent set of information requirements on sellers and suppliers. If they are not complied with the consumer has a period to exercise his or her right to cancel the transaction. The result of doing so means that the consumer must be reimbursed his or her costs within 30 days. Under regulation 10, cancellation has the effect of treating the agreement as if never made, *i.e.* void. The European influence is clear and the remedy different from the normal common law rule that the contract might be rescinded at the option of the party not in breach.[83] The impact of these regulations on traders is backed up by the use, since June 2001, of Stop Now Orders[84] which allow the Office of Fair Trading, other qualifying bodies and trading standards officers to seek court orders in the county courts and High Court against those who infringe a range of regulations which affect the collective interest of consumers.[85] Qualifying bodies may also seek an undertaking from businesses against continued use of terms and processes of information which break the regulations. As such, the enforcement is primarily of a public regulatory type rather than merely a private law remedy in contract law. The expanding number of European directives also lead to a widening of the divide between consumer contracts to which they apply and commercial contracts which are largely excluded.[86] The requirements of information in durable form or writing also put into reverse a process of reducing formalities in contract law to a minimum.[87]

The key issue, however, in relation to distance selling is not answered by these regulations. In this chapter we have been discussing formation issues around the issue of offer and acceptance. The Distance Selling Regulations give a right of cooling off to the consumer once a contract is formed. It is assumed that advertising by some but not all means of distance communication must therefore be an offer rather than an invitation to treat. This would of course be at odds with existing common law principles. If case law under the regulations confirms this to be true then a third category of communication rules for offer and acceptance, depending upon the means used, will have come into effect.

(4) The EU directive on electronic commerce[87a]

4.20   The European Union adopted the e-commerce directive in June 2000. This seeks to regulate business transactions on the Internet, and to reduce legal impediments to doing so such as writing and signature. There is a requirement on Member States to ensure that laws applicable to the contractual process neither create obstacles for the use of electronic contracts nor result in such contracts being deprived of legal effectiveness and

---

[83]   See Chap. 23.
[84]   Stop Now Orders (EC Directive) Regulations 2001 (5.1.2001/1422).
[85]   Contracts concluded away from Business Premises Regulations 1987, Consumer Credit Act 1974, Package Travel, Package Holidays and Package Tours Regulations 1992, Time Share Act 1992, and the Unfair Terms in Consumer Contracts Regulations 1999, among others.
[86]   See Chap. 15.
[87]   See Chap. 11.
[87a]   Directive 2000/311 EC on certain legal aspects of information society services, in particular electronic commerce, in the internal market.

validity on account of their having been made by electronic means.[88] Under article 10 prior to an order being placed, information must be given by the service provider to the recipient of the service "clearly, comprehensibly and unambiguously". This must include: (a) the different technical steps to follow to conclude the contract; (b) whether the contract will be filed by the service provider and whether it will be accessible; (c) the technical means for identifying input errors; and (d) the languages offered by the conclusion of the contract. Contract terms and general conditions provided to the recipient must be made available in a way that allows him or her to store and reproduce them. These provisions do not apply to contracts made by interchange of e-mails or "equivalent individual communications". It is interesting to note that contracts made by modern forms of information technology may be developing in a different direction to the rest of contract law by adding to the list of formal requirements for making such contracts. The common law over the years had gradually reduced formal written requirements to a minimum. Consumer protection appears to necessitate a different approach, in the twenty first Century.

When Communication of Acceptance is not Necessary

Unilateral contracts and waiver

Unilateral contracts represent the most important category of offers in which communication of acceptance is not required. The offeror does not have to be notified that the person has embarked upon the requested conduct and the offer can be revoked in theory by the offeror at any time.[89] The right to communication of acceptance is deemed to be waived. In *Carlill v. Carbolic Smoke Ball Co. Ltd*[90] acceptance was completed by performance in taking the purported cure without the need to communicate acceptance to the Smoke Ball Company. The relationship between a bank and retailer when you use a credit card is usually regarded as a unilateral contract. In *First Sport Ltd v. Barclays Bank plc*[91] Evans L.J. stated that: "The card conveys to the retailer, or to any other person to whom it is presented, an offer made by the bank which, if accepted, establishes contractual relations between them. This strictly is a unilateral contract and it is unnecessary for the retailer's acceptance to be communicated to the bank.[92] The offeror may waive also his or her right to communication of the acceptance in a bilateral contract. This may be express or implied. Implied waiver of communication will not be lightly inferred. **4.21**

Acceptance by silence

The offeror cannot impose, or assume, acceptance by silence by the offeree. The leading case is *Felthouse v. Bindley*[93] in which the plaintiff and his nephew who lived in **4.22**

---

[88] Art. 9.
[89] However, see discussion in Chap. 3.
[90] [1893] 2 Q.B. 163.
[91] [1993] 1 W.L.R. 1229 (at pp. 1234–5).
[92] Citing *United Dominions Trust (Commercial) Ltd v. Eagle Aircraft Services* [1968] 1 W.L.R. 74.
[93] (1862) 11 C.B.(N.S.) 869; 142 E.R. 1037.

Tamworth were negotiating a sale of the nephew's horse. In a letter he wrote "If I hear no more about him I consider the horse is mine". The nephew did not reply, although he did in fact subjectively believe he was accepting the offer. The Court held there was no contract between the Felthouses. Acceptance was not to be construed from silence alone. There may however be acceptance by silence if: (i) as we have discussed, the offeror waives the right to have communication; (ii) communication is merely for the benefit of the offeror; (iii) the offeree solicited the offer in the first place; or (iv) in exceptional circumstances, *e.g.* the abandonment of arbitration.[94] In exceptional circumstances inaction on the part of the offeree may allow or should lead the offeror to infer that the offer has been accepted. In *Rust v. Abbey Life Assurance Co. Ltd*[95], the plaintiff Christine Rust sold her hotel for £75,000 and paid the money into her account at the National Westminster Bank. She then decided to put her money into Abbey Life Property Bonds, and completed an application form which included questions more appropriate to life insurance including the name and address of her GP. A cheque for £91,000 was paid over to the insurers. The Court of Appeal rejected the plaintiff's claim for the return of her money. She had claimed there was no contract because the offer could not be accepted by silence. The Court held there was acceptance on either of two grounds. First, that her application form was an offer to invest the money followed by the act of the insurers in allocating units in their property bond fund. Brandon L.J. saw some difficulty about holding that the allocation of itself constituted acceptance: "I would prefer to say that the issue of the policy constitutes acceptance".[96] This constituted an acceptance of the plaintiff's offer. The selling off of the agreement was no more than a record of the agreement and the terms of it. There was a second ground as an alternative, namely that "the plaintiff having had the policy in her possession since October 1973 had raised no objection to it." Brandon L.J. stated[97] that: "Although silence or inactivity was not evidence of acceptance, having regard to the circumstances or facts of the case between the parties there was an inevitable inference from the conduct of the plaintiff in doing and saying nothing for seven months that she accepted the policies as a contract between herself and [her insurers] the first defendants".

4.23   Even in commercial matters silence can amount to acceptance. In *Minories Finance Ltd v. Afribank Nigeria Ltd*[98], a contract was made "by inaction or silence". On the question of whether acceptance must always be communicated, Longmore J. stated that the ordinary rule about silence did not apply "because both sides agree that by the custom and practice of banking a contract can and does come into existence by doing nothing, in other words without the necessity for the acceptance to be communicated".[99] The Judge also gave another example, that of a wine merchant who offers a case of claret which the recipient "accepts" by drinking it. In *Weatherby v. Banham*[1] the publishers of a book called the "Racing Calendar" continued to send copies to a person after he had died. The defendant who had moved into the deceased's house did not return them to the publishers. It was held that a contract was made simply by

---

[94] Discussed earlier in Chap. 2.
[95] [1979] 2 Lloyd's Rep. 334.
[96] At p. 340.
[97] At p. 340.
[98] [1995] 1 Lloyd's Rep. 134.
[99] At p. 140.
[1] (1832) C and P 228, 172 E.R. 950.

keeping the books in question. These were contracts by inaction rather than conduct and no words of acceptance were deemed necessary. Silence can also be treated as acceptance of a repudiatory breach.[2]

Silence may also be regarded as merely equivocal. In *Re Selectmove*[3] it was argued by Selectmove that it's offer to pay off its debts in instalments had been accepted by the Inland Revenue's silence. The Court of Appeal accepted that *Felthouse v. Bindley* was correct when the offeror tries to impose acceptance by silence on the offeree. However, if the offeree indicates that there is to be agreement, if he [the offeree] has not said otherwise within a specified time, the situation was less clear cut. Peter Gibson L.J. stated that: "I can see no reason in principle why that should not be an exceptional circumstance such that the offer can be accepted by silence".[4] He added however that it was not necessary to have a concluded view on the point. Gibson L.J. approved a statement[5] of Evans J. in an earlier case that: "The significance of silence, as a matter of law, may also be different when there is an express undertaking or an implied obligation to speak, in the special circumstances of a particular case".   **4.24**

"Inertia selling"

The Unsolicited Goods and Services Act 1971 was enacted to deal with the situation which was common before the passing of the Act, namely that of sending goods to unsuspecting members of the public, who were informed that if they wished to keep the goods then they would have to pay for them, or they could return the goods at their own expense. In other words, silence was deemed to be consent to the sale and acceptance of the goods. The practice was deemed unsatisfactory and indeed open to abuse. The Act reversed this principle in favour of the recipient. The onus was on the sender to show that a sale was made and the court of recovery on the supplier. The 1971 Act is further amended by the Consumer Protection (Distance Selling) Regulations 2000.[6] The recipient of goods to which the regulations apply, if he or she has no reasonable cause to believe that they were being sent with a view to their being acquired for the purposes of a business and he or she has neither agreed to acquire or return them, may treat the goods as an unconditional gift.[7]   **4.25**

THE REVOCATION OF A PREVIOUSLY POSTED ACCEPTANCE BY THE OFFEREE

The postal rule and the rule on revocation collide if it is the offeree rather than the offeror who changes their mind and rejects the offer after posting a letter indicating their acceptance of the offer before the letter does. Although this must be quite a   **4.26**

---

[2] See *Vitol SA v. Norelf Ltd (The Santa Clara)* [1996] AC 800, see Chap. 23.
[3] [1995] 1 W.L.R. 474.
[4] At p. 478.
[5] *Gebr. van weelde Scheepvaart Kantor Bv. v. Compania Naviera Sea Orient* [1985] 2 Lloyd's Rep. 496 at p. 509.
[6] Regs 22 to 24.
[7] Reg. 24(1), (2). There may now be a potential challenge to this under the Human Rights Act 1998.

common situation in everyday life, there is no English authority on the point. So let us say Janice has received an offer for a training contract from a local firm of solicitors by letter and posts a letter of acceptance off to them, then changes her mind. She immediately sends another letter rejecting the offer which arrives before her first letter arrives. Janice also telephones the firm and says there is a letter of acceptance in the post but she wants the firm to ignore it, that she has now decided to reject their offer. In principle there is a contract because this was made as soon as the letter of acceptance was posted. A subsequent communication of revocation must be too late after this event. The contract has been concluded and both sides must be bound. If the offeree was allowed to change her mind, only the offeror would be bound by the posting of the acceptance not the offeree. This view applies the rules in a logical way but seems impractical and on occasion will lead to absurd results, particularly if, as we have suggested, the postal rule is based on practical convenience. Nevertheless in most jurisdictions the posting of the acceptance precludes revocation.[8] In the United States the authorities tend to support the view that once posted the acceptance is complete and cannot be taken back by other means.[9] [10]

4.27   The view that an acceptance can be revoked after an earlier posted acceptance has been sent is often supported by citing the Scots law case of *Countess of Dunmore v. Alexander*.[11] The Countess of Dunmore was looking for a servant and heard that the pursuer Betty Alexander was leaving the service of Lady Agnew. After an initial enquiry the Countess wrote on November 5 to Lady Agnew asking her to engage Betty Alexander at a salary of £12 for one year. This was to be sent on to the plaintiff Miss Alexander. On the following day, November 6, 1826, she sent another letter saying that she no longer needed Miss Alexander's services after all. Both letters arrived at Lochnaw where the plaintiff lived and were delivered at the same moment to her. The Court of Session held that there was no contract. The judgment is sometimes cited for the proposition that a postal acceptance can be revoked by a subsequent communication which arrives earlier (or simultaneously).[12] [13] The better view seems to be that the original inquiry by the Countess was merely an invitation to treat and Lady Agnew's response an offer of employment on behalf of Betty Alexander. The letter of November 5 was the offer which was then successfully revoked by the letter of November 6 when the two arrived together. The case therefore really stands as an example of revocation of offers. On either view the Court agreed there was no completed contract and the servant was not entitled to her wages. On a practical and common sense level there appears no point in forcing a person to go ahead with a contract which she already immediately regrets. Reliance theory would argue that there was little justification for holding parties to a totally unexecuted contract, such as here, so the parties should not be regarded as bound. Modern "cooling off" periods for consumers adopt this approach giving the customer time to reconsider, for instance on the terms a consumer credit agreement or timeshare

---

[8] See the New Zealand case of *Wenkheim v. Arendt* (NZ) 1 JR 73 (1973).

[9] See *Morrison v. Thoelke* (1963) 155 So. 2d 889.

[10] See Farnsworth, *Contracts* (2nd ed., Little brown and Co, Boston, 1990), p. 182. Like most points of American law, cases can be found on both sides in the sheer weight of authorities from 50 jurisdictions.

[11] 1830 9 S.C. 190.

[12] Based on a Scots law text *Gloag on Contracts* who regarded the letter from Lady Agnew as an offer. The Countess's first letter (of November 5) was therefore an acceptance. However, this view is generally rejected.

[13] See McBride, *Contract* (1987, W Green and Sons, Edinburgh), p. 56, on the present position in Scots law.

agreement.[14] On the other hand, in the interests of certainty it may be that the postal acceptance should be final after all. Perhaps the problem the postal rule itself. No universal answer to this question seems entirely satisfactory.

Flowchart B: Acceptance

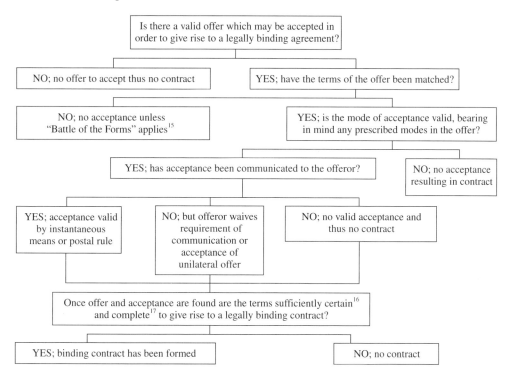

[14] The Consumer Protection (Distance Selling) Regulations 2000 allow consumers to have a change of heart and cancel although the contract in such cases is already formed. The effect of cancellation within the prescribed time limits is to treat the agreement as if no contract was ever formed, subject to various rules, see earlier pp. 55–56
[15] See Chap. 5.
[16] See Chap. 5.
[17] See Chap. 5.

Chapter 5

PROBLEMATIC AGREEMENTS

DIFFICULT CASES

It may be difficult to extract a precise offer or acceptance from lengthy correspondence, **5.1** complex negotiations or a multitude of communications. Nevertheless, the courts will try to look for a clear offer and acceptance, even in complicated commercial dealings. For instance in *Thorensen Car Ferries Ltd v. Weymouth Portland BC*[1] there was a dispute over providing services at a terminal for "a roll-on/roll-off" ferry between Weymouth and France. Donaldson J. found that there was a contract from the correspondence by offer and acceptance. The Court could see no reason why Thoresen should not have acted as they did and treated the harbour master's letter as "the acceptance of a legally binding commitment to make the slot available to them in the summer of 1975".[2] Equally, many everyday situations can be difficult to analyse as offer and acceptance. Lord Denning had to deal with this in the mundane setting of a car park in *Thornton v. Shoe Lane Parking.*[3] The analysis of offer and acceptance at the barrier divided the Court of Appeal.[4] Situations like car parks, boarding a bus or purchasing a ticket or a soft drink from an automatic vending machine are everyday situations where offer and acceptance remains problematic. The world of agreement cannot be fitted with ease into a single theory. For example, take the case of cross-offers. Alison writes to Lydia offering to sell her car at a stated price and Lydia writes to Alison offering to buy the vehicle at exactly the same price. The two letters cross in the post and are on identical terms. In the Court of Exchequer Chamber in *Tinn v. Hoffman & Co.*[5] it was stated *obiter* that cross offers do not make a contract. The plaintiff, Joseph Tinn, was an iron manufacturer at Ashton in Bristol, who exchanged identical offers with the defendant, an iron merchant in Middlesborough. The majority were of the "strong opinion" that such cross-offers did not make a binding contract and that the offer in one of the letters could not amount to an acceptance of the offer contained in the other. Honeyman J. dissented believing that the parties were *ad idem* at one and the same moment. Another problematic area is the rules of clubs or associations and whether these are contractually binding among the members. Depending on the circumstances, rules incorporated into contracts can be

---

[1] [1977] 2 Lloyd's Rep. 614.
[2] At p. 619.
[3] [1971] 2 Q.B. 163.
[4] See Chap. 2.
[5] (1873) 29 L.T. 271.

legally binding.[6] In company law the memorandum and articles of association of the company are a contract between that person and the company and also constitute a contract between the person and another shareholder of the company.[7]

5.2   In a judgment concerning the "long hours" culture of British employment relations and for health and safety regulations in general, it was held in *Barber v. RJB Mining (UK) Ltd*[8] that the Working Time Regulations 1998, which impose a maximum working week of 48 hours (unless there had been derogation from their implementation), imposed a contractual obligation on an employer to ensure that an employee worked no more than the statutory limit. If an employee were forced to work longer than, this he could bring action in the courts for breach of contract, rather than resolve the matter at an employment tribunal.

On the other hand, in *Clansmen Sporting Club v. Robinson*,[9] it was held that as a matter of construction something could be required to be done in conformity with a rule, without the rule itself becoming a term. In this case, the defendant was a boxer who argued World Boxing Organisation rules had been incorporated into his contract with the promoters. The High Court held they were not part of the contract, either as an implied term or otherwise. The regulations were apparently frequently ignored even by the WBO itself. The Court also said that was not the task of the Court to enforce regulations by means of incorporating them into a contract. In *Anderton v. Rowland*,[10] it was held that a member of the Showmen's Guild was not entitled to compensation from another member for breach of the Guild's rules as these did not generally create a contractual remedy between members.[11] However, in *Clark v. University of Lincolnshire and Humberside*,[12] it was held that a new University was a statutory corporation with legal personality and capacity to make contracts within it's powers.[13] The arrangement between the institution and a fee paying student was contractual. The claimant alleged that disciplinary actions brought against her had been in breach of University rules. The fact that an action for judicial review would be the normal remedy did not rule out a contractual claim, according to the Court of Appeal. The case also illustrates the developing relationship between contract and public law.

5.3   A contract concluded through a single intermediary also poses difficulty for the analysis of offer and acceptance. In *Pagnan SpA v. Feed Products*[14] Lloyd L.J. said that he did not consider it helpful to consider offer and counter-offer when considering a contract negotiated through a single intermediary: "the only question in such a case is whether there comes a point in time when the intermediary has obtained the agreement of both parties." A fictitious third party has a role to play in contract law. This idea forms the basis of implying terms in contract,[15] indeed an entire contract may be implied by the

---

[6]   See *Clarke v. Earl of Dunraven, The Satanita* [1897] AC 59.
[7]   See *Rayfield v. Hands* [1960] Ch.1. However this was largely based on a statutory provision, the Companies Act 1985 s. 14.
[8]   [1999] 2 C.M.L.R. 823.
[9]   *The Times*, May 22, 1995.
[10]   *The Times*, November 5, 1999.
[11]   *The Satanita* may now be seen as an exceptional case.
[12]   [2000] 1 W.L.R. 1988.
[13]   On capacity see Chap. 12.
[14]   [1987] 2 Lloyd's Rep. 601.
[15]   See Chap. 12.

courts.[16] This in itself is difficult to reconcile with offer and acceptance. In *Upton-on-Severn RDC v. Powell*,[17] the defendant was a farmer in Worcestershire whose Dutch barn went on fire in November 1939. He telephoned the emergency services and asked them to send "the fire brigade". The operator contacted the local fire service in Upton-upon-Severn. The defendant's farm was actually in Strensham in the Pershore fire district, not Upton. The Upton fire fighters nevertheless extinguished the blaze. The plaintiff was entitled to a free service from his own district but not from that of another. Upton therefore claimed boundary charges by way of contract from the defendant. It was held that there was an implied contract to pay for the service rendered. Lord Greene MR held that the defendant was to be treated as having requested the Upton fire brigade to be sent to his farm and the fact that the plaintiffs believed the fire to be in their own area did not prevent a contractual relationship, for which he had to pay, being formed with the defendant. The case may be regarded as having been decided on grounds of public policy as much as applying to doctrines of contract law. In *Lockett v. A. and M. Charles Ltd*[18], the plaintiffs, a husband and wife, stopped for lunch at the defendant's hotel and restaurant at Bray. Mrs Lockett swallowed a few mouthfuls of whitebait and was taken ill.[19] It was held that there were contracts with both of them. There was no evidence that either the husband or the wife had ordered the meal. The court concluded that, even if the husband ordered, there was a separate implied contract with Mrs Lockett. She was entitled to recover damages for breach of the implied condition that the food supplied was fit for eating. The contract was also seen as a sale of goods rather than services, *i.e.* the preparation of the meal by the chef.[20]

TAKING A MORE RELAXED VIEW OF OFFER AND ACCEPTANCE

The discussion of cases in the previous section leads some to argue that offer and acceptance in it's traditional form may not be necessary in every case.[21] Lord Denning, in *Gibson v. Manchester City Council*[22] put forward a more flexible attitude to finding agreement. In the Court of Appeal he rejected too formal a test, stating[23]:   **5.4**

> "To my mind it is a mistake to think that all contracts can be analysed into the form of offer and acceptance. I know in some textbooks it has been the custom to do so; but, as I understand the law, there is no need to look for a strict offer and acceptance. You should look at the correspondence as a whole and at the conduct of the parties and see therefrom whether the parties have come to an agreement on everything that was material."

---

[16] This was formerly the basis of recovery in restitution or quasi-contract, see Chap. 26.
[17] [1942] 1 All E.R. 220.
[18] [1938] 4 All E.R. 170.
[19] On implied terms see Chap. 17.
[20] See also Chap. 12.
[21] See Adams and Brownsword, *Key Issues in Contract* (1995, Butterworths, London).
[22] [1978] 2 All E.R. 583.
[23] At p. 586.

The House of Lords disagreed and held that the parties had not concluded a binding contract because the Council had never made an offer capable of acceptance. Lord Diplock stated[24] that:

> "there may be certain types of contract, though I think they are exceptional, which do not fit easily into the normal analysis of a contract as being constituted by offer and acceptance; but a contract alleged to have been made by an exchange of correspondence between the parties in which the successive communications other than the first are in reply to one another is not one of these".

However, the realistic approach of Lord Denning was endorsed by Lord Wilberforce in *New Zealand Shipping Co. v. Satterthwaite*[25] who took a practical view. The world did not always conform to textbook categories. He listed some of the problem areas many of which we have already encountered:

> "It is only the precise analysis of this complex of relations into the classical offer and acceptance, with identifiable consideration, that seems to present difficulty, but this same difficulty exists in many situations of daily life, *e.g.* sales at auction; supermarket purchases; boarding an omnibus; purchasing a train ticket; tenders for the supply of goods; offers of rewards; acceptance by post; warranties of authority by agents; manufacturers' guarantees; gratuitous bailments; bankers' commercial credits. These are all examples which show that English law, having committed itself to a rather technical and schematic doctrine of contract, in application takes a practical approach, often at the cost of forcing the facts to fit uneasily into the marked slots of offer, acceptance and consideration."[26]

Contract is more likely if parties have started performance

5.5   It is sometimes suggested that the courts are more likely to find agreement if there has been reliance by the parties, *e.g.* the agreement is acted upon or has been performed to some extent. In *G. Percy Trentham Ltd v. Archital Luxfer Ltd*[27] the defendants were building and civil engineering contractors employed as main contractors on the construction of industrial units at Farnborough. The plaintiffs were subcontractors installing aluminium walling, doors, screens and windows. Much of the work had been carried out before any formal contractual relationship had been established (a not uncommon phenomenon in the building trade.) The issue was whether a contract had been formed by offer and acceptance. The Court of Appeal held that it had, a contract coming into force during performance, and this impliedly governed pre-contractual performance. The parties always intended to enter into binding contractual relations. Steyn L.J. emphasised that "one must not lose sight of the commercial character of the transaction".[28] He said that there were four main points to the approach to formation in

---

[24] At p. 974.
[25] [1975] A.C. 154.
[26] At p. 167.
[27] [1993] 1 Lloyd's Rep. 25.
[28] At p. 29.

such cases. First, the court had to take an "objective" view. The governing criterion was "the reasonable expectations of honest men" and the yardstick was the "reasonable expectations of sensible businessmen".[29] This did not include the "subjective expectations and unexpressed mental reservations of the parties". Secondly, Lord Steyn noted in the "vast majority" of cases "the coincidence of offer and acceptance was the mechanism of contract formation". It is so in a contract alleged to have been made by an exchange of correspondence, but "it is not necessarily so in the case of a contract alleged to have come into existence as a result of performance".[30] Thirdly, was the impact of the fact that a contract was "executed rather than executory",[31] *i.e.* if performance has already started: "The fact that a contract is performed on both sides will often make it unrealistic to argue that there was no intention to create legal relations". Finally, "if a contract only comes into existence during and as a result of performance of the transaction it will frequently be possible to hold that the contract impliedly and retrospectively covers pre-contractual performance".[32] Steyn L.J. concluded that the judge had analysed the matter in terms of offer and acceptance. He agreed with his conclusion, but said:

> "I am in any event satisfied that in this fully executed transaction a contract came into existence during performance even if it cannot be precisely analysed in terms of offer and acceptance. And it does not matter that a contract came into existence after part of the work had been carried out and paid for. The conclusion must be that when the contract came into existence it impliedly governed pre-contractual performance".[33]

Reliance, in other words, can be a factor in determining whether there really was agreement. Reliance alone is not yet a substitute for offer and acceptance. The limited scope for reliance is illustrated by *British Steel Corporation v. Cleveland Bridge & Engineering Co. Ltd*[34]. Although some work had been done, there was never a contract. Instead the plaintiff recovered a reasonable sum in remuneration for what they had done in a claim in restitution for *quantum meruit*.[35] Even after some performance, there was still no contract. A contract had not been created by the plaintiffs carrying out the work since the terms of the contract were still in negotiation. The parties had ultimately been unable to reach final agreement on the price or other essential terms as to performance.

The conclusion is that offer and acceptance matters. Offer and acceptance is a con- **5.6** venient and practical instrument for finding agreement, but agreement is the vital requirement. Offer and acceptance will be manipulated if agreement is obviously present, or there is some reliance by the parties so that a contract can more easily be inferred. The courts still look for offer and acceptance as the talisman of agreement. In *Hispanica de Petroleos SA v. Vencedora Oceanica Navegacion SA "The Kapetan*

---

[29] At p. 27.
[30] At p. 27.
[31] See Chap. 8.
[32] See *Trollope & Colls Ltd v. Atomic Power Construction Ltd* [1963] 1 W.L.R. 333; *Ball* (1983) 99 L.Q.R. 572.
[33] At p. 29–30.
[34] [1984] 1 All E.R. 504.
[35] See Chap. 26.

Markos",[36] in which it had been argued that a collateral contract was to be implied, Mustill L.J. asked the pertinent question[37] "What was the mechanism for offer and acceptance?" Without it there was no contract. In *Blackpool and Fylde Aero Club v Blackpool Borough Council*[38] the Court of Appeal took a similar view. The vital factor was for the court to be able to conclude with confidence that "the parties intended to create contractual relations and that the agreement was to the effect contended for. It must also, in most cases, be able to answer the question posed by Mustill L.J. [above]".[39] Like other technical areas for the formation of contracts, disputes over offer and acceptance or consideration of contracts may arise after the relationship has broken down. In other words, when one of the parties no longer wishes to be bound by the agreement. The argument that no contract ever came into existence, because of lack of offer and acceptance, would not have been raised if the parties had remained on good terms.

"THE BATTLE OF THE FORMS"

5.7   As we have discussed, the analysis of offer and acceptance can be artificial and lead to practical difficulty. The widespread use of standard form contracts[40] often results in an impasse known as the "battle of the forms". This occurs when both parties have their own standard terms and purport to use these as the basis for their contract. In other words, if Adams Ltd offers on their terms and Benjamins Ltd reply on the basis of agreeing to their own, on traditional principles, if Benjamin's reply is construed as a counter offer then no contract will be formed. The parties agreement (if any) is only complete when one accepts the other's final counter offer. There may in fact be several exchanges within this process before agreement is reached, or awkwardly, each may believe they are dealing on their own terms. This is obviously a practical issue where legal theory has difficulty coming to terms (literally) with the real world. When this occurs (as it frequently does) there are the various possibilities for dealing with two sets of standard terms. The obvious answer is that there never was a contract formed at all because, applying the traditional rules of offer and acceptance, there was no agreement.[41] In order to avoid this conclusion a number of approaches have developed to deal with the problem.

"The first blow" approach

The terms of the contract are those of the original offer. This will apply if the offeree's terms are different only in details which may be ignored. It does not apply if there are substantial changes to the offer. In *Butler Machine Tool Company Ltd v. Ex-Cell-O Corporation (England) Ltd*[42] Lord Denning commented:

---

[36] [1987] 2 Lloyd's Rep. 321.
[37] At p. 331.
[38] [1990] 1 W.L.R. 1195.
[39] At p. 1205.
[40] Discussed later in Chap. 17.
[41] See *Johnson Matthey Bankers v. Stock Trading Corporation of India* [1984] 1 Lloyd's Rep. 427 (at p. 433).
[42] [1979] 1 All E.R. 965.

"In some cases, however, the battle is won by the man who gets the blow in first. If he offers to sell at a named price on the terms and conditions stated on the back and the buyer orders the goods purporting to accept the offer on an order form with his own different terms and conditions on the back, then, if the difference is so material that it would affect the price, the buyer ought not to be allowed to take advantage of the difference unless he draws it specifically to the attention of the seller."

Lord Denning also favoured a wider view of the process, to which we return in due course.[43]

The "last shot" doctrine

The contract is concluded on the terms of the party whose final counter offer was   **5.8** accepted. The party who fired the last shot wins the argument, and the agreement will be on that party's standard terms. In *British Road Services Ltd v. Arthur V. Crutchley and Co. (Factory Guards Ltd)*,[44] there was a theft of a lorry load of whisky in the Liverpool dock area in the summer of 1963. The plaintiffs delivered a consignment of whisky to the defendants for storage. Their driver gave the defendants a delivery note containing the words "all goods are carried on the [plaintiffs'] conditions of carriage, copies of which can be obtained upon application to plaintiffs' offices. The note was stamped by the defendants: "Received under AVC *i.e.* [the defendants'] conditions." The Court of Appeal held that this amounted to a counter-offer which the plaintiffs had accepted by handing over the goods. The contract in other words was on the defendants' and not the plaintiffs' conditions. The "last shot" doctrine means that if a contract finally results, it is on the terms of the final document which has been accepted and results in a contract.[45] The last shot is the most widely used test but it can be criticised. In it's favour it gives relatively greater certainty, is based upon a traditional common law approach and is relatively straight forward to apply. However against this there are a number of disadvantages. Firstly it produces an "all or nothing" answer to whether there is a contract and on whose terms, secondly it is rigid in it's approach and encourages parties to be adversarial and seek to contract entirely on their own terms, on a "take it or leave it" basis. The contract is either on one set of terms or else there is no contract at all. This is a stark choice.

The flexible approach

In *Butler Machine Tool Co Ltd v. Ex-Cell-O Corporation (England) Ltd*[46] the Court of Appeal concluded in an argument over the battle of the forms that the contract was on the buyer's terms, but for different reasons. Lawton and Bridge L.J. held that the buyer's order was a counter offer which the sellers had accepted by completing and returning an acknowledgment. This applied a traditional common law analysis. Lord Denning took an alternative approach:

[43] At p. 968.
[44] [1968] 1 All E.R. 811.
[45] See also *Zambia Steel and Building Supplies Ltd v. James Clark and Eaton Ltd* [1986] 2 Lloyd's Rep. 225.
[46] [1979] 1 All E.R. 965.

"There are yet other cases where the battle depends on the shots fired on both sides. There is a concluded contract but the forms vary. The terms and conditions of both parties are to be construed together. If they can be reconciled so as to give a harmonious result, all well and good. If differences are irreconcilable, so that they are mutually contradictory, then the conflicting terms may have to be scrapped and replaced by a reasonable implication."[47]

This involves an interventionist role by the court, similar to that adopted in America, which we discuss shortly.

The "knock out" approach

This is becoming popular in other jurisdictions.[48] The knock out is a variation of the flexible approach. If the differences in the terms are so great then the court may adopt its own approach and construe agreement from the terms the parties have in common.[49] The knock out principle has been adopted in the Unidroit principles[50] and the "Lando" Commission for European Contract Law.[51]

"The loudest shout" wins the argument

A fourth possibility to be found in France, but not yet adopted in England, is referred to as the "loudest shout" doctrine. If the provisions are conflicting but not completely contradictory, the one which is most clearly expressed governs.[52]

5.9   Agreement on essential points is sometimes sufficient

In *Pagnan SpA v. Feed Products Ltd*[53] a contract was formed only on the basis of essential terms, while other terms remained to be negotiated. Lloyd L.J. stated that failure to agree on the outstanding matters would not necessarily invalidate the existing contract. It would do so, however, if the contract was unworkable without them in which case it would be void for uncertainty. Bingham J. stated:

"just as it is open to parties by their words and conduct to make clear that they do not intend to be bound until certain terms are agreed, even if those terms (objectively viewed) are of relatively minor significance, the converse is also true. The parties may by their words and conduct make it clear that they do intend to be bound, even though there are other terms yet to be agreed, even terms which may often or usually be agreed before a binding contract is made."[54]

---

[47] At pp. 968–969.
[48] See Hondius and Mahé, "The Battle of Forms: Towards a Uniform Solution" (1998) 12 J.C.L. 268.
[49] At p. 968.
[50] Principle of European Contract Law Article 2.22.
[51] See Chap. 1.
[52] See Hondius and Mahé *(supra)* p. 270.
[53] [1987] 2 Lloyd's Rep. 601.
[54] At p. 611.

A different view was taken in *Metal Scrap Trade Corporation v. Kate Shipping Co Ltd "The Gladys" (No 2)*.[55] It was held that even if the terms still to be agreed were fairly trivial, there was no agreement until they had been clarified, if that appeared to be the parties' intention. In this case the Court held that there was no contract. Potter J. stated that by the time negotiations ended "either as a matter of construction of the documents, or on the basis of the oral evidence I have heard that the parties shared a common intention to make a binding contract prior to agreement of the final form.[56]

Contract "on the usual terms" by course of dealings?

Many contracts are on a repetitive basis between parties who know each other well. If so, contracts can be made on the basis of a course of dealings.[57] It will be a matter of proof which party's terms have formed the basis of their business dealings in the past.

A new approach?

The discussion of the battle of the forms illustrates that merely applying traditional rules to modern practices does not always work, and leaving matters to the courts can result in confusion with alternative views cancelling each other out.[58] There may be scope for a new approach either through the case law or by legislation to deal with the battle of the forms problem. In the United States, the Uniform Commercial Code[59] provides that a "definite and seasonable expression" of acceptance or a written confirmation within a reasonable time will be an acceptance even though it contains different or additional terms "unless acceptance is expressly made conditional on assent to the additional or different terms". Between "merchants" they will become part of the contract unless: (a) the offer expressly limits acceptance to the terms of the offer; (b) they materially alter it; or (c) notification of objection to them has already been given or is given within a reasonable time after notice of them is received. In *Matter of Doughboy Industries Inc*,[60] the Supreme Court of New York held that an arbitration clause was a material term and could not be incorporated under the code provision in a dispute over conflicting sets of conditions. Under the UCC, even if no contract is initially formed by applying the code rule, there may still be a contract as a result of "acceptance by conduct". In *Northrop Corp. v. Litronic Industries*,[61] Chief Judge Richard Posner stated that "The battle of the forms in this case takes the form of something very like a badminton game".[62] The code provision allows the courts to adopt more flexibility in the question of offer and acceptance and avoids the mirror image rule and traditional approaches still followed in England. The American and English positions on the battle of the forms were discussed

5.10

---

[55] [1994] 2 Lloyd's Rep. 402.
[56] At p. 410.
[57] See *Kendall Sons v. Lillico and Sons Ltd* [1969] 2 A.C. 31.
[58] See Hondius and Mahé, "The Battle of Forms: Towards a Uniform Solution" (1998) 12 J C L at 268–275 on European and also the UNIDROIT solution to the question.
[59] 2–207(1).
[60] (1962) 233 N.Y.S. 2d 488.
[61] 29 F.3rd 1173 (1994).
[62] At p. 1175.

in *OTM Ltd v. Hydranautics*.[63] Parker J. considered the relevant provisions of the Californian Commercial Code and English law, and concluded that English law applied to the dispute in question.

Certainty as a Formation Requirement

5.11   An agreement which lacks certainty is void. Certainty applies to both (a) the contract as a whole and (b) any important terms. In *Loftus v. Roberts*[64] the plaintiff was a well known actress, Miss Kitty Loftus, who sued Arthur Roberts, a theatre owner, over the terms of a contract to perform in a play at two theatres in the West End of London. She had received a letter which said "I hereby agree to engage you for the principal lady's part "*Victoria Chaffers*" in my play "*HMS Irresponsible*" for a suburban tour at the salary which we have agreed to. In the event of the piece coming to town under my West End management I engage you to play the part . . . "at a West End salary" to be mutually arranged between us". The defendant argued that the phrase "West-end salary" was too uncertain as salaries varied enormously. The court held that there was no contract as there were many salaries for actresses in the West End of London, and the phrase "to be agreed between us" suggested the parties had not yet reached a final agreement and were still in a state of negotiation. The case therefore illustrates both (a) uncertainty and (b) incompleteness. Generally speaking the courts are reluctant to find (a), but strict about the need for (b).

The law reports are full of judicial statements on the need for certainty. They also reveal a reluctance to find uncertainty which will lead to the agreement being void (compare this with the attitude to incompleteness).[65] In *Greater London Council v. Connolly*,[66] Lord Denning MR stated[67]: "The courts are always loath to hold a condition bad for uncertainty. They will give it a reasonable interpretation wherever possible". Most judges require more than a reasonableness approach. The starting point is usually the ordinary rules of construction of contracts. In *G. Scammell and Nephew v. H. C. and J. G. Ouston*[68] the House of Lords held that a clause as to hire purchase terms was too vague. There was no contract. The House of Lords was put off not only by the vagueness or unintelligibility of the words but by the "startling diversity of explanations" of what the bargain was between the parties. Lord Wright stated that uncertainty should only be found when:

> "the language used was so obscure and so incapable of any definite or precise meaning that the court is unable to attribute to the parties any particular contractual intention . . . But the test of intention is to be found in the words used. If these words, considered however broadly and untechnically and with due regard to all just implications, fail to evince any definite meaning on which the court can safely act, the court has no choice but to say that there is no contract. Such a position is not often found. . . ."[69]

[63] [1981] 2 Lloyd's Rep. 211.
[64] (1902) 18 T.L.R. 532.
[65] See later p. 74.
[66] [1970] 2 Q.B. 100.
[67] At p.108.
[68] [1941] A.C. 251.
[69] At p. 268.

Uncertainty is not always the result of inadvertence by the parties. In long term rela- **5.12**
tional contracts the parties often leave the contract open to ensure later flexibility. They
also frequently provide for this by means of arbitration clauses. There are a number of
factors relevant to the question of certainty. If performance of the contract has begun,
the courts are more likely to find agreement. This is a good example of reliance theory
at work. If the parties have acted on the agreement, the courts are more likely to try to
avoid uncertainty and find there was agreement. In *Hillas & Co. Ltd v. Arcos Ltd*[70] the
Court was prepared to consider that there was a contract if it had been performed even
partially and also if there was a course of dealings between the parties. The phrase in
question, "of fair specification", could also be interpreted with the aid of evidence. If
there are several different meanings or ambiguous or disputed terms in the agreement,
the courts are more likely to find it void for uncertainty. In *G. Scammell and Nephew v.
Ouston*[71] there was no contract. The House of Lords held that the phrase "on hire purchase terms" was too uncertain to be enforced. The Court could find no guidance to its
meaning and the relationship was essentially a "one off". No fewer than five different
meanings of the words were put forward. If uncertainty can be cured by an arbitration
mechanism in the contract then that should be used.[72] In *Kings Motors (Oxford) Ltd v.
Lax*[73] an option in a lease for a further term "at such a rental as may be agreed between
the parties" made the contract unenforceable. This was held to be too uncertain and the
agreement was void because there was no arbitration or other means available for resolving the matter. Meaningless words and phrases may, however, be ignored. In *Nicolene
Ltd v. Simmonds*[74], the acceptance contained the words "I assume that we are in agreement that the usual conditions of acceptance apply." There were no usual conditions of
acceptance between the parties so it was not certain what this meant. The Court of
Appeal held that the phrase was meaningless, but could be severed from the rest of the
contract. Denning L.J. stated[75]:

> "In my opinion, a distinction must be drawn between a clause which is meaningless
> and a clause which is yet to be agreed. A clause which is meaningless can often be
> ignored, while still leaving the contract good, whereas a clause which has yet to be
> agreed may mean that there is no contract at all, because the parties have not agreed
> on all the essential terms."

The price is for many people the most important term in any contract. If the price is not **5.13**
agreed, the contract may be too uncertain to be enforced. Statute tries to deal with this
problem. For instance, the Sale of Goods Act 1979 provides that the buyer must pay a
"reasonable price".[76] This is a question of fact depending on the circumstances of each

---

[70] (1932) 147 L.T. 503.
[71] [1941] A.C. 251.
[72] See *Sudbrook Trading Estate Ltd v. Eggleton* [1983] 1 A.C. 444.
[73] [1969] 3 All E.R. 665.
[74] [1953] 1 All E.R. 822.
[75] At p. 825.
[76] S. 8(2).

particular case.[77] The Supply of Goods and Services Act 1982 provides that where the price is not agreed, or left to determine by a manner agreed in the contract or by course of dealings between the parties, there is an implied term that the party contracting with the supplier will pay "a reasonable charge".[78] The remuneration for services rendered may also be dealt with in restitution law.[79] Generally speaking, lack of a price is fatal to a contract. In *May and Butcher Ltd v. R*[80] the House of Lords held that there was no contract because there was no agreement on price. On the other hand (in *Foley v. Classique Coaches Ltd*[81]), "the price was to be agreed by the parties in writing and from time to time". This was held to be sufficient to avoid uncertainty. It is quite common in commercial arrangements to have a "fluctuation" or "variations of price" clause. This allows the parties to vary the term.[82] House buyers with a mortgage are usually subject to their mortgage repayment rate changing from time to time. This is usually enforceable because one party is allowed to vary the price unilaterally.[83] Unilateral variation is normally unenforceable without fresh consideration.[84]

5.14   The bare essentials may be all that is required. The courts will usually try to find a contract even if the agreement only deals with the bare essentials. The issue boils down to whether or not the parties really intended to make a contract. In *Malcolm v. Chancellor, Masters and Scholars of the University of Oxford*[85] the Court of Appeal held that an oral agreement between publishers, Oxford University Press, and an author, Andrew Malcolm, to publish a book was an enforceable contract, even though matters such as royalties had not been agreed upon. The plaintiff had already relied on the agreement by starting to write his book on philosophy called *Making Names*. Equally, in *Rafsanjan Pistachio Producers Cooperative v. Kaufmanns Ltd*[86] Rix J. held in the commercial court that even if an important term had been omitted from the contract, a contract could be formed if the term still to be agreed was certain enough and the parties intended to create legal relations. Finally, gapfilling by custom, trade practice, course of dealings or implied terms may be used to supply what is missing. It may be possible to find terms by other means which we will discuss later.[87]

INCOMPLETENESS

5.15   Contract law requires the agreement to be final and complete. In commercial life there are many examples of parties trying to bind other persons into a relationship short of making a contractual obligation. The examples of incompleteness mostly stem from a different root to those which we have discussed under uncertainty. In the former case, the

---

[77] S. 8(3).
[78] S. 15.
[79] See Chap. 26.
[80] [1934] 2 K.B. 17.
[81] [1934] 2 K.B. 1.
[82] See also Chap. 8.
[83] See *Lombard Tricity Finance Ltd v. Paton* [1989] 1 All E.R. 918.
[84] See later in Chap. 8.
[85] 1994 E.M.L.R. 17.
[86] *The Independent*, January 12, 1998.
[87] See later Chaps 12 and 16.

purported agreements are deliberately drafted and use wording which is designed to have a legal effect, albeit one which is not fully contractual. Uncertainty is usually associated with inadvertence. The courts are less tolerant of incomplete agreements. The tendency is for such arrangements to fail. Traditionally agreements for the sale of land made "subject to contract" are not binding until formal contracts have been exchanged by the parties.[88] This leaves homebuyers vulnerable to "gazumping", in other words an increase of the price in the period between agreeing to a sale and exchanging completed contracts.[89] The practice of gazumping, allowed by English law, was described by Kilner Brown J. in *Cohen v. Nessdale Ltd*[90] as a "social and moral blot on the law". The "subject to contract" rule remains in spite of criticism of its effect.[91] There are many examples of modern commercial devices which attempt to bind parties together. Contracts often include phrases such as to "negotiate in good faith", "use best endeavours", or "reasonable" endeavours. Such agreements are vulnerable to allegations of lack of certainty or completeness, or fail because there is no consideration.

Agreements to agree

A contract to make an "agreement to agree", or simply to negotiate, lacks both certainty and completeness and is not enforceable. In *Courtney & Fairburn Ltd v. Tolaini Bros (Hotels) Ltd*[92] Lord Denning stated: "If the law does not recognise a contract to enter into a contract (when there is a fundamental term yet to be agreed) it seems to me that it cannot recognise a contract to negotiate. The reason is because it is too uncertain to have any binding force. It seems to me that a contract to negotiate, like a contract to enter into a contract, is not a contract known to the law."[93] The law did not recognise a contract to negotiate and where a fundamental matter was left to negotiate there was no contract. The deal to develop the Thatched Barn Hotel in Hertfordshire therefore fell through.

"Lock-in" and "lock-out" agreements

A "lock-in" agreement is an attempt to make one party negotiate exclusively with another person. Lock-in arrangements are generally unenforceable (see above). A "lock-out" agreement, on the other hand, is an undertaking not to negotiate with a third party, and it is possible for such agreements to be enforceable in special circumstances. In *Pitt v. PHH Asset Management Ltd*[94] there was an oral agreement between the parties that the vendors would not consider any offers from third parties in return for the other party exchanging contracts within two weeks of receiving a draft contract. The Court of

---

[88] See *Von Hatzfeldt-Wildenburg v. Alexander* [1912] 1 Ch. 284.
[89] The Government has made proposals to deal with this and the "subject to contract" rule, Green Paper, December 1998. Legislation to deal with this is likely in future.
[90] [1981] 3 All E.R. 118.
[91] See Kay, "Protecting the Consumer in the Home Buying Process" National Association of Estate Agents, 1998. The Homes Bill 2001 which would have required the preparation of a "seller's pack" failed to become law.
[92] [1975] 1 W.L.R. 297.
[93] At p. 301.
[94] [1993] 4 All E.R. 961.

Appeal held this was an agreement capable of being enforced as a binding "lock-out agreement". The agreement did not lack certainty because it had a time limit attached to it. There was also consideration for the agreement in promising to exchange contracts within two weeks. Lock-out agreements are popular in commercial relationships. The essence of a lock-out is that it is negative in nature, unlike an attempt to lock a party in. There has to be certainty provided by the time limit, and some consideration must be provided.

Agreement to "negotiate in good faith"[95]

5.16   An agreement to "negotiate in good faith" was held to be not a binding contract in *Walford v. Miles.*[96] The House of Lords held that the term "negotiate in good faith" was unenforceable as a contractual obligation because it lacked the necessary certainty. Lord Ackner stated that,[97] "the concept of a duty to carry on negotiations in good faith is inherently repugnant to the adversarial position of the parties when involved in negotiations . . . How is the court to police such an agreement? A duty to negotiate in good faith is as unworkable in practice as it is inherently inconsistent with the position of a negotiating party".[98] However, if there was consideration, an agreement not to negotiate with any other third party for a specified period could be binding.[99] It is necessary that there is a time limit on such an agreements. An agreement to negotiate in good faith in the event of disputes arising over a contract for software design was not enforceable in *Halifax Financial Services Ltd v. Intuitive Systems Ltd.*[1] The High Court held that on its true construction the clause in question was optional only. However, the judge went on to state *obiter dictum* that had it been regarded as obligatory by the parties, it would still be unenforceable on the principle of *Walford v. Miles*, since a duty to negotiate in good faith was too uncertain. The courts would not compel parties to engage in co-operative processes. The expression "we are fixed in good faith" was held as evidence of an intention to create a contract in *Hanjin Shipping Co. Ltd v. Zenith Chartering Corporation "The Mercedes Envoy".*[2]

A promise "to use best endeavours"

5.17   A promise to use best endeavours to a particular end can be enforceable. In *Little v. Courage Ltd,*[3] Millett L.J. stated that there was an important distinction between an undertaking "to use one's best endeavours" to do something (for instance to obtain planning permission, or an export licence, which was sufficiently certain and therefore capable of being enforced) and on the other hand, an undertaking "to use one"s best

---

[95] [1993] 4 All E.R. 961.
[96] [1992] 2 A.C. 128.
[97] At p. 138.
[98] The House of Lords declined to follow the American case of *Chanel Home Centers, Division of Grace Retail Corporation v. Grossman* (1986) 795 F.2d.291.
[99] Good faith in general is discussed later in Chap. 14.
[1] [1999] 1 All E.R. (Comm) 303.
[2] [1995] 2 Lloyd's Rep. 559. On intention to create contractual relations, see Chap. 11.
[3] (1995) 70 P and CR 469.

endeavours to try to agree", which was no different from an undertaking to agree, to try to agree or to negotiate with a view to reaching agreement. The latter were equally uncertain and incapable of giving rise to an enforceable legal obligation.[4] In *Little v. Courage* the plaintiff James Little, was the tenant of a public house, *The Alexandra*, in Norwich of which Courage Ltd, the defendants, were the landlords. The issue was over an option to renew their Business Agreement for a further five years. There were suggestions of various implied terms that the parties "take all reasonable steps to reach agreement" and "to use its best endeavours to reach agreement". The Court of Appeal applied the distinction between an undertaking to use one's best endeavours to achieve an objective which was enforceable and an undertaking to use one's best endeavours to agree. The latter was no different from an undertaking to negotiate. In *Obagi v. Stanborough Developments Ltd*[5] the obligation to use best endeavours to obtain planning permission for a building was held to mean such reasonable steps as a prudent and determined man acting in his own self interest and anxious to obtain such permission would have taken. It was enforceable as a binding obligation. In *Gamerco SA v. KM/Fair Warning (Agency) Ltd*[6] a term was implied to give business efficacy to a commercial contract. The implied term was to use "all reasonable endeavours" to obtain a safety permit for a football stadium in Madrid to hold a rock concert. It was not necessary to require an absolute obligation to obtain the permits and licences in question. Garland J. therefore held that the "proper implication would be to use all reasonable endeavours".[7][8] Such a term was a binding contractual obligation.

Promise to "use all reasonable endeavours" to procure a contract with a third party

This type of term was held to be enforceable in *Lambert (Rae) v. HTV Cymru (Wales) Ltd*[9] in which the plaintiff was the author of a series of stories and drawings of cartoon characters called *The Furlings*. The defendants were supposed to "use all reasonable endeavours" to obtain rights of negotiation with other parties to enable the plaintiff to establish himself in publishing in other countries including North America. The Court of Appeal held that a distinction could be drawn between a contract to do something and a contract to use all reasonable endeavours to procure that some third party does the same thing. The latter was sufficiently certain and the clause in question was enforceable.

---

[4] At p. 476.
[5] [1995] 69 P and CR 573.
[6] [1995] 1 W.L.R. 1226.
[7] At p. 1231.
[8] The case is also important for it's discussion of the effect of frustration, see later in Chap. 22.
[9] [1998] F.S.R. 874.

THE EFFECT OF FAILURE TO AGREE OR LACK OF FINALITY

What if no contract results?

5.18 If no contract is ever formed as a result of uncertainty or failure of offer and acceptance, there can be no contractual remedy. The answer then depends upon restitution law.[10] Where the parties are still negotiating a contract but have not yet formalised the agreement, any costs incurred may be at that party's own risk. This would apply to a sale of property still "subject to contract". In *Regalian Properties v. London Dockland Development Corp.*[11] Rattee J. held that "subject to contract" meant that each party had to bear their own costs in meeting the contract and there could be no restitutionary claim for expenses. On the other hand, this is to be contrasted with *British Steel Corporation v. Cleveland Bridge Engineering Co Ltd*[12] where a restitutionary remedy was available.

Can incompleteness be dealt with by estoppel?[13]

In *Attorney-General of Hong Kong v. Humphreys Estate (Queens Gardens Ltd)*[14] Lord Templeman stated that:

> "it is possible but unlikely that in circumstances at present unforeseeable a party to negotiations set out in a document expressed to be "subject to contract" would be able to satisfy the court that the parties had subsequently agreed to convert the document into a contract or that some form or estoppel had arisen to prevent both parties from refusing to proceed with the transactions envisaged by the document."[15]

Estoppel could in future provide an alternative to be used to deal with incomplete agreements including the problem of "gazumping" house prices.

---

[10] See Chap. 26.
[11] [1995] 1 All E.R. 1005.
[12] [1984] 1 All E.R. 504.
[13] See Chap. 9.
[14] [1987] A.C. 114.
[15] At pp. 127–28.

Chapter 6

Mistake in Relation to Agreement

Introduction: one for dog lovers

The front page of *The Times*, February 2, 1996 contained the following story: **6.1**

> "A tearful and acrimonious battle over the ownership of JJ, a playful and potentially valuable Irish setter pup, was decided yesterday when a judge decided that it could remain with the couple who had bought it. But the six-month-old bitch. . . will have to return in 18 months to where it was born to give birth to a litter. In a settlement which mirrors complicated divorce case access agreements, both sides will have the right to visit the dog when it is not with them. The saga began last October when Margaret Webb of Swindon, Wiltshire, was presented with the puppy by her children who had raised £350 to buy it to help her overcome a serious illness. Three days later, Biddy Evans, who with her husband, George, runs the Fosse Dogotel and Cattery near Cirencester, rang to say she had mistakenly sold them a bitch instead of a dog and wanted it back. . . After the agreement Mrs Webb, 48, said: I am delighted. These past few months have been a nightmare. We love JJ and she has bonded with our other red setter. Mrs Evans claimed she would never have sold JJ to the couple if she had known that they were unemployed because she claimed keeping a pedigree dog costs hundreds of pounds a year."

The case was settled out of court prior to a hearing so we are denied a judgment. What would the county court have decided about the dispute between the Fosse Dogotel and Cattery and the children of Margaret Webb? The answer lies mainly in the rules of agreement mistake. After we have looked at this doctrine, we shall discuss, at the end of this chapter, what the judgment might have been.

"Agreement Mistake"

Offer and acceptance wears an interesting disguise in relation to mistake in contract law. **6.2** There are three categories of mistake, which break down into two distinct doctrines. First, both parties may make the same mistake at the time of contracting. This is a "common mistake" (sometimes confusingly called "mutual mistake") which "nullifies" the agreement. The parties may have agreed but they were both wrong about some fundamental matter at the time of formation. Offer and acceptance match, but common mistake robs the agreement of its substance.[1] Secondly, contractual mistake may also arise if only one of the parties makes a mistake, or the parties do not reach agreement at all, because, as objectively understood, both take a different meaning. These are called unilateral and mutual mistake respectively. Unilateral and mutual mistake are also called "agreement mistake" or "mistake negativing agreement." There is no meeting of the minds or *consensus ad idem* based on a corresponding offer and acceptance.

Mistake requires more than the parties be at cross purposes or that one party, in his or her own mind, gets something wrong. This would be too open ended a principle. It would also provide an easy escape route from contracts. A subjective mistake by one party only is not a sufficient ground for mistake. In contract law the parties are taken to have agreed what they appeared to agree, not what each privately in their own mind believed they had done. However, in relation to mistake in contract law, the analysis is not entirely objective either. The basic objective test allows for a subjective element. Unfortunately there is a scarcity of modern case law on mistake. Mistake has atrophied through lack of recent case law, and much of the law is over 100 years old. This reflects the perceived narrowness of the doctrine, and also the development of more popular and effective remedies such as misrepresentation which may arise on the same facts, give better remedies and are wider in their application.

Mistake has to be treated as two doctrines in another important respect. There are separate principles for mistake at both common law and in equity, and different remedies for each in the two systems. Mistake at common law renders a contract void from the beginning. If the contract is not void, the second possibility is that equity may intervene to allow or refuse a remedy applying a different approach to that of the common law narrow grounds.[2]

The narrow doctrine of mistake

- If Trevor is selling something which Sally believes to be a different object, the contract is not void for mistake. Sally has made the mistake in her own mind.

- The mistake must be as to a promise made by the other. If a promise was expressly made, this will be a breach of warranty. Mistake arises if one party believes the other is promising when that person knows they is not. If Sally thinks Trevor is promising something whereas Trevor knows he is not, Sally is contracting on a different basis. The contract will be void for mistake. Sally was mistaken as to what she thought was Trevor's promise.

- There is some debate as to whether it would it be sufficient if a reasonable person should have known the facts, even if subjectively that person did not know the true state of the other's mind.

- Even if Trevor knows Sally is making a mistake, he is normally under no legal duty to tell her otherwise.[3] If Trevor did not induce the contract by any misrepresentation, he is under no obligation to tell Sally the truth.

[1] We discuss this category separately in Chap. 21.
[2] See Chap. 21, where remedies for contractual mistake are discussed in greater detail.
[3] See later Duty of Disclosure, Chap. 15.

The test for mistake is objective, but with a subjective element

The general rule is that a mere subjective mistake does not make a contract void. The **6.3** parties continue to be bound by their agreement. If on an objective basis, a reasonable person would have believed that the other party is offering X, when subjectively he was really offering Y, there is still a contract. The over-riding objective approach in contract law is well expressed by Blackburn J. in *Smith v. Hughes*[4] where he stated, "Whatever a man's real intention may be, he so conducts himself that a reasonable man would believe he was assenting to the terms proposed by the other party and that other party on that belief enters into the contract with him, the man thus conducting himself would be equally bound as if he had intended to agree to the other party's terms". This represents the first of three subtly different views expressed by the judges in *Smith v. Hughes*, a case which we shortly discuss. The subjective element in mistake is doubted by those who would adhere to a strictly objective approach in contract law. The question is whether mistake arises when one party makes a mistake and the other: (a) is actually aware or should in fact have been aware, *i.e.* subjective or (b) a reasonable person in her shoes should have been aware, *i.e.* objectively, that a mistake has been made? If the answer is (a), there is an element of a subjective approach. If it is (b), it is objective. It appears that (a) has the stronger support. The normal objective test in contract law may be displaced by subjective element of knowledge in mistake cases. This is illustrated by *Hartog v. Colin and Shields*[5] where hare skins were sold at a price "per pound" rather than "per piece". There had been a course of dealings based on the latter arrangement between the parties over a period of years. It was held that the contract was void for mistake as the plaintiffs should have realised that the defendant was mistaken. Although mistake contains a subjective element, the test remains largely objective.

The farmer and the racehorse trainer: "old oats", "new oats" or just "oats"?

Smith v. Hughes[6] is one of the most discussed cases in contract law. It is often cited in **6.4** support of a more subjective approach to mistake in contract law. Both Blackburn J. and Hannen J. seem to say that a contract is void for mistake if one party enters into it under a fundamental mistake and the other knows of the mistake (we have already quoted Blackburn J.). The answer to this remains the key to any discussion of agreement mistake. The reported judgment in *Smith v. Hughes* concerns an appeal to the Queen's Bench from the County Court at Epsom (not surprisingly, considering the subject matter.) The plaintiff was a farmer who had sold some oats to the defendant, a race horse trainer. The plaintiff showed the defendant some oats which he had for sale. The defendant kept the sample (it appears for a couple of days) then bought 16 quarters of

---

[4] (1871) LR 6 Q.B. 597.
[5] [1939] 3 All E.R. 566.
[6] (1871) LR 6 Q.B. 597.

oats at 34s. per quarter. Later he discovered that the oats were "new" oats, not "old" oats,[7] so he refused to accept the oats or to pay for them.

Although *Smith v. Hughes* is about the legal meaning of mistake, the main issue, and ultimately the outcome of the case, depended on a straightforward question of fact. The truth remains a mystery to the present day. Was the word "old" ever used? The plaintiff farmer's view was that in July of the previous year (1870) he had a quantity of new winter oats for sale which he was keen to get rid of, the price being high as oats were in short supply. He took a sample of these to the defendant's manager, Hughes, and asked if he bought oats. The latter said he was "always a buyer of good oats". After delivering a sample, the plaintiff sold the oats to the defendant. The defendant's version of the same conversation was that he (the defendant) said "I am always a buyer of good old oats" and the plaintiff replied "I have some good old oats for sale". Hence the dispute. Was the word "old" mentioned or not? The outcome depended on it. The issue was what was being sold, just "oats" or "old oats"? The appeal was against the judge's direction to the jury. At the trial he had asked the jury to consider two questions. If they answered yes to these, they had to find for the buyer, *i.e.* the race horse training defendant. Had the world "old" been used by the plaintiff or the defendant in making the contract? If so, they had to give their verdict to the defendant. The words used had to be construed as a warranty or express term of the contract. However, if they thought the word "old" had not been used, then the second question applied: did the seller believe the buyer was contracting for old oats? If he was, then the verdict had to be for the defendant and the contract void for mistake. If the evidence was that the seller, *i.e.* the plaintiff, did not know this, then the contract should stand.

6.5   The jury at first instance found for the buyer, *i.e.* there was no contract. It was void for mistake. However, the jury did not say which question they had answered in the buyer's favour. The Court of the Queen's Bench found that there had been a misdirection by the judge on the second question and so ordered a re-trial. The Court held that the record of the Judge's directions to the jury failed to clarify the key distinction. There would only be an agreement mistake if the seller know of the buyer's mistake, that he wanted old oats and had mistakenly taken this to be a term of the contract. If the buyer thought the oats were warranted to be old and the seller knew this but was making no such claim, then the contract was void for mistake. The seller's knowledge was vital. If the buyer merely thought they were old, this was his own mistake and the contract was valid. The correct question to the jury should have been: (a) did the buyer agree to take the oats believing them to be old. In this case the contract remains valid. However, if the seller knew that the buyer was only contracting for old oats, he had knowledge that the buyer understood the contract differently from how he (the seller) understood it. The contract was then void for mistake. According to Hannen J., the seller should not be able to hold the buyer to "that which was only the apparent, and not the real bargain".[8] If this were the case, the sale was void for mistake. If, on the other hand, the buyer wrongly supposed the oats were old, or not new, and took this view without any promise or statement by the seller, the contract had to stand. In order to render the contract void for mistake,

---

[7] New oats are likely to give racehorses colic and are therefore not what racehorse trainers would normally wish to purchase. Did or should the farmer have known this? The farmer claimed, "I do not know that trainers never use new oats; a trainer has since this transaction offered me money for new oats" (at p. 598).
[8] At p. 610.

according to Hannen J.[9] it must be: (a) not merely that the plaintiff believed the defendant to believe he was buying old oats, but also (b) that he believed the defendant to believe that he, the plaintiff, was contracting to sell old oats. Finally there is a third view, that of Cockburn C.J. that:

> "the two minds were not *ad idem* as to the age of the oats; they certainly were *ad idem* as to the sale and purchase of them. Suppose a person was to buy a horse without a warranty believing him to be sound; and the horse turns out unsound, could it be contended that it would be open to him to say that, as he had intended to buy a sound horse, and the seller to sell an unsound one, the contract was void, because the seller must have known from the price the buyer was willing to give, or from his general habits as a buyer of horses, that he thought the horse was sound? The cases are exactly parallel. The result is that, in my opinion, the learned judge of the county court was wrong in leaving the second question to the jury, and that, consequently, the case must go down to a new trial."[10]

The contract was valid or void for mistake depending on the answer to the relevant questions. On the facts, the judges on appeal seemed to favour the plaintiff's argument that the contract was valid, hence sending the case back for retrial. Hannen J. appeared to be so inclined: **6.6**

> "I am the more disposed to think that the jury did not understand the question in this last sense because I can find very little, if any, evidence to support it a finding upon it in favour of the defendant. It may be that the defendant believed the oats were old, and it may be suggested that the plaintiff thought and so believed, but the only evidence from which it can be inferred that the plaintiff believed that the defendant thought that the plaintiff was making it a term of the contract that the oats were old is that the defendant was a trainer, and that trainers, as a rule, use old oats; and that the price given was high for new oats, and more than a prudent man would have given."[11]

Finally, the defendant having admitted he bought the oats after having had the sample for two days, the Court held there was not sufficient evidence for the jury to find for the defendant on the second question "if they rightly understood it". The rule in *Smith v. Hughes* is contained on the final page of Hannen J.'s judgment: "In order to relieve the defendant it was necessary that the jury should find not merely that the plaintiff believed the defendant to believe that he was buying old oats, but that he believed the defendant to believe that the plaintiff, was contracting to sell old oats". Of course, if Blackburn J.'s view is correct that an objective view is taken, *i.e.* that of a reasonable person in the position of the favour, then would a reasonable farmer know or have reasonable grounds for believing that racehorses do not enjoy "new" oats? The plaintiff claimed there was no such general knowledge and that he had recently sold new oats for racehorses. If the reasonably objective view would be that they would be useless and he should have known this, the contract should be void for mistake. The result of the case illustrates the

---

[9] At p. 611.
[10] At p. 606.
[11] At p. 611.

unwillingness of nineteenth century English judges to admit the possibility of mistake at all. It also shows that this area has not moved very far since Victorian times as there is a lack of modern case law. Of course a case like *Smith v. Hughes* might still be set aside on terms in equity and this might be the result today in light of *Solle v. Butcher*.[12]

THE CATEGORIES OF AGREEMENT MISTAKE

The cases where mistake arises through lack of agreement are broken down into two categories.

Mutual mistake

6.7 The parties have a different understanding, applying objective criteria. Since the parties were never in agreement, there is no contract. However, if, objectively, there was no doubt or possible misunderstanding about the agreement, then the contract will be upheld. Cases which are universally acknowledged as involving mutual mistake are few. The parties are essentially at cross purposes. The most famous example is *Raffles v. Wichelhaus and Busch*.[13] In a contract for the sale of cotton, the plaintiffs described the goods as "ex the ship Peerless" from Bombay. The buyers contracted to buy, thinking that they were buying goods from the ship "Peerless" which had sailed from Bombay in December. In fact, the sellers intended to sell cargo on board a ship of the same name which had sailed from Bombay in October. The defendants refused to take the cotton and the plaintiffs sued for damages of non-acceptance. The Court of Exchequer held the buyers were not liable as there was no contract. Was this due to mutual mistake? The case has been subject to much scrutiny.[14] There was no reasoned judgment, so it has been left to commentators to turn the case into a principle. As there was no evidence as to which ship the contract truly related to, the ambiguity prevented any *consensus ad idem* and therefore a contract coming into existence.[15] The judgment in the case is short, consisting of a mere seven words (albeit *per curiam*), namely that: "There must be judgment for the defendants". This was on hearing counsel's argument for the defendants that there was "latent ambiguity" as to which "Peerless" was correct,[16] and that therefore there was no consensus *ad idem* and so no binding contract. This argument prevailed. It is regarded by some as the high point of a purely subjective view of formation which was rapidly taken over by objectivity. There was no contract because subjectively there never was a meeting of the parties minds. Nowadays a purely subjective test is no longer tenable.

"If only he'd put the word escorte before the word begloom instead of after it"

---

[12] See Chap. 21.
[13] (1864) 2 H and C 906, 159 E.R. 375.
[14] See Simpson, *The Beauty of Obscurity: Leading Cases in the Common Law* (1995, Oxford), Chap. 6.
[15] This famous case is now regarded as an historical curiosity, and scholarship has revealed that more has been read into it than is justified. For an interesting deconstruction of this case see Grant Gilmore, *Death of Contract (1974,* Ohio State), pp. 35–44.
[16] Parol evidence was admissible to prove this (see Chap. 12).

Ambiguity, indeed incomprensibility, was the issue in the following case, which is probably   **6.8**
as good an example of mutual mistake as there is. In *Falck v. Williams*[17] the plaintiff Falck
was a shipowner living in Norway who sued the defendant, a shipbroker in Sydney, over a
contract to load the ship "Semiramis" with a cargo of copra in Fiji for delivery to the United
Kingdom or some port in Europe. Williams took this to be a proposal for carriage of a cargo
of shale to be loaded at Sydney and delivered to Barcelona, and he accepted the proposal
under this impression. At the trial it transpired that both parties appeared to have acted in
good faith, and that "any mistake was unintentional, whoever might be to blame for the misunderstanding"(according to Lord Macnaghten later in the House of Lords). The mistake
arose because there had been two contracts under negotiation, one to do with the copra, the
other a contract for shale. The Privy Council on appeal from New South Wales held there
was no contract. The confusion stemmed from the fact that negotiations were taking place
through an agent, Buch, who used a telegraphic code for messages. The dispute was as to
whether the word "escorte" was to be read with what had gone before or what followed? In
code, the message which was sent read, "Shale Copyright Semiramis Begloom Escorte
Sultana Brilliant Argentina Bronchil". This was meant to read as "Shale, your rate is too
low, impossible to work business at your figures, Semiramis, have closed in accordance with
your order, confirm, two ports Fiji Islands, keep a good look-out for business for this vessel,
wire us when anything good offers". Unfortunately the parties had different interpretations
of this message, and over the word "escorte" in particular.

The Privy Council held there was no conclusive evidence pointing one way or the other.
It was impossible to find that there was a contract, as the parties were not "at one". The
acceptance by Williams, as he meant it to be understood, had no connection with "or reference to the proposal which Buch intended to make and thought he was making". The
fault lay with the appellant's agent, Mr Buch, according to Lord Macnaghton sounding
exasperated by the whole business:[18] "If he had spent a few more shillings on his message,
if he had even analysed the words he used more carefully, if he had only put the word
estcorte before the word begloom, instead of after it, there would have been no difficulty".[19] The judgment of the Privy Council was that there was no contract. It was not for
the Court to determine what was the true construction of the telegram.[20] It was the duty
of the appellant as plaintiff to make out that the construction which he put upon it was
the true one. In this he failed as the Privy Council held the message to be ambiguous.
Indeed, even if the respondent had tried to maintain his own interpretation he would have
failed also. It was for the plaintiff to show that the contract was clear and unambiguous so
that the defendant could not have misunderstood it, and not for the Court to construe.

Unilateral mistake

Unilateral mistake applies if: **6.9**

    (i)   one party is mistaken and he or she would not have entered into the contract
           had he or she known their mistake;

---

[17] [1900] A.C. 176.
[18] At p. 181.
[19] The code word "escorte" acquires an extra letter "estcorte" in Lord McNaughton's speech. Even that great
judge was confused.
[20] It is worth noting that the Court was refusing to put its own objective construction before that of the parties
(discussed Chap. 2).

(ii)   the mistake ought reasonably to have been known to the other party; and

(iii) the mistaken party is not at fault.

Many of the leading cases on unilateral mistake are about the mistaken identity of one of the parties, which we discuss in a separate section shortly. However, if we apply the basic principle of unilateral mistake to this issue, a contract will be void for unilateral mistake only if:

(a)   Avril believes she is contracting with Bob; and

(b)   in fact she is contracting with Clive.

Their contact will be void provided that:

(a)   Clive is aware of the mistake; and

(b)   Avril herself is not at fault in making the mistake.

An application of these rules is to be found in *Boulton v. Jones*[21] where Pollock C.B.[22] stated:

> "It is a rule of law that if a person intends to contract with A, B cannot give himself any right under it. Here the order was given to Brocklehurst. Possibly Brocklehurst might have adopted the act of the plaintiff in supplying the goods and maintained an action for their price. But since the plaintiff has chosen to sue, the only course the defendants could take was to plead that there was no contract with him."

Martin B. held that if there was any contract at all, it was not with the plaintiff. The Court added: "If a man goes into a shop and makes a contract, intending it to be with one particular person, no other person can convert that into a contract with him".[23] Normally identity is not such a vital ingredient of a contract, particularly in face to face retail transactions. The identity of the other person must be important enough to be a term, indeed a term of significance, to the contracting party. In *Boulton v. Jones*[24] the importance of only dealing with a person called Brocklehurst was sufficient to make the contract void for mistaken identity. On the other hand, in *Citibank NA v. Brown Shipley and Co.*[25] (discussed later), a bankers' draft issued to a person claiming false authority was nonetheless held to be a contract, although it could have been voidable. It is usual to classify the situation according to the physical presence of the parties. So if the parties are not in each others' presence, called *inter absentes, i.e.* contracting by letter, telephone or fax, then there is an assumption that the party only intended to deal with the person

---

[21] (1857) 2 H and N 563, 157 E.R. 232.
[22] At p. 233.
[23] At p. 233.
[24] (1857) 2 H and H 564, 157 E.R. 232.
[25] [1991] 2 All E.R. 690.

with whose name and address they are in communication. This can of course be proved to be otherwise. If, however, the parties are face to face, called *inter praesentes*, as in the case of customer and shopkeeper or retailer, the presumption is that the trader intended to deal with whoever entered the premises. The shopper's name is not usually vital, merely their ability to pay for any goods they take away. It is for the seller to prove that the identity of the customer was central to the transaction and that mistaken identity is sufficient to render the contract void.

Mistake and misrepresentation are to be contrasted though they may overlap

Many unilateral mistake cases also involve misrepresentation (often fraudulent) about the person's identity. There will generally be both possibilities for the plaintiff to chose from if they was deceived into contracting. Normally they will opt for misrepresentation as the remedies are better.[26] However, since misrepresentation makes the contract voidable, and this will not be available if a third part has acquired goods (as is often the case), the plaintiff may be forced to fall back on unilateral mistake. This is frequently a last resort. The action is not against the fraudster who induced the contract, but against the third party who has possession of the goods, in the tort of conversion. This action is brought to prove a better title in the plaintiff than that of the person in possession. The key is the issue of mistake. If there was a mistake, the contract is void and therefore the other party acquired no title to pass on. The Latin maxim, *nemo dat quod non habet*, applies. This means that no one can give a good title who does not himself have a title to give. The original owner is entitled to his or her goods back. However, if mistake does not apply, then the third party (who is also an innocent victim having acquired the goods in good faith, without notice and for value) wins out. It is usually an unfortunate choice the courts are led to make between two innocent parties. Hence the difficulties the courts have encountered in resolving such questions. There are good reasons to reform the law in the area of mistake.[27]

6.10

There are major conceptual differences between mistake and misrepresentation. A misrepresentation is an untrue statement of fact; mistake on the other hand relates to the terms of the agreement.[28] The effect of the doctrines also differs. Misrepresentation renders a contract voidable, unless one of the bars to rescission applies. At common law a contract is void for mistake in equity. Making the correct choice of doctrine may be vital to the plaintiff. If the contract is void *ab initio* (as in the case of non-existent goods) then the plaintiff cannot choose misrepresentation as there is nothing to avoid. This was the point of *McRae v. Commonwealth Disposals Commission*.[29] If the misrepresentation induces a non-fundamental mistake, only the misrepresentation claim arises. However, if the misrepresentation induces a fundamental mistake, or one actionable in equity, both claims may be feasible.[30]

[26] See Chap. 18.
[27] See Chap. 21, and later p. 92.
[28] We discuss the distinction between terms and representations in Chap. 13.
[29] (1950) 84 C.L.R. 377, discussed in Chap. 21.
[30] See *Leaf v. International Galleries* [1950] 2 K.B. 86.

Mistaken Identity[31]

Contracts concluded at a distance or "inter absentes"

6.11 The general rule is that the identity of a person with whom one contracts at a distance may be important enough to avoid the contract. It is only a *prima facie* rule which can be rebutted by evidence to the contrary. In *King's Norton Metal Co. Ltd v. Edridge Merrett & Co Ltd*[32] a fraudster named Wallis dishonestly used headed notepaper in the name of Hallam and Co., a firm in Sheffield, to obtain goods from a company in Birmingham. The action between the parties was in the tort of conversion for return of the goods. The tort action was the only ground for recovering the goods from the third party as there was no contract between the sellers and the innocent third party purchaser. The plaintiffs claimed they only intended to deal with Hallam and Co, not with the person calling himself Wallis. The Court of Appeal held there was a concluded contract albeit one voidable for fraud. The plaintiffs had intended to contract with the writer of the letter. To one member of the Court of Appeal, A. L. Smith L.J., the "law seems well settled . . . If a person, induced by false pretences, contracted with a rogue to sell goods to him, and the goods were delivered the rogue could until the contract was disaffirmed give a good title to the goods to a bona fide purchaser for value". The question was: "with whom . . . did the plaintiffs contract to sell the goods? . . . If it could have been shown that there was a separate entity called Hallam and Co. and another entity called Wallis then the case might have come within the decision in *Cundy v. Lindsay*". In *King's Norton* there was a contract with the person who wrote the letters by which the property passed to him. The contract was voidable for fraud, but not void for mistake.

The classic authority on an "inter absentes" mistaken agreement is *James Cundy and T. Bevington v. Thomas Lindsay*.[33] The plaintiffs received an order from a person calling himself Blenkarn giving his address as 37 Wood Street, Cheapside. The signature was made to appear as if it was "Blenkiron and Co.", a company who traded at No. 123 in the same street. Without checking the number, the plaintiffs posted off the goods. They were successful in their tort claim in conversion against a third party who had obtained the goods, a set of cambric handkerchiefs, from the fraudster. The contract between the plaintiffs and Blenkiron was void for mistake as they intended to deal with a different person and the identity of that person was a term of the contract. The holding of *Cundy v. Lindsay* was analysed by Waller J. in *Citibank NA v. Brown Shipley and Co.*[34] as circumstances in which a contract is void for unilateral mistake: "(i) A thinks he has agreed with C because he believes B, with whom he is negotiating is C; and (ii) B is aware that A did not intend to make any agreement with him; and (iii) A has established that the identity of C was a matter of crucial importance". Waller J. in *Citibank* stated[35] that the *Cundy v. Lindsay* principle would apply "only if the precise identity of the bailee and possibly also the identity of the person to whom the banker's draft was to be delivered were mistaken *and* proved to be of fundamental importance." In *Citibank* the identity was held not to be sufficiently crucial.

---

[31] See Goodhart, "Mistake as to Identity in the Law of Contract" (1941) 57 L.Q.R. 228.
[32] (1897) 14 T.L.R. 98.
[33] (1878) 3 App. Cas. 459.
[34] [1991] 2 All E.R. 690 (at p. 699).
[35] At p. 702.

Instances of cases where mistaken identity invalidates an agreement are like gold dust,   **6.12**
not easy to find. A rare modern example, however, is *Shogun Finance Ltd. v. Hudson,*[36]
where a fraudster tried to obtain a vehicle on hire purchase terms from the plaintiffs by
impersonating a third party, producing his driving licence and forging his signature. This
was sufficient for the plaintiff's credit granting facilities and they let him have the car. He
then sold the car to the defendant who had no knowledge of the fraud. The plaintiffs
claimed the vehicle back or damages in the alternative arguing that the identity of the
buyer was fundamental to the agreement and that the false signature made the contract
void. The defendant had two good, well worn, arguments. The identity of the fraudster
was not crucial to the agreement which was, at most, voidable. This had not occurred
before the sale to the defendant who, as a private purchase in good faith, was entitled
(under the Hire Purchase Act 1964, s. 27) to obtain a good title, and so keep the car. The
County Court Judge in Leicester held that because there had been no face to face
contact, and the agreement was in writing, this was not an *inter praesentes* agreement[36a],
the identity of the hire purchaser of the car was crucial and the agreement rendered void
at common law.[37]

The Court of Appeal upheld the judgment. The purchaser did not obtain a good title
as the fraudster was not a "debtor" under the agreement with whom the finance
company had intended to contract. The dealer had not been active as the fraudster's
agent for the purpose of the sale.

The contracting parties are face to face or "inter praesentes"

If the parties are in each other's presence, there is a presumption that they intended to   **6.13**
contract with each other. This is the normal rule in a consumer retail transaction. The
retailer has to take reasonable steps to check the person's identity however. The identity
of the person contracting is less significant when they are in each other's presence as it is
assumed a party knows with whom they are dealing. So the issue becomes whether reasonable steps were taken to check who the other party was and the importance (if any)
of that person's stated identity to the transaction. If the mistake is merely as to the other
person's attributes, this does not count. Their true identity must be a fundamental term.
In practice it is usually a person's ability to pay, rather than the individual's true identity
that is crucial to the seller.

As we have seen in *Shogun Finance* (above) a fraud is also committed by the impersonator.
If he immediately sells the goods on to a third party, the third party may think he is entitled
to the goods, but the original owner may argue that the contract with the "rogue" or fraudster is void. No good title was ever passed because of the rule that only a person with a good
title can do so. The action by the original owner is in the tort of conversion. Both parties are
innocent, but sadly one must lose as the law now stands. Hence the dilemma, revealed in the
reported cases. The modern tendency to pay by credit card further complicates matters since
the payer is the credit card company, who will bear the losses of a fraudulent transaction.
Many thousands of such cases annually are nowadays governed by banking and criminal

---

[36] [2000] All E.R. (D) 306.
[36a] In the Court of Appeal, Sedley L.J., disserting, took the view that the case should be treated as *inter praesentes.*
[37] *Kings Norton Metal* and *Cundy v. Lindsay* were applied.

law principles so it is regrettably rare for a pure contract law point to arise. There is a need to clarify some points in need of attention. Like the rest of mistake, this is an area calling out for reform and clarifications, as the following cases illustrate.[38]

(1) The classic "rogue" cases

6.14

The preponderance of the reported authorities tend to favour the third party and hold the contract valid, rather than void for mistake at common law. In *Phillips v. Brooks Ltd*[39] a fraudster named North obtained some pearls and a ring from a jeweller's claiming that he was "Sir George Bullough" who lived in St. James' Square. He then pledged the ring to a firm of pawnbrokers, the defendants, who gave him a sum of money in security. The Court held that there was no mistake and the contract must stand, as the plaintiff intended to deal with the person in front of him. The mistake related to the honesty or creditworthiness of the person concerned. Horridge J. stated:

> "although the plaintiff believed the person to whom he was handing the ring was Sir George Bullough, he in fact contracted to sell and deliver it to the person who came into his shop, and who was not Sir George Bullough, but a man of the name of North, who obtained the sale and delivery by means of the false pretence that he was Sir George Bullough".[40]

As between the two parties, innocent seller or third party, it was the seller who had to suffer the loss. The Court used as authority, in particular, the judgment of Morton C.J. in *Edmunds v. Merchants' Despatch Transportation Co*[41], an American case. Horridge J. concluded: "I think the seller intended to contract with the person present, and there was no error as to the person with whom he contracted, although the plaintiff would not have made the contract if there had not been a fraudulent misrepresentation".[42] In *Lewis v. Averay*[43] there was a similar outcome when the plaintiff, a post graduate chemistry student in Bristol, sold his Austin Cooper car to a rogue who claimed that he was the well known actor Richard Greene who had appeared as "Robin Hood" in the television series of that name. The identity was held to relate only to the honesty of the payment rather than the contract as a whole. Lord Denning argued that the better principle would be for a contract to be voidable,[44] not void, in such cases, so long as the plaintiff was able to do so before third parties in good faith acquired rights under it for value.

Lord Denning was critical of some of the earlier authorities. The French jurist Pothier is often quoted as authority for error as to the person (*i.e.* mistaken identity in civil law systems). Lord Denning felt this had "given rise to such refinements that it is time it was dead and buried altogether". He described the distinction between a mistake as to identity which rendered a contract void and a mistake merely as to attributes which did not, as "a distinction without a difference", adding that: "These fine distinctions do no good to the law".[45] On balance, Lord Denning's sympathies lay with the third party buyer. He

---

[38] We discuss this later in Chap. 13.
[39] [1919] 2 K.B. 243.
[40] At p. 246.
[41] (1883) 135 Mass. 283.
[42] At pp. 248–49.
[43] [1972] 1 Q.B. 198.
[44] *i.e.* in equity.
[45] At p. 206.

had acted "with complete circumspection, and entire good faith". Whereas the seller "had let the rogue have the goods and thus enable him to commit the fraud". The true principle emerging from the case law was:[46]

> "when two parties have come to a contract — or rather what appears on the fact of it to be a contract — the fact that one party is mistaken as to the identity of the other does not mean that there is no contract, or that the contract is a nullity and void from the beginning. It means only that the contract is voidable, that is, liable to be set aside at the instance of the mistaken person, so long as he does so before the parties have in good faith acquired rights under it".

This is in accordance with the presumption suggested by Devlin L.J.[47]

Lord Denning's views, sensible as they may be, cannot yet be said to be good law. Nor can the holding of *Lewis v. Averay* be said to be a rule. This is clear from the following case. *Ingram v. Little*[48] was described by Lord Denning in *Lewis v. Averay*[49] as a case which "cannot be reconciled" with *Phillips v. Brooks*. The facts, it must be admitted, are very similar, but not however identical. This time the plaintiffs were three women, Elsie and Hilda Ingram and a Mrs. Badger, who jointly owned a car and advertised it for sale in the *Bournemouth Echo*. A person who called himself P. G. M. Hutchison answered the advertisment. Before accepting his cheque one of the women went out of the room to check his name in the telephone directory and discovered it was listed as he had stated. The person who signed the cheque was not who he said he was and sold the car a few days later to Reginald Little, a car dealer in Blackpool. This time the Court of Appeal held the contract void for mistake, though Devlin L.J. dissented. His dissent is probably the most interesting of all the judgments in the three cases.[50] The holding of the majority in *Ingram v. Little* was that the plaintiffs had demonstrated that the identity of the buyer was an essential term and that their investigation of the telephone directory was sufficient to prove this. Also they had not been careless and done everything that could be asked of them to verify the identity of the buyer. Nevertheless, Phillimore L.J. in *Lewis v. Averay*[51] distinguished the facts in *Ingram v. Little* as: **6.15**

> ". . . being special and unusual facts . . . which had sufficiently shown that in the particular circumstances . . . contrary to the prima facie presumption, the lady who was selling her motor car was not dealing with the person actually present".

Thus, it looked as if *Ingram v. Little* could be "distinguished on its facts" and so marginalised to stand alone. This is no longer the case. The Court of Appeal judgment in *Shogun Finance Ltd v. Hudson*[51a] (discussed earlier) adds a significant authority to the balance in favour of voidness in such circumstances.[51b]

---

[46] At p. 207.
[47] Darlin L.J. dissenting in *Ingram v. Little*, [1961] 1 Q.B. 31 (at p. 66).
[48] [1961] 1 Q.B. 31.
[49] At p. 205.
[50] See later pp. 92–93.
[51] At p. 208.
[51a] [2000] All E.R. (D) 306.
[51b] See *Finucane* (2000) 151 N.L.J. 1217.

6.16   A similarly disputed case is *Sowler v. Potter*[52], in which the defendant, Ann Robinson, had been convicted of permitting disorderly conduct at the Swan Café in Great Swan Alley in London. She changed her name to Ann Potter and entered into a lease with the plaintiff, Helen Sowler, for premises at Coleman Street in London to run as a restaurant. Later she officially changed her name to Ann Potter. The lease was held to be void because of the false identity. The plaintiff's agent had believed himself to be dealing with someone other than Ann Robinson whose case had been reported in the newspapers. Tucker J. stated that:[53]

> "This case of landlord and tenant is clearly one where the consideration of the person with whom the contract was made was a vital element in the contract, and that therefore, if there was any mistake on the part of the plaintiff with regard to the identity of the person with whom she was contracting, the contract is void *ab initio*".

The authority of this case has been doubted.[54]

The series of "rogue" cases were discussed by Waller J. in *Citibank NA v. Brown Shipley and Co.*[55] who emphasised three points of importance. First, that each of these cases rested on their own facts; secondly, that in order to prove no title had passed it was necessary to prove there was never a contract; and thirdly, that this can only happen if it is fundamental to the contract that one party should be who he said he is. This is easier to establish where contracts are made entirely by documents, and is less so in an *inter praesentes* position, according to Waller J.

Finally, the only case relevant to this type of mistake to have reached the House of Lords so far is *Lake v. Simmons*[56] in which the fraudster was a woman, Esmé Ellison, who obtained goods by deception from jewellers in Exeter by claiming she was a Mrs van der Borgh who lived at a large house nearby in Dawlish and that her sister was "engaged to Commander Digby". Suitably impressed, the jeweller let her have some necklaces on approval. She stole ten of these and was later convicted of theft and sentenced to imprisonment with hard labour. The House of Lords held that there was never a contract with Esmé Ellison, who was "a mere intermediary, little more than a porter", as far as the sale to her "husband" was concerned. However the case was really about the construction of an exemption of liability in the seller's insurance policy against loss by theft or dishonesty by a customer in respect of goods entrusted to them. The House of Lords held that the jeweller did not intend to sell to her and that she was not a "customer". The issue was, therefore, not purely one of mistake.

(2) The state of the law on unilateral mistake

6.17   In *Ingram v. Little*,[56a] Devlin L.J. dissented and would have held that a contract was formed. He would have followed *Phillips v. Brooks Ltd* (it is interesting that if either Sellars or Pearce L.J. had joined with Devlin L.J. in all three cases, Phillips, Ingram and Lewis would have reached a similar conclusion). Devlin L.J. also drew on American case

---

[52] [1940] 1 K.B. 271.
[53] At p. 275.
[54] The decision has been criticised several times by the courts, see *Solle v. Butcher* [1950] 1 K.B. 691 and *Lewis v. Averay* [1972] 1 Q.B. 206.
[55] [1991] 2 All E.R. 690.
[56] [1927] A.C. 487.
[56a] [1961] 1 Q.B. 31.

law[57] and the New Zealand case of *Fawcett v. Star Car Sales Ltd*.[58] He concluded with a plea for law reform saying that the distinction between void and voidability is a fine one and the rights of parties should not depend upon it. Rather, there should be apportionment of the loss between them under statutory reform.[59] Mistaken identity is an area lacking clear guiding authority. It is not surprising that most cases are dealt with by misrepresentation. In 1966 the Law Revision Committee proposed that contracts be made voidable rather than void for mistaken identity. They described the distinction between void and voidable for mistake to be "a very fine one, which has led to the greatest dissatisfaction with the present state of the law".[60] This might be a step in the right direction, but nothing has yet been done to implement this recommendation.

The dispute over JJ the Irish setter puppy: how should the court have decided?

Our discussion of mistake has emphasised the narrowness of the doctrine of mistake, at both common law and in equity. In general, it is more likely that a contract will remain valid if challenged on the grounds of mistake, and this probably applies to the subjective mistake of the sellers, Mr and Mrs Evans in selling a bitch rather than a dog. This would not be sufficient to set the contract aside. It was their own mistake and they were also at fault. Nor would the fact that the ultimate recipient of the puppy was unemployed be likely to succeed in court. It was not up to the purchasers to tell them anything about their financial circumstances.[61] There are, however, arguments which could be put forward on behalf of the Dogotel and Cattery including questions of fact which could have a bearing on their claim for the return of the animal on the ground of mistake. How was the dog identified at the time of sale, did the buyers inspect it, was the sale of merely "an Irish setter puppy" or "a puppy" or "a dog"? Did the word "dog" mean a male animal or would it be taken as any one of that species, male or female? How would a reasonable person of the age of the children (or were they adults?) buying the puppy understand the sale? If there was a promise that the sale was of an Irish setter bitch, was this ever stated? There are also the questions that the sellers did or did not ask, for instance about the job of the eventual owner of the dog, or whether she was well enough physically and financially capable to look after JJ. If the answer was in the affirmative, then the outcome could be that the contract was void for mistake. In other words, what did each party know, or should reasonably have known, about the other party's state of mind, and was either at fault? Other facts we do not know include whether the sale was *inter preasentes* (presumably it was) and whether the sellers knew that the recuperating mother of the children was to be owner of the dog. We also would need to know if there had been any misrepresentation to ground a claim under that heading,[62] if there were oral promises or a written contract containing

6.18

---

[57] Referred to at p. 66 of the judgment.
[58] [1960] N.Z.L.R. 406.
[59] See Reform of Mistake, Chap. 21.
[60] Twelfth Report of the Law Reform Committee, Cmrd. 2958 (1966), *Transfer of Title to Chattels*, paras 6 and 7, pp. 4–7.
[61] See Chap. 15.
[62] See Chap. 18.

express terms which would amount to a breach of contract by either party.[63] The case is complicated by the fact that the buyers were the children of Mrs Webb. If they were younger than 18, did they have capacity to contract[64] and how is the state of mind of children to be ascertained (on an objective basis)? They after all were the purchasers who were giving JJ as a gift to their mother. If they were older than 18, did they mention for whom the puppy was intended? This might raise the possibility of third party rights (see Contracts (Rights of Third Parties) Act 1999).[65] Might Mrs Webb have an action against the sellers if the dog was not of satisfactory quality?[66] On balance, it was almost certainly right that the contract should stand. The complicated visiting and breeding arrangement was not something a Court could normally order in a dispute over property of this kind, but rather a compromise solution.

---

[63] See Chap. 23.
[64] See Chap. 11.
[65] See Chap. 10.
[66] See Chap. 12.

Chapter 7

BASIC DOCTRINES OF CONSIDERATION

PROMISE AND CONSIDERATION

Any developed legal system must have a clear set of rules to determine which promises **7.1** are enforceable as contracts. Promises may be enforced on the basis of four alternative principles.[1]

First, that contracts must be put in writing. English law has had an ambivalent attitude to formalities. In the days when many people were illiterate, deeds were commonplace. Writing was seen as a bulwark against fraud. The Statute of Frauds 1677 provided six different categories of contracts which were required to be written or evidenced in writing. The Statute of Frauds has all but disappeared in England.[2] There are more recent requirements of writing, for instance in modern consumer legislation, and while these remain exceptional their number and importance is growing. Form is not a great indicator of enforceability in English law. Elsewhere, the civil law systems of Europe, under the influence of Roman law, place greater emphasis on formalities in the making of contracts. This also applied in Scots law, though the need for writing there has recently been curtailed.[3] In practice, most commercial contracts are put into writing, even though there is no formal requirement to do so, since commercial contracts are simply too important to leave as oral agreements, subject to the vagaries of mental recall.

The second principle upon which contracts may be enforced is that of the intention of the parties. In many legal systems intention to create legal relations is paramount. Once again the obvious illustration being the European legal systems in the civilian tradition. A gratuitous promise, seriously intended, is enforceable in most jurisdictions with a Roman law background. Until just over a hundred years ago, English law had no such rule that there had to be an intention to create contractual relations. This is now a factor in the formation of contracts under English law but remains a subsidiary requirement, and some traditionalists would still argue that it is not a pre-requisite of making a contract in English law.[4] If consideration were ever to be substantially reformed, or indeed abolished, intention to create legal relations could replace it as the main requirement for contract formation.

The third possibility for enforcing promises is that adopted by English law, namely the rules of consideration as the badge of enforceability. Consideration mainly applies to

---

[1] Fuller, "Consideration and Form" (1941) Col. L.R. 799.
[2] See Chap. 11.
[3] Requirements Of Writing (Scotland) Act 1995.
[4] Discussed in Chap. 11. The requirement of intention to create legal relations owes its origin to *Carlill v. Carbolic Smoke Ball* [1893] 2 Q.B. 163, see Chap. 2.

simple contracts. In one rare example where the writing is contained in a deed, a gratuitous promise, *i.e.* a gift, is enforceable without consideration. Finally, there is the test of
reliance by the promisee, usually linked with detriment by acting upon the promise. Under
this theory, promise becomes enforceable because of detrimental or reasonable reliance
without the need for consideration. In English law, the most notable example of this is to
be found in the doctrine of promissory estoppel.[5] Reliance alone is not yet a ground for a
cause of action based on a promise, though it has become so in other common law
systems.[6] All four tests of enforceability are therefore to be found in English law.

7.2   In this chapter, we consider the traditional approach of English contract theory – the
classical notion of consideration. Consideration is more than a single doctrine. It is a
series of doctrines each with a set of rules, which developed incrementally and later collectively merged by the nineteenth century to become a general requirement that in order
to make a contract there had to be consideration provided by the promisee. Promise is the
starting point for the formation of a contract. A promise is only enforceable as a contract
if it is supported by consideration. Consideration is defined as something of value in the
eyes of the law, given or promised by one party to the contract which makes the other
party's promise enforceable as a contract. The theory is that contract is an exchange or
bargain between two persons.

Historically, consideration has proved to be capable of changing its meaning. It is a
kind of legal chameleon. Modern contract law had its origins in the medieval system of
writs, in particular the writ of *assumpsit*. Consideration in return for a promise can be
found as early as Tudor times.[7] When Lord Mansfield became Chief Justice of the King's
Bench in the Eighteenth century, the great judge took a liberal attitude towards consideration as an essential requirement. In *Pillans and Rose v. Van Mierop and Hopkins*[8] he
rejected the idea that a written contract without consideration was not a contract.
Consideration was only evidence of the parties' intention; if this could be found by other
means, consideration was unnecessary. Lord Mansfield stated that "the ancient notion
about the want of consideration was for the sake of evidence only; for when it is reduced
into writing as in covenants, specialities and bonds etc. there was no objection to the
want of consideration . . . in commercial cases among merchants the want of consideration is not an objection". Lord Mansfield also argued that a previous moral obligation
was sufficient consideration for a future gratuitous promise. In *Hawkes v. Saunders*,[9]
Lord Mansfield stated "when a man is under a moral obligation, which no court of Law
or Equity can enforce, and promises, the honesty and rectitude of the thing is consideration . . . The ties of conscience upon an upright mind are a sufficient consideration".

In liberalising and rationalising commercial law, Lord Mansfield was ahead of time,
and his views did not prevail. As early as *Joseph Rann v. Isabella Hughes*[10] the reaction
had set in, and consideration was seen as necessary to all contracts unless made under
seal. The views of Lord Mansfield were explained in *Wennall v. Adney*,[11] a case we discuss

---

[5] See Chap. 9.
[6] See Chap. 9.
[7] *e.g. Joscelin and Shelton's case* (1557) 3 Leonard 4, 74 E.R. 503. The requirement of consideration was recognised in *Slade's case* (1602) 4 Co. Rep. 92a 76 E.R. 1072 and 1074. Thereafter, modern contract law based upon
consideration may be said to have developed.
[8] (1765) 3 Burr 1663, 97 E.R. 1035.
[9] (1782) 1 Cowp 289, 98 E.R. 1091.
[10] (1778) 7 Term Rep 350, 2 E.R. 18.
[11] (1802) 3 P and P 249, 127 E.R. 137.

later and which may be the starting point of the present era of consideration. Eventually, in *Eastwood v. Kenyon*,[12] consideration in the sense of something of economic worth or value was definitively established as the test of enforceability of promises in contract law. Consideration had became the golden rule in contract law and the key to enforceable promises. *Eastwood* also established that motives such as love and affection were not the same as consideration. Although consideration is nowadays under attack, the doctrine is still the lynchpin of contract law.

There are three main functions of the rules governing consideration. First, to mark **7.3** out the enforceability of promises. Secondly, to deal with the important problems of evidence and establishing the existence of contracts. Thirdly, as a means by which the courts could strike out various promises on grounds of public policy. Public policy is still a factor in the enforcement of promises. For instance, fear over extortion led to the rule that a promise to do something to which one is already contractually bound cannot be sufficient consideration.[13] Consideration is a useful and malleable doctrine for determining the enforceability of promises. In *Ward v. Byham*,[14] the father of an illegitimate child separated from his partner then offered the mother, £1 per week maintenance for the child so long as the child was "well looked after and happy". The defendant ceased the payments when the mother re-married. Denning L.J. took the unorthodox view that a promise to perform an existing duty could be good consideration.[15] The two other members of the Court of Appeal held that the mother did owe an existing duty to maintain the child, under the National Assurance Act 1948. There was consideration in the mother's undertaking to keep the child happy and to allow her to choose where to live. Morris L.J. held that the mother had provided sufficient consideration as she had promised to do more than the law required.[16] The idea of value in the eyes of the law is a very flexible instrument to do justice. The rule that consideration need not be adequate reflects the common law position that the courts will resist interfering with the parties own bargain and will not renegotiate a contract. The parties' are left free to determine their own price, in accordance with the market or their own subjective valuation.[17] The law upholds the position of free market capitalism.[18]

The problem of evidence is also at the core of the development of consideration. Medieval common lawyers were concerned that not only seriously intended but also provable promises should be enforced; the question was how to do so. The obvious answer was to put every contract in writing, but this was impractical in the days when the majority of people could neither read nor write and so this approach was both unsatisfactory and also open to abuse.[19] Elizabethan lawyers opted instead for the formality of the sealing of a deed, rather than signature, as sufficient proof indicating agreement to a promise. In the

---

[12] (1840) 11 A and E 438, 113 E.R. 482, discussed later p. 108.
[13] See Chap. 8.
[14] [1956] 1 W.L.R. 496.
[15] The standard view is that this is not good consideration, see Chap. 8.
[16] See also *Williams v. Williams* [1957] 1 ALL E.R. 305. Both of these cases were cited as authority for a wider and more liberal definition of consideration in relation to varying an existing contract in *Williams v. Roffey Brothers and Nicholls (Contractors) Ltd.* [1991] 1 Q.B. 1 (see p. 100 and Chap. 8).
[17] For the idea that in the eighteenth century there was a "sound price" doctrine which gave way to freedom of contract principle, see "The Transformation Debate", Chap. 14.
[18] This rule survives in the Unfair Terms in Consumer Contracts Regulations 1999 where the adequacy of the price is not subject to the fairness requirement, see Chap. 15.
[19] See the doctrine of *non est factum*, Chap. 21.

absence of sealing of a contract, consideration developed as the next best alternative. As early as *Sharington v. Strotton*[20] it was stated that "the law has often provided that a contract by words, shall not bind without consideration". It is from this that the doctrine of consideration developed.

When consideration is lacking

7.4   It is often only after the parties have fallen out with one another, and wish to find a means of escape from their relationship, that the question of consideration is raised retrospectively. Consideration may be used as a mere technical device in other words. Reliance theorists would argue that this exposes the essential emptiness of the doctrine and that detrimental reliance is a better measure of enforceability.[21] In *Thorensen Car Ferries Ltd v. Weymouth Portland BC*[22] Donaldson J. seemed to agree that consideration was not always the real reason for the dispute: "A defence of lack of consideration rarely has merit . . . The realities of the dispute were always known to both parties and they did not include the question of whether there was consideration for the contract". On the same theme, in *Bob Guiness Ltd v. Salomonsen*[23] Denning J. stated "It must be remembered that that which amounts in legal theory, to consideration, is sometimes a real consideration and sometimes not. Consideration in law is sometimes the real purchase price of a promise, and sometimes it is a mere fiction devised to make a promise enforceable".[24] This adds fuel to the critical view that it is time for the rules governing consideration to be reformed.[25]

A finding of insufficient consideration makes the contract unenforceable, not void. In *Dorimex v. Visage Imports Ltd*[26] Sir Richard Scott V.C. stated that:

> "A lack of consideration does not render an agreement void; it renders it unenforceable. If an agreement, unenforceable for want of consideration, is carried into effect by the parties, there is an end of the matter; unless of course there is some other vitiating feature. If A agrees with B to do a job for £100 and does it so well that B agrees to pay him an extra £50, the agreement as to the extra £50 is unenforceable, but it is not void; and if B does pay the £50 he cannot get it back".

What is Consideration?

A benefit, detriment or forbearance

7.5   Consideration is usually defined as either a benefit to the promisor *or* a detriment, or forbearance, by the promisee. This is the classic view, of which there are two famous statements. Patteson J. in *Eleanor Thomas v. Benjamin Thomas*[27] stated that consideration

---

[20]   (1565) 1 Plowd 300, 75 E.R. 454.
[21]   See Chap. 10. This is also a good example of the relational theory of contracts, see Chap. 1.
[22]   [1977] 2 Lloyd's Rep. 614 (at p. 619).
[23]   [1948] 2 K.B. 42 (at p. 45).
[24]   At p. 45.
[25]   See Chap. 9.
[26]   (unreported, Court of Appeal, 18 May 1999).
[27]   (1842) 2 Q.B. 851, 114 E.R. 330.

meant "something which is of some value in the eye of the law, moving from the plaintiff: it may be of some detriment to the plaintiff or some benefit to the defendant; but at all events it must be moving from the plaintiff". The second famous definition of consideration is that in *Currie v. Misa*,[28] where Lush J. stated that: "A valuable consideration, in the sense of the law, may consist either in some right, interest, profit or benefit accruing to one party, or some forbearance, detriment, loss or responsibility given, suffered or undertaken by the other". The benefit or detriment interchange represents the traditional idea of contract as being an exchange based upon a reciprocal obligation.

This remains the standard theory. A party seeking to establish the presence of consideration may do so by proving either that they conferred a benefit upon the promisee in return for the promise or that they incurred a detriment in so doing. In either case, there is "something of value in the eyes of the law" given in return for a promise. Consideration may be *either* a "benefit" to the promisor or a "detriment" to the promisee. It need not be both. Benefit or detriment are essentially different sides of the same coin. The benefit to one party is a detriment to the other. The consideration provides the antidote to each. In *Williams v. Roffey*[29] a practical benefit to both parties was held sufficient to vary an existing contract. This test would not be sufficient to create a contract however.[30] This is the reverse of the traditional approach whereby detriment to the promisee is the key factor. The courts are generally less concerned with finding benefit to the promisor if the promisee undertook some detriment in the form of an obligation or burden. The consideration must be causally connected with the promise. The promisor must have requested or accepted the detriment or benefit in return for their promise.

The judicial task of finding either benefit or detriment is illustrated by *Tanner v. Tanner*,[31] in which the plaintiff, Eric Tanner, was a milkman during the early hours of the day and a croupier in the evening. He had been married for many years and had a daughter and son, but he got "fed up" with married life and decided to go out to have a "good time". He met a woman, Josephine MacDermott, with whom he had two children. When the relationship ended she claimed to be entitled to remain in the house they had shared. The Court of Appeal held that there was a contract giving the plaintiff and her children a licence to remain in the property. She had suffered a detriment, which provided the necessary consideration, in giving up her rented flat to live with the plaintiff. The defendant had implicitly promised to allow her to live in their shared home, and this was irrevocable until the children were 16. As well as benefit or detriment, consideration may also consist of a forbearance. The promisee gives up, or promises to give up, something which they have "a right" to do. We return to the question of forbearance later in our discussion of the sufficiency doctrine.[32] **7.6**

The price given in return for a promise

This definition of consideration is particularly appropriate to contracts for the sale of goods. Consideration is viewed as the price requested by the promisor, in return for their **7.7**

---

[28] (1875) LR 10 Exch 153 (at p. 162).
[29] [1991] 1 Q.B. 1.
[30] See Chap. 8.
[31] [1975] 1 W.L.R. 1346.
[32] See pp. 102–104.

promise. In *Dunlop Pneumatic Tyre Co Ltd v. Selfridge & Co Ltd*,[33] Lord Dunedin adopted the definition of the great Oxford contract lawyer Sir Frederick Pollock,[34] that consideration was "an act or forbearance of one party, or the promise thereof is the price for which the promise of the other is bought, and the promise thus given for value is enforceable."[35] Consideration is the price paid for the promise. It is this which makes a contract into a binding agreement, rather than merely a voluntary arrangement. In practical terms, consideration is a brilliant idea which enables millions of contracts to be formed without cumbersome legal formalities. As a flexible and effective tool, consideration still has a great role part to play in modern contract law. However, admiration for it's practical simplicity has to be tempered with doubt. This was noted by Lord Dunedin in the *Dunlop Tyre* case who began his judgment,[36] with the observation that:

> "I confess that this case is to my mind apt to nip any budding affection which one might have had for the doctrine of consideration. For the effect of that doctrine in the present case is to make it possible for a person to snap his fingers at a bargain deliberately made, a bargain not in itself unfair and which the person seeking to enforce it has a legitimate interest to enforce."[37]

Consideration as a bargain between the parties

Consideration may alternatively be defined as a bargain based upon reciprocal obligations to which each party must therefore give something to the other by way of exchange. Bargain theory is influential in the United States. In the American Restatement (Second) of Contracts s. 71, in order to constitute consideration a performance or a return promise must be "bargained for". Under s. 71(2) "a performance or return promise is bargained for if it is sought by the promisor in exchange for his promise and is given by the promisee in exchange for that promise". This statement represents another view of contract as an exchange.

A practical benefit or mutual advantage

7.8   The fourth and most controversial definition of consideration which may apply in relation to a variation of a contract but not yet to its formation is that adopted by the Court of Appeal in *Williams v. Roffey Bros and Nicholls (Contractors) Ltd.*[38] A new definition of consideration as any practical benefit giving mutual advantage to each party might be sufficient to vary a contract. The case was largely about the question of a pre-existing contractual duty between a builder and sub-contractor. The Court of Appeal held that an additional payment to the plaintiff, a carpenter, to secure completion of work he was doing on a block of flats was enforceable. There was a benefit to the defendants in (i)

---

[33] [1915] A.C. 847.
[34] *Pollock on Contracts* (1876, 8th ed.), p. 175.
[35] At p. 855.
[36] At p. 855.
[37] Lord Dunedin, it might be pointed out, was a Scots lawyer whose contract law exists (proudly in the opinion of most) without the need for consideration. See Chap. 11.
[38] [1991] 1 Q.B. 1.

seeking to ensure that the plaintiff continued work and did not stop in breach of the subcontract, (ii) avoiding a penalty clause for delay and (iii) avoiding the trouble and expense of engaging a third party to complete the carpentry work. These were the practical benefits from the agreement to pay the bonus, and the Court of Appeal held that such practical benefits were capable of being sufficient consideration.[39] So far this definition has attracted mixed reactions.[40]

Any judicial reason for enforcing a promise

Public policy may have a hand in finding consideration or its absence. Consideration is an example of judicial policy making by which the courts shape contract law. This involves a wider view of the enforcement of promises that looks beyond the technical rules of the consideration. Consideration is therefore the reason for the promise, and can be applicable to a wide range of factors.[41] This view allows consideration to break free from it's historic boundaries to reflect modern commercial and social conditions and realities. Judges determining cases on grounds of policy is currently unfashionable, and viewed with suspicion, at best kept under firm control. Nevertheless, policy is never far from the surface of contract law.

THE BASIC RULES IN RELATION TO CONTRACTUAL FORMATION

Flowchart C (see p. 109) shows how the basic rules are applied leading to the formation   **7.9** of a contract.

Consideration may be executed or executory

Executed consideration means that a party's obligation has been performed. If consideration is executory, it remains to be performed in the future. In both cases there is good consideration. A promise to perform in the future is sufficient. Reliance theorists would limit the scope for recovering damages if the contract was entirely executory, *i.e.* unperformed by both parties, at the time of breach.

Consideration need not be adequate

The law does not enquire into the true worth of the contract, or strike out the price as being unfair. That has not traditionally been the role of the courts. The risk of making a good or a bad bargain rests on the party herself. Even before the present system of free-enterprise developed, the value of goods was recognised as being personal. In 1651, the philosopher and political scientist Thomas Hobbes wrote in *Leviathan* that: "The value of all things contracted for, is measured by the Appetite of the Contractors: and therefore the just value, is that which they be contented to give." The law reflects this position. Consideration does not have to be adequate, in other words, a true reflection of the

---

[39] Discussed in more detail in Chap. 8.
[40] See Chap. 8.
[41] See Atiyah, "Consideration: A Restatement" in *Essays on Contract* (1986, Clarendon Press, Oxford), Chap. 8.

worth value of what was given in exchange for the promise.[42] Even a nominal sum will be sufficient to make a contract. This is one of the great anomalies of the doctrine. Any token sum provided can amount to good consideration. In *Mountford v. Scott*[43] the defendant granted the plaintiffs a six month option to purchase his house for £10,000 in consideration of the sum of £1. This tiny sum amounted to valuable consideration which was sufficient to form a contract.[44] In the sixteenth century case *Sir Anthony Sturlyn v. Albany*[45] it was stated: "for when a thing is to be done by the plaintiff be it never so small, this is a sufficient consideration to ground an action".

7.10   Historically, there is scope for arguing that the price of a commodity was relevant to the enforceability of a sale in contract law. This was known as the "sound price" doctrine in the eighteenth century; an equitable notion that a "sound price warrants a sound commodity". The sound price doctrine was rejected at an early date, giving way to the idea of *caveat emptor, i.e.* let the buyer beware[46]. It was not the common law's role to remake a bargain for the parties.[47] Nevertheless, if there is something of value given by the promisee, the courts will usually try to find that there is sufficient consideration. Even apparently trivial items can amount to consideration if they have been accepted or requested by the promisor. In *Chappell & Co. Ltd v. Nestlé Co Ltd*[48] wrappers for chocolate bars were held to amount to part of the consideration.[49] At the other end of the scale, a party who has agreed over generous terms is not entitled to escape from the agreement on this ground alone. In *Newbold v. Leicester City Council*,[50] the Court of Appeal held that a Council which had agreed to pay lump sums in compensation to employees for reduction in earnings was not allowed to get out of the agreement because they had been "irrationally generous". The rule also applies under the modern regulation of consumer contracts. The fairness requirement is not imposed on terms relating to the price of goods and services under the Unfair Terms in Consumer Contracts Regulations 1999, with regard to the adequacy of the price or remuneration.[51]

Consideration must be sufficient in law

7.11   Sufficiency of consideration means satisfying the legal rules necessary to provide good consideration at law. This is usually something of economic value. If the consideration has a monetary worth, there is usually little problem, even if the consideration is apparently trivial. Intangible values, such as love and affection, or moral values do not generally amount to sufficient consideration. In *White v. Bluett*,[52] it was held that there

---

[42] The principle that the court will not, in general, investigate the adequacy of consideration is recognised and preserved by Unfair Terms in Consumer Contracts Regulations 1999. (See Chap. 15.)
[43] [1975] Ch. 258.
[44] Russell L.J. at p. 264.
[45] (1587) Cro. Eliz 78 E.R. 327 (at p. 328).
[46] An example of the "Transformation" from equity to law in Horowitz, *The Transformation of American Law* (1977, Harvard), p. 180 (discussed later, Chap. 14).
[47] See *Stuart v. Wilkins* (1778) 1 Doug 18, 99 E.R. 15.
[48] [1960] A.C. 87.
[49] See also *Esso Petroleum Co Ltd v. Customs and Excise Commissioners* [1976] 1 W.L.R. 1.
[50] *The Times*, August 20, 1999.
[51] Reg. 6(2). The rule only applies, however, if the term is written in "plain and intelligible language" (see Chap. 15).
[52] (1853) 23 L.J. Ex 36.

was no consideration for a promise by a father not to sue for money owed to him, if the son would stop complaining to him about how he would distribute his property. Parke B. asked counsel, "is an agreement by a father in consideration that his son will not bore him, a binding contract?" Counsel had argued that the son had a right to make the complaints mentioned, and his agreeing to forego that right was good consideration. There was a detriment in "not being able to continue his well-grounded complaint". The court rejected the argument. According to Pollock C.B.: "In reality, there was no consideration whatever. The son had no right to complain, for the father might make what distribution of his property he liked; and the son's abstaining from doing what he had no right to do can be no consideration."[53] A forbearance to act can be sufficient consideration. Giving up a right to do something which he is entitled to do can be a detriment to the promisee. In the American case *Hamer v. Sidway*[54] an uncle promised his nephew $5,000 if the nephew would refrain from "drinking liquor, using tobacco, swearing and playing cards or billiards for money until he should become 21 years of age". The nephew avoided all these temptations until he came of age in 1875 but the uncle's executors refused to pay the $5,000. The Court of Appeals in New York held that there was sufficient consideration because the nephew had a right to do all of these things and he had given up something of value by refraining from doing so. The nephew had provided consideration to support the promise to pay. Parker J. stated that consideration meant not so much that one party had benefitted as that the other had abandoned some legal right, or limited his legal freedom of action in the future, as an inducement for the promise of the other party. It was sufficient that he "restricted his lawful freedom of action within certain prescribed limits upon the faith of his uncle's agreement, and now, having fully performed the conditions imposed, it is of no moment whether such performance actually proved a benefit to the promisor, and the court will not inquire into it".[55] The promise was enforceable as the forbearance provided good consideration.

What is the present position in English law on forbearance? In *White v. Bluett* it was held that the son had no right to complain. He therefore gave up nothing by not doing so. However, if the American view of *Hamer* is preferred, the nephew did provide consideration. The modern approach suggests that *Hamer* might now be the better authority. In *Hamer v. Sidway* the New York court noted that the nephew had used tobacco and drunk liquor in the past. What if he never had done so, nor ever intended to do so? The issue was discussed in *Arrale v. Costain Civil Engineering Ltd*,[56] in which the plaintiff, Abdullah Arrale, was a worker who had to have his left arm amputated as a result of an industrial accident while building a harbour wall at Dubai. He obtained a sum of money under a state statutory compensation scheme while in Dubai, and, when accepting, signed a receipt accepting the amount in "full satisfaction and discharge of all claims in respect of personal injury whether now or hereafter to become manifest arising directly or indirectly from the accident". Later he came to England and issued a writ claiming damages for negligence at common law. Lord Denning[57] thought there was no true

7.12

---

[53] At p. 37.
[54] (1891) 27 NE 256.
[55] The New York Court cited the English case of *Shadwell v. Shadwell* (1860) 9 C.B.N.S. 159, 142 E.R. 62, as authority.
[56] [1976] Lloyd's Rep. 98.
[57] At p. 102.

agreement between the parties to compromise all future claims. According to Geoffrey Lane L.J.: "It is no consideration to refrain from a course of action which it was never intended to pursue."[58] The plaintiff had provided no consideration for the compromise which was not therefore enforceable.

Compromise of claims is a widespread practice in relation to civil litigation whereby one party settles and the other compromises a dispute without admitting liability. This arrangement differs from a forbearance where the party gives up a right of action. Compromise agreements are generally enforceable, since both parties give up something and thereby provide fresh consideration.[59] This applies even if the claim would not have succeeded. The rule does not apply if the party knew that their claim was bound to fail, however.[60] A release from further claims of which a party was unaware at the time of the agreement can be set aside in equity for unconscionability.[61]

Consideration must be causally related to the promise

7.13   There has to be a causal connection between the promise given and the consideration provided, in other words, one must have been given in return for the other. The mere conferment of a benefit by chance will not suffice. Consideration is usually given either at the request or with the acceptance, express or implied, of the promisor. In *Combe v. Combe*[62] a husband promised his wife whom he was divorcing that he would pay her a sum of £100 a year. She refrained from proceedings for financial provision but this was held not to be a forbearance amounting to consideration as the husband had not requested her to do so. The causal connection between promise and consideration is illustrated by *Wigan v. English and Scottish Law Life Assurance Association*[63] in which William Hackblock took out life insurance on his own life for £5000. The insurance coverage did not apply if he died, "by his own hands, by duelling or by the hands of justice". Hackblock was in financial straits and owed Sir Frederick Wigan £15,000. As security Hackblock delivered the policy to solicitors with instructions to assign the policy to Wigan, but to use their discretion as to whether they told Wigan of the assignment to him. In fact the solicitors obtained a promise of more time to repay the debt from Wigan and, acting on Hackblock's instructions, destroyed the assignment of the insurance policy. William Hackblock committed suicide, without notice of the assignment of the policy having been given either to Wigan or the insurers. In an action by Wigan's estate to recover the policy money it was held that there was no valuable consideration for the assignment. The existence of an antecedent debt was not consideration for security given by the debtor. Consideration and promise must be causally linked in that one is given in response to the other. Since that was not the case here, the plaintiffs' action failed.

---

[58] At p. 106, citing as authority *Cook v. Wright* (1861) 1 B & S 559, 121 E.R. 822.
[59] *BCCI v. Ali* [2001] 2 W.L.R. 735.
[60] *Callisher v. Bischoffsheim* (1869) LR 5 Q.B. 449.
[61] *BCCI v. Ali* [2001] 2 W.L.R. 735. (Regarding damages for loss of commercial reputation in this case, see Chap. 25).
[62] [1951] 2 K.B. 215.
[63] [1909] 1 Ch. 291.

Consideration must not be past

The rule that consideration must be given in return for the promise is related to the rule **7.14** that consideration must not be past. This is one of the oldest aspects of the doctrine of consideration. A promise given after the consideration has been provided is gratuitous. In *Roscorla v. Thomas*,[64] a case from the Cornwall Assizes, the plaintiff bought a horse from the defendant who promised the plaintiff that the horse "did not exceed five years old" and "was sound and free from vice".[65] In fact "on the contrary thereof" it was found by the Court that the horse was "vicious, restive, ungovernable and ferocious" and the plaintiff sued for breach of the promise. The action failed since the consideration provided by the plaintiff was already past when the promise by the defendant that the horse was "free from vice" was made. The warranty was not given in return for the promise of payment made for the horse and, being made after the sale, was gratuitous and therefore insufficient consideration. Denman C.J. stated the rule[66] that "the promise must be coextensive with the consideration . . . the precedent sale without a warranty, though at the request of the defendant imposes no other duty or obligation on him. It is clear therefore that the consideration stated would not raise an implied promise that the horse was sound or free from vice". It is interesting to note that although the judgment was given two years after that in *Eastwood v. Kenyon*[67] which rejected the idea, the Court was still prepared to countenance moral obligations as providing consideration. The exceptions where there was insufficient consideration to support an implied promise, but which would support an express one, were voidable contracts subsequently ratified, statute barred debts subsequently revived and "equitable and moral obligations which but for some rule of law, would of themselves have been sufficient to require an implied promise".[68]

The past consideration rule applied in more modern times in *Re McArdle*,[69] in which a will executed by William McArdle left property to his wife Holly in trust for their four children. One of his sons, Monty McArdle, and his wife, Marjorie, took over a bungalow at Wimborne and did it up at a cost of £488. Later Monty and Marjorie presented a document containing a promise that "In consideration of your carrying out certain alterations and improvements to the property" the other McArdle children would pay Monty and Marjorie £488 for their expenditure. This was held to be unenforceable as all the work had been done before the promise was made. The Court of Appeal held that the alterations and improvements completed before the signing of the undertaking by the children amounted to past consideration. "The true position" (according to Jenkins L.J.) was that "the work had in fact all been done and nothing remained to be done by Mrs Marjorie McArdle at all, the consideration was a wholly past consideration, and therefore the beneficiaries' agreement for the repayment to her of the £488 out of the estate was a *nudum pactum* [a bare promise], a promise with no consideration to support it".[70]

The fact that the consideration precedes the promise does not necessarily make the **7.15** consideration past. The conduct may be such as to raise a presumption that there

---

[64] (1842) 3 Q.B. 235, 114, E.R. 496.
[65] At p. 497.
[66] At p. 498.
[67] (1840) 11 A and E 438, 113 E.R. 482.
[68] At p. 498.
[69] [1951] Ch. 669.
[70] At p. 678.

should be an implied term for payment. The service must be both requested by the promisor and on the understanding that it would be paid for by him. An example, from Jacobean times is *Lampleigh v. Brathwait*,[71] in which the defendant, Thomas Brathwait, having murdered a man, Patrick Mahume, asked the plaintiff, Anthony Brathwait, to travel from London to Royston where King James I was staying and attempt to obtain a Royal pardon. The plaintiff duly obtained the requested pardon at his own expense. The defendant then promised to pay him £100 but later changed his mind and refused to do so. The defendant argued that there was no consideration for the promise. The Court held that the plaintiff was entitled to recover because the request for the service provided included an implied promise to pay. In *Pao On v Lau Yiu Long*,[72] the Privy Council laid down the requirements for an action completed before a promise could be recognised as consideration:

(i)   the service must have been rendered at the promisor's request;

(ii)   the parties must have understood that the act was to be paid for or result in some benefit to the other party; and

(iii) the payment, or the conferment of a benefit, would have to have been legally enforceable had it been promised in advance.
       If these conditions apply, a later promise to pay is enforceable if rendered at the request of a party and on a clear understanding that payment would be made in due course so long as the payment would be legally enforceable if it had been promised in advance.

Consideration must move from the promisee but need not move to the promisor

7.16   The promisee has to prove that the consideration was provided by them and not a third party. The consideration does not have to move to the promisor, however, but may go to a third party instead. In *Pearl Carriers Inc v. Japan Lines Ltd (The Chemical Venture)*[73] payments were made by the charterers of the ship to the crew of the vessel. It was held that these were consideration for a promise made by the shipowners to the charterers. The rule that consideration must move from the promisee still exists in relation to the formation of any contract. In theory, the promisee must still provide consideration before any contract comes into existence. However, the application of the rule that only the parties to the original contract may benefit is now subject to the Contracts (Rights of Third Parties) Act 1999. The rule that consideration must move from the promisee is effectively abolished as far as third parties are concerned unless the parties choose to exclude the Act in making their contract.[74]

---

[71] (1615) Hobart 105, 80 E.R. 255.
[72] [1980] A.C. 614.
[73] [1993] 1 Lloyd's Rep. 509 (at p. 522).
[74] See Chap. 10.

Consideration distinguished from related concepts

(1) Motive is not the same as consideration

Motive and consideration are closely linked, both being a reason for agreeing and hence making the promise enforceable. The motive of a party for contracting is subjective, however, and consideration which is defined as "something of value in the cases of the law" is regarded as objective. Usually the latter will be an economic value of worth rather than merely a personal motivation for action. In *Thomas v. Thomas*[75] Patterson J. stated: "Motive is not the same thing [as] consideration."[76] In *Bob Guiness Ltd v. Salomonsen*[77] Denning J. stated: "The real consideration for the promise was the antecedent betting debt. The motive which prompted the promise was the desire that the winner should forbear, but motive is not the same thing as consideration".[78] The difficulty of ascertaining the motives of an individual may account for the law's reluctance to allow motive alone to count. Consideration must therefore be more than the subjective reason for contracting.[79]

(2) Gratuitous promise or gift.

A gift is not a contract in English law. In *Colonia v. Amoco Oil*[80] the issue was whether   **7.17**
payments made were a gift or to settle disputed claims. Potter J. stated: "Far from being a windfall the payment was made pursuant to an enforceable agreement . . . and could in no sense be regarded as a gift".[81] Gifts are an example of gratuitous promises, known in the old days as *nudum pactum* (literally a bare promise). They are enforceable if made by deed. The words *ex gratia*, *i.e.* without obligation, are often used to denote no liability, contractual or otherwise.[82]

(3) Condition distinguished from consideration

Consideration must be distinguished from the fulfilment or occurrence of a condition.[83] So if Cynthia promises Brian "I shall pay you £1000 if you score a century playing cricket for your club this season", this is not a contract, but a gratuitous promise subject to a condition. However, if A promises B "if you contract influenza after buying and using my Smokeball . . ." then this is a contract. The catching influenza is a condition but consideration is provided by using the Smokeball. The condition entitles the party to enforce the promise which is supported by consideration.[84]

(4) Consideration must be more than a moral obligation   **7.18**

This brings us back to the great debate over the nature of consideration. Lord Mansfield had tried to liberalise the definition of consideration so that the making of a promise

---

[75] (1842) 2 Q.B. 851, 114 E.R. 330.
[76] At p. 341.
[77] [1948] 2 K.B. 42.
[78] At p. 47.
[79] However, in *Williams v. Roffey* [1991] 1 Q.B. 1, subjective or practical benefit to both parties appeared to be sufficient. (See earlier p. 100, and Chap. 8.)
[80] [1995] 1 Lloyd's Rep. 570.
[81] At p. 577.
[82] See Chap. 11 on intention to create legal relations.
[83] On the various meanings of the word "condition" in contract law, see Chap. 13.
[84] See *Carlill v. Carbolic Smoke Ball Co.* [1893] 2 Q.B. 163 (discussed Chap.2).

would be sufficient consideration because of the moral imperative to perform according to one's word. No other material detriment had to be shown. This view was rejected in the case which enthroned consideration as the ultimate requirement of a contract in England to the present time. In *Eastwood v. Kenyon*[85] the plaintiff was the executor of the will of John Sutcliffe, who died leaving a daughter Sarah, a small child. Sarah later married the defendant. In the meanwhile, Sarah's guardian until she reached adulthood, spent £140 in looking after and improving the estate, using money borrowed from another party, Blackburn, to whom he had provided a promissory note. When Sarah married the defendant, he promised to repay the loan but when he failed to do so was sued by the plaintiff. The issue was whether the claim showed sufficient consideration for the promise. The plaintiff argued that a moral consideration was sufficient to support a promise. Lord Denman, in one of the most important judgments in the history of contract law, held that a moral obligation was not enough to provide consideration.[86] If a moral obligation to act were sufficient "the doctrine would annihilate the necessity for any consideration at all, in as much as the mere fact of giving a promise creates a moral obligation to perform it". Having rejected this view, Lord Denman went on to point out its dangers and consequences:

> "The enforcement of such promises by law, however plausibly reconciled by the desire to effect all conscientious engagements, might be attended with mischievous consequences to society; one of which would be the frequent preference of voluntary undertakings to claims for just debts. Suits would therefore be multiplied . . . to the prejudice of real creditors".

7.19   It is interesting to note that Lord Denman's authority for this view of consideration, which has lasted for more than 150 years, is the earlier case of *Wennall v. Adney*[87], a case which rejected the moral obligation test of consideration. Lord Denman approved an editors note to that case which read as follows:

> ". . . an idea has prevailed of late years that an express promise, founded simply on an antecedent moral obligation, is sufficient to support an *assumpsit*. It may be worth consideration, however, whether this proposition be not rather inaccurate, and whether that inaccuracy had not in a great measure arisen from some expressions of Lord Mansfield . . . which if construed with the qualifications fairly belonging to them, do not warrant the conclusion, which appears to have been rather hastily drawn from thence". The present law may therefore correctly be said to be based on this view of *Wennall v. Adney* in 1802."

---

[85] (1840) 11 A and E 438, 113 E.R. 482.
[86] The notion of *pacta sunt servanda, i.e.* that promises create a moral imperative to perform, has a long history. It is still relevant today, see the "performance interest" in damages, Chap. 24.
[87] (1802) 3 B and P 249, 127 E.R. 137.

Flowchart C: Consideration in the Formation of a Contract

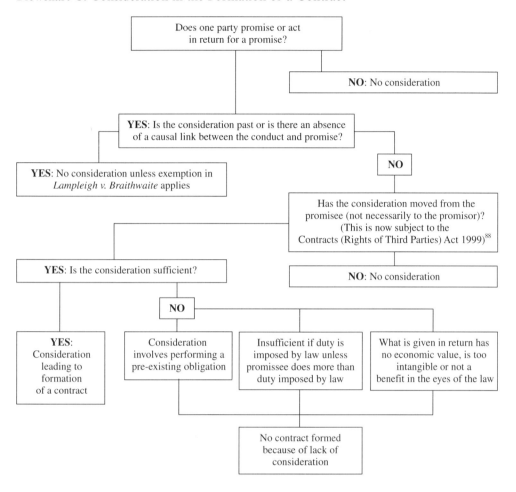

Chapter 8

Varying the Contractual Nexus

Introduction

Consideration is required for the variation of a contract as well as in its formation. If one party promises to modify their obligations without a fresh consideration being provided in return, the promise to vary the original agreement is gratuitous and therefore unenforceable. This is an unsatisfactory aspect of the sufficiency doctrine and often leads to unfairness or inconvenience. The rule also tends to defeat a key objective of contract law, namely, that of fulfilling the reasonable expectations of the parties.[1] This leads to a discussion of reforming consideration, a debate which has been in progress for many decades.

Giving Extra

It is not sufficient consideration to promise more or undertake additional acts if there already exists a pre-existing legal, statutory or contractual duty. The promise to give an extra amount is gratuitous, unless something additional is given in return, and so the promise to pay extra is unenforceable. This can often create difficulties and misunderstandings in practice. **8.1**

Performing a duty imposed by law or by statute

A legal or statutory duty to perform some act will render a subsequent promise to do the same, thing or to pay extra, ineffective as the promise lacks consideration. In *Collins v. Godefroy*[2] it was held that a promise to pay a witness who was already subpoenaed to attend a trial was not supported by consideration. He was unable to recover his fee or compensation for his loss of time. Under modern statutory rules, a contract to pay fees to an expert witness is valid.[3] If a person does, or promises to do, more than they are

---

[1] See Chap. 1.
[2] (1831) 1 Ad 950, 109 E.R. 1040.
[3] See *Goulden v. Wilson Barca, The Times*, August 20, 1999. Nowadays there are statutory rules allowing payment of expenses to witnesses. Under the Civil Procedure Rules 1999 r. 34.7, a witness must be offered a reasonably sufficient sum to cover their expenses travelling to and from the court.

required to do by law, that may have the effect of providing fresh consideration. For instance, in *Glasbrook Brothers v. Glamorgan County Council*,[4] during a strike, extra police protection was called for by the owners of a coal mine. Although the police were under a duty to maintain law and order, they were held to be entitled to payment for the increased level of policing provided which went beyond their normal duties. Similarly, in *Harris v. Sheffield United Football Club Ltd*,[5] where the issue was the provision of "special police services" under the Police Act 1964 at a football ground, Bramall Lane, in Sheffield, the Court of Appeal held that these were services for which payment had to be made. Neill L.J. laid down four guidelines in the form of questions as to when the cost of the additional services provided were recoverable:

(i) "Are the police officers required to attend on private premises or in a public place?";

(ii) "Has some violence or other emergency already occurred or is it immediately imminent?";

(iii) "What is the nature of the event or occasion at which the officers are requested to attend?"; and

(iv) "Can the provision of the necessary amount of police protection be met from the resources available to the Chief Constable without the assistance of officials who would otherwise be engaged in other duties or off duty?"[6]

Pre-existing contractual obligations

8.2 The rule with regard to pre-existing duties and consideration applies with equal force to a contractual duty to perform a contract. The classic case is *Stilk v. Myrick*,[7] the judgement in which is capable of two interpretations, depending upon which report is used. The Espinasse report stresses the policy aspects of the judgment, the other by Campbell has, however, been more influential.[8] The contract in question was between the master and crew of a vessel on a round trip between London and the Baltic. At Kronstadt near St Petersburg in the Gulf of Finland, two crew members deserted. The captain promised to distribute the wages of the two men among the remaining members of the crew if they did the extra work required to get the vessel home. The owners refused to pay the money to the sailors when they returned to England. The Court found in favour of the defendants. The crew were already contractually bound to operate the ship, so a promise to pay more was not good consideration. The public policy argument behind this was to prevent contractual variations by extortion or economic duress.[9] Lord Ellenborough, on the other hand, said that the reason for the judgment was that there was no consideration for the agreement, the seamen being under

---

[4] [1925] A.C. 270.
[5] [1987] 2 All E.R. 838.
[6] At pp. 846–847.
[7] (1809) 2 Camp 317, 170 E.R. 1168, 6 Esp 129, 170 E.R. 851.
[8] Espinesse has a low reputation as a Court Reporter. He actually appeared as Counsel in this case. For an account of the case and its reports see Luther, "Campbell, Espinesse and the Sailors: text and context in the common law" (1999) 19 Legal Studies 526.
[9] See Chap. 19.

an existing contractual duty to the ship owner. The fear of economic duress and public policy were present in the background nevertheless. The issue had already been litigated upon, with a similar outcome.

In an earlier case *Harris v. Watson*[10] the plaintiff, a seaman, was promised five guineas "over and above his common wages" to perform some extra duties in navigating a ship, the *Alexander*, to Lisbon. The plaintiff stated that this had been done because the ship was in danger and the master wished to encourage the crew to "exert themselves". The plaintiff was nonsuited, *i.e.* he had no claim. Lord Kenyon based his judgment on policy, stating that:

> "If this action was to be supported it would materially affect the navigation of this Kingdom. This rule is founded on a principle of policy for if sailors were in all events to have their wages and in times of danger entitled to insist on an extra charge on such a promise as this, they would in many cases suffer a ship to sink, unless the captain would pay any extravagant demand they might think proper to make."[11]

The exceptions to the rule in *Stilk v. Myrick*

8.3 The rule does not apply in three cases. First, if exceptional and unforeseen risks have arisen and require the extra payment, this may be binding.[12] Secondly, if a new agreement is made at a higher rate of pay or to settle a dispute, this may be binding. This is a form of discharge by agreement[13] and substitutes a new contract, in place of the old, so this is not a true exception. Thirdly, if one party is in breach of the agreement but promises extra to the other to continue, this will be binding. In *Turner v. Owen*[14] Cockburn C.J. told the jury that when a seaman signed articles "he cannot claim extra remuneration for the same services as are included in the articles . . . If, before the ship sets sail, the seaman discovers that she is one in which he cannot safely embark, he can refuse to do so and enter into a new contract".

The pre-existing contract rule does not apply to promises made to third parties.

If one party, Andy, is already obliged to do something for the other party to a contract, Ben, and promises to do the thing for a third party, Chris, then his promise does not lack consideration. Andy suffers a detriment by making the second contract because he may now be subject to two actions for breach of contract. The leading case *Scotson v. Pegg*[15] in which it was already held that the performance of an act which a person has already agreed with another to perform, was good consideration for a contract with a third party.

---

[10] (1791) Peake 102, 170 E.R. 94.
[11] At p. 94.
[12] See *Hartley v. Ponsonby* (1857) 7 E and B 872.
[13] See p. 124.
[14] (1862) 3 Fed F 176, 176 E.R. 79 where a sailor received extra wages for continuing to discharge his duties on an unseaworthy ship returning from the Falkland Islands.
[15] (1861) 6 H and N 295, 158 E.R. 121.

The third party must, however, gain a benefit from the performance. This rule is now subject to the Contracts (Rights of Third Parties) Act 1999.[16]

Revisiting the pre-existing contract rule: the carpenter who was offered extra to finish the job

8.4   The issue of a pre-existing contract and promises to pay more to complete the work arose in a case we have already encountered, *Williams v. Roffey Brothers and Nicholls (Contractors) Ltd.*[17] The Court of Appeal held that a promise to pay more money under an existing contract could amount to enforceable consideration. In doing so, the Court also suggested a new, more liberal, definition of consideration for contractual variations.[18] It is one of the most discussed cases in contract law of modern times. Views on the judgment range from enthusiasm to cynicism or downright opposition. Time will tell whether this is to be regarded as a landmark decision or "confined to its facts", *i.e.* consigned to the waste paper bin.

The plaintiff, Lester Williams, entered into a subcontract with the defendants to do carpentry work to refurbish a block of 27 flats in West London for £20,000. After the plaintiff had completed only nine of the flats, he found himself in financial difficulties, due in part to the agreed price being too low and also his own failure to supervise properly the work. The defendants, meanwhile, were potentially liable under a "penalty clause" if their own main contract was not completed on time. The defendants therefore agreed to pay the plaintiff an extra £10,300 at a rate of £575, on completion of each flat. Seven weeks later the plaintiff had substantially completed eight further flats and the defendants made one further payment of £1,500. At this point the plaintiff stopped work. The plaintiff sued for the extra money agreed. The defendants argued that there was no consideration because the plaintiff was already contractually bound to finish the job.

The Court of Appeal held that the promise to pay extra was binding. There was consideration for the second agreement to make the additional payment, even although there was an existing contractual obligation between the parties, so long as the defendants had either secured a benefit, or avoided a detriment or disbenefit. The defendants obtained a commercial advantage from the plaintiff agreeing to complete the flats and this was good consideration. This was, however, subject to the promise not being secured by economic duress (which did not arise in this case) or fraud.

8.5   The Court of Appeal did not regard themselves as overruling *Stilk v. Myrick*, which was "distinguished". Glidewell L.J. stated in reference to *Stilk v. Myrick* that the holdings in *Williams* "refine and limit the application of that principle, but they leave the principle unscathed".[19] The Court of Appeal relied on several earlier authorities to support its holding. Glidewell L.J. stated that, following the decision of the majority in *Ward v. Byham,*[20] the whole court in *Williams v. Williams,*[21] and the Privy Council in *Pao*

---

[16] See Chap. 10.
[17] [1991] 1 Q.B. 1.
[18] Or, by extension, to formation of contracts at some future date.
[19] At p. 16.
[20] [1956] 1 W.L.R. 486.
[21] [1957] 1 W.L.R. 148.

On v. Lau Yiu Long,[22] the present state of the law on this subject could be expressed as follows:

> "(i) If A has entered into a contract with B to do work for, or supply goods or services to, B in return for payment from B; and (ii) at some time before A has completely performed his obligations under the contract, B has reason to doubt whether A will, or will be able to, complete his side of the bargain; and (iii) B thereupon promises A an additional payment in return for A's promise to perform his contractual obligations on time; and (iv) as a result of giving his promise, B obtains in practice a benefit, or obviates a disbenefit; and (v) B's promise is not given as a result of fraud or economic duress on the part of A; then (vi) the benefit to B is capable of being consideration for B's promise, so that the promise will be legally binding."[23]

The Court of Appeal held that since the plaintiff had substantially completed eight of the flats, he was entitled to part of the extra sum as promised.[24] Since he had not been paid for this work, he was entitled to down tools and was not himself in breach of contract in so doing. The case is of considerable importance because it advances the arguments about consideration and appears to fly in the face of earlier authorities. It also has significant practical and legal ramifications, particularly for construction contracts. There are, therefore, three important strands to the judgment in *Williams v. Roffey:* (a) the finding of consideration for a subsequent variation of a pre-existing contract; (b) the re-definition of consideration; and (c) the possibility of raising other doctrines in argument. We shall discuss each of these in turn.

(1) Finding consideration in a promise to pay more under an existing contract

This is the hub of the argument over *Williams v. Roffey*. Counsel for the plaintiff argued **8.6** that "it is in the interest of commercial reality that the parties should be allowed to agree that if the contract price for a subcontracted job is too low it should be increased". There was (he claimed) a common practice in the building industry for main contractors to increase subcontractors payments. He cited *Finland Steamship Co Ltd v. Felixstowe Dock and Railway Co*[25] as authority for agreed variations of a contract. In *Williams,* according to the plaintiff, the agreement could have legal effect for three reasons. First, there were benefits and detriments to both parties, for instance, in the avoidance of the penalty clauses. Secondly, that *Stilk v. Myrick* was distinguishable on this basis. Furthermore, *Stilk* did not apply to the building trade where such variations were said to be commonplace. Finally, with the development of the concept of economic duress,[26] the rule in *Stilk v. Myrick* was "neither necessary nor desirable" and should no longer be regarded as good law.[27] In reply the defendants' argument was based on traditional legal principles. The benefits conferred on the defendants, *i.e.* (i) that the plaintiff continued work and did not breach the contract; (ii) the avoidance of the penalty clause; and (iii) avoiding

---

[22] [1979] A.C. 614.
[23] At pp. 615–616.
[24] On the doctrine of substantial performance, see Chap. 23.
[25] [1980] 2 Lloyd's Rep. 287.
[26] See Chap. 14.
[27] [1991] 1 Q.B. 1 (at p. 4).

having to go elsewhere to engage other persons to finish the work, were all of a "practical nature". The defendants "derived no benefit in law since the plaintiff was promising to do no more than he was already bound to do by his subcontract". To allow variations such as that in the present case would undermine agreed contracts, particularly in the construction industry. The Court found that there was sufficient consideration for the promise to pay more. In so doing they also softened the requirement of what amounts to consideration at least as a requirement for varying an agreement.

(2) The meaning of consideration reconsidered: a pragmatic approach

In order to find for the plaintiff, the Court of Appeal had to find fresh consideration in the new arrangement. The narrower definitions of consideration in the past were rejected.[28] Russell L.J. stated: "I do not believe that the rigid approach to the concept of consideration to be found in *Stilk v. Myrick* is either necessary or desirable. Consideration there must still be but, in my judgment, the courts nowadays should be more ready to find its existence so as to reflect the intention of the parties to the contract where the bargaining powers are not unequal and where the finding of consideration reflects the true intention of the parties."[29]

8.7   Russell L.J. saw benefits to both parties in the renegotiation because the original price, it was accepted, was too low to complete the work profitably, and the defendants were able to continue with the services of the plaintiff without having to search for another subcontractor. There was a new formalised method of payment to replace the previous haphazard scheme. These were all "advantages" to the defendant "which can fairly be said to have been in consideration of their undertaking to pay the additional £10,300."[30] Russell L.J. stated:

> "True it was that the plaintiff did not undertake to do any work additional to that which he had originally undertaken to do but the terms upon which he was to carry out the work were varied and, in my judgment, that variation was supported by consideration which a pragmatic approach to the true relationship between the parties readily demonstrates."

Purchas L.J. was prepared to look for "mutual advantages" which would amount to sufficient consideration to support the second agreement to pay the extra amount: "There is clearly a commercial advantage to both sides from a pragmatic point of view . . . As a result of the agreement the defendants secured their position commercially".[31]

8.8   Purchas L.J. described the idea that a party could claim that by not breaching a contract he had provided consideration for carrying on as "distinctly unattractive". The test was whether each party obtained commercial practical benefits even if neither suffered any detriment as a result:[32]

> "I consider that the modern approach to the question of consideration would be that there were benefits derived by each party to a contract of variation. Even

---

[28] See Chap. 7.
[29] At p. 18.
[30] At p. 19.
[31] At p. 22.
[32] At p. 23.

though one party did not suffer a detriment this would not be fatal to the establishing of sufficient consideration to support the agreement. If both parties benefit from an agreement it is not necessary that each also suffers a detriment."[33]

Stilk v. Myrick was not overruled however, it was distinguished. Glidewell L.J. stated:[34]

"If it be objected that the propositions above contravene the principle in *Stilk v. Myrick*, I answer that in my view they do not; they refine, and limit the application of that principle, but they leave the principle unscathed *e.g.* where B secures no benefit by his promise. It is not in my view surprising that a principle enunciated in relation to the rigours of seafaring life during the Napoleonic wars should be subjected during the succeeding 180 years to a process of refinement and limitation in its application in the present day."

Russell L.J.[35] added:

"For my part I wish to make it plain that I do not base my judgment upon any reservation as to the correctness of the law long ago enunciated *Stilk v. Myrick*. A gratuitous promise, pure and simple, remains unenforceable unless given under seal. But where, as in this case, a party undertakes to make a payment because by so doing it will gain an advantage arising out of the continuing relationship with the promisee the new bargain will not fail for want of consideration".

Finally, Purchas L.J. was not convinced by counsel's arguments that both *Stilk v. Myrick* and *Harris v. Watson* were cases of *nisi prius* in the Court of King's Bench in Guildhall and could therefore easily be overruled by the Court of Appeal.

(3) Could other doctrines have been raised in argument?

(a) Promissory estoppel

In *Williams* the Court of Appeal might have grasped the nettle and allowed promissory   **8.9**
estoppel to create a cause of action to enable the plaintiff to claim his extra money.[36] There were two compelling reasons why they were unable to do so. First, promissory estoppel was not pleaded at first instance, so there were procedural reasons for not being able to raise the matter on appeal. Secondly, the Court of Appeal was bound by precedent to reject such an argument. However, one detects a note of sympathy for the use of promissory estoppel in this situation. As well as re-iterating the point that the plaintiff might have used promissory estoppel in his claim as an additional weapon (so long as it was not his only argument), Russell L.J. would have:

---

[33] In (1996) *Journal of the Chartered Institute of Arbitrators*, "Arbitration", p. 296, the reaction to the judgment in *Williams* was negative: "This judgment would appear incomprehensible to the average planning engineer for it would be inconceivable, that, when working on the refurbishment of a number of flats that a sub-contractor would not complete his work progressively on a flat-by-flat basis. That he should receive a 50% mark up for doing what anyone would naturally expect, must appear unbelievable."

[34] At p. 16.

[35] At p. 19.

[36] Promissory estoppel cannot be used as a cause of action in England at present, see Chap. 10.

"welcomed the development of argument, if it could have been properly raised in this court, on the basis that there was here an estoppel and the defendants, in the circumstances prevailing, were precluded from raising the defence that their under-taking to pay the extra £10,300 was not binding".[37]

An opportunity was therefore sadly missed.

(b) Economic duress

The question of economic duress was not an issue in *Williams* as the initiative for paying the extra money came from the defendants, not from the plaintiff. If economic pressure amounting to duress had been applied by the plaintiff in threatening not to finish the work unless paid extra for doing so, this would have rendered the agreement to pay voidable.[38]

(4) The aftermath of *Williams*

(a) Distinguished or explained

8.10   In *Re Selectmove Ltd*[39] the Court of Appeal refused to extend the principle laid down in *Williams v. Roffey Bros* to part payment of a debt.[40] A company had offered to pay its arrears by instalments to the Inland Revenue who said that they would let them know in due course if this was acceptable. The company heard nothing further, but paid some instalments believing an agreement to be in place. This was premature because they then received a threat of legal proceedings by the Inland Revenue if the full arrears were not paid immediately. The Court of Appeal was not prepared to allow *Williams v. Roffey* to overrule the House of Lords in *Foakes v. Beer*[41] that part payment of a debt cannot be good consideration.[42] The company, Selectmove, had argued that it had provided con-sideration, in that it was to the "practical benefit" of the Inland Revenue for the company to stay in business and continue to make payments, rather than go into liquidation, which would mean the Revenue recovering even less. Peter Gibson L.J., rejected Selectmove's argument and declined to follow *Williams*[43]:

"I see the force of the argument [that *Foakes v. Beer* be reconsidered],[44] but the dif-ficulty that I feel with it is that if the principle of *Williams'* case is to be extended to an obligation to make payment, it would in effect leave the principle in *Foakes v. Beer* without any application. When a creditor and a debtor who are at arm's length reach agreement on the payment of the debt by instalments to accommodate the debtor, the creditor will no doubt always see a practical benefit to himself in so doing. In the absence of authority there would be much to be said for the enforce-ability of such a contract. But that was a matter expressly considered in *Foakes v.*

---

[37] At p. 17.
[38] See Chap. 19.
[39] [1995] 1 W.L.R. 474.
[40] See p. 120.
[41] (1884) 9 App. Cas 605.
[42] See p. 121.
[43] At p. 481.
[44] Referring to a cited article, Adams and Brownsword, "Contract, Consideration and the Critical Path" (1990) 53 M.L.R. 536.

Beer yet held not to constitute good consideration in law. *Foakes v. Beer* was not even referred to in [*Williams*], and it is in my judgment impossible, consistently with the doctrine of precedent, for this court to extend the principle of *Williams'* case to any circumstances governed by the principle of *Foakes v. Beer*."

The Court of Appeal suggested that had to be done either by the House of Lords, or Parliament after consideration by the Law Commission.

In *Re C (A Debtor)*,[45] Bingham M.R. stated *obiter dicta* that all the relevant authori-   **8.11** ties had not been referred to in *Williams v. Roffey*.[46] This suggested an invitation to view the judgment as *per incuriam*. The Master of the Rolls also took the view that there was an important difference between promises to pay extra and promises to pay a lesser sum. The "factual context" could provide a basis for distinguishing *Williams* from *D & C Builders*.

> "Although *Williams v. Roffey Bros.* appears to have stimulated considerable commentary among academic jurists there is, so far as I can see, no discussion of the interrelationship between these two principles [*i.e.* a promise to pay extra or take a lesser sum on a debt owed]. In any event, it seems to me that there are significant factual differences . . . The rule in *Williams* if such it is, does not therefore apply to a promise to accept less for a pre-existing debt".

(b)   Williams v. Roffey *applied*

Williams v. Roffey Brokers was applied in *Simon Container Machinery Ltd v. Emba*   **8.12** *Machinery AB*,[47] in which the contract was to supply machinery to equip eight factories in the former Soviet Union, manufacturing cardboard boxes to pack food products. The plaintiffs were sub-contractors of the original suppliers, the defendants. As a result of economic changes during the collapse of the Soviet Union in 1991, the defendants were unable to continue payments after some of the equipment had been shipped to them. The plaintiffs brought action against the defendants over payments they had received from their credit insurers. They claimed an express term of the purchase orders required the defendants to pay such sums over to the plaintiffs. They claimed that the defendants only held such money in trust, and also that they should pay over their profits on a basis of restitution or unjust enrichment.[48] On the contract claim, the defendants argued that such a term did not have the construction placed upon it by the plaintiffs and that the agreement in any case lacked consideration.

In the Commercial Court it was held that there was intention to create legal relations and that there was consideration for the agreement. The test laid out in *Williams v. Roffey* was applied. There was consideration for the terms set out in the second agreement. The first contractors (the defendants) had reason to believe that the plaintiff might wish to withdraw from the agreement, otherwise they might not make further purchase

[45] *The Times*, May 11, 1994.
[46] Citing *D and C Builders Ltd v. Rees* [1966] 2 Q.B. 617, *Pinnels Case* (1602) 5 Co. Rep 117a, 77 E.R. 237 and *Foakes v. Beer* (1884) 9 App. Cas. 605.
[47] [1998] 2 Lloyds' Rep. 429.
[48] See Chap. 26.

orders. There was therefore a practical benefit to the defendants. According to Judge Raymond Jack,[49] applying the principles set out by Glidewell L.J. in *Williams*:

> "Emba had reason to think that Simon might seek to withdraw from the contract constituted by Simon's acceptance of the first purchase order if the additional terms were not agreed. Further, if no agreement was reached in relation to the first purchase order, Emba put at risk Simon's acceptance to such further purchase orders as Emba wished to place. Consideration is therefore to be found for the addition to the first purchase order of the terms set out in the additional agreement."

8.13   There was also support for *Williams* in an earlier case, *Anangel Atlas Compania Naviera v. Ishikawajima-Harima Heavy Industries*[50] where Hirst J. stated that:

> "where there is a practical conferment of benefit or a practical avoidance of disbenefit for the promise, there is good consideration, and it is no answer to say that the promisor was already bound; where, on the other hand, there is a wholly gratuitous promise *Stilk's* case remains good law".[51]

On the evidence there was a very substantial practical avoidance of disbenefit to the defendants which constituted good consideration.

TAKING A LESSER SUM

Part payment of a debt is not sufficient consideration

8.14   It is one of the curiosities of English contract law that a promise by a creditor to take less than is owed to them by the debtor is not legally binding, as such a promise lacks consideration. In *Couldery v. Bartrum*[52] Jessel M.R. pointed out that:

> "a creditor might accept anything in satisfaction of his debt except a less amount of money. A creditor could accept a horse, or a canary, or a tomtit if he chose. That would be good consideration for the promise; but, by a most extraordinary peculiarity of the English Common Law, he could not take 19s. 6d. in the pound; that was *nudum pactum* [*i.e.* a gratuitous promise]. Therefore, although the creditor might take a canary, yet, if the debtor did not give him a canary together with his 19s 6d, there was no accord and satisfaction; if he did, there was accord and satisfaction. That was one of the mysteries of English Common Law".[53]

---

[49] At p. 435.
[50] [1990] 2 Lloyd's Rep. 526.
[51] At p. 545.
[52] (1881) 19 Ch. 394.
[53] At p. 399.

The classic example of this rule in operation is *Foakes v. Beer*.[54] The defendant, Dr John Weston Foakes, owed Julia Beer a sum of over £2,000 on a judgment debt. Mrs Beer agreed to accept £500 immediately, with the remainder to be paid in instalments, and promised that she would thereafter not take any further proceedings against Dr Foakes. He paid the money as agreed, but Mrs Beer went back on her word. She then went on to claim interest on the judgment. The defendant claimed that he was not obliged to pay interest as this was covered by the promise of the plaintiff not to sue. The House of Lords held that there was no consideration for the agreement and that Dr Foakes was still bound to pay the additional sum.[55] There was no rule preventing Mrs Beer from enforcing payment of the interest on the judgment. Even then, not all the Law Lords were enthusiastic about the decision to which the House of Lords had arrived. Lord Fitzgerald expressed the view that "it would have been wiser and better if the resolution in *Pinnel's Case* had never been come to . . . We find the law to have been accepted as stated for a great length of time, and I apprehend that it is not now within our province to overturn it".[56] This was, of course, in the days before 1966 when the House of Lords was bound by its own precedents.

Exceptions to the rule in *Foakes v. Beer*

(1) Consideration may be found in payment by a different means: The rule in *Pinnel's* case, "a horse, hawke or robe"

The history of this rule goes back to *Pinnel's Case*[57] (and even earlier). This famous case was heard in the Court of Common Pleas. Pinnel brought an action of debt against Cole for £8 10s on a bond due on the November 11, 1600. Cole argued that he had paid him £5 2s 2d on October 1, which Pinnel had accepted in full satisfaction of the £8 10s. The plaintiff obtained judgment because of insufficient pleading by the defendant. However, the point of law was established nevertheless. A payment at the request of the creditor on an earlier date or by a different method provided a fresh element, and was sufficient to discharge the debt. **8.15**

> "The gift of a horse, hawk or robe, etc in satisfaction is good. For it shall be intended that a horse, hawk or robe, etc might be more beneficial than money in respect of some circumstance, or otherwise the plaintiff would not have accepted of it in satisfaction."[58]

The question is whether something in addition which counts as consideration has been given as a benefit to the creditor for her promise to take a lesser amount. So if Jason owes Louise £100, is supposed to meet her in Bristol to re-pay the money and at Louise's request pays her £75 on the same day at Gloucester, the payment at Gloucester may be

---

[54] (1884) 9 App Cas. 605.
[55] *Foakes v. Beer* still has its supporters. See O'Sullivan, "In Defence of Foakes v. Beer" (1966) 55 C.L.J. 219.
[56] At p. 630.
[57] (1602) 5 Co Rep. 117a, 77 E.R. 237.
[58] At p. 237.

sufficient consideration, if it is a benefit to Louise. (She may now live there having moved from Bristol). However, it is up to Louise. She must accept or reject the change of venue, which cannot be forced upon her. The debtor cannot compel the creditor to take a different mode of payment. Any additional element of value may be regarded as consideration for the promise to forego what is owed, for instance, payment at another place or an earlier date if this is requested or agreed to by the creditor.

8.16   In *Vanbergen v. St Edmunds Properties Ltd*[59] the plaintiff by agreement paid money owed into a bank in Eastbourne rather than to the London offices of the defendants' solicitors in order to avoid bankruptcy proceedings against him. The Court of Appeal held that the change of venue was a concession to oblige the plaintiff and the defendants accrued no benefit from it. It therefore provided no fresh consideration. Lord Hanworth M.R.[60] found that there was:

> ". . . no advantage which the creditors could reap out of that made of payment from Eastbourne . . . 'I find it quite impossible to say that those terms fulfilled the qualification laid down by Lord Selborne [in *Foakes v. Beer*], that it is 'some independent benefit, actual or contingent, of a kind which might in law be a good and valuable consideration for any other sort of agreement not under seal' ".[61]

It is now established that payment by cheque or direct debit is not different from payment by cash. In *Goddard v. O'Brien*[62] it was held that payment by a promissory note was different from payment in cash. If accepted, by the creditor, this could discharge the obligation by providing fresh consideration to make a promise to take less binding. This proposition was rejected in *D and C Builders v. Rees*.[63] Lord Denning considered that:

> "no sensible distinction can be taken between payment of a lesser sum by cash and payment of it by cheque. The cheque, when given, is conditional payment. When honoured, it is actual payment. It is then just the same as cash. If a creditor is not bound when he receives a payment by cash, he should not be bound when he receives payment by cheque."[64]

This was approved by the Court of Appeal in *Re C (A Debtor)*.[65]

8.17   Payment by direct debit was considered in *Esso Petroleum Co Ltd v. Milton*.[66] The defendant was the licensee of two of the plaintiffs' service stations in Exeter. He alleged that it was impossible to conduct business in the light of the conditions imposed on him by Esso, so he regarded the contract as at an end. One of the issues for the Court of Appeal was whether direct debit was to be treated in the same way as cheques. The Court of Appeal held that modern commercial practice treated direct debit in the same way as a

---

[59] [1933] 2 K.B. 223.
[60] At p. 233.
[61] At p. 233.
[62] (1882) 9 Q.B.D. 37.
[63] [1966] 2 Q.B. 617.
[64] At p. 623.
[65] *The Times*, May 11, 1992.
[66] *The Times*, February 13, 1997.

payment by cheque and was, therefore, the equivalent of cash or cheque. It might be argued that direct debit is a considerable benefit to the payee.

(2) Part payment by a third party

The rule in *Foakes v. Beer* does not apply where the part payment is made by a third party, so long as the creditor accepts this as final settlement. In *Hirachand Punamchand v. Temple*,[67] Lieutenant Temple borrowed money from the plaintiffs who demanded payment, but when he did not pay in full they told his father, Sir Richard Temple. The father offered a lesser sum than the debt in full settlement of his son's debt. It was held that acceptance of the father's cheque extinguished the debt even though for a lesser amount. The creditor could not sue the debtor for the balance which remained unpaid."[68]

(3) Composition agreements between a debtor and creditors

When a person goes bankrupt or a company goes into liquidation, the creditors may meet together and agree to accept a percentage of what is owed to each. This type of agreement is binding between the creditors, yet each appears to be accepting less than their due and it is doubtful if there is consideration between each creditor. **8.18**

   This is an example of the elastic concept of consideration being stretched for practical reasons. In *Boyd v. Hind*[69] it was stated that a composition with creditors was binding because "for such agreement there is good consideration to each creditor viz the undertaking of the other compounding creditors to give up a part of their claim".[70] In *Good v. Cheeseman*[71] the reason for holding such agreements to have consideration was to be found in each of the creditors forbearance to sue each other.

   Denning J. in *Bob Guiness v. Salomonsen*[72] described why such agreements were treated as binding (in his opinion). The reason was not consideration, but equitable estoppel[73]:

> "The new promise in such case stands on the same footing as other promises which are enforced without the existence of any real consideration, such as promises by creditors under a composition arrangement to accept less than their due and promises of a bank which, at the buyers request and expense notifies a seller that it has opened a credit in his favour [bankers commercial credit]. These promises are enforced when they are intended to be legally binding, intended to be acted upon, and are in fact acted on, even though it may be difficult in legal theory to find any real consideration for them. There is in truth no real consideration unless the fact of acting on the promise is regarded as consideration . . . it now seems clear that these cases must be treated as exceptions to the doctrine of consideration. Ingenuity may suggest consideration, so as to appear to make the law logically consistent, but on some occasions . . . it is necessary to shed fictions."[74]

[67] [1911] 2 K.B. 330.
[68] At p. 339.
[69] (1857) 1 H and N 938, 156 E.R. 1481.
[70] At p. 1485.
[71] (1831) 2 B and Ad 328, 172 E.R. 805.
[72] [1948] 2 K.B. 42 (at pp. 47–48).
[73] See Chap. 10.
[74] At pp. 47–48.

(4) Promise is made by deed

8.19 If the promise to take less is contained in a deed, no question of consideration need arise and the promise will be binding. This is an example of an alternative to consideration operating to resolve a practical problem, one which occurs not infrequently in business relations.

CONTRACTUAL VARIATIONS

Discharge by agreement

8.20 The rule is that a contract cannot be varied unilaterally. To be effective, a variation requires the agreement of both parties and consideration. Contracts are often discharged by agreement when both parties either give extra or give up something to the other in an exchange of promises.

If neither party has performed, *i.e.* the consideration is executory, there is no difficulty as each party gives up their rights in return for the other doing so. If the contract has been executed by one party then there must either be: (a) fresh consideration, called "accord and satisfaction"; (b) a release "under seal"; or (c) promissory estoppel may apply. An accord and satisfaction is the purchase of a release from a contractual obligation in return for fresh consideration. The accord is the agreement by which the obligation is discharged. The satisfaction is the consideration which makes the new agreement. Therefore an accord without satisfaction is not effective. In *British Russian Gazette and Trade Outlook Ltd v. Associated Newspapers Ltd*[75] the plaintiff, Talbot, agreed to settle two actions brought by himself and the *Russian Gazette* against the *Daily Mail* for libel. His promise to compromise was set out in a letter stating "I accept the sum of one thousand guineas . . . in full discharge and settlement of my claims". Before the money had been paid, Talbot disregarded the promise and proceeded with his defamation action. He argued that there was no breach of the agreement until there was actual payment. The Court of Appeal disagreed. The letter was an agreement in which there was consideration in the form of a promise for a promise: You promise to pay the one thousand guineas, if I promise to discontinue proceedings. This constituted a good accord and satisfaction, and therefore a discharge of the claims by agreement. Far more claims are settled by agreement between the parties than ever reach the courts.

The contract itself provides for variation

8.21 A contract may provide for unilateral variation by one of the parties. For instance, in *Lombard Tricity Finance Ltd v. Paton*[76] the rate of interest payable on a credit agreement could be changed in accordance with an agreed term. This was held to be valid. Mortgage repayments normally fluctuate at the option of the lending bank or building society in this way. However, if there is no unambiguous provision allowing for unilateral

---

[75] [1933] 2 K.B. 616.
[76] [1989] 1 All E.R. 918.

variation in the contract, then any attempt to do so will be unenforceable. In *Hayes v. Securities and Facilities Division*,[77] employees were given subsistence allowances of £62.50 per day within London and £60 for the rest of the country. This was reduced unilaterally to £50 by the employers. The Court of Appeal held that the employer's attempt to do so was unlawful.

The rule in *Pigot's* case[78]

If a deed or written contract is altered, or words struck out, without the consent of the other party, the contract is discharged except as against the party making or agreeing to the alterations. However, in *Raiffeisen Zentralbank Oesterreich AG v. Crossseas Shipping Ltd.*,[79] the Court of Appeal held that the rule in *Pigot's* case should only be applied when the change was potentially prejudicial to the other parties rights and obligations.

Other forms of variation

Variation may also occur by means of waiver, *i.e.* suspending a right,[80] by rescission in certain situations[81] or by novation. This latter ground is created by making a new agreement between some parties or between different parties on the same terms.[82] **8.22**

Varying a third party's right

The power of contracting parties to rescind or vary a third party right to a benefit in a contract between two others is severely limited by the Contracts (Rights of Third Parties) Act 1999 s.2.[83]

Variation by waiver and promissory estoppel

There are two further means by which a contract may be varied. The doctrine of waiver as applied in *Hughes v. Metropolitan Railway Co.*,[84] allowed a forebearance by one party to be relied upon by the other party. This merely suspends the operation of a contractual right but nevertheless gives the other party an important breathing space, and one which is legally enforceable. The doctrine of promissory estoppel is an equitable notion established by Denning J. in *Central London Property Trust Ltd v. High Trees House*[85] This allows a promise which is intended to be acted upon, and is in fact relied upon, to be enforced if it is equitable to do so. The doctrine applies in the absence of consideration,

---

[77] *The Times*, April 26, 2000.
[78] *Henry Pigot's case* (1614) 11 Co. Rep. 266, 77 E.R.
[79] [2000] 3 All E.R. 274.
[80] See Chap. 10.
[81] See Chap. 23.
[82] See *Rasbora Ltd v. JCL Marine Ltd.* [1977] 1 Lloyd's Rep. 645.
[83] See Chap. 10.
[84] (1877) 2 App Cas. 439, see Chap. 9.
[85] [1947] K.B. 130, see Chap. 9.

but only in the variation of an existing contractual obligation. Promissory estoppel does not create a cause of action. We discuss waiver and promissory estoppel in greater detail in Chapter 9. However before leaving variation of contract, it is important to rationalise the various rules and principles which we have encountered so far and attempt to establish the relationship between them.

The relationship between *Foakes v. Beer*, *Williams v. Roffey*, the doctrine of waiver in *Hughes v. Metropolitan Railway* and promissory estoppel.

8.23   Denning J. relied on *Hughes v. Metropolitan Railway Company* as a basis for the doctrine of promissory estoppel. Although decided seven years previously, *Hughes* was not considered in *Foakes v. Beer*.

There is no question therefore that *Foakes* could have been overruled by *Hughes* but was not. What then is the relationship between *Foakes v. Beer*, promissory estoppel and *Williams v. Roffey*?

Foakes v. Beer remains good law. A promise to take a lesser sum is not binding in the absence of fresh consideration. The doctrine of waiver as expressed in *Hughes v. Metropolitan Railway* does not supersede the rule in *Foakes*. Promissory estoppel, when it applies, can mitigate the rigours of the common law. Promissory estoppel is an equitable doctrine. It does not apply to pre-existing debts (although Denning expressed the view it could).

Like waiver, promissory estoppel only suspends the operation of a promise, it does not extinguish it. *Williams v. Roffey* allows a promise to pay extra to be enforced if there is a mutual benefit to both parties and no economic duress. It does not apply to *Foakes v. Beer* situations of pre-existing debts (see *Re Selectmove*). Promissory estoppel was not pleaded in *Williams v. Roffey*. Russell L.J. suggested that if it had been he might have been, interested in pursuing the argument as an additional element in the plaintiff's claim. The rule that it could not be used as a cause of action was too firmly fixed by precedent to be overturned in the Court of Appeal. The relationships in question are set out in tabular form opposite.

Legal quadrilateral: the relationships between four rules and doctrines

8.24   Waiver and promissory estoppel are discussed later in Chapter 9. The reader may wish to consult this diagram again after having looked at these two doctrines:

(1) the rule in *Foakes v. Beer* Waiver: *Hughes v. Metropolitan Railway.*[86]
(2) the judgment in *Williams v. Roffey Brothers.*[87]

What is the relationship between various rules and doctrines in the above diagram? If we call *Foakes v. Beer* "A", *Hughes v. Metropolitan Railway* "B", *Williams v. Roffey* "C" and Promissory Estoppel "D" then the following relationships apply:

- **A to B**: Though decided seven years earlier, *Hughes* was not discussed in *Foakes v. Beer*. Neither overrules the other and both remain good law.

---

[86] See Chap. 9.
[87] See Chap. 9.

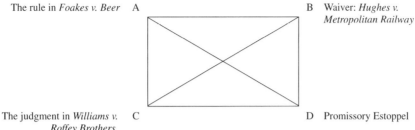

The rule in *Foakes v. Beer*   A

B   Waiver: *Hughes v. Metropolitan Railway*

The judgment in *Williams v. Roffey Brothers*   C

D   Promissory Estoppel

- **A to C**: The approach of *Williams v. Roffey* does not apply to pre-existing debts (see the judgment of the Court of Appeal in Re *Selectmove*). *Foakes v. Beer* was not discussed in *Williams*.

- **A to D**: Promissory estoppel applies only to future conduct not to discharging pre-existing debts (though there are dicta of Lord Denning to the contrary).

- **B to C**: Waiver only suspends existing rights which can be re-invoked within a reasonable time on giving notice. So far it has not been applied to promises to pay more.

- **D to C**: Promissory estoppel was not an issue in *Williams*.[88] The doctrine could, however, be extended to such situations in future.[89]

- **B to D**: Waiver and promissory estoppel may or may not be regarded as the same principle.[90]

REFORMING CONSIDERATION

The radical reform of the rule that consideration must move from the promisee as a result of the Contracts (Rights of Third Parties) Act 1999 puts the spotlight on the entire doctrine of consideration. We have noted some of the criticisms of consideration as we have proceeded. Consideration tends to be a topic which divides opinion. For some it is the bastion of traditional English contract law, others would like to see it done away with completely. Lord Wright thought consideration "riddled with illogicality, fiction and anomaly".[91] Lord Goff in *White v. Jones*[92] expressed the view that: **8.25**

> "It is true that our law of contract is widely seen as deficient in the sense that it is perceived to be hampered by the presence of an unnecessary doctrine of consideration and (through a strict doctrine of privity of contract) stunted through a failure to recognise a *quaesitum tertio*."

---

[88] See earlier p. 117.
[89] See Chap. 9.
[90] See Chap. 9.
[91] (1939) 55 L.Q.R. 189 (at p. 202).
[92] [1995] 1 ALL E.R. (at p. 705).

His criticisms as far as the latter doctrine is concerned have now been dealt with in the Contracts (Rights of Third Parties) Act 1999. Is it time to adopt a similarly radical approach and reform consideration? Part of the criticism stems from the perceived inconvenience of many of the aspects of consideration when applied to practical situations, for instance: (i) Promises to take less, and contractual variation is made difficult and complex; (ii) Gratuitous promises are unenforceable unless made by deed; and (iii) The status of many types of arrangement such as compositions with creditors and consumer guarantees may be questionable.

8.26   It may seem strange that the legal status of something as mundane as a guarantee of consumer goods given usually by a manufacturer could be in doubt. Nevertheless, it remains hard to find consideration even although they are usually regarded as legally binding. When a consumer fills in the guarantee card and returns it to the manufacturer, the consideration is past as far as the contract with the retailer is concerned. In addition the buyer is suffering no detriment in returning the guarantee card since the Unfair Contract Terms Act 1977 s. 5 prevents taking away rights from consumers by means of guarantees.[93] Equally, the manufacturer does not appear to benefit. However, there may be benefit and detriment; the manufacturers gain something in return ("goodwill" is probably too intangible) and the customer may benefit by receiving additional benefits, such as repair or replacement beyond the normal common law or statutory rights. The situation where the customer pays an additional sum for the guarantee is simpler. Consideration is then provided for a contract with the manufacturer in which the guarantee contains a set of promises.[94]

The arguments for and against consideration

8.27   The main arguments against consideration are that it enshrines the formality of exchange, prevents a general reliance theory developing, is overtechnical, can be subverted by providing even a nominal consideration and causes huge problems for those who wish to vary a contract. It is artificial and out of date, and often acts to undermine and disappoint the reasonable expectations of the parties. There are equally good arguments in favour of consideration. The doctrine epitomises the basic nature of English contracts as being exchanges. It is flexible and can take account of public policy. It is infinitely variable and yet gives certainty to contract law. Consideration is an adaptable principle, capable of many meanings, allowing or preventing promises being enforced for many reasons. It is not necessarily some ancient hangover from a bygone era, but a useful and subtle lawyers' tool. The alternatives to consideration, from the formality of putting contracts in writing, requirements of evidence as to parties' intentions, or a principle of detrimental reliance, are all much worse.

Consideration has already been reformed in part in the Contracts (Rights of Third Parties) Act 1999. The rule that consideration must move from the promisee is effectively abolished.[95] In 1937, the Law Revision Committee, in its Sixth Interim Report (Cmd 5449) made some proposals for the reform of consideration. There were four main

---

[93] See Chap. 17.
[94] The implementation in the United Kingdom of the European Directive on Consumer Guarantees in 2002 adds to consumer rights in this area.
[95] See Chap. 10.

recommendations: (i) any promise in writing should be binding, even if there is no consideration for it; (ii) past consideration should be sufficient; (iii) performance of an existing duty should be a good consideration; and (iv) the abolition of the rule in *Pinnel's case* which would provide that a promise to accept part payment of a debt should be binding. Nothing came of this proposal. We explain the background and reform of the privity rule later.[96] The Law Commission in its attempted codification of contract law would have retained consideration; however the codification came to nothing,[97] and at present there are no proposals to tackle the reform of consideration as a whole.

There are two possibilities for reform. First, that consideration redefined as a less strin- **8.28** gent test, such as "practical benefit", could be applied. Earlier in this chapter we discussed a liberalised version of the meaning of consideration in the Court of Appeal's judgment in *Williams v. Roffey Brothers*. Were a "subjective benefit to both parties" test to gain approval as the requirement for formation of a contract as well as in its variation, then consideration could be found in a far wider range of transactions and arrangements. This would meet many of the criticisms, but, also render the principle less certain, and open to abuse. It would also be possible to simply abolish consideration. A single sentence Act could read: "The rule that consideration is required for the formation of a contract is hereby abolished". The courts would then be left with the question of what to put in it's place. Alternatively, the reforming statute might attempt to do so itself. What might be the alternatives to consideration? We shall discuss these in future chapters:

(i)   Greater use of the requirements of formalities[98];

(ii)   Greater importance attached to the intention of the parties,[99] so that any promise seriously intended to be binding could be enforceable;

(iii)   An expanded and redefined doctrine of economic duress to protect promisors[1];

(iv)   Unconscionability allowed to develop as a ground for refusing to enforce promises[2];

(v)   Public policy play a more overt role in the types of promises enforceable;

(vi)   "Detrimental" reliance becomes the guiding principle for enforcement;

(vii)   "Reasonable" reliance (a wider version of above);

(viii) Promissory estoppel used as a cause of action.

We turn to these three latter possibilities in our next chapter.

---

[96] See Chap. 10.
[97] See Chap. 1.
[98] See Chap. 11.
[99] See Chap. 11.
[1] See Chap. 19.
[2] See Chap. 14.

Chapter 9

EQUITABLE ESTOPPEL[1]

Introduction: Reliance on promises

The clearest example of reliance theory in modern English contract law is the doctrine **9.1** of promissory estoppel. When promissory estoppel emerged into the world in 1946 in Lord Denning's landmark *ex tempore* judgment in the *High Trees* case reported later in 1947,[2] contract law entered a new era. In *Syros Shipping Co. v. Elaghill Trading Co. "The Proodos C"*, Lloyd J. described *High Trees* as "the case which marked the turning point in the modern law of equitable estoppel".[3] Promissory estoppel deals with an apparent deficiency in the common law and allows for the variation of a contract to be given a limited effect without the need for fresh consideration. The broader importance of this doctrine is that it is an example of reliance which may one day develop as the guiding theory of English contract law, replacing the existing exchange principle based upon the need for consideration. Though potentially an important supplement to contract law where consideration is lacking, promissory estoppel does not purport to provide a viable alternative to consideration as a whole. The words of Denning L.J. in *Combe v. Combe*[4] reflect the limited nature of waiver and promissory estoppel in this respect: "The doctrine of consideration is too firmly fixed to be overthrown by a side wind. It's ill effects have been largely mitigated of late though it still remains a cardinal necessity of the formation of a contract".[5] Promissory estoppel is one species of equitable estoppel which has grown up within the confines of contract law. Other varieties of equitable estoppel which exist on the periphery or strictly outside of contract law are: (i) proprietary estoppel; (ii) estoppel by convention; (iii) estoppel by representation; and (iv) estoppel by conduct. Each of these is linked to promissory estoppel, being equitable in nature, but in a number of key ways the rules of each remain different. This has led to the suggestion originally made by Lord Denning in *Amalgamated Investment and Property Co. Ltd v. Texas Commerce International Bank Ltd*[6] and now taken up by the High Court of Australia that the different types of estoppel be merged into single doctrine of equitable estoppel linked

---

[1] Elizabeth Cooke, *The Modern Law of Estoppel* (2000, Clarendon Press, Oxford) for an excellent account of this area.
[2] *Central London Property Trust Ltd v. High Trees House Ltd* [1947] K.B. 130.
[3] [1980] 2 Lloyd's Rep. 390 (at p. 391).
[4] [1951] 2 K.B. 215.
[5] At p. 220.
[6] [1982] Q.B. 84.

to the concept of unconscionability.[7] We shall consider this prospect and the various types of estoppel in turn. First we shall begin with the most important doctrine for contract lawyers, promissory estoppel.

THE BACKGROUND TO PROMISSORY ESTOPPEL

9.2 The idea of promissory estoppel can be illustrated by the outline of a simple case. In *H.M. 24 Hour Vehicle Recovery v. Hall*[8] the defendant's car was towed away by recovery services as an abandoned vehicle on the instructions of the police. In order to recover her car she wrote a cheque which she later cancelled once the car had been returned to her. It was held by Bolton County Court that it was contrary to public policy to allow someone to cancel a cheque in these circumstances. The plaintiff had relied on her promise to pay by returning the seized car. Promissory estoppel applied to prevent the defendant going back on her word to pay the penalty charge. The historical origins of this doctrine derive from two separate streams: (a) estoppel and (b) waiver, which converged to create the doctrine we know today.

Estoppel

Estoppel is a common law rule of evidence which prevents a person denying a fact which she had previously asserted to be true. Estoppel was defined by Lord Birkenhead in *Maclaine v. Gatty*[9] as arising where "A has by his words or conduct justified B in belieiving that a certain state of facts exists and B has acted on such belief to his prejudice, A is not permitted to affirm against B that a different state of facts existed at the same time". It is notable that B must have acted on the words in question. Historically, estoppel could only apply to a statement of fact, but not to a promise. The House of Lords affirmed this rule in *Jorden v. Money*.[10] This was unfortunate and closed off an avenue of development for many years until the present doctrine of promissory estoppel was established. The judgment in *Jorden v. Money* may well have been inevitable (albeit unfortunate) given the long standing distinction between a statement of fact and a promise of future intention which is a fundamental feature of English contract law.[11] Although estoppel is usually seen as a defence it may be used by a plaintiff to add an element to his claim which, by way of an additional argument, might assist the action to succeed.

Waiver

9.3 As we discussed earlier, the rule in *Foakes v. Beer*[12] prevents[13] a debtor enforcing a promise by a creditor to accept a lesser sum than is owed to her.[13] Depending upon one's point of

---

[7] See Spence, *Protecting Reliance: The Emergent Doctrine of Equitable Estoppel* (1999, Hart Publishing, Oxford).

[8] (1996) C.L.Y. 1128.

[9] [1921] 1 A.C. 376 (at p. 386).

[10] (1854) 5 H.L. Cas 185, 10 E.R. 868.

[11] See Chap. 13.

[12] (1884) 9 App. Cas 605.

[13] See Chap. 8.

view, the result of *Foakes v. Beer* is potentially unfair, certainly from the debtor's perspective.[14] The common law developed the doctrine of waiver as a way of mitigating the harshness of the rule requiring fresh consideration for a promise to take less. The leading authority in this area is the House of Lords judgment in *Hughes v. Metropolitan Railway Co.*[15] (a case decided seven years earlier than *Foakes v. Beer*). The plaintiff, Thomas Hughes, was the landlord of property leased to a railway company situated in Euston Road, London, near the present station. He told the defendants that they had six months to repair the property or he would take steps to forfeit their lease. Negotiations then took place to purchase the lease between the parties but these broke down. Hughes sought possession of the property at the end of the six months claiming that he was entitled to do so because of his original notice. The railway company argued that they had done nothing while the negotiations were continuing as they took this to mean that the notice was in abeyance. The House of Lords applied the doctrine of waiver to suspend the notice until the negotiations had reached their conclusion. The defendants were entitled to relief against the forfeiture of the lease. Cairns L.C. stated the rule which has been applied regularly since that time:

> "It is the first principle upon which all Courts of Equity proceed, that if parties who have entered into definite and distinct terms involving certain legal results . . . afterwards by their own act or with their own consent enter upon a course of negotiations which has the effect of leading one of the parties to suppose that the strict rights arising under the contract will not be enforced or will be kept in suspense or held in abeyance, the person who might otherwise have enforced those rights will not be allowed to enforce them where it would be inequitable, having regard to the dealings which have thus taken place between the parties."[16]

The notion that waiver merely suspends the strict insistence on a right in *Hughes* leads into the modern doctrine of equitable estoppel.

Another, rather less famous case, is *Birmingham and District Land Co. v. London & NW Railway*,[17] in which Lindley L.J. stated that the legal principle applicable had been settled by *Hughes*, and was applicable to a case in which building operations were suspended, which thereby "raised an equity" against the landlord to prevent him ejecting the tenants until they had a reasonable time to complete the work. Bowen L.J. went further than this, however. According to one of the great nineteenth century judges in the Court of Appeal the rule was not confirmed to relief against forfeiture or indeed the rule laid down in *Hughes*. Bowen L.J. stated a wider test closer to the doctrine of promissory estoppel, and wider than the rule in *Hughes v. Metropolitan Railway*. Bowen L.J.'s statement of principle might well be regarded as the true source of the modern law[18]:

> "The truth is that the proposition is wider than cases of forfeiture. It seems to me to amount to this, that if persons who have contractual rights against others induce

---

[14] Not everyone agrees, see O'Sullivan (1996) 55 C.L.J. 219.
[15] (1877) 2 App. Cas 439.
[16] At p. 448.
[17] (1888) 40 Ch. 268.
[18] At p. 286.

by their conduct those against whom they have such rights to believe that such rights will either not be enforced or will be kept in suspense or abeyance for some particular time, those persons will not be allowed by a Court of Equity to enforce the rights until such time has elapsed, without at all events placing the parties in the same position as they were before. This is the principle to be applied. I will not say it is not a principle that was recognised by Courts of Law as well as of Equity. It is not necessary to consider how far it was always a principle of common law."

In *Emmanuel Ajayi v. R.T. Briscoe (Nigeria) Ltd*[19] the Privy Council applied the principle of promissory estoppel "as defined by Bowen L.J. in the *Birmingham Land Co. Case*."

Promissory Estoppel and Waiver

9.4   Waiver is still conventionally regarded as distinct from promissory estoppel but there is authority for saying that the two have now merged,[20] or may indeed be the same thing. In *Durham Fancy Goods Ltd v. Michael Jackson (Fancy Goods)*[21] Donaldson J. stated "the principle of equity upon which the promissory estoppel cases are based is applicable to and bars the plaintiffs claim. This principle was formulated by Lord Cairns in *Hughes v. Metropolitan Railway Co.*" In *Prosper Homes v. Hambro's Bank Executor & Trustee Co.*,[22] Browne-Wilkinson J. stated:

> "I do not think it matters whether it is expressed as being a waiver of contractural rights or a promissory estoppel. In my judgment, they are really two ways of saying exactly the same thing. If a party has represented that he is not going to rely on his strict contractural rights he is taken as being waived them, that is to say he is estoppel from relying on them ... But whether one expresses the doctrine as one of waiver or as one of estoppel it is in my judgment essential that the statement or conduct relied on unequivocally show that the party is not relying on his contractual rights."[23]

Finally in *Charles Rickard Ltd v. Oppenhaim*[24] Denning L.J. stated:

> "Whether it be called waiver or forbearance on his part, or an agreed variation or substituted performance does not matter. It is a kind of estoppel. By his conduct he evinced an intention to effect their legal relations. He made, in effect, a promise not to insist on his legal rights. That promise was intended to be acted on and was in fact acted on. He cannot afterwards go back on it ... It is a particular application of the principle which I endeavoured to state in *Central London Property v. High Trees House*".[25]

[19] [1964] 1 W.L.R. 1326.
[20] Care has to be taken over judicial terminology, in this case using the word "waiver" when the judge is really speaking of promissory estoppel.
[21] [1986] 2 Q.B. (at p. 847).
[22] (1980) 39 P & CR 395.
[23] At p. 401.
[24] [1950] 1 K.B. 616.
[25] At p. 623.

The drawback with this view is that promissory estoppel is seen in the corseted form of the traditional Victorian doctrine of waiver, rather than the more modern concept of equitable estoppel capable of expansion and development.[26] There are also differences between waiver and promissory estoppel which cannot be entirely glossed over. Waiver does not appear to require reliance, nor does it have to be inequitable to go back on one's promise. Waiver can also be used in a separate meaning as an election between rights, for example whether to rescind a contract for breach.[27] If the innocent elects to affirm he has waived his right to rescind the contract and this right is extinguished, it may be better to regard this latter aspect of waiver as being a different meaning of the same word. If these two doctrines have in fact now merged, or there is a good case for their doing so, then the *Birmingham Land Co* case is the origin of the doctrine. In which case we should call our subject the *Birmingham Land* principle.[28] It is still conventional however to treat the following case as the origin of the modern law of promissory estoppel.[29]

Lord Denning and *High Trees*.

Central London Property Trust Ltd v. High Trees House Ltd[30] is one of the most famous cases in the whole of contract law, yet it is only a judgment of the High Court at first instance and the judgment of Denning J. a mere three pages in length. Furthermore, the gist of the principle of promissory estoppel is largely *obiter dicta* rather than being the ratio of the case itself. *High Trees* marks a watershed in contract law and to this day the ambit of the principle established remains a topic for debate. In July 1946, therefore, English contract law took an important step forward. The case concerned a lease made under seal in 1937 of a block of flats for a period of 99 years. The defendants were in fact a subsidiary of the plaintiffs who owned the property. The rent was set at £2,500 a year but as a result of the disruption caused by the Second World War, few flats were let so the defendants were unable to pay as agreed. After some discussion between the parties, a letter was sent by the plaintiffs in January 1940 which stated "we confirm the arrangement made between us by which the ground rent should be reduced. . . to £1250 per annum". This half rate was paid during the war until the beginning of January 1945 when the flats were fully let again. In September 1945 the receiver of the plaintiffs demanded full rent be paid, from that time onwards and also arrears for the period of half rent. An action was commenced for £625, the quarterly rate at the original rent of £2500. The plaintiff succeeded on the basis that the full rent was payable from January 1945. What of the intervening period between 1940 and 1945? That of course is the subject of one of the most famous pieces of *obiter dicta* in English law. Denning J. based his judgment on the principle that where parties enter into an arrangement intended to create legal relations and one party makes a promise to vary the agreement which he knows will be acted upon and is acted upon, then the promise is binding even although

9.5

---

[26] We discuss the possible development of promissory estoppel later pp. 145–148.

[27] See Chap. 23.

[28] In *Combe v. Combe* [1951] 2 K.B. 215 (at p. 219) Lord Denning described promissory estoped as "first stated" in *Hughes* and "enlarged" in *Birmingham Land*.

[29] In *The Post Chaser* [1982] 1 All E.R. (at p. 27). Goff J. stated that Denning J. had simply "breathed new life into the doctrine of equitable estoppel". Of course, as a judge of first instance given the limitations of precedent, even Denning J. was not at liberty to invent entirely new ideas of his own creation.

[30] [1947] K.B. 130.

there is no consideration. The person making the promise is not allowed to act inconsistently with it. This was the doctrine of promissory estoppel. In this case, the promise only remained operative so long as the conditions giving rise to it continued, *i.e.* the lack of tenants and income from rent. With the ending of the war, and the building being fully occupied by tenants again, the original rent was payable. There were two strands to the doctrine at common law, estoppel and waiver, which were then married to equity. Surveying the period following *Jorden v. Money* when "the law has not been standing still", he noted that what had occurred was a "natural result of the fusion of law and equity".[31] Denning J. also expressed the view that the new doctrine ought also to apply to promises to take a lesser sum, as in *Foakes v. Beer*,[31a] and could extinguish a debt. Both of these views of Denning J.'s have failed to gain later approval by the courts. However, the central element was established in *High Trees* that "a promise intended to be binding, intended to be acted on, and in fact acted on, is binding so far as its terms properly apply".[32]

9.6   Another early example of the doctrine is *Robertson v. Minister of Pensions*,[33] in which once again Denning J. was the judge at first instance. Colonel Robertson received a letter from the War Office describing his disabilities as having been caused by "military service". Relying on this he did not seek independent medical advice but assumed this would qualify him for disability benefits. The Ministry of Pensions (another Government department) went back on the War Office's assurance and declared his injuries not caused by action in warfare. The Court held that the assurance fell within the newly established principle of promissory estoppel. Denning J. stating that "if a man gives a promise or assurance which he intended to be binding on him and to be acted on by the person to whom it is given, then once it is acted upon, he is bound by it".[34]

THE BASIC RULES OF PROMISSORY ESTOPPEL

The two key principles:

- The element of a promise: This must be "clear and unequivocal" and to have been intended to be acted upon by the other party.

- The reliance factor: The promise must have been acted upon in fact by the promisee. The reliance need not be detrimental. There is no requirement of consideration moving from the promisee.

There are also a number of limiting factors:

- Promissory estoppel alone does not create a cause of action, but merely acts as a defence. It is a "shield but not a sword".

---

[31]   At p. 134.
[31a]   (1884) 9 App. Cas 605.
[32]   At p. 136.
[33]   [1949] 1 K.B. 227.
[34]   At p. 231.

- It must be equitable (or not unconscionable) to rely on the promise.

- A pre-existing contract or legal relationship is necessary.

- Promissory estoppel does not extinguish but only suspends an obligation.

Flowchart D sets out the rules leading to promissory estoppel.

Flowchart D: Promissory Estoppel

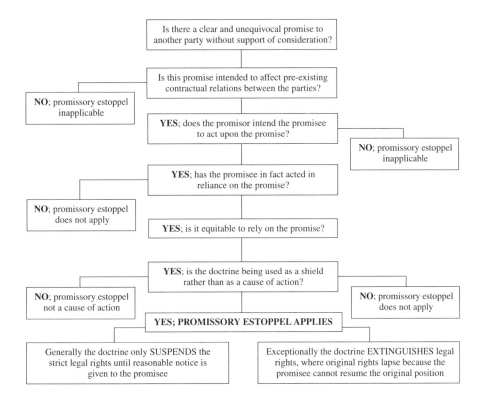

The basic principles of the doctrine

(1) There must be an unequivocal promise which was intended to be acted upon.

The promisee must make it clear that the promisor does not intend to enforce his strict **9.7** contractual rights. The requirement of a clear promise distinguishes promissory from proprietary estoppel.[35] In *Scandinavian Trading Tanker Co. v. Flota Petrolera Ecuatoriana "The Scaptrade"*[36] Goff J. described the first criterion for establishing equitable estoppel in a particular case[37]: "First they had to establish that the owners had represented unequivocally that they would not enforce their strict legal right, under the contract

---

[35] See later p. 145.
[36] [1983] 1 All E.R. 301.
[37] At p. 304.

between the parties, to withdraw the vessel from the charterers' service in the event of a default in payment of an instalment of hire".[38] The test for establishing Goff J.'s first requirement is based on promisee objectivity.[39] This first requirement could be fulfilled "if a reasonable man in the shoes of the charterers would have inferred from the owners' conduct that they were making such a representation.[40] The words used must be more than "mere acts of indulgence," according to Viscount Simonds in *Tool Metal Manufacturing Co. Ltd v. Tungsten Electric Co.*[41] where he stated that "the gist of the equity lies in the fact that one party has by his conduct led the other to alter his position. I lay stress on this, because I would not have it supposed particularly in commercial transactions, that mere acts of indulgence are apt to create rights . . . ".[42]

(2) There must be Reliance by the Promisee

9.8   The reliance factor is vital to promissory estoppel. The promise must have been intended to be acted upon, and in fact acted upon, by the promisee.[43] The issue which has caused most difficulty is whether the reliance in question must have been detrimental. There are contradictory judicial views on this point. In *W.J. Alan and Co v. El Nasr Export and Import Co.*[44] Lord Denning rejected the need for detriment in addition to reliance.[45] In this instance Lord Denning represents the mainstream view:

> "I know that it has been suggested in some quarters that there must be detriment. But I can find no support for it in the authorities cited by the judge. The nearest approach to it is the statement of Viscount Simonds in the *Tool Metal* case,[46] that the other must have been led 'to alter his position'. . . But that only means that he must have been led to act differently from what he otherwise would have done. And if you study the cases in which the doctrine has been applied, you will see that all that is required is that the one should have *acted* on the belief induced by the other party. That is how Lord Cohen put it in the *Tool Metal* case,[47] and that is how I would put it myself . . . "[48]

The Law Commission in their Report on Privity of Contract noted:

> "A useful analogy is the doctrine of promissory estoppel . . . There, the debate has ranged for many years as to whether the promisee needs to have merely relied, or must have detrimentally relied, on the promise in order to fall within the doctrine. Although the matter cannot be regarded as entirely settled, there seems to be an emerging consensus to the effect that mere reliance is sufficient."[49]

---

[38] Citing *Woodhouse AC Israel Cocoa Ltd SA v. Nigerian Marketing Co. Ltd* [1972] A.C. 74).
[39] See Chap. 2.
[40] Citing *Bremer Handelsgesellschaft mbH v. Vanden Avenne-Izegem PVBA* [1978] 2 Lloyd's Rep. 109 at p. 126 per Lord Salmon.
[41] [1955] 1 W.L.R. 761 (at p. 764).
[42] At p. 764.
[43] See the Privy Council's judgment in *Emanuel Ajahi v. R.T. Briscoe (Nigeria) Ltd* [1964] 1 W.L.R. 1326.
[44] [1972] 2 Q.B. 189.
[45] At pp. 213–214.
[46] [1955] 1 W.L.R. 761 (at p. 764).
[47] At p. 799.
[48] See also Goff J. in *Societe Italo-Belge v. Palm Oils (The Post Chaser)* [1982] 1 ALL E.R. 19.
[49] Law Commission No. 242 "Privity of Contract: Contracts for the Benefit of Third Parties"p. 106 para 9.19. (The Report is discussed more fully in Chap. 10).

An alternative view was expressed by the Court of Appeal in *Goldsworthy v. Brickell*[50] when Nourse L.J. stated *obiter dicta* that detriment is a requirement of promissory estoppel.[51] After reviewing the requirements of the doctrine, the third of which was "that the defendant, in reliance on the representation, acted to his detriment, or in some other way which would make it inequitable to allow the plaintiff to go back on this representation",[52] Nourse L.J. added that "it is very difficult to see how, on the evidence, the defendant did in fact act to his detriment or in some other material way".[53] On balance the better view is that reliance alone is sufficient, without the need for a detriment to be shown. It should be noted that detriment in this context is different from that used in the definition of consideration.[54] Detrimental reliance remains a requirement of proprietary estoppel.[55]

The limitations of the doctrine

(1) Promissory estoppel does not create a cause of action.

This is sometimes expressed by the phrase that the doctrine acts as "a shield but not a **9.9** sword". Promissory estoppel can be used as a defence but not as a cause of action alone. This is an important limitation on the doctrine in England. In *Combe v. Combe*,[56] the Court of Appeal held that a wife could not enforce her ex-husband's promise to pay her £100 a year free of tax because promissory estoppel could not create a cause of action. Lord Denning began his judgment[57] with words of warning:

> "Much as I am inclined to favour the principle stated in the *High Trees* case it is important that it should not be stretched too far, lest it should be endangered. The principle does not create new causes of action where non existed before. It only prevents a party from insisting on his strict legal rights, when it would be unjust to allow him to enforce, them having regard to the dealings which have taken place between the parties."

The rule is illustrated by *Syros Shipping Co. v. Elaghill Trading Co. "The Proodos C"*[58] where a promise by various consignees in a contract for the carriage of 82 Volvo tractors to pay for the return of a vessel to the port of Hodeidah in the Yemen was held to be unenforceable. There was no consideration for the purported agreement, so there was no pre-existing contractual relationship on which to base estoppel. Promissory estoppel could not be used as the owners were seeking to rely on this as an "independent cause of action" which could not be done.

---

[50] [1987] 1 ALL E.R. 853 (this is also a case on undue influence, see Chap. 19).
[51] At pp. 872–73.
[52] At p. 873.
[53] At p. 873.
[54] See Chap. 8.
[55] See later p. 146.
[56] [1951] 2 K.B. 215.
[57] At p. 219.
[58] [1980] 2 Lloyd's Rep. 390.

Other jurisdictions such as the United States and Australia have now crossed this Rubicon and allowed promissory estoppel to create a cause of action.[59] We discuss some of the more important case law later.[60] Although it cannot be used alone as a cause of action, the plaintiff may use promissory estoppel as part of his action, thereby enabling the claim to succeed. In *Amalgamated Investment v. Texas Commerce Bank*[61] Brandon L.J. stated:

> "In this way the bank, while still in form using the estoppel as a shield would in substance be founding a cause of action on it. This illustrates what I would regard as the true proposition of law, that while a party cannot in terms found a cause of action on an estoppel, he may, as a result of begin able to rely on an estoppel, succeed on a cause of action on which, without being able to rely on that estoppel, he would necessarily have failed."

(2) The equitable factor

9.10   It must be inequitable for the promisor to go back on his promise and enforce his strict legal right. The essence of this equitable doctrine is unconscionability. In *Scandinavian Tanker v. Flota Petrolera "The Scaptrade"*[62] Goff J. stated: "since the equitable estoppel is founded on representation, it can only be unconscionable for the representor (here the owners) to enforce his strict legal right if the conduct of the representee (here the charterers) has been so influenced by the representation as to call for the intervention of equity." Although promissory estoppel is based upon the equitable notion of unconscionability, it is not strictly co-extensive with that doctrine.[63] The rule is that it must be equitable for the promisee to rely on the promise. The judge has a discretion as to what he considers equitable in the circumstances. In *D & C Builders v. Rees*[64] the plaintiffs were in Lord Denning's words "a little company, "D" stands for Donaldson, a decorator, and "C" for Casey, a plumber. They were a firm of jobbing builders doing building work for the defendant at their premises in Brick Lane, in the East End of London. They rendered a bill for just over £746 of which £250 was paid. The plaintiffs, who were in "desperate financial straits", were induced to accept an offer made by the defendant's wife (acting as the defendant's agent) of a cheque for £300 in full settlement of the claim which was worth £482.13s. 1d. (*i.e.* 65p), telling them that "My husband will offer you £300 in settlement. That is all you'll get. It is to be in satisfaction". The Court of Appeal held that the plaintiff builders could recover the balance of what they were owned. They were not estopped, because the conduct of Mrs Rees, the defendant's wife, was not equitable in the circumstances.[65] The Court of Appeal also disposed of any doubt established that

---

[59]   See Murphy and Speidal, *Studies in Contract Law* (1991, 4th ed., The Foundation Press, New York) pp. 468–476. In the United States the basis for promissory estoppel as a cause of action is the Restatement (Second) Contracts s. 90. (see later p. 144).

[60]   See *Waltons Stores (Interstate) Ltd v. Maher* (1988) 164 C.L.R. 387 and *Hoffman v. Red Owl Stores* 133 N.W. 2d 267.

[61]   [1982] Q.B. 84 (at p. 131).

[62]   [1983] 1 All E.R. 301 (at pp. 304–305).

[63]   See Chap. 14.

[64]   [1966] 2 Q.B. 617.

[65]   The case is also relevant to the question of economic duress, see Chap. 9.

payment by cheque was the same as payment by cash.[66] In *Re Selectmove Ltd*[67] there was further discussion of the equitable element. The company had argued that it would be inequitable for the Inland Revenue to go back on its promise to allow them to pay their tax liabilities in instalments. The Court of Appeal rejected the argument, as Selectmove had failed to act equitably by not in fact making the requested payments to the Inland Revenue under the new arrangement. In *Societe Italo-Belge pour le Commerce et l'Industrie SA v. Palm and Vegetable Oils (Malaysia) Sdn Bhd, The Post Chaser*,[68] the court stated that the main requirement of promissory estoppel was that some "inequity" could be shown to result. If this was proved, there was no need to show a detriment. Goff J. stated:[69]

> "The fundamental principle is that stated by Lord Cairns [in *Hughes*]. The representor will not be allowed to enforce his rights 'where it would be inequitable having regard to the dealings which have thus taken place between the parties'. To establish such inequity, it is not necessary to show detriment; indeed, the representee may have benefited from the representation, and yet it may be inequitable, at lease without reasonable notice for the representor to enforce his legal rights . . .".

(3) Promissory estoppel only applies to an existing contractual relationship.

In order to prevent it expanding into the realm of consideration, the courts have **9.11** restricted promissory estoppel to situations where there is an existing contract. Promissory estoppel raises a "defensive equity" only, to vary an existing obligation. In *Ajayi v. Briscoe*,[70] Lord Hodson spoke of promissory estoppel as "applying when one party to a contract in the absence of fresh consideration agrees not to enforce his rights",[71] and in such cases "an equity will be raised in favour of the other party".[72] There is some support for a broader doctrine, however. Lord Denning in *Evenden v. Guildford City AFC Ltd*[73] considered that the doctrine was not limited to situations in which the parties were already contractually bound to one another. Lord Denning considered that it was not necessary for a contractual relationship to exist: "I do not think it is so limited. It applies whenever a representation is made, whether of fact of law, present or future, which is intended to be binding, intended to induce a person to act on it, and he does act on it".[73a] His Lordship cited *Durham Fancy Goods Ltd v. Michael Jackson (Fancy Goods) Ltd*[74] as authority. In this case the Court held that the plaintiffs were bound by the equitable principle of promissory estoppel. Donaldson J. held that "a pre-existing contractual relationship between the parties was not essential, provided that there was a pre-existing legal relationship which could in certain circumstances give rise to liabilities and penalties".[75] Basing his definition of promissory estoppel on Lord Cairns' speech in

[66] See Chap. 8.
[67] [1955] 1 W.L.R. 474.
[68] [1982] 1 All E.R. 19.
[69] At pp. 26–27.
[70] [1964] 1 W.L.R. 1326.
[71] At p. 1330.
[72] At p. 1330.
[73] [1975] Q.B. 917.
[73a] At p. 924.
[74] [1968] 2 Q.B. 839.
[75] At p. 847.

Hughes v. Metropolitan Railway, Donaldson J. took the view that the Lords had "assessed a pre-contractual relationship between the parties but this does not seem to me to be essential".[76] All that was required was a pre-existing legal relationship which could give rise to liabilities and penalties. However in *Syros Shipping Co. v. Elaghill Trading Co., "The Proodos C"*[77] an attempt to use promissory estoppel failed partly because the promise was based on an "agreement" which lacked consideration. There was therefore no pre-existing contractual relationship upon which to attach the doctrine.

(4) Suspended But Not Extinguished: The Original Obligation may be Revived on Giving Reasonable Notice

9.12   For many years there was a debate as to whether the doctrine brings an end to a future obligation or merely suspends it's operation. The settled view now is that promissory estoppel is merely suspensory. Lord Denning took the view that promissory estoppel could discharge an obligation. In *W.J. Alan v. El Nasr Export and Import Co.*[78] it was stated that "there are cases where no withdrawal is possible. It may be too late to withdraw: or it cannot be done without injustice to the other party. In that event he is bound by his waiver. He will not be allowed to revert to his strict rights. He can only enforce them subject to the waiver he has made". However, Lord Denning noted that the usual effect was that a party's strict rights are at least suspended as long as the waiver lasts. In *Tool Metal Manufacturing Co Ltd v. Tungsten Electric Co Ltd*[79] the House of Lords took a similar view. According to Lord Tucker:

> "There are some cases where the period of suspension clearly terminates on the happening of a certain event, or the cessation of a previously existing state of affairs, or on the lapse of a reasonable period thereafter. In such cases no intimation or notice of any kind may be necessary. But in other cases, where there is nothing to fix the end of the period which may be dependent on the will of the person who has given or made the concession, equity will, no doubt require some notice or intimation together with a reasonable period for re-adjustment before the grantor is allowed to enforce his strict rights."[80]

The House of Lords made it clear that in most cases rights are only suspended, not extinguished, by waiver or promissory estoppel. In *E.A. Ajayi v. R.T. Briscoe (Nigeria) Ltd,*[81] the Privy Council held that the promise was only intended to have a suspensory effect.[82] The equitable nature of promissory estoppel allows the courts flexibility in dealing with the effect of the doctrine. In *Tool Metal*, Viscount Simonds pointed out[83] that: "Equity is not held in a strait jacket. There is no universal rule that an equitble arrangement must always be determined in one way". The courts have a discretion in the application of the

---

[76] At p. 847.
[77] [1981] 3 All E.R. 189.
[78] [1972] 2 Q.B. 189 (at p. 213).
[79] [1955] 2 All E.R. 657.
[80] At p. 675.
[81] [1964] 3 All E.R. 566.
[82] If promissory estoppel is based on the principle of waiver in *Hughes*, then this makes the two doctrines similar in effect.
[83] At p. 661.

doctrine and as to its effect. This would be fettered by treating all rights affected as either suspended or extinguished. In *Roebuck v. Mungovin*[84] Lord Browne-Wilkinson stated that "the effect of such an estoppel is to give the court a power to do what is equitable in all the circumstances". Finally, in *Crabb v. Arun District Council*[85] the Court of Appeal emphasised that the nature of the relief to be given when an equitable estoppel is raised was flexible. The courts had to decide if anything was necessary to achieve an equitable result in the circumstances of the particular case. Of course many of the cases hinge on the construction of what was promised. Did the parties intend the right to be extinguished or merely suspended? In most cases the intention will be to give the other party more time to pay, rather than to wipe out any contractual liability in its entirety for the future. In the United States promissory estoppel can extinguish a right. The doctrine that evolved from the Restatement of Contracts in 1933 not only permitted promissory estoppel to create a cause of action, but also to extinguish rights.[86]

Promissory Estoppel as a Cause of Action in other Common Law Jurisdictions

One of the key issues in reliance theory is whether promissory estoppel should be permitted to outflank consideration and provide a remedy on its own, in other words, to create a caution of action. As we have discussed, in England this has not yet occurred. Promissory estoppel is only a defence. This is not so in other common law jurisdictions. In the hands of the High Court of Australia in their judgment in *Waltons Stores (Interstate) Ltd v. Maher*,[87] the doctrine of promissory estoppel became a sword. A promise to go ahead with a lease of property at Nowra in New South Wales was relied upon to the extent of one of the parties demolishing an existing building in order to redevelop the site. No contract was made, however, and eventually the defendants changed their mind knowing that the other party had taken steps to proceed with their projected agreement. This was held to be unconscionable and the plaintiffs were allowed to use promissory estoppel as their cause of action. The test was whether there was a "departure from the basic assumption underlying the transaction which could be regarded as unconscionable". Mason L.J. and Wilson J. held that:

9.13

> "The appellant's inaction, in all the circumstances, constituted clear encouragement or inducement to the respondents to continue to act on the basis of the assumption which they had made. It was unconscionable for it, knowing that the respondents were exposing themselves to detriment by acting on the basis of a false assumption, to adopt a course of action which encouraged them in the course they had adopted. To express the point in the language of promissory estoppel the appellant is estoppel in all the circumstances from retreating from its implied promise to complete the contract."[88]

---

[84] [1994] 2 A.C. 224 (at p. 235).
[85] [1976] Ch. 179.
[86] See *Farnsworth Contracts* (1990, 2nd ed, Little Brown and Co.), pp. 95–102.
[87] (1988) 164 C.L.R. 387.
[88] At p. 401.

It appears that in the Australian Court's view there had to be "detrimental reliance" for a promise to found a cause of action. The requirements of promissory estoppel as a cause of the action were set out by Brennan J.:

"(i) The plaintiff assumed that a particular legal relationship then existed between him and the defendant or expected that a particular legal relationship would exist between them and, in the latter case, that the defendant would not be free to withdraw from the expected legal relationship; (ii) the defendant induced the plaintiff to adopt that assumption or expectation; (iii) the plaintiff acts or abstains from acting in reliance on the assumption or expectation; (iv) the defendant knew or intended him to do so; (v) the plaintiff's action or inaction will occasion detriment if the assumption or expectation is not fulfilled; and (vi) the defendant has failed to act to avoid that detriment whether by fulfilling the assumption or expectation or otherwise".[89]

The High Court of Australia's approach is fairly narrow and also cautious suggesting that the concept has to be treated with care.[90] It is certainly not a licence to enforce any promise which is relied upon. Mason C.J. pointed out that[91] "mere reliance on an executory promise to do something, resulting in the promisee changing his position or suffering detriment, does not bring promissory estoppel into play. Something more would be required." He cited the Privy Council case of *A-G of Hong Kong v. Humphreys Estates (Queens Gardens) Ltd*[92] that this might be found, if at all, in the creation or encouragement by the party estoppel, of an assumption in the other person that a contract will come into existence or a promise will be performed and that the other party relied on that assumption to this detriment and to the knowledge of the first party. Mason C.J. derived authority from the American Restatement of Contracts s. 90 that the principle should be expressed in terms of a "reasonable expectation" on the part of the promisor that the promise will induce action or forbearance by the promisee and that it will be unconscionable to go back on his word. Injustice can therefore only be avoided by holding the promisor to his word. The Australian doctrine has it's foundation in the equitable doctrine of unconscionability.[93]

9.14   The United States Restatement (Second) of Contracts allows promissory estoppel to operate as a cause of action. The courts are given a discretion to determine the appropriate remedy so that there may not be full enforcement of the promise. Section 90(1) states that "a promise which the promisor should reasonably expect to induce action or forbearance on the part of the promisee or a third person and which does induce such action or forbearance is binding if injustice can be avoided only by enforcement of the promise. The remedy granted for breach may be limited as justice requires." Section 90 does not require that the promise giving rise to action must be the equivalent of an offer that would become a contract if accepted by the promise. There are three questions to answer in applying the doctrine:

---

[89] As to whether damages should be based upon the reliance or expectation principle, see Chap. 23.
[90] See Spence, "Protecting Reliance", (1999, Hart Publishing, Oxford).
[91] At p. 406.
[92] [1987] 1 A.C. 114.
[93] As to whether damages should be awarded to promissory estoppel on an expectation or a reliance test, see Chap. 26.

(a)   Was the promise one which the promisor should reasonably expect to induce action or forbearance of a definite and substantial character on the part of the promisee?

(b)   Did the promise induce such action or forbearance?

(c)   Can injustice be avoided only by enforcement of the promise?

In *Hoffman v. Red Owl Stores Inc.*[94] the plaintiff, Hoffman, owned a bakery near the town of Green Bay, Winsconsin. He was told he could get a franchise with a supermarket chain if he took steps to gain experience in the business and invested $18,000 dollars. He relied on this by taking steps to sell his bakery, acquiring another store and moving to another town. The arrangement fell through and the plaintiff recovered reliance damages on the basis of a claim in promissory estoppel. The Court held that promissory estoppel should give the plaintiffs their action: "We conclude that injustice would result here if plaintiffs were not granted some relief because of the failure of defendants to keep their promises which induced plaintiffs to act to their detriment". The plaintiff was therefore able to use promissory as a cause of action. The insertion of s. 90 into the first Restatement represented the victory of reliance theorists over the exchange based view of traditional contract theory.[95] To counterbalance this, the American view of the meaning of consideration has been traditionally narrower than that in England.[96]

THE VARIETIES OF EQUITABLE ESTOPPEL

The remaining categories of equitable estoppel have developed separately from contract law. In *Crabb v. Arun District Council* Lord Denning, referring to the many headed varieties of estoppel, stated[97]: "When counsel for Mr Crabb said that he put his case on an estoppel, it shook me a little: because it is commonly supposed that estoppel is not itself a cause of action. But that is because there are *estoppels and estoppels*. Some do give rise to a cause of action. Some do not". We shall now look briefly at the different types of equitable estoppels.

9.15

Proprietary estoppel

It is proper to regard proprietary estoppel doctrine as being within the province of land law. This arises when the owner of land creates an understanding in another person that he will acquire rights to the property. Proprietary estoppel does not require a promise (unlike promissory estoppel) but can also be constituted by acquiescence, in other words, by allowing the person to persist in a notion knowing this be unwarranted. There are clearly similarities between proprietary and promissory estoppel, but there are also important differences. Both are equitable in nature and therefore discretionary depending

---

[94] (1965) 133 N.W. 2d 267.
[95] See Chap. 1.
[96] See Farnsworth, "Contracts", (1990, 2nd ed., Little Brown, Boston).
[97] [1975] 3 All E.R. 865 (at p. 871).

on the conduct of the parties. However, proprietary estoppel only arises in relation to property and requires detrimental reliance to be shown. Proprietary estoppel can create a cause of action. A good example of proprietary estoppel is *Re Basham (Deceased)*,[98] in which the plaintiff, Joan Bird, and her husband had helped her mother and stepfather for many years without any remuneration on the understanding that she would inherit her stepfather's property at Great Hockham, Norfolk when he died. He repeated that she was to have the cottage in question, and that "she would lose nothing by her help". She was held to be entitled to the property of the stepfather, Henry Basham who died intestate, on the basis either of proprietary estoppel or of a constructive trust.[99] Proprietary estoppel was defined by Judge Edward Nugee[1] as arising where "one person, A, has acted to his detriment on the faith of a belief which was known to and encouraged by another person B, that he either has or is going to be given a right I or over B's property B cannot insist on this strict legal rights if to do so would be inconsistent with A's belief." However, in *Gillett v. Holt*[2] Robert Walker L.J. noted the fluid nature of proprietary estoppel, and rejected the notion that the doctrine of proprietary estoppel could be treated as subdivided into three or four watertight compartments: ". . . the fundamental principle that equity is concerned to prevent unconscionable conduct permeates all the elements of the doctrine. In the end the court must look at the matter in the round". Unlike the doctrine of promissory estoppel, detrimental reliance must be shown for proprietary estoppel. Balcombe L.J. in *Wayling v. Jones*[3] stated the relevant principles of detrimental reliance for proprietary estopped as being:

(a) there is a "sufficient link" between the promises relied on and the conduct constituting the detriment[4];

(b) the promises relied on do not have to be the sole inducement so long as they are an inducement[5]; and

(c) once it is proved that promises were made and conduct by the plaintiff the burden of proof shifts to the defendant to prove that he did not rely on the promise.[6]

In *Wayling v. Jones* the plaintiffs conduct in helping run a café and two hotels in Barmouth according to the Court "for what was at best little more than pocket money", was "conduct from which his reliance on the deceased's clear promises could be inferred."[7]

9.16   The need for unconscionability is an element of the equitable nature of this doctrine. In *Taylor's Fashions v. Liverpool Trustees*[8] Oliver J. reiterated the view that the doctrine

---

[98] [1986] 1 W.L.R. 1498.
[99] On this and the wider aspects of reliance upon wills, see Nield, "If you look after me, I will leave you my estate", (2000) 20 Legal Studies 98. This article also includes discussion on New Zealand law.
[1] At p. 1503.
[2] [2001] Ch. 210 (at p. 225).
[3] (1995) 69 P and CR 170 (at p. 173).
[4] He cited *Eves v. Eves* [1996] C.L. 638.
[5] *Amalgamated Investment v. Texas Commerce Bank* [1982] Q.B. 84.
[6] See *Greasley v. Cook* [1985] 1 W.L.R. 1306.
[7] At p. 173.
[8] [1982] Q.B. 133.

was based on unconscionability. Proprietary estoppel was directed as ascertaining whether, in particular individual circumstances, "it would be unconscionable for a party to be permitted to deny that which, knowingly or unknowingly, he has allowed or encouraged another to assume to his detriment than to enquiring whether the circumstances can be fitted within the confines of some preconceived formula serving as a universal yardstick of unconscionable behaviour."[9] In *Taylor v. Dickens*[10] the plaintiff, Bob Taylor, worked for the defendant, Maisie Parker, as a part-time gardener. The defendant promised him that, now she was widowed, the plaintiff would become owner of the house at Crownthorne when she died. Later it was discovered that she had changed her will. Judge Weekes in the Chancery Division stated that the equitable jurisdiction would not hold a person to a promise merely because it was unfair, unconscionable or morally objectionable for him to go back on his word. The plaintiff should have known that wills were revocable and that Mrs Parker could change her mind. Even the plaintiffs' wife admitted that Mrs Parker had told him "not to count his chickens before they are hatched". The judgment was however described by Robert Walker L.J. in *Gillett v. Holt* as "clearly wrong":

> "The judge seems to have forgotten that the whole point of estoppel claims is that they concern promises which, since they are unsupported by consideration, are initially revocable. What later makes them binding, and therefore irrevocable, is the promisee's detrimental reliance on them. Once that occurs, there is simply no question of the promisor changing his or her mind."

Proprietary estoppel was successfully argued in *Gillett v. Holt*.[11] The defendant, Kenneth Holt, a wealthy farmer in Lincolnshire, was 38 when he first met the claimant, Geoffrey Gillet, who was then 12 years of age. The claimant worked for the defendant for many years and when he married, Holt made various statements about leaving his property to the claimant, when he [*i.e* the defendant] died. The plaintiff continued to work for the defendant but their friendship broke down and the defendant, by now having formed a relationship with a local solicitor, changed his mind and left the house and property to the solicitor in a new will. At first instance the claim based on proprietary estoppel failed but this was overturned in the Court of Appeal. The Court of Appeal held that the claimant should inherit the £300,000 farm when the defendant died on the basis of proprietary estoppel, but not the rest of his property. There had been a detriment which established a proprietary estoppel creating a right of action for the claimant.

The remedies for proprietary estoppel are various as befits an equitable power. The promisor may be required to convey the property to the other person, merely allow the person to stay on the property, or pay damages to compensate him for his reliance expenditure. The courts will consider the conduct of the promisor in doing so, and whether it was unconscionable or otherwise. The objective of equitable relief was described by Sir Arthur Hobhouse in *Pinner v. Mayor of Wellington*[12] as being to determine in what way "equity can be satisfied". This depends on the circumstances of each case. Equity is

---

[9] At p. 151.
[10] [1998] 1 F.L.R. 806.
[11] [2000] 2 All E.R. 289.
[12] (1884) 9 App. Cas 699 (at p. 714).

usually restricted to the minimum to do justice (or even simply to avoid injustice) to the plaintiff. Equitable doctrines such as proprietary estoppel or constructive trust can also sometimes be used to remedy a defect in form, as for instance where land was sold by oral agreement, thereby failing to comply with the law of the Property (Miscellaneous Provisions) Act 1989 s. 2, which requires writing.[13]

Estoppel by convention

9.17   Estoppel by convention applies when both parties to a transaction act on a shared assumption that certain facts are true. They are estopped from denying this later if it would be unconscionable for them to do so. There does not have to be a promise or representation for estoppel by convention to apply.[14] In *Amalgamated Investment v. Texas Commerce Bank* the common assumption was that the parties had entered into a contract of guarantee made by a subsidiary of the defendants. This was not true though it was believed by both parties at the time. On an action for the declaration that the defendants were not entitled to use the money, estoppel by convention was applied as a defence to defeat the action. Lord Denning stated *obiter dicta* that estoppel by convention could be used as a cause of action, Brandon L.J. however would have used the contract as the cause of action instead. In *Norwegian American Cruises v. Paul Mundy, "The Vistafiord"*[14a] the Court of Appeal held that estoppel by convention prevented a party raising a different interpretation upon which the parties had acted.

Estoppel by representation

If a person makes a clear and unambiguous representation of fact, he may be prevented from denying the truth of the statement if the person to whom it was made acted upon the statement to her detriment, as was the intention of the representor.[15]

Estoppel by conduct

This is an under-developed idea but one which could, in due course, have a far reaching impact. Unlike promissory estoppel, it is not an aspect of waiver and is to be regarded as a separate doctrine. Estoppel by conduct first appeared in *Panchaud Freres SA v. Ets. General Grain Company*,[16] where it was described by Lord Denning[17]:

> "The basis of it [estoppel by conduct] is that a man has so conducted himself that it would be unfair or unjust to allow him to depart from a particular state of affairs which another has taken to be settled or correct." Applied to the rejection of goods, the principle may be stated thus: If a man, who is entitled to reject goods on a

---

[13]   See *Yaxley v Gotts* [2000] Ch. 162; [1999] 2 F.L.R. 941, noted in *Imogen Moore* (2000) 63 M.L.R. 912.
[14]   See *Amalgamated Investment and Property Co v. Texas Commerce International Bank* [1982] Q.B. 84.
[14a]   [1988] 2 Lloyd's Rep. 343.
[15]   See *Low v Bouverie* [1891] 3 Ch. 82 and *Lombard North Central plc v. Stobart* [1990] 9 Tr. L.R. 105.
[16]   [1970] 1 Lloyd's Rep. 53.
[17]   At p. 57.

certain ground, so conducts himself as to lead the other to believe that he is not relying on that ground, then he cannot afterwards set it up as a ground of rejection, when it would be unfair or unjust to allow him so to do."[18]

In the same case, Winn L.J. perceived estoppel by conduct as not restrained by the requirements of waiver or estoppel to promises to vary an existing agreement:

"I respectfully agree with my Lord that what one has here is something perhaps in our law not yet wholly developed as a separate doctrine – which is more in the nature of a requirement of fair conduct – a criterion of what is fair conduct between the parties. There may be an inchoate doctrine stemming from the manifest convenience of consistency in pragmatic affairs, negativity an liberty to blow hot and cold in commercial conduct."[19]   **9.18**

In a later case, *Toepfer v. Peter Cremer*,[20] Lord Denning described the doctrine as follows: "When one person has led another to believe that a particular transaction is valid and correct, he cannot thereafter be allowed to say that it is invalid and incorrect where it would be unfair and unjust to allow him to do so. It is a kind of estoppel. He cannot blow hot and cold as it suits his book". The existence of such a wide doctrine is doubted by many and there have been criticisms of the "*Panchaud Freres*" principle, and whether it should be developed. In *Syros Shipping v. Elaghill Trading Co. "The Proodos* C"[21] Lloyd J. stated: "the principle established by *Panchud Freres* has not yet been fully worked out by the courts; in particular it is uncertain whether it is to be regarded as based on estoppel or whether it is based on a kind of estoppel or whether it is a kind of waiver, and if so what its limits are. But one thing is quite certain. It cannot be used to create a new cause of action".[22] Whether *Panchaud Freres* is really equitable estoppel is open to debate though it was regarded as such by Lord Denning.[23] The alternative view is that it is based on waiver, though this was expressly rejected in the judgment. Two requirements of equitable estoppel, representation and reliance upon it, do not appear to be present. The argument of estoppel by conduct failed in *Glencore Grain Rotterdam BV v. LORICO*,[24] in which Evans L.J.[25] regarded *Panchaud Freres* as based on a acceptance of goods and whether or not a party could rely on a matter which he did not raise at the time. He reviewed Lord Denning's version of estoppel by conduct as being based on whether it was "unfair or unjust to allow a person to depart from a particular state of affairs".[26] As far as Winn L.J.'s "separate doctrine" was concerned, it had received "no support", in his judgment,

---

[18] Lord Denning cites an earlier case, *Central Newbury Car Auctions Ltd v. Unity Finance Ltd* [1957] 1 Q.B. 371, and authorities listed at p. 380.
[19] At p. 57.
[20] [1975] 2 Lloyd's Rep. 118 at p. 123.
[21] [1980] 2 Lloyd's Rep. 390.
[22] At p. 392.
[23] In *Proctor and Gamble Philippine Manufacturing Co. v. Peter Cremer "The Manila"* [1988] 3 All E.R. 843. Hirst J. (at p. 852) preferred the estoppel explanation "since it has the greater weight of authority behind it."
[24] [1997] 2 Lloyd's Rep. 386.
[25] At p. 396.
[26] At p. 395.

"from any of the later authorities".[27] The Court of Appeal approved Goff J.'s statement in *BP v. Hunt (No. 2)*[28] that this was "an argument of last resort when they [counsel] find it difficult to bring their case within the established principles of estoppel, waiver or election." Evans L.J.[29] rejected any "separate doctrine" derived from *Panchaud Ferers* alone. Without some promise or representation "no estoppel or waiver can arise, and there is no general rule that what the Court or tribunal may perceive as "unfairness or injustice" has the same effect. The single doctrine of estoppel being worked out in Australia is grouped around a central notion of estoppel by conduct, although the phrase is not the same as that used in the *Panchaud Freres* principle.

A SINGLE DOCTRINE OF EQUITABLE ESTOPPEL?

9.19   Promissory estoppel has developed slowly in England. There is an argument for taking the doctrine a few stages further. The main developments could be that:

(i)   Promissory estoppel be allowed to create a cause of action in clearly defined circumstances;

(ii)   Promissory and proprietary estoppel brought together perhaps in one all embracing principle of equitable estoppel;

(iii)   The courts lay down clear guidelines for unconscionability to prevent the doctrine getting out of control; or

(iv)   Promissory estoppel apply even without a pre-existing contract.

Equitable estoppel is an interesting ground for debate.[30] A more developed reliance based general doctrine of estoppel, as a supplement to consideration, would allow the latter doctrine to continue in something like it's traditional form. The strongest arguments against an overindulgence in equitable estoppel are the fears of uncertainty and the traditional "flood gates" argument, as simply too many commercial arrangements might be caught up in the still rather vague notions of reliance and unconscionability. The Australian cases show how careful any such development has to be. On the other hand, the growth of an equitable principle to stand alongside but not replace consideration allows the traditional bulwark of the enforcement of promises to be preserved. This area of discussion on the limits of promises is likely to remain an interesting battleground in years to come. In *Crabb v. Arun DC*[31] Scarman L.J. took the view that the distinctions between promissory and proprietary estoppel were unhelpful. His Lordship stated that: "I do not find helpful the distinction between promissory and proprietary estoppel. This distinction may indeed be valuable to those who have to teach or expound the law, but I do not think that, in solving the particular problem raised by a particular case, putting the law into categories is of the

---

[27]   At p. 396.
[28]   [1979] 1 W.L.R. 788 (at p. 811).
[29]   At pp. 397–8.
[30]   See Halliwell, "Estoppel: Unconscionability as a cause of action" (1994) 14 Legal Studies 15.
[31]   [1976] Ch. 179.

slightest assistance".[32] Scarman L.J. also drew a wider picture of the basis for equitable intervention. There were three questions to ask based upon the conduct and relationship of the parties,[33] "First, was an equity established? Second, what is the extent of the equity, and third what relief is appropriate to satisfy the equity?" Lord Denning supported the view that the varieties of estoppel might be reduced to a single principle doctrine in *Amalgamated Investment and Property Co. Ltd v. Texas Commerce International Bank*.[34] The various rules and doctrines could be: "seen to merge into one general principle shorn of limitations. When the parties to a transaction proceed on the basis of an underlying assumption – either of fact or of law – whether due to misrepresentation or mistake makes no difference – on which they have conducted the dealings between them – neither of them will be allowed to go back on that assumption when it would be unfair or unjust to allow him to do so. If one of them does seek to go back on it, the courts will give the other such remedy as the equity of the case demands."[35] This view was rejected by Millett L.J. in *First National Bank plc v. Thompson*,[36] who stated that "Spencer Bower's valiant attempt to demonstrate that all estoppels other than estoppel by record are now subsumed in the single and all-embracing estoppel by representation and that they are all governed by the same requirements, has never won general acceptance. Historically unsound, it has been repudiated by academic writers and is unsupported by authority".[37][38] However, in *Woodhouse AC Israel Cocoa SA v. Nigerian Produce Marketing*[39] Lord Hailsham expressed the view that "the time may soon be when the whole sequence of cases based on [promissory] estoppel may need to be reviewed and reduced to a coherent body of doctrine by the courts".

Other common law jurisdictions have taken tentative steps towards a general principle **9.20** of equitable estoppel but the difficulties are considerable and the resulting effect debatable. In Australia, estoppel has taken steps towards a merger and is developing a single doctrine based around the equitable notion of unconscionability.[40] Australian law was late by common law standards in adopting promissory estoppel in *Legione v. Hateley*.[41] Having done so, they now have taken to estoppel with enthusiasm.[42] In *Commonwealth v. Verwayen*,[43] which was not strictly speaking a contract case, the High Court of Australia expressed support for bringing the various doctrines and remedies in the field of estoppel under a "single overaching doctrine". Mason C.J.[44] stated that the "consistent trend in the modern decisions points inexorably towards the emergence of one overarching doctrine of estoppel rather than a series of independent rules". Among English cases cited by Mason C.J. were *Taylor's Fashions Ltd v. Liverpool*

---

[32] At p. 193.
[33] At p. 193.
[34] [1982] Q.B. 84 (at p. 122).
[35] At p. 122.
[36] [1996] 1 All E.R. 140.
[37] Spencer-Bower and Turner, *The Law Relating to Estoppel by Representation* (1977, 3rd ed, Butterworths).
[38] At p. 144.
[39] [1972] 2 All E.R. 271 (at p. 282).
[40] Spence, "Australian Estoppel and the Protection of Reliance" (1997) 11 Journal of Contract Law 203.
[41] (1983) 152 C.L.R. 406.
[42] See Spence, *Protecting Reliance*, (1999, Hart Publishing, Oxford), p. 15. See also *Australian Securities Commission v. Marlborough Gold Mines Ltd* (1993) 177 C.L.R. 506.
[43] (1990) 170 C.L.R. 394.
[44] At p. 410.

Trustees Co,[45] *Amalgamaged Investment v. Texas Bank,*[46] and *AG (Hong Kong) v. Humphreys Estate (Queen's Garden) Ltd*[47]. Dean J.[48] stated that "there is reason in principle for refusing to accept promissory estoppel as but an emanation of the general doctrine of estoppel by conduct". The elements of estoppel were described by Chief Justice Mason as being united by common characteristics[49]: "there is but one doctrine of estoppel, which provides that a court of common law or equity may do what is required, but not more, to prevent a person who has relied upon an assumption as to a present, past or future state of affairs (including a legal state of affairs), which assumption the party estoped has induced him to hold, from suffering detriment in reliance upon the assumption as a result of the denial of its correctness. A central element of that doctrine is that there must be a proportionality between the remedy and the detriment which is its purpose to avoid". In doing so, Mason L.J. appeared to endorse Lord Dennings views in *Texas Commerce International Bank.* Deane J.[50] agreed that "there is no reason in principle for refusing to accept promissory estoppel as but an emanation of the general doctrine of estoppel by conduct".

9.21   Oliver J. in *Taylors Fashions* and Robert Goff J. (at first instance) in the *Texas Bank Case* have convincingly explained why it is undesirable to seek to restrict equitable estoppel to certain defined categories such as promissory estoppel, proprietary estoppel and estoppel by acquiescence: "It appears to me that the courts of this country should recognise a general doctrine of estoppel by conduct which encompasses the various categories of 'equitable estoppel' and which operates throughout a fused system of law and equity."[51] It is worth noting the number of English authorities cited above. Perhaps English law is not so far away from following the Australian lead.[52] Reviewing earlier authorities, Mason C.J. took the view that recent developments in both England and Australia had brought "a greater underlying unit to the various categories of estoppel . . . "Indeed the consistent trend in the modern decisions points inexorably towards the emergence of one overarching doctrine of estoppel rather than a series of independent rules".[53] The general principle of estoppel in Australian law is based upon unconscionability. "The basis of equitable estoppel, according to Mason CJ is "the relief necessary to prevent unconscionability and to do justice between the parties".[54] Brennan J.[55] defined the wider doctrine of equitable estoppel as one which "yields a remedy in order to prevent unconscionable conduct on the part of the party, who having made a promise to another who acts on it to his detriment, seeks to resile from the promise". In *Verwayen* the Australian High Court was not unanimous, with both Dawson J. and McHugh J. dissenting on the point of whether there was a general equitable doctrine. McHugh J. took the view that once the detriment has ceased, or been paid for, there was "nothing

---

[45] [1982] Q.B. 133.
[46] [1982] Q.B. 84 A.R. 122.
[47] [1987] A.C. 114.
[48] At p. 440.
[49] At p. 413.
[50] At p. 400.
[51] At p. 440.
[52] Care has to be taken with the expression "estoppel by conduct" in *Verwayen* which is cited in it's traditional sense rather than Lord Denning's version in *Panchaud Freres,* (see earlier p. 148).
[53] At pp. 410–411.
[54] At p. 411.
[55] At pp. 428–429.

unconscionable in a party insisting on reverting to his former relationship with the other party and enforcing his strict legal rights". In a later case, *Giumelli v. Giumelli*,[56] the High Court of Australia treated promissory and proprietary estoppel as merged. They did not however make clear to what extent there was a single doctrine of estoppel in Australian law.[57] The process of merger has therefore still some way to go before it is complete, in Australia, and is yet to take root in English law. It is an interesting project, which could alter the basis of the enforceability of promises.

---

[56] [1999] H.C.A. 10. Australian and other developments are fully discussed in Cooke, "The Modern Law of Estoppel" O.G.P. 2000.
[57] See Wright [1999] C.L.J. 476.

Chapter 10

THIRD PARTIES

Introduction

The Contracts (Rights of Third Parties) Act 1999 transformed one of the traditional **10.1** corner-stones of contract law, the doctrine of privity of contract. The old common law rule has been rendered ineffectual as a result of the Act, which provides that from May 2000 a third party who satisfies the conditions laid down in the legislation may obtain an enforceable benefit under a contract to which they are not party. The 1999 Act has been hailed as potentially one of the most radical watersheds in the history of English contract law, and dismissed by others as a white elephant. The Act allows the parties to supersede the privity rule, if they wish, by giving a third party an enforceable benefit. The privity rule is not abolished, however, if the parties wish to retain it or the third party falls outside the Act. The common law survives if that is what the parties intend.

The mischief which the statute were designed to supplant was the difficulties associated with the long-standing privity rule. In *Panatown Ltd v. Alfred McAlpine*, Lord Goff stated[1] that "the existence of these problems led first of all to the recognition of a number of exceptions to the rule and ultimately only last year to its abolition by the Contracts (Rights of Third Parties) Act 1999". Lord Goff explained this stating that:

> "The rule, seen in the abstract is rational and very understandable in a law of contract which includes the doctrine of consideration; but it has given rise to great problems in practice - because, both in commerce and in the domestic context, parties do enter into contracts which are intended to confer enforceable rights on third parties, and a rule of law which precludes a right of enforcement by a third party can therefore fail to give effect to the intention of the contracting parties and to the reasonable expectations of the third party".

It was not beyond the wit of lawyers to devise a legal system without privity of contract, indeed it took legal intelligence to invent it. Privity certainly had it's own rationale. Having developed privity into a predominant position, English law clung tenaciously to the idea after most other common law jurisdictions had either abandoned or reformed

---

[1] [2000] 4 All E.R. 97 (at p. 120).

the doctrine down to a minimum.[2] In other European civilian systems, including Scots law,[3] privity is displaced by a *ius quaesitum tertio*, giving a third party an enforceable right to sue if that is the intention of the contracting parties. There were arguments for and against privity of contract, and reforming the rule proved to be no easy matter. Essentially there are two elements to the privity doctrine. First, that a third party cannot benefit from a term in a contract between two others, and secondly, cannot have a detriment imposed upon him or her. As a result of the 1999 Act, the first element is now possible, but the second part of the privity rule remains. Although privity of contract is considerably reduced in importance, a great deal of the old law survives. Many contracting parties may conclude that they wish to exclude the Act altogether as they are allowed to do, and a number of third parties will fail to qualify or fall outside of it's provisions. Some considerable historical background is therefore still necessary to an understanding of the new régime.

THE BACKGROUND OF THE PRIVITY OF CONTRACT RULE

10.2   Historically, privity of contract performed some very important functions for contract law. Like the doctrine of consideration, the main purpose of the privity rule was to determine which promises were to be regarded as contractual. In other words, to act as a wall or boundary fence of enforceability. The second function was evidentiary, *i.e.* to prove that obligations were seriously intended, and, the third to control fraud and false claims. The privity rule and consideration are closely entwined, indeed the rule that consideration must move from the promisee and the doctrine of privity are really aspects of the same thing. The former is concerned with whether there is a contract at all, the latter about which person or persons may benefit. In one of the leading early cases, *Price v. Easton,*[4] two different reasons for the judgment were given. Denman L.J. based his judgment on consideration: "the declaration cannot be supported, as it does not shew any consideration for the promise moving from the plaintiff to the defendant".[5] On the other hand, Littledale J. concluded that "No privity is shown between the plaintiff and the defendant".[6] Could privity be reformed without doing the same for consideration?[7] The answer from other jurisdictions appeared to be in the affirmative.[8] The doctrine of consideration is nonetheless clearly undermined in the process.

Privity of contract is not an ancient rule. It was only finally established in English law in *Tweddle v. Atkinson,*[9] in which Wightman J. said that no "stranger" could take advantage of a provision in a contract even though it was made for his benefit. Crompton J. came to the same conclusion but based his decision on the rule that "consideration must move from the promisee."[10] The doctrine of privity of contract has two strands: a

[2] The Americans discarded privity of contract at an early date in *Lawrence v. Fox.* (1859) 2 N.Y. 268 by giving third parties an enforceable right in a contract between two others. The Restatement (Second) Contracts s. 302 also gives third party beneficiaries a right, if that is the intention of the parties.
[3] See *Carmichael v. Carmichael's Executrix* 1920 S.C. (HL) 195.
[4] (1833) 4 B and Ad. 433, 110 E.R. 518.
[5] At p. 519.
[6] Patteson J. added a third ground: "There is no promise to the plaintiff alleged".
[7] On reforming consideration as a whole, see Chap. 8.
[8] *e.g.* In New Zealand, the Contracts (Privity) Act 1982.
[9] (1861) 1 B & S 393, 121 E.R. 762.
[10] See Chap. 7.

"benefit" rule and a "detriment" rule. The privity rule prevented a third party enforcing a promise in a contract to which they were not a party, nor could they use the contract as a defence to an action by one of the two contracting parties. The contract could not avail a party against a claim brought by a third party.[11] Equally, however, a contracting party could not enforce terms in their favour against the third party, thereby imposing a detriment upon them. At one time the mere existence of a contract prevented action by a third party in tort.[12] This restriction was removed by the House of Lords in *Donoghue v. Stevenson*.[13] Lord Denning supported enforceable third party rights in *Smith and Snipes Hall Farm Ltd v. River Douglas Catchment Board*[14] and *Drive Yourself Hire Co (London) Ltd v. Strutt*.[15] However, the House of Lords in *Midland Silicones Ltd v. Scruttons Ltd*,[16] took the view that reform of the privity rule, if it was to be undertaken, had to be done by Parliament.

10.3 *Scrutton v. Midlands Silicones Ltd*[17] is a good example of how the privity rule operated, and also of it's practical inconvenience. A bill of lading which incorporated the United States Carriage of Goods by Sea Act 1936 contained a limitation of liability of $500 for loss, damage or delay for any drum containing chemicals shipped from the United States to England. The stevedores unloading the vessel, *The American Reporter*, in the London docks negligently dropped and damaged a drum, and its contents, worth £593, were lost. The consignees, *i.e.* the party to whom the goods were being delivered, sued for the value of the lost chemicals. The stevedores argued that their liability was limited to £179 (*i.e.* the sterling equivalent of $500 in 1957). The House of Lords (with Lord Denning dissenting) held that the stevedores were third parties to the main contract and that they could not claim a benefit or be protected under it. The House of Lords stated that "it was a fundamental principle that only a person who is party to a contract can sue upon it".[17a] A stranger to a contract could take advantage of provisions of the contract between two others, even where it is clear from the contract that some provision in it were intended to benefit him.[18]

10.4 Privity of contract is an example of an unpopular or inconvenient common law rule which the courts strove to avoid by the invention of exemptions or the use of alternative doctrines. An illustration of this is the House of Lord's judgment in *Beswick v. Beswick*.[19] Old Peter Beswick, aged 70, and in poor health, agreed with his nephew John, the defendant, to transfer the goodwill and trade utensils of his coal round business. The consideration was to pay Uncle Peter £6.50 per week as a consultant and after Peter Beswick died £5 a week for life to Peter Beswick's widow, Ruth, the plaintiff. When the nephew refused to pay the widow she brought action against him, though not a party to the original contract. The House of Lords held that in her personal capacity she could not

---

[11]   See *Dunlop Pneumatic Tyre Co Ltd v. Selfridge and Co* [1915] A.C. 847.
[12]   See *Winterbottom v. Wright* (1842) 10 M and W 109, 107 E.R. 171.
[13]   [1932] A.C. 562.
[14]   [1949] 2 K.B. 500.
[15]   [1954] 1 Q.B. 250.
[16]   [1962] A.C. 446.
[17]   [1962] A.C. 446.
[17a]   At p. 494.
[18]   Lord Denning disagreed: "First of all let me remind your Lordships that this 'fundamental principle' was a discovery of the nineteenth century. Lord Mansfield and Buller J. knew nothing of it. But in the nineteenth century it was carried to the most extravagant lengths".
[19]   [1968] A.C. 58.

succeed because of the privity rule, since a third party could not enforce a contract between two others. However, as administratrix of a party to the contract she was entitled to an order for specific performance of the promise by her nephew and was not limited to merely nominal damages for loss to the deceased's estate.

REFORMING THE PRIVITY RULE

10.5   Prior to the Contracts (Rights of Third Parties) Act 1999, judges were often prepared to criticise privity of contract but were not prepared (or able) to avoid or abolish it altogether. In *Forster v. Silvermere Golf and Equestrian Centre Ltd*[20] Dillon J. was forced to conclude that the plaintiff who had not entered into a contract as trustee or agent for her children could only recover damages for herself and not for the rights of occupation after her death which her children should have enjoyed.[21] He commented that: "if that conclusion was correct it was a blot on our law and thoroughly unjust but the court was bound by the decision". In *Swain v. Law Society*,[22] Lord Diplock said that the "lacuna" resulting from the non recognition of third party rights was "an anachronistic shortcoming that has for many years been regarded as a reproach to English private law". In *White v. Jones*[23] Lord Goff said, "It is true that our law of contract is widely seen as deficient in the sense that it is perceived to be hampered by the presence of an unnecessary doctrine of consideration and (through a strict doctrine of privity of contract) stunted through a failure to recognise a *jus quaesitum tertio*". Finally in *Darlington Borough Council v. Wiltshier Northern Ltd*[24] Steyn L.J. stated that the case for recognising a contract for the benefit of a third party was "simple and straightforward".[25] To emphasise his point Steyn J.,[26] observed: "The genesis of the privity rule is suspect. It is attributed to *Tweddle v. Atkinson*. It is more realistic to see that the rule originated in the misunderstanding of *Tweddle v. Atkinson*".[27]

10.6   This lack of enthusiasm for the rule by the courts is shown by the numerous exceptions and means of avoidance developed by the judges.[28] There have been earlier attempts at law reform in this area. In 1937 the Law Revision Committee in its Sixth Report[29] recommended that a third party be allowed to benefit from contracts between two others, however, no legislative action resulted from this. Since then despite the criticisms the rule has remained intact. In 1991 the Law Commission undertook a review of the rule starting with a Consultation Paper[30] followed by a Report published in 1996.[31] There are

---

[20] (1981) 125 S.J. 397.
[21] As a result of the House of Lord's judgment in *Woodar Investment v. Wimpy Construction UK* [1980] 1 W.L.R. 277.
[22] [1983] 1 A.C. 598 (at p. 611).
[23] [1995] 2 A.C. 207 (at pp. 252–3).
[24] [1995] 1 W.L.R. 68 (at p. 76).
[25] At p. 76.
[26] Also at p. 76.
[27] Steyn L.J. citing Atiyah, *The Rise and Fall of Freedom of Contract* (1979, Clarendon Press, Oxford).
[28] See later pp. 170–177.
[29] (Cmnd 5449, paras 41–48).
[30] Consultation Paper and Report No.121 "Privity of Contract: Contracts for the Benefit of Third Parties" (1991).
[31] Law Commission No. 242 "Privity of Contract: Contracts for the Benefit of Third Parties", CM 3329, HMSO July 1996.

arguments both for and against the privity of contract rule.[32] They are fairly evenly divided. In favour of privity is the intellectual and historical connection with consideration. Both doctrines set limits on which promises are enforceable and by whom and prevent gratuitous promises being enforced. Both give the law a reasonable certainty, and enforce the view of contract as a bargain or exchange for which one party only gets an enforceable right if they gave something in return. Supporters of privity also argue that any injustice involved can usually be met by invoking one of numerous exceptions or means of avoiding the rule.

Further arguments in favour of keeping privity of contract are set out by the Law Commission Consultation Paper which described four main reasons for doing so:

> "First, that reform was unnecessary because the rule caused few problems in practice given that those who were affected by it could use various devices, to get round the third party rule. Secondly, that no legislative reform could hope adequately to deal with all the diverse situations where the third party rule is relevant. Thirdly, that the existing legal regime, while complicated, achieved certainty, and that reform would only result in uncertainty and litigation. Fourthly, that the proposals for reform might lead to contracting parties being bound to third parties when this was not their true intention."[33]

These arguments were not however sufficient to win the debate. The arguments against the privity rule have prevailed. As set out in the Law Commission Report, they are: **10.7**

(i)   that the intentions of the parties to the contract are frustrated by the rule;

(ii) that injustice may result to third parties;

(iii) that the exceptions to the rule and means of avoiding it[34] are so numerous that the rule itself "has to be questioned as impractical and unfair";

(iv) the exceptions have made the law in this area "artificial, uncertain and complex";

(v)   the rule has been reformed or abolished in most other common law jurisdictions;[35]

(vi) "in the interests of harmonisation with other Member States of the European Union differences in contract law should be minimised". In most European legal systems third parties can be given enforceable rights[36]; and

(vii) the third party rule causes difficulties in commercial life. This is particularly apparent in construction contracts and insurance law.[37]

---

[32] See Adams, Beylefeld and Brownsword, "Privity of Contract - The Benefits and Burdens of Law Reform" (1997) 60 M.L.R. 238 and Mitchell, "Privity reform and the nature of contractual obligations" (2000) 19 Legal Studies 229.

[33] Paras. 4.3–4.4. See also Law Commission Report para. 1.7. Arguments in favour of change are set out in Part III of the Report.

[34] See p. 170–177.

[35] In the United States the recognition of a third party's right to enforce a contract goes back to *Lawrence v. Fox* 20 NY 268 (1859). See Restatement of Contracts 3.302. In New Zealand, see Contracts (Privity) Act 1982, and in Australia, the Western Australia Property Law Act 1969.

[36] For example, in France under the Civil Code, Art. 1121 and in Germany under the Civil Code, Art. 328 BGB.

[37] See Law Commission Report pp. 39–52.

The inconvenience of privity of contract in commercial law led Steyn L.J. in *Darlington Borough Council v. Wiltshier Northern Ltd*[38] to comment[39]: "While the privity rule was barely tolerable in Victorian England, it has been recognised for half a century that it has no place in our more complex commercial world". The balance of these arguments seemed weighted in favour of reform. In 1996 the Law Commission Report proposed abolishing the benefit aspect of the privity rule while leaving the detriment rule intact. The Law Commission took the view that privity has become so enshrined as to make judicial reform very difficult. They concluded that legislation was required but with some scope for judicial development in certain areas:

> "... we believe that a detailed legislative scheme is the best means of reforming privity, we have no desire to hamper judicial creativity in this area. For example, we have left to the developing common law, what the rights of promisees should be in contracts for the benefit of third parties; and we have left open for the judges to decide what the rights of a joint promisee, who has not provided consideration, should be."[40]

They also recommended that the existing exceptions and means of avoiding the rule at common law largely be retained.

10.8   The 1999 Act follows closely, but not exactly, the Law Commission's Draft Bill[41]. It is a law reforming statute but not a code. This leaves scope for judicial developments and interpretation and a considerable amount of the pre-existing law remains. The guiding principles however radically change the law. The Act modifies but does not abolish privity of contract, but its effect leaves the old doctrine in tatters. Many of the old cases on privity are now of doubtful authority as a result of the Act. A large number would have to be decided differently or on a completely different basis. It is arguable *Tweddle v. Atkinson,*[42] and *Beswick v. Beswick*[43] that would now be decided differently. *New Zealand Shipping Co v. AM Satterthwaite and Co Ltd,*[44] which would result in a similar conclusion but by a very different route. The plaintiff's family in *Jackson v. Horizon Holidays*[45] would also have a strengthened claim because of the Act. Finally, cases such as the House of Lord's judgment in *Linden Gardens Trust Ltd v. Lenesta Sludge Disposals*[46] showed that the common law could deal with complex commercial arrangements but that there was a need for major law reform of this area. Gradual judicial interpretation will develop the relationship between the old law and the new.

---

[38] [1995] 1 W.L.R.
[39] At p. 76.
[40] Para. 1.10.
[41] See Law Comm Rep (No 242) pp. 173–182.
[42] (1861) 1 B and S 393, 121 E.R. 762.
[43] [1968] A.C. 58.
[44] [1975] A.C. 154.
[45] [1975] 1 W.L.R. 1468.
[46] [1994] 1 A.C. 85.

THE CONTRACTS (RIGHTS OF THIRD PARTIES) ACT 1999

The Contracts (Rights of Third Parties) Act 1999 received the Royal Assent on **10.9** November 11, 1999 and came into force on that day.[47] The Act applies to contracts made after that date if the parties choose to do so. Otherwise after May 11, 2000 the Act applies unless the parties decide to exclude it by showing a contrary intention.[48] Many contracts will therefore write out the Act in order to avoid the potential uncertainties that it brings. There are two foundation stones upon which the edifice of the Act is erected: (i) The contracting parties intentions should determine to extent of third parties rights and (ii) The reasonable expectations of third party beneficiaries should be protected. The first of these two principles allows the parties' intentions to determine who shall receive an enforceable benefit and the extent of that right. The parties may retain their right to vary the third parties' benefit if they choose to do so, and to exclude the operation of the 1999 Act entirely.[49] The second principle is illustrated by the rules determining when the third parties' rights may not be varied or rescinded without their consent once it has "crystallised". The traditional concepts of acceptance and the more modern alternative notion of reliance both have a part to play in this respect.[50]

The Act in outline:

The benefit rule of the doctrine of privity of contract is fundamentally altered in **10.10** favour of third parties covered by the Act. A third party may now have an enforceable benefit conferred on him or her in a contract between two others. The third party may either be expressly identified or the contract purport to confer an enforceable benefit upon him or her. Once the benefit has been conferred the parties may not vary or take it away from them without their consent, unless the parties agree otherwise or a court exercises its discretion within the provisions of the Act. Third parties falling outside the Act are still subject to the privity rule. Defences available against contracting parties, including exemption clauses, still apply to third parties. The existing common law exceptions and means of avoiding the doctrine of privity of contract are not abolished so the third party may bring a tort action or the promisee seek a remedy such as damages to enforce the contract on behalf of the third party. The rule that the contracting parties may not impose a detriment on a third party is retained. The rule that consideration must move from the promisee is reformed, as far as third parties are concerned. A promise in the original contract must still be supported by consideration given by the promisee. To that extent the rule still survives, but otherwise it is rendered nugatory.

---

[47] See Macmillan, "A Birthday Present for Lord Denning: The Contracts (Rights of Third Parties) Act 1999" (2000) 63 M.L.R. 721.
[48] S. 10.
[49] Ss 1 and 2.
[50] See later p. 166.

The tests for an enforceable benefit

(1) Who may benefit?

10.11 The most important issue raised by the Act is the definition of who is entitled to benefit as third parties and whether that right is intended to be enforceable. The rule reflects a balance in relation to third parties. On the one hand to be fair and flexible to potential third parties, but on the other a desire to prevent the number of potential third party beneficiaries getting out of hand.

(a) The first limb: express provision

The contract may expressly provide that the third party with benefit. This may be by name as a member of a class or by answering a particular description.[51] Express provision is a matter of construction of the contract. An obvious example would be that "Mrs Sandra Maxwell has a right to sue to enforce the term in this contract made for her benefit". The person does not however have to be named. The Act provides that the third party may be identified in the contract: (i) by name: (ii) as a member of a class, *e.g.* sub-contractors or employees; or (iii) answer a particular description *e.g.* Mrs Maxwell's, executor. The person need not even be in existence when the contract is made,[52] *e.g.* the third party could be an unborn child, a future spouse or a company as yet unformed.[53] The Law Commission was in favour of the creation of a rebuttable presumption in favour of an enforceable third party right where the person was expressly identified.[54] There is no further requirement under the first limb. The promise need not be proved to have been intended to be enforceable by the third party nor even for their own benefit, *i.e.* it could be conferred on him to be held as trustee for a fourth party. Express provision is likely in relation to the benefit of being covered by an exemption clause such as that in *Adler v. Dickson*.[55] This would be covered by s. 1(a) (as well as s. 1(6)).

(b) The second limb: purporting to confer a benefit

10.12 This is the most important section of the Act and likely to cause the greatest uncertainty in future. A term may "purport to confer a benefit" upon the third party.[56] This section is subject to s. 1(2).[57] From the construction of the contract as a whole it must appear that the parties intended the benefit to be enforceable by the third party. The "second limb" is restricted by two requirements, first that the parties intended the third party to receive the benefit, and second that they intended to create a right enforceable by him or her. Merely receiving a benefit is not enough under the second limb. Enforceability is a question to be ascertained from a proper construction of the contract as a whole.[58] Although the third party may enforce the term; he or she is not to be treated as a party to the contract for any other reason or Act.[59]

---

[51] S. 1(i)(a).
[52] S. 1(3).
[53] This is a clear deviation from the past consideration rule (see Chap. 7).
[54] See para 7.17.
[55] [1955] 1 Q.B. 158.
[56] S. 1(1)(b).
[57] See Roe, "Contractual Intention Under Section 1(1)(b) and 1(2) of the Contracts (Rights of Third Parties) Act 1999" (2000) 63 M.L.R. 887–894.
[58] S. 1(2).
[59] S. 7(4).

The Act expresses the Law Commission Report's recommendation that in order to satisfy the second limb the contracting parties must have both intended the third party to benefit and also that this be enforceable by him or her. The most interesting aspect of the new law is who falls inside or outside of the second limb of section 1. The 1999 Act is not a code and therefore leaves much to be developed and determined by the courts. No guidelines are given, though the Law Commission report gives seventeen hypothetical examples of situations which it considers either fall inside or outside the line.[60] If we select ten of these as illustrations, collectively, they help to paint a clearer picture of how the Act will apply, in future:

(a)   A promises B, his father that in return for transferring the family home to him (A), he will pay an annuity to C for life after B dies.[61] According to the Law Commission Report, C will now have an enforceable right under the Act;

(b)   A buys land from B and promises to pay one third of the price to C. C has an enforceable right. This is subject, as in the first example, to A being unable to rebut the presumption that he did not intend to give C the right;

(c)   B owes money to C and promises to pay A to carve a sculpture of C. A fails to carve the sculpture having promised B to do so. C may sue A for failure to confer a benefit on her under the Act;

(d)   B asks A and Co solicitors to draft a will leaving his estate to a charity C. D, a partner in the firm, negligently fails to take any measures to do so before B dies. C seeks to bring action against A and Co. In the view of the Law Commission it cannot do so because the promise in the contract between A and B did purport to confer a benefit on C, but was only to allow B to confer a benefit on C. C, the intended beneficiary, therefore does not have any right of enforcement under the Act and must rely on a tort action as in *White v. Jones*[62];

(e)   B takes out a life insurance policy with A Ltd naming C, his co-habitee, as beneficiary. When B is killed in an accident, C has been identified by name and has an enforceable right to claim her benefit;

(f)   B employs A to build a conservatory as an extension to his daughter's house as a birthday present. The work is badly done and the house suffers structural damage and a valuable collection of flowers are damaged. C has a direct action against the builders for breach of contract;

(g)   B takes his wife and family away on holiday to a hotel owned by A. The family suffers inconvenience and disappointment in their holiday as they were moved to another hotel. B's wife and children, so long as expressly identified, will have their own action for breach of action;

(h)   B buys an expensive suite of furniture from A Ltd, a well known central London department store, for his friends Mr & Mrs C who have just got

---

[60]   See paras 7.28 to 7.44, pp. 85–89.
[61]   *i.e.* as in *Beswick v. Beswick* [1968] A.C. 58.
[62]   [1995] 2 A.C. 207.

married. He makes it clear the purchase is for them and the delivery instructions show it is to be sent to C's house. The suite of furniture is not of satisfactory quality. The C's may sue A Ltd. for breach of an implied term of quality as they have been expressly identified. However, if the furniture is sold to B who says nothing about it being for anyone else then no other party has any enforceable right;

(i)   B and Co have a standard form contract which excludes liability for the liability of "agents, servants, employees and subcontractors". C a surveyor employed by B and Co is negligent in carrying out a survey of the site. C is protected by the exemption clause[63]; and

(j)   B agrees to carry A's packages by road. There is a "deemed value" clause that no package is worth more than £100, *i.e.* liability is limited to that amount. B subcontracts the carriage of goods to C (without the knowledge of A). C has not been identified and cannot claim protection if he loses a package worth more than that sum.[64]

There is no special test of enforceability for consumers as a group. The Law Commission rejected such a special rule of enforceability for such a wide category.[65] Consumers in general do benefit greatly from the Act. So, for instance, manufacturers may now confer rights on consumers allowing the purchaser a remedy if the person they bought goods from went out of business.

(2) The importance of the parties' intention

10.13   The third party's right depends upon the intention of the parties. Even if the contract purports to benefit the third party, the contracting parties can argue that it was never their intention to give the third party an enforceable right. Section 1(2) provides that subsection 1(1)(b) does not apply if on a proper construction of the contract it appears that it did not intend the term to be enforceable by the third party.[66] The normal rules of construction apply, including the "parol evidence rule",[67] *i.e.* that oral evidence is not admissible to prove or vary the terms of a written contract. Section 1(4), which was added during the passage of the Bill through Parliament, makes it clear that the third party only receives their right via the contracting parties and therefore cannot be better off than the parties intended. The Law Commission's view was that there should be a rebuttable presumption in favour of a third party right wherever a contract term purported to confer a benefit on a third party who was expressly identified. The promisor must therefore satisfy the court that this was not the parties' intention.

(3) The benefit conferred

10.14   Section 1(5) provides that the third party shall have any remedy that would have been available to them in an action for breach of contract if they had been a party to the contract. This includes a claim for damages, specific performance and injunctions, but

---

[63] See also discussion in Chap. 16.
[64] All examples from Law Commission Report pp. 85–89.
[65] See paras 7.54–7.55.
[66] See *Roe* (2000) 63 M.L.R. 887.
[67] See Chap. 12.

excludes other remedies such as the self help remedy of rescission and restitutionary remedies.[68] The third party is also subject to restrictions on their claim such as the remoteness rule and the duty to mitigate.[69] Essentially the third party is given the same rights to enforce a term for their benefit as a contracting party, but is not to be placed in a better position than either of the parties to the original contract. Although the third party may enforce a term in the contract, he or she is not regarded as a party to the contract itself for any other purpose.[70] The benefits to third parties include exemption clauses. Section 1(6) provides that benefits to the third party shall include the right to be protected by an exclusion or limitation of liability. This is one of the main aspects of the Act which has done away with much tangled case law.[71] Exemption clauses and third parties are dealt with later.[72]

(4) The third party's right is subject to vitiating factors

The promisee must still perform his or her side of the contract and the third parties'   **10.15**
rights are subject to all the main vitiating factors, *e.g.* misrepresentation, duress, undue influence and mistake.[73]

(5) The other main provisions of the Act

(a) Securing the third parties' right: the rules for "crystallisation"

Once a benefit has been conferred on a third party, the parties' right to vary or rescind that benefit is restricted. In order to protect third parties, the Act limits the right of the   **10.16**
contracting parties to vary or cancel the right of third parties once the benefit has "crystallised". This is an aspect of the second principle underlying the Act, that of "reasonable expectations". A benefit has crystalised protecting the right of the third party if:

(i) the third party has communicated his or her assent to the term, *i.e.* by acceptance;

(ii) the promisor is aware that the third party has relied on the term; or

(iii) the promisor can reasonably be expected to have foreseen that the third party would rely on the term and the third party has in fact relied on it.[74]

Reliance theory[75] underpins the 1999 Act. Under s. 2(2) assent may be by words or conduct,[76] but if the postal services are used the assent is not communicated until the letter is received.[77] The postal rule is therefore excluded.[78] There are five principles to consider in relation to the crystallisation of the third party's right.

---

[68] See Chap. 26.
[69] See Chap. 25.
[70] S. 7(4).
[71] See Chap. 16.
[72] See p. 168 and Chaps 16 and 17.
[73] See Chaps 18, 19 and 21.
[74] S. 2(1)(c).
[75] See Chap. 1.
[76] S. 2(2)(a)
[77] S. 2(2)(b)
[78] See Chap. 4.

(i) Acceptance: The rule here mirrors that of formation by offer and acceptance. Acceptance in this context means, according to the Law Commission Report, "an assent by words or conduct communicated by the third party to the promisor". If there is acceptance, this alone is sufficient. Reliance does not also have to be shown.

10.17 **(ii) Reliance in fact:** Reliance is capable of two meanings. First, that the promisor is aware that the third party has relied on the term.[79] The reliance does not need to be detrimental.[80] Even trivial reliance is sufficient. The Law Commission Report rejected the alternative approach of the New Zealand Contracts (Privity) Act 1982 s. 5(1)(a) which requires that "the position of the third party been materially altered by the reliance . . . on the promise." The Law Commission took the view that "the importance of reliance is in indicating that expectations have been engendered in the third party and the triviality of the reliance seems irrelevant to that".[81]

(iii) Reasonable expectation of reliance: If the promiser could reasonably be expected to have foreseen that the third party would rely on the term and that it has in fact been relied upon, then the benefit has attached to the third party.[82] The Law Commission Report suggested this would be met by conduct induced in the expectation that the promise would be performed, or at least entitled to performance of the promise.

10.18 **(iv) The parties may agree to their own test, or rule out the need for consent to a variation:** The parties to the contract may by their own agreement allow for the variation or rescission of the third party, without their consent, or lay down their own different conditions for consent by the third party.[83] Consent may be dispensed with entirely if: (i) it cannot be obtained because a third party's whereabouts cannot reasonably be ascertained or (ii) he is mentally incapable of consenting.[84] If the parties apply to the court, consent may be dispensed with under the reliance rule if "it cannot reasonably be ascertained whether or not the third party has in fact relied on the term." If the court decides to dispense with a third party's consent altogether it may do so but may also impose other conditions "as it thinks fit", which may include the payment of compensation to the third party.[85] Under s. 2(3) the parties retain the right to make their own provisions concerning cancellation or variation. The intention of the parties is therefore protected. If they wish to do so by express term of the contract, they may agree to rescind or vary the contract without the consent of the third party or make their own rules as to when the consent of the third party is or is not required for cancellation or variations. Contract lawyers are quite likely to advise their clients to exercise this power to avoid future difficulties.

(v) The courts' discretion: The courts have a wide discretion under the Act and will undoubtedly have an important role in interpreting the Act in years to come. The Law Commission believed that such a limited judicial discretion "is most unlikely to create any significant degree of uncertainty." Time, of course, will tell if this is true.

---

[79] S. 2(1)(b)
[80] Para. 9.19, p. 106 "A useful analogy is the doctrine of promissory estoppel. Although the matter cannot be regarded as entirely settled, there seems to be an emerging consensus to the effect that mere reliance is sufficient." (See, Chap. 9) e.g. Lord Denning in *W. J. Alan & Co Ltd v El Nasr Export and Import Co* [1972] 2 Q.B. 189.
[81] Para 9.31, p. 109.
[82] S. 2(1)(c)
[83] S. 2(3).
[84] S. 2(4).
[85] S. 2(6).

(b) Defences

(i) Available To the Promisor: Defences available between the parties including exemp-   **10.19**
tion clauses still apply to third parties. The promisor is entitled to all the defences or
set-off which would have been available against the promisee, which arose from the
contract or which would have arisen if the third party had been a party to the contract.
The parties are free to modify any defences or set-offs if they choose to. The most likely
defences in this situation viz-à-viz the third party are misrepresentation, undue influence, mistake or frustration. The promisor is entitled to any defence or set off that
arises in connection with the contract and is relevant to the term,[86] and also defences
which would have been available to him in proceedings brought by the promisee.[87] The
promisor is also entitled to a defence arising from an express term of the contract, providing that it be available against the third party and those which would have been
available because of any express term against the promisee[88] or would have been available if the third party had been a party to the contract.[89] Under s. 1(6), where the third
party seeks to enforce a term of the contract (including an exemption clause) they may
not do so if they could not have done had they been a party to the contract.[90] The
promisor is not, however, allowed to bring a counter claim against the third party even
if it is available against the promisee. This would be imposing a detriment on the third
party.

(ii) Defences available to the third party: Section 3(6) only allows the third party to rely   **10.20**
on a term to the extent they could if they were a party to the contract. The third party
is not to be treated better than if he or she were a party. The third party has similar
defences available to the parties including being able to rely on an exclusion or limitation
clause. If, however, the exclusion clause could not have been relied upon by either the
promisor or promisee, then it is also unenforceable by the third party.[91]

(c) Enforcement by the promisee

Section 4 provides that the Act does not affect the right of the promisee to enforce any
term of the contract. This preserves the common law position, though how far this will
remain of importance in the future remains questionable. We discuss enforcement by the
promisee later.[92] Where the promisee does enforce the contract, the Act prevents "double
indemnity" where the promisee takes action in respect of the third party's loss. Section 5
provides that where the promisee has recovered "a sum in respect of the third party's loss
in respect of the term", or the expense to the promisee in making good the default of the
promisor, to the third party, the court "shall reduce any award to the third party to such
extent as it thinks appropriate to take account of the sum recovered by the promisee".
The usual means of enforcement by the promisee is a claim for substantial damages but
this can also include equitable remedies.[93]

---

[86] S. 3(2)(a).
[87] S. 3(2)(b).
[88] S. 2(4).
[89] S. 2(4).
[90] Exemption clauses and third parties are dealt with later, see Chap. 16.
[91] S. 1(6).
[92] See later pp. 173–176.
[93] For equitable remedies, see Chap. 26.

(d) Exceptions: contracts not covered by the act

10.21   There are a number of contracts not covered by the 1999 Act. The list includes bills of
exchange, promissory notes and negotiable instrument.[94] These are also existing statutory exceptions to the privity rule in the Bills of Exchange Act 1882[95] and the Companies
Act 1985 s. 14.[96] The 1999 Act does not apply to contracts of employment against an
employee, home worker or agency worker.[97] The Act also confers no third party rights in
the case of carriage of goods by sea, rail or road, or by air (if subject to the rules of
international transport convention).[98] However, significantly the third party may rely on
s. 1 of the Act to confer a benefit on him if the term is an exclusion or limitation of liability in such a contract.[99] The necessity for the convoluted reasoning of such cases as
New Zealand Shipping Co. Ltd v. Satterthwaite is therefore rendered redundant in relation to international trade law[1].

The 1999 Act and other related areas of contract law

(1) Exemption clauses and third parties

10.22   There was discussion by the Law Commission as to the extent to which the Unfair
Contract Terms Act 1977[2] should be modified to take account of the 1999 Act. The 1977
Act limits or restricts the right of parties to exclude their liability to one another for negligence and also breach of contract. In the case of exemptions for personal injuries, these
are void under s. 2(1) and remain so in relation to third parties. On balance, the Law
Commission concluded that restrictions of liability for negligence for other types of loss
such as damage to property should not be extended to claims by third parties under the
1999 Act. Such limitations on liability will therefore be valid and not subject to s. 2(2) of
the Unfair Contract Terms Act.[2a] The 1977 Act imposes a reasonableness test and one of
the difficulties would be ascertaining what would be reasonable in relation to the wide
range of third parties covered by the Act. Third parties can however claim the protection
of exemption clauses under the 1999 Act. There is an important difference drawn
between the third party relying on an exemption clause and it being used against them.
If A excludes liability for himself and third party, C to B, the other contracting party,
then the clause is subject to a reasonableness test as judged against the promisor who
has the protection of the Unfair Contract Terms Act.[3] However, if the exemption clause
is used by A against B, the other contractor, and C, the third party, UCTA will be available for claims involving personal injuries but not under s. 2(2) for claims for other types
of injury, *e.g.* loss of property. The scope of UCTA s. 2(2) does not extend to this case.

---

[94] S. 6(1).
[95] See later p. 176.
[96] S. 6(2).
[97] S. 6(3).
[98] S. 6(5).
[99] S. 6(5)(b).
[1] [1975] A.C. 154, see also Chap. 2.
[2] See Chap. 17.
[2a] S. 7(4), 1999 Act.
[3] S. 1(6).

The important question of exemptions of liability covering third parties is discussed later.[4]

(2) Arbitration provisions

The Law Commission recommended that arbitration agreements be excluded from the Act. This was not accepted and the 1999 Act applies to third parties who are beneficiaries of arbitration clauses and are now able to enforce them.[5] This allows them to be governed by the Arbitration Act 1996.

(3) The 1999 Act and the rule that consideration must move from the promisee

The Act reforms two basic rules of consideration: (i) the rule that consideration must **10.23** move from the promisee and (ii) past consideration as far as third parties are concerned.[6] The parties to the original contract must still provide consideration, in other words consideration is necessary to make an initial contract. To that extent, the rule that consideration must move from the promisee survives. However, a benefit can now be conferred on a third party without any consideration moving from the third party. For practical purposes, therefore, the common law rule is rendered nugatory. Even under the 1999 Act, however, the third party beneficiary does not become a party.[7] According to the Law Commission, the new Act must affect the old common rule: "The rule that consideration must move from the promisee, in so far as it means that consideration must move from the *plaintiff*, had to be departed from if our reform of privity were to bring about any real change". Section 1 of the Act must therefore be interpreted as also reforming the rule that consideration must move from the plaintiff.

As for reforming consideration itself, the Law Commission accepted that giving a third party rights which could not be varied by the parties "lessens the importance of consideration". As to future reform of the doctrine: "The recognition of exceptions [i.e. by deeds and promissory estoppel], allied to academic criticisms of the requirement of consideration (in its classic sense of there needing to be a requested-performance or counter-promise) suggests that the doctrine of consideration may be a suitable topic for future separate reviews by the Law Commission."

As to the past consideration rule, a third party may now acquire an enforceable right after the main contract is made. The third party does not even have to be in existence when the contract was formed, *e.g.* an unborn child or someone answering a particular description under s. 1(3). Otherwise, however, as between the parties, the past consideration rule remains intact.

---

[4] See Chap. 17.
[5] S. 8.
[6] See Chap. 8.
[7] Paras 6.3–6.8. The Law Commission proposal is that "legislation should ensure that the rule that consideration must move from the promisee is reformed to the extent necessary to avoid nullifying other proposed reform".

THE SURVIVING COMMON LAW

The detriment rule continues

10.24 The contracting parties may still not impose a detriment on the third party. However, the parties can make conditions on the benefits conferred on the third party by the contract The rule against imposing burdens on third parties is different in land law. In *Tulk v. Moxhay*[8] it was held that restrictive covenants may bind subsequent purchasers of the land so long as they are negative in character and the subsequent purchaser has notice or knows of the covenant. The rule in *Tulk v. Moxhay* may also apply to personal property.[9] This view was challenged by Lord Diplock as being incorrect in *Port Line Ltd v. Ben Line Steamers Ltd.*[10]

The pre-existing exceptions and means of avoiding privity are preserved

The common law developed many ways of getting round privity. Indeed the exceptions probably outnumber the applications of the rule itself. The existing exceptions and means of avoidance are preserved by the 1999 Act. Section 7(1) provides that the Act "does not affect any right or remedy that exists or is available apart from this Act". According to the Law Commission it was preferable to keep the previous exceptions rather than sweep them all away:

> "Some of those exceptions give third parties more secure rights than do our reforms and it is no part of our thinking to render third parties worse off than they already are. Nor do we anticipate any difficulty . . . in allowing existing exceptions to coexist along with our new wide-ranging exceptions. Of course, it can readily be anticipated that some of the artificial techniques that have been evolved to by-pass privity will wither away and the same may also occur in respect of other exceptions which give third parties no advantages over our proposed reform. This is only to be welcomed in rendering the law simpler."[11]

(1) Action in tort by the third party.

10.25 An action in the tort of negligence, by or against a third party is the simplest means of avoiding the privity rule. The famous case of *Donoghue v. Stevenson*[12] provides a classic example. An action for negligence was successful against the manufacturer of a bottle of ginger beer which allegedly contained a decomposed snail. The pursuer, May Donoghue, drank some of the contents of the bottle then claimed that the bottle also contained the remains of a decomposed snail. She became ill as a result of drinking the liquid. She had not bought the ginger beer herself, which had been purchased by a friend at a café in Paisley, near Glasgow in August 1928. The pursuers action had in negligence against the

---

[8] [1848] 2 Ph 774, 41 ER 1143.
[9] See *Lord Strathcona Steamship Co v. Dominion Coal Co. Ltd* [1926] A.C. 108.
[10] [1958] 2 Q.B. 146.
[11] Law Commission Report para. 6.3.
[12] [1932] A.C. 562.

manufacturers rather than in contract against the retailer to be. The House of Lords held in favour of Mrs Donoghue, and established that the ultimate consumer of a product could take direct action against a manufacturer in the tort of negligence. As applied to English law, the doctrine of privity of contract was no longer an impediment to such a claim in tort. By their judgment the House of Lords transformed the law of negligence and the whole of the common law in the twentieth century. The old privity case of *Winterbottom v. Wright*[13] was overruled. The 1999 Act may prove a fertile source of claims, and provide a more versatile action than one in tort. Some third parties who fall within s. 1 are bound to prefer the option of action under the Act rather than face the difficulties of proving fault in a negligence action. Consumers in general, however, are not likely to be covered as third parties. An action in tort is likely to remain consumers' main means of legal redress. Before we leave this topic it should be remembered that on action in contract and tort can co-exist on the same facts. In *Daniels v. R. White and Tarbard*,[14] the husband, a street trader, purchased a bottle of lemonade from the defendant, Mrs Tabard, licensee of a pub, the "Falcon Arms", in Battersea. The bottle contained 38 grains of carbolic acid disolved in the lemonade. Both Mr and Mrs Daniels consumed some of the contents. The husband, as the person who bought the lemonade, was able to sue the seller in contract. Mrs Daniels was prevented by privity of contract (as she would still remain under the 1999 Act) from bringing an action in contract and so sued the manufacturer in negligence. Mrs Daniels failed to prove a lack of reasonable care. Her husband succeeded in contract for breach of the strict duty to provide a product reasonably fit for use under the Sale of Goods Act 1979.[14a]

(2) Trustee of a promise

The trust concept in this context was described by Lord Wright in *Vandepitte v. Preferred Accident Insurance Corporation of New York*:   **10.26**

> "A party to a contract can constitute himself a trustee for a third party of a right under a contract and thus confer such rights enforceable in equity on the third party. The trustee can then take steps to enforce performance to the beneficiary by the other contracting party as in the case of other equitable rights. The action should be in the name of the trustee; if however he refuses to sue, the beneficiary can sue, by joining the trustee as defendant."[15]

To take an example, if Angela promises Beatrice that she will to pay a sum of money to Beatrice on behalf of her daughter Carolyn, Beatrice may be considered a trustee for the benefit of Carolyn. Carolyn, now the beneficiary of the trust, may in certain circumstances be able to enforce the promise between Angela and Beatrice. This is because a third party can enforce a contract if there is a trust in her favour. This avoids the privity rule because the third party is not relying on being a party to the original contract. The useful device of the equitable trust is kept under firm control, however. It has been applied to promises to pay money or to transfer property, but it is not universally applied

---

[13]   (1842) 10 M and W 109, 152 E.R. 402.
[14]   [1938] 4 All E.R. 258.
[14a]   See Chap. 12.
[15]   [1933] A.C. 70 (at p. 79).

to contractual obligations. The courts usually require a clear intention by the parties to create a trust in favour of the third party.[16] In *Re Schebsman, Official Receiver v. Cargo Superintendents (London) Ltd and Schebsman*[17] Lord Greene M.R. stated: "It is not legitimate to input into the contract the idea of a trust when the parties have given no indication that such was their intention. To interpret this contract as creating a trust would in my judgment be to disregard the dividing line between the case of a trust and the simple case of a contract made between two persons for the benefit of a third." On the other hand, the trust concept succeeded in *Re Flavell*.[18] The device of a trust is limited in scope. This means of avoiding the doctrine of privity is likely to atrophy in light of the 1999 Act.

(3) Agency

Agency is a type of contract whereby one person, the principal, employs another person, an agent to act on his or her behalf. An agent is not the same as an employee, indeed very different rules apply to each of these relationships. A principal may acquire rights and liabilities under contracts made by their agent with third parties. Agency avoids the privity doctrine. The agent and principal are effectively the same party. The agency device is apparent when one party books a holiday on behalf of another.[19] Agency may be used to allow third parties to take advantage of an exclusion clause in contracts to which they were not the main contracting party.[20]

(4) Collateral contracts

10.27   This is a useful practical device to avoid the privity rule by finding another antecedent contract.[21] The consideration for the collateral agreement is entering into the main contract. In *Shanklin Pier Ltd v. Detel Products Ltd*[22] the plaintiffs owned a pier on the Isle of Wight. They had an agreement with a firm of contractors to have the pier painted with two coats of bituminous paint. The defendants, who were paint manufacturers, promised that their paint known as DMU would be suitable for the work and would last for seven to ten years. Relying on this promise, the plaintiffs told the contractors to use the defendant's product. The paint proved unsatisfactory and lasted only about three months. McNair J. held that there was a contract between the plaintiffs and the manufacturers as to the durability of the paint. This was a collateral contract, a contract between the pier owners and the paint manufacturers, and privity was thereby avoided.[23]

(5) Joint promisees

The common law developed rules allowing persons to be treated as benefiting from the fact that they were "jointly" promising with another.[24] Curiously, joint promises are not

---

[16] See *Les Affréteurs Réunis SA v. Leopold Walford (London) Ltd* [1919] A.C. 801.
[17] [1944] Ch. 83 (at p. 89).
[18] (1884) 25 Ch. D 89.
[19] See *Jackson v. Horizon Holidays* [1975] 1 W.L.R. 1468.
[20] See *New Zealand Shipping Co. Ltd v. AM Satterthwaite and Co. Ltd* [1975] A.C. 154.
[21] It is also a means of incorporating an exemption clause, see Chap. 16, or avoiding the parol evidence rule, see Chap. 12.
[22] [1951] 2 K.B. 854.
[23] See also in the context of hire the purchase of a car, *Brown v. Sheen and Richmond Car Sales Ltd* [1950] 1 All E.R. 1102.
[24] See the Australian case of *Coulls v. Bagot's Executor and Trustee Co. Ltd* (1967) 119 A.L.R. 461.

included in the 1999 Act. The original draft Bill in the Law Commission's Report stated that they were not to be considered as third parties.[25] This was withdrawn in the Government Bill in December 1999 and there is no mention of them in the 1999 Act. Joint promisee appear still to have to rely on their existing common law rules for avoiding the old privity doctrine, however. It is likely, however, that by interpretation they will be treated as third parties under the Act.

(6) Assignment

Contractual rights may be assigned to a third party. This is widespread in commercial relationships, for example, unpaid debts to debt collecting agencies. The creditor transfers it's right of recovery in return for a sum of money and the debt collecting company steps into the company's shoes. A promisor is also allowed to subcontract the performance of the contract to another person, so long as the contract does not require personal services by the other party. This is known as vicarious performance.[26] The main contractor normally remains primarily liable under the contract.

10.28

(7) Enforcement of the contract by the promisee

The promisee may normally only recover substantial damages if he has suffered a loss. If the loss is suffered by the third party, the promisee is only entitled to a nominal award. Privity of contract will prevent the third party enforcing the contract in his own right. In order to avoid a "black hole" where neither third party nor promisee may enforce the contract, the promisee may, in certain circumstances, be entitled to enforce the contract, thereby benefitting the third party.[27] In some cases the promisee and third party may have agreed such an arrangement between themselves. The promisee may have a variety of remedies. He may recover: (i) nominal damages for his own loss; (ii) in certain circumstances, damages for the third party; (iii) his own "performance interest"; (iv) specific performance[28]; or (v) an injunction[29] on behalf of the third party. These possibilities are retained by the Contracts (Rights of Third Parties) Act 1999.

In most cases where a loss is suffered by a third party, the promisee is only entitled to nominal damages. A number of exceptions have been built up over the years including "the rule in *Dunlop v. Lambert*."[30] A quantity of Scotch Whisky on board a vessel the *Ardincaple* en route from Leith to Newcastle was thrown overboard during a storm. It was held that the consignor of the goods was entitled to substantial damages even though he was no longer the owner of the goods, title to which had passed to the consignee. This was based on a special contract of bailment, providing an exception to the privity rule.[31] Lord Denning in *Jackson v. Horizon*[32] applied this exception to allow a

10.29

---

[25] In the Draft Law Commission Bill, Clause 8(1) "where the persons to whom a contractual promise is made include a person who does not provide consideration for the promise, that person shall not be treated as a third party for the purposes of this Act".

[26] See *Davies v. Collins* [1945] 1 All E.R. 247.

[27] See Treitel, "Damages in Respect of a Third Party's loss", (1998) 114 L.Q.R. 527; Wallace; "Third Party Damages: No Legal Black Hole" (1999) 115 L.Q.R. 394.

[28] *Beswick v. Beswick* [1968] A.C. 58.

[29] *Snelling v. John G. Snelling* [1973] Q.B. 87.

[30] (1839) 6 Cl and Fin 600, 7 E.R. 824. This case is discussed at length by several law Lords in *Panatown Ltd v. Alfred McAlpine Construction Ltd* [2000] 4 All E.R. 97.

[31] See Lord Clyde in *Panatown v. Sir Alfred MacAlpine* [2000] 4 All E.R. (at p. 105).

[32] [1975] 1 W.L.R. 1468.

father to recover for the disappointed expectations of himself, his wife and children when a holiday in Sri Lanka turned into a disaster. The House of Lords in *Woodar Investment Ltd v. Wimpey Construction UK Ltd*[33] questioned *Jackson*, however, stating that a contracting party might only recover for his or her own disappointment and the *Jackson* situation was to be treated as a special case. The Law Lords were critical of the law as it then stood. Nevertheless, the *Dunlop v. Lambert* exception has continued to be applied in other contexts,[34] particularly building contracts. In *The Albazero*[35] Lord Diplock stated the basis for the rule as being that:

> "In a commercial contract concerning goods where it is in the contemplation of the parties that the proprietary interests in the goods may be transferred from one owner to another after the contract has been entered into and before the breach which causes loss or damage to the goods, an original party to the contract, if such be the intention of them both, is to be treated in law as having entered into the contract for the benefit of all persons who have or may acquire an interest in the goods before they are lost or damages, and is entitled to recover by way of damages for breach of contract the actual loss sustained by those for whose benefit the contract is entered into."[36]

10.30   The reasoning of the *Albazero* was extended to the construction of defective buildings in *St Martins Property Corporation v. Sir Robert McAlpine Ltd*[37] in which an action arose over buildings constructed by the parties to the contract, but which was on land belonging to a third party. Did C (the third party) or A (the employer, *i.e.* client) have a remedy against the builders B? A had suffered no substantial loss as a result of the defective buildings and C was not a party to the contract with B. Therefore privity of contract would prevent C from recovering.[38] In the *St Martins* case, the land upon which the building was erected was transferred to the third party before the date of breach. In order to avoid the situation in which neither party had a claim against the builders, the House of Lords extended the principle of *Albazero* to contracts relating to land, not just personal property.[39] The House of Lords held that if it was envisaged by the parties that the property would be transferred to a third party and the consequences of the breach of contract suffered would therefore fall elsewhere, then the contracting party had a cause of action to recover the losses suffered. The majority of the House of Lords made it clear that, as a result of *St Martins* and also the *Albazero*, the contracting party was accountable to the third party for damages recovered, and would not be able to recover substantial damages if the third party had a direct remedy against the building contractors. Lord Griffiths disagreed with the latter suggesting that the contracting party might bring an action even if the third party had a direct remedy against the builders.

---

[33] [1980] 1 W.L.R. 277.
[34] It was applied in *Linden Gardens Trust Ltd v. Lenesta Sludge Disposals Ltd* [1994] A.C. 85.
[35] [1977] A.C. 774.
[36] At p. 847.
[37] Heard with *Linden Gardens Trust Ltd v. Lenesta Sludeg Disposals Ltd* [1994] A.C. 85. See also the Court of Appeal judgment in *Darlington BC v. Wilshier Northern* [1995] 1 W.L.R. 68.
[38] The third party might have a claim under s. 1 of the 1999 Act if the case were to arise today, if the parties intended to confer an enforceable benefit on the building owner.
[39] See Unberath, "Third Party Losses and Black Holes: Another View" (1999) 115 L.Q.R. 535.

The point arose again in *Panatown Ltd v. Alfred McAlpine Construction Ltd*[40] where the House of Lords held by a majority of three to two that where the third party had a direct remedy, in this case a "duty of care deed" with the builders, the employer had no right to substantial damages under the main contract. The majority of the Law Lords saw no reason to extend the exception in *Dunlop v. Lambert* to situations in which the third party has a right of action himself. The duty of care deed gave the ultimate owners of the defectively built office block (and future owners) a direct action for bad workmanship against the contractors. There was therefore no justification for allowing the employer under the original contract to claim substantial damages. Lords Goff and Willett dissented. The fact that the third party had an action under a specially executed deed should not deflect from the principle that a contracting party had a performance interest in the contract being properly performed. This interest originally set out by Oliver J. in *Radford v. De Froberville*[41] had been further established as a basis of damages by Lord Griffiths in *St Martins Property Corp*. The contracting party had a right to substantial damages if the contract has not performed to his expectations.[42] The two dissenting Law Lords would therefore have allowed the employers action against the contractors to succeed.

This is an important issue and area of contract law which had divided judicial and   **10.31**
academic opinion. It is likely to lead to further developments in years to come. Many cases will continue to fall outside of the 1999 Act. The right of the promisee to sue is preserved by the 1999 Act. The Law Commission Report proposed that a promisee retains his right to sue on the contract made for the third party's benefit:

> ". . . we saw no reason to remove a contractual right from the promisee merely because the .contract gives rights of enforcement to a third party. Indeed we have gone further in emphasising that we would not wish our reform to be construed as casting any doubt on those important recent decisions in which a promisee has been held able to recover a third party's loss. Such developments will remain important because there will be many contracts where a third party stands to benefit and yet will not have a right of enforceability under our proposals."[43]

Section 4 of the 1999 Act preserves the right of the promisee "to enforce any term of   **10.32**
the contract". In order to prevent a double indemnity s. 5 provides that where a term of a contract is enforceable by a third party, and the promisee has recovered a sum for "(a) the third party's loss in respect of the term or (b) the expense to the promisee of making good to the third party the default of the promisor", then the court "shall reduce any award to the third party to such extent as it thinks appropriate to take account of the sum recovered by the promisee".

(8) Damages and third parties

The issue of damages, third parties' rights and assignment arose in the Commercial Court in *Total Liban SA v. Vitol Energy SA*.[44] The buyer of a quality of gasoline, which

---

[40] [2000] 4 All E.R. 97.
[41] [1977] 1 W.L.R. 1262.
[42] We return to discuss this important view of contract damages in Chap. 26.
[43] The Law Commission gives the example of *Linden Gardens Trust Ltd v. Lenesta Sludge Disposals Ltd* [1994] 1 A.C. 85.
[44] [2000] 1 All E.R. 267.

turned out to be defective, got into financial difficulties and did not have the finances to pursue or defend any action against the sellers. The buyers therefore assigned their rights to a third party. The arbitrator decided that the third party could not obtain damages against the seller as it had not made any payments to their assignors, the buyers. The High Court held this was wrong. The buyer had an action for substantial damages and the uncertainty over the quantum could be dealt with by existing techniques to prevent a windfall for the third party.

(9) Statutory exceptions to the privity rule

10.32   There are many exceptions created by statute.

- The Package Travel, Package Holidays and Package Tours Regulations 1992[45] based upon a European directive allow a holidaymaker to pursue an action for breach of contract against the other contracting party "irrespective of whether such obligations are to be performed by that other party or by other suppliers of services".[46]

- The Companies Act 1985, s. 14 gives individual shareholders a right to sue one another,[47] although there is no contract between the shareholders *inter se*.

- Under the Bills of Exchange Act 1882, the privity rule is inappropriate to negotiable instruments such as bank notes, which have their own set of rules, and therefore privity of contract does not apply.

- In the context of life and other types of insurance contracts, such as the Married Women's Property Act 1882 s. 11, where a person may insure his or her life in favour of their spouse and children. The policy creates a trust for the beneficiaries. The 1999 Act does create a right for others such as dependents or co-habitees who were not covered until now. Insurance law contains many other statutory exceptions to the privity rule, *e.g.* the Road Traffic Act 1988 which allows a third party to a car insurance policy to be enforced against the insurer.[48]

- The Law of Property Act 1925 s. 56 provides that "a person may take an immediate or other interest in land or other property, or the benefit of any condition, right of entry, covenant or agreement over or respecting land or other property, although he may not be named as a party to the conveyance or other instrument". This exception is within the province of land law.

---

[45]   Also discussed in Chap. 12.
[46]   Reg. 15.
[47]   See also Chap. 5.
[48]   See the Third Parties (Rights Against Insurers) Act 1930.

Chapter 11

INTENTION, CAPACITY AND FORM

INTENTION TO CREATE LEGAL RELATIONS

The third requirement of contractual formation in English law is that the parties have an **11.1** intention to create legal relations.[1] On the surface, intention to contract does not appear to be necessary. An alien who landed in a high street full of shoppers would not recognise much discussion of formation of contract, nor would it elicit much from the shoppers themselves (apart from surprise), many of whom would be unaware that they had been making contracts, although they were, of course, doing so. Contracts can be formed by conduct alone, and if the conduct shows an intention to create legal relations, that in itself is sufficient. Contract law assumes intention to create legal relations in most commercial matters and intention to contract does not have to be proved. Other areas such as agreements within the family and social arrangements are kept out of the law of contract for reasons of public policy. As times change the barriers against enforcing purely private arrangements are gradually breaking down. The minimal requirement of intention has led to some to doubt whether such a principle exists, or is necessary, at all.[2] Two distinct meanings have to be distinguished. Intention is relevant throughout contract law to determine what the parties said or did, for example to differentiate an offer from an invitation to treat,[3] or to contract a condition from a warranty.[4] Intention to create legal relations, on the other hand, is a requirement of the formation of contracts as a whole.

The requirement of intention to create legal relations owes its origin to the judgment of the Court of Appeal in *Carlill v. Carbolic Smoke Ball Co. Ltd*[5] in which a newspaper advertisement was held to be an offer showing contractual intention to create a unilateral contract. Intention was affirmed by the House of Lords in *Heilbut, Symons & Co. v. Buckleton*,[6] in which Lord Moulton stated that, "Not only the terms of such contracts but the existence of an *animus contrahendi* [*i.e.* intention to create contractual relations] on the part of all the parties to them must be clearly shown." Later in *Balfour v. Balfour*,[7] intention (or lack of it) became an essential question in the formation of contracts in

---

[1] For an account of the development of the various doctrines, see Simpson, "Innovation in 19th Century Contract Law" (1975) 91 L.Q.R. pp. 247–278.
[2] Tuck (1943) Can. Bar Rev. 123; Hedley (1985) O.J.L.S. 391; Unger (1959) M.L.R. 96.
[3] Chap. 3.
[4] Chap. 13.
[5] (1893) 2 Q.B. 163. See Chap. 2.
[6] [1913] A.C. 30 (at p. 47).
[7] [1919] 2 K.B. 571.

general. Since *Balfour* the issue of intention has turned into a negative question as to which arrangements the law will *not* recognise as contracts. This is mainly a policy decision leaving various types of agreement outside the ambit of the law. The limits of contract law ebb and flow with public policy. The issue of intention to create legal relations and public policy arose in *Robinson v. Commissioners of Customs and Excise*.[8] The claimant argued that he had made a contract for confidential information to be given to Customs and Excise leading to the arrest or seizure of other persons or goods for which he would receive a remuneration and expenses. It was held by Brown J. that no contract was formed, as there was no intention to create legal relations. First, because it had been made clear to the plaintiff that the reward was not a certainty, there was no amount of reward fixed; he had been told that money would only be paid by results and that it was not a matter for the informants contact but for that person's supervisor. The Court held that the plaintiff's claim was not actionable on grounds of public policy.

The presumption of contractual intention in commercial arrangements

11.2 In transactions of a commercial nature it is not necessary to prove that the parties intended to create contractual relations. Instead there is a rebuttable presumption that legally binding relations were intended. The usual means of avoiding contractual liability is by an express statement to that effect, *e.g.* the agreement is "binding in honour only" or merely a "memorandum of understanding". On the other hand, where a contract has been formed, the parties may not avoid the courts altogether. To do so would oust the jurisdiction of the courts and this is void on the grounds of public policy.[9] Football pools are not a contract between the organisers and those who submit their completed coupon. In *Appleson v. Littlewoods Ltd*,[10] the competition was subject to a rule that the competition was not covered by "any legal relationship, rights, duties or consequences or be legally enforceable or be subject of litigation". This was sufficient to negative any contractual intention. It was held that the conditions of the competition prevented the plaintiffs from bringing any action to enforce payment.[11] In *Rose and Frank Co. v. J.R. Crompton & Bros*[12] there was an "honourable pledge clause" which was held to rule out contractual relations. Equally, the Court of Appeal in *Kleinwort Benson Ltd v. Malaysia Mining Corporation Bhd*[13] held that a "letter of comfort" was only a statement of present intention drafted by lawyers and was not a contract. There is generally no intention to create contractual liability in advertisements, leaflets, signs or notices, even if these are overtly commercial in nature. This may be reversed by showing a definite intention to contract.[14]

The presumption in favour of contractual intention is difficult to rebut. It was not rebutted in *Edwards v. Skyways Ltd*[15] where the words *ex gratia* failed to negative contractual relations. However, in *Orion Insurance Co. v. Sphere Drake Insurance*[16] Hirst J.

---

[8] *The Times*, April 28, 2000.
[9] See Chap. 20.
[10] [1939] 1 All E.R. 464.
[11] On the National Lottery, see Chap. 20.
[12] [1925] A.C. 445.
[13] [1989] 1 All E.R. 785.
[14] See *Bowerman v. ABTA* [1996] C.L.C. 451; *Carlill v. Carbolic Smoke Ball Company* [1893] 2 Q.B. 163.
[15] [1964] 1 All E.R. 494.
[16] [1990] 1 Lloyd's Rep. 465.

held that the plaintiff had succeeded in satisfying the "heavy burden" which rested upon them to prove, on the balance of probabilities, that the agreement was made without intention to contract. Generally the courts require a high standard of proof before they will conclude that any commercial agreement lacks contractual intention. The phrase that "we are fixed *in good faith*" arising during negotiations was held not to rule out a contract for a charter party in *Hanjin Shipping Co. Ltd v. Zenith Chartering Corp. "The Mercedes Envoy"*[17]. Contractual intention may, be negatived if on an objective view, the statement is made in jest or in anger. In *Licences Insurance Corporation v. Lawson*[18] at an angry meeting the defendant made a statement in the heat of the moment which could have been regarded as a contract. It was held that it was not, because on an objective view, a person at the meeting would not reasonably take it to have been intended as such.[19]

Social and domestic arrangements

(1) Family affairs

The relationship of husband and wife or partners living together has traditionally been treated as a private area, beyond the scope of the contract law. In *Balfour v. Balfour*[20] Atkin L.J. held that there was no intention to create legal relations in family affairs. The plaintiff and defendant were a married couple living in Sri Lanka. The defendant held a Government appointment as Director of Irrigation, but his wife suffered from a physical condition, rheumatoid arthritis, which was affected by the climate on the island, so on medical advice she decided to return to England where she remained. The defendant agreed to pay his wife £30 a month by way of maintenance until she could return to Sri Lanka. Later the Balfours decided on a permanent separation and she sued the husband on his promise. The Court of Appeal held that the promise of maintenance was unenforceable as there was no intention to create legal relations. The couple were still living as man and wife, albeit separately, so the arrangement was not a binding contract. According to Atkin L.J., "agreements such as these are outside the realm of contracts altogether. The common law does not regulate the form of agreements between spouses. Their promises are not created with seals and sealing wax. The consideration that really obtains for them is that natural love and affection which counts for so little in these cold Courts".[21]

11.3

On the other hand, if the parties are spouses with an intention to separate permanently, contractual relations may be created. In *Merritt v. Merritt*[22] the husband deserted his wife to live with another woman. The Court of Appeal held that an agreement with his wife about maintenance was a contract because it was made after the marriage between John and Millicent Merritt had already broken down. The Court of Appeal stated *per curiam* that in deciding whether or not an agreement was intended to establish legal relations, the surrounding circumstances must be looked at in order to see whether

---

[17] [1995] 2 Lloyd's Rep. 559.
[18] (1896) 12 T.L.R. 501.
[19] See also *Lucy v. Zehmer* (1954) 196 V.A. 493, 84 S.E. 2d 516, discussed in Chap. 2.
[20] [1919] 2 K.B. 571.
[21] At p. 579.
[22] [1970] 1 W.L.R. 1211.

reasonable people would regard the agreement as intended to be legally binding. However, in *Xydhias v. Xydhias*[23] the Court of Appeal held that ordinary contractual principles were not applicable to an agreement for ancillary relief in divorce proceedings. An agreement for the compromise of ancillary relief was held not to give rise to a contract enforceable in law. One of the reasons being that the parties to such an agreement could not sue for specific performance.

If the arrangement is purely commercial between husband and wife then there may be a contract. For instance in *Pearce v. Merriman*,[24] it was held that a husband could be his wife's tenant. There is a presumption against an intention to create legal relations in agreements between parent and child. In *Jones v. Padavatton*[25] the mother, Violet Jones, had an arrangement with her daughter, Ruby, to continue living with the mother who provided for her maintenance while the daughter studied for the Bar. The daughter failed her Bar examinations and then had a dispute with her mother which led to her bringing an action for possession of the house requiring her daughter to leave by notice to quit. The Court of Appeal held that there was no contract allowing the daughter to remain because intention to create legal relations was lacking. A member of a family might enter into a legally binding contract with regard to family affairs but there was a presumption against such an intention. On the facts the arrangements over the house were without contractual intention. The daughter therefore had no defence to her mother's action for possession of the home. Dankwaerts L.J. described the action as "really deplorable[26] . . . The points of difference between the two parties appear to be comparatively small, and it is distressing that they could not settle their differences amicably and avoid the bitterness and expense . . . carried as far as this court".

(2) Personal and social relationships[27]

11.4 Inviting a friend to dinner does not amount to a contract and this also applies to most social arrangements, although changes in contract law with regard to some domestic arrangements are already afoot. Prenuptial contracts made in contemplation of marriage are still not enforceable in English law, although they are enforceable in France, Germany, Sweden and in certain American States such as New York and California. A Government Green Paper in November 1998 proposed that in future legal effect be given to pre-nuptial agreements, so the position in England may be subject to change.[28] Similarly, cohabitation contracts are not legally enforceable as contracts. In 1991, a private members' Bill "The Cohabitation (Contract Enforcement) Bill", was introduced to the House of Commons but failed to become law. Such arrangements are essentially within the sphere of family law rather than contract, the legal consequences of which have to be determined in light of modern attitudes and public policy. A contract for IVF fertility treatment was deemed to be a contract in *Patricia Thompson v. Sheffield Fertility Clinic*[29] The grounds of enforceable contracts are therefore widening. On the other hand,

---

[23] [1999] 2 All E.R. 386.
[24] [1904] 1 K.B. 80.
[25] [1969] 1 W.L.R. 328.
[26] At p. 329.
[27] See Freeman, "Contracting in the Haven *Balfour v. Balfour* Revisited" in "Exploring The Boundaries of Contract" (1996, ed. Halston, Dartmouth Publishing, Aldershot).
[28] *The Times*, November 5, 1998 ran the headline "With this ring and contract, I thee wed".
[29] Hooper J., November 24, 2000 (QB, unreported).

breach of promise of engagement was once a fruitful source of litigation between fiancés, but the action no longer exists. The Law Reform (Miscellaneous Provisions) Act 1970 s. 1(1) swept away this action and with it the contractually binding nature of persons being engaged to be married.

An arrangement between partners or housemates over rotas for cooking meals or house cleaning would clearly be thrown out as not being contractually binding if one of parties attempted to claim it was enforceable, but persons who share house together may make a contract with one another if it is for commercial purpose. In *Simpkins v. Pays*[30] the defendant lived with her granddaughter, Esme, and the plaintiff, a rent paying lodger in a house in Wrexham. The three housemates entered into a competition in their joint names in a newspaper the *Sunday Empire News* to place eight fashion items and ladies attire in order of merit. They won the prize of £750 but there was a dispute over sharing out the prize money. The plaintiff claimed her third of this sum. It was held that there was a contract to share the prize winnings and this was legally binding.[31] House sharing agreements whereby a friend stays for a period in your home does not create a contract. However, in *Parker v. Clark*[32] the plaintiffs Dudley and Madeleine Parker made an agreement with Herbert and Jane Clark to leave their own house *The Thimble* and live with the Parkers at their much larger house *Cramond*. An agreement was made whereby the plaintiffs were to make various contributions such as buying a new television set and car in return for which the Parkers promised they would leave them the house when they died. When the parties became estranged the Parkers claimed breach of contract. It was held that they would succeed. Devlin J. held that "the parties intended to enter into an agreement therefore binding in law and not a mere unenforceable family agreement".

Car sharing arrangements to work have also led to contractual disputes. In *Coward v. Motors Insurers Bureau*[33] the Court of Appeal rejected the idea that the parties intended their arrangement to be legally binding. Upjohn L.J. stated that if the parties had been asked if they intended to enter into a legal relationship with the other they would probably have answered "I never gave it a thought". The House of Lords came to a different conclusion in *Albert v. Motor Insurers Bureau*[34] where their Lordships equated lifts to work with a taxi service, and therefore a service for which payment had to be made.

(3) Intention to create legal relations is relevant in other areas of contract law

The distinction between contracts of employment and contracts for services is an impor-   **11.5**
tant area for employment lawyers.[35] In modern times, with the changing nature of the employment relationship and flexible working practices, many persons are employed without a traditional contract of employment. In *Diocese of Southwark v. Coker*[36] the applicant to an employment tribunal, Dr Alexander Coker, was an assistant curate of the Church of England at a church in Belsize Park. He claimed unfair dismissal from his

---

[30] [1955] 3 All E.R. 10.
[31] Although prizes and gaming are generally contrary to public policy and unenforceable, properly drawn up agreements to share a prize, *e.g.* the National Lottery, may be enforceable. (See Chap. 20).
[32] [1960] 1 W.L.R. 286.
[33] [1963] 1 Q.B. 259.
[34] [1971] 2 All E.R. 1345.
[35] The distinction is important for many purposes including income tax, national insurance, employment rights, health and safety regulation and vicarious liability. The leading case is *Ready Mixed Concrete v. Min of Pensions and National Income* [1968] 2 Q.B. 497.
[36] [1998] I.C.R. 140.

post after he failed to obtain a permanent parish and was removed from the diocesan payroll. The Court of Appeal held that he did not have a contract of employment, since not every agreement involving work constituted a binding contract. The claimant, as an ordained priest, held an office with functions designated by law and set out in the Book of Common Prayer. The relationship of the applicant with his bishop was governed by the law of the church and was not a contractual arrangement. The relationship was not therefore covered by legislation. The position is not the same for all religious faiths. Jewish rabbis are regarded as employed by their community.

CAPACITY TO CONTRACT

Capacity to contract is an interesting area of contract law rarely taught at undergraduate level but which raises many difficult and complex questions. The capacity to contract of limited companies, unincorporated associations, public authorities and government departments is a major subject of detailed rules of great interest to commercial lawyers. There are also rules on capacity for those who are weak and less capable of looking after themselves such as children, the mentally disabled and others temporarily lacking mental capacity. The rules governing capacity exist on behalf of those who may be vulnerable but also to protect others who make contracts with those of limited capacity. Persons over the age of 18 have full contractual capacity, if they are of sound mind and not suffering from a factor ruling out capacity such as drunkenness. The latter must be sufficiently severe to render the party incapable of understanding the transaction into which they had entered.[37]

Minors contracts

11.6   The age of capacity to contract for minors was reduced from 21 to 18 by the Family Law Reform Act 1969 s. 1. Until 1969 anyone under the age of 21 was legally termed an infant. Generally speaking, a person is not bound by a contract entered into under the age of 18 even if the other party contracting does not know of this fact or the minor has lied about their age. There are three exceptions. First, a minor is bound by a contract to supply necessaries to them if the contract is for their benefit. A minor must pay a "reasonable" price for these rather than their actual cost of the "necessaries" supplied. Under the Sale of Goods Act 1979 s. 3(3), "necessaries" means "goods suitable to the condition in life of the minor or other person concerned and to his actual requirements at the time of the sale and delivery." In *Nash v. Inman*,[38] the plaintiff, a tailor, supplied clothing to the defendant, a first year student at Trinity College, Cambridge, to the value of over £145, including 11 fancy waistcoats. The defendant refused to pay for the waistcoats arguing (rather cheekily) that he was a minor, and that the waistcoats supplied were not "necessaries". The Court of Appeal held that they were necessaries to an undergraduate at Cambridge in Edwardian days. Necessaries at common law take account of the status of the minor and that person's needs at the time of making the contract. Nowadays that would no doubt include ownership of a mobile phone, for instance.

---

[37] *Gore v. Gibson* (1843) 13 M and W, 623 153 E.R. 260.
[38] [1908] 2 K.B. 1.

A minor is also bound by a contract of employment, but only if it is for their benefit.[39] The point about benefit to the minor arose in *Aylesbury Football Club v. Watford Association Football Club*.[40] The claimants, Aylesbury FC, brought an action for damages against the defendants alleging that the defendants had induced a young footballer, Lee Cook, who was under 18, to break his contract with them. The issue was whether Lee Cook's contract with Aylesbury FC was enforceable as being to the minor's benefit. Poole J. held that it was not beneficial so the contract could not be enforced. There were a number of reasons: Lee Cook did not receive extra training or experience because of the contract, and he did not receive a workable player's contract as the contract was not registerable under FA rules, indeed it was in breach of these rules prohibiting contracts with those under 17, or 18 in full time education. The contract was extremely onerous and restricted his main interest which was the freedom to pursue his football career. The payment of wages depended on the will of his employer. Therefore, the contract could not "sensibly or realistically be described as being for his benefit" and was unenforceable.

Thirdly, ceratin contracts made by a minor may be voidable rather than void. The minor may ratify the contract upon reaching 18 years of age or within a reasonable time thereafter. The contract is binding on the other party without the option given to the minor to ratify or rescind. The minor who rescinds will not be liable to perform in future but will only be able to recover any money paid under the contract if there has been a total failure of consideration.[41] Under the Minor's Contracts Act 1987 s. 3(1), a court may, if it is just and equitable to do so, require the minor to transfer to the plaintiff any property acquired by the minor under the contract. The law on minors' contracts is still a complex mixture of common law and statute, attempting to strike the right balance between the protection of the minor and those who deal with them. There may still be a need for some law reform in this area.

Mentally incapacity and intoxicated persons

Persons of unsound mind generally lack the capacity to make a contract. A person who is defined as mentally disturbed within the meaning of the Mental Health Act 1983 is incapable of contracting. Any contract is voidable by such persons though binding upon the other party.[42] Where the person is not a patient under the 1983 Act, then mental incapacity is not a ground for setting aside a contract unless known to the other party.[43] A contract may, however, be set aside on the equitable ground of unconscionability or applying the old rules on "poor and ignorant persons". [44] Similar rules apply to contracts entered into by a person who has consumed too much alcohol. It is a question of fact whether a person's mind was so impaired by intoxication as to invalidate the contract, and also that the other person knew of the incapacity. The presumption is that a person is sober. For both the inebriated and those suffering from periods of mental disorder, a contract made while sober or during a "lucid interval" will be valid. The effect of this type of incapacity

11.7

---

[39] See *Doyle v. White City Stadium* [1935] 1 K.B. 110.
[40] Poole J., June 12, 2000 (QB, unreported).
[41] *Steinberg v. Scala (Leeds) Ltd* [1923] 2 Ch. 452.
[42] *Re Walker* [1905] 1 Ch. 160.
[43] *Hart v. O'Connor* [1985] A.C. 1000.
[44] *Cresswell v. Potter* [1978] 1 W.L.R. 255 (see Chap. 14).

is to make any contract voidable, not void.[45] Like minors, persons suffering mental incapacity or drunkenness must pay a reasonable price for necessaries.[46] In *Gore v. Gibson*[47] the
defendant pleaded that when he signed a bill of exchange he was "so utterly deprived of
sense, understanding and the use of his reason" that he was unable to understand the
"meaning, nature or effect of the contract thereby". It was held that in cases of complete
inebriation a contract is void. However, where drunkenness is only partial it is not a case
where equity should give relief as this would only encourage anti-social behaviour.

Companies

An incorporated company may contract being a legal person distinct from its shareholders. The company must act within the limits of it's memorandum of association. If
it acts beyond this then that will be *ultra vires* and void.[48]

FORM

11.8 Formality has long since ceased to be an important requirement in English contract law.
The general rule at common law is that contracts can be made orally and without the formality of writing. Under the Statute of Frauds 1677, designed to control fraud, a series
of six named contracts had to be in writing, or evidenced in writing. The doctrine of consideration came under threat through this, but writing failed to take hold, except of
course in land law where it is still paramount. The list of contracts requiring a written
form was reduced to two categories in 1954. Although writing is largely seen as an
archaic device for enforcing contracts it is a requirement which is increasingly being used
in relation to modern protective legislation, for consumer contracts, particularly under
directives made by the European Union. Form is therefore still an important element of
contract law.[49] Formalities are an ancient device to achieve two main functions in contract law. First, to provide evidence to prove the existence and terms of contracts. This is
both an aid to memory as a safeguard to assist later recall and also provides a crucial
defence against fraudulent claims. Secondly, formalities exercise a "cautionary" function,
namely to bring home to contracting parties the effect of what they may be signing or to
what they have agreed. Thirdly, there is the so called "channelling function", in other
words to determine which agreements are to be regarded as contracts in certain types of
transaction. This assists in marking out the boundaries of contract.

Form was given a huge increase in status by the Statute of Frauds 1677 but since then
its importance has declined and the doctrine of consideration replaced form as a contractual requirement in most cases. Formalities of writing tend to be inconvenient and
time consuming. Despite this, most commercial contracts, though generally not required
to be in writing, are nevertheless mostly put in carefully drafted written form.

---

[45] See *Lucy v Zehmer* (1954) 196 V.A. 493, 84 S.E. 2d. 516, discussed Chap. 2.
[46] Sale of Goods Act 1979 s. 3(2).
[47] (1845) 13 M and W 621, 153 E.R. 260.
[48] See *Ashbury Railway Carriage and Iron Co. v. Riche* (1875) LR 7 H.L. 653; *William Cory and Son Ltd v.
London Corporation* [1951] 2 K.B. 476 (discussed Chap. 23).
[49] See Fuller, "Consideration and Form" (1941) Columbia Law Review 799.

Contracts required to be in writing

By statute a small number of contracts must be in writing to be enforceable, *e.g.* the Bills **11.9** of Exchange Act 1882 s. 3(1) and the Bills of Sale Act 1878. These are specialised areas of commercial law, where formality has remained necessary. Contracts for sale or other disposition of an interest in land can also only be made in writing. The Law of Property (Miscellaneous Provisions) Act 1989 s. 2 repealed s. 40 of the Law of Property Act 1925 which for decades had made it necessary for the sale of other disposition land to be merely evidenced in writing. Contracts for the sale of land must now be made in writing to include all the terms. At one time the doctrine of part performance mitigated the writing requirement but the courts now appear to adhere to the necessity of writing.[50] Unless such contracts are in writing they will not be enforceable. However, the doctrine of estoppel may now be used to remedy a defect in form.[51] Contracts for the sale of land at auction do not have to be in writing.[52]

Contracts requiring to be evidenced in writing

A guarantee for the debts or liabilities of another must be evidenced in writing. This is the one remaining category of the Statute of Frauds 1677 to have survived. Section 4 requires that a contract of guarantee must be evidenced by some note or memorandum in writing and signed by the party against whom the contract is being enforced. Failure to comply with the requirements of s. 4 will make the contract unenforceable. The Statute of Frauds 1677 define a contract or guarantee as a "promise to answer for the debt, default or miscarriage of another person".

Deeds

A deed is a specific type of legal document which must bear the word "deed" or an indi- **11.10** cation that the document is intended to have that effect. The document must be signed by the maker of the deed and signature must be attested by a witness (or two witnesses if the deed is signed at the members direction). The deed has to be delivered, showing intention to be bound by the document.[53] The requirement of a deed being sealed with wax has been abolished.[54] Leases for more than three years must be by deed and also gratuitous promises. In the latter case this does away with the requirement of consideration. Otherwise formalities are in addition to the need for consideration.

Writing as a protection for consumers

Consumer law now includes the use of writing as a means of protecting consumers and notifying parties of their liabilities and rights. For instance, the Timeshare Act 1992

---

[50] See *Firstpost Homes Ltd v. Johnson* [1995] 1 W.L.R. 1567.
[51] See *Yaxley v. Gotts* [1999] 2 F.L.R. 941 and Tee (2000) 59 C.L.J. 23.
[52] See Sale of Goods Act 1979, s. 57(2). A sale by auction is complete when the auctioneer announces its completion by the fall of his hammer
[53] Law of Property (Miscellaneous Provisions) Act 1989 s.1(2)(3).
[54] S. 1.

requires that those offering timeshares of houses and flats tell their would-be customers in writing of various matters relating to the contract, such as the services to which the customer would have access and the exact period for which the customer's rights may be exercised. The Consumer Credit Act 1974 ss 60, 61 require certain details of consumer credit and hire purchase agreements to be provided in writing. There are three conditions which must be satisfied if a regulated agreement is to be treated as properly executed. The document must be in a prescribed form containing all the prescribed terms and signed both by the debtor or hirer and the creditor or person on their behalf. The document must also include all the terms of the agreement other than implied terms and when sent to the debtor be in such a state that all its terms are readily legible.

11.11   These rather mundane and unexciting provisions have now led to what may be English Contract Law's first brush with the Human Rights Act 1998. In *Wilson v. First County Trust*[55] the Court of Appeal held that an agreement governed by the 1974 Act was unenforceable by the creditor because a "document fee" of £250 had been improperly treated as credit. Since the amount of credit was wrongly stated, the agreement was not a properly executed registered agreement. The defendant creditors were therefore unable to enforce the contract. The Court of Appeal found for the claimant on the main issue but made a declaration that s. 127(3) of the 1974 Act which restricted the right to enforce the agreement was incompatible with the creditor's rights under the European Convention of Human Rights and the Human Rights Act 1998. The formalities put into place by European directives for consumer protection herald a new return to requirements informational, albeit in electronic form. The Consumer Protection (Distance Selling) Regulations 2000 require contracts with consumers made at a distance to be put in hard copy and sent to consumers within seven days of their formation. The writing must contain details of the transaction including addresses of the seller and supplier of the goods.[56]

Formalities: for and against

11.12   In Scots law, lacking a doctrine of consideration, formalities have always played an important role. There was greater use of writing and evidence was provided usually by writ or oath. Such rules are tedious and inconvenient, not to say often impractical. Scots law did away with most of these in the Requirements of Writing (Scotland) Act 1995. There is now no written requirement for a contract or unilateral obligation apart from the creation, transfer or variation of an interest land[57] (as in England) or for a gratuitous unilateral promise not in the course of a business.[58] In modern times informality has largely won the day in the United Kingdom, even in a system like Scots law lacking the doctrine of consideration, however, the arguments associated with the rules for e-commerce across the European Union may mean a re-awakening of the importance of terms of agreements being in a permanent recorded form.[59]

---

[55] [2001] 2 W.L.R. 302, see Lawson (2001) 151 N.L.J. 882.
[56] See Chap. 4.
[57] S. 1(2)(a)(i).
[58] S. 1(2)(a)(ii).
[59] See Chap. 4.

Chapter 12

The Parameters of the Contract

Determining the Contents of a Contract

In determining the contents of a contract and its proper interpretation we enter a **12.1** complex, but practical, area of contract law. Many words, letters and documents may have been exchanged between the parties before and indeed after the contract was made. The scope of the contract must be ascertained in light of what was actually agreed at the time of formation. This depends upon whether the contract was oral, written or a combination of both. If the contract is made up entirely of spoken words, its terms are a question of fact. The burden of proof is on the plaintiff, who will normally be the person alleging that there is a contract, or that a contract contains a particular term. The party must prove his case on the balance of probabilities and evidence is crucial. For instance, proving that a letter was actually sent for the purposes of the postal rule will be vital to the existence and terms of any purported contract. Many contracts which appear to be entirely oral, *e.g.* many consumer transactions, are in reality on written standard terms and have been incorporated by notice.[1] With only a small number of exceptions, contracts can be made orally.[2] In commercial contracts it remains normal to put the terms in writing. As Samuel Goldwyn, the famous Hollywood film producer, is once apochryphally said to have remarked, "an oral contract ain't worth the paper its written on". The parties usually wish to ensure that their contract is a detailed and accurate record of agreement. The writing may include several documents, including standard terms and annexing many different terms.

If documents are incorporated into the main contract they must be identified and referred to in the main agreement. This is called joinder of documents. Joinder may be effected by an intermediate document however it must be clear that the two documents are intrinsically connected.[3] Many commercial documents may be joined into the principal agreement. This can make the final contract voluminous. It is not uncommon for inconsistencies to occur whereby details of a document conflict with the main contract. In such situations the courts have to ascertain the intention of the parties.[4] They will usually try to find agreement on the terms if possible. A clause may also be incorporated into a contract without specific reference to the clause itself on the basis of an implied

---

[1] See Chap. 16.
[2] See Chap. 11, for the written and other requirements of "Form".
[3] *"The Anemone"* [1987] 1 Lloyd's Rep. 546.
[4] *Adamastos Shipping Co. v. Anglo Saxon Petroleum Co.* [1959] A.C. 133.

term. In *Extrudakerb (Maltby Engineering) Ltd v. White Mountain Quarries Ltd*,[5] an arbitration clause was incorporated into a building sub-contract by the implication of a term.[6] Carsewell J. held that if an officious bystander had asked the parties whether they considered that the arbitration clause should apply in the event of a dispute, the answer would be clear that it would. Normally such clauses can only be incorporated by specific reference.[7] If the contract is partly oral and partly written, the parol evidence rule applies. This governs the admissibility of oral evidence. We discuss this shortly. First, however, we shall consider the rules of admissibility of evidence of terms and the interpretation and construction of contracts.

THE ADMISSIBILITY OF EVIDENCE

The surrounding circumstances of the contract: "the factual matrix"

12.2   There are a number of rules of admissibility and construction applying to determine the scope and meaning of the terms of a contract.[8] Some of these rules exclude matters which might at first sight appear relevant in the interests of fairness and completeness. For instance, in construing a written contract, the preliminary negotiations between the parties are inadmissible,[9] as also are the parties' words after the contract was formed,[10] subsequent actions cannot be taken into account in determined whether a term is really a condition,[11] and the parties own subjective intentions and meanings attributable to words are inadmissible.[12] However, if there is ambiguity in the written contract, the parties own intention may be considered in evidence. Questions most often arise in relation to the factual or commercial background against which the contract was made. This is sometimes called the "factual matrix". Traditionally the background to the contract was not admissible in evidence. The words alone had to be interpreted to construe by meaning of any document. This view has now been abandoned in favour of a wider approach. Lord Wilberforce in *Reardon Smith Line v. Hansen-Tangen The Diana Prosperity*[13] described the factual matrix as a concept which "can be illustrated but hardly defined". In a commercial contract this included "the commercial purpose of the contract". This in turn presupposed knowledge of "the genesis of the transaction, the background, the context, the market in which the parties are operating".

The extent to which surrounding circumstances should be admitted is a matter of lively judicial debate. Bingham L.J. in *Harrods v. Schwartz-Sackin*[14] was in favour of a wider admissibility and a liberal approach to the inclusion of surrounding facts:

---

[5] *The Times*, July 10, 1996.
[6] See later p. 205.
[7] *T. W. Thomas and Co. Ltd v. Portsea Steamship Co. Ltd* [1912] A.C. 1 where an arbitration clause was not incorporated into a charterparty.
[8] See Lewison *The Interpretation of Contracts* (1997, Sweet and Maxwell, London).
[9] *Prenn v. Simmonds* [1971] W.L.R. 1381.
[10] *James Miller v. Whitworth Estates* [1970] 2 W.L.R. 728.
[11] *Schuler AG v. Wickman Machine Tool Sales Ltd* [1973] 2 All E.R. 39.
[12] See Lord Hoffman in *Investors Compensation Scheme v. West Bromwich Building Society* [1998] 1 W.L.R. 896.
[13] [1976] 1 W.L.R. 989 (at pp. 995–996).
[14] [1991] 18 F.S.R. 209

"The rule that the intention of parties to a written agreement is to be elicited from an objective construction of the language they have used, read in its factual context, and not from evidence of their subjective intentions, is not in my view an obstacle to fair construction of contracts but is a rule which ensures that the court gives effect to the parties' own contemporaneous bargain rather than to their *ex post facto* statements as to what they intended or would with the benefit of hindsight have intended. This is because the interests of contracting parties are often divergent if not conflicting, and the agreement may represent the only overlapping area of interest and thus the only area of consensus".[15]

An even wider view of admissibility is that proposed by Lord Hoffman in *Investors Compensation Scheme v. West Bromwich Building Society* who stated:

"The background was famously referred to by Lord Wilberforce as 'the matrix of fact', but this phrase is, if anything, an understated description of what the background may include. Subject to the requirement that it should have been reasonably available to the parties, and to the exception to be mentioned next, it includes absolutely anything which would have affected the way in which the language of the document would have been understood by a reasonable man".[16]

Such an approach would allow the parties scope to argue for a wider inclusion of terms. This goes beyond the traditional rules which aim to keep the parameters of the contract and corresponding disputes over its contents within sustainable boundaries.[17] There was some support for this new approach by the majority of the Court of Appeal in *MDIS Ltd v. Swinbank*[18] and in recent law. There is also judicial support for a more conservative attitude or at least a critical view of allowing too much factual matrix to encroach into the contract itself.

In general the courts are reluctant to go as far as Lord Hoffman's dictum would suggest. **12.3** In *Scottish Power plc v. Britoil (Exploration) Ltd*,[19] the Court of Appeal, held that the surrounding circumstances should only be considered to ascertain facts in the minds of both parties at the relevant time of contracting to look for the common intention of the parties. Evidence of one party's subjective intention was inadmissible. Equally inadmissible was evidence of negotiations leading up to the contract. Staughton L.J. criticised counsel for trying to include a "large volume of additional background material". This did not assist an understanding of the contract and added to the cost of litigation:

"The factual matrix to which a court was to have regard in construing a contract meant the immediate context of the contract. Consideration of the surrounding circumstances should be confined to the facts which both parties would have had in

---

[15] At p. 219.
[16] [1998] 1 W.L.R. 896 (at p. 912).
[17] For a critical view of the Hoffman approach to interpretation, see Malcolm Clarke, "Interpreting Contracts - The Price of Perspective" (2000) 59 C.L.J. 18. The Hoffman view is also applicable to the question of interpretation (see later p. 197).
[18] [1999] 1 Lloyd's Rep I.R. 98. See also *A.G. Europe v. International Insurance, The Times*, June 22, 2001 and *Biggin Hill Airport v. Bramley LBC, The Times*, January 9, 2001.
[19] (1997) 94(47) LSG 30.

mind and known that the other had in mind when the contract was made . . . A wide definition of surrounding circumstances tends to add to the cost of litigation but contribute little to the understanding of the contract."[19a]

The Court was there to ascertain the common intention of the parties, so evidence of one party alone, or pre-contractual negotiations were both inadmissible:

"It was often difficult to restrain counsel from producing a great deal of evidence under the heading of matrix, which on examination contributed little or nothing to the true understanding of the parties' contract. All, or almost all, judges were now concerned about the huge costs of litigation. Such a wide definition of surrounding circumstances, background or matrix seemed likely to increase the cost to no very obvious advantage."[19b]

In *Youell v. Bland Welch and Co Ltd*[20] Staughton L.J. would have limited admissibility to "what the parties had in mind . . . what was going on around them at the time when they were making the contract", and he approved Lord Kirkland in *Bank of Scotland v. Dunedin Property Investment Ltd*[21] who limited admissibility to "facts which both parties would have had in mind and known that the other party had in mind, when the contract was made". Staughton L.J. in *Youell* expressed his own view of the court's task in relation to admissibility:

"It is now, in my view, somewhat old fashioned to approach the problem armed with the parol evidence rule, that evidence is not admissible to vary or contradict the words of a written contract. The modern approach of the House of Lords is that on the positive side evidence should be admitted of the background to the contract, the surrounding circumstances, the genesis and aim. Almost every day in these courts there is a contest as to what comes within that description. The notion is what the parties had in mind, and the court is entitled to know what was going on around them at the time when they were making the contract. This applies to circumstances which were known to both parties, and to what each might reasonably have expected the other to know."[22]

The amount of admissible evidence of surrounding circumstances as an aid to interpreting a contract is therefore an important issue. Practitioners and judges are constantly called upon to consider the background to the words of the contract.

THE PAROL EVIDENCE RULE

12.4   Despite Staughton L.J.s *dicta*,[23] the parol evidence rule remains the usual starting point on the admissibility of evidence as an aid to constructing a contract. The parol

---

[19a]   At p. 48.
[19b]   At p. 52.
[20]   [1992] 2 Lloyd's Rep. 127 (at p. 133).
[21]   (1998) S.C. 657 (at p. 670).
[22]   At p. 133.
[23]   See above, at p. 191.

evidence rule was stated by P.O. Lawrence J. in *Jacobs v. Batavia and General Plantations Ltd*:

> "It is firmly established as a rule of law that parol evidence cannot be admitted to add to, vary or contradict a deed or other written instrument. Accordingly, it has been held that (except in cases of fraud or rectification, and except, in certain circumstances, as a defence to an action for specific performance) parol evidence will not be admitted to prove that some particular term, which had been verbally agreed upon, had been omitted (by design or otherwise) from a written instrument constituting a valid and operative contract between the parties."[24]

It has been observed that the parol evidence rule is neither about parol contracts, *i.e.* oral, nor is it even a rule these days. It is in fact a rule of evidence, an example of the "best evidence" rule. The situation would be better described by saying that there is a rebuttable presumption that, a written document is intended to be the whole contract between the parties. If so evidence of oral terms cannot be allowed. The parol evidence rule operates to exclude not only oral evidence, but other forms of evidence as well, such as previous negotiations, drafts of earlier contracts, or other associated documents, not properly joined. The rule only applies if the contract is intended to be entirely in writing. As we shall discuss, this allows numerous exceptions and means of avoiding the rule.

There are a number of sensible reasons for the parol evidence rule.[25] First, it narrows the issues arising from a contractual document, and keeps any disputes within reasonable limits. Secondly, the rule promotes certainty, and reduces the possibility of contracts being modified by later evidence, so that contracting parties rights and obligations were undermined. Thirdly, the rule attempts to control fraud, and, finally, it aims at finality which is what any written contract is expected to achieve. Despite this array of good arguments the rule has not been applied in many cases, indeed one has to work hard to find any reported judgments. It was applied in *Newman v. A and S Gatti*,[26] where the plaintiff, Ethel Newman, an actress, signed a written agreement to appear as understudy for a well known star of the Edwardian stage, Miss Edna May, in "*The Belle of May Fair*". Before signing she claimed to have been told by the defendant's manager that if Edna fell ill she would get the role for the rest of the run of the operatta. This statement was not, however, put into the written agreement. When Miss May was taken ill, the plaintiff was at first given the main part, but later this was taken over by another actress. The judge found that the oral undertaking had been made, and therefore she was entitled to damages. This was reversed on appeal. Vaughan Williams L.J. held that the question of construction should not have been put to the jury as a question of fact, *i.e.* oral evidence. The construction of a written contract was for the judge *i.e.* a question of law. Oral evidence could not be admitted. The Court expressed sorrow for the plaintiff but in the absence of a collateral contract she could not succeed. This is a rare example of the rule, which is significantly outnumbered by it's exceptions.

12.5

---

[24] [1924] 1 Ch. 287 (at p. 295).
[25] See McLauchlan, "The admissibility of parol evidence to interpret written contracts" (1974) N.Z.U.L.R. pp. 121–139.
[26] (1907) 24 T.L.R. 18.

Exceptions to the parol evidence rule

(1) Contract partly written partly oral

12.6   If a party can show that their intention was to treat the contract as only partly in writing with other oral terms included, the parol evidence rule does not apply. There is a presumption that a written document represents the whole contract, but this can be rebutted, and oral terms may be admissible.[27] This is the major exception which allows many cases to slip by the rule. A good example of this is the Scots law case of *Irons v. Partick Thistle Football Club Ltd*,[28] in which David Irons was a professional footballer who signed for Patrick Thistle FC and later alleged that certain terms were agreed between himself and the manager, John Lambie, relating to a signing on fee and a bonus of £20,000 if Patrick Thistle achieved promotion. These statements were not recorded in the standard form written contract which he signed. Different figures were later filled into blank spaces in the contract. Patrick Thistle later alleged that only lower bonuses had been agreed and these were the figures stated in the document. The Outer House of the Court of Session held that while normally oral evidence was not admissible to contradict the terms of a written contract, as a result of the football clubs admission that a bonus of some sort was payable, oral evidence was admissible because both parties had agreed that the written document was not the entire agreement between them.[29]

(2) Existence of a condition precedent

Oral evidence is admissible to prove that the contract is not yet in force because of a condition precedent to the agreement. In *Pym v. Campbell*[30] there was a written contract for the sale of a share in a new invention, a "Crushing, Washing and Amalgamating Machine". Parol evidence was admitted to show that the contract did not come into force until the invention had been approved by two engineers, one of whom, Abernethie, could not be found. This was a condition precedent which was an admissible question of fact to be left to the jury.

(3) To identify the subject matter of the contract

12.7   In *Margo Freeguard v. Ingrid Rogers*,[31] in a dispute concerning a house and garden in Chichester, the Court of Appeal held that in construing an option agreement whereby vendors granted purchasers an option to buy "the property known as" at a given address, the Court was entitled to take into account extrinsic evidence as to what exactly the property was and whether, for example, it included an adjoining garage. This was an exception to the parol evidence rule. According to Peter Gibson L.J.: "The rule's operation was not confined to oral evidence and had been taken to exclude extrinsic matter in writing. The exception to that rule was that extrinsic evidence might be admitted to identify the subject-matter of a contract where there was doubt as to what that was, or to determine the extent or boundaries of land which were the subject of the document."

---

[27] See Lord Russell of Killowen C.J. in *Gillespie v. Cheney Eggar & Co.* [1896] 2 Q.B. 59.
[28] [1997] S.L.T. 983.
[29] For an English example of the same principle see *Couchman v. Hill* [1947] K.B. 554 as to whether or not a heifer was in fact "unserved".
[30] (1866) 6 El and Bl 370, 119 E.R. 903.
[31] *The Times*, October 22, 1998.

(4) To show the purpose of the contract

In *Krell v. Henry*[32] parol evidence was admitted to show that the purpose of making a contract to take a room in Pall Mall was in order to view the Coronation procession of King Edward VII, not merely to have use of the rooms for the two days in question.

(5) A collateral contract has been formed

The device of the collateral contract can be used to avoid the parol evidence rule. For instance, if William makes a promise to Yvonne about a certain matter and she then contracts with William on the strength of William's undertaking, or indeed enters into a contract with a third party Zoë on the basis of William promise, there may be a binding collateral contract with William. The consideration for this is entering into the main agreement, and evidence of the statement made by William is admissible. This is not caught by the parol evidence rule because there are in fact two contracts, not one, the first being entirely oral and not subject to the rule. This is illustrated by *City and Westminster Properties (1934) Ltd v. Mudd*[33] in which the tenant of a greengrocers shop, Dixon Horace Mudd, was assured that he could continue to sleep on the premises if he signed a new lease. The oral promise was admissible as a collateral contract separate from the lease itself. The consideration for the oral promise was entering into the main agreement. Collateral contracts may also be binding where the main contract is with a third party.[34] Collateral contracts are often important in hire purchase cases involving cars which appear to be purchased from dealers, but where the customer's contract is concluded with a finance company. The buyer may hold the dealer to an oral undertaking if this amounts to a collateral contract. In *Andrews v. Hopkinson*,[35] the defendant in extolling the virtues of a second hand car stated "it's a good little bus. I could stake my life on it. You will have no trouble with it". The car was defective and the dealer was held liable, being in breach of a collateral warranty as to the quality of the car.

(6) Miscellaneous grounds upon which oral evidence is admissible

Parol evidence is also admissible on other grounds which are discussed elsewhere: **12.8**

    (i)   Evidence of a custom or implied term is admissible to add to or explain a written agreement;[36]

    (ii)   The equitable remedy of rectification operates in relation to documents which do not correctly record an agreement. Parol evidence may be admitted to prove this point. This is considered in relation to remedies for mistake[37];

    (iii)   Parol evidence is admissible to show the existence of a vitiating factor such as misrepresentation or undue influence[38];

---

[32] [1903] 2 K.B. 740. See further Chap. 22.
[33] [1959] Ch. 129.
[34] *Shanklin Pier Ltd v. Detel Products* [1951] 2 K.B. 854.
[35] [1957] 1 Q.B. 229.
[36] See later pp. 198–208.
[37] See Chap. 21.
[38] See Chaps 18 and 19.

(iv) Evidence of lack of capacity to contract is admissible by parol evidence[39]; and

(v) An oral statement may vary a written exemption clause. We shall discuss this later.[40]

(7) Attempts to avoid the parol evidence rule by draftsmanship

It is not uncommon for one party to attempt to exclude oral statements and other terms in standard form contracts. The clause usually states that the written document is the "entire agreement" between the parties and no other matters are admissible to add to, or vary, the writing. Entire agreement or "watertight" clauses are designed to deal with situations like that which arose in *Curtis v. Chemical Cleaning and Dyeing*[41] where a shop assistant misrepresented a written exemption clause to a customer. The shop was held liable because the oral statement superseded the written term. Such clauses do not always succeed in their intent in the modern world of contract law.

12.9   In 1998 the Office of Fair Trading stated their opinion that "entire agreement" clauses were potentially "unfair" in consumer contracts.[42] Also in *Thomas Witter v. TBP Industries Ltd*[43] an attempt to list representations in a schedule to the contract and thereby exclude all other statements as not being part of the contract, was unsuccessful. Other representations could be relied upon as included in the contract. In *Deepak Fertilisers and Petrochemical Corporation v. Davy McKee (London) Ltd*[44] an entire agreement clause stated that "This contract comprises the entire agreement between the parties . . . and there are not any agreements, understandings, promises or conditions, oral or written, expressed or implied, concerning the subject matter which are not merged into this contract and superseded hereby". The Court of Appeal took a strict construction of the clause as exempting liability and held that this was effective to exclude liability for any collateral warranty but was not sufficient in it's wording to exclude liability for misrepresentation.

An entire agreement can also succeed in its desired effect of keeping extraneous statements out of a contract. In *Inntrepreneur Pub Company Ltd v. East Crown Ltd*[45] an entire agreement not only rendered evidence of a collateral warranty inadmissible, it deprived what would otherwise have been a valid collateral warranty of it's legal effect. Lightman J. described the purpose of such clauses as being "to preclude a party to a written agreement from threshing through the undergrowth and finding a chance remark or statement on which to found a claim".

The rule survives proposals for its reform

12.10   Criticism of the parol evidence rule has led to the Law Commission reviewing its status on two occasions. In a Working Paper[46] the Law Commission recommended the

---

[39] See Chap. 11.
[40] See Chap. 16.
[41] [1951] 1 K.B. 805.
[42] Discussed Chap. 15.
[43] [1994] T.L.R. 145.
[44] [1999] B.L.R. 41.
[45] *The Times*, September, 5, 2000.
[46] (No. 70), 1976 para. 43.

abolition of the rule, saying: "It is a technical rule of uncertain ambit which, at least, adds to the complications of litigation without affecting the outcome and, at worst, prevents the courts getting at the truth". A decade later the Law Commission Report of 1986 decided against recommending abolition:

> "The consequences of abolishing the parol evidence rule would be that very many cases would be decided exactly as they are today, either where the writing prevails over oral evidence (not because the oral evidence is excluded but because this gives effect to what the parties are found to have agreed) or where the oral evidence prevails over the writing (not because the courts have discovered an exception to the parol evidence rule but again because this gives effect to what the parties are found to have agreed)."[47]

The Law Commission concluded that "there is *no rule of law* that evidence is rendered inadmissible or is to be ignored solely because a document exists which looks like a complete contract. Whether it is a complete contract depends upon the intention of the parties, objectively judged, and not on any rule of law."[48] It has been suggested[49] that the parol evidence rule amounts to no more than a presumption that a document which looks like the whole contract really is so. This presumption can be rebutted to show that the parties' intention was the contract would be partly written but also partly oral, in which case the parol evidence rule ceases to apply. In *Gillespie v. Cheney Egar & Co.*[50] Lord Russell of Killown C.J. said: "When parties have arrived at a definite written contract, the presumption is that the writing was intended to contain all the terms of the contract; but it is a presumption only, and either party may allege an antecedent express stipulation intended to continue in force with the written contract, and may contend that the written contract was not intended to include all the terms".

The parol evidence rule is still applied

Despite calls for it's abolition the rule remains alive (if not exactly kicking) today, particularly in land law. In *W. F. Trustees Ltd v. Expo Safety Systems Ltd*,[51] in the Chancery Division, Jonathan Sumption Q.C. stated that the parol evidence rule, "remained a valuable rule of evidence in the construction of documents, particularly conveyancing documents . . . Transfers of interests in land were documents which subsequent purchasers of the same or neighbouring interests should be entitled to read and understand for themselves without the assistance of the parties' recollections. There could be few fields in which the exclusion of parol evidence served a more valuable purpose". The parol evidence rule was also applied in *Woolls v. Powling*.[52] The Court of Appeal held that where a conveyance was clear as to the boundary lines between two properties, extrinsic evidence about the boundary line was not admissible. However, a plan of the land "for the

12.11

---

[47] "Law of Contract: The Parol Evidence Rule" (No. 154), Law Commission (Cmnd 9700, 1986).
[48] Para. 2.17.
[49] *Wedderburn* [1959] C.L.J. 58.
[50] [1896] 2 Q.B. 59.
[51] *The Times*, May 24, 1993.
[52] *The Times*, March 9, 1999.

purposes of identification only" could be used to determine where the boundary lay. The basic need for certainty in written documents lies at the heart of both of these examples.

THE RULES OF INTERPRETATION AND CONSTRUCTION

12.12 Interpretation[53] and construction are, strictly speaking, two different processes.[54] Interpretation is the process whereby a court gives meaning to the language used by the parties. This can involve technical meanings, trade practices and course of dealings between them. The object is usually to ascertain the true meaning of the words as used by the parties themselves. Construction, on the other hand though it is often used in same sense, really means giving legal effect or meaning of the words. The latter is for the courts to decide, for instance, whether a term is to be treated as a condition or a warranty. If we make this distinction, then the construction of a contract begins with the interpretation of it's language but does not end with it. The process of interpretation, meanwhile, stops short of a determining of the legal effect of the words used. In practice the two processes are inextricably linked. The main rule of interpretation of contracts is based on the intention of the parties as evidenced by the contract itself. The approach is once again objective. The parties' subjective intentions are relevant, but not conclusive. In *Zoan v. Rouamba*,[55] the Court of Appeal emphasised that it was the intention of both parties that was relevant to the construction of a document, not simply the meanings which are partly contended. The courts should apply the plain and ordinary meaning of the words used, unless a special meaning was intended. The courts are allowed to look beyond the literal words in cases of technical words, ambiguities and absurdities. This really involves going back to the surrounding circumstances.[56] The literal meaning will give way or be restricted, increased or changed if it does not give effect to the intentions of the parties. This means, usually, a literal meaning to the words used. Apart from this there are a mass of technical aids to construction.[57] The interpretation of contracts is both a practical art and an important aspect of everyday contract law. According to Sir Christopher Staughton:[58]

> "For anyone who intends to practise commercial law, the interpretation of contracts is a topic of vital importance. Formation of contracts, mistake and misrepresentation, . . . frustration are all interesting topics which were taught in this University [*i.e.* Cambridge] with enthusiasm 44 years ago and no doubt still are; but I have rarely ever heard of them since. It is interpretation which is far more important in practice. There is a shortage of academic work on the subject, perhaps because it would be a great labour to assemble the definitive work from a great mass of material."[59]

---

[53] See Lewison, *Interpretation of Contracts* (1997, 2 ed. Sweet and Maxwell, London), for a full and detailed account of the many rules and techniques of interpretation of contracts.
[54] See Patterson, "Interpretation and Construction of Contracts" 62 Col L.R. 833 and Farnsworth, "Meaning in the Law of Contracts" (1967) 76 Yale Law Journal 939.
[55] [2000] 1 W.L.R. 1509.
[56] See *Clarke* [2000] C.L.J. 18. In *HSBC plc v. Mutual Insurance (UK) Ltd, The Times*, June 11, 2001 surrounding circumstances were used to show that something had gone wrong in drafting a wrong document.
[57] See Lewison, *Interpretation of Contracts* (1997, 2nd ed, Sweet and Maxwell, London).
[58] "How do the Courts Interpret Commercial Contracts?" [1999] C.L.J. 303–313.
[59] At p. 303.

Staughton identified four main principles of interpretation. First, to look for the intention   **12.13**
of the parties by considering the wording of the contract to see what it says. It is not correct
to ask the parties what they thought the contract meant (*i.e.* a purely subjective approach).
Secondly, the court must look at the surrounding circumstances known to both parties
when they made the contract, *i.e.* "the factual matrix" (discussed earlier). Thirdly, if the
ordinary meaning leads to an absurd conclusion, the judge must consider whether it must
bear some other meaning. Finally, the court is entitled to look at evidence of how the
market works, such as custom or trade practice but not at "what people in the market think
it means except where the words are used in a special or technical meaning".[60] Contract
lawyers also need to be familiar with a wide range of rules for interpretation and construction which apply in relation to particular types of terms, *e.g.* exemption clauses applying the "*contra proferentem*" rule[61] and also to rules of interpretation based upon implied
terms and trade practices in particular kinds of contracts.

IMPLIED TERMS AND GAPFILLING

It would be unrealistic to expect every term in a contract to be written down or expressed   **12.14**
in words. This would be inconvenient and impractical, leave control of the terms entirely
in the hands of the parties, or more commonly, just one of them, and require contracts
to be absurdly lengthy documents.[62] In the days when solicitors and notaries were paid
by the word this was often sadly the case. Today standard form contracts drafted by one
of the parties are often extensively worded. Even so there may be gaps to fill. The ideology of freedom of contract meant that it was for the parties to make their own terms. It
was not for the courts to re-write contracts nor to do the job of draftsmanship for the
parties. In theory the judges should not intervene in the formation of terms.

By the end of the nineteenth century a new doctrine emerged in the form of the
implied term. To some this was a fiction, to others an ingenious tool. Either way, it
allowed the courts to get involved in the contents of contracts without infringing the
principle of freedom of contract. Based on the theory that the courts were merely interpreting the presumed intention of the parties, they could incorporate new terms where
the contract was silent. The technique of the implied term had other functions. Implied
terms became legal rules and could be used as a means of achieving substantive fairness.
Implied terms could also be used as a theoretical underpinning for setting aside or discharging a contract for common mistake or frustration,[63] or to resolve contractual disputes when the contract could not deal with the matter. In *Paula Lee Ltd v. Robert Zehil
Ltd*[64] a contract to distribute clothing in certain countries in the Middle East was held to
be subject to an implied term. The defendant's freedom of choice to select the garments
should be limited to those methods of performance which could be regarded as reasonable in all the circumstances. The contract itself was silent on the matter.

---

[60] See later p. 200.
[61] See Chap. 16.
[62] See Schwartz, "Relational Contracts in the Courts" (1992) 21 J.L.S. 278–81).
[63] See Trakman, "Frustrated Contracts and Legal Fictions" (1983) 46 M.L.R 39 and Smith, "Contracts-
Mistake, Frustration and Implied Terms" (1994) 110 L.Q.R. 400.
[64] [1983] 2 All E.R. 390.

12.15   Statute has also taken up the idea of implied terms, most notably in relation to implying conditions into contracts for the sale of goods. The idea of the courts using implied
terms to supplement that which is unexpressed is sometimes known as "gapfilling".
Gapfilling is necessary because contracts are left incomplete. There may be many reasons
for this. The parties may simply not have the time or energy to list all the possible circumstances which might arise during the contract, they may not foresee events, or deliberately
say nothing for fear of putting the other party off contracting in the first place. It may be
that the language used was vague or ambiguous or the cost of dealing with the matter was
greater than the risk, *e.g.* taking out expensive insurance to cover a remote possibility.

Terms implied "in fact" and "in law"

12.16   Terms may be implied into contracts on two fundamentally different bases. Terms are
implied "in fact" in order (i) to try to arrive at the parties "actual" intention on matters
which they omitted to express in the contract or (ii) to find the "presumed" or hypothetical intention of the parties, over matters about which they may not have thought at the
time of contracting. Terms implied "in fact" are designed to supplement the unexpressed
but supposed actual intentions of the parties in a contract which is likely to be personal
to them, *i.e.* usually a one-off contract, not of a particular type, and concerning a term
not commonly found in contracts in general. On the other hand, terms will be implied
"in law" where precedent or statute has incorporated such terms into particular types of
contract. As an illustration of the latter, in contracts of employment there will be an
implied term that the employer has to take reasonable care to protect the health and
safety of their employees.[65] Such implied terms are used to incorporate certain basic rules
of law. The courts may often do so to achieve greater fairness or for other policy
considerations.

     The distinction between terms implied "in law" or "in fact" was explained by Lord
Wright in *Luxor (Eastbourne) Ltd v. Cooper*,[66] in which he stated that:

> "The expression 'implied term' is used in different senses. Sometimes it denotes some
> term which does not depend on the actual intention of the parties but on a rule of law,
> such as the terms, warranties or conditions which, if not expressly excluded, the law
> imports, as for instance under the Sale of Goods Act and the Marine Insurance Act.
> But a case like the present is different because what it is sought to imply is based on
> an intention imputed to the parties from their actual circumstances."

If a term is implied "in fact" it must give way to the parties' own expressed or "actual"
intention. In the case of terms implied in law, their effectiveness depends on whether the
term is based upon (a) a default rule, *i.e.* the parties may agree otherwise or (b) is
mandatory. In the latter case the parties' own intentions are secondary. Such implied
terms are legal rules imported into contracts for reasons of public policy. Good examples of this are the implied conditions as to quality in contracts for the sale of goods
where one party "deals as consumer". Such conditions are implied even if the parties

---

[65] *Lister v. Romford Ice and Coal Storage Co* [1957] A.C. 555.
[66] [1941] A.C. 108 (at p. 137).

attempt to exclude them.[67] The process of implication applies only to bilateral contracts. In *Little v. Courage*[68] the judge stated that it would not be right to imply a term into a unilateral contract, a view with which the Court of Appeal agreed.

(1) Terms implied by custom

Terms can be implied (a) by custom or (b) by the usage of a particular trade or business. Category (a) is generally of ancient or certainly long standing origin whereas (b) can include many modern, up to date practices of particular business industries. Custom may be implied into a contract so long as it is not inconsistent with an express term nor contrary to a common law rule. Customary rules also have to be reasonable and most will have existed for a very long time, even to the limit of legal memory, "time immemorial".[69] In *Hutton v. Warren*,[70] Parke B said:

   12.17

> "It has long been settled that in commercial transactions extrinsic evidence of custom and usage is admissible to annex incidents to written contracts, in matters with respect to which they are silent. The same rule has also been applied to contracts in other transactions of life, in which known usages have been established and prevailed; and this has been done upon the principle of presumption that, in such transactions, the parties did not mean to express in writing the whole of the contract by which they intended to be bound, but to contract with reference to those known usages."

Customs are often local and frequently, rather than reasonable, quite idiosyncratic. In *Smith v. Wilson*[71] the expression "one thousand rabbits" was held by custom to mean 1,200.[72] If both parties understood that the custom was incorporated as a term, it may be enforceable. Trade usages are customary rules in modern clothing which generally arise out of numerous similar transactions and course of dealings between parties in the same business over many years. They become so commonplace that the parties assume they are dealing on this basis and do not bother to put them in their contracts. Usually trade practices must be both certain and reasonable to be implied into the contract. They also have to be well recognised not only by the parties themselves but also more generally in a trade, industry or locality. To be implied it has to be shown that the parties intended to be bound by the practice but largely omitted to mention it in their contract because it "went without saying".

   12.18

The idea of a trade practice was discussed in *Cunliffe-Owen v. Teather and Greenwood*[73] where the usages in question were those of the Stock Exchange. The judge,

---

[67] See the Unfair Contract Terms Act 1977 s. 6. See also Chap. 17.

[68] (1995) 70 P and C.R. 469.

[69] *i.e.* from the death of King Henry II on September 3, 1189, the period of limitation for limits of right laid down by the Statute of Westminster 1275. (See Pollock and Maitland, *History of English Law* (1968, 2nd ed, Cambridge University Press), Vol. 1, p. 168, for the reasoning behind this rule.)

[70] (1836) M and W 466, 150 E.R. 517.

[71] (1832) 3 B and Ad 728 E.R.

[72] According to Sir Carleton Kemp Allen, *Law in the Making* (1958, Oxford University Press), quoting Pollock, *Principles of Contracts* (13th ed) p. 202: "the rabbit merchants 1,200 is ten long hundreds of six score each". In other words, this old custom goes back to the ancient British practice of counting in dozens rather than in tens. The system derived from the Romans. The "bakers dozen", *i.e.* 13 instead of 12, is another numerical curiosity of customery practice.

[73] [1967] 1 W.L.R. 1421.

Ungood-Thomas J., identified two requirements of usage: (a) a practice and (b) one which the court will recognise. This latter is a mixed question of fact and law. To be a recognised usage it must be: (i) certain, in the sense that it is reasonably established; (ii) "notorious", *i.e.* so well known in the market in which it is alleged to exist that those who conduct business, contract with the usage as an implied term; and (iii) it must be reasonable.[74] The practice has to consist of a "community of acts, established by persons familiar with them, though it is not necessary to have a detailed recital of instances". The court will not enforce a usage which is unreasonable. However, if a party knows of such a usage and agrees to it even if unreasonable, he is bound by it. The Court also stated *per curiam*, that: "The practice that is essential to establish usage is not a matter of opinion, of even the most highly qualified expert, as to what it is desirable that the practice should be . . . For a practice to be a recognised usage it should be established as a practice having binding effect".

12.19   The courts have long recognised that trade practices are not always for the public good. In *Robinson v. Mollett*,[75] Brett J. said of trade customs:

> "When considerable numbers of men of business carry on one side of a particular business, they are apt to set up a custom which acts very much in favour of their side of the business. So long as they do not infringe some fundamental principle of right and wrong, they may establish such a custom; but if, on dispute before a legal forum, it is found that they are endeavouring to enforce some rule of conduct which is so entirely in favour of their side that it is fundamentally unjust to the other side, the courts have always determined that such a system, if sought to be enforced against a person ignorant of it, is unreasonable, contrary to law, and void."

12.20   This has a distinctly modern ring to it and suggests that even in the middle of Victorian times the courts were not as oblivious to fairness as some would suggest. It is also interesting to see this phenomenon viewed as "custom". The statement could well be the basis of a test of inequality of bargaining power.[76] Custom, therefore, had a role to play as a fairness principle in an earlier era of the common law.

(2) Terms implied by statute

The Sale of Goods Act 1979 implies a number of terms into all contracts for the sale of goods. At their core is a series of implied conditions as to the quality of items purchased. The idea of implying terms did not begin with the original Sale of Goods Act, as drafted by a Birmingham County Court judge, Sir Mackenzie Chalmers in 1893. This was intended to be a codification of the existing common law. The nineteenth century courts implied terms into particular types of contracts before 1893 (rather mirroring Lord Denning's view 100 years later).[77] For example, in *Jones v. Just*[78] it was held by Mellor J. that if a buyer had not had the opportunity of examining goods, in this case manilla hemp from Singapore, they should be of merchantable quality.[79] Nevertheless the 1893

---

[74] At p. 1438.
[75] (1875) LR 7 H.L. 802 (at p. 818).
[76] See Chap. 14.
[77] See p. 208.
[78] (1868) LR 3 Q.B. 197.
[79] A phrase which survived in the Sale of Goods Act until 1994, when it was replaced by "satisfactory quality".

Act is generally taken to be the starting point of the modern law and with it, consumers' rights.

The Act was amended and re-enacted in 1979 and lays down a series of implied conditions which apply, unless excluded, to all contracts, whether the buyer is a private individual or a business. The seller must to be acting in the course of business. The first implied term is that the seller must have title to sell the goods,[80] secondly there is an implied warranty of "quiet possession" (*i.e.* no one else has a right over the goods which they may wish to assert), and thirdly, an implied condition that goods must strictly correspond with their description.[81] Finally, the Act lays down a cluster of implied conditions as to the quality of the goods. Goods sold must be of "satisfactory quality"[82] and be "reasonably fit for purpose".[83] In 1994 the definition of s. 14(2) was changed from merchantable to "satisfactory quality". This now includes fitness of the goods for their common purpose, appearance and finish, freedom from minor defects, safety and durability. There is also an implied condition that when goods are sold by sample, the bulk of the goods must correspond with the sample in quality.[84] At one time, these implied terms could all be excluded by the seller, but this is now subject to the Unfair Contract Terms Act 1977.[85]

An example of the Sale of Goods Act being used for consumer protection is *Godley v.* **12.21** *Perry*[86] in which the defendant was a newsagent, James Perry, who sold a catapult to a six year old boy, Nigel Godley. The toy broke when the plaintiff used it and badly injured his eye in the process. The catapult had been imported from Hong Kong by suppliers, and sold to the newsagent by sample, the defendant's wife testing its strength by pulling on the elastic. The defendant sought indemnity against the suppliers who were joined in the action as defendants. It was held that the boy could recover damages for breach of the implied condition that the catapult was not reasonably fit for purpose. He was able to rely on the seller's skill and judgment in this matter. The retailer meanwhile recovered against the supplier under s. 15 since the goods were sold by sample (Mrs Perry having tested it). The Court held that the bulk of the goods were made of unsuitable brittle material and did not correspond with the sample and therefore breach of this implied condition was established.

Breach of the implied conditions relating to quality is strict, *i.e.* there is no require- **12.22** ment of proving fault by the seller. So even if goods are sold in a sealed bottle which the retailer could not have opened, the retailer will be strictly liable even if the fault lay with the manufacturer of the product who was negligent. In *Daniels v. R White and Sons and Tarbard*[87] a bottle of lemonade was sold which contained a quantity of carbolic acid probably coming from the manufacturers disinfecting plant. The plaintiff, a street trader, drank some of the contents. The defendant, Mrs Tarbard, who was landlady of a pub in Battersea, *The Falcon Arms*, sold the lemonade to the plaintiff in a sealed bottle and was held liable to the plaintiff who drank some of the liquid, even though the defendant had

---

[80] S. 12.
[81] S. 13.
[82] S. 14(2A) and (2B) as amended in 1994.
[83] S. 14(3)(b).
[84] S. 15(2)(a).
[85] See Chap. 17.
[86] [1960] 1 W.L.R. 9
[87] [1938] 4 All E.R. 258

no opportunity to test the contents of the bottle. The manufacturers, R. White Ltd, were not liable, because negligence could not be proved against them. It was held that they had taken reasonable care at their plant. On the facts this appears difficult to believe.

In *Chaproniere v. Mason*[88] the plaintiff was a solicitor, with an office in the Haymarket, London. The defendant was a baker and confectioner carrying on business in Charles Street, Piccadilly. The plaintiff sent his articled clerk to the defendant's shop to buy a Bath bun and meat pie. When the plaintiff bit into the bun his tooth struck a stone and broke, causing an abscess to be formed in his mouth. The Master of the Rolls (no pun intended) stated that: "the presence of a stone of considerable size in a Bath bun is a very untoward incident and . . . such a bun is not reasonably fit for mastication". The Court of Appeal found for the plaintiff. The fate of the boy who made the bun is recorded in the report. He was no longer in the employment of the baker but was now "at sea". The fate of the articled clerk, *i.e.* trainee solicitor, who bought the bun for the solicitor is not recorded.

12.23   In order to import particular statutory terms into different types of contract it is necessary to be clear about the nature of transaction, for instance whether a contract to eat a meal at a restaurant is a sale of goods or a contract for services. In *Lockett v. Charles*[89] it was held to be a sale of goods. This was important because it meant that the relevant set of implied conditions from the Sale of Goods Act could be implied into the contract. In this case a married couple became ill from eating a quantity of whitebait at a hotel restaurant. The Court not only implied terms between the restaurant and the husband who ordered the meal but also an implied contract between the restaurant and the female plaintiff, who was entitled to damages in breach of contract for the food poisoning caused by the meal. A similar issue over the kind of contract arose in *St Albans District Council v. International Computers Ltd*[90] where computer software was held to be a product and therefore subject to the Sale of Goods Act, while maintenance, facilities management and out-sourcing were contracts for services. Depending upon the type of contract, different implied terms will apply. Contracts for services are governed by the Supply of Goods and Services Act 1982. There are two Parts to this Act. Part (a) deals with contracts which transfer goods (but not property or ownership in them) in which there are implied terms as to quality or fitness similar to the 1979 Act. This Part covers such contracts as bailment, hiring or rental arrangements. Part (b) deals with contracts for the supply of services, in which there are three implied terms: (i) that the service be carried out with reasonable skill and care[91]; (ii) that it will be carried out within a reasonable time[92]; and (iii) that the party contracting will pay a reasonable charge when the consideration has not been fixed.[93] It is worth noting that these are "intermediate terms" rather than terms fixed as conditions or warranties.[94]

(3) Terms implied by the courts: the tests for implying terms at common law

12.24   The courts have traditionally implied terms sparingly, so as not to infringe freedom of contract and to interfere with the parties' autonomy in making their own agreements. In

---

[88] (1905) 21 T.L.R. 633.
[89] [1938] 4 All E.R. 170.
[90] [1996] 4 All E.R. 481.
[91] S. 13.
[92] S. 14.
[93] S. 15.
[94] See Chap. 13, for a discussion of the construction of the nature of terms.

Hamlyn and Co. v. Wood and Co. Kay L.J. stated: ". . . it is a dangerous thing lightly to imply what they [the parties] have not expressed . . . [T]he court ought not to imply a term into a contract unless there arises from the language of the contract itself . . . such an inference that the parties must have intended the stipulation in question [so] that the Court is necessarily driven to the conclusion that it must be implied".[95] Despite this warning, the courts have not proved reluctant to use implied terms, indeed the idea has blossomed over the years. Lord Denning took the widest view, that the courts should imply terms based on "the presumed intention" of the parties (one of his favourite concepts) and this should include taking into account the reasonableness of all the circumstances surrounding the case. Reasonableness included the merits of the case, the type of contract in question, the likely impact on other contracts of a similar type and public policy. This allowed a great interventionist judge like Lord Denning enormous latitude. The majority of judges take a more cautiously conservative position. Implied terms have to be necessary, in order to supplement the parties intention, but not to subvert them. It is not the function of the court to write the contract for the parties.

Implied terms have provided an interesting battleground for judicial policy making in contract law. The tests for implying terms have a subjective element, in that the question of what the parties themselves would have agreed is relevant and admissible. Therefore there will be no implied term if a party (a) does not know of the matter; (b) the facts on which the implication is based; (c) would not have agreed the term anyway; (d) would not have accepted the precise formulation offered by the other; or (e) had no clear term in mind. For once, objectivity is not the complete answer in contract law.

(a) The test of necessity: The Moorcock *principle*

The most traditional test which was laid down in the case of *The Moorcock*[96] is that a term will only be implied to save the consideration for the contract. A term will only be implied to prevent a failure of the consideration or if the contract would not work without it, in other words, a test of necessity. This was said to be based on the presumed intention of the parties and "upon reason". *The Moorcock* has been used again and again over the years. The court may imply a term but only to give effect to the parties unexpressed intention. According to Bowen L.J. in *The Moorcock*, the test was "the presumed intention of the parties with the object of giving to the transaction such efficacy as both parties must have intended that at all events it should have".[97]   **12.25**

(b) The "business efficacy" and "officious bystander" tests.

These are really different shades of the same test applying "business efficacy" and the "officious bystander" tests as to what was required to make the contract work, but nothing more complex. In *Reigate v. Union Manufacturing Co.*[98] the business efficacy test was described by Scrutton L.J. in the following dictum:

"... it is such a term that it can confidently be said, that if, at the time the contract was being negotiated, some one had said to the parties, 'What will happen in such a

---

[95] [1891] 2 Q.B. 488 (at p. 494).
[96] (1889) 14 P.D. 64.
[97] At p. 68.
[98] [1918] 1 K.B. 592 (at p. 605).

case?' they would both have replied: 'Of course, so and so will happen; we did not trouble to say that; it is too clear.' Unless the court comes to some such conclusion as that, it ought not to imply a term which the parties themselves have not expressed."

The "officious bystander" test for an implied term, was put forward by Mackinnon L.J. in *Shirlaw v. Southern Foundries*[99]: "*Prima facie* that which in any contract is left to be implied and need not be expressed is something so obvious that it goes without saying; so that, if while one of the parties were making their bargain, an officious bystander were to suggest some express provision for it in the agreement, they would testily suppress him with a common, 'oh, of course'." Both these tests import a subjective element into the question. Would both parties actually agree to the same clear term if it were suggested to them at the time of making the contract? Unless it is clear they would have done, there is no implied term.

12.26   The reluctance of the courts to imply a term based on "necessity" or "business efficacy" test is shown by *Easton v. Hitchcock*.[1] The plaintiff was a female private detective who was employed by the defendant, a married woman, to keep an eye on her husband. The fact that he was being watched was divulged to an intermediary by one of the plaintiffs employees who then told the husband. It was claimed that there was an implied term of confidentiality in the contract. The court held that even although it was essential that the business of a private inquiry agent should be conducted with secrecy, there was no implied warranty that former employees would not disclose information about the work they had been involved in to others. It was of course open to the parties to expressly agree this beforehand and they had clearly not done so. There was therefore no reason for the courts to imply such a term.[2] Confidentiality or "gagging" clauses are a common feature of many modern contracts. They are now made void in employment contracts as a result of the Public Interest Disclosure Act 1998.[3]

(c) "Reasonableness in all the circumstances"

As we have mentioned, Lord Denning took a wide view of the judicial function in relation to implied terms. Indeed, it was one of the central themes of his view of contract law that the courts should adopt the position of the reasonable man or woman. Rather than being dependant on the parties alone, the court should look at all the circumstances of the case and imply terms for broader reasons depending upon whether it was reasonable or otherwise to do so. For Lord Denning, the courts had been implying terms for years under such a theory while pretending that they were only doing what the parties intended. Applying a transparency argument, it was time, according to Lord Denning, that the judges were more honest about what they were up to. Lord Denning thought the officious bystander implying terms "in fact" "should be sent from the field, he had held up the game too long".[4] According to the former Master of the Rolls this placed too limited a role on the judge. The courts should go back to the earlier doctrine of the implied term in law, and impose a term whenever it is reasonable to do so, to do justice

---

[99] [1939] 2 K.B. 206 (at p. 227).
[1] [1912] 1 K.B. 535.
[2] See Chap. 20.
[3] The Act prevents detriments in employment, such as dismissal to "whistleblowers".
[4] See Denning, *The Discipline of Law* (1979, Butterworths, London).

and in order to do what was fair between the parties. Lord Denning expressed his view judicially in *Greaves and Co (Contractors) v. Baynham Meikle and Partners*[5] and in the Court of Appeal in *Liverpool City Council v. Irwin*.[6]

(d)   The test in Liverpool City Council v. Irwin

The House of Lords rejected reasonableness in all the circumstances test in *Liverpool*   **12.27**
City Council v. Irwin.[7] The issue in *Liverpool Council* was whether a covenant should be implied into the leases of council tenants in three high-rise tower blocks. This would require the defendants to maintain the common parts of the buildings, *i.e.* lifts, staircases and toilets in a decent state of repair. This question, of course, had implications not only for the parties themselves but also for all council tenants and local authorities throughout the country. In the Court of Appeal, Lord Denning dissenting held that there was an implied duty on the landlord to take reasonable care to keep the common parts of the building "reasonably fit for use by the tenants and their visitors". The tenants had not been able to show a breach of this on the facts. The other two members of the Court of Appeal, Roskill and Ormrod L.J.J.s, held that there was no implied duty on the basis that the Court ought not to imply any such onerous and novel obligation where it was not necessary to give business efficacy to the contract. The House of Lords agreed with Lord Denning that there had to be an implied duty on the Council to maintain the building, but disagreed on the reasoning. The obligation to take reasonable care was based on what was "necessary having regard to the circumstances".

The House of Lords rejected Lord Denning's wide ranging approach of reasonableness as an attempt to kill off the officious bystander. Lord Wilberforce stated that he would not endorse his general principle: "indeed it seems to me, with respect, to extend a long and undesirable way beyond sound authority".[8] The term to be implied had to be reasonable but also had to be based on necessity as an "incidental" to the particular type of contract. It was not sufficient to say that the court could imply the term merely because they considered it reasonable to do so. In a later case, *Scully v. Southern Health and Social Services Board*,[9] Lord Bridge stated that:

> "A clear distinction is drawn in the speeches of Viscount Simonds in *Lister v. Romford Ice and Cold Storage Company Ltd*[10] and Lord Wilberforce in *Liverpool City Council* . . . between the search for an implied term necessary to give business efficacy to a particular contract, and the search based on wider consideration, for a term which the law ill imply as a necessary incident of a definable category of contractual relationship . . . I fully appreciate that the criterion to justify an implication of this kind is necessity, not reasonableness".

The House of Lords held that the terms in question in a contract of employment between doctors and their Northern Ireland Health Boards were not merely reasonable, but necessary in the circumstances.

[5] [1975] 1 W.L.R. 1095.
[6] [1976] 1 Q.B. 319.
[7] [1977] A.C. 239.
[8] At p. 253.
[9] [1992] 1 A.C. 294 (at p. 307).
[10] [1957] A.C. 555.

12.28   Lord Denning took the initiative again in a later case where he justified his approach to reasonableness by suggesting that there are two categories of contracts. In *Shell v. Lostock Garages*[11] he stated that the first comprised relationships of common occurrence such as consumer and retailer, employer and employee, landlord and tenant etc. in which (a) the obligations were not based on the intentions of the parties, actual or presumed, but on more general considerations and (b) the question was whether the law had already defined the obligation or the extent of it. Lord Denning would follow the implied term as laid down in such cases otherwise he would look to see what would be reasonable in general. That was the process in *Liverpool City Council v. Irwin*. The Court should look to wider considerations. The second category consisted of cases which are not of common occurrence. Here, the implication was based on the intention imputed to the parties from the surrounding circumstances. The traditional test applied to this more limited group, *i.e.* necessity to give the contract business efficacy and make it workable.[12] Lord Denning's two categories have attracted a measure of judicial support, indeed he may be expressing a widely shared view. Implied terms as rules of law are common in many transactions. These are rules of law unless the parties exclude or override them by express terms. As a general proposition, however, the test remains that as laid down in *Liverpool City Council* by the House of Lords.

(e)   The five "BP Westernport" criteria

12.29   At the same time as *Liverpool City Council* was in the Apellate Committee of the House of Lords, in *BP (Westernport) Pty Ltd v. The President, Councillors and Ratepayers of Shire of Hastings*[13] on appeal from the Supreme Court of Victoria in Australia, the Privy Council laid down another set of rules on implying terms. This was a compilation of the rules already described but was also a subtly different list from that in *Liverpool City Council*. The criteria are a synthesis of the existing rules. In order to imply a term it must be: (i) reasonable and equitable; (ii) required for business efficacy; (iii) obvious; (iv) capable of clear expression; and (v) not contradict any express turn of the contract. The first, of course, is not universally acknowledged indeed it was distinguished and qualified by the House of Lords in *Liverpool City Council*. Lord Simon in the Privy Council pointed out that the five tests "may overlap". It is not certain whether every criteria has to be met in each case, although it would appear they are all required. Nevertheless, in *Ashmore v. Corporation of Lloyds (No. 2)*[14] Gatehouse J. held that a term may be implied on one test but not on another. In *Phillips Electronique v. BSky Broadcasting Ltd*[15] Sir Thomas Bingham accepted the *BP (Westernport)* criteria as "an accurate and comprehensive statement of the law on the implication of terms into commercial contracts". Acknowledging the list, Sir Thomas Bingham commented that:

> ". . . its simplicity could be almost misleading . . . the implication of contract terms involves a different and altogether more ambitious undertaking: the interpolation of

---

[11] [1977] 1 All E.R. 481.

[12] As an example of a "one off" contract, not belonging to a definite type or category, and the question of implying terms in the circumstances, see *National Bank of Greece SA v. Pinios Shipping Co "The Maira"* [1989] 1 All E.R. 78.

[13] (1978) 52 A.L.J.R. 20, heard April 1977. Speeches in *Liverpool* delivered March 1976.

[14] [1992] 2 Lloyd's rep. 620.

[15] [1995] 3 E.M.L.R. 472 (at pp. 480–481).

terms to deal with matters for which, ex hypothesi, the parties themselves have made no provision. It is because the implication of terms is so potentially intrusive that the law imposes strict constraints on the exercise of this extraordinary power. . . . The question of whether a term should be implied, and if so what, almost inevitably arises after a crisis has been reached in the performance of the contract. So the court comes to the task of implication with the benefit of hindsight, and it is tempting for the court then to fashion a term which will reflect the merits of the situation as they then appear. Tempting but wrong".[16]

Sir Thomas Bingham would nevertheless have been prepared to imply a term of good faith into the contract in question.[17]

(i) The "reasonable and equitable" test: This is the most debatable of the *BP Westernport* **12.30** tests, as the extent to which reasonableness and equity should be taken into account. In *BP Refinery (Westernport)* the plaintiff oil company entered into a contract with a rating authority in Victoria to build an oil refinery. This agreement provided for the local taxes to be payable by the plaintiffs. The tax rate was high and the plaintiffs argued that there was an implied term that the tax rate should cease to apply in the event of the plaintiffs no longer occupying the refinery premises. The Privy Council held that there was no such implied term on the basis that it could not be regarded as reasonable and equitable. An implied term based on reasonableness alone was rejected in *Marsh v. Thomson Tour Operators*[18] in which tour operators promised that if they failed to fulfil the promises in their brochure they would "spend 24 hours trying to put things right. If they failed to do so, they would fly customers home free of charge and refund the cost of the holiday. The operators argued there was an implied term that the customers' complaints had to be reasonable, and their right to return home must also be reasonable in the circumstances. The judge in Colchester County Court refused to imply such a term based upon reasonableness. The operators could have made an express term to deal with this when they gave the guarantee.

(ii) The "business efficacy" test: We have already considered this test, which merely restates the common law rule over the last century.[19]

(iii) The compelling test: it must be so obvious that it "goes without saying". This is a restatement of the mythical nosey third party "bystander"; the classic statement of which is that of MacKinnon L.J. in *Shirlaw v. Southern Foundries (1926) Ltd.*[20] In *Little v. Courage*[21] Millett L.J. in the Court of Appeal stated that if the officious bystander had asked the question ". . . they [the parties] would have told him not to be silly . . . the hypothetical bystander must be persistent as well as obvious. If he had persisted in his question, I have no doubt what answer the parties would have made." The obviousness of the term is also an important factor. In *Hughes v. Greenwich LBC*[22] the House of Lords held that the courts should only imply a term into a contract when there was a compelling reason to do so. In this case the plaintiff was the headmaster of a school who moved into school

---

[16] At p. 482.
[17] At p. 484, see also Chap. 14, for a discussion of the good faith issue in this case.
[18] [2000] C.L.Y. 4044.
[19] See earlier p. 205.
[20] [1959] 2 K.B. 206.
[21] (1995) 70 P and CR 469 (at p. 479).
[22] [1994] 1 A.C. 170.

accommodation. The House of Lords held that the only compelling reason for implying a term would be if living at the school was essential to the performance of his duties under his contract, rather than being merely conclusive to the better performance of his duties. On the judges finding that it was not necessary for him to live there in order to do his job, no term could be implied in his contract of employment.

(iv) The clarity test: "capable of clear expression": The court is less likely to imply a term if the parkes cannot agree. In *Lister v. Romford Ice and Cold Storage Co Ltd*[23] as many as half a dozen different versions of the term to be implied were put forward. This argued against implying any term. The courts look for clear evidence of what the parties "presumably" would have agreed.

(v) The "non-contradictory" test: Freedom of contract requires that the parties' intentions should be paramount. If there is an express term which contradicts any suggested implication, there is no room for implying a term. In *Tamplin Steamship Co Ltd v. Anglo Mexican Petroleum Products Co Ltd*,[24] Lord Parker of Waddington stated that: "It is, of course, impossible to imply in a contract any term or condition inconsistent with its express provisions, or with the intention of the parties as gathered from those provisions". If the implied term is mandatory by statute, *e.g.* the implied conditions as to quality under s. 14(2) and (3) of the Sale of Goods Act 1979, then this supersedes the parties' own intentions. The express term may be treated as a disclaimer or exemption clause and subject to the appropriate rules.[25] This was discussed in *Johnstone v. Bloomsbury Area Health Authority*,[26] in which the Court of Appeal held that an express term that a junior hospital doctor be on call beyond his normal working week, did not prevent the implication of a term that the employers must not damage the doctor's health by requiring him or her to work excessive hours. The term could be seen as an exemption clause and so subject to the Unfair Contract Terms Act 1977 s. 2(1) which renders exclusions of liability for personal injuries void.[27] The general rule remains that an express term will prevent an implied term being read into a contract.

---

[23] [1957] A.C. 555.

[24] [1916] 2 A.C. 397 (at pp. 422–423).

[25] See Chaps 16 and 17.

[26] [1991] 2 All E.R. 293.

[27] See Chap. 17. Hours of work in the United Kingdom are now covered by the Working Time Regulations 1998 (S.I. 1998/1833). Under Regulation 18, doctors in training remain an exception to the rule. Regulation 20, provides that the working time rules also do not apply to managers or executives with "unmeasured working time". This includes academics writing textbooks.

Chapter 13

The Classification of Terms

For contract lawyers, the classification of terms takes us to the doorstep of breach of contract. The type of term determines the nature of the breach and therefore the remedy. Terms have proved a fertile ground for judicial policy making and academic debate. In particular, the relationship between the competing aims of certainty and justice in contract law has been a subject for much discussion.

Terms and Representations

The distinction between terms and "mere" representations is an historic and important **13.1** one in contract law. Terms are promises which form part of a contract, whereas representation are statements of fact which induce a contract. It is often hard to distinguish a term from a representation. If George tells Michelle that the dishwasher he is willing to sell her is in "excellent condition", is this a term or a representation?[1] Does this give Michelle a right to sue for breach of contract, or merely to seek a remedy for actionable misrepresentation because the statement is untrue? The answer depends on the legal construction of George's words. This has to be viewed objectively, *i.e.* by a reasonable person in Michelle's position. Objectivity is determined from the evidence, at the time of making the contract. Did George intend his words to be a promise or only an inducement to buy?

The courts have developed a number of tests for distinguishing terms and representations based on the intention of the party making the statement. None of these offer infallible guidance. If a statement is important, it is more likely to be construed as a promise, in other words, a term. A statement is also more likely to be a term if an oral statement is put into writing. This suggests that the parties intended it to be significant. A statement will be a term if the person making the statement is in a better position to know the truth than the other party. For instance, in *Couchman v. Hill*[2] an oral statement that a calf was "unserved" was held to be a term as only the seller could know whether or not it was true, and the buyer had to rely on his knowledge. If the words are immediately followed by a contract, they are likely to be part of the "offer" which was accepted, *i.e.* a term. In this case the rules of offer and acceptance will be applied. This factor is also quite capable of the opposite construction. The words may have been the vital inducement to contract.

---

[1] See *Oscar Chess v. Williams* [1957] 1 W.L.R. 370 and *Dick Bentley Productions Ltd v. Harold Smith (Motors) Ltd* [1965] 1 W.L.R. 623.
[2] [1947] K.B. 554

Special skill or knowledge will usually make a statement into a term.[3] Equally, lack of special skill or knowledge may reduce the words to a representation, as for example, in *Routledge v. McKay*.[4] If one party asks the other to verify the statement this probably means that it is meant to be taken seriously, *i.e.* it is a term. It could equally be that the person doubts the other's word or wishes to have it clarified, in which case it is likely to be a representation. A number of the traditional tests are, therefore, frankly ambivalent. Finally, the statement may amount to a promise binding as a collateral contract.[5]

13.2   The distinction between terms and representations is now of less practical importance as a result of the Misrepresentation Act 1967, s. 1. At common law, if a statement became a term of the contract, the right to rescind for misrepresentation was lost. The actions for breach and misrepresentation were also mutually exclusive. If the plaintiff chose the wrong option, their action would fail. The Misrepresentation Act 1967, s. 1 removed this bar. Even if the statement became a term, the right to sue for misrepresentation was not automatically lost. For the first time a statement could be actionable as either a term or a misrepresentation. In *Pennsylvania Shipping Co v. Compagnie Nationale de Navigation*[6] a charterparty of a tanker, the *Vendemiare*, contained certain statements which might have been actionable either as terms or misrepresentations. The plaintiffs brought action for misrepresentation. Branson J. held that the statements had become terms. The plaintiffs' claim for misrepresentation had become merged with the higher right of breach of contract and therefore lost. Such a position would not apply today. The Misrepresentation Act 1967 s. 1 removed two bars on rescission for misrepresentation. First, that the misrepresentation had become a term and secondly, that the contract had been performed. In either of these cases the right to sue for misrepresentation remains. The plaintiff has a choice, as long as the statement is capable of being both. In the past, plaintiffs were often keen to prove the statement was a term since remedies for breach were generally superior to those for misrepresentation. As a result of the 1967 Act and the common law development of negligent misstatement, this is no longer true. Misrepresentation may indeed be a more effective weapon.

13.3   The impact of European law has altered the common law distinction between terms and representations. As a result of implementation in the United Kingdom of the Package Travel, Package Holidays and Package Tours Regulations 1992, statements in holiday brochures are now treated as terms. In the past these would normally have been treated as mere advertising or at most representations. Regulation 4 provides that "no organiser or retailer shall supply to a consumer any descriptive matter concerning a package, the price of a holiday or any other conditions applying to the contract which contain misleading information". The retailer or organiser will be liable for breach of contract if he does so.[7] Liability on the tour operator for personal injuries to a holiday maker is not strict.[8] The information provided to potential customers in brochures is also required to be "legible, comprehensive, and accurate", in so far as it relates to the price and other matters required to be specified.[9] The Package Travel Regulations have

---

[3] *Esso Petroleum v. Mardon* [1976] Q.B. 801.
[4] [1954] I W.L.R. 615.
[5] See Chap. 12.
[6] [1936] 2 All E.R. 1167.
[7] This provision cuts across the common law rule of privity of contract (see Chap. 10).
[8] See *Hone v. Going Places Leisure Travel, The Times,* August 6, 2001.
[9] Reg. 5(1).

developed as an important piece of consumer protection law and have led to a large volume of claims by holidaymakers. The principle underlying these actions illustrates one of the objectives of contract law, namely compensation for disappointed expectations.[10]

CONTRACTUAL OBLIGATIONS

A contract is made up of reciprocal obligations based upon one another. Contractual obligations are mutually dependant upon one another. Thus Sarah promises to do X, if Mary promises to do Y in return. Sarah's promise may be either an obligation undertaken by her to perform certain acts or an obligation warranting the truth of a statement. Contractual obligations are usually further broken down into (a) primary and (b) secondary obligations. Primary obligations are duties imposed or undertaken by the parties to the contract. They create the binding obligations on each of the parties. Secondary obligations to pay damages arise when the contract is breached.[11]   **13.4**

From a realist jurisprudential perspective, the true nature of contractual obligation is that it is a prediction of liability to pay damages if a party breaks their promise.[12] Contracts are made up of various types of terms, the most important of which are known as conditions. The word "condition" is capable of two quite different meanings in contract law. The first is as an important term of a contract, one which will give rise to a right to rescind in the event of breach. This is a "promissory" condition forming part of the contract and creating primary obligations. The second meaning is nearer to that used in everyday language. If I say something is "conditional" it means it depends on something happening. I promise to deliver the goods to you on Friday "if it is a nice day" or "if I am not too busy writing this book". In each of these cases, assuming the parties intended to create a contractual obligation, my promise is subject to the two conditions. In contract law these are known as "contingent" conditions. They are contingencies or events upon which the existence of my promise, or a part of it, depends. The two contingencies were not the same. In the "nice day" example, this is something beyond my control, it may or may not take place, but if it does, I am bound. On the other hand, writing a book is in my own hands, I may choose to do so or not as I please, so the contingency in this case is at my "option". This distinction between promissory and contingent terms is basic to contract law. If a promissory term is broken, the remedies are those for breach of contract, *i.e.* damages as of right and potentially rescission.[13] However, if a contingent condition happens, this brings the contracts into being (a condition precedent) or in some cases the occurrence of a condition subsequent means the contract is no longer binding. Neither party may sue the other for breach if the event in question is a contingent condition. We shall look at these two examples in turn.

[10] See Chap. 25.
[11] The distinction is set out by Lord Diplock in *Photo Production v. Securicor Transport Ltd* [1980] A.C. 827 (at p. 849). Lord Denning commented on Lord Diplock's words in *George Mitchell (Chesterhall) v. Finney Lock Seeds* [1983] 1 All E.R. (at p. 116): "No doubt it is logical enough, but it is too esoteric altogether. It is fit only for the rarefied atmosphere of the House of Lords. Not at all for the chambers of the practitioner. Let alone for the student at the university." It remains a precise description of contractual obligations nevertheless.
[12] Holmes, *The Common Law* (1963, Little Brown, Boston).
[13] See Chaps 24–26.

Condition precedent

13.5   Many of the older cases use the expression "condition precedent" as meaning a condition which relieves a party of their own performance. Contracts usually depend upon each party performing in return for the other's promise. Each party's performance is therefore a condition precedent to performance by the other party. One party's failure to perform entitles the innocent party to withhold their own performance. The modern meaning of condition precedent is quite different however. This is an occurrence which brings a contract, or part of it, into existence. Neither party has actually promised to do the thing in question, so a failure of a condition precedent is not a breach of contract. Contingent terms can also be activated by the act or default of either party, not by just external events. This is sometimes called an "option", when one party exercises a right to take up a contract, for example when a commodity such as sugar trades at a particular price. There are two types of condition precedent. The first prevents a contract being formed at all, the second merely suspends the operation of some of the contract's main obligations until the event in question either does or does not take place. In *Pym v. Campbell*[14] the plaintiffs agreed to sell a share of the invention of a "Crushing, Washing and Amalgamating Machine", which was subject to the approval of two engineers, one of whom, Abernethie, could not be found. Since his approval had not be given, the Court held there was no contract. The contract had failed to come into existence because approval by the third party was a condition precedent to formation.[15]

13.6   Arbitration clauses are a common type of term which act in most cases as a condition precedent to litigation. Such clauses provide that disputes between the parties will be resolved by arbitration rather than the courts.[16] Arbitration procedures cannot oust the jurisdiction of the courts entirely as a rule of public policy.[17] If the arbitration clause is binding it must be used before any litigation takes place, and a party who jumps the gun may be restrained by a stay of proceedings.[18] Such clauses are commonly known as *"Scott v. Avery* clauses" after the leading case in which their validity was first considered.[19] In *Halifax Financial Services Ltd v. Intuitive Systems Ltd*[20] the parties made a written contract for the supply of software design services. By clause 33 the parties agreed a dispute mechanism which provided that within 10 days of written notices senior representatives of the parties would meet "in good faith" and attempt to reach a resolution without recourse to the courts. When the plaintiff commenced legal action, the defendant sought to have the proceedings stayed on the ground that the clause was a condition precedent, like an arbitration clause. The Court held that on it's construction clause 33 was optional only and merely provided a mechanism for the parties to negotiate. The Court also considered the obligation to negotiate in good faith and applied the holding of *Walford v. Miles*[21] that this was unenforceable because of a lack of certainty

---

[14] (1856) El and Bl 370 119 E.R. 903

[15] A condition precedent can be proved by oral evidence. See exceptions to the parol evidence rule, Chap. 12.

[16] Arbitration clauses for less than £5000 may be ignored by consumers. See Arbitration Act 1996. Consumers are free to use the County Courts if they prefer, see Applebey, *A Practical Guide to the Small Claims Court* (1999, 2nd ed, Tolley Buttend).

[17] See Chap. 20.

[18] *Reichhold Norway ASA v. Goldman Sachs* [2000] 1 W.L.R. 173.

[19] (1856) 5 H.L.C. 811, 10 E.R. 1121.

[20] [1999] 1 All E.R. (Comm) 303.

[21] [1992] 2 A.C. 128.

and also that good faith was not generally recognised in English law.[22] If the condition precedent is for one party's benefit, only that party may waive it.[23] A condition precedent will also be in effective if it lacks certainty.[24]

Condition subsequent

A condition subsequent operates to bring to an end an existing contract. The classic example of this is *Head v. Tattershall*,[25] an action for breach of warranty *(i.e.* a promise) that a horse had been hunted with the "Bicester and Duke of Grafton's hounds". The defendant backed up this statement by adding that if the horse did not comply with this undertaking, it could be returned at any time before 5 o'clock on the following Wednesday. The plaintiff took delivery of the horse, but it was injured when it took flight and seriously injured itself against the bar of a carriage. There was no fault on the plaintiff's part. The injury decreased the value of the horse and shortly thereafter the plaintiff discovered that the horse had never in fact hunted with the fox-hounds in question. The Court held he was entitled to return the horse. The sale was subject to a condition subsequent that if the statement was untrue, the plaintiff's promise to buy was no longer binding. The case is also worth noting for the fact that the groom in charge of the horse told the plaintiff at the time that the horse had not in fact hunted with the Bicester hounds. The plaintiff may not have acted in good faith, although Cleasy B. thought that he did, as there was "nothing proved but a loose statement by the groom who had charge of the horse".[26] The conduct of one of the parties may give the other party the right to terminate the contract. In *Bland v. Sparkes*[27] it was held that a contract could be brought to an end if the other party was convicted of a serious criminal offence, even though the conduct leading to conviction had taken place before the contract was formed.

13.7

PROMISSORY TERMS

Promises in a contract are also categorised into "conditions and warranties". This dichotomy only took hold following the Sale of Goods Act 1893 which classified implied terms in contracts for the sale of goods as either conditions or warranties. Every promissory term had to belong to one category or the other and the meaning of terms ascertained when the contract was formed. Conditions were generally terms of a more serious nature. The real importance of condition was that, in the event of breach the other party was entitled to rescind the contract, whereas a breach of warranty led only to damages. Applying this system, every term had to be labelled from it's birth. In *Wallis, Son and Wells v. Pratt and Haynes*[28] the House of Lords adopted the division of conditions and

13.8

---

[22] See Chaps 5 and 14.
[23] *Heron Garage Properties Ltd v. Moss* [1974] 1 W.L.R. 148.
[24] *Lee-Parker v. Izzet (No. 2)* [1972] 2 All E.R. 800.
[25] (1871) LR 7 Ex. 7.
[26] The concept of good faith (or lack of it in English law) is discussed in Chap. 14.
[27] *The Times*, December 17, 1999.
[28] [1911] A.C. 394.

warranties as a guiding principle not only in contracts for the sale of goods, but in contracts generally. Since then the situation has become more complex. We illustrate this in Flowchart E.

Flowchart E: The Classification and Effect of Promissory Terms

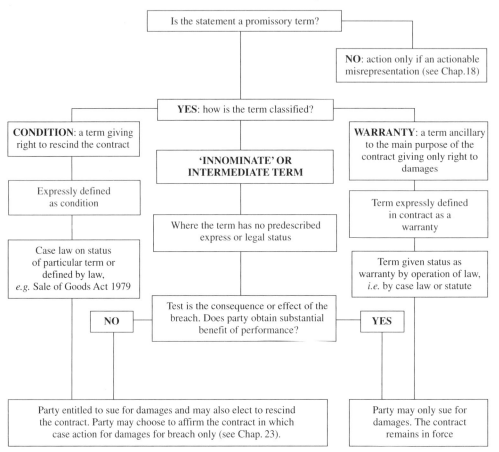

THE MODERN APPROACHES TO THE CLASSIFICATION OF PROMISSORY TERMS

The importance of the term

13.9   This is the oldest test but is now subject to the various rules of construction which we shall discuss in due course. The more important the term, the more likely it is to be a condition. This is illustrated by two similar, but contrasting, cases. In *Poussard v. Felix Spiers and Christopher Pond*,[29] Madame Poussard was an opera singer and the defendants were producers of events,[30] in this case the production of an opera *Friquette* at the Criterion Theatre. The plaintiffs' wife (her husband was suing on her behalf in those days) agreed in writing to take part in the opera which was due to begin on November 28, 1874. She took ill in November and did not recover until December 4. She returned to take up her role only to be told that a Miss Lewis had taken her place. She brought an action for breach of contract. The question to be answered was whether being absent for the first six days amounted to a breach sufficient to justify the defendants bringing Madame Poussard's contract to an end. The answer depended on how important her appearance at each night's performance would be to the defendants. The answer given was that "the failure of consideration was great". In other words, it was a breach entitling the defendants to rescind. Under normal circumstances, absence from employment leads to frustration and not breach as it is brought about by an event beyond the parties' control, *i.e.* ill-health.[31] Blackburn J. alludes to this possibility: ". . . this inability having been occasioned by sickness was not any breach of contract by the plaintiff and no action can lie against him [the singer's husband] for the failure thus occasioned." The effect on the defendants was that the singer's illness amounted to a breach of a condition. They were therefore entitled to bring the contract to an end and free to employ a substitute. Without this the show could not have gone ahead. The breach was therefore an important one from the plaintiff's perspective.

On the other hand, in *Bettini v. Gye*[32] the defendant was Frederick Gye, a famous **13.10** manager of the Covent Garden Opera House. He agreed with Bettini, an Italian singer, to give various performances, in public and private, of concerts and an opera. The period of the engagement was to last some 15 weeks. It was a term of the contract that the plaintiff should be in London six days in advance of the first performance for rehearsals. He failed to attend the rehearsals so the defendant terminated his contract. Bettini sued for wrongful dismissal, *i.e.* unjustified breach of contract. This time the Court held the term breached was only the equivalent of a warranty. The defendant could have claimed damages but was not entitled to bring the contract to an end. The appearance of the singer at the rehearsal was minor compared to the overall length of the contract as a whole and could not be said to be a significant breach. Blackburn J. stated that the classification of the term "depends on the true construction of the contract taken as a whole". In neither case was the term in question strictly a condition or warranty. Rather, it was the importance of the term and the effect of breach that counted. A view that was taken up later and, as we shall see, is now the key test.

The term is classified by statute

If a statute classifies a term as a condition or warranty then that will govern unless the **13.11** parties are free to modify the legislation in question. Normally they will not be allowed

---

[29] (1876) 1 Q.B.D. 410.
[30] Among other things, England's first cricket tour to Australia in 1861, see Frith, *The Trailblazers* (1999, Boundary Books, Goosetrey, Cheshire).
[31] See Chap. 22.
[32] (1876) 1 Q.B.D. 183.

to do so. The implied conditions under the Sale of Goods Act 1979 have traditionally been strictly applied, particularly those relating to the contractual description of the goods under s. 13. Any breach of the rule about description, however slight, was often regarded as a breach of condition. Two examples illustrate the draconian nature of the section. In *Arcos Ltd v. Ronaasen and Son Ltd*[33] timber was supplied which was one sixteenth of an inch thinner than specified. This in no way impaired it's purpose which was the manufacture of barrels, but nevertheless the buyer was entitled to reject the goods. Similarly in *Re Moore and Landauer and Co.*[34] there was a dispute over Australian canned fruit which was sent in cases which contained the incorrect number of tins. The total number of tins of fruit was in conformity with the contract. Nevertheless, the Court held that there was a breach of the contractual description. This was a condition, and the buyers were entitled to reject the goods.[35] The common law position has now been modified by an amendment to the Sale of Goods Act in 1994. A new s. 15A inserted into the 1979 Act provides that if a breach of implied condition under ss 13, 14 or 15 of the 1979 Act is so slight that it would be unreasonable for the buyer to reject the goods, then the breach is to be treated as merely a breach of warranty. The subsection does not apply in consumer sales, so any breach of implied terms of the relevant sections will still amount to a condition, giving a right to the consumer to rescind. The rule in s. 15A is not mandatory. The parties are free to exclude or modify it in their contract, if they wish to do so. Section 15(2) provides that the section will not apply if a contrary intention appears from the contract, or if it is to be implied from the parties' own agreement. It is for the seller to show that the breach falls within section s.15A.[36]

The intention of the parties

13.12   The parties themselves may expressly classify the term as a condition or warranty. The courts will normally uphold this construction. In *Lombard North Central plc v. Butterworth*[37] a computer was leased from a finance company. By clause 2(a) of the agreement punctual payment of each quarterly rental was to be of the essence of the contract. The time of payment of the rental was made a condition by express term. The Court of Appeal held that the parties were free to make a term a condition if they wished to do so and this would be upheld by the courts, in the absence of any other clear compelling rule. The courts will however look at the substance of the clause rather than merely the form. The term must truly state the parties intention, rather than simply use the word "condition" itself. In *Schuler AG v. Wickman Machine Tool Sales Ltd*[38] a German company which manufactured engineering products entered into a distribution agreement with an English company, for a period of 4½ years. The contract laid out a strict timetable requiring representatives to visit six firms in every week in order to solicit orders for the panel presses. The clauses in question were stated to be "conditions" giving a right to terminate the agreement. The plaintiffs failed to make a tiny number of the

---

[33] [1933] A.C. 470.
[34] [1921] 2 K.B. 519.
[35] On the justification for these cases (or lack of it), see pp. 226–227.
[36] S.15A(3).
[37] [1987] 1 Q.B. 527.
[38] [1974] A.C. 235.

agreed visits and the defendants rescinded the contract. The House of Lords held that they were not entitled to terminate the agreement. There was a presumption that if the word "condition" was used, it was mean to be a term which gave a right to repudiate, no matter how small the breach. The word would not be given that meaning if such a construction produced a result "so unreasonable that the parties could not have intended it, or if there was some other possible and reasonable construction. The House of Lords also stated *per curiam* that in construing a contract, to determine the meaning of condition, "the court was not entitled to take into account the conduct of the parties subsequent to the making of the contract as throwing light on the meaning to be given to it".

Legal precedent or widespread trade usage

If there is a precedent classifying a term as a condition or warranty, the parties are taken   **13.13** to know the law and the clause will be given it's legally established construction. Similarly, if there is a well known trade usage that the term is always treated as belonging to one category or the other. This is illustrated by the leading case of *Maredelanto Compania Naviera SA v. Bergbau-Handel GmbH "The Mihalis Angelos"*[39] in which a charterparty provided that the vessel in question would be "expected ready to load" on July 1 1965. The ship was to carry a cargo from Haiphong but military activity during the Vietnam War had resulted in delays in loading in the port. The ship remained in Hong Kong meanwhile. The Court of Appeal held that the charterers were entitled to cancel the contract on July 20. The "expected ready to load" clause was to be treated as a condition. The phrase had a clear legal meaning which both parties understood when making the contract. There was a precedent in that previous judicial decisions had characterised the "expected ready to load" clause as a condition. The Court of Appeal further stressed the advantages of holding the clause to be a condition. According to Megaw L.J. in commercial law it was preferable to have a firm and definite rule for a particular class of legal clause in common use. It was better for both parties to be able to say: "If a breach is proved, then the charterer can put an end to the contract".[40] Other examples of prior judicial rules classifying terms in a particular way are numerous. Thus clauses dealing with the time goods are shipped[41] and the date of payment of hire of a charterparty[42] are treated as conditions under normal circumstances.

The term is fundamental to the contract[43]

A term will inevitably still be a condition when it is fundamental to the contract. In   **13.14** *Barber v. NWS Bank plc*[44] the Court of Appeal held that a term that the seller at the time

---

[39] [1971] 1 Q.B. 164.
[40] At p. 205.
[41] *Bowes v. Shand* (1877) 2 App. Cas 455.
[42] *Mardorf Peach and Co Ltd v. Attila Sea Carriers of Liberia* [1977] A.C. 850.
[43] This category is an abolished doctrine relating to exemption clauses (but see Chap. 16). It may however be resurrected or re-appear in due course in a different context. See Smith, "Concurrent Liability in Contract and Unjust Enrichment: The Fundamental Breach Requirement" (1999) 115 L.Q.R. 245, in which the author proposes a changed relationship between contract and restitution law (see Chap. 26).
[44] [1996] 1 W.L.R. 641.

of a conditional sale agreement was owner of the car must be a condition. This was so because it was fundamental to the agreement. This was already supported by a similar statutory rule under the Hire Purchase Act 1964, s. 27(3). Sir Roger Parker stated: "In my judgment there can be no doubt that the term was a condition. It was fundamental to the transaction that the bank had the property in the Honda at the time of the agreement and would retain it until paid in full the moneys due under the agreement. Only on this basis could the agreement operate".[45] He went on to reject counsel's argument that this might be an innominate term. "This term is not one which admits of different breaches some of which are trivial, for which damages are an adequate remedy and others which are sufficiently serious to warrant rescission. There is here one breach only."[46] The concept of the "fundamental term" was once influential in relation to exemption clauses but is now subject to ss 3 and 9 of the Unfair Contract Terms Act 1977 which effectively abolished the doctrine.

Only one type of breach is possible

If only one breach is possible and the effect is likely to be identical in every case, the term will be strictly a condition or a warranty. An example is the classification of time terms in certain commercial contracts which we discuss later in this chapter.

The new flexibility: innominate or intermediate terms

13.15   The rigid classification of conditions and warranties has now been abandoned. The final demise of this dichotomy and recognition of a new category, or "third way", came in the Court of Appeal's judgment in *Hong Kong Fir Shipping Co Ltd v. Kawasaki Kisen Kaisha Ltd*.[47] A merchant vessel had been chartered for two years and was described as being "fitted for ordinary cargo service". However, after the voyage had started it was found that the engine room was undermanned and the crew badly trained. The engines were in such a bad state that it required two spells of repairs of five and then 15 weeks. The charterers repudiated the contract on the basis that the ship was not seaworthy. In a counterclaim the owners sued for wrongful repudiation. The issue was whether the term as to seaworthiness was a condition or a warranty. The Court of Appeal held it was neither. The clause belonged to a third category, of "innominate" or intermediate terms.[48] The intermediate term approach applied where the breach could be trivial or serious depending on the circumstances. The status of the term depended on the facts and, crucially, on the effect or consequences of the breach, not the classification at the date of formation. The flexible nature of such a term was justifiable, according to Upjohn L.J., "if a nail is missing from one of the timbers of a wooden vessel, or if proper medical supplies or two anchors are not on board at the time of sailing, the owners are in breach of the seaworthiness stipulation. It is contrary to common sense to suppose that, in such circum-

---

[45] At p. 646.
[46] On "international terms" see this page "The new flexibility".
[47] [1962] 2 Q.B. 26.
[48] See Applebey and Meisel, "Hong Kong Fir Revisited: The House of Lords and Certainty in Contracts" [1982] 4 L.M.C.L.Q. 592.

stances, the parties contemplated that the charterer should at once be entitled to treat the contract as at an end for such trifling breaches".[49] The test for "innominate" terms was laid down by Diplock L.J.: "[Did] the occurrence of these events deprive the charterers of substantially the whole benefit which it was the intention of the parties as expressed in the charterparty that the charterers should obtain from the further performance of their own contractual undertakings."[50]

The court has to look at the seriousness of the consequences and determine the effect of the breach of the term. The innocent party must lose the substantial benefit of the contract to be entitled to rescind. Unclassified or "innominate terms" are now usually known as "intermediate" terms. Diplock L.J. described these as:

"undertakings of a more complex character which cannot be categorised as being 'conditions' or 'warranties' ... [A]ll that can be predicated is that some breaches will and others will not, give rise to an event which will deprive the party not in default of substantially the whole benefit which it was intended that he should obtain from the contract; and the legal consequences of a breach of such an undertaking, unless provided for expressly in the contract, depend upon the nature of the event to which the breach gives rise and do not follow automatically from a prior classification of the undertaking as a 'condition' or a 'warranty'".[51]

(1) The meaning and definition of an intermediate term

The question of which terms were to be regarded as intermediate and which would continue to be regarded conditions was discussed by the House of Lords in *Bremer Handelsgesellschaft v. Vanden Avenne-Izegem PVBA*,[52] in which two clauses, (a) a prohibition of export clause and (b) a clause setting down a schedule for notifying, and acting upon, a *force majeure* occurrence, had to be construed and classified. The first clause was held to be an innominate term because it would give rise to many varying breaches. The second was held to be a condition, since terms relating to time required punctual compliance.[53] The House of Lords took the view that they would not regard any clause as a condition unless there was a good reason for doing so. According to Lord Wilberforce, whether a clause was a condition or intermediate term depended on (i) the form of the clause itself; (ii) the relation of the clause to the contract as a whole; and (iii) general considerations of law. It is evident from Lord Wilberforce's speech that questions of fairness and public policy also have a part to play in any classification.

    The category of intermediate term was applied in *Rice t/a Garden Guardian v. Great Yarmouth Borough Council*[54] in which a local authority had contracted with the plaintiff, to provide ground maintenance and leisure management for a period of four years. The contract was a standard form produced by the Association of Metropolitan Local Authorities. The council argued that the contract should be read literally so as to give them the right to terminate the agreement for any breach of obligation other than the

13.16

---

[49] At pp. 62–63.
[50] At p. 72.
[51] At p. 70.
[52] [1978] 2 Lloyd's Rep. 109.
[53] See later pp. 224–226.
[54] (2001) 3 L.G.L.R. 4.

trivial. The Court of Appeal disagreed. Lady Justice Hale held that contract had to be read in a "common sense, commercial interpretation". As in *Hong Kong Fir*, *i.e.* the cumulative effect of many slight breaches, the court should look at the effect as a whole. This included looking at the contractor's performance over the duration of the contract and whether the cumulative breaches showed that there would be a continuing below standard performance. In other words, would the council be "deprived of a substantial part of the totality of that which it had contracted for during the period. The contract contained "multi-faceted obligations which could be broken in many different ways". It was held that the council had obtained the substantial benefit of the contract so they were not therefore entitled to rescind.

(2) The swinging pendulum of policy: the Intermediate approach is now the rule

13.17   The old system of conditions and warranties was too rigid and could lead to unfairness. Flexibility in construing the terms can deal with this, but can run the risk of uncertainty in turn. This is a serious matter, particularly for businesses who may be faced with a difficult choice over rescinding a contract. By making the wrong decision, a party may leave themselves open to a claim for wrongful repudiation. It also leaves the status of the term to be determined ultimately to the courts. This could be years after the contract has effectively ceased to exist. The fear of uncertainty led to a reaction in the courts against intermediate terms for some years. The pendulum has now swung again and intermediate terms again appear to have the upper hand. A term will now be treated as an intermediate term unless some other factor prevails. Intermediate terms are not just a "residual" category but a general principle subject to the rules which we have already described in this chapter.

The intermediate term approach has been applied many times since 1962.[55] In the House of Lords in *Rearson Smith v. Hansen Tangen "The Diana Prosperity"*,[56] Lord Wilberforce described the old sale of goods cases as "excessively technical" and in need of reconsideration by the Law Lords. This point was taken up in the Court of Appeal in *Cehave NV v. Bremer Handelsgesellschaft MbH*, "*The Hansa Nord*",[57] where the plaintiffs were a Dutch company who agreed to buy a large quantity of Florida citrus pulp pellets for use as animal feed. The defendants were the German sellers who promised that the goods would be shipped in "good condition", and would be of merchantable quality. The price was £100,000. When the cargo arrived in the port of Rotterdam it was found that some of the goods had deteriorated due to overheating, but those in the second hold were satisfactory. In the meantime, the price which would be obtained from re-selling the pulp pellets, (as the buyers had intended to do) had fallen. The buyers rejected the entire cargo, but then re-purchased them for £30,000 when they were sold at the dock to an importer who was acting as their agent. This was too clever by half for Lord Denning. The question for the Court of Appeal was whether the buyers were right to reject. The Court of Appeal found that there was no breach of the requirement of merchantability, *i.e.* they could be resold. The other term, "in good condition", was classified as an intermediate term. The consequences of the breach did not go to the root of the contract, as the buyers still had the substantial benefit of the contract. The Court of Appeal relied on s. 61(2) of the original Sale

---

[55] *Federal Commerce and Navigation Ltd v. Molena Alpha* [1976] 1 Lloyd's Rep. 201.
[56] [1976] 1 W.L.R. 989 (at p. 998).
[57] [1976] Q.B. 44.

of Goods Act 1893 which preserved the existing common law rules prior to the Act. This meant that conditions and warranties were not a rigid dichotomy. The Court was therefore able to hold that the particular express term about "good condition" was an innominate term. The 1979 Act was not a complete code requiring every term to be a condition or warranty after all. Even in contracts for the sale of goods there was scope for intermediate terms.

There has been criticism over the years of the rigidity of the law in this area, particularly in relation to sale of goods. In 1983 the Law Commission concluded that the classification of statutory implied terms as conditions or warranties was inappropriate and liable to produce unreasonable results. It should therefore be replaced by the neutral expression "term". This would enable courts to construe the meaning in each case.[58] This was not adopted in the Law Commission's Final report on the matter in 1987,[59] nor in the succeeding legislative changes.[60] The idea of intermediate terms is, however, given a statutory approval in the Supply of Goods and Services Act 1982, ss 13-15. The obligations to provide services with reasonable skill and care, and within a reasonable time, are classified as terms, not conditions or warranties.[61] The modern policy can therefore be said to be of general support for intermediate terms. Flexibility, if not triumphant, is back in favour. In *Tradax Export v. Goldschmidt SA*[62] Slynn J. stated: ". . . in the absence of any clear agreement or prior decision that this was to be a condition, the Court should lean in favour of construing [the term in question] as an intermediate term, only a serious or substantial breach of which entitled rejection". In *Bunge Corporation v. Tradax Export*[63] Lord Roskill recognised the modern approach as not being "over-ready to construe terms as conditions, unless the contract clearly requires the court to do so". Nonetheless, "the basic principles of construction for determining whether or not a particular term is a condition remain as before". The judgment in this case shows that the courts still take certainty seriously, particularly in relation to time terms. Lord Roskill pointed out the need for certainty on the one hand, and on the other the desirability of not allowing rescission where the breach was technical and damages would be an adequate remedy.

There is one category of contract which is not subject to the intermediate term approach. In *United Dominions Trust (Commercial) Ltd v. Eagle Aircraft Services Ltd*[64] the Court of Appeal held that in unilateral contracts the terms imposed by the promisor had to be adhered to and performed accordingly by the other side. They were therefore conditional in this strict sense, and could not be analysed to see if they were "intermediate" on the *Hong Kong Fir* approach.

13.18

---

[58] Sale and Supply of Goods (Law Commission Working Paper No. 85) para. 2.37.
[59] Sale and Supply of Goods (Law Commission No. 160) Cmnd 137, 1987.
[60] Sale and Supply of Goods Act 1994 amending the Sale of Goods Act 1979.
[61] On the 1982 Act and implied terms in contracts for services, see Chap. 12.
[62] [1977] 2 Lloyd's Rep. 604 (at p. 612).
[63] [1981] 1 W.L.R. 711 (at p. 727).
[64] [1968] 1 All E.R. 104.

TIME IN CONTRACT LAW: HOW VITAL IS PUNCTUALITY?

Commercial contracts

13.19   Time of performance is frequently crucial in commercial contracts. The date of completing the contract will be written into the agreement and parties are generally aware that this is a condition. The importance of certainty was spelt out by Lord Roskill in his 1981 Holdsworth Club Presidential Address, "Half a Century of Commercial Law",[65] where he stated as two guiding principles of contract law:

> "First, that law should be certain. Secondly, whilst being certain it must be adaptable to the changing needs of the particular period. Those two principles are not contradictory. On the contrary, they are complementary. As to the first, business men make their contracts by reference to certain legal rules. Those rules must be certain."

The same point was made by Lord Bridge who stated in the *Chikuma*:

> "Where, as here, [the parties] embody in the contracts common form clauses, it is, to my mind, of overriding importance that their meaning and legal effect should be certain and well understood. The ideal at which the courts should aim, in construing such clauses, is to produce a result, such that in any given situation both parties seeking legal advice as to their rights and obligations can expect the same clear and confident answer from their advisers and neither will be tempted to embark on long and expensive litigation in the belief that victory depends on winning the sympathy of the court."[66]

13.20   The need for certainty in commercial matters runs counter to the flexible approach to terms which we have discussed. The question of punctuality has been stressed by the courts particularly in commercial contracts. In two cases, the House of Lords reiterated the need for parties to treat time clauses with the utmost respect or suffer the consequences. In *A/S Awilco of Oslo v. Fulvia Spa di Navigazione of Cagliari, The Chikuma*,[67] the facts appear to lead to an extraordinary result. A charterparty involving a Norwegian charterer and shipowners in Genoa provided that if the charterers failed to make "punctual and regular payment" to the owner's bank in Italy, the shipowners would be entitled to withdraw the vessel. After 80 payments had been made, the 81st happened to fall on a Friday, in this case January 22, 1976. The charters' bank in Norway arranged to make a credit transfer to the owner's bank in Italy. This was done by telex. Interest did not begin to run on the sum in question until the Monday under Italian law, so the owners withdrew the ship. They lost interest on the sum of between $70 and $100 dollars which would have been accured to their account. The charters counterclaimed for

---

[65]   The Holdsworth Club, the University of Birmingham 1981.
[66]   *A/S Awilco of Oslo v. Fulvia Spa di Navigazione di Cagliari* [1981] 1 W.L.R. 314 (at p. 322).
[67]   [1981] 1 W.L.R. 314.

more than $5 million. The House of Lords held the owners were entitled to terminate because the term as to payment was a condition and the charterers were in breach. *Per curiam*, the House of Lords stated that it was of overriding importance that the meaning and legal effect of such standard terms be certain and well understood.

A similar conclusion was reached in *Bunge Corporation v. Tradax Export SA.*[68] The **13.21** House of Lords held that the *Hong Kong Fir* approach was inapplicable to stipulations as to time in mercantile contracts. Here time terms were generally to be treated as conditions, the breach of which, no matter how minor, should entitle the other party to treat the contract as at an end. They were not intermediate terms because in relation to time in commercial contracts, there was only one kind of breach possible, namely, to be late. Lord Wilberforce commented that to such cases the gravity of the breach approach was unsuitable. In *Bunge Corporation* the delay was merely two days in nominating a port. This was nonetheless sufficient to entitle the sellers to treat themselves as discharged.

In *Societe Italo-Belge v. Palm and Vegetable Oils (Malaysia) Sdu. Bhd. The Post Chaser*[69] a "declaration of ship" clause was held to be an essential step in the performance of a contract of carriage of goods by sea. Although a time had not been fixed, the contract required that the declaration be made "as soon as possible after the vessel's sailing". This indicated that a speedy declaration was necessary and that the term was a condition, not intermediate. Goff J.[70] approved a statement that apart from express agreement or notice, the courts would require precise compliance with stipulations as to time. The test was to consider whether the circumstances of the case indicated that this would fulfil the intentions of the parties. Broadly speaking, time was considered of the essence in mercantile contracts, and in other cases where (i) the nature of the contract, (ii) the subject matter or (iii) the circumstances of the case, required precise compliance.

Time terms in commercial contracts may still be regarded as intermediate, however. In **13.22** *Torvald Klaveness A/S v. Arni Martime Corporation, The Gregos*,[71] the House of Lords held that a clause stating the date of re-delivery of a chartered vessel was not a condition. The obligation to re-deliver on time was an intermediate term. Lord Mustill stated that whether a term was a condition or innominate was to be determined by it's practical importance in the scheme of the contract. The effect of a few days delay was likely to be variable.

The question of time in other types of contract

At common law, time is generally regarded as "of the essence", *i.e.* a condition, but in equity this was not so. These are only general principles and the test includes looking at the parties' intentions. Even if time is not originally of the essence, it may be made so by giving notice to perform within a reasonable time. In *British and Commonwealth Holdings v. Quadrex Holdings Inc*[72] the Court of Appeal said that there were three requirements of such a notice: (i) the party serving notice has to be ready willing and able to perform, (ii) the other party must have been guilty of unreasonable delay and (iii)

---

[68] [1981] 1 W.L.R. 711.
[69] [1981] 2 Lloyd's Rep. 695.
[70] At p. 699.
[71] [1994] 4 All E.R. 998.
[72] [1989] 3 All E.R. 492.

reasonable time must be given to complete the sale. This is an important question in land law. A notice making time of the essence was also issued in relation to the special man-ufacture of a motor car in *Rickards (Charles) Ltd v. Oppenhaim.*[73] It was held by the Court of Appeal that time had been made of the essence and that the defendants could cancel the order because of late delivery.

13.23   The rules with regard to time vary from one contractual context to another and indeed within a particular kind of contract. For instance, in contracts for the sale of goods it was established in *Hartley v. Hymans*[74] that time of delivery is normally a condition. On the other hand in the Sale of Goods Act 1979, s.10 provides that, unless a contrary inten-tion appears from the contract, time of payment is not of the essence of a contract of sale. Section 10(2) makes clear that the question of time in other stipulations depends on the terms of the contract. In other areas, like construction contracts, the treatment of time is very different. Here the parties want the work to be completed. They do not, gen-erally speaking, want to terminate the agreement and leave themselves stranded or looking for someone else to complete the job. The question of delay is carefully worked out in "penalty clauses" in which the contractor agrees to pay pre-estimated damages if they does not finish on time. If these are a reasonable pre-estimate they are enforceable.[75] If delay is inordinate or stretches on far too long, it may lead to frustration of the con-tract.[76] Equity can relieve against contractual penalties and forfeiture. This discretion is not unfettered, however, according to the House of Lords in *Scandinavian Trading Tanker Co AB v. Flota Petrolera Ecuatoriana.*[77] So in contracts for the sale of land, the courts can intervene to prevent a party rescinding a contract because of lateness, and can order specific performance of the contract. However, in *Union Eagle Ltd v. Golden Achievement Ltd*[78] the Privy Council refused specific performance even although the pur-chase was a mere ten minutes late in completion. The time and date for completion was very clear. Since the contemplated purchase had been a long running affair, the vendor was entitled to rescind.[79]

EFFICIENT BREACH, GOOD FAITH AND RESTITUTION

13.24   This chapter has shown some very clear examples of a fundamental issue for contract lawyers. How far should the parties be allowed to break a contract, or terminate, purely for their own economic self interest? Does the existence of a contract involve a higher, even moral, duty to perform? In the *Chikuma* case the owners had a financial incentive to get out of their contract because the market was rising and they could make a greater profit elsewhere; it was more advantageous to rescind the contract than to continue. This is sometimes called "efficient breach".[80] Economists tend to see such behaviour as moral

---

[73] [1950] 1 K.B. 616.
[74] [1920] 3 K.B. 475.
[75] See further Chap. 25.
[76] See Chap. 22.
[77] [1983] 2 A.C. 694 (at p. 700).
[78] [1997] A.C. 514.
[79] See Stevens, "Having your Cake and Eating it?" [1998] 61 M.L.R. 255.
[80] See MacNeil, "Efficient Breach of Contract: Circles in the Sky" (1982) 68 VA LRev 947.

and rational. English contract law allows the parties to pursue their own advantage, and to act in an adversarial way towards the other party if they deem it in their own best interests. This position may be criticised as being ethically unacceptable and also because it allows the law of contract to be abused.

There are two alternatives to allowing the parties freedom to use their contractual obligations as they see fit. First, the introduction of a rule of good faith in breach, or a narrower version of this could be a rule prohibiting bad faith in breach. If a party acted for an illegitimate motive in rescinding a contract, they should not be allowed to do so without suffering a penalty.[81] The question of breach would then be judged against the reasons for the breaching or rescinding party acting as they had. If the reasons were not justifiable, then they would have acted wrongfully and be liable in damages. The main argument against this is that it would interfere with the freedom of the market place to tie people into contracts they do not want, and that any attempts by the courts and law to do so would be unworkable in practice. Commercial parties would normally be able to circumvent any such rules if they wished, but unfairly. A further alternative could be to require the re-payment of profits made as a result of breach of contract to the other party on the basis of an unjust enrichment or restitutionary principle.[82] The view that a contract is a promise with a moral imperative attached has its adherents in Anglo-American law but has largely dropped out of favour.[83] The issue shows that contract is not just a set of rules but a human activity in which standards of behaviour, ethics and even psychology have a part to play in shaping the contours of its subject matter.[84]

[81] There are of course strong arguments on both sides. See Forte, *Good Faith in Contract and Property Law* (1999, Hart Publishing, Oxford) and Chap. 14.

[82] This was taken a step nearer in the House of Lords judgment in *Attorney-General v. Blake* [2001] 1 A.C. 268. We discuss this later in Chap. 26.

[83] See Fried, *Contract as Promise* (1981, Harvard University Press, Cambridge, Massachusetts).

[84] Trebilcock, *The Limits of Freedom of Contract* (1993, Harvard University Press, Cambridge, Massachusetts); Kronnan and Posner, *The Economics of Contract Law* (1979, Little Brown and Co, Boston and Toronto).

Chapter 14

CONCEPTS OF FAIRNESS IN CONTRACT LAW

LAW AND EQUITY

> "Equity is a Roguish Thing ... Equity is according to the Conscience of him that is Chancellor, and as it is larger or narrower so is Equity. Tis as if they should make the Standard for the Measure we call a Foot, to be the Chancellor's Foot; what an uncertain Measure would this be; One Chancellor has a long Foot another a short Foot a third an indifferent Foot; tis the same thing in the Chancellor's Conscience."[1]

14.1 This famous quotation by John Selden represents the most traditional common lawyer's distrust of principles of equity and fairness. Equity grew up as a system of natural justice which depended on the particular case. As such, it could be regarded as wayward and lead to uncertainty. The relationship between law and equity is one of the oldest debates in jurisprudence and one which exists in some form in most legal systems. In the hands of judges like Lord Eldon, equity became even more conservative than the common law in the nineteenth century. In England, common law and equity maintained their own separate courts and rules until 1873. Law and equity remain divided, for example in relation to contractual mistake or remedies, so the process of fusion is not yet complete. This chapter looks at various "fairness" or equitable principles emerging in contract law. One recurring theme of this book is the gradual re-emergence of equity in the guise of unconscionability and fairness rules. A carefully analysed definition of unconscionability could provide a different approach to the enforcement of promises, and would obviate the need for consideration in every case.

14.2 Does English contract law pay sufficient to heed fairness?[2] The answer depends on one's point of view. There is no golden rule and as times change, so does the law. In the eighteenth century, equity had a part to play in contracts. Later freedom of contract allowed the parties to pursue (even to exploit) their own self interest. Individualism was ideologically sound and seen as paramount.[3] The early twentieth century saw adherence to rules as uppermost in contract law and certainty a primary objective. Under the

---

[1] Selden, *A Brief Discourse Concerning the Lord Chancellor of England* (1672 (first published in 1617), W. Dugdale, London). The "Chancellor's foot" has been a metaphor for equity since the seventeenth century.
[2] See in general, Willett, *Aspects of Fairness in Contract* (1996, Blackstone Press Ltd, London).
[3] Atiyah, *The Rise and Fall of Freedom of Contract* (1979, Clarendon Press, Oxford), The association with free enterprise liberalism is obvious..

pressure of consumerism, contract law has given way to notions of reasonableness, equality of bargaining power and fairness. The pendulum is still swinging. Equitable notions are now back in vogue.

For 200 years the common law had one overriding ideal, that of freedom of contract. This encouraged parties in business to do things for themselves without interference from government, judges or other forms of regulation. The role of the courts was to ascertain the intention of the parties and act as an umpire between two free and rational individuals who were regarded as capable of looking after themselves. It was not for the law to adopt a paternalistic role, apart from in cases of vulnerable groups such as children or persons of unsound mind. Today unconscionability, good faith and fairness point towards a new set of principles. Most legal systems in Europe have adopted an overarching principle of good faith. The United States has both "good faith" and "unconscionability", although it must be said that their impact has not been without criticism, nor entirely successful.

14.3   Fairness can be divided into two broad categories: (a) procedural and (b) substantive.[4] Procedural fairness looks at the means whereby a person enters into a contract. In English law there is procedural fairness in the rules governing duress, undue influence, misrepresentation and in the "reasonable steps" rules for incorporating exemption clauses. Substantive fairness can be seen in the rules on exemption clauses, penalty clauses, the restraint of trade doctrine and in the intervention of public policy generally. Procedural and substantive fairness can sometimes unite in the same area, for instance the idea of "manifest disadvantage" in relation to undue influence and in the statutory and regulatory requirements for exemption clauses and unfair terms in consumer contracts.[5] In English contract law fairness falls far short of being a general requirement.

As an antidote to the equitable notion of fairness, the common law perceived certainty as a key objective of contract law. Lord Roskill, in his Presidential Address to the Holdsworth Club of the University of Birmingham, summed up the guiding principles of commercial law as being:

> "First that law should be certain. Secondly, whilst being certain it must be adaptable to the changing needs of the particular period. Those two principles are not contradictory. On the contrary, they are complementary. As to the first, business men make their contracts by reference to certain legal rules. Those rules must be certain."[6]

In one of the cases cited by Lord Roskill in his Birmingham address, the *Chikuma*,[7] Lord Bridge stated[8]:

> "The ideal at which the courts should aim, in construing such clauses, is to produce a result, such that in any given situation both parties seeking legal advice as to their rights and obligations can expect the same clear and confident answer from their

---

[4] The distinction is set out in *Hart v O'Connor* [1985] A.C. 1000.
[5] See Chaps 19, 17 and 15, respectively.
[6] "Half-a-century of Commercial Law", The Holdsworth Club of the University of Birmingham, 1981.
[7] [1981] 1 W.L.R. 314.
[8] At p. 322.

advisers and neither will be tempted to embark on long and expensive litigation in the belief that victory depends on winning the sympathy of the court."

The tensions between certainty and justice lie at the root of many of the issues in contract law.

A brief excursion into the past: "the transformation debate"

Was there historically a more equitable side to contract law? Legal history is not our **14.4** topic in this book, but the equitable nature of contract law is of a wider theoretical interest. The issue was discussed by a Morton Horwitz in his book *The Transformation of American Law 1760–1860*,[9] a work which is also concerned with English law during the same period. Horwitz claims, in what is now called the "Transformation Thesis", that before the industrial revolution, the common law was much more influenced by equity than is normally supposed and that this included the law of contracts. Conceptions of natural justice and equity were found in contract law quite widely before the 1780's, such as the idea of a "sound price" being a warranty for a "sound commodity" giving a buyer a right to sue for faulty goods such as a horse which they had purchased. These equitable notions were swept away by freedom of contract and *caveat emptor*. In 1790, John Joseph Powell's *Essay upon the Law of Contracts and Agreements* placed law firmly ahead of equity:

> "It is absolutely necessary for the advantage of the public at large he said that the rights of the public should depend upon certain and fixed principles of law, and not upon rules and constructions of equity, which when applied ... must be arbitrary and uncertain, depending on the extent of their application upon the will and caprice of the judge."

Horwitz's thesis reflects a broadly Marxist viewpoint linked with the critical legal studies **14.5** movement (which developed out of a conference in Wisconsin in 1967). Law and ideology are connected and contract law succumbed to capitalism following the industrial revolution. Law is therefore a product of an economic system which it reflects. Contract law on this basis became the tool of the free market *laissez faire* system and individualism in the nineteenth century. His views have not gone unchallenged and have been subjected to detailed scholarly criticism.[10] An interesting attempt to take the development of contract law even further back to its deepest roots is Gordley, *The Philosophical Origins of Modern Contract Doctrine*.[11] In his book Professor Gordley argues that the common law of contract was influenced by European natural law theory deriving through Aquinas from Aristotle, and then mixed with Christian doctrine. The origins of the common law are traced to a group of teachers at the University of Salamanca in Spain in the sixteenth century. Their work then influenced the French jurist Pothier whose impact on English

[9] (1977, Harvard University Press), especially Chap. 6 "The Triumph of Contract".
[10] See Simpson, "The Horwitz Thesis and the History of Contracts" (1979) 46 University of Chicago Law Review 533–601 and Williams (1978) 25 U.C.L.A. Law Review 1187–1218.
[11] (1991, Clarendon Law Series, Oxford).

law in the eighteenth century is well established.[12] This is an interesting question, but largely one for the Jurisprudence classroom. However, it does emphasise that contract law, moral and political philosophy and justice, have always had a relationship, but one which has changed over the centuries, and will continue to do so in the future.

FAIRNESS AT COMMON LAW

The notion of reasonableness

14.6   The test of reasonableness is the common law's response to an over zealous attachment to rules. The discretion attaching to the word "reasonable" or "reasonableness" gives the court a power to do justice in a myriad of different situations. This usually depends on the merits of the particular case. Reasonableness in contract law is to be found in implied duties to take "reasonable care",[13] the requirement of "reasonable to believe" under the Misrepresentation Act 1967 s. 2(1),[14] "reasonableness" as the test for exemption clauses under the Unfair Contract Terms Act 1977,[15] the test for liquidated damages as being a "reasonable" pre-estimate loss[16] and the rule requiring "reasonable steps" to be taken to incorporate terms into an unsigned contract.[17] Reasonableness is an open-ended concept.[17a] In the hands of intervention judges such as Lord Denning, "reasonableness" took on an added meaning. Lord Denning based his concept of reasonableness on the "presumed intention of the parties". This allowed the former Master of the Rolls enormous discretion in legal doctrine. It was sometimes used to advance Lord Denning's own views on the best way to do justice between the parties, as well as to develop the law.

14.7   Reasonableness permeates the common law. It is also the guiding principle behind the modern law of negligence where it has been turned into a tool of public policy. Over the years reasonableness has proved a useful device for achieving fairness. Reasonableness is not a new idea. It has been around contract law since Victorian times. A reasonableness test is to be found as early as the Railway and Canal Traffic Act 1854. Free market entrepreneurs of the day complained vigorously against it.[18] In *Clarke v. West Ham Corporation*[19] an embryonic test of reasonableness can be discerned. In this case the Tramways Act 1870, which governed local tramways, authorised the companies running services to charge two sets of fares. The lower one allowed the companies to limit their liability (a modern equivalent, differential pricing, is discussed later).[20] In *Clarke* no such alternative had been offered to passengers. Although "reasonableness" did not arise on the wording of the Act, Kennedy L.J.[21] stated:

---

[12] Treatise on the Law of Obligations (1764) translated into English in 1806. It had an impact on notions such as agreement and free will in the formation of contracts.
[13] See Chap. 12.
[14] See Chap. 18.
[15] See Chap. 17.
[16] See Chap. 25.
[17] See Chap. 16.
[17a] The "open texture of rules" is described by Hart, *The Concept of Law* (1985, Clarendon Press, Oxford).
[18] See Cornish and de Clark, *Law and Society in England 1750–1950* (1989, Sweet and Maxwell, London).
[19] [1909] 2 K.B. 858.
[20] See Chap. 17.
[21] At pp. 883–884.

"if it were necessary or relevant to consider the question of reasonableness, I think that the proposed contract would be clearly unreasonable ... there is in fact no option given to the passengers to pay a higher toll and retain fully his common law right to damages. No such alternative appears in the conspicuously exhibited tolls. No such alternative is in fact offered to any passengers".

Under the Unfair Contract Terms Act 1977, reasonableness is central to assessing the fairness of exemption clauses.[22]

The discarded general principle of inequality of bargaining power

In the 1970's, a general overarching principle to achieve both procedural and substantive **14.8** fairness in contract law was proposed in Lord Denning's attempt to establish a doctrine of inequality of bargaining power. Such a principle was potentially far-reaching. The disadvantaged person could be anyone, including those who understood the nature of the transaction, and the principle might apply without any disability in the weaker party. The concept of inequality of bargaining power emerged out of two cases of undue influence. In *Lloyd's Bank v. Bundy*[23] Lord Denning propounded his general principle of inequality of bargaining power, to which there were five key elements:

(a)   lack of independent advice;

(b)   inadequate consideration;

(c)   the bargaining power of the party had been impaired by reason of his own needs or desires;

(d)   ignorance or infirmity; and

(e)   there was undue influence or pressure brought to bear for the benefit of the other.

Lord Denning described the requirements as follows:

"By virtue of it, the English law gives relief to one who without independent advice, enters into a contract on terms which are very unfair ... or transfers property for a consideration which is grossly inadequate, when his bargaining power is grievously impaired by reason of his own needs or desires, or by his ignorance of infirmity, coupled with undue influences or pressures brought to bear on him by or for the benefit of the other."[24]

There was no need for actual wrongdoing by the stronger party. According to the Master of the Rolls: "The one who stipulates for an unfair advantage may be bound solely by his own self-interest unconscious of the distress he is bringing to the other."[25] Nor was

---

[22] See Chap. 17.
[23] [1975] Q.B. 326. For the facts of this case, see Chap. 19.
[24] At p. 339.
[25] At p. 339.

there a need for domination or one party overcoming the other party's will. A general principle of inequality of bargaining power had been created out of the doctrines of undue influence, consideration and unconscionable bargains, and turned into a new common law doctrine.

14.9   In a later case, *Backhouse v. Backhouse*,[26] the common law doctrine was married to it's equitable partner, unconscionability. Lord Denning also linked inequality of bargaining power to undue influence in *Avon Finance Co Ltd v. Bridger*.[27] A son brought undue influence to bear on his parents by giving them an entirely misleading account of documents he wanted them to sign. The parents' bargaining power was impaired by their own ignorance. The Court of Appeal held that the transaction should be set aside on this basis. In *Avon Finance* Lord Denning added a sixth element to the definition of inequality of bargaining power; that the document to be signed was not properly explained, or a misleading account was given to the other party. Lord Denning's concept may just have been too wide and likely to create excessive uncertainty for it to last. It did not do so. In requiring no element of wrongdoing, the concept offered too much scope for undermining agreements. Hence it had to fall by the wayside.

A general principle of inequality of bargaining power was rejected by Lord Scarman in *National Westminster Bank v. Morgan*[28] and again by the Privy Council in *Boustany v. Pigott*.[29] Nevertheless, bargaining power remains a key to making contracts and equality lies at the root of fairness. Equilibrian of bargaining power remains in relation to the statutory control of exemption clauses in the Unfair Contract Terms Act 1977 in which Schedule 2, para (a) provides that the reasonableness or otherwise of the exemption clause may be judged according to "the strength of the bargaining positions of the parties relative to each other".[30]

Some "straws in the wind": a common law test of fairness?

14.10   A ground breaking case on fairness at common law is the judgment of Sir Thomas Bingham M.R. in *Interfoto Picture Library v. Stiletto Visual Programmes Ltd.*[31] The plaintiffs owned a library of photographs, from which the defendants had requested a number of transparencies to assist them in an advertising campaign. The slides were sent in a jiffy bag along with a note containing conditions among which was a provision for a holding charge of £5 per day for every transparency retained after a period of two weeks. The defendants were unaware of this term and forgot about the slides for several weeks before returning them. They subsequently received a bill, which they refused to pay, for £3,783 for keeping the slides beyond the agreed date. The Court of Appeal held that the holding charge was particularly "onerous and unusual" and would not generally be known to the other party. It had not been fairly and reasonably brought to the other party's attention and therefore had not been incorporated into the contract. The plaintiffs were not allowed to rely on the term but they were entitled to a sum assessed as "fair remuneration" for their

[26] [1978] 1 W.L.R. 243.
[27] [1985] 2 All E.R. 281.
[28] [1985] A.C. 686.
[29] (1995) 69 P. and C.R. 298.
[30] We discuss strength of bargaining power in consumer and non-consumer contracts later in Chap. 17.
[31] [1989] Q.B. 433.

services to the defendants. This was a claim for *quantum meruit*, an example of restitution in the context of contract law.[32]

Sir Thomas Bingham's judgment in *Interfoto* is particularly interesting. The question **14.11** of incorporation was based on the requirement of having reasonable notice, but could extend to a general principle of fairness. So far this has failed to develop. There have, however, been two further references to the possibility of fairness at common law, the first being another judgment of Sir Thomas Bingham. In *Timeload Ltd v. British Telecom plc*[33] he stated:

> "As I ventured to observe in *Interfoto Picture Library v. Stiletto Visual Programmes Ltd*,[34] the law of England, while so far eschewing any broad principle of good faith in the field of contract, has responded to demonstrated problems of unfairness by developing a number of piecemeal solutions directed to the particular problem before it. It seems to be at least arguable that the common law could, if the letter of the statute [*i.e.* the Unfair Contract Terms Act] does not apply, treat the clear intention of the legislature expressed in the statute as a platform for invalidating or restricting the operation of an oppressive clause in a situation of the present, very special, kind".

The Master of the Rolls' dictum in *Interfoto* was considered again in *Zockoll Group Ltd v. Mercury Communications Ltd*,[35] where the Court of Appeal held that the defendant's conduct in allowing the plaintiffs to build up a market of alphanumeric numbers of value to travel agents then withdraw the number later, rendered their contract substantially different, The term allowing them to do so was subject to the requirement of reasonableness under the Unfair Contract Terms Act 1977. The Court also considered that there might be a wider power to consider the reasonableness of the term outside the Act. Phillips L.J., observed: ". . . nor would it be right to ignore the Master of the Roll's observations on the potential operation of the common law".[36] The *Interfoto* test was applied to incorporate the rules of a scratchcard game run by the *Daily Mirror* in *O'Brien v. MGN Ltd*.[36a] The rule in question was held to be neither "onerous nor outlandish".

The development of a special notice test

The *Interfoto* principle was applied by the Court of Appeal in *AEG (UK) Ltd v. Logic* **14.12** *Resource Ltd*,[37][38] a case which raised two important fairness points. The question was whether the defendant had received sufficient notice of terms to incorporate them into the contract of sale and, if so, whether or not they were reasonable within the meaning of the Unfair Contract Terms Act 1977.[39] Hirst L.J. considered that the terms in question were "extremely onerous" and also "unusual" in the absence of any evidence

---

[32] Discussed later in Chap. 26.
[33] [1995] E.M.L.R. 459 (at p. 468).
[34] [1989] Q.B. 433, 439.
[35] [1998] F.S.R. 354.
[36] At p. 363.
[36a] *The Times*, August 8, 2001.
[37] [1996] C.L.C. 265.
[38] See Bradgate, "Unreasonable Standard Terms" (1997) 60 M.L.R. 582.
[39] Exemption clauses and the rules of incorporation of terms are discussed in Chaps 16 and 17.

that they were standard or common terms. The Court held that because of this, the terms had not been fairly brought to the other party's attention. A word of caution was added by Hobhouse L.J. however, who suggested that the courts should be unwilling to take this approach too far:

> "In my judgment, it is desirable as a matter of principle to keep what was said in the *Interfoto* case within its proper bounds. A wide range of clauses are commonly incorporated into contracts by general words. If it is to be the policy of English law that in every case those clauses are to be gone through with, in effect, a tooth comb to see whether they were entirely usual and entirely desirable in the particular contract, then one is completely distorting the contractual relationship between the parties and the ordinary mechanisms of making contracts. It will introduce uncertainty into the law of contract."[40]

The *Interfoto* principle is novel in that it is possible it may apply to a range of terms, not just exemption clauses. A general principle of fairness at common law remains unlikely as it would undermine certainty in commercial contracts. In relation to consumer contracts, the rule is now different.[41]

The common law doctrine of restraint of trade

14.13   This is often used as a fairness principle, though that is not it's primary object. Rather it is to ensure greater competition in the market place. Restraint of trade acts such as concepts and undue influence, unconscionability, inequality of bargaining power and reasonableness (which is it's guiding principle) are often linked together.[42] The test for restraints of trade which render a covenant *prima facie* void at common law is whether they are reasonable between the parties and also in the public interest. A reasonableness test therefore permeates this doctrine; historically one of the most basic public policy areas in contract law. The determination of reasonableness rests with the courts. It therefore has an important role in the judicial development of the law.

FAIRNESS IN EQUITY

The equitable doctrine of unconscionability

14.14   In theory, fairness and justice lie at the heart of equity. It is the equitable doctrine of unconscionability that has perhaps the greatest potential for expansion into an overarching principle in modern contract law.[43] Unconscionability also has an historical pedigree in English law and has been adopted throughout the common law world, for instance in Australia and the United States. The doctrine had it's origins in a narrow set of rules designed to protect those who expected to inherit property and who sold their rights

---

[40]   At p. 277.
[41]   Fairness is now a general requirement of consumer contracts under the Unfair Terms in Consumer Contracts Regulations 1999 (see Chap. 15).
[42]   Discussed in Chap. 18.
[43]   See Halliwell, *Equity and Good Conscience in a Contemporary Context* (1997, Old Bailey Press, London).

at an undervalue.[44] The essence of unconscionability was that advantage had been taken of "poor, ignorant or weak minded persons". This represented an example of paternalistic protection for those who were infirm or disabled, but was not a universal principle.

The definition of unconscionability has changed over the years, with the poverty aspect being replaced by considerations of wider disability such as age, gender, mental incapacity or illiteracy. In this form it still remains a narrow doctrine in England. Unconscionability is also linked to the doctrine of equitable fraud. The leading case under the heading of "poor and ignorant" persons is *Fry v. Lane*,[45] in which two men sold their interests in property to a person who knew it's true value for a sum considerably less than the property was worth. They had not received any independent advice. Kay J. set the transaction aside for unconscionability.

This category is still applied but has become increasingly rare in modern times. In *Cresswell v. Potter*[46] unconscionability was used to protect a woman because of her lack of education and low income. She had received no independent advice and had given away her rights in the matrimonial home at an under value. Megarry J. held that the plaintiff, Hilda Cresswell, a female telephone operator, should have the contract set aside. This was based upon the old "poor and ignorant" category, though strictly speaking she was neither. Indeed the expression itself smacks of a by-gone era. In *Backhouse v. Backhouse*[47] the conveyance of a house by a woman to her former husband was set aside because of the emotional strain of divorce proceedings and the advantage enjoyed by the husband in negotiating with her. Balcombe J. expressed doubts about the requirement that the party must be "poor and ignorant". In this case the plaintiff was "certainly not wealthy" but neither was she poor and was described as an intelligent woman. He set the transaction aside preferring to make reference to the concept of inequality of bargaining power as a better and more contemporary approach.

14.15

(1) The modern version of unconscionability

The power of equity to act against unconscionability now extends into other areas. In *Bank of Credit and Commerce International SA v. Ali*[48] a release of claims against a former employer under statute, common law and equity was held to be ineffective in relation to claims of which the claimant was unaware. Equity had the power to intervene in certain circumstances to prevent the beneficiaries from relying on the express words of such a release when it would be unconscionable for them to rely on the words of general release of claims. Unconscionability now includes a wider power to relieve against certain kinds of conduct. There are said to be three factors which are essential:

14.16

(a) reprehensible conduct on the part of the person obtaining the advantage;

(b) an outcome which "shocks the conscience of the court"; and

(c) it must be unconscionable or inequitable for the party to keep the benefit so obtained.[49]

---

[44] *Earl of Chesterfield v. Janssen* (1750) 2 Ves. Sen 125 28 E.R. 82 and *Earl of Aylesford v. Morris* (1873) L.R. 8 Ch. App 484, where Lord Chancellor Selbourne stated that there was "hardly any older head of Equity".

[45] (1889) 40 Ch. D. 312.

[46] [1978] 1 W.L.R. 255.

[47] [1978] 1 W.L.R. 243.

[48] [2000] 3 All E.R. 51.

[49] *Fry v. Lane* (1888) 40 Ch. 312.

In *Alex Lobb (Garages) Ltd v. Total Oil G B Ltd*[50] the Court described the elements of unconscionability in a slightly different way:

(a) serious disadvantage of one party to the other, such as extreme inequality of bargaining power, because of poverty, ignorance, lack of advice, age, ignorance, or even difficulties with language;

(b) these weaknesses are exploited by the stronger party in a morally culpable manner; and

(c) the resulting agreement is not merely hard or improvident, but overreaching and oppressive.

The judge stated that there had to be:

"... impropriety, both in the conduct of the stronger party and in the terms of the transaction itself (though the former may often be influenced from the latter in the absence of an innocent explanation) which in the traditional phrase 'shocks the conscience of the court' and makes it against equity and conscience of the stronger party to retain the benefit of a transaction he has unfairly obtained".[51]

14.17 The traditional view of *Fry v. Lane* that there are three requirements may have been expanded but there is still no general rule against "unconscionability".[52] In *Kalsep Ltd v. X-Flow Bv*,[53] Pumfry J. held that in order to obtain relief against the agreement as an unconscionable bargain, the party has to show impropriety in both the terms of the agreement and the manner in which the agreement was made. This involved more than harshness or the agreement being improvident. There had to be some form of coercion or other improper pressure. The Court therefore had to "look at the transaction as a whole". In the Court of Appeal in *Alec Lobb v. Total Oil Great Britain Ltd*,[54] Dillon L.J. rejected a general concept based on unfairness alone or inequality of bargaining power. It is only if the conduct of the party seeking to rely on the transaction is unconscionable, coercive or oppressive that it will be set aside.

14.18 Unconscionability looks at the conduct of the dominating party. The courts still tend to require more than just unfairness. The High Court of Australia in *Commercial Bank of Australia v. Amadio*[55] laid down their own basic requirements for a general principle of unconscionability. The person obtaining the benefit must know of the other person's disadvantage. Like undue influence, this can include constructive knowledge. Mere inequality of bargaining power was not enough, nor was the fact that the contract was harsh in it's provisions. One party must impose the objectionable terms in a morally reprehensible way, and in a manner shocking to the conscience.[56] The burden is on the victim to prove unconscionable conduct. However, there may be a presumption of uncon-

[50] [1983] 1 W.L.R. 87.
[51] At p. 95.
[52] Australia now appears to have done so following *Commercial Bank of Australia v. Amadio* [1983] 151 C.L.R. 447.
[53] *The Times*, May 3, 2001.
[54] [1985] 1 All E.R. 303.
[55] [1983] 151 C.L.R. 447.
[56] In England, see *Multiservice Book Binding Co Ltd v. Marden* [1978] 2 All E.R. 489.

scionability if there is extreme weakness on one side and exploitation of this by the other party.[57]

In *Boustany v. Pigott*[58] the Privy Council considered an appeal from the High Court of Antigua and Barbados. Lord Templeman agreed with counsel for the appellant on a list of points which together could constitute unconscionable conduct:

(a) objectionable terms are imposed on the weaker party in a reprehensible manner;

(b) the behaviour of the stronger party is morally culpable or reprehensible;

(c) inequality of bargaining power or objectively unreasonable terms are not enough; there must be actual or constructive fraud or other unconscionable conduct; and

(d) the stronger party must take unconscientious advantage of the weaker party's disabling condition or circumstances.

This was summed up in the principle that it should be unfair to allow "the strong to push the weak to the wall".

(2) Statutory controls

Unconscionable transactions can also be struck down by legislation. Various types of extortionate or unconscionable transactions are controlled by statute. For instance, under the Consumer Credit Act 1974, ss 137-140, a court has the power to reopen "extortionate credit bargains . . . if it thinks just".[59] This is a particularly helpful ruling for striking down agreements with high rates of interest. A reform of this area is pending in the United Kingdom.[59a] The Fair Trading Act 1973 also gives wide powers but none approaching the wide supervisory role given in other jurisdictions to control unconscionability.

In the United States, the Uniform Commercial Code s. 2-302 provides a general control of commercial contracts, such as sale of goods, on the ground of unconscionability.[60] The UCC contains a wide power, though this approach is certainly not without it's critics. Unconscionability may exist in a contract as a whole or merely in relation to a particular clause at the time the contract was made. The courts may refuse to enforce the contract or may enforce the remainder of the contract without the unconscionable clause. There is also a power to limit the scope of contract terms to avoid resulting unconscionability. The principle of UCC 2-302 is said to be based on "the prevention of oppression and unfair surprise and not of disturbance of allocation of risks because of superior bargaining power". There is no precise definition of unconscionability provided by the UCC. However, there is general guidance on interpretation.[61]

14.19

---

[57] See also *Commonwealth of Australia v. Verwayen* [1990] 170 C.L.R. 394 linking the doctrine with equitable estoppel (see Chap. 9). See Spence, *Protecting Reliance: The Emergent Doctrine of Equitable Estoppel* (1999, Hart Publishing, Oxford). For an account of estoppel linked to a principle of unconscionability, see Halliwell (1994) 14 Legal Studies 15 Finn, "Unconscionable Conduct" (1994) 8 Journal of Contract Law; 37.

[58] (1995) 69 P. and C.R. 298.

[59] *Ketley v. Scott* [1981] I.C.R. 241; *Davies v. Directloans* [1986] 2 All E.R. 783.

[59a] See "New credit laws will crack down on loan sharks", *The Times,* July 26, 2001.

[60] See Goldsmith (1996) 11 Journal of Contract Law; Farnsworth, *Contracts* (1990, 2nd ed., Little Brown, Boston) pp. 323–343; Leff (1967) 115 U. of Pennsylvania LR 485.

[61] For an example of the Uniform Commercial Code's application, see Ramsay, *Law in Context: Text and Materials on Consumer Protection* (1989, Weidenfeld, London) at p. 102 (this contains a case study on *Toker v. Westerman* (1969) 274 A. 2d 78).

14.20   It is recognised that there are two aspects to the doctrine: (i) procedural and (ii) substantive fairness. Both factors must be present although not necessarily in equal measure. The provision therefore covers two different aspects of fairness, both of which are already covered in English law. In *Williams v. Walker Thomas Furniture Co*[62] the court defined unconscionability as "an absence of meaningful choice on the part of one of the parties together with contract terms which are unreasonably favourable to the other party." Farnsworth[63] describes this as the most durable dictum on the meaning of unconscionability.

GOOD FAITH: A NEW OVERARCHING PRINCIPLE OF CONTRACT LAW?[64]

Introduction

14.21   Good faith is an important element of contract law in the European civil law systems.[65] In a sense it is the equivalent of equity, reasonableness and indeed much more. Good faith also applies in other common law jurisdictions. In the United States Uniform Commercial Code, s. 1–203 provides that: "Every contract or duty within this Act imposes an obligation of good faith in its performance or enforcement." Section 205 of the American Law Institute, Restatement (Second) of the Law of Contracts states that "Every contract imposes upon each party a duty of good faith and fair dealing in its performance and its enforcement."

Good faith is not a general requirement of English law. This was discussed by Bingham L.J. in *Interfoto Picture Library v. Stilletto Visual Programmes*,[66] where he referred to the civilian idea of good faith:

> "This does not simply mean that they should not deceive each other, a principle which any legal system must recognise; its effect is perhaps most aptly conveyed by such metaphorical colloquialisms as 'playing fair', 'coming clean' or 'putting one's cards face upwards on the table'. It is in essence a principle of fair and open dealing. English law has, characteristically, committed itself to no such overriding principle but has developed piecemeal solutions in response to demonstrated problems of unfairness."[67]

---

[62] (1965) 350 F. 2d 445.
[63] Farnsworth, *Contracts* (1990, 2nd ed., Little Brown, Boston).
[64] For a comparative account of good faith in other jurisdictions and also articles on English law see Beatson and Friedmann, *Good Faith and Fault in Contract Law* (1995, Clarendon Press, Oxford); Nolan (1996) 59 M.L.R. 603; Brownsword, *Good Faith in Contract — Concept and Context* (1999, Hird and Howells, Ashgate), and Forte, *Good Faith in Contract and Property Law* (1999, Hart Publishing). The literature on good faith is extensive. See Mason, "Contract, Good Faith and Equitable Standards in Fair Dealing" (2000) 116 L.Q.R. 66; Teubner, "Legal Irritants: Good Faith in British Law or How Unifying Law Ends Up in New Divergences" (1998) 61 M.L.R. 11.
[65] See Collins, "Good Faith in European Contract Law" (1994) 14 O.J.L.S. 229.
[66] [1989] Q.B. 433.
[67] At p. 439.

The issue of whether or not good faith would be a good idea in English contract law is a matter for current debate. The introduction of good faith would develop new doctrines in contract law and change the way English contract law works in practice. Impetus for the introduction of such a principle comes from the fact that good faith exists throughout the legal systems of the European Union and is increasingly likely to become a part of English law as a result of the implementation of European directives.

The meanings of good faith

The key difficulty with good faith lies in it's definition.[68] There are a number of different possibilities. First, it could be a duty to act fairly and equitably towards the other party, in other words to act in on open and honest way in contractual relations. Secondly, it could be a duty of trust and confidence with the other party. Thirdly, it may be a set of standards of reasonable behaviour in contractual relations. This could provide detailed rules governing the formation, performance and breach of contracts. Good faith could also include substantive fairness in the content of contracts as well as the way in which the parties acted fairly or otherwise towards one another.[69] Good faith might only apply in a certain set of situations to cover particular areas of contractual behaviour. This could be done by means of interpretion, *e.g.* breaching a contract for economic reasons might be regarded as wrongful.[70] Good faith could also include a duty to disclose information to the other party. This would overule cases like *Turner v. Green*.[71] Finally, the law could respond by defining a set of examples of "bad faith". This would be nearer to the unconscionability test discussed earlier.
14.22

The Court of Appeal in *Director General of Fair Trading v. First National Bank plc*[72] discussed the meaning of good faith as that phrase is used in the Unfair Terms in Consumer Contracts Regulations 1994 (revised these were subsequently in 1999). This is now the leading authority on good faith in a substantive area of contract law.[72a] The Court noted that the concept had it's roots in the civil law, on which the European directive was based. A prime example being the German Civil Code (BGB) s. 242 and the German Standard Contract Terms Act 1976, which allow a term to be set aside if it is "unreasonably disadvantageous".[73] The Court of Appeal approved the view that three key elements of good faith were the:
14.23

    (a)   promotion of fair and open dealing;

    (b)   prevention of unfair surprise; and

    (c)   absence of real choice.

---

[68] See Steyn, "Fulfilling the Reasonable Expectations of Honest Men" (1997) 113 L.Q.R. 433.

[69] The Unfair Terms in Consumer Regulations 1999, in keeping with the original EU directive, no longer attempt to define "good faith". The now repealed 1994 Regulations incorporated the first three factors under schedule 2 of the Unfair Contract Terms Act 1977 (see Chap. 17), and a further guideline: "the extent to which the party had acted fairly and equitably with the consumer". This has now been removed under the updated version of the rules in 1999.

[70] See Chap. 26.

[71] See Chap. 15.

[72] [2000] 2 All E.R. 759.

[72a] See Chap. 15.

[73] *Cf* the test of manifest disadvantage for undue influence (see Chap. 19).

The Court also made reference to Sir Thomas Bingham in *Interfoto*.[74]

Does good faith already exist in English law?

(1) Existing examples of good faith in contract law

14.24   The expression "good faith" appears in isolated instances of English contract law, for instance in insurance contracts. Insurance is the leading example of a small group known as contracts *uberrimei fidei* or of "utmost good faith", of which a requirement of disclosure is imposed. Good faith also applies elsewhere, *e.g.* to buyers in contracts for sale of goods and other modern examples imported from Europe, through European directives *e.g.* Commercial Agents (Council Directive) Regulations 1993.

Implied terms may also be a vehicle for good faith in English law. An implied term of something close to good faith in performance was discussed in *Scully v. Southern Health and Social Services Board*.[75] The House of Lords held that there was an implied duty on the employers to take reasonable steps to bring to the attention of doctors employed by a health authority notice of a right to "add on" contributions which could give them more valuable pensions when they retired. In *Malik v. Bank of Credit and Commerce International SA*[76] the device of the implied term was used to incorporate a duty not to damage the relationship of trust and confidence between employer and employee. The employees obtained damages for the stigma attaching to their commercial reputations as a result of their employer's dishonest behaviour. The House of Lords accepted that the contracts of the employees contained an implied term that the defendants would not "without reasonable or proper cause, conduct themselves in a manner likely to destroy or seriously damage the relationship of confidence and trust between employer and employee".[77]

14.25   The courts have been open to the suggestion of an implied term of good faith. In *Ashmore v. Corporation of Lloyds (No. 2)*[78] Gatehouse J. upheld a duty of good faith. The Court stated that "Lloyd's accepted (obviously correctly) an unqualified duty to act in good faith".[79] Also in *Phillips Electronique v. BSkyB*[80] Sir Thomas Bingham M.R. stated, "For the avoidance of doubt we would add that we would, were it material, imply a term that BSB should act with good faith in the performance of this contract."

A duty of good faith was considered and recognised between mortgagors and mortgagees in relation to consent to letting the mortgaged property in *Imperial Group Pensions Trust Ltd v. Imperial Tobacco Ltd*.[81] A breach of such a duty of good faith required proof of dishonesty or improper motive, it was held in *Medforth v. Blake*.[82] Without proof of either of these, the duty of good faith was unworkable in practice. The

---

[74] See p. 238.
[75] [1992] 1 A.C. 294.
[76] [1995] 3 All E.R. 545.
[77] At p. 609.
[78] [1992] 2 Lloyd's Rep. 620.
[79] At p. 631.
[80] [1995] E.M.L.R. 472 (at p. 484).
[81] [1991] 1 W.L.R. 589.
[82] [1999] 3 W.L.R. 922.

allegation of such a duty without proof of dishonesty was struck out by the Court of Appeal in *Starling v. Lloyds TSB Bank plc*.[83]

In the context of a construction contract it was stated by Sir Thomas Bingham in *Balfour Beatty v. Docklands Light Railway Ltd*:

> "... the Employer was not only bound to act honestly but also bound by contract to act fairly and reasonably even where no such obligation was expressed in the contract ... If the Contractor can prove a breach of this duty it will be entitled to a remedy."[84]

Incrementally, there is now a burgeoning requirement of good faith in English contract law as a result of the implementation of European directives. The Unfair Terms in Consumer Contracts Regulations 1999 impose good faith in the requirement of "fairness". Good faith is also to be found in the Commercial Agents (Council Directive) Regulations 1993.[85] Regulation 3(1) provides that a commercial agent in performing his activities "must look after the interests of his principal and act dutifully and in good faith". By reg. 4(1), a principal in his relations with his commercial agent "must act dutifully and in good faith". The EU directive on Distance Selling[86] is now implemented in the United Kingdom in the Consumer Protection (Distance Selling) Regulations 2000. Article 4.2 of the Directive requires information to be provided "with due regard to the principles of good faith".[87]

14.26

(2) Good faith in English contract law: The same outcome by different means?

This is the "equivalency" argument. English contract law already has good faith by applying notions in other ways or using other doctrines. The requirement of reasonableness, doctrines of promissory estoppel, duress, undue influence and the use of implied terms all achieve good faith by other means. In other situations also, for instance whether there has been a repudiatory breach of contract, the state of mind and intentions may play a part whether or not there is an intention to repudiate.[88] Essentially, questions of motive do involve some consideration of good faith. However, this is still not the crucial question in breach of contract which is still largely viewed objectively.[89] A duty of good faith may now be implicit in the tendering process as a result of *Blackpool and Fylde Aero Club v. Blackpool Borough Council*[90] and *Fairclough Building Ltd v. Port Talbot Borough Council*.[91] In the latter case, Parker L.J. approved the judge at first instance, Michael Davies J., who stated:

14.27

> "The duty of the defendants was to act in good faith — not to issue a sham invitation to the plaintiffs or anyone else, for example, which here they did not do. Then

---

[83] *The Times*, October 29, 1999.
[84] [1996] 78 B.L.R. 42 (at p. 58.)
[85] SI 1993 No. 3053.
[86] (Directive 97/17/EC)
[87] See Chap. 4.
[88] *Woodar Investment v. Wimpey and Vaswani v. Italian Motors (Sales and Services) Ltd* [1996] 1 W.L.R. 270. See Chap. 23.
[89] See Chap. 23.
[90] [1990] 1 W.L.R. 1195.
[91] (1991) 62 B.L.R. 82 (see also Chap 3).

it was the duty, in my judgment, of the defendants honestly to consider the tenders of those whom they had placed on the shortlist, unless there were reasonable grounds for not doing so."

The arguments for and against good faith

(1) A radical suggestion

14.28   Let us become law reformers and propose a major change in English contract law. A Good Faith in Contracts Act 2010, s. 1 might run something like this: "Unless a contrary intention appears from the contract, there is to be implied into every contract governed by English law an implied duty to act in good faith in the formation, performance or breach of contract in dealing with the other party." The impact of such a provision would be far reaching. The attraction of an implied term approach is that it would leave the question of good faith in the hands of the parties. It would also leave the definition or the development of the detailed content of good faith to the judges, in keeping with English legal tradition. The parties would be free to exclude good faith, though this would not be likely to be looked upon with approval, or agreed to, in many cases.

(2) Against good faith

14.29   The English courts still reject a duty to negotiate in good faith as a result of the House of Lord's judgment in *Walford v. Miles*.[92] A general right of good faith in negotiation still remains a live issue.[93] In *Halifax Financial Services v. Intuitive Systems Ltd*[94] an agreement to provide software design stated that if disputes arose, the parties would within ten business days "meet in good faith" and try to resolve the matter without going to the law over the matter. The Court held that on it's construction the provision was not binding. The agreement was also unenforceable as lacking certainty as well as consideration.

The rejection of good faith here was not just in pre-contractual negotiations but in post-contractual dispute resolution. This was an unfortunate development in a situation in which *Walford* could have been distinguished. The argument against a duty of good faith to which we refer was stated by Lord Ackner in *Walford v. Miles*:

> "The concept of a duty to carry on negotiations in good faith is inherently repugnant to the adversarial position of the parties when involved in negotiations . . . A duty to negotiate in good faith is as unworkable in practice as it is inherently inconsistent with the position of a negotiating party. It is here that the uncertainty lies. In my judgment, while negotiations are in existence either party is entitled to withdraw from these negotiations, at any time and for any reason. There can be thus no obligation to continue to negotiate until there is a 'proper reason' to withdraw."[95]

---

[92] [1992] 2 A.C. 128. (Discussed in Chap. 5).
[93] See Carter and Furmston, "Good Faith and Fairness in the Negotiation of Contracts" (1994) 8 Journal of Contract Law pp. 1–15, 93–119 and comments by others in the same volume at pp. 120–153.
[94] [1999] 1 All E.R. Comm 303.
[95] [1994] 1 All E.R. 453 (at pp. 460–461).

As well as Lord Ackner's view that good faith is "repugnant" to the adversarial nature **14.30** of English law, there are other arguments against good faith.[96] First, the self interest of the parties would be limited, and it would radically change the adversarial nature of English contract law, as well as undermine freedom of contract. Good faith would require investigations into motive, *i.e.* why parties had acted in a particular way and whether they had done so for good or bad reasons. This would be likely to be subjective and difficult for the courts to assess. Above all it would make contract law uncertain since fairness is ultimately about the ethics of commercial dealings. How are ethics in this context to be defined or judged? There is also the problem of definition. What does good faith really mean? The final argument against such an overarching principle is that good faith would encourage the courts to become too interventionist in their dealings with the parties.[97]

(3) In favour of good faith[98]

Supporters claim that good faith is an idea whose time has come. Good faith would give the judges a useful tool to use in cases of unfairness. Good faith would force businesses to deal more fairly with one another, and this would change commercial practice for the better. Trust and cooperation are now key business and economic concepts.[99] It is claimed that economies where trust and cooperation exist to a high degree, perform more efficiently.[1] Trust is a better way of dealing with business partners then by the use of the law and legal sanctions. Finally, the European Union will gradually require good faith in more and more transactions within the single market. It is time for English contract law to come to terms with the concept.

The Choice of Fairness Concepts

The fairness principles which we have discussed in this chapter differ from each other. **14.31** Each has its own rationale. The reasonableness concept at common law is objective and the standard of behaviour set by the law.[2] Unconscionability looks at the behaviour of the party gaining an advantage and refuses to enforce any contract where this would lead to injustice. Unconscionability is a doctrine ripe for development in contract law. With a carefully defined scope it could provide a vehicle for a different basis for enforcing promises. The High Court of Australia is already inching towards such a position.[3] It also has its origins historically within the traditions of equity, and fits in with English tradition.

---

[96] For interesting discussions of both sides of the arguement, see Brownsword, *Good Faith in Contract* (1999, Hird and Howells, Ashgate).
[97] I am grateful to have had the opportunity to attend the conference on Good Faith at the Sheffield University Institute of Commercial Law at Easter 1997 and to interpret the views expressed. In particular, thanks to Professor Roger Brownsword for his cogently expressed arguments in favour of the doctrine.
[98] Discussed by Adams and Brownsword, *Key Issues in Contract* (1995, Butterworths,) pp. 198–254.
[99] See Fukayama, *Trust: The Social Virtues and the Creation of Prosperity* (1995, Free Press, New York).
[1] On trust and cooperation in contract law, see the special issue on Contracts and Cooperation (1997) 21 Cambridge Journal of Economics No. 2, March 1997.
[2] Traditionally in Bower L.J.'s famous phrase, test of "the man on the Clapham Omnibus"?
[3] See Chap. 9.

Good faith, the European principle, is certain to have an increasing role though the implementation of directives and the gradual harmonisation of law across the continent. In England, notions of good faith are taking hold. Whether or not contract law will be the better for this remains the key debate. The outcome will depend upon how it is defined and the circumstances within which it is applied.

Chapter 15

ASPECTS OF FAIRNESS: DISCLOSURE AND CONSUMER CONTRACTS

THE ABSENCE OF A GENERAL DUTY OF DISCLOSURE

Informational disadvantage, in other words, one party knowing less than the other about the relevant background and detail of the transaction is one of the biggest problems in contract law. English contract law does not, in general, require someone to disclose facts to the other party, even if that knowledge would have materially influenced his or her decision to contract. In contacts for sale of goods or land, for instance, the maxim *caveat emptor* or "let the buyer beware", prevails. Each party must discover the truth for themselves, rather than rely on the other party volunteering information. In European systems the duty of good faith often requires such disclosure.[1] **15.1**

The lack of a duty of disclosure is illustrated by *Turner v. Green*.[2] Shortly before an inter- **15.2** view between solicitors in Portsmouth to arrange for the compromise of an action, the plaintiff's solicitor, Fowler, received a telegram telling him of the result of proceedings in the action which were favourable to the defendant. However, he did not disclose this to the other side when they made their agreement to settle the action. The defendant claimed that the agreement was not binding because a material fact had not been disclosed. It was held that there was no obligation on the plaintiff's solicitor to disclose what he knew to the defendant. The agreement therefore stood, since failure to disclose information was not a ground for rescission, nor a defence to specific performance. Chitty J.[3] stated:

> "It cannot be contended that Fowler was under any obligation to disclose the result of the telegram; therefore [Counsel] . . . was driven to say that it was *a shabby trick* on Fowler's part not to disclose the information he had received, because the course adopted in this case would be generally condemned by high-minded men. I find myself unable to act judicially on any such ground."

The rule is also illustrated by more recent examples. It was held that a University had no duty to disclose to a member of staff that he would receive a higher pension if he had delayed his early retirement for a month in *University of Nottingham v. Eyett (No. 1)*.[4]

---

[1] See Chap. 14.
[2] [1895] 2 Ch. D 205.
[3] At p. 208.
[4] [1999] 2 All E.R. 437.

The pensioner had all the relevant information and he could have read and understood this on his own. There was therefore no breach of the obligation of trust and confidence[5] in failing to do so. On the other hand, in *Scally v. Southern Health and Social Services Board*[6] the House of Lords implied such a term in the situation where employees were otherwise ignorant as to benefits to which they were entitled.

15.3   There is no requirement to disclose to the other party a change of intention if this had been truthfully expressed at the time. This is not a statement of fact. If a contracting party subsequently changes their intention, there is no duty to communicate this to the other party. In *Wales v. Wadham,*[7] at the time of their divorce Vivien Wales promised to pay his wife Avril £13,000 as financial support. The latter re-married and became Mrs Avril Wadham. By re-marrying, the defendant would forfeit her right to maintenance, and the husband would have been under no obligation to support her. He claimed that by making the agreement she was guilty of fraud since the defendant had said that she did not intend to remarry. Tudor Evans J. in the Family Division held that the wife had made an honest representation of her intention. It was not a statement of fact or an intention which she did not actually hold at the time. The Court stated that she was under no duty to disclose her change of mind. Tudor Evans J. stated:

> "a statement of intention is not a representation of existing fact, unless the person making it does not honestly hold the intention he is expressing, in which case there is a misrepresentation of fact in relation to the state of that person's mind. That does not arise on the facts as I have found them. On the facts of this case, the wife made an honest statement of her intention which was not a representation of fact, and I can find no basis for holding that she was under a duty in the law of contract to tell the husband of her change of mind."[8]

15.4   Relationships such as employment often raise the issue of disclosure. In *Bank of Credit and Commercial International v. Ali,*[9] at first instance the court refused to extend any duty of disclosure to employment contracts.[10] A group of employees of the Bank, which had been guilty of fraudulent and dishonest conduct, had signed a compromise agreement to settle claims against their former employer, which was by now in liquidation. One part of the claim was based upon non-disclosure of material facts about the business which would have been relevant to their claim for damages for loss of commercial reputation.[11] The judge held that neither compromise agreements nor employment contracts required disclosure at common law. This had been established in *Bell v. Lever Brothers*[12] in which the House of Lords held that the employees in that case, Bell and Snelling, had been under no obligation to divulge breaches of their service contracts which could have resulted in summary dismissal. In *BCCI v. Ali* Lightman J. held that no duty of

---

[5] See Chap. 25. This developing duty could eventually outflank the non-disclosure rule in employment contracts.
[6] [1990] 4 All E.R. 563.
[7] [1977] 1 W.L.R. 199.
[8] At p. 211.
[9] [1999] 2 All E.R. 1005.
[10] The judgment was overturned by the House of Lords on other grounds.
[11] See Chap. 25.
[12] [1932] 1 A.C. 161. (See also Chap. 21.)

disclosure of wrongdoing arose as a result of breach of the implied term of trust and confidence in a contract of employment.[13] In *Bell v. Lever Brothers* Lord Atkin had denied there was any duty of disclosure in employment contracts: "It seems to me clear that master and man negotiating for an agreement of service are as unfettered as in any other negotiation".[14]

15.5 The plaintiffs had sought to have the compromise agreement set aside on three grounds, namely, for non-disclosure, misrepresentation and mistake. In a later episode of this protracted litigation the House of Lords held that the employees had not given up their claims of which they were unaware at the time.[15]

In other contexts too there is no requirement of disclosure. This is particularly true in the confidential world of banking contracts. In *Christofi v. Barclays Bank plc*[16] the Court of Appeal held that, in the absence of an express agreement between a bank and it's customer, the law would not impose an implied duty on the bank not to disclose to a person making a claim against the customer's property, over which the bank itself had a security, the fact that a claim was not protected by the entry of a caution in the Land Registry.

15.6 Disclosure of wrongdoing is now protected by law. Employees who may not be subjected to any detriment, including dismissal, if they reveal breaches of the law by their employers. The Public Interest Disclosure Act 1998 was passed to protect "whistleblowers" in the workplace and amends the Employment Rights Act 1996[17] to prevent employers imposing sanctions on employees who reveal wrongdoing. The Act enshrines the notion of trust and confidence in the employment relationship.

When Disclosure is Required or Non Disclosure is Actionable

If the statement is misleading because it is only partially true

15.7 A claimant may have an action in misrepresentation if a statement is only partially true because of non-disclosure. In *Dimmock v. Hallett*[18] property was described as "let to Hickson". It was claimed that he had let a farm "Creykes Hundreds" for £130 a year and let another to Wigglesworth for £160. In fact both had given notice to quit. The statement that the farms were let was misleading. The silence over the fact that the tenants were leaving distorted what had been said and amounted to a misrepresentation. Cairns L.J. regarded the point as of importance to the purchaser "for if the tenants leave he must either find new tenants or make allowances to the outgoing tenants. I think therefore that the omission is very material." A half truth can therefore amount to a misrepresentation.

---

[13] See also Chap. 25.
[14] At pp. 227–228.
[15] *BCCI v. Ali (Assessment of Costs)* [2001] 2 W.L.R. 735.
[16] [2000] 1 W.L.R. 937.
[17] S. 43A-L.
[18] (1866) L.R. 2 Ch. App. 21.

Concealment of the truth or simply remaining silent can also be a misrepresentation. In *Gordon v. Selico*[19] a firm of estate agents acting for vendors of the property told builders to bring a flat at Frognal "up to scratch" before putting it on the market. The contractor papered over cracks in the hall, covering up some patches of dry rot. The Court of Appeal held that concealment of the dry rot amounted to a misrepresentation. The management agents were held to be vicariously liable for misrepresentation. Goulding J. stated (at first instance): "I am satisfied that the plaintiffs would not have entered into a contract or accepted the lease had they known there was dry rot". He added: "The law must be careful not to run ahead of popular morality by stigmatising as fraudulent every trivial act . . . to make buildings or goods more readily saleable . . . but it is to my mind quite a different matter for an intending vendor to hide so sinister and menacing a defect as active dry rot."[20]

The rules and meaning of the wider concept of misrepresentation are discussed later.[21]

Statement becomes untrue after contract made

15.8   If a statement which was true later becomes untrue before the contract is made, then the representor is under a duty to tell the other of a change in circumstances. In *With v. O'Flanagan*[22] during negotiations of the sale of a medical practice the vendor made statements which by the time the contract was signed became untrue. The value of the practice had in fact fallen due to the vendor's illness and consequent inability to carry out his duties. It was held that he should have notified the purchaser of the situation.[23] In an earlier case *Davies v. London and Provincial Marine Insurance Co.*,[24] Fry J.[25] stated: "if a statement of fact has been made which is true at the time but which during the course of negotiations becomes untrue, then the person who knows that it has become untrue is under an obligation to disclose to the other the change of circumstances."

Contracts *uberrimae fidei* or of utmost good faith

15.9   The principle exception to the rule against disclosure is insurance contracts. These are said to be *uberrimae fidei* or contracts of utmost good faith. There is a duty on the insured to disclose material facts. A policy of life insurance must give accurate details of a person's known medical history. The contract is voidable if they do not do so. The duty of disclosure is not confined to the insured; the insurer is also required to disclose to the insured facts relevant to the insurance contract. In *Banque Financière de la Cité v. Westgate Insurance Co Ltd*[26] Slade L.J. quoted Lord Atkin in *Bell v, Lever Brothers*[27]:

---

[19] (1986) 278 E.G. 53.
[20] At p. 57.
[21] See Chap. 18.
[22] [1936] Ch. 575.
[23] See also *Spice Girls Ltd v. Aprilla World Service* [2000] E.M.L.R. 478, in which the fact that one of the girls had decided to leave the group had not been disclosed.
[24] (1878) 8 Ch. 469.
[25] At p. 475.
[26] [1989] 2 All E.R. 952.
[27] At p. 988.

> "Ordinarily the failure to disclose a material fact which might influence the mind of a prudent contractor does not give the right to avoid the contract. The principle of *caveat emptor* applies outside contracts of sale. There are certain contracts expressed by the law to be contracts of the utmost good faith, where material facts must be disclosed; if not, the contract is voidable. Apart from special fiduciary relationships, contracts for partnership and contracts of insurance are the leading instances. In such cases the duty does not arise out of contract; the duty of a person proposing an insurance arises before a contract is made, so of an intending partner".[28]

Slade J. went on to note that "in the case of commercial contracts broad concepts of honesty and fair dealing, however laudable, are an uncertain guide when determining the existence or otherwise of an obligation".

In *Joel v. Law Union & Crown Insurance Co*[29] Fletcher Moulton L.J. said: "Insurers are thus in the highly favourable position that they are entitled not only to bona fides on the part of the applicant, but also to full disclosure of all knowledge possessed by the applicant that is material to the risk." The law in this area goes back two centuries to the judgment of Lord Mansfield in *Carter v. Boehm*.[30] A more modern example of this principle in operation is *Lambert v. Cooperative Insurance Society Ltd*[31] in which the plaintiff took out an insurance policy on her own and her husband's jewellery. No questions were asked about previous convictions and she gave no information about this. In fact her husband had been convicted of theft. When some of her jewellery was stolen the insurers refused to pay on the ground that she had not disclosed a material fact. It was held that the insurers were entitled to so do as Mrs Lambert had a duty to disclose such relevant information.[32]   **15.10**

"Fiduciary duties"

Fiduciary relationships also attract a need for increased honesty.[32a] If the relationship between the parties is of a fiduciary nature, then greater disclosure and trust between the parties is required. This can be found in various types of commercial contracts. For instance, if an agent acts for two parties, each as his principal, there is obvious opportunity for conflict. This is sometimes said to be expressed as a "no conflict" rule in the dealings of the agent or manager with the two other parties. A good example of this is the manager of a pop group who is acting for different members of the group. They may end up in dispute or at least have different interests from each other. In *Martin-Smith v. Williams*[33] the plaintiff was acting for various members of the band *Take That* had contractual agreements. The judge, Ferris J., characterised the manager's duty as a "duty of good faith". He quoted Millett L.J. in *Bristol and West Building Society v. Northern*[34] in respect of the duty of good faith where the Court of Appeal stated: **15.11**

---

[28]   [1932] A.C. 161 (at p. 227).
[29]   [1908] 2 K.B. 863.
[30]   (1766) 3 Burr 1905, ER.
[31]   [1975] 2 Lloyd's Rep. 485.
[32]   See also *Pan Atlantic Insurance Co. Ltd v. Pine Top Insurance Co.* [1994] 3 All E.R. 581.
[32a]   A Solicitor is under a duty to observe fiduciory obligations to a client, see *Longstaff v. Birtles*, *The Times*, September 18, 2001.
[33]   [1998] E.M.L.R. 334.
[34]   [1996] 4 All E.R. 699 (at pp. 710–712).

> "Even if a fiduciary is properly acting for two principals with potentially conflicting interests he must act in good faith in the interests of each and must not act with the intention of furthering the interests of one principal to the prejudice of those of the other . . . But it goes further than this. He must not allow the performance of his obligations to one principal to be influenced by this relationship with the other. He must serve each as faithfully and loyally as if he were his only principal."

The Court held that there had been no breach of such a duty on the facts.

15.12   Even if there is a fiduciary element in the relationship, such as exists in a contract of employment, that does not necessarily import a duty of disclosure. In *Nottingham University v. Fishel*[35] Elias J. held that the employee's fiduciary duty not to pursue his own interests where he was bound to work for his employers, only arose if the employee had undertaken to work solely for the employer, and not other remunerative work. The employee was not bound to inform the employer when he was doing work elsewhere. In this case a clinical embryologist at Nottingham University had undertaken work for private clinics without telling his employers. The fiduciary duty did not arise automatically in contracts of employment and so there was no duty of disclosure.

Guarantees

15.13   In *Associated Japanese Bank v. Credit du Nord*[36] it was argued that a guarantee was voidable because the plaintiffs failed to disclose to the defendants a material fact which related to the "intrinsic features of the principal transaction" (in the case of a sale and leaseback transaction). Steyn J. took as authority for this *London General Omnibus Co Ltd v. Holloway*.[37] However, he held the plea of non disclosure was not sustainable.

Statutory exceptions where disclosure required

By various measures Parliament has made provision for the disclosure of information in contract law. A good example is the Consumer Credit Act 1974, s. 55 requiring disclosure of rules of interest charged to consumers. The Consumer Protection (Distance Selling) Regulations 2000 also require disclosure of information in sales of consumer goods and services when made exclusively by means of distance communication.[38]

Sales of residential property

The traditional rule in house sales has been the old adage of "let the buyer beware". In 1988 the Law Society suggested changing this rule.[39] The Homes Bill which was dropped as a result of the election in 2001 would have required vendors to provide a survey and "information pack" for potential purchasers. This would include a survey of the prop-

---

[35] [2000] I.C.E. 1462.
[36] [1989] 1 W.L.R.
[37] [1912] 2 K.B. 72 (at pp. 85–88).
[38] See Chap. 4.
[39] "Caveat Emptor in Sales of Land", Law Society, 1988.

erty. While short of reversing the common law rule this would have been an important addition to the need for disclosure in contract law. It is likely that some major changes will occur in this area in the near future.

Should there be a wider general duty of disclosure?

The main argument against disclosure is that contracts might be too easily set aside. A **15.14** duty to disclose would also be contrary to the "adversarial" approach of English contract law, whereby each party looks after his or her own self interest. It would be unworkable, and would also be hard to define and difficult to apply. On the other hand, a duty to disclose information would lead to greater trust, would counteract the inbuilt advantage given to the party with superior information, would lead to greater fairness in contract law, and would be a step towards adopting a principle of good faith in English contract law as we discussed earlier.[39a]

THE UNFAIR TERMS IN CONSUMER CONTRACTS REGULATIONS 1999[40]

An important and wide ranging example of fairness in English contract law is that **15.15** imposed by the Unfair Terms in Consumer Contracts Regulations 1999. Consumer contracts involving the purchase of goods and services are the most numerous and familiar species of contracts for most people. As a result of a European Union Directive, the United Kingdom implemented the Unfair Terms in Consumer Contracts Regulations in 1994.[41] These were amended in 1999 to reflect more closely the aims of the Directive. The regulations impose a requirement of fairness in most consumer contracts. This represents an important step in the widening division of contract law into two distinct subjects, commercial contract law and consumer law. We discuss this development later in this chapter. The Unfair Terms in Consumer Contracts Regulations are the most important European Union initiative to affect our domestic contract law.[42]

The parties

Since the 1999 Regulations are a consumer protection measure, they only apply if one **15.16** party is a consumer and the other is a seller or supplier acting for a commercial purpose. Consumer is defined as any "natural person who, in contracts covered by these Regulations, is acting for purposes which are outside his trade, business, or profession".[43]

[39a] See Chap. 14.
[40] Bright, "Winning the battle against Unfair Contract Terms" (2000) 20 Legal Studies 331; see generally Lockett and Egan, *Unfair Terms in Consumer Agreements* (1995, Willey).
[41] 93/13/EEC. The Treaty power to pass directives on the area of consumer protection is now contained, post Amsterdam, in Article 95. Most European contract directives are based upon the need for harmonisation within the single market.
[42] Dean (1993) 56 M.L.R. 581–90; Smith (1994) Current Legal Problems 5; MacDonald (1994) J.B.L. 44.
[43] Reg. 3.

A natural person means a human being; not a legal person such as a company or person trading as a business.[44] The consumer must be buying for their own private needs. On the other side the party dealing with the consumer must be "a seller or supplier". This means "any natural or legal person who, is acting for purposes relating to his trade, business, profession or whether privately owned or publicly owned".[45] The wording of the Regulations was changed in 1999 to omit reference to "goods" so it appears that contracts covering sales of land sale are now included.[46] The definitions of the parties differ from that under the Unfair Contract Terms Act 1977. It can be argued that this adds unnecessary complexity to the law.

Non-individually negotiated terms

The regulations are aimed at the abuses of standard form contracts. They focus on the question of whether the consumer had any part in agreeing to the terms. If they did not, then the regulations will come into play. Even if a particular term is negotiated, the rest of the contract may still be within the regulations if the overall assessment indicates that the contract was pre-formulated.[46a] A term is not "individually negotiated", according to reg. 5(2), if it has been drafted in advance and the consumer has not been able to influence the substance of the term. Under reg. 5(4), the burden is on the supplier or seller to show that the term was not individually negotiated.

When the regulations do not apply: The "core" exceptions

15.17   There are two exclusions to the overall requirement of fairness. Significantly these only apply if the term in question is written in plain intelligible language. First, any term which defines the main subject matter of the contract[47] and secondly, any term which deals with the adequacy of the price or remuneration.[48]

The adequacy of the price is a reflection of the common law rule on consideration.[49] The courts are not in a position to overturn the agreed price even if one of the parties made a bad bargain. Whether a term is part of the price, or not, may be an interesting question. In *Director General of Fair Trading v. First National Bank plc*[50] one of the issues was the statues of a clause in a standard form loan agreement. This provided that if the borrower defaulted and he had to pay in instalments, interest on the outstanding principal sum would be payable at the contractual rate even after all other instalments had been paid. The term concerning the rate of interest payable could not be challenged as unfair because that concerned the adequacy of the consideration. It was held that the default provision for the payment of interest could be assessed for fairness.

---

[44] This definition is narrower than the equivalent provision dealing with consumers under the Unfair Contract Terms Act 1977, under which a business may "deal as consumer" (see Chap. 17).
[45] Reg 3.
[46] This point, which was debatable, appears to have been confirmed in *Zealander v. Laing Homes Ltd* (2000) 2 T.C.L.R. 724.
[46a] Reg. 5(3).
[47] Reg. 6(2)(a).
[48] Reg. 6(2)(b).
[49] See Chap. 7.
[50] [2000] 1 All E.R. 240.

The Court of Appeal agreed with the Judge[51] that the term in question was not a "core **15.18** term". Peter Gibson L.J. stated that:

> "The test in respect of the relevant term is not whether it can be called a "core term" but whether it falls within one or both of paras (a) and (b) of reg 3(2). Neither paragraph is in our opinion apt to cover the relevant term, which certainly does not define the main subject matter of the contract and which cannot, in our view, realistically be said to concern the adequacy of the remuneration, relating as it does to a case where the borrower is in default and then merely providing for the continuation of the contractual rate after judgment. As the Solicitor General pointed out, if the bank was right almost any provision containing any part of the bargain would be capable of falling within the reach of reg 3(2). There is nothing in the directive to require so wide an interpretation."[52]

Plain intelligible language and construction of the contract

Sellers and suppliers have to ensure that the terms must be written in plain intelligible lan- **15.19** guage.[53] As we have seen, this requirement is also necessary for the core exceptions to apply. If there is any doubt about the meaning of the term, the interpretation most favourable to the consumer shall prevail.[54] In its Second Bulletin on the monitoring of fairness, the Office of Fair Trading discussed this requirement. The well known phrase "does not affect your statutory or common law rights" was regarded as "meaningless" to most people.[55] The OFT also warned against "double negatives", and suggested short sentences should be used whenever possible. When lengthy clauses were unavoidable, these should be split up to deal with each issue in sequence. Cross references should be reduced as should the use of terms defined elsewhere. The contract should be written in such a way that related topics are brought under the same sub-headings. There should be an avoidance of statements not defining the extent of rights and duties under the contract. There is no doubt this provision has led to some major contractual re-drafting of contracts involving consumers.

The meaning of fairness

Apart from the "core" exceptions, the regulations impose a test of fairness on all the terms **15.20** of consumer contracts. The assessment of unfairness must take account of: (i) the nature of the goods and services contracted for; (ii) the time the contract was made; (iii) "all the circumstances attending the conclusion of the contract"; and[56] (iv) all the other terms of the contract, or any other contract on which it is dependent (reg. 6). Four important matters relating to fairness are set out in reg. 5: (a) the test only applies to terms not individually negotiated, and such terms will be unfair if (b) they are contrary to the requirement of good faith, (c) they cause significant imbalance in the parties' rights and obligations under the contract, and (d) these are to be detriment of the consumer.[57]

---

[51] [2000] 2 All E.R. 759.
[52] At p. 768.
[53] Reg. 7(1).
[54] Reg. 7 (except under Reg. 12).
[55] It is ineffective and redundant in light of the Unfair Contract Terms Act 1977, s. 5 (see Chap. 17).
[56] This may be regarded as another exception to the parol evidence rule, (see Chap. 12).
[57] Reg. 5(1).

Under the 1994 regulations there was a schedule giving guidance on the meaning of the phrase "good faith". This contained the first three items in Schedule 2 of the Unfair Contract Terms Act 1977 on reasonableness[57a] and in addition a further element, namely "the extent to which the seller and supplier has dealt fairly and equitably with the consumer". This has now been omitted in the revised 1999 Regulations.[58] There is now no regulatory guidance on the matter. Good faith in the area of consumer contracts becomes an important part of English law as a result of this provision. Rather than restrict the definition of good faith, the intension appears to have been to expand it. The development of the meaning of good faith is now placed in the hands of the judge.

15.21   Schedule 2 contains an "indicative and illustrative list" of terms which may or may not be regarded as "unfair". The list does not define terms as fair or unfair, rather it lists terms which may be unfair, known colloquially as the "grey list". The Schedule can be broken down into, first, terms already covered by the Unfair Contract Terms Act. These include terms (i) excluding or limiting death or personal injury, (ii) excluding or limiting contractual obligations for total or partial non-performance and (iii) excluding the consumer's right to take legal action or exercise a remedy, restricting evidence available to him or imposing a different burden of proof on the consumer.

15.22   The second and wider group are terms definitely not covered by the 1977 Act. The regulations widen the scope of fairness beyond any single type of term, *e.g.* exemption clauses. So terms may or may not be fair which provide that: (i) an agreement is binding only on the consumer but only at the seller or supplier's option, (ii) the consumer pays a disproportionately high compensation, (iii) the seller may dissolve the contract, *i.e.* terminate unilaterally or without reasonable notice, as well as terms which (iv) automatically extend contracts of fixed duration and (v) automatically bind the consumer where he or she had no opportunity of becoming aware of those terms before the contract. Similarly, terms may or may not be fair which (vi) allow the seller to unilaterally vary the contract or vary the goods or services provided, or which (vii) allow the seller to increase the price, (viii) give the seller the exclusive right to interpret the contract, (ix) limit the seller's obligation for commitments by agents or (x) make commitments subject to particular formality. This latter category has potentially outlawed "entire agreement clauses" in consumer contracts.[59] Arbitration clauses are also potentially unfair. In England, arbitration clauses involving consumers can be treated as unfair by a consumer if they are for less than £5000 (the small claims limit in the county courts.) This is therefore one example of a blacklisted term.[60]

Director General of Fair Trading v. First National Bank plc

15.23   *Director General of Fair Trading v. First National Bank plc*[61] is the main authority on the interpretation of the meaning of fairness.[62] At first instance the judge found the clause in

[57a] See Chap. 17.
[58] On the 1999 Regulations, see Beresford (2000) 59 C.L.J. 242.
[59] See Chap. 12.
[60] Arbitration Act 1996, ss 89–92. Section 91 provides that an arbitration agreement is unfair in a consumer contract if for less than the small claims limit. The consumer may prefer to use the County Court.
[61] [2000] 2 All E.R. 759, reported at first instance [2000] 1 All E.R. 240, Evans-Lombe J.
[62] For other briefly reported decisions on fairness, see *Zealander v. Laing Homes Ltd* (2000) 2 T.C.L.R. 724; *Camden LBC v. McBride* [1999] 1 C.L. 284; *Broadwater Manor School v. Davis* [1999] 5 C.L. 208.

question was fair. The Court adopted the approach of first asking what the consumer would have thought at the time:

> "It seems to me to be appropriate to stand back, and without reference to statute of authority, consider whether, had a potential borrower had the effect of the provisions of cl. 8 drawn to his attention immediately after entering into a loan agreement containing that clause, he would reasonably have replied to the question that they were unfair. It seems to me that if a borrower in those circumstances was informed that the provisions of cl. 7 required him to pay to the bank the contractual rate of interest on so much of the sum advanced as remained outstanding for so long as it remained outstanding he would not have regarded that as unfair."[63]

According to the judge, the next issue was to consider whether there was a breach of the requirement of good faith. This would happen if the term "unfairly deprived customers of benefits or advantages which they might probably have expected to receive" fitted the facts. Evans-Lombe J. adopted the test of "reasonable expectations". The question of fairness applied in three stages depending upon whether it was (a) inherently, (b) proceduraly or (c) substantively unfair, and also based on the avoidance of "unfair surprise". According to Evans-Lombe J.:   **15.24**

> "a court considering whether a given term of a contract is an 'unfair term' will look at all the circumstances of the case and its judgment will be based on an amalgam of perceived substantive and procedural unfairness . . . It seems to me that a term not inherently unfair can still constitute a breach of the requirement of good faith if it unfairly deprives consumers of a benefit or advantage which they may reasonably expect to receive".[64]

Evans Lombe J. held the clause in question was not unfair. The only advantage which borrowers lost was their statutory exemption from paying interest on the amount of any judgment obtained against them as a result of default. There was nothing in the statute preventing charging interest in the way the lenders had done and no public policy against it. Procedural unfairness was not made out, although the Court noted that "it may well be that those institutions take more active steps than does the bank to ensure that their borrowers are not subject to unfair surprise".

The Court of Appeal reversed the judge's decision on the fairness point.[65] The key to fairness was the element of good faith. Peter Gibson L.J.[66] described this as follows: **15.25**

> "A term to which the consumer's attention is not specifically drawn but which may operate in a way which the consumer might reasonably not expect and to his disadvantage may offend the requirement of good faith. Terms must be reasonably transparent and should not operate to defeat the reasonable expectations of the

---

[63] At pp. 249–250.
[64] At p. 251.
[65] [2000] 2 All E.R. 759. See Beresford (2000) 59 C.L.J. 242; Bright, "Winning the Battle Against Unfair Terms" (2000) 20 Legal Studies 331.
[66] At p. 769.

consumer. The consumer in choosing whether to enter into a contract should be put in a position where he can make an informed choice. The element of significant imbalance would appear to overlap substantially with that of the absence of good faith. A term which gives a significant advantage to the seller or supplier without a countervailing benefit to the consumer (such as a price reduction) might fail to satisfy this part of the test of an unfair term."

15.26   The Court of Appeal concluded that the judge had been wrong on the fairness question, stating that "the test of fairness is not to be judged by personal concepts of inherent fairness apart from the requirements of the directive and regulations".[67] The term was held to be unfair because:

> "The bank, with its strong bargaining position as against the relatively weak position of the consumer, has not adequately considered the consumer's interests in this respect. In our view the relevant term in that respect does create unfair surprise and so does not satisfy the test of good faith, it does cause a significant imbalance in the rights and obligations of the parties by allowing the bank to obtain interest after judgment in circumstances when it would not obtain interest . . . and no specific benefit to compensate the borrower is provided, and it operates to the detriment of that consumer who has to pay the interest."[68]

The key elements in good faith according to the Court of Appeal were therefore (i) fair and open dealing, (ii) the prevention of unfair surprise, (iii) the absence of real choice to the consumer and (iv) significant imbalance to the detriment of the consumer.[68a]

The judge's decision on the fairness question was overruled specifically on the grounds that fairness was not to be deemed a subjective issue, that the term had not been brought to the customers attention and the bank was in a stronger bargaining position in drafting terms which were to their own advantage.

An arbitration clause contained within a contract for the purchase of a house was held to be unfair by a judge in the Technology and Construction Court in *Zealander v. Laing Homes Ltd*.[69] The purchase was covered by the National House Builders Council "Blue Mark" agreement which included the arbitration clause at issue. This was struck out as unfair on the grounds that the purchaser was unaware of the clause, there was inequality of bargaining between the parties and the consumer was placed at a disadvantage. Arbitration clauses are not covered by the Unfair Contract Terms Act 1977, as not being regarded as a species of exemption clause.[70]

The effect of unfair terms in a consumer clause

15.27   If a term is unfair, it does not bind the consumer, *i.e.* it is unenforceable[71] rather than void.[72] However, if the contract is capable of continuing without the unfair term, then

---

[67]   At p. 770.
[68]   At p. 770.
[68a]   The concept of good faith is dealt with in greater detail in Chap. 14.
[69]   (2000) 2 T.C.L.R., Judge Harvey.
[70]   S. 13(2). (See Chap. 17).
[71]   Reg. 8(1).
[72]   For a discussion of the distinction, see Chap. 18.

the rest of the contract can continue. The fairness requirement is basically a self help remedy for consumers.[72a] If the term is unfair it is not binding and the consumer may ignore it. It is up to the seller to show it is fair. The issue of fairness is largely an administrative decision as part of the regulatory role of the OFT and other qualifying bodies. The OFT responds to complaints and then negotiates, re-drafting in the bulk of cases. Individual consumers do not have to act.

Excepted contracts

The 1994 Regulations contained a number of exempted contracts namely employment, succession, family law or company law.[73] Although the list is now repealed, such contracts were already regarded as being outside of consumer contract law by the European directive. The Schedule was merely a redundant provision and has been omitted in the 1999 regulations. The listed contracts therefore remain outside the regulations in practice.

The role of the office of fair trading and qualifying bodies

The regulations create an important regulatory public role for the Office of Fair Trading.   **15.28**
The powers of the OFT as contained in regs 10-15 are to:

(a)   consider any complaint that a term in general use is unfair, unless the complaint is "frivolous or vexatious" or a "qualifying body has notified the Director that it agrees to consider the complaint[74];

(b)   bring proceedings for an injunction or interlocutory injunction against the party[75];

(c)   seek an undertaking against the continued use of unfair terms[76]; and

(d)   take proceedings to obtain an injunction which the court may grant on any terms it "thinks fit".[77]

The Director General is also empowered to disseminate information and advice about his monitoring of unfairness "as may appear to him to be expedient". This occurs through regular bulletins and press briefings.[78]

The 1999 Regulations made significant changes in the powers of the Director General of Fair Trading. From October 1999 the revised rules allow the new qualifying bodies,[79] such as statutory Regulators, trading standards departments and the Consumers

---

[72a]   On self-help remedies, see Chap. 26.

[73]   Schedule 1, 1994 Regulations (repealed).

[74]   Reg. 10.

[75]   Reg. 12.

[76]   Reg. 14.

[77]   Reg. 12(3).

[78]   Reg. 15. The Office of Fair Trading also publishes general guidance on Unfair Terms (the latest was issued in February 2001).

[79]   Qualifying Bodies are listed in Schedule 1. The Unfair Terms in Consumer Contracts (Amendment) Regulations 2001 add the Financial Services Authority as a qualifying body.

Association to apply for injunctions to prevent the continued use of an unfair term, provided they give the Office of Fair Trading 14 days notice of their intention to do so.[80] Traders must also now produce copies of their standard form contracts and give information about their use to the OFT. This is designed to facilitate the investigation of complaints and assist compliance with undertakings.[81]

15.29   The Office of Fair Trading has the right to supply enquirers about particular standard terms with details of relevant undertakings and court orders. This area is now largely public interest regulation rather than contract law itself, but the effect on individual contracts can nevertheless be considerable. For instance, the Office of Fair Trading supported the Consumers Association in their action to prevent the continued use of so called "lock-in" mortgages, *i.e.* having to stay with the same leader on the same terms for many years or incur a penalty.[82] As we have discussed, the powers of the Director General of Fair Trading were used in *Director General of Fair Trading v. First National Bank*.[83] Until now the Office of Fair Trading had contented itself with using its power to obtain undertakings as to future conduct as sufficient enforcement. The 1999 regulations are likely to be more widely used, particularly as the authorities are armed with new powers to which we now turn.

The Stop Now Orders (EC Directive) Regulations 2001

15.30   The enforcement powers of the Office of Fair Trading[84] are simplified and streamlined in regulations which came into force in June 2001. Under the regulations, a "qualifying body", such as trading standards officers or others who may apply for such powers, may direct a business to refrain from infringing European Union law in the area of consumer protection. The body seeking to enforce the provision must normally give the recipient two weeks to comply, after which they may apply to a county court or High Court for a Stop Now Order. This acts as an injunction, failure to obey being contempt of court. The qualifying enforcement authority may ask for an undertaking that the business cease engaging in conduct which breaches the regulations. Anyone who gives such an undertaking may be liable in civil proceedings if they fail to adhere to or fulfil the undertaking. The Stop Now Order Regulations also apply to breaches of other pieces of European and UK Consumer Protection law. This includes the Consumer Protection (Cancellation of Contracts Concluded Away from Business Premises) Regulations 1987,[85] the Package Travel, Package Holidays and Package Tours Regulations 1992,[86] the Consumer Protection (Distance Selling) Regulations 2000[87] and the Unfair Terms in Consumer Contracts Regulations 1999.[88] Stop Now Orders are

---

[80]   Reg. 12.
[81]   Reg. 13.
[82]   See "Courts Set to Ban Lock-in Mortgages", *The Sunday Times*, July 25, 1999.
[83]   [2000] 1 All E.R. 240; 2 All E.R. 759.
[84]   There are also a number of other "UK Qualified Entities" (Schedule 3, 2001 Regulations).
[85]   See Chap. 4.
[86]   See Chap. 13.
[87]   See Chap. 4.
[88]   The powers under Stop Now Orders were described by the spokeswoman for the Institute of Directors as being "the World of Alice, sentence first, verdict afterwards". There is no doubt they strengthen the powers of consumer regulators.

likely to be used extensively as an alternative to prosecution in the magistrates courts. The existence of this enforcement mechanism may also produce a knock-on effect on many consumer contracts.

SHOULD CONSUMER CONTRACTS AND COMMERCIAL CONTRACTS BE REGARDED AS DIFFERENT SUBJECTS?

There has always been a debate over whether a general contract law really exists,[89] or whether there is merely a series of rules for different contracts, each having it's own discrete body of law. Modern contract law is a mixture of general doctrines, *e.g.* offer and acceptance, misrepresentation and consideration, and case law drawn from every field and type of contract from shipping law to plumbing contracts. Some would assert that a new classification has developed whereby contract law pays increasing attention not to the type of contract but to the contracting parties. There are a number of reasons for this insight.

   First, the use of standard form contracts in which goods or services are offered on a "take it or leave it" basis. This has led to the recognition of the concept of inequality of bargain power. Such a situation is not restricted to consumers, however, but applies also in the commercial context. In consumer law, standard form pose a greater threat to fairness.

   Secondly, the lack of information or disparity of knowledge between the contracting parties is recognised as a problem in contract law, especially where one of the parties is a consumer. The need for protection in the market place in commercial contracts is less pressing. Indeed it may be regarded as both unnecessary and counter productive. The parties are likely to have access to legal advice or should have incorporated the expenses of professional help as part of the transaction costs of their business overheads. Consumers rarely have this benefit.

   Thirdly, there are now many special rules for consumer contracts as a result of intervention by Parliament and the European Union. The European Union does not, in general, legislate on private commercial contracts, although this may be seen in isolated instances.[90]

   Fourthly, a separate development is visible between consumer contracts and the main body of commercial law. The courts and judges now recognise greater fairness rules, particularly in contract law.[91] If a separate and distinct consumer contract law exists, it dates from 1973. This was the year in which a small claims procedure appeared in the county courts (a procedural matter) and the year when "consumer sales" were recognised as different from other contracts for the sale of goods in the now repealed Supply of Goods (Implied Terms) Act 1973. The main differences have blossomed since that time. Among the special differences between the two areas include:

15.31

15.32

---

[89] See Chap. 1.
[90] *e.g.* Commercial Agents (Council Directive) Regulations 1993.
[91] See Chap. 17.

(a) the separate treatment of "consumer" and "non-consumer" contracts in the Unfair Contract Terms Act 1977, ss 3, 6, 7 along with the notion of "consumer" and "non-consumer" sales;

(b) the right to rescind for trivial breach of conditions under the Sale of Goods Act 1979 s. 15A[92] (commercial contracts have now lost this power);

(c) the "fairness" requirement in consumer contracts under the Unfair Terms in Consumer Contracts Regulations 1999;

(d) special legislation for consumers, *e.g.* the Consumer Credit Act 1974, the Timeshare Act 1992[93] and the Package Holiday Regulations 1992. This has overturned the common law distinction between terms and representations[94]; and

(e) European Directives which will also lead to further changes in English law, *e.g.* the Guarantees of Goods in Consumer Sales Directive 2000, implemented in 2002;

15.33 The main arguments for having a separate law for consumers are:

(a) it is already happening, especially as a result of European directives for consumers;

(b) in consumer contracts there is generally inequality of bargaining power;

(c) commercial contracts are often professionally drafted and certainty is a paramount consideration; and

(d) commercial parties can afford to go to court.

This is how the law has developed over the centuries. Consumers mostly end up in small claims procedures where cases are not reported. It would be better for the rational development of contract law as a whole if consumer law developed it's own discrete set of rules. The two systems have already drifted apart in the last decades. On the other hand, consumer law enlarges and enriches contract law. Contract law should be allowed to develop as an embracing set of principles eclectically draw from all types of contracts. Traditionalists can fairly argue that rules of contract law is distorted in a consumer contract. Most consumer contracts are executed transactions, *i.e.* they take place immediately. Business contracts are more often long term relational contracts so the parties have a greater stake in good will towards each other. There is a need to intervene to provide for greater fairness on behalf of consumers, but less so or none at all in commercial matters which should be left to the market and freedom of contract.

15.34 The law of contract is two separate areas to which different rules apply because the character of the parties and context are different. It can be argued that a consumer law would be easier to understand and could be more coherent if there was a separation of consumer contracts. This is what happens in other countries such as the United States.

---

[92] See Chaps 13 and 23.
[93] See Chap. 13.
[94] The Timeshare Act 1992 may also be enforced by the Stop Now Orders (EC Directive) Regulations 2001.

In commercial contracts there is a need for certainty. This does not apply so much in consumer law where the paramount objective is restoring a balance of fairness. The two categories are drifting apart at this point.

On balance, there is much to be said for maintaining contract law as a whole. Formal equality should be preserved. The principles of contract law already exist in many contexts, including consumers. Distinctions based on the parties, subject matter and terms have existed for nearly 200 years in contract law and the various different elements have added to the wider picture of the subject as a general theory of contractual obligations. Contract law is a rich and varied subject, and is enhanced by cases involving consumers, as well as the commercial contracts. The problems of inequality of bargaining power, imperfect information and standard terms also apply to small business, and exist throughout contracts. Contract law remains intact, for the present at least.

Chapter 16

EXEMPTION CLAUSES AT COMMON LAW

Introduction

The concept of inequality of bargaining power revealed that unfettered freedom of con- **16.1**
tract could lead to unfairness, particularly where standard form contracts were used by
sellers and suppliers of goods to exclude liability in their dealings with consumers. This
led to the courts developing a number of techniques to strike down attempts to avoid or
limit liability in contracts. Parliament has also taken a hand with the enactment of the
Unfair Contract Terms Act 1977. This is one of the most important pieces of legislation
in contract law. The definition and legal effect of an exemption clause was once a relatively simple concept. The Unfair Contract Terms Act 1977 has gradually extended the
meaning of such clauses beyond their common law roots.[1] An exemption or exclusion
clause (the expressions are usually regarded as synonymous) is a term in a contract which
takes away one party's liabilities or the other party's rights or remedies under a contract.
A limitation clause is another species of the same type of term. This restricts the liability of one party to a fixed sum of money, smaller than any reasonable pre-estimate of
loss. Exemptions and limitations of liability are treated alike, except that the rules of construction of each may be different.[2] Exemptions of liability or consent to risk are not the
exclusive province of contract law. Disclaimers of liability in signs and notices are also
to be found in relation to negligence and other legal wrongs.[3] Exemptions for negligence
are also subject to the Unfair Contract Terms Act 1977.

(1) The uses and abuses of standard form contracts

The widespread use of exemption clauses is associated with the growth of standard term **16.2**
contracts, which probably account for more than 90 per cent of all contracts made. The
use of standard terms is commonplace in consumer contracts, although it is also a
general practice throughout industry. Contracts for travel, parking a car, drycleaning,
theatre tickets, insurance and package holidays are all regularly accompanied by standard printed terms. Most sellers and suppliers of goods have their own terms which are
routinely used in every transaction. Apart from casual oral arrangements, such as an
agreement with a private house owner to repair a roof, for instance, it is relatively uncommon to find a contract not governed by standard terms. Standard form terms and

---

[1] We discuss this later, see Chap. 17.
[2] See later p. 276.
[3] *e.g.* wrongful interference with goods. See *Vine v. Waltham Forest* [2000] 4 All E.R. 169. Discussed later p. 273.

conditions are found usually in the "small print" of contracts and drafted by one side of the transaction in advance. There is usually no discussion of the contents of the contract and the other party simply agrees to the terms offered, a phenomenon sometimes described as "take it or leave it".

Standard forms appear to be an abuse of freedom of contract, and are by their nature potentially unfair. Their widespread use has led contract lawyers to review the concept of inequality of bargaining power, which, though generally linked to consumer contracts, applies throughout commercial contracts. It is in fact relatively uncommon to find equality of bargaining power in the market place. Even in the same business context, a party may have superior bargaining power in one situation, and inferior power in another. To take a simple example, a farmer in Herefordshire who grows apples as his only crop, is probably able to determine the wages he pays to casual pickers and also their terms of work. However if he sells his entire produce to a large chain of supermarkets then the balance of bargaining power is certainly on the other side. The farm's scope to negotiate with the supermarket may be very limited or non existent. In both situations there is inequality of bargaining power. Standard form contracts tend to institutionalise this inequality.

16.3   There are also advantages to standard terms which have to be included in any balanced appraisal of their functions. The fact that terms are so widespread suggests they are successful and useful. Sellers and suppliers of goods and services in commercial contracts would argue that their greatest advantage is in reducing "transaction costs", that is, the overhead expenditure in making and negotiating contracts and dealing with disputes arising thereafter. Standard forms reduce the time taken to make a contract since the parties do not have to discuss or argue over the main terms or even points of detail. For business they are effective in controlling risk factors in advance so the parties know where they stand. Standard terms can be used universally for transactions so thousands of new contracts can be agreed using a simple format. Agents and employees can be authorised to contract on the standard terms only, so there is no risk of them making a deal which is out of line with the firm's policy. The conclusion is that they give control of the bargaining process to the party with the standard terms. They can also be drafted by lawyers to suit the firms' own needs. In so far as they reduce the price to the other party, they can be said to be an advantage to both sides. Indeed many standard forms are produced not by individual firms but their trade or professional association, and everyone in that business uses them. Such terms have often been agreed with all the major parties involved, including customers and parties likely to be on the other side. The potential unfairness stemming from the abuses of standard form contracts and the impact of inequality of bargaining power led the common law to control a particular type of term, exemption clauses.[3a]

(2) The extent to which the common law survives the 1977 Act

16.4   The courts developed a number of techniques and common law doctrines to control exemptions of liability. These were:

(a)   the rules for incorporating exemption clauses into contracts;

[3a] See Trebilcock and Dewees, "Judical Control of Standard Form Contracts", in Burrows and Veljanowski, *The Economic Approach to Law* (1981, Butterworths, London).

(b)   the strict construction of terms which exempted a party from liability;

(c)   the debate over the effect of a "fundamental breach" of contract;

(d)   the use of the doctrine of privity of contract to limit the scope of exemption clauses; and

(e)   the possibility (in at least a vestigial form) of a common law test of reasonableness.

Before we proceed to consider each of these in turn it is necessary to determine the extent to which each of these common law rules have survived or continue in importance following the enactment of the Unfair Contract Terms Act 1977. The answer in each case is different.

The incorporation rules at common law remain important for two reasons, first, to determine whether the clause is included as part of a contract. If the exemption is not properly incorporated into the contract then it may be ignored as contract law, although it may nevertheless be effective to exclude liability in negligence. Incorporation is also a factor under the Unfair Contract Terms Act 1977. The old common law case law still provides useful guidance on the question of whether it is reasonable to incorporate the term into the contract. The strict construction applied by the courts to avoid having to apply a particularly harsh exemption, the so called *contra proferentum* rule, is now less important where the 1977 Act applies, since the courts now have a wide discretion on the various factors in the test of reasonableness. Nevertheless, the courts still regularly adopt a literal or strict approach even under the Act and of course many contracts fall outside the statute. The common law case law on the rules of interpretation therefore remains highly relevant. The doctrine of fundamental breach was formally laid to rest by the Unfair Contract Act ss 3 and 9. The old doctrine may have life in it yet in relation to the question of reasonableness under the 1977 Act as we shall discuss.[4] The doctrine of privity of contract may now be circumvented as a result of the Contracts (Rights of Third Parties) Act 1999.[5] Privity may no longer be used to strike out a third party exemption clause if the parties to the original contract so wish. The relationship between the 1999 Act and the Unfair Contract Terms Act 1977 is discussed elsewhere.[6] Finally, the common law rules remain in force where the 1977 Act does not apply. Apart from the types of contract excluded by Schedule 1 of the Act, there are also contracts which fall outside of the Act because they are neither in "written standard terms of business" nor does either party "deal as consumer". Many important commercial agreements between parties of equal bargaining power fall outside the Act. There are indications that a common law test of reasonableness remains a possibility in this area. In conclusion, is that the common law remains relevant particularly in relation to many contracts between businesses.

[4] Discussed later p. 280. See also Chap. 17.
[5] See Chap. 10.
[6] See Chaps 10 and 17.

THE INCORPORATION OF EXEMPTION CLAUSES AT COMMON LAW

The effect of signature

16.5   Signature normally operates as definitive of agreement to the terms of a written contract. In *L'Estrange v. F Graucob Ltd*[7] it was held that the terms were binding even if the signatory Harriet L'Estrange, owner of a café in Llandudno, had neither read nor understood the conditions. The only exceptions were misrepresentation, a mistakenly signed document or one which was only a memorandum of a previous oral agreement which did not include the clause. What is now described as the rule in *L'Estrange v. Graucob* goes back to earlier law. In *The Luna*,[8] the Master of a Dutch fishing vessel the *Luna*, who spoke very little English and could not read the language well, signed an agreement with the tug *Kingston* to tow his vessel from the mouth of Humber into Hull for 15 shillings (75p). The parties orally agreed the terms and a document was signed. The printed conditions provided that the owners of the vessel undertook to indemnify the tug owners against all liabilities and costs and changes in respect of any actions that might be brought, in performing the towage. The Dutch master of the vessel was not aware that printed conditions contained this indemnity clause when he signed the contract. The tug towed the *Luna* into another vessel, the *Frances and Jane*. It was held that even the inability to read English could not avail him. The contract was binding although he could not have understood the terms when he signed the document. The rule is linked to objective theory and is really a practical one to avoid allowing parties to deny documents clearly bearing their signature. Hill J. held that the master was bound by the contract whether he had read it or not and, as their agent, the owners of the *Luna* were also bound.

(1) The modern approach to restrictive or onerous terms

16.6   Although signature normally leads to a party being bound by the terms of a contract, a different approach to signature is now developing both through case law and under statute. In *Harvey v. Ventilatoren-Fabrik Oelde GmbH*[9] the Court held that a set of printed conditions had not been incorporated because, according to Kerr L.J., "[v]iewed objectively, a reasonable person in the position of the plaintiff could naturally conclude that the printed material on the back, which he did not understand, could be regarded as irrelevant". The plaintiff, a scrap metal dealer in Fleetwood, Lancashire, contracted with the German defendants for two machines for his business. The contract was made orally and the negotiations were in English as the plaintiff could not speak German. The machines were defective and the plaintiff claimed they were unfit for purpose. The issue was where the contract was formed and whether the official referee was correct to allow the plaintiff to issue a writ and serve it on the plaintiff in Germany. The oral agreement was confirmed by a contract in writing. There were two sets of terms (a common occurrence known as the "battle of the forms")[10] and (unnecessarily) the plaintiff signed both of them. The terms returned to the defendants contained, in German, a jurisdiction

---

[7]   [1934] 2 K.B. 394. By an irony of history, counsel for the defendant, who successfully relied on the exemption clause, was A. T. Denning. As a judge, Lord Denning spent 40 years seeking to control exemption clauses of the sort applied in the *L'Estrange* case.
[8]   [1920] p. 22.
[9]   [1989] Tr L.R. 138.
[10]   See Chap. 5.

clause that disputes would be settled by the court at the town of Oelde. The set retained by the plaintiff had nothing at all printed on the back of it.

The issue was both the construction of the document and the effect of signature. The Court of Appeal held that even when the document was signed there was scope for inquiry as to whether the person signing was misled and whether this negatived his assent to one or more terms of the document. The judgment applied two of the exemptions in *L'Estrange v. Graucob,* that there was misrepresentation and that the writing did not reflect the oral agreement between the parties.[11] The Court held that "since one set of documents was blank on the reverse, he [the plaintiff] was entitled to assume that the printed matter on the other set, which he did not understand and which had never previously been discussed between the parties, was not intended to form part of the accepted orders which the documents purported to acknowledge."

Given the exceptions and the development of different approaches it is probably better   **16.7**
to say that signature is no longer automatically binding in many transactions. For instance, some types of contract, *e.g.* timeshare agreements, give the consumer a "cooling off" period to read the small print or repent of their bargain. The biggest exception occurs where the Unfair Contract Terms Act 1977 applies. Under the Act it is no longer reasonable to rely solely on a party's signature as indicating agreement to all the terms.[12] The treatment of signature under the Act is therefore closer to that in the following case, where a party's signature was held not to be binding because the proper procedural steps had not been taken to bring the exemption clause to the customer's attention. In the Canadian case of *Tilden Rent-a-Car v. Clendenning*[13] the defendant rented a car at Vancouver Airport. The contract was made at speed with a view to delivering the car to the customer as quickly as possible. The conditions in the small print of the agreement provided that the vehicle was not to be driven in breach of the terms of the agreement, on the back of which was stated that the car must not be driven by anyone who had consumed any amount of alcohol, not just within the legal limit. The defendant signed the document without reading and paid the premium for insurance against damage. The car was damaged while the defendant was driving it and it transpired that he had consumed some alcohol. The Ontario Court of Appeal refused to hold him bound by the signature. It was held that this could only be relied upon as manifesting agreement when it was reasonable for the party relying on the signed document to believe that the person signing really did agree to the document's contents. In a car rental contract where speed was of the essence, onerous and unusual printed terms ought to be brought to the others party's attention by more reasonable measures. Mere signature was not enough. This might involve special notice by pointing out the terms in question to the other party. This is close to the test for incorporation in relation to exemption clauses under the reasonableness test of the Unfair Contract Terms Act 1977[14] and also to the requirement of knowledge of onerous terms suggested by Sir Thomas Bingham's approach in *Interfoto Picture Library v. Stilletto Visual Programmes.*[15]

---

[11] The earlier case of *Roe v. R. A. Naylor Ltd* (1917) 1 K.B. 712 was considered, but the plaintiff was not excused on this ground because here there were two sets of conditions to sign.
[12] We discuss this in Chap. 17.
[13] (1978) 83 D.L.R. (3d) 400.
[14] See Chap. 17.
[15] [1989] Q.B. 433, see Chap. 14 and later p. 273.

16.8   The courts are nevertheless reluctant to abandon the signature rule entirely or to undermine the importance of signature. Dillon L.J. in *Interfoto* noted that the situation in which one party signs and then contracts on the other party's standard terms of business is notoriously one where the contract contains a fictional element of consent, which nevertheless has to be accepted by contract law in the interests of having a coherently objective scheme. Signature is the manifestation of objective agreement which still forms one of the cornerstones of contract law.[16] There is also a view that signature of a document means that a party is prevented from denying it's validity or knowledge of the contents of the contract by the doctrine of estoppel by representation.[17] The judicial basis for this argument is the judgment of Blackburn J. in *Harris v. Great Western Railway.*[18] However, the correctness of the estoppel approach was questioned by Lord Devlin in *McCutcheon v. David MacBrayne Ltd*[19] suggesting that this view be re-examined by the House of Lords at a later date. Lord Devlin believed the estoppel view was wrong.

16.9   For a signature to be effective to incorporate terms and to bind a party, the document signed must be regarded as contractual. A mere receipt or piece of paper for some other purpose is not enough. In *Grogan v. Robin Meredith Plant Hire*,[20] a civil engineering firm were laying pipes in Wales.[21] Their site agent hired a machine and driver from Meredith Plant hire, and each week the site agent signed the drivers "time sheet", a paper which kept a record of the hours that he had worked. The time sheet contained the words "all hire undertaken under CPA [Contractors Plant Association] conditions. Copies available on request," above the space for signature. At the time of hiring no terms had been mentioned and there had been no suggestion that the contract was on CPA conditions. Pill J. held that the contract had been varied by the site agent's signature of the time sheets and so the conditions applied. The Court of Appeal disagreed. The relevant question to ask was whether the time sheet was within the class of document which the party receiving it knew contained, or which a reasonable person would expect to contain, relevant contractual conditions.

In this case documents such as a time sheet, invoice or statement of account did not normally have contractual force to make or vary a contract. The purpose of time sheets was to record the performance of the contract by one of the parties, not to contain or evidence the terms of a contract. Time sheets were administrative or accounting documents which did not have the power to incorporate the CPA conditions into an existing contract. A similar rule applies to the incorporation of terms generally. A ticket, in many cases, is merely evidence of payment. So for instance, the till receipt you receive at the check-out in a supermarket listing items purchased and prices paid is there to provide proof of purchase. A ticket is not a contractual document *per se*. It becomes so if the ticket contains or refers to contractual terms of which reasonable steps have been taken to bring the conditions to the other party's attention. Receipts have a practical purpose in that in most shops insist on them if you wish to return items purchased or complain

---

[16] See Spencer, "Signature, Consent and The Rule in *L'Estrange v. Graucob*" [1973] C.L.J. 103; Samek, "The Objective Theory of Contract and The Rule in *L'Estrange v. Graucob*" (1974) 52 Can BR 351; and also Chap. 2.

[17] See Chap. 9.

[18] (1876) 1 Q.B.D. 515.

[19] [1964] 1 W.L.R. 125.

[20] [1996] 53 Con L.R. 87; 15 Tr. L.R. 371.

[21] Singleton (1996) 15 Tr. L.R. 323.

about faulty or defective goods. The receipt provides evidence of a contract with the retailer and may be vital to the successful outcome of the consumer's complaint.

(2) Oral statements varying written terms

If an oral statement by one of the parties misrepresents or varies a written exemption **16.10** clause then the oral statement supersedes the writing. This is a further exception to *L'Estrange v. Graucob* and also to the parol evidence rule.[22] In *Curtis v. Chemical Cleaning and Dyeing Co.*,[23] the plaintiff took a white satin wedding dress trimmed with beads and sequins to a firm of dry cleaners, the defendants. She was given a piece of paper headed "Receipt" and asked to sign. On asking the reason for her signature being required, the plaintiff was told by the shop assistant that the shop did not accept liability for specific risks including damage to beads and sequins. The "receipt" actually contained written terms that the cleaners accepted no liability at all. The Court of Appeal held that the cleaners could not rely on the written terms because spoken words had misrepresented the written terms.[24]

The rule described has led to the drafting of "entire agreement" or "watertight" clauses in contracts which seek to exclude other evidence, including oral statements by employees at the time of formation of the contract.[25] In consumer contracts such clauses run the risk of being regarded as unfair and may be unenforceable under the Unfair Terms in Consumer Contracts Regulations 1999. In commercial contracts entire agreement clauses are widespread, and in most cases, enforceable.[26]

Unsigned contracts and notices excluding liability

(1) Tickets and contractual documents

If no document is signed but a party wishes to incorporate written terms into the agree- **16.11** ment between the parties, they must take reasonable steps to bring the writing to the other party's attention or knowledge. The burden of showing that the terms have been incorporated is on the party seeking to rely upon them. An objective standard is applied, based upon the average person, not upon the particular individual with their own characteristics, peculiarities or knowledge of the facts. The requirement is on the party to take reasonable steps, and if they did so, it does not matter that the plaintiff did not in fact read or understand the terms if reasonably sufficient notice was given. If the document only looks on it's face like a receipt, then greater steps have to be taken to bring the terms to the other party's attention.

The leading case which established these rules is *Parker v. S.E. Railway Co.*[27] in which the plaintiffs each deposited bags at a station cloakroom of the defendants' railway station and paid 2 pence.[28] The plaintiffs' luggage was lost while in the defendant's possession.

---

[22] See Chap. 12.
[23] [1951] 1 K.B. 805.
[24] See also *J. Evans and Son (Portsmouth) Ltd v. Andrea Merzario Ltd* [1976] 2 All E.R. 930.
[25] Discussed in Chap. 12.
[26] *Watford Electronics v. Sanderson CFL Ltd, The Times*, March 9, 2001 (reported at first instance [2000] 2 All E.R. (Comm) 984) and *Inntrepreneur Pub Company v. East Crown Ltd* [2000] 2 Lloyd's Rep. 611.
[27] (1877) 2 C.P.D. 416.
[28] There were in fact two actions, one by Parker and another by a plaintiff named Gabell.

Parker received a paper ticket, on one side of which was written a number, a date, printed words as to when the office would be open and the words "See back". On the reverse of the ticket were several terms including one which stated that "The company will not be responsible for any package exceeding the value of £10". The Court of Appeal held that the correct question for the jury should have been "whether the company did that which was reasonably sufficient to give the plaintiff notice of the condition". The Court of Appeal overturned the judgment at first instance and ordered a retrial. The railway company had done sufficient in the circumstances to bring the conditions to the plaintiff's attention. This is probably still good enough today. By having terms and conditions of travel at railway stations available on demand, the train operating companies are taking reasonable steps to bring their standard terms to the notice of members of the travelling public.

16.12   Mellish L.J. in *Parker v. S.E. Railway Co.*[29] stated that the correct approach was to ask three questions. First, whether the person receiving the ticket saw or knew that there was writing on the ticket. If they did not, then they were not bound by the conditions. Secondly, if the answer was that they knew there was writing, and knew, or believed, that the writing contained conditions, they were bound by the conditions. Finally, the Court had to ask whether, as a question of fact, the other party had been given "reasonable notice that the writing contained conditions". The conditions, including the exemption clause, to the attention of the plaintiff. By handing in his bag and tendering his money, the plaintiff made an offer. The ticket with the conditions was not an unqualified acceptance but a counter-offer, so when Parker took the ticket and left his luggage at the cloakroom he had accepted this counter-offer by conduct. The application of the offer and acceptance rule here has not gone unchallenged.[30]

Other ticket cases involving railway companies over the years have largely depended on their facts. In *Thomson v. LMS Railway*[31] the words on the face of the ticket were "Excursion, for conditions see back". On the back was written "Issued subject to the conditions in the company's timetables, notices, and excursions and other bills". This was held to be sufficient even though in the case of a timetable this would have had to be purchased in those days. Nowadays free booklets are supposed to be available on request at railway stations. In *Parker* the Court took the view that the railway company was entitled to make certain "assumptions" about the person depositing luggage with them, that the person could read and understand English, and that the customer paid "such attention to what he is about as may reasonably be expected from a person in such a transaction". The standard of care required was only that of the average man or woman in the street. The railway had to "take mankind as they find them, and if what they do is sufficient to inform people in general that the ticket contains conditions . . . a particular plaintiff ought not to be in a better position than other persons on account of exceptional ignorance or stupidity or carelessness". There is no higher standard to cope with special categories unless the circumstances demand it, *e.g.* in foreign languages at a port or airport. In *Henderson v. Stevenson*[32] the steps taken were held not to be reasonably

[29] (1877) 2 C.P.D. 416 (at p. 423).
[30] For another analysis of offer and acceptance in a ticket case see *Thornton v. Shoe Lane Parking* [197] 2 Q.B. 163 (See Chap. 2)
[31] [1930] 1 K.B. 41.
[32] (1875) LR 2 H.L. Sc. App. 470.

sufficient. The ticket in question given to the passenger on boarding a ship merely stated on the front "Dublin to Whitehaven". On the reverse of the ticket were words exempting the company for loss of luggage. It was held that the conditions on the back did not form part of the contract of passage. The plaintiff had neither seen these, nor had his attention been properly directed to them, so the Court held that the plaintiff had not agreed to their incorporation. Modern train and bus passenger tickets routinely state on their face that they are "subject to conditions". This minimum phrase is probably sufficient in most cases.

(2) Signs and notices excluding liability

Exclusions of liability are commonly displayed on signs or notices. This may be an effective disclaimer of liability if reasonable steps are taken to bring the notice to the attention of those affected, either in negligence or by contract. If a contract is formed the notice must be visible before the contract is made. In *Olley v. Marlborough Court Ltd*[33] the defendants were owners of the Marlborough Court Hotel in Lancaster Gate, London. A notice in the hotel bedroom stated that: "The proprietors will not hold themselves responsible for articles lost or stolen unless handed to the management for safe custody." While the porter in charge for the day was cleaning a bust of the Duke of Marlborough at the foot of the staircase, a thief broke into the plaintiff's room and stole furs, jewellery and articles of personal clothing belonging to Mrs Olley. It was held that the terms of the notice in the room did not form part of the contract made between the guests and the proprietor of the hotel. The contract had been made before the guests had an opportunity to see the notice and hence the defendants were liable.[34] Similarly, in *Chapelton v. Barry Urban DC*[35] the plaintiff went to the beach in South Wales where, beside a stack of deck chairs, was a sign stating "Hire of chairs 2d, per session of 3 hours". The plaintiff paid his 2 pence to an attendant who came round and gave him a piece of paper on the back of which was stated that the council would not be liable for any accident or damage arising from the hire of the chair. The chair broke and the plaintiff was injured. It was held that the words on the ticket did not protect the defendants, as they came after the contract was formed. The plaintiff was entitled to assume that only the words on the notice formed the terms of the contract. It is interesting to note that the court treated the notice as an offer not merely as an invitation to treat. This is a different rule than that applying to similar statements that goods are for sale.[36] It is no longer possible to exclude liability for personal injuries under the Unfair Contract Terms Act 1977 s. 2(1).[37]

A notice may also have a direct effect in forming a unilateral contract with a customer, if it is construed as an offer which the customer accepts. In *Bowerman v. ABTA*[38] the plaintiff went on a holiday organised by her school. A notice displayed in the travel agents set out the terms of a scheme to protect against the bankruptcy of travel agents.

16.13

---

[33] [1949] 1 K.B. 532.
[34] The strict liability of innkeepers for their guests' property is one of the oldest forms of liability in the common law going back to the Middle Ages. Liability may be limited to a total sum of £100, and £50 per item by the Hotel Proprietors Act 1956. See Berry (1981) N.L.J. 795.
[35] [1940] 1 K.B. 532.
[36] See Chap. 3.
[37] See Chap. 17.
[38] [1995] 145 N.L.J. 1815. See also Chaps 2 and 11.

It was held by the Court of Appeal that the notice created a contract between the plaintiff and the defendants, there being sufficient intention to create legal relations and also offer and acceptance. The Court of Appeal found different grounds for holding, but Hobhouse L.J. took the view that the notice was an offer to a member of the public, stating that "it satisfies the criteria for a unilateral contract and contains promises which are sufficiently clear to be capable of legal enforcement. The principles established in *Carlill* apply." Like *Carlill*, the *Bowerman* example has to be handled with care. It is a rare specimen dependant on it's own unusual facts.

(3) Even a prominently displayed notice may not be sufficient.

16.14   In *Vine v. Waltham Forest LBC*[39] a plaintiff returning from a hospital appointment got out of her car to be sick in a car park and when she returned to the vehicle found that it had been clamped. She had to pay £100 to have the car returned. The Court of Appeal agreed with the judge's conclusion that even though the notice was clearly visible, the plaintiff had not read it and therefore had not agreed to it's terms. She was entitled to recover, in restitution,[40] for the money paid to get back the car. The action here was in tort for wrongful interference with goods, rather than an exemption of liability in contract. The legal context of the notice was therefore different.

Special notice of "onerous or unusual" terms

16.15   The courts are slowly moving towards a rule that "special notice" may be required for certain types of term. This means that if a term or notice is onerous or unusual, greater steps may be required to incorporate it into a contract or give effect to it's provisions.[41] In *Spurling v. Bradshaw*[42] Denning L.J. called this the "red hand test": "Some clauses I have seen would need to be printed in red ink on the face of the document with a red hand pointing to it before the notice could be held to be sufficient." Although precedent can be found for such a rule, it cannot yet be said to amount to a general principle. In *Circle Freight International Ltd v. Medeast Gulf Exports Ltd*[43] Taylor L.J. stated that normally it is sufficient if adequate notice is given identifying and relying upon the conditions and if they are available on request. However, stricter requirements may apply if the condition or any of them are particularly onerous or unusual. In *Interfoto Picture Library v. Stiletto Visual Programmes*[44] the Court of Appeal held that greater steps were required for the incorporation of an onerous holding charge provision.[45] Similarly, in *Thornton v. Shoe Lane Parking Ltd*[46] Megaw L.J.[47] stated the question of incorporation should be based on the notice of the particular condition on which the defendant wished to rely, rather than consideration of the conditions in general.

Until recently, special notice of individual terms has not been required.[48] In *Interfoto*,

---

[39] [2000] 4 All E.R. 169.
[40] See Chap. 26.
[41] See MacDonald (1992) Legal Studies 277.
[42] [1956] 1 W.L.R. 461 (at p. 466).
[43] [1988] 2 Lloyd's Rep. 427 (at p. 433).
[44] See Dillon L.J. [1989] Q.B. 433 (at p. 437).
[45] Discussed in Chap. 14.
[46] [1971] 2 Q.B. 163.
[47] At pp. 172–73.
[48] See however *Tilden Rent-a-Car v. Clendenning* (earlier p. 269).

(a non-exemption clause case) Bingham L.J. stated that: "The defendants are not to be relieved of liability because they did not read the condition, although doubtless they did not; but in my judgment they are to be relieved because the plaintiffs did not do what was necessary to draw this unreasonable and extortionate clause fairly to their attention."[49] This may be a pointer to the future direction of the common law. There is, however, less need now for the courts to put too a strained meaning on the traditional incorporation rules as a result of the Unfair Contract Terms Act 1977, given that the reasonableness test, where applicable, may be used to avoid the incorporation of unusual or onerous terms.[50] In *AEG (UK) Ltd v. Logic Resource Ltd*,[51] the Court of Appeal found on alternative grounds that an exemption clause could not be relied upon by the plaintiffs. Two members of the Court of Appeal, Hirst and Waite L.J.J. based their judgments on the common law, finding that the clause in question was not incorporated because it was unusual or onerous, and applying the reasoning of *Interfoto v. Stiletto Visual Programmes*, that there had to be a greater effort to incorporate such terms. According to Hirst L.J.: "the defendants had been confronted with Hobson's choice in their contractual terms. The case fell within the *Interfoto* class".[51a] The judge had failed to apply this principle and had also treated the clause in isolation and not in context. The clause had not been incorporated because insufficient steps had been taken to bring it to the other party's attention. Waite L.J. agreed, holding that the clause was "a particularly onerous or unusual condition which AEG as suppliers were under a duty to draw fairly and reasonably to the attention of Logic as buyers; a duty which was not discharged by the generalised conditions". Hobhouse L.J. rejected the use of an extended incorporation test at common law but held that the contents of the clause, imposing on the buyers an obligation to pay for the cost of returning the goods, were unreasonable under the Unfair Contract Terms Act 1977. This was "extremely onerous, and also unusual in the absence of any evidence that it is a standard or common term".

Hobhouse L.J. warned against too wide a use of any special notice test stating that: **16.16**

> "It is desirable as a matter of principle to keep what was said in the *Interfoto* case within its proper bounds. A wide range of clauses are commonly incorporated into contracts by general words. If it is to be the policy of English law that in every case those clauses are to be gone through with, in effect, a toothcomb to see whether they were entirely usual and entirely desirable in the particular contract, then one is completely distorting the contractual relationship between the parties and the ordinary mechanisms of making contracts. It will introduce uncertainty into the law of contract. In the past there may have been a tendency to introduce more strict criteria but this is no longer necessary in view of the Unfair Contract Terms Act."[51b]

Hobhouse L.J. found that the clause was unreasonable under the 1977 Act.

On the other hand, in *O'Brien v. MGN Ltd*[51c] the rules of a scratchcard game were

---

[49]   [1989] Q.B. 433 (at p. 445).
[50]   See Chap. 17.
[51]   [1995] CCH Commercial Law Reports 265. See Bradgate, "Unreasonable Standard Terms" (1997) 60 M.L.R. 582.
[51a]   At p. 278.
[51b]   At p. 278.
[51c]   *The Times*, August 8, 2001.

incorporated by reference in the newspaper which organised the competition. The *Interfoto* test was applied but satisfied since the rules governing a "windfall prize" were neither "enorous" nor "outlandish".[51d]

A consistent course of dealings between the parties

16.17   If the parties have dealt with each other on the same terms on a number of previous occasions, it is reasonable to suppose that each has had the opportunity to know the terms of their contract. Thus the terms can be incorporated by a "course of dealings". How many dealings and in what circumstances depends on the facts of the case. In *Hardwick Game Farm v. Suffolk Agricultural Poultry Produces Association*[52] the parties had dealt with each other three or four times a month for three years and a "sold note" was sent to the buyer containing terms. This was sufficient to incorporate the terms even if the buyer had never actually read them. On the other hand, in *Spurling (J) Ltd v. Bradshaw*[53] the defendant deposited eight barrels of orange juice with the defendants who owned a warehouse. The invoice stated that goods were stored at "owners risk". A further document stated that conditions on the reverse side were incorporated into the contract. The clause in question[54] exempted the warehousemen from liability for "loss damage or deterioration [of the goods] however, whensoever and wheresoever occasioned" (a clause unlikely to satisfy the test of reasonableness today). The clause was designed to apply even if caused by negligence or the wrongful act of the defendants. The orange juice was ruined by bad storage. It was held that the clause applied because the defendants had received similar terms in a number of previous transactions. They had adequate opportunity to take careful note of the terms, so were deemed to contract on similar conditions. The exemption clause applied by "constructive" notice, *i.e.* the defendants ought to have been aware of them.

16.18   In *British Crane Hire Corporation Ltd v. Ipswich Plant Hire Ltd*[55] conditions which had been used previously were incorporated on the "common understanding of the parties". The parties were in business and had dealt with each other on previous occasions on similar terms. The courts are less willing to incorporate terms on this basis in consumer contracts. In *Hollier v. Rambler Motors (AMC) Ltd*[56] Salmon L.J. declined to imply a term into an oral consumer contract on the strength of a course of dealing which consisted of "at most three or four transactions over a period of five years". The course of dealings must be consistent. If the course of dealings is not the same on every occasion then the rule does not apply. In the Scottish case of *McCutcheon v. David MacBrayne Ltd*[57] the pursuer's car sank, along with the ferry the *Lochiel*, travelling from Islay to the Scottish mainland. The pursuer had travelled before and also shipped cattle on board. When he and his brother in law, Mr McSporran, booked their passage

---

[51d] The incorporation issue was described by Hale L.J. as "an excellent question in contract law examination. Like all good questions, it is easy to ask, but difficult to answer".
[52] [1969] 2 A.C. 31.
[53] [1956] 1 W.L.R. 461.
[54] Notoriously referred to by Lord Denning in his "Red Hand test" (see earlier para. 16.15).
[55] [1975] Q.B. 303.
[56] [1972] 1 All E.R. 399.
[57] [1964] 1 Lloyd's Rep. 16.

he was not asked to sign the usual "risk note" as on previous occasions. The House of Lords held that there was no consistent course of dealings, as on the day in question when the accident occurred, the pursuer was offered an oral contract without reference to the conditions. Lord Pearce stated that: "It is the consistency of a course of conduct which gives rise to the implication that in similar circumstances a similar contractual result will follow. When the conduct is not consistent, there is no reason why it should still produce an invariable contractual result."[58] [59]

THE CONSTRUCTION OF EXEMPTION CLAUSES *CONTRA PROFERENTEM*

The rule of interpretation adopted to deal with exemption clauses is that the courts should construe each term narrowly against the party seeking to rely upon them. This is illustrated by *Andrews Brothers (Bournemouth) Ltd v. Singer and Co. Ltd*[60] in which an exemption clause read ". . . all conditions, warranties and liabilities implied by statute, common law or otherwise are excluded". This was held not cover an express term in the contract that the vehicle in question was a "new Singer car", when in fact this was untrue.[60a] This narrow view of construction was necessary in the old days to limit the scope of exemption clauses. Ambiguities would be resolved against the user of the standard terms, and a narrow meaning would usually be given to words and expressions in the contract. The Latin expression *contra proferentem* means that the term is to be interpreted against the party seeking to rely upon it, if the meaning or effect of the term is in doubt. So, for instance, if words of exclusion were listed in the contract, they would be seen as final and exhaustive and other words would not be added to the list. A literal interpretation of the clause would be adopted. The courts would also adopt their own meaning on occasion based on the true intention of the parties. The construction rules were described by Lord Denning in *George Mitchell (Chesterhall) Ltd v. Finney Lock Seeds*[61] as the "secret weapon used to strike down the idol of freedom of contract". The weapon was called "the true construction of the contract." According to Lord Denning, the courts "used it so as to depart from the natural meaning of the words of the exemption clause and to put upon them a strained and unnatural construction". Since the Unfair Contract Terms Act 1977, there is far less need for the courts to adopt such a rigorous attitude to the construction of exemption clauses. The reasonableness test allows the courts a power to interpret the substance of exemption clauses without recourse to special or distorted rules of construction. The need for too much use of straining of language is not necessary where the Act applies. The modern approach is to give words in commercial contracts their ordinary and natural meaning if possible.[62] Of course, in

16.19

---

[58] At p. 27.

[59] See Evans (1964) 27 M.L.R. 354. The theory being an implied term that the contract remains the same on each occasion (see Chap. 12).

[60] [1934] 1 K.B. 17.

[60a] On implied terms in contracts for the sale of goods, see Chap. 12.

[61] [1983] Q.B. 284 (at p. 297). This was the former Master of the Roll's final judgment, delivered in July 1982.

[62] See Lord Diplock in *Photo Production v Securicor Transport Ltd* [1980] A.C. 827.

consumer contracts a narrower view of the scope of the exemption clause may still be preferred.[63]

16.20   The courts are generally unwilling to allow a party to exclude liability for his or her own negligence unless express words are clearly used. In *White v. John Warwick and Co.*[64] the plaintiff hired a tricycle and was injured when the saddle tipped up and threw him on to the road. The contract exempted the defendant from liability for "any personal injuries". It was held that the words only exempted from liability for breach of contract on his part, *i.e.* breach of an obligation to maintain the machine fit for purpose. The alternative of liability in the tort for negligence remained, and this had not been excluded. The common expression "owners risk" is often found in car parks and cloak-rooms and means that liability in negligence is excluded. This is usually sufficient to exempt from liability in negligence. In *Canada Steamship Lines Ltd v. The King*,[65] in an appeal from Quebec, Lord Morton of Henryton in the Privy Council said that if negligence was expressly excluded, effect had to be given to that provision. However, he went on to state[66] that: "If there is no express reference to negligence, the court must consider whether the words used are wide enough, in their ordinary meaning, to cover negligence. If a doubt arises at this point, it must be resolved against the *proferens*": He then stated the basic *contra proferens* position "in cases of doubt the contract is interpreted against him who has stipulated and in favour of him who has contracted the obligation". If the words used are wide enough for the above purpose, the court must then consider whether "the head of damage may be based on some ground other than that of negligence".[67] However, the other ground must not be so "fanciful or remote" that the party relying on the clause cannot be supposed to have desired protection against it. The existence of a possible head of damages, other than that of negligence, was fatal to the *proferens* even if the words used were *prima facie* enough to cover negligence on the part of the party's servants. Lord Morton cited *Alderslade v. Hendon Laundry Ltd*[68] as authority. In this case, the plaintiff took ten Irish linen handkerchiefs to be cleaned by the defendants. The terms of the contract contained a clause limiting liability to 20 times the maximum charge. The handkerchiefs were lost but the Court of Appeal held that there was a duty on the laundry to take reasonable care of the items. This was a duty of care in negligence and since there was no other liability which could attach, the clause was therefore effective to exclude the defendants' liability.

16.21   Indemnity clauses (another type of exemption clause) by which one party promises to meet the liabilities, expenses and claims of the other party under the contract were discussed in *EE Caledonia v. Orbit Valve plc.*,[69] a case involving the aftermath of the North Sea *Piper Alpha* tragedy in 1988 when many workers were killed as a result of an explosion. The Court of Appeal considered Lord Morton's three rules in *Canada Steamship* (above). The third rule was "simply an aid in the process of construction". The ordinary

---

[63] A quite different régime is introduced to provide for "fairness" under Reg. 7(2) of the Unfair Terms Regulations 1999 which provides: ". . . if there is any doubt about the meaning of a written term, the interpretation most favourable to the consumer shall prevail". This is in effect the old common law *contra proferentem* rule of construction. (See Chap. 15.)

[64] [1953] 2 All E.R.

[65] [1952] A.C. 192.

[66] At p. 208.

[67] Interpreting the Civil Code of Lower Canada, but also the English common law rule.

[68] [1945] 1 K.B. 189.

[69] [1995] 1 All E.R. 174.

meaning of the words in their contractual setting was "the dominant factor" according to Steyn L.J.[70] In *Deepak Fertilisers and Petrochemical Corporation v. Davy McKee (London) Ltd*[71] the Court of Appeal adopted the view of the House of Lords in *Photo Production* that courts should avoid a strained construction of exemption clauses and give them their natural and ordinary meaning if possible. The Court of Appeal nevertheless applied a *contra proferentum* approach to the phrase "any and all liabilities" which was stated to be a "very wide" phrase; "very clear words must be used in order to bring liability for express contractual obligations within the scope of an indemnity clause".

The construction of limitation clauses

Limitations of liability are less narrowly construed than exemption clauses. The former **16.22** are more likely to be given their ordinary and natural meaning since there is a greater possibility they represent the intention of the parties, particularly in commercial contracts. The leading case is *Ailsa Craig Fishing Co. Ltd v. Malvern Fishing Co. Ltd*[72] in which the defendants made a contract to guard two fishing boats in Aberdeen harbour. The House of Lords held that limitation clauses in the contract were wide enough to cover liability in negligence. The clause had to be construed "in the context of the contract as a whole, it must be most clearly and unambiguously expressed, and in such a contract as this, must be construed *contra proferentum*".[73] However, the courts should not go too far according to Lord Wilberforce: "One must not strive to create ambiguities by strained construction. The relevant words must be given, if possible, their natural, plain meaning.[74] Lord Wilberforce added that: "Clauses of limitation are not regarded by the courts with the same hostility as clauses of exclusion: this is because they must be related to other contractual terms, in particular to the risks to which the defending party may be exposed, the remuneration which he receives, and possibly also the opportunity of the other party to insure".

In *EE Caledonia Ltd* (see earlier) Steyn L.J. stated the view, *obiter dicta*, that the law takes an "indulgent attitude" to limitation clauses compared with *exemption* and indemnity clauses.[75] The House of Lords confirmed this approach to limitation clauses in *Bovis Construction (Scotland) Ltd v. Whatlings Construction Ltd*[76] a case involving the construction of the Royal Concert Hall in Glasgow. Limitation clauses were to be construed with a degree of strictness, but less narrowly than exemption or indemnity clauses. The analogous concept of a limitation based on time period rather than monetary value was considered in *BHP Petroleum v. British Steel plc.*[77] in which the plaintiffs ordered an oil pipeline to be built in North Wales, the contract excluding all liability except for defects becoming apparent within two years of purchase. The High Court held the clause was effective to exclude the liability in question. Rix J. stated that the Court should look at

---

[70] At p. 181.
[71] [1999] B.L.R. 41.
[72] [1983] 1 Lloyd's Rep. 183.
[73] At p. 184.
[74] At p. 184.
[75] [1995] I All E.R. 174 (p. 179).
[76] 1995 SLT 1339.
[77] [1999] 2 All E.R. (Comm) 544.

the wider construction of the clause and consider the contract as a whole. The principles of construction applicable to a limitation clause could equally apply to limitations of time periods. Reliance may also be a factor in the extent to which a court will allow a party to have the protection of a limitation clause. In *Watford Electronics Ltd v. Sanderson CFL Ltd*[78] it was held that in determining the scope of a limitation of liability in a contract which contained an "entire agreement clause"[79], no statements or misrepresentations had been relied upon by either party in making the contract. The extent of the reliance in acknowledgment of this undertaking was an important element in the construction of the limitation clause.

Exemptions of liability for fraud

16.23   An exemption clause will not be construed as applying to fraud at common law. In *S. Pearson and Son Ltd v. The Lord Mayor and Dublin Corporation*[80] the Privy Council held that exemptions could only be construed on the basis of "contemplated honesty" on both sides. They could not therefore apply in relation to fraudulent representations. In *Motis Exports Ltd v. Dampskibsselskabet AF 1912,*[81] Court of Appeal held that a clause in a bill of lading, exempting the shippers from liability for loss or damage to goods in their possession before loading or after discharge, did not cover deliberately delivering up forged documents.

THE DOCTRINE OF FUNDAMENTAL BREACH

16.24   The origin of the idea of fundamental breach is to be found in *Chanter v. Hopkins*[82] in which the defendant, Richard Hopkins, of the Vine Inn, at St Ives in Huntingdon ordered "Chanter's Smoke Consuming Furnace" from the plaintiff, an invention patented by the latter. The furnace was delivered but found to be of no use for it's intended purpose in the brewing of beer so it was returned as being unsuitable. Since he had ordered it, the defendant was bound to pay, having taken the risk that it might not be workable. In the judgment a seed was sown by Lord Abinger C.B.,[83] that "If a man offers to buy peas of another, and he sends him beans, he does not perform his contract; but that is not a warranty; there is no warranty that he should sell him peas; the contract is to sell peas, and if he sends him anything else in their stead, it is a non performance of it". A new category of breach developed out of this dictum. A party who performed it in an entirely extraneous way stepped outside of the contract. This was non-performance or a fundamental breach. The idea was rooted in English tradition that somehow there was a core obligation, the consideration for the contract, which was more fundamental then any condition or warranty. A fundamental breach was therefore a total failure of consideration by another name.[84]

[78] *The Times*, March 9, 2001, reported at first instance [2000] 2 All E.R. (Comm) 984.
[79] See Chap. 12.
[80] [1907] A.C. 351.
[81] [2000] 1 All E.R. (Comm) 91. (See also p. 282.)
[82] (1838) 4 M and W 399, 150 E.R. 1484.
[83] At p. 1487.
[84] See Chap. 26.

Shipping law later took up this idea in the twentieth century with the rule that if a ship deviated from it's agreed route, the charterers had stepped out of the contract and any clauses in the contract exempting liability could no longer be relied upon. Marrying this rule to that in *Chanter v. Hopkins* produced a result that was a potent device to use against exemption clauses. A party could not rely on an exemption clause to protect themself against non performance or for a totally different performance of the contract to that agreed. In *Karsales (Harrow) Ltd v. Wallis*[85] an exemption clause was struck down in a contract to sell a second hand car that was so full of defects that it could not be driven. The Court of Appeal held that the thing delivered was not a car, which by definition had to be capable of movement. This constituted non performance of the agreement and the exemption clauses could not apply as a rule of law. The contract having ceased to exist, so also did the exemption clause. In *George Mitchell (Chesterhall) Ltd v. Finney Lock Seeds* Lord Denning applied the idea to cabbages. The variety sold to a farmer did not grow causing him a considerable loss of profits. The seedsmen could not rely on his limitation clauses because the vegetables which emerged were not cabbages at all, they were "heartless" cabbages, a different thing altogether. *Chanter v. Hopkins* and peas and beans had come full circle.

The House of Lords finally rejected this argument on appeal in *George Mitchell*   **16.25**
(Chesterhall) Ltd v. Finney Lock Seeds Ltd.[86] According to Lord Bridge: "In my opinion, this is not a 'peas and beans' case at all. The defective seeds in this case were seeds sold and delivered, just as clearly as they were seeds supplied, by the appellants to the respondents. The relevant condition, read as a whole, unambiguously limits the appellants' liability to replacement of the seeds or refund of the price".[87] The House of Lords was not prepared to apply a rigorous doctrine of fundamental breach to exemption clauses.[88] The House of Lords re-affirmed their earlier judgment in *Suisse Atlantique Société d'Armement Maritime SA v. NV Rotterdamsche Kolen Centrale*,[89] in which it was held that the doctrine of fundamental breach was only a rule of construction and not a rule of law. The rule of construction meant that the parties would not normally intend to do so, but could, if the language was clear enough, exclude liability for a "fundamental" breach of contract. In *Photo Production v. Securicor Transport Ltd*,[89a] the House of Lords rejected the view espoused by Lord Denning and the Court of Appeal since *Harbutt's "Plasticine" Ltd v. Wayne Tank and Pump Co Ltd*[90] that it was a rule of law that the parties could never exclude liability for a fundamental breach. The rule of construction approach was therefore affirmed by the Law Lords. The arguments and debate over this common law doctrine were finally brought to an end by the Unfair Contract Terms Act 1977 ss 3 and 9 which applied a reasonableness test to exclusion clauses even if there had been a fundamental breach.

---

[85]   [1957] 1 W.L.R. 936.
[86]   [1983] 2 A.C. 803.
[87]   See Adams, "Fundamental Breach - Positively Last Appearance" (1983) 46 M.L.R. 771.
[88]   Their Lordships found the clause in question to be unreasonable, however. See Chap. 17.
[89]   [1967] 1 A.C. 361.
[89a] [1980] A.C. 827.
[90]   [1970] 1 Q.B. 447.

Phoenix from the ashes: The re-incarnation of fundamental breach

16.26   Lord Denning's view of fundamental breach was rooted in his own view of reasonableness and of the presumed intention of the parties. In *Levison v. Patent Steam Carpet Cleaning Company Ltd*[91], Lord Denning defended the doctrine which he had developed and nurtured for over a quarter of a century; *obiter dicta* he suggested that the concepts of reasonableness and fundamental breach could be equated. If a clause was wide enough to include a breach of so serious a character or of such disastrous consequences as to involve a fundamental breach, it must be regarded as unreasonable. Equally, if a clause were to be held to be reasonable, it could not on the face of it exclude liability for a fundamental breach. A fundamental breach would simply not be covered on a proper construction of the exemption clause. This argument could easily have saved the doctrine from extinction but had a single flaw. Fundamental breach was an example of a breach which had to be construed in light of it's consequences.[92] The Act required that reasonableness be determined on the construction of the clause and contract when formed. This meant that taking into account the effect of the breach was inadmissible.[93] The doctrine foundered as a result.

16.27   There may be scope once again for arguing that reasonableness and fundamental breach are really different ways of arriving at the same conclusion. In *Edmund Murray Ltd v. BSP International Foundations Ltd*[94] it was stated that an exemption attempting to exclude or restrict liability could not be rejected on the grounds of a "fundamental breach". This approach had to give way to a test of reasonableness under s. 11 of the Unfair Contract Terms Act 1977. However, reasonableness and fundamental breach may still prove to have much in common. In *Lease Management Services v. Purnell Secretarial Services*[95] the Court of Appeal held that it could not be reasonable to exclude liability for breach of a warranty or condition expressly given or for an implied term which was fundamental to the contract. This would be to bring the common law doctrine back under the guise of the statutory test. Such a judicial approach is not unknown in the history of English law.

There may further support for equating a finding of unreasonableness with a construction of a contract which appears to exclude liability for breach of fundamental obligations is to be found in *Sovereign Finance Ltd v. Silver Crest Furniture Ltd.*[96] Longmore J. held in the Queen's Bench Division that the plaintiffs could not rely on an exemption clause which he stated was *prima facie* unreasonable becaute it attempted to exclude all liability. Such a clause was too wide and excluded the core obligations to perform. This view comes close to equating unreasonableness with the common law doctrine of fundamental breach. There remains the possibility of applying the common law doctrine of fundamental breach to contracts outside of the Act.[97] Many commercial contracts which are not made on standard form, are not covered by the 1977 Act. The common law rules may still remain relevant in this context.

---

[91] [1978] Q.B. 69.
[92] See Chap. 13.
[93] This was an important change in the original Bill during it's passage through Parliament in 1977.
[94] (1994) 33 Con L.R. 1.
[95] [1994] Tr. L.R. 337.
[96] [1997] C.C.L.R 76.
[97] See Chap. 17.

One of the most interesting cases in recent times is *Motis Exports Ltd v.* **16.28**
Dampskibsselskabet AF 1912,[98] where the Court of Appeal affirmed a decision by Rix J.
The carriers in a carriage of goods by sea misdelivered goods to fraudsters who stole
them by presenting forged bills of lading. The judge applied the reasoning of the fundamental breach cases that a clause which exempted from liability for such a loss could not
be construed to cover an obligation of such fundamental importance to deliver up the
goods only by providing the genuine bill of lading. The Court of Appeal agreed. On it's
construction the clause did not cover misdelivery to criminals but also, even if it had
done so, this "was not a construction which ought to be adopted having regard to the
fundamental importance of the obligation to deliver to the correct person". Stuart-
Smith L.J. stated[99]: " . . . even if the language was apt to cover such a case, it is not a construction which should be adopted, involving as it does excuse from performing an
obligation of such fundamental importance. As a matter of construction the courts lean
against such a result if adequate content can be given to the clause". The idea of fundamental breach in a different meaning, that of determining the relationship between contract and restitution, has recently been resurrected.[1] A remedy based upon restitutionary
rather than contractual principles could apply if a fundamental breach had terminated
a contract. Currently there must be no existing contract before a remedy in restitution is
permitted. We discuss this later.[2]

EXEMPTION CLAUSES AND THIRD PARTIES

The doctrine of privity of contract[3] was used extensively in the past to control exemp- **16.29**
tion clauses. In *Adler v. Dickson*,[4] the Master and Boatswain of a vessel *The Himalaya*
were held not to be covered by exemption clauses entered into between passengers and
the "P and O" Steamship Company when a passenger slipped on a gangway going on
board a ship and suffered a personal injury. The Court of Appeal held that the clause on
it's construction did not apply to the defendants but *obiter dicta*, even if it had, the fact
that they were third parties would prevent the servants of the company taking advantage
of the exemption clause in their favour. Privity of contract was therefore used as a device
to control the scope of exemption clauses and prevent third parties gaining their advantage in a contract between two others. In *Scruttons v. Midland Silicones Ltd*[5] the House
of Lords reaffirmed the doctrine of privity, although later a technical and carefully
drafted contract seeking to protect independent contractor third parties prevailed in *New
Zealand Shipping Co v. A. M. Satterthwaite & Co. Ltd (The Eurymedon)*.[6]

The need for such complexity has now been done away with as a result of the
Contracts (Rights of Third Parties) Act 1999 which allows the parties to confer an
enforceable benefit, including the right to the protection of an exemption clause on a

---

[98] [2000] 1 All E.R. (Comm) 91.
[99] At p. 98.
[1] See Smith, "Concurrent Liability in Contract and Restitution" (1999) 113 L.Q.R.
[2] See Chap. 26.
[3] See Chap. 10.
[4] [1955] 1 Q.B. 158.
[5] [1962] A.C. 446.
[6] [1975] A.C. 154, see Chap. 2.

third party.[7] In recent years, the courts in this country and also in other common law jurisdictions have been inclining towards giving third parties protection of exemption clauses.[8] The Contracts (Rights of Third Parties) Act 1999 allows third parties to be protected by exemption clauses made in their favour. The Act allows the parties to confer a benefit on a third party. Section 1(6) states that "where a term of a contract excludes or limits liability [this extends] . . . to the third party enforcing the term", then this "shall be construed as references to availing himself of the exclusion of limitation". Exemption clauses are therefore covered by the 1999 Act which allows third parties such as *Adler v. Dickson* to be covered.[9] A general exemption of employees or agents as a class would probably suffice to extend the protection of an exemption clause to such a group.[10] The 1999 Act does not permit unlimited use of the Unfair Contract Terms Act 1977, however. Under s. 7(2) of the 1999 Act, the reasonableness test s. 2(2) of the 1977 Act does not apply. In other words, there is to be no determination of the reasonableness of the excluding term between the promisor and the third party. Exclusion of liability for personal injury under s. 2(1) remain void in relation to third parties as well as with the promisee. Third parties seeking to bring action will not, however, be able to challenge an exemption clause made between the parties on reasonableness grounds.

A COMMON LAW TEST OF REASONABLENESS FOR TERMS FALLING OUTSIDE THE UNFAIR CONTRACT TERMS ACT

16.30 In *Timeload Ltd v. British Telecommunications plc*[11] Sir Thomas Bingham hinted that there might be scope for a general test of fairness for certain types of clause even in commercial contracts. In considering whether s. 3(2) of the 1977 Act applied to the term in question, the Court observed:

> "It seems to me at least arguable that the common law could, if the letter of the [Unfair Contract Terms Act] does not apply, treat the clear intention of the legislature expressed in the statute as a platform for invalidating or restricting the operation of an oppressive clause in a situation of the present, very special, kind. I say no more than that there is, I think, a question here which has attracted much attention in Commonwealth jurisdictions and on the continent and may well deserve to be further explored here."

The need for judicial creativity expanding the rate of the common law is, of course, much reduced in light of the unfair Contract Terms Act 1977.

---

[7] The judgment in *The Eurymedon* is also superseded by the enactment of the Carriage of Goods by Sea Act 1992.

[8] See *Southern Water Authority v. Carey* [1985] 2 All E.R. 1077; *Norwich City Council v. Harvey* [1988] 1 W.L.R. 828; and in Canada, *London Drugs Ltd v. Kuehne and Nagle International* (1992) 97 D.L.R. (4th) 261.

[9] The type of clause in *Adler v. Dickson* still leads to litigation. See *Lotus Cars Ltd v. Southampton Cargo Handling plc* [2000] 2 All E.R. (Comm) 705.

[10] S. 1(3) of the 1999 Act. This is the intention of the legislation.

[11] [1995] E.M.L.R. 459.

Chapter 17

THE UNFAIR CONTRACT TERMS ACT 1977

THE BACKGROUND TO THE LEGISLATION

The Unfair Contract Terms Act 1977 is one of the two most important pieces of legislation in the field of general contract law.[1] The common law techniques described in the previous chapter proved to be either flawed or ineffective. Parliament therefore acted on behalf of consumers and others who lack equality of bargaining power to regulate the use of exemption clauses in standard term contracts. The modern statutory era begins with the Misrepresentation Act 1967, s. 3 of which provided that disclaimers of liability for misrepresentation must be just and reasonable.[2] This section remains in force though was later amended to conform with the "reasonableness" test under the Unfair Contract Terms Act 1977.[3] The Law Commission's First Report on Exemption Clauses in 1969 resulted in the Supply of Goods (Implied Terms) Act 1973. Although repealed and replaced by the 1977 Act, the 1973 Act, in retrospect, was a watershed in the development of the present law. The Act only applied to contracts for the sale of goods, providing that sellers could no longer exclude or limit their liability for the quality of the goods. This represented the biggest single advance for buyers, particularly consumers, since the original Sale of Goods Act in 1893. A distinction was introduced between "consumer" and "non consumer" sales. In the former exemptions were void, and in "non consumer" sales, *i.e.* between two businesses, exemption clauses were made subject to a reasonableness requirement. If there is a separate and developing law of contract for consumers then it dates from this time.[4]

17.1

The Unfair Contract Terms Act 1977 was enacted following the second Report on Exemption Clauses of the Scottish and English Law Commissions.[5] The name of the Act is misleading in several crucial ways. It only deals with exemption clauses and does not impose a fairness test. It is not restricted to contract law but deals with liability for negligence and other forms of liability, such as that of occupiers of business premises. Although it was created largely as a measure of consumer protection, the 1977 Act, in several important areas, also deals with some exemptions where both parties are in business. A more accurately descriptive title would therefore be the Void

17.2

---

[1] The other being the Misrepresentation Act 1967.
[2] Discussed in Chap. 18.
[3] This explains the fact that there is no s. 8 in the 1977 Act. This was repealed when the modified s. 3 of the 1967 Act was introduced.
[4] Discussed earlier in Chap. 15.
[5] Exemption Clauses: Second Report Law Comm No. 69 (1975).

and Unreasonable Exemptions Act. By giving the courts a power to strike down even freely agreed commercial contracts on the ground of unreasonableness, the Act allowed considerable judicial intervention. It's greatest practical benefit as far as consumers are concerned has been to force sellers and suppliers of goods and services to amend the small print in many of their contracts to comply with the Act.

Even today, many signs and notices are still visible in car parks, theatres and restaurants but the situation has changed vastly since the Act was passed. The Act is really about law making by persuasion rather than simple regulation. It also recognises that many exemption clauses are perfectly fair and justifiable. If we compare the 1977 Act and the Unfair Terms in Consumer Contracts Regulations 1999,[6] it is clear the ambit of each is different. The 1999 Regulations apply only to consumer contracts and define consumer narrowly to mean "natural" persons, *i.e.* a business can never be a consumer.[7] The 1977 Act looks at the type of contract in question but only regulates a particular category of terms, exemption clauses. On the other hand, the "fairness" test covers all the terms of a consumer contract with two notable exceptions.[8] The Unfair Contract Terms Act applies not only to contracts, it also covers negligence and occupiers liability. Neither the Act nor the Fairness Regulations may be excluded by the parties. The two regimes do overlap, however, and terms in consumer contracts which are exemption clauses can be subject to both sets of rules. An opportunity was missed to introduce a comprehensive single code in this area, and the failure to do so adds some unnecessary confusion. Table Y sets out the main differences between the 1977 Act and the 1999 Regulations.

The Act reflects the view that not all exemptions of liability are bad. Where the parties voluntarily and deliberately allocate the risks of the activities of contracting and limit their liabilities in the process, there is no reason to disturb this by statutory intervention. This is particularly true of commercially agreed contract terms. The Act envisages the need for some statutory control, flexible enough to fit the facts of different situations. This is expressed in the "reasonableness" test which can be applied selectively to the individual circumstances of each case. The result is two degrees of control along with a third area where the Act does not apply. A blanket prohibition on exemptions was seen as neither justified nor desirable.

Exemptions of liability rendered void

17.3   A number of exemptions of liability are rendered void by the Act, in situations in which it was regarded as wrong in principle to allow exemption clauses to apply. The main examples being:

(a)   death or personal injuries caused by negligence[9];

(b)   title to goods in both consumer and non-consumer sales[10];

(c)   quality of goods in consumer sales[11];

---

[6] See Chap. 15.
[7] Unlike the 1977 Act, as we shall see later pp. 293–296.
[8] Discussed in Chap. 15.
[9] S. 2(1).
[10] S. 6(1)(a).
[11] S. 6(2).

Table Y: Relationship between the Unfair Contract Terms Act 1977 Act and the Unfair Terms in Consumer Contracts Regulations 1999.

	1977 Act	1999 Regulations
Applies to:	Exemptions, limitations or disclaimers of liability only	Most terms in consumer contracts
Types of liability:	Both contract and negligence	Consumer contracts only
Parties:	One party must act as business, other deals as consumer but also applies to many business contracts where standard written terms used	Must be a seller or supplier in business and a consumer who is not in business
Consumer:	Wide definition, can include a business if "dealing as consumer"	Only "natural persons", *i.e.* never a business
Effect:	Void or subject to satisfying the "reasonableness" test	Not binding on the consumer, *i.e.* unenforceable
Excluded Contracts or Terms:	Various types of contract (see Schedule 1) and under s. 3 if neither party is a consumer nor contract on standard written terms	"Core" term exemptions only, *i.e.* (i) main subject matter and (ii) adequacy of consideration (so long as written in plain intelligible language)
Scope of coverage:	Depends upon type of liability and looks at contract as a whole	Fairness requirement for each term not individually negotiated
Language of contract:	None required, but must satisfy reasonableness test (if applicable)	Written in plain and intelligible language
Burden of proof:	Person relying on clause, must prove reasonableness, may be subject to strict construction	On seller or supplier to show that it is fair. Ambiguities resolved in favour of consumer
Definition of main test:	Reasonableness (s.11 & Schedule 2) (latter only strictly applies to s. 6)	Regs 5 and 6 and in non-binding "Grey List" (Schedule 2)

    (d)   exclusions by manufacturers in consumer guarantees[12]; and

    (e)   exemption clauses in miscellaneous consumer contracts where possession or ownership of goods is transferred.[13]

The reasonableness test

17.4   The Law Commission argued for a reasonableness test, but only in selected circumstances. There were certain advantages in a reasonableness criterion, according to the 1975 Report: "It would operate flexibly, enabling account to be taken of the great variety of situations to which any general control must apply and without interfering unduly with arrangements which have long operated to the advantage of suppliers and consumers alike . . . It would not be exclusive but would leave room for special treatment for selected cases."[14] The reasonableness test applies to five types of exemption:

    (a)   loss or damage to property caused by negligence[15];

    (b)   exemptions of liability for the quality of goods in non consumer sales[16];

    (c)   breach of contract in two situations:

        (i)   where one party; and deals as consumer or on written standard terms of business

        (ii) where one party renders a substantially different performance than reasonably expected or no performance at all[17];

    (d)   exclusions in non consumer contracts under which possession of goods is transferred[18]; and

    (e)   indemnity clauses where one party deals as consumer.[19]

Free from control

Finally, there are situations where no statutory control is deemed justified. If neither party deals as a consumer or on standard terms, a commercial contract is subject only to the common law rules. The common law does remain in these cases however and subject to the pattern of controls on exemption clauses developed by the courts. The 1977 Act also excludes from it's ambit certain types of contract.[20]

---

[12] S. 5(1).
[13] S. 7(1).
[14] Law Commission 2nd Report on Exemption Clauses, 1975, paras 65 and 66.
[15] S. 2(2).
[16] S. 6(3).
[17] S. 3. This is a further example of the "reasonable expectations" principle in modern contract law (see Chap. 1).
[18] S. 7(3).
[19] S. 4(1).
[20] See Schedule 1, and later p. 290.

THE SCOPE OF THE ACT

Obligations covered

The scope of the Act is set out in s. 1. This covers most contractual obligations, *i.e.* **17.5**
arising from the express or implied terms, or to take reasonable care or exercise reasonable skill in the performance of a contract. Negligence liability, in other words the
common law duty to take reasonable care or exercise reasonable skill, is also covered.
The Act, in addition, encompasses things done in the course of a business or for business purposes by the occupier under the Occupiers Liability Act 1957. A later piece of
legislation, the Occupier's Liability Act 1984, s. 2 allows occupiers of premises used for
recreational or educational purposes to give warnings and disclaim liability by exemptions. This is not regarded as business liability. The 1984 Act circumvents the 1977 Act
in this respect. The right to exclude relates specifically to the dangerous state of the
premises.[21] The 1977 Act does not cover strict liability (*i.e.* liability without fault).

"Business liability"

The main sections of the Act (ss 2–7) only apply to business liability carried out by a
person in the course of business. This can be their own business or that of another
person. There is one notable exception to this, private sales being included in the Act.
Under s. 6(4) any contract of sale of goods or hire purchase, even one not involving a
business, must satisfy the requirements of the Act. This includes one in which the seller
is a private individual not acting as part of a business.[22] Business liability is defined by
s. 14 as including "a profession and the activities of any government department or
local or public authority".[23]

The nature of the breach or obligation

The Act lays down that it is immaterial for the purposes of the Act whether the breach **17.6**
is inadvertent or intentional, or whether liability arises directly or vicariously.[24] Vicarious
liability is a type of strict liability where one party is held responsible for the conduct of
another person. Most commonly this applies to employers for their employees acting in
the course of their employment. In *Photo Production Ltd v. Securicor Transport Ltd*,[25]
Securicor were held vicariously responsible for the wrongful acts of their employee, the
night watchman George Musgrove, who out of boredom lit a small fire in a waste paper
basket and accidentally set fire to the factory he was supposed to be guarding in "the
course of his employment".[26] The factory was completely destroyed as a result.

---

[21] See Rogers, *Winfield and Jolowicz on Tort* 15th ed, (1998, Sweet and Maxwell), pp. 305–309.
[22] We discuss this later, p. 294.
[23] See later p. 291.
[24] S. 1(4).
[25] [1980] A.C. 827.
[26] See also Chap. 16, on the doctrine of fundamental breach in this case.

The coverage of the core obligations

The key provisions of the Act are contained in ss 2 to 7 which lay down the basic obligations and rules for controlling exemptions of liability. These rules may also be restricted in their application to parties "dealing as consumer" or "on written standard terms of business".[27]

Contracts not covered by the Act

Excluded contracts are listed in Schedule 1. The Act does not apply to (i) contracts of insurance, and also any contract "so far as it relates" to (ii) the creation transfer or termination of an interest in land, (iii) creation or transfer of rights or interests in trade mark, patent, copyright or other intellectual property, (iv) formation or dissolution of a company, including any body corporate or partnership or (v) the creation or transfer of securities. Contracts of insurance are the only category which is entirely exempted.[28] Otherwise the exceptions apply only those parts of contracts so far as they relate to each of the contracts in question. So an exclusion clause relating to intellectual property for instance is excluded from the Act but not the entire contract.[29] In *Electricity Supply Nominees Ltd v. IAF Group Ltd*[30] a clause in a lease which stated that rent had to be paid "without any deduction or set-off whatsoever" was held to be excepted from the main provisions of the 1977 Act. By para. 2 certain contracts such as marine salvage or towage,[31] charter parties and contract of carriage of goods by sea are subject to s. 2(1) but exempted from the remainder of s. 2. By para. 5 contracts for the international maritime carriage of goods are excepted. The requirement of reasonableness would not therefore apply to a *New Zealand Shipping Co Ltd v. AM Satterthwaite* type situation involving damage to goods transported by sea.[32] Such contracts are however subject to the Hague – Visby Rules which lay down provisions for limitation of liability by international convention.

17.7   Under para. 4, ss 2(1) and 2(2) of the 1977 Act do not cover contracts of employment, "except in favour of the employee". This means an employer cannot restrict his or her liability for personal injuries to an employee, but employees are allowed to restrict their liability to others. The Act does now appear to extend to employees who are deemed to "act as consumers" entitling them to the protection of s. 3.[33] The largest area not covered by the Act is contracts between businesses not on standard form conditions. These fall through the provisions of s. 3. Such contracts are governed on common law rules alone.[34] Contracts for the international sale of goods are not covered by the Act.[35] Finally, by s. 27(1) (as amended by the Contracts (Applicable Law) Act 1990, s. 5) contracts which are only governed by English law because of a choice of law clause, and which otherwise

---

[27] See later on pp. 289–291.

[28] *cf.* the Unfair Terms in Consumer Contracts Regulations 1999 where they are now included. Such contracts often contain a long list of excepted risks and exemptions of liability.

[29] See *Salvage Association v. CAP* [1995] F.S.R. 654.

[30] [1993] 1 W.L.R. 1059.

[31] *e.g. The Luna* [1920] P 22 (see Chap. 16).

[32] [1975] A.C. 154. See Chaps 2 and 16.

[33] See *Brigden v. American Express Bank Ltd* [2000] 1 R.L.R. 94, see on p. 295.

[34] See Chap. 16.

[35] S. 26, see also Burbridge (2000) N.L.J. 1544.

would be subject to another jurisdiction, are not covered. Many commercial contracts made by foreign parties include a clause agreeing to make English law the proper law of the contract. Section 27(2) does not permit the parties to choose a foreign law just to avoid the provisions of the Act.[36] The Act also applies where one party is a consumer habitually resident in the United Kingdom, and "the essential steps for the making of the contract were taken there "whether by him or by others on his behalf".[37]

THE KEY PROVISIONS OF THE ACT

Negligence liability (s. 2)

Liability for personal injury or death caused by negligence cannot be excluded or **17.8** restricted and any attempt to do so is rendered void. Injury leading to liability for loss or damage to property caused by negligence is subject to a reasonableness test. The common law defence of assumption of risk, or *volenti non fit injuria*, no longer applies. In other words, a person's awareness of risk does not indicate a voluntary acceptance that another person should not be liable if injury occurs.[38] The practice in the past of asking a party to sign a disclaimer of liability in the event of mishap loses its validity.

Contractual liability (s. 3)

When liability arises in contract (other than the named contracts set out in ss 5, 6, and 7), any exemption clause in which either one party (a) "deals as consumer" or (b) deals on the other's "written standard terms of business", must satisfy the reasonableness test. If neither of these conditions apply, the contract is outside the Act. A party in breach cannot exclude or restrict any liability to (a) render a contractual performance substantially different from that which was reasonably expected of them or (b) render no performance at all except in so far as the term satisfies the requirement of reasonableness. This provision appears to render the common law doctrine of fundamental breach obsolete.[39]

Contracts of sale of goods and hire purchase (s. 6)

The effect of an exclusion clause will depend on whether the contract is a "consumer **17.9** sale", which are rendered void under ss 13, 14 and 15, or a "non consumer sale", in which case any exemptions are subject to the reasonableness test. Exceptions of liability under s. 12, *i.e.* for the seller's implied undertaking as to title, cannot be excluded in any contract, whether a consumer or non consumer sale.

---

[36] S. 27(2)(a).
[37] S. 27(2)(b).
[38] S. 2(3).
[39] However, see Chap. 16.

Miscellaneous contracts under which goods pass (s. 7)

Other contracts under which possession of goods pass have similar requirements to those described above imposed upon them under this section. If one party "deals as consumer", any exemption covered by s. 7 is void. In non-consumer contracts these are subject to satisying the reasonableness test.

Other provisions affecting liability

Under s. 4 the reasonableness test is applied to indemnity clauses, where one party "deals as consumer". Indemnity clauses are considered to be exemptions from liability for the purposes of the Act. Section 5 renders guarantees of consumer goods which seek to take away the buyer's rights void. The section does not apply to the original contracting parties, *i.e.* retailer and consumer, but between consumer and manufacturer. The status of such agreements has been questioned in the past over the consideration provided for the manufacturer's guarantee.[40] The phrase commonly found on guarantees that "this does not affect your common law or statutory rights" is therefore now redundant. Section 5 would treat any attempt to do so as a nullity, which the consumer may ignore.

Clauses dealing with the effect of breach

Section 9 provides that where the contract is either terminated or by election is treated as a repudiated, the terms of the contract remain and have to meet the requirement of reasonableness (if relevant).[41] This section along with s. 3 (above) was designed to abolish the common law doctrine of fundamental breach. No lingering common law rule should allow the Act to be outflanked. However, there may again be case law and judicial dicta to suggest that reasonableness and fundamental breach may coincide.[42]

Further varieties of exemption clause (s. 13)

17.10   The Act spells out a number of additional examples of coverage. Originally thought of as a residual category, s. 13 has now been liberally interpreted to develop the concept of an exemption clause within the meaning of the Act. Section 13(1) sets out three further instances as exemptions of liability: (a) making liability or enforcement subject to restrictive or onerous conditions, (b) restricting a right or remedy or subjecting any person to prejudice in doing so and (c) excluding or restricting rules of evidence or procedure. This subsection also prevents terms or notices restricting or excluding the relevant obligation or duty arising.[43] It is from this section that the flowering growth of the meaning of the concept of an exemption clause now stems.[44]

---

[40] See Chap. 7.
[41] See Chap. 23 on breach of contract.
[42] See Chap. 16.
[43] *Harris v. Wyre Forest District Council* [1990] A.C. 831, see p. 298.
[44] See pp. 296–299.

Arbitration clauses are not exemption clauses

Section 13(2) identifies a type of clause which is definitely not an exemption clause and is not covered by the Act. These are arbitration clauses which are governed by the Arbitration Act 1996 and a considerable body of case law.

Avoiding the Act by means of secondary contract

This section deals with another kind of device for avoiding liability, namely a secondary contract which takes away rights under the primary contract. Section 10 provides that exemption clauses under the second contract are covered by the Act.[45]

Definitional sections

Section 11 deals with the meaning of reasonableness and Schedule 2 also gives guidance on the meaning of this phrase, specifically in the context of s. 6. We turn to the interpretation of words and phrases used in the Act in the next section.

INTERPRETING THE ACT

The Act leaves open many key concepts for interpretation by the Courts, and in particular the meaning and scope of some important words and phrases which form the basic structure of the legislation. This has led to a growing jurisprudence from the case law interpreting the Act.

The parties

(1) "Business liability"

The Act only applies to "business liability" (apart from s. 6(4) which can cover private   **17.11**
sellers of goods). This means things done in the course of one's own or another's business, or from the occupation of premises used for business purposes by the occupier.[46] "Business" is defined in s. 14 as including "a profession and the activities of any government department or local or public authority".[47] The definition of business liability has been given meaning by judicial interpretation which has had the knock on effect of extending the idea of a "consumer". This leads to a broader coverage of the Act's provisions. A slightly different approach was applied in *Stevenson v. Rogers*[48] to the analogous phrase used in the Sale of Goods Act 1979 "in the course of a business".[49] In this case a fisherman sold his fishing boat secondhand to the plaintiff. The question was whether he had done so "in the course of a business"? The Court of Appeal concluded

---

[45] See *Tudor Grange Holdings Ltd v. Citibank NA* [1991] 4 All E.R. 1.
[46] S. 1(3).
[47] See *St Alban's City and District Council v. ICL* [1995] F.S.R. 686.
[48] [1999] 1 All E.R. 613.
[49] See Sealy (1999) 58 C.L.J. 276.

that he did, and that the sale satisfied the statutory test of "in the course of business" even although fishing, not selling boats, was the plaintiff's trade. The sale of the fishing vessel therefore had to satisfy the 1979 Act requirements relating to quality of goods sold. The meaning of the two connected phrases covering business liability are treated differently under each Act and this is something which should be made more consistent in future.

(2) "Dealing as consumer"

17.12   The Act provides some meaning to the phrase in s. 12. There are three statutory requirements:

(a)   the party does *not* make the contract in the course of a business nor hold themself out as doing so[50];

(b)   the other party *does* make the contract in the course of a business (hence the importance of the meaning of that expression)[51]; and

(c)   in the case of sale of goods or hire-purchase, the goods are "of a type ordinarily supplied for private use or consumption".[52]

It should be noted that it is not the goods themselves, nor the purchaser's own purpose, but rather the type of goods that is significant. Two other rules are contained in the section. The burden of proof is on the person alleging that someone does not deal as a consumer.[53] In other words, it is not for a party to prove that they are a consumer. Secondly, persons buying at auction sales cannot be regarded as consumers.[54] This applies whether they are in fact buying privately or otherwise. Determining the status of the buyer and the purpose of purchasing can pose difficulties in this context. Is the antique vase for one's own mantelpiece, or to trade or sell later?

The definition of a consumer has been extended by case law to a somewhat surprising extent. Even a large company or partnership, and many businesses, may on occasions deal as a consumer.[55] In *Peter Symmons and Co v. Cook*[56] a sale of a Rolls Royce car to a partner in a firm of surveyors was held to be a consumer sale for which statutory rights could not be excluded. For a sale to fall outside of the category of a consumer sale it had to be an "integral part of the buyers business or a necessary incident of the business". Only then could the buyer be said to be on an equal footing with the seller. Since the car also had it's private uses, this amounted to a consumer transaction. So if a firm of solicitors purchased a new coffee maker for the office of one of their partners on normal retail terms this would be a consumer sale. They would be in no better a position than an ordinary member of the public, even though the firm was not a private individual. Coffee makers satisfy the test as being normally supplied for private use.

---

[50]   S. 12(1)(a).
[51]   S. 12(1)(b) (see p. 293).
[52]   S. 12(1)(c).
[53]   S. 12(3).
[54]   S. 12(2).
[55]   *cf.* the Unfair Terms in Consumer Contracts Regulations 1999, where only natural persons may obtain the benefit of the regulations. Other legal persons such as companies or partnerships can never do so.
[56]   (1981) 131 N.L.J. 758.

There was a similar outcome in *Rasbora Ltd v. JCL Marine*[57] in which a company, reg-   **17.13**
istered in Jersey in the name of the plaintiff as sole owner, purchased a yacht. When the
yacht sank, after catching fire off the Kent coast due to faulty electrical wiring, the plaintiff was able to avail himself of the protection of the Supply of Goods (Implied Terms)
Act 1973 (since repealed and now s. 6, 1977 Act) to claim this was a consumer sale and
the exemption clause in question was void. The judgment of Lawson J. in this case, if not
actually wrong, certainly pushes the idea of "consumer" a stage further. The object of
the plaintiff in purchasing the yacht in his company name had been to avoid paying VAT
(legitimately). The ultimate purpose of the yacht was private use and enjoyment and it
was this which counted.

Guidance on "dealing as consumer" is to be gleaned from *R and B Customs Brokers Co
Ltd v. United Dominions Trust Ltd*[58] in which the issue was the phrase "in the course of a
business". The Court of Appeal held that a firm of custom brokers had dealt as a consumer when it purchased a four-wheel-drive vehicle for one of it's directors. The Court
applied the reasoning of a case decided under the Trades Descriptions Act 1968, and an
earlier case *Davies v. Sumner*[59] that in order to be in the course of a business a sale must be
(a) an integral part of the business, (b) incidental to it or (c) of a type regularly carried out
by the buyer. In the absence of any of these, the sale was more likely to be a consumer sale.
The key issue was the regularity of the transactions. If these were regular then the contract
was more likely to be a business contract. Things required for business purposes tend to be
ordered on a regular basis. Consumer sales are generally lacking such frequency and are
more likely to be in the nature of "one-off" arrangements. The authority of *R and B
Customs Brokers* may now be questioned following *Stevenson v. Rogers.*[60]

The definition of "dealing as consumer" was extended to include employees in
Brogden v. American Express Bank Ltd.[61] The High Court held that an employee could
be considered a consumer under s. 3 of the Act, however, the clause in question dealing
with payments in lieu of notice was held by Morland J. not to be an exemption clause.[62]

The key factors in the meaning of "deal as consumer"[63] are:

- The type of goods in a contract for sale or services. Was the purpose of the sale
  for business or for private use or enjoyment?

- Whether integral to the business, *i.e.* for the purpose of increasing business
  profits.

- The regularity of similar transactions (if any).

- Equality of bargaining power. Did the business simply get the same price and
  conditions as a private consumer?

---

[57] [1977] 1 Lloyd's Rep. 645.
[58] [1988] 1 All E.R. 847.
[59] [1984] 1 W.L.R. 405.
[60] See earlier p. 291.
[61] [2000] 1 R.L.R. 94.
[62] The Court relied on *obiter dicta* in two earlier cases: *Micklefield v. SAC Technology Ltd* [1990] 1 R.L.R. 218
and the Scot's law case of *Chapman v. Aberdeen Construction Group* [1991] 1 R.L.R. 505. See also Watson,
"Employees and the Unfair Contract Terms Act" (1985) 1 L.J. 323.
[63] It is to be noted that the Unfair Terms in Contracts Regulations 1999 adopt very different criteria for the
parties and in particular for the meaning of consumer. See Chap. 15. Under the influence of increasing
European directives applying only to "natural persons", the meaning of consumer under the 1977 Act is likely
to change.

(3) Private sales and the Unfair Contract Terms Act

17.14   Unlike the Sale of Goods Act 1979, sales between two private individuals are covered by the 1977 Act. Section 6(4) applies the provisions of the 1977 Act to "any contract of sale of goods or hire purchase agreement". The status of an exemption clause is complicated if two private individuals are involved. If the seller is a private individual, the buyer cannot be regarded as dealing as consumer. The private seller may exclude liability for any express terms or misrepresentations, although this will be subject to the reasonableness requirement as the sale, though covered by the 1977 Act, is regarded as a non-consumer sale. For example, Stella sells her second hand washing machine to Barry, claiming that it is "practically brand spanking new" (which it is not). She disclaims any liability "if it is not up to scratch, or if anything goes wrong". Barry says "ok, that's fine". The machine turns out to be on it's last legs, does not spin dry properly and is quite useless for washing clothes. Can Barry sue Stella for the state of the machine? The Sale of Goods Act does not apply between private individuals, however, if Stella's words are either terms of a contract or actionable misrepresentations,[64] Stella's disclaimer is subject to the Unfair Contract Terms Act, s. 6(4) or the Misrepresentation Act 1967, s. 3. In the former case, Barry is not "dealing as consumer" because in order for him to deal as a consumer, Stella must deal as a business.[65] Clearly Stella does not do so unless one wishes to follow the lead of *Stevenson v. Rogers.*[66] The exemption clause in this case is not void, but subject to the reasonableness test. In other words, Stella and Barry are treated as if both are in business rather than being (as they really are) private individuals.

"Written standard terms of business"

17.15   If neither party is a consumer, s. 3 only applies to the contract if the parties use "written standard terms of business".[67] The latter is a question of fact. In *St Alban's City and District Council v. International Computers Ltd*[68] a contract to purchase computer software was held to be on "standard terms" even though there had been negotiation over the terms which were all one party's own terms drafted by them in advance. The judge at first instance, Scott-Baker J. held that the parties had in fact contracted on the defendant's written standard terms.[69] This was a question to be determined on the facts of a particular case. In this case not all terms had to be fixed by the supplier. The Court stated that some clauses, such as price, might be negotiated individually and the contract will still remain on standard terms of business. Although there had been negotiations in the *St Alban's* case, they left the defendant's conditions largely untouched.

   On the other hand, in *Flamar Interocean Ltd v. Denmac Ltd The Flamar Pride,*[70] there had been negotiations and "a number of alterations to fit the circumstances of the

---

[64] See Chap. 18.

[65] S. 12(1)(b).

[66] [1999] 1 All E.R. 613. See earlier p. 293.

[67] See Lawson, "Controlling Written Standard Terms: The Scope of s. 3 of the Unfair Contract Terms Act 1977" [1998] T LR 487.

[68] [1995] F.S.R. 686.

[69] The case also discussed the question of reasonableness at first instance and in the Court of Appeal (1996) 15 Tr. L.R. 444 (see p. 305).

[70] [1990] 1 Lloyd's Rep. 434, Potter J. at p. 438.

plaintiff's case before its terms were finalised between the parties" in the defendants standard terms to suit the plaintiff. The result was that the terms were not standard and the case fell outside of s. 3. This was also the finding in *Salvage Association v. Cap Financial Services*[71] where it was held that standard terms were not being used. The pre-drafted contractual terms were only a "starting point in the negotiations"; there had been legal advice, negotiations went on for some time and the parties were of roughly equal bargaining power. According to Judge Thayne Forbes,[72] the test of standard terms was "a question of fact and degree to be decided in all the circumstances of the particular case". The Court suggested the following list without claiming that this was an exhaustive list of all the factors to be taken into consideration:

> "(i)   the degree to which the 'standard terms' are considered by the other party as part of the process of agreeing the terms of the contract;
> (ii) the degree to which the 'standard terms' are imposed on the other party by the party putting them forward;
> (iii) the relative bargaining power of the parties;
> (iv) the degree to which the party putting forward the 'standard terms' is prepared to entertain negotiations with regard to the terms of the contract generally and the 'standard terms' in particular;
> (v)   the extent and nature of any agreed alterations to the 'standard terms' made as a result of the negotiations between the parties;
> (vi) the extent and duration of the negotiations."

In *Chester Grosvenor Hotel Co. Ltd v. Alfred McAlpine Management Ltd*[73] there were **17.16** variations on the normal standard terms used to fit the arrangement between the parties. The Court held that the contract could nevertheless still be covered by s. 3 as standard written terms. This was a question of fact in the particular circumstances. Terms dealing with price and also dates of performance or delivery will clearly be negotiable or allowed to differ from contract to contract, yet other terms remain in standard form.

Under the 1977 Act, the question to be determined is whether the contract as a whole is on standard terms. The fact that a particular term, even the term in question, was negotiated while the rest of the contract was pre-drafted by one party may not save the contract from the scrutiny of s. 3 of the Act. In the Scottish case of *McCrone v. Boots Farm Sales Ltd*[74] the pursuer was a farmer who purchased weed killer from the defenders which failed to control weed growth in his crop. In the outer House of the Court of Session, Lord Dunpark held that a party who argued that standard terms were used from the fact that the other party invariably used them, had to satisfy the Court that each party had led the other "reasonably to believe" that it was intended that such a document was to be used. This involved spelling out the nature, subject matter and terms of the prior transactions. The phrase "standard form contract" was not limited to written contracts but could include any contract, even one partly oral, which included a set of fixed terms or conditions. Therefore, where general conditions were relied on, the party doing so could not deny that was what they were simply because the contract was entered into

---

[71] [1995] F.S.R. 654.
[72] At p. 672.
[73] (1991) 56 B.L.R. 115.
[74] 1981 S.C. 68.

orally. It should be noted by way of contrast that the Unfair Terms in Consumer Contracts Regulations 1999 apply to any term which has not been individually negotiated. The contract as a whole does not have to be in standard form. Under the 1999 Regulations this will be the case where any term was drafted in advance and the consumer was unable to influence the substance of the term.[75]

What is an exemption clause?

There is no simple definition which provides a test in every case. Rather there are several different tests, each of which have been influential over the years.

(1) A defence to an action for breach of contract

17.17   An exemption clause may be regarded as a defence to an action for breach of contract or negligence. In *Owners of Istros Steamship v. FW Dahlstroem and Co.*[76] Wright J. approved this approach to the nature of an exemption clause. The clause's "appropriate effect" was stated to be "a shield to a claim for damages".[77] On such a view, exemption clauses continue to exist after the breach and act to limit or exclude potential liability to pay damages for breach of contract. This approach has largely atrophied in recent years.

(2) Qualifying or modifying an obligation

The second purported test is that any disclaimer operates to modify or define the obligation undertaken by the party relying on the term. The exemption clause has to be read alongside the contract as a whole to see if what occurs does amount to a breach of contract. For instance, if Felicity, a professional surveyor and valuer, promises to do a survey of a house but disclaims any liability in negligence, she has never promised a non-negligent survey in the first place, so no duty of care was undertaken. This approach was often taken in the old fundamental breach cases. Academically, this theory is associated with the New Zealand Law Professor Brian Coote.[78] A contract, therefore, should be construed to read what was promised against what was excluded. On this basis, if covered by the clause, the conduct of the party in question might not be a breach. This "qualifying" of the obligation approach received the judicial seal of approval in Lord Diplock's judgment in *Photo Production Ltd v. Securicor Transport Ltd*,[79] in which he stated: "Parties are free to agree to whatever exclusion or modification of all types of obligation as they please within the limits that the agreement must retain the legal characteristics of a contract." The view that one could prevent a duty of care arising at all by means of a disclaimer was firmly rejected by the House of Lords in *Harris v. Wyre Forest District Council*.[80] This reversed the Court of Appeal's holding to the contrary effect that obligations could be prevented from arising by excluding them at the date of contract.

---

[75] See Chap. 15.
[76] [1931] 1 K.B. 247.
[77] At p. 253.
[78] See Coote, *Exemption Clauses* (1964, Sweet and Maxwell, London).
[79] [1980] A.C. 827 (at p. 848).
[80] [1990] A.C. 831.

(3) "By nature" exemption clauses[81]

The third approach is to treat exemption clauses as having a nature or essence. In *Photo* **17.18**
Production Ltd v. Securicor Transport Ltd[82] Lord Wilberforce took the view that exemption clauses were a type of clause in their own right. The existence and meaning of such a
clause was a matter of construction of both the contract and the clause itself. The question to be asked was "what have the parties bargained for?"[83] This was really a variation of
the previous view looking at the contract as a whole. The "by nature" argument has been
criticised and has lost ground of late. In *Phillips Products Ltd v. Hyland*,[84] Slade L.J. stated:
"it is not relevant to consider whether the form of a condition is such that it can aptly be
given the label of an 'exclusion' or 'restriction clause'. There is no mystique about 'exclusion' or 'restriction' clauses. To decide whether a person excludes liability by reference to a
contract term, you look at the effect of the term – you look at its substance". The Court
of Appeal looked at the effect or purpose of the clause in question. This approach has now
become a useful test for exemptions of liability under the 1977 Act.[85]

(4) Exemption clauses under the 1977 Act

The definition of an exemption clause is vital under the Act, which only applies to
exemptions of liability and not to fairness in general. The Act does not give a definitive
list, but in it's various sections it provides for ten categories of exemptions, without treating these as exhaustive. We have already illustrated many of these. The key to the Act
is s. 13(1)(c) which extends it's scope beyond the mere exclusion or restriction of liability
to "terms and notices which exclude or restrict a relevant obligation or duty".
Originally, s. 13 was thought of as a residual category of perhaps limited importance.
This subsection has opened up a fruitful new opportunity for fresh claims and arguments
over the true meaning of exclusion clauses.[86] The importance of the section is that it's
wording widens the scope of the Act to include clauses of a type which might not have
been considered exemption clauses at one time, and in doing so fuels further speculation
as to what is an exemption clause. As a result of judicial interpretation, there are now
three further theories as to the meaning and extent of exemption clauses. No single one
of these has won the day at present and all may be said to be competing for support.

(a) The "but for" test

A "but for" test applies if there would be an obligation, and therefore liability, without **17.19**
the clause in question. The Act will then apply as a result of s. 13 since the clause has
taken away a pre-existing right from the other party. There is judicial acknowledgement
of this test in *Johnstone v. Bloomsbury Health Authority*[87] and by the House of Lords in
Smith v. Eric Bush.[88] In the latter, Lord Griffiths stated "the existence of the common law

[81] See MacDonald, "Exemption clauses: the ambit of s. 14(1) of the Unfair Contract Terms Act 1977" (1992)
12 Legal Studies 277.
[82] [1980] A.C. 827.
[83] At p. 843.
[84] [1987] 2 All E.R. 620.
[85] See later p. 300.
[86] For an interesting discussion, see MacDonald, "Exclusion Clauses: the Ambit of s. 13(1) of the Unfair
Contract Terms Act 1977" (1992) 12 Legal Studies, 277.
[87] [1991] 2 All E.R. 293.
[88] [1990] 1 A.C. 831.

duty to take reasonable care . . . is to be judged by considering whether it would exist 'but for' the notice excluding liability."[89] The House of Lords stated that the correct approach was to look at the contract or duty in care in negligence without the exemption clause or disclaimer. If the clause or notice took away an obligation which would have otherwise existed, it would be subject to s.13 of the Act. The "but for" test now appears to be the current approach. This arguably extends the concept of an exemption clause beyond the protective girdle envisaged by the draftsmen of the 1977 legislation. (Though the courts' task is to interpret the will of Parliament, not re-write the law.)

A good example of a clause now caught by the Act is to be found in *Stewart Gill Ltd v. Horatio Myer and Co. Ltd*,[90] involving a "set-off clause" under which a party could deduct payments against incorrect or defective performance. This was held to be an exemption clause. The Court of Appeal took the view that s. 13(1)(b) of the Act had extended the meaning of exemption clauses to include rights which would be available "but for" the clause. The clause was an exemption clause despite appearances. It was subject to the reasonableness test and this was not satisfied in the contractual context in question. A "no set off" clause was also treated as an exemption clause in *Overland Shoes Ltd v. Shenkers Ltd*.[91] This time the Court of Appeal held that the "no set off" clause in the standard trading conditions of the British International Freight Association satisfied the reasonableness test. A contractual term dealing with a right of set off was also treated as an exclusion clause in *WRM Group Ltd v. Wood*.[92] In the Court of Appeal Morritt L.J. held that a set of clauses applicable to claims for up to £300,000 satisfied the reasonableness test. The contract had been a bargain made at arm's length and was fair.

(b)   The purpose of the clause

17.20   The same clause in a similar contract can be an exclusion clause in one context and not in another. The difference being that the courts will look at the purpose as well as the nature of the clause involved. This approach was used in the following two cases which, although lending weight to the "but for" test discussed earlier, also add an alternative approach of their own. In *Thompson v. T. Lohan (Plant Hire) Ltd*[93] the defendants hired an excavator along with a driver to a third party to do some work at Bigby quarry, South Humberside. The contract was in standard form produced by the Contractor's Plant Association. Two clauses stated that the hirer had to indemnify the owners of the equipment if they had claims made against them for personal injury or damage to property. The husband of the plaintiff was killed by the negligence of a driver working at the site. His widow, Christine, obtained damages for her husband's death from the defendants and they then sought to recover from the third party, J W Hurdiss, who were also second defendants. At the time both parties involved in the accident were employed by the first defendants, T. Lohan (Plant Hire) Ltd. The third party claimed that the clauses in conditions 8 and 13 excluded liability for personal injuries and were therefore void under s. 2(1). The Court of Appeal rejected this argument. The clauses were there to transfer liability from one party to another, not to exclude liability towards an injured party. The plaintiff herself was not prejudiced in any way by the effect of the clause; so far as she

---

[89]   [1989] 2 All E.R. 514 (at p. 530).
[90]   [1992] 2 All E.R. 257.
[91]   [1998] 1 Lloyd's Rep. 498.
[92]   [1998] C.L.C. 189.
[93]   [1987] 2 All E.R. 631.

was concerned it was not an exemption clause. The conditions stood, therefore, and were not exemption clauses within the meaning of the Act. The outcome was different however in *Phillips Products Ltd v. Hyland*[94] in which the conditions in question were similar to *Thompson*. This time the hired driver damaged the plaintiff's property. The Court of Appeal held that the condition was governed by the 1977 Act and that s. 2(2) rendered the clause unreasonable. The test for an exclusion clause was based upon the nature of the clause and it's effect, not merely the form of the clause.

(c) A "reasonable expectations" test

The "reasonable expectations" test contains potentially the widest possibility for extending the concept of an exemption clause. This would regard any term as an exemption if it interfered with any performance of the contract which a party could reasonably expect. There is statutory authority for this approach in s. 3 of the Act which speaks of "rendering a contractual performance substantially different from that which was reasonably expected of him". This question of expectation hinges on the parties' intentions when making the contract. Reasonable expectation is the beating heart of contract law.[94a] There is less judicial support for such a broad and all embracing approach at present, probably based upon the fear that such a principle could lead to significiantly more terms being caught by the Act, and therefore great uncertainty. In another context, however, a reasonable expectations text in relation to fairness under the Unfair Terms in Consumer Contracts Regulations 1999 received judicial support from Evans-Lombe J. in *Director General of Fair Trading v. First National Bank plc*[95]. The requirement of good faith contained in the regulation was described as dependent upon whether the term in question "unfairly deprived consumers of benefits or advantages which they might reasonably have expected to receive".[96]

17.21

The concept of reasonableness

The idea of the courts having to intervene in contracts to judge reasonableness under statute goes back to the Railway and Canal Traffic Act 1854.[97] In the nineteenth century this was anathema to many judges, politicians and businessmen at that time, as it flew in the face of freedom of contract. Lord Bramwell in *Manchester, Sheffield and Lincolnshire Rly Co v. Brown*,[98] a case involving a fishmonger from Grimsby, commented,[99] "For here is a contract made by a fishmonger and a carrier of fish who know their business, and whether it is just and reasonable is to be settled by me who am neither fishmonger, nor carrier, nor with any knowledge of their business".[1] The task of the judges is just as slippery today. However times have changed, and it is now regarded as acceptable and proper that the courts should have a role in policing contracts in this way.

17.22

---

[94]   [1987] 2 All E.R. 620.
[94a] See Chap. 1.
[95]   [2000] 1 All E.R. 240
[96]   See Chap. 15.
[97]   *Peck v. North Staffordshire Railway Co* (1862–3) 10 H.L.C. 473 11 E.R. 1109. Lord Bramwell in *Manchester Sheffield and Lincolnshire Rly Co. v. Brown* (below) had harsh words for this case: "Until now I thought it was wrongly decided . . . if it were within my competency to overrule it, I would do so."
[98]   (1883) 8 App. Cas. 703.
[99]   At p. 716.
[1]   Quoted by Atiyah, "The Rise and Fall of Freedom of Contract" (1979, Oxford), at p. 559. The background to the legislation in the nineteenth century is discussed at p. 559.

There are two elements to the reasonableness test under the 1977 Act. First, whether it is reasonable to incorporate the term taking into account the procedural aspects of reasonableness such as the rules of incorporation and secondly, is it reasonable to rely on the exemption term? The two aspects of reasonableness enable the court to consider both formation issues and the contents or substance of the term. The common law was only able to deal with the former. The 1977 Act gives the courts a stronger and more effective weapon to deal with exemption clauses than that wielded by the judges. A wider range of reasonableness factors can also be brought into play.[2] The courts determine reasonableness as a question of fact. There is a wide discretion to determine the question, subject to guidance from the Act itself[3] and the precedents of a quarter of a century of case law. The key to the Act is equality of bargaining power. In consumer contracts there is a tendency to treat exemptions as unreasonable. In commercial contract the trend is the reverse since such clauses should have been freely agreed. Parties in business should also be aware of terms and be more evenly matched.

The Act has had a dramatic effect in changing the contents of contracts forcing sellers and suppliers of goods to draft more reasonable terms in contracts. Reasonableness is really an attempt to legislate by persuasion rather than purely by regulation. The test of reasonableness is objective. It does not depend upon the parties acting in an equitable way, nor having gained an unfair advantage over the other party through undue influence or unconscionable conduct.[4] It is not necessary for a plaintiff to plead the issue of reasonableness. In *Kristina Sheffield v. Pickfords Removals Ltd*[5] Lord Woolf M.R. held that a defendant who intended to rely on his own standard conditions should as a matter of practice have to include in his defence a statement that his conditions were reasonable.

(1) Statutory guidance on reasonableness

There are two main statutory sources of guidance on reasonableness.

(a) Section 11

17.23   The Act provides only general help on the meaning of reasonableness, indeed it was debated whether any guidance should be laid down at all in case these fossilised into the only rules applicable. The result is a compromise, giving some assistance to lawyers and the courts but leaving matters open textured for later interpretation by the courts. Section 11 sets out a number of important provisions on reasonableness. The burden of proof is on the person relying on the clause. It is not for the consumer to prove the clause unreasonable. Reasonableness is to be judged at the time of making the contract. This prevents considering the nature and effect of the breach in all the circumstances as was the test for fundamental breach.[6] Reasonableness for negligence, however, is judged at the time the liability arose. Two factors are listed in s. 11 to be taken into account. First, the question of insurance and secondly, in the case of limitation clauses, the resources available

---

[2] Lawson, "The reasonableness test: recent case law under the Unfair Contract Terms Act 1977" (1999) 18 T.L.R. 18.

[3] S. 11 and Schedule 2.

[4] See Chap. 14.

[5] [1997] T.L.R. 337.

[6] The original Bill from which the 1977 Act emerged would have judged reasonableness in all the circumstances, *i.e.* the consequences and extent of the breach, rather than the circumstances at the time the contract was made. This would have allowed the common law doctrine of fundamental breach a new lease of life.

to meet liability. The first is clearly important, the second is a curious provision which seemed for years destined never to be taken seriously by the courts. However, it was treated as a factor in *The Salvage Association v. CAP Financial Services*[7] in which a limitation clause of £25,000 was not regarded as adequate against the insurance cover of the defendants. Indeed the defendants had subsequently increased the figure of coverage to £1,000,000. The Court also concluded that CAP had resources sufficient to meet possible liabilities for amounts greatly in excess of £25,000.

(b) Schedule 2 "guidelines" for the application of the reasonableness test

The guidelines were originally introduced in 1973 in an Act now repealed to deal with exemption clauses in sale of goods. The guidelines were re-enacted as Schedule 2 of the 1977 Act, however, they still strictly only apply to exclusions of liability under s. 6 *i.e.* contracts for the sale of goods. In *Overseas Medical Supplies Ltd v. Orient Transport Services Ltd*[8] it was held that the guidelines in Schedule 2 were relevant to the question of reasonableness throughout the Act. The factors in all other cases (indeed in sale of goods cases themselves) are not limited to the list set out in Schedule 2. The guidelines show that common law is still relevant and follow many of the judge made rules. Paragraph (a) refers to equality of bargaining power, para. (b) deals with situations such as differential pricing and para. (c) allows reference to many of the rules on incorporation of terms, knowledge and awareness, *i.e.* were reasonable steps taken, and course of dealings between the parties. These were all discussed under the common law in the previous chapter. The common law is therefore still guidance on reasonableness. In particular, the extent of knowledge or agreement to the exemption clause and the common usage of such clauses either by course of dealings or standard form are key factors. Indeed it may be that even the doctrine of fundamental breach gives some guidance.[9]

17.24

(2) Judicial interpretation of the reasonableness test[10]

The factors on reasonableness are open, *i.e.* new ones may always emerge, and no element is necessarily decisive. This means that there is no "weighting of factors", and reasonableness remains a matter of judicial impression. Among the main grounds for determining reasonableness discernible from the case law are the following 15 factors:

17.25

(a) Was it reasonable to incorporate or rely on the clause?

(b) Was there equality or inequality of bargain power? In other words, did one party impose their terms on a weaker party?

(c) Was this a standard form contract offered on a "take it or leave it" basis?

(d) Did the party have a choice or were alternative contracts available?

(e) Did one party deal as a consumer? If so, exceptions of liability are likely less reasonable, whereas in commercial contracts exemption clauses are looked upon more favourably.

---

[7] [1995] F.S.R. 654.
[8] [1999] 2 Lloyd's Rep. 273.
[9] See Chap. 16.
[10] See Adams and Brownsword, "The UCTA: A Decade of Discretion" (1988) 104 L.Q.R.

(f)   The burden of proof is significant to the outcome of many cases.

(g)   Knowledge of the term is important. Did the party really agree to the exemption clause and was he or she aware of the clause before the contract was signed?

(h)   Did the parties have a previous course of dealings?

(i)   The possibility of either party being covered by insurance against liability or the risk involved. The courts are generally willing to give effect to the allocation of risk by the parties themselves in commercial contracts.

(j)   The consideration or price paid for the contract. Did this take into account the exemption clause?

(k)   Were there two alternative prices offered? Differential prices can shift the balance towards reasonableness.

(l)   The question of negligence and whether this was expressly excluded.

(m)   The "proportionality" of the breach to the clause.

(n)   The amount of any limitation clause.

(o)   The wider public policy implications of holding a term reasonable or unreasonable, in a particular type of contract.

(a) Commercial contracts failing the reasonableness test

17.26   There have been two leading judgments by the House of Lords on the reasonableness issue. In *George Mitchell (Chesterhall) Ltd v. Finney Lock Seeds Ltd*[11] the plaintiffs were farmers in East Lothian who purchased a quantity of cabbage seeds which turned out to be the wrong variety of cabbages and germinated and grew but were commercially useless and had to be ploughed in. It was held that this was due to the seller's fault. A limitation clause provided a maximum liability of no more than the price of the seeds which was just over £200. The farmer claimed the loss of his profits calculated at £61,000. The House of Lords held the limitation clause failed the reasonableness test in the circumstances. There were four main reasons given for the holding:

(i)   the clause had been inserted by one side, and there was no real negotiation over the terms;

(ii)   loss was caused by the negligence of the seller[12];

(iii) the sellers were in a better position to insure against losses from defective seeds than the farmer; and

(iv)   the sellers had suffered complaints in the past and settled disputes at a higher figure than their own limitation clause.

---

[11] [1983] 2 A.C. 803.
[12] The courts have traditionally been reluctant to allow exclusions for negligence (see Chap. 16).

This suggested that even the defendants did not consider it a reasonable sum. It was not, according to Lord Bridge,[13] accurate to describe reasonableness as an exercise in discretion. The Court had to entertain a whole range of considerations, put them in the scales on one side or the other, and decide on which side the balance came down.

The second significant judgment of the House of Lords on reasonableness is *Smith v.*   **17.27**
Eric S Bush,[14] a case on negligent misstatement in a survey carried out for the bank which had been asked to provide a loan for the purchase of a residential property. One of the key issues was the reasonableness or otherwise of disclaiming liability. The House of Lords found the disclaimer unreasonable. Lord Griffiths thought the following should "always be considered":[15]

    (i)   Were the parties of equal bargaining power?

    (ii)   In the case of advice, would it have been reasonably practicable to obtain the advice from an alternative source taking into account considerations of costs and time?

    (iii)   How difficult is the task being undertaken for which liability is being excluded?

    (iv)   What are the practical consequences of the decision on the question of reasonableness? This must involve the sums of money potentially at stake and the ability of the parties to bear the loss involved, which, in it's turn, raises the question of insurance.

In *St Albans City and District Council v. International Computers Ltd*[16] a limitation clause was held unreasonable and therefore could not be relied upon in a contract for computer software. The defendants supplied both product and services to a local authority to enable it to calculate it's council tax paying population for the purpose of striking a rate for tax. The defendants had limitation clauses in the contract limiting their liability to £100,000. The software provided was not fit for purpose and so was in breach of the Sale of Goods Act 1979. The computers were to work out the local population as a preliminary to calculate the proper rate of council tax. This led to St Albans District failing to recover significant revenue which led to a shortfall of £484,000.[17] Section 3 of the Act applied because although neither party was a consumer, "standard terms of business" were used. At first instance, Scott Baker J.[18] found the clause unreasonable[19] for the following reasons: (i) the defendants had substantial resources to meet liability (applying s. 11); (ii) they had a very large insurance policy; (iii) the limitation was disproportionate to their insurance coverage; (iv) the defendants were in a much stronger bargaining position than the defendant local authority; (v) other companies also offered

---

[13] At pp. 815–816.
[14] [1990] 1 A.C. 831.
[15] At pp. 858–859.
[16] [1996] T.L.R. 444.
[17] The plaintiffs also suffered other losses, *e.g.* a precept from the local county council of £1.7m. The court held that some of the shortfall in revenue could be recovered in a higher tax in subsequent years, and therefore was not recoverable in damages.
[18] [1995] F.S.R. 686.
[19] The Court of Appeal agreed with the judge's conclusion on reasonableness, see [1995] F.S.R. 686 (at pp. 707–711).

similar standard terms so the plaintiffs had little choice; and (vi) the wider implications of the finding of reasonableness were taken into account. If the plaintiff had to cover the loss, the result would mean an increase in the following year's council taxes, whereas the defendants could claim on their insurance policy.

17.28   The Court of Appeal in upholding the judge noted the approach set out by Lord Bridge in *George Mitchell (Chesterhall) Ltd v. Finney Lock Seeds,*[20] that even if there was room for legitimate difference of judicial opinion, where it was impossible for the higher court to treat one view as "demonstrably right" or "demonstrably wrong" the appellate court should treat the judge's holding of reasonableness or otherwise with the "utmost respect". The appellate court should refrain from interference unless it (a) proceeded on some erroneous principle or (b) was plainly and obviously wrong.

The photocopier leasing industry provides two good examples of unreasonableness. In *Danka Rentals Ltd v. Xi Software Ltd*[21] the plaintiff's exemption clauses were held to be unreasonable. In *Danka* the defendants had leased a photocopier which was a complete disaster and repeatedly broke down, so they stopped paying rental and were sued by the plaintiffs, who were suppliers of the machine. The judge decided that the exemption clause had been incorporated. The defendant "did at least briefly look at or read the clauses in question and therefore probably understood the nature of what he was signing".[22] The clause excluding liability was held to be unreasonable. It was enormously wide, attempted to exclude liability for any express representation or warranty and it amounted to a total exclusion of all liability. According to the Court:

> "the natural meaning is offensive to reason . . . any clause with that meaning, is therefore *prima facie* unenforceable. The fact that the clause is too wide to be reasonable means that the clause as a whole must be regarded as unenforceable even if the parties relying on the clause may wish to rely on an obligation which it might be reasonable to exclude if it were excluded on its own".[23]

The customer was surrendering his rights against the owner and relying instead on a possible remedy against his supplier. This would prove problematic and awkward in the circumstances. "There existed therefore . . . a very strong general reason for holding that the exclusion clauses were too wide and are unreasonable."[24]

17.29   Also in *Lease Management Services Ltd v. Purnell Secretarial Services Ltd,*[25] [26] the defendant Mrs Berry leased a photocopier for her company. She wished to have the facility for paper plates and dealt with a Mr Brokers, believing him to be employed by Canon Ltd. In fact he was employed by the plaintiffs. The copier delivered did not have the facility for which Mrs Berry was looking. The Court of Appeal held that there was a warranty that the copier could make the appropriate paper plates. The exemption clauses relied on by the plaintiffs were unreasonable. The term was fundamental to the

---

[20] [1983] 2 A.C. 803 (at p. 816).
[21] (1998) 17 T.L.R. 74.
[22] At p. 85.
[23] This comes close to Lord Denning's (now abolished) fundamental breach approach.
[24] At p. 92.
[25] [1994] T.L.R. 337.
[26] See Phang, "Of Paper Plates, Estoppel and Reasonableness" (1995) 14 Trading Law 378.

transaction as far as Mrs Berry was concerned. It could not be fair or reasonable to exclude liability for such a term (the old doctrine of fundamental breach rears it's head again). The clause in question embraced "virtually all liability for any shortcomings in the equipment, irrespective of seriousness and irrespective of how the warranty or condition arose. Self evidently it cannot be reasonable to exclude liability for a breach of warranty or condition which has been expressly given."[27]

(b) Exemption clauses in commercial contracts satisfying the reasonableness test

When the parties choose to allocate the risk in full knowledge of the facts and their rights in doing so, then the courts will usually give effect to clauses as being reasonable.[28] The strong trend at present is towards upholding exemptions and limitations in commercial contracts. In *Watford Electronics Ltd v. Sanderson CFL Ltd*[29] the Court of Appeal overturned the judges' finding in a contract to supply software packages for telemarketing that a limitation clause was unreasonable. Chadwick L.J. stated that: **17.30**

> "Where experienced businessmen representing substantial companies of equal bargaining power negotiate an agreement, they may be taken to have regard to the matters known to them. They should, in my view, be taken to be the best judge of the commercial fairness of the agreement which they have made; including the fairness of each of the terms of that agreement . . . Unless satisfied that one party has, in effect, taken unfair advantage of the other – or that a term is so unreasonable that it cannot properly have been understood or considered – the court should not interfere."[29a]

In *Sonicare International Ltd v. East Anglia Freight Terminal Ltd*[30] a limitation of liability in the standard term contract of the National Association of Warehouse Keepers which restricted liability to £100 per tonne was held to be reasonable. The judge considered the facts to be nicely balanced.[31] Against the term was the fact that the sum in question was a "derisory" figure in relation to liner business concerning containerised, rather than bulk, cargo. On the other hand, the conditions represented a long course of dealings between the parties and reflected the commercial reality of the contract, but the risk had been previously allocated and covered by insurance. Finally, the owners of the goods would not only be insured but would have the primary remedy against the carriers. The Court stated that it would be regrettable to strike down standard terms recommended by a responsible organisation but that it's decision was applicable only between the parties and on the facts of the case. However, between different parties and on different facts, the Court might well conclude that the clause was unenforceable.

In *Stag Line Ltd v. Tyne Shiprepair Group, The Zinnia*[32] one clause in a commercial contract held reasonable, while another was not a reasonable clause. On the question of   **17.31**

---

[27] There are commercial and practical reasons for such clauses in the type of leasing arrangements in question set out in *Danka Rentals Ltd* (1998) 17 Tr.L.R. (at p. 87).

[28] See Barker, "A return to freedom of contract?" (2001) N.L.J. 344.

[29] *The Times*, March 9, 2001. Reported at first instance [2000] 2 All E.R. (Comm) 984.

[29a] 2001 WL 171981 (at para. 55).

[30] [1997] 2 Lloyd's Rep. 48.

[31] At p. 55.

[32] [1984] 2 Lloyd's Rep. 211.

reasonableness, Staughton J. stated[33]: "I would have been tempted to hold that all the conditions are unfair and unreasonable for two reasons: first, they are in such small print that one can barely read them; secondly the draftsmanship is so convoluted and prolix that one almost needs an LL.B. to understand them." In the commercial setting of the contract, and given the parties had equality of bargaining power, the terms were held reasonable. In *McCullagh v. Lane Fox and Partners Ltd*[34] an action for negligent mis-statement, *i.e.* in tort, against an estate agent contained a disclaimer which was held to be reasonable. The purchaser was a "sophisticated" member of the public who had ample opportunity to regulate his conduct having regard to the disclaimer and who was assumed to have had legal advice before exchanging contracts. The use of disclaimers by estate agents was commonplace and the normal basis on which house sales were carried out. The Court of Appeal held that it would not therefore be unreasonable for the estate agents to rely on the disclaimer. Insurance is obviously an important factor in assessing reasonableness. This arose in *Flamar Interocean v. Denmar "The Flamar Pride"*[35] where Potter J. discussed the question of insurance cover. In assessing reasonableness, the Court would assume that the parties contracted on the basis that insurance was available. The judge noted that the Court did not have to assume what the insurance arrangements were, nor what either party took the insurance arrangements of the other to be, if there had been no discussion of the point. Nevertheless, insurance was an important factor as evidence of allocation of risk and therefore reasonableness.

(3) Residual issues on the reasonableness test

17.32   It is open to a court to determine the question of reasonableness differently from a finding in a previous case. The facts of every case are different even when involving a similar contract. In *R. W Green Ltd v. Cade Brothers Farms*[36] a clause similar to that in *George Mitchell (Chesterhall) Ltd* was held to be reasonable. In the latter case, of course, the House of Lords held it was not. This shows the discretionary nature of the task facing the judges and how on the facts it is permissible to reach different conclusions. The basis for the judgment in *Green* was set by Griffith J.:

> To my mind the contract in clear language places the risk in so far as damage may exceed the contract price, on the farmer. The contract has been in use for many years with the approval of the negotiating bodies acting on behalf of both see potato merchants and farmers, and I can see no grounds upon which it would be right for the Court to say in the circumstances of this case that such a term is not fair or reasonable."[37]

This case also illustrates that one clause can be reasonable and another not in the some contract. In *Green* the Court held that a clause requiring complaints about defects in the seeds purchased to be notified to the seller within three days was regarded as have too short a time frame to be reasonable. The rest of the exemption clauses was nevertheless

[33] At p. 222.
[34] *The Times,* December 22, 1995.
[35] [1990] 1 Lloyd's Rep. 434.
[36] [1978] 1 Lloyd's Rep. 602.
[37] At p. 608.

held to be reasonable. Exemption clauses are severable under the Act. The A⟨ "except in so far as" the clause satisfies the reasonableness test. It remains whether a court might enforce part of clause while finding the remainder sonable. In *Cade Brothers Farms* the terms of a contract were severed an⟨ unreasonable while the other part of the clause satisfied the statutory test. I *Ltd v. Horatio Myer & Co. Ltd*,[38] the Court of Appeal did not sever unreaṣ⟨⟨⟨ in a clause when determining whether or not it was reasonable.

The issue is really whether the term can stand alone and be judged separately from the rest of the contract. If it can, severance is possible. What the courts will not do is re-write the clause or substitute a more reasonable term or financial limit. That would be making the contract afresh for the parties, something the courts are not willing to do. Indeed this would be impermissible under the principle of freedom of contract. In construing reasonableness, the courts are required to look at the clause as a whole. In *AEG (UK) Ltd v. Logic Resources Ltd*[39] the question of reasonableness arose not only at common law but also under the 1977 Act.[40] Reasonableness under the Act had to be dealt with by looking at the clause as a whole. It was not right to take any part of the clause in isolation. According to Hobhouse L.J., the key question on reasonableness was the reality of the consent of the party who would be bound by the exemption clause. The Court considered the term and the nature of the contractual relationship between the parties. This raised the issue of equality of bargaining power which, in the case of AEG, "militated strongly" against the plaintiffs. They were a large multi-national company, the defendant was a one man business. The plaintiffs failed to satisfy the burden of proving reasonableness. **17.33**

(4) Consumer contracts involving reasonableness

Most consumer claims which end up in court take place in the county courts under the small claims procedure where they tend to be heard in private.[41] There are, therefore, far fewer reported cases involving consumer contracts. In general, exemption clauses in consumer contracts are less likely to satisfy the test of reasonableness.[41a] However, many well drafted exemption clauses will do so. There are reported exceptions. In *Woodman v. Photo Trade Processing*[42] the plaintiff recovered 13 photographs from a 36 exposure film of pictures of a friend's wedding.[43] A clause in the terms of the contract for developing and printing of the film limited liability to the value of replacing the firm. This was held to be unreasonable because there was no realistic alternative offered to the plaintiff. The key factors were taken to be the strength of price, alternatives available and bargaining power between the parties. The plaintiff could have been offered two levels of pricing. There was a Code of Practice in the business that a "two tier" pricing service ought to be suggested to consumers and this had not been offered. This is known as "differential **17.34**

---

[38] [1992] 2 All E.R. 257.
[39] [1995] CCH Commercial Law Reports 265.
[40] Two members of the Court of Appeal found the clause not incorporated at common law. Therefore no question of statutory reasonableness arose (see Chap. 16).
[41] See Applebey, *A Practical Guide to the Small Claims Court* (1999, 2nd ed., Tolley Butterworth, London).
[41a] See Lawson (1981) 131 N.J.L. 935.
[42] (Exeter County Court, 1981, unreported).
[43] This case is discussed in Ramsey, *Consumer Protection: Text and Materials* (1989, Weidenfeld Paperbacks, London), pp. 107–112.

pricing". If a lower price is offered and accepted then any limitation clauses may become more reasonable as a result.

In *Wight v. British Railways Board*[44] the holding of *Parker v. South East Railway Company*[45] was upheld and an exemption clause held to be reasonable. The plaintiff left her suitcase subject to "owners risk" and a limitation of liability based on the weight of the suitcase. This was held to be reasonable because the plaintiff should have realised there would be no "come back" if the suitcase was lost. By displaying a clear coloured poster close to the parcel referring to conditions and the monetary limitation, the Board had done all they reasonably could to bring the conditions to the plaintiffs attention. It was not reasonable for the Board to bear the cost of insurance. Similar limitations based on weight were in common use among the Board's competitors, sometimes with less generous financial limitations. The holding mirrors the factors set out in Schedule 2 to the Act. Properly drafted terms in consumer contracts often pass the reasonableness test. For instance, in *Sargant v. CIT (England) t/a Citalia*[46] a term in a contract for a holiday which required complaints to be made within 28 days of returning was held reasonable because delay was "genuinely prejudicial" to defending a claim against the operators.[47]

(5) "No refunds"

17.35   Numerous notices containing exemption clauses are still visible, many of which have no effect, *e.g.* "No liability for personal injury". These are misleading and designed to deter claims. In this respect many may be successful because consumers and others are not aware of their rights. In the area of retail transactions the law now makes it a regulatory offence to mislead the public in this way. If a sign in a shop purports to take a consumer's rights away (specifically restricted to s. 6 of the 1977 Act), the retailer now commits an offence infringing the Consumer Transactions (Restrictions on Statements) Order 1976.[48]

---

[44] (1983) C.L.Y. 424.
[45] See Chap. 16.
[46] [1994] C.L.Y. 566.
[47] Such terms must also pass a fairness test under the Unfair Terms in Consumer Contracts Regulations 1999 (see Chap. 15).
[48] This was made under the Fair Trading Act 1973 (S.I. 1976/1813). Examples of these misleading statements can be prosecuted by trading standards departments in local authorities. Why the order has not been extended to all exemption clauses is a mystery.

Chapter 18

MISREPRESENTATION

FLAWED AGREEMENTS

Void, voidable and unenforceable

In this, and succeeding chapters, we shall discuss a variety of situations in which a contract may fail to be formed, give grounds for setting aside or be unenforceable at law. If no contract ever properly came into existence, or is vitiated at birth by some factor, it is said to be void. Any purported agreement is therefore a nullity, even if the parties believed there was a contract and acted upon it. The old phrase void *ab initio*, from the beginning, is sometimes used to emphasise that the agreement never materialised from the outset. The phase "void contract" is, logically, a "meaningless expression",[1] being a contradiction in terms. Nevertheless, the expression is normally used to denote an agreement which is a nullity. The clearest example is common mistake.[2] A contract may also be void for illegality[3] or certain terms may be rendered void by statute.[4] It must be borne in mind that even if the transaction is nullified as a contract, it may still lead to remedies and therefore legal consequences in the law of restitution.[5]

18.1

If a contract comes into existence but contains a vitiating factor, which provides a ground for setting the agreement aside at the option of one of the parties, it is said to be voidable. A valid contract exists between the parties until one party brings it to an end by rescission. A voidable contract starts it's life as valid until it is set aside. Rights can therefore pass meanwhile between the parties or even to a third party. In the latter case, if title to goods passes to a third party the right to rescind the contract may be lost. Contracts are voidable for misrepresentation,[6] duress,[7] undue influence[8] and for mistake in equity[9] where the process is more selective however.

Finally, a contract may also be unenforceable. The courts will not enforce the agreement even though a contract of sorts may be said to exist. This occurs when the parties

18.2

---

[1] See Devlin J. in *Ingram v. Little* [1961] 1 Q.B. 31 (at p. 64).
[2] See Chap. 21.
[3] See Chap. 20.
[4] *e.g.* the Public Interest Disclosure Act 1998 inserted a new subsection into the Employment Rights Act 1996, s. 43J. There are also a number of examples in the Unfair Contract Terms Act 1977 (see Chap. 17).
[5] Discussed later Chap. 26.
[6] See later this Chapter.
[7] See Chap. 19.
[8] See Chap. 19.
[9] See Chap. 21.

do not comply with formalities,[10] in some circumstances in relation to illegality,[11] for lack of consideration[12] and against a consumer in relation to unfair terms in consumer contracts.[13] The effect of unenforceability is variable. For instance, lack of consideration does not render a promise void, but only unenforceable. If the parties go ahead and perform the contract, money paid is not recoverable in contract. If the failure of consideration is total there may be recovery in restitution if paid but not enforcement of the "agreement" itself. A contract which is described as void for illegality or unenforceable may not be wholly ineffective for all purposes. Once again the courts may allow a remedy in restitution or for property rights to pass if the parties are not equally blameworthy. The status of unenforceable contracts has now been placed under the scrutiny of the Human Rights Act 1998. In *Wilson v. First County Trust*[14] a document fee had been wrongly included as part of a loan under the Consumer Credit Act 1974. The agreement had been improperly executed so the contract did not comply with the formal requirements of the Act. The Court of Appeal held that since the provision meant that the agreement was unenforceable by the leading institution, the Court would exercise it's power to declare that section of the Act incompatible with the creditor's rights under the European Convention of Human Rights.

In the following chapters we shall discuss the important words void, voidable and unenforceable in greater depth and in the context of specific doctrines for dealing with flawed agreements. The variety of effects are illustrated in Table Z.

MISREPRESENTATION

18.3 Generally speaking contracts do not arise spontaneously. One of the parties may be deceived, misled, encouraged or otherwise induced to enter into a contract by another person's words upon which they relied. If the words used become terms of a contract between the parties, they may be regarded as promises and give rise to an action for breach of contract.[15] A statement of fact which proves to be untrue may lead to any resulting contract being rendered voidable for misrepresentation. This is an important device for procedural fairness.[16] The common law has been supplemented by the Misrepresentation Act 1967, one of the most important statutes in contract law. An actionable misrepresentation is: (a) an untrue statement or assertion of fact by a person ("the representor") which (b) does *not* fall into one of the categories which are not regarded a misrepresentation, (c) induces the other person to enter into a contract that is (d) relied upon by the representee and (e) normally has to be "material". The misrepresentation need not, however, be the only reason for entering the contract. We shall consider each of these requirements in turn.

---

[10] See Chap. 11, particularly the requirement of writing under the Law of Property (Miscellaneous Provisions) Act, s. 2. However, also see *Yaxley v. Gotts* [1999] 2 F.L.R 941, discussed in Chap. 9.
[11] See Chap. 20
[12] See Chap. 7.
[13] See Chap. 15.
[14] [2001] 2 W.L.R. 302.
[15] See Chap. 13, on the distinction between terms and representation, and Chap. 23 on discharge by breach of contract.
[16] See Chap. 14.

Table Z: Void, Voidable and Unenforceable

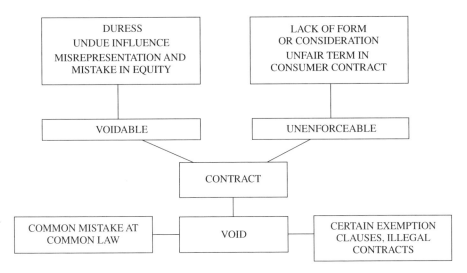

A statement or other assertion of fact which is untrue

Spoken words and written statements make up the most obvious type of misrepresenta- **18.4**
tion. The false statement of fact must be clear and on an objective test[17] intended to be
relied upon by the representee. The courts may now be less willing to find misrepresentation in light of the extensive nature of damages awarded under s. 2(1) of the 1967
Misrepresentation Act.[18] In *Avon Insurance v. Swire Fraser*[19] Rix J. stated that: "In the
present state of the law relating to the measure of the loss, where there was room for an
exercise of judgment a misrepresentation should not be too easily found, and a broad
approach should be taken." A misrepresentation can also be made by conduct as well as
words, such as the concealment of defects from a prospective purchaser.

In *Ridge v. Crawley*[20] the plaintiff purchased a house with insecure foundations. The
Court of Appeal upheld the judge at first instance, that concealing or disguising under-
lying problems with the property could amount to an actionable misrepresentation.[21]
Even a misleading image or photograph can be a misrepresentation. In *Spice Girls v.
Aprilla World Service*[22] a photograph of a motorcycle along with the image of five Spice
Girls was held to be an actionable misrepresentation since by the time the picture was
taken, one member of the quintet was known to be leaving. In *St Marylebone Property*

---

[17] See Chap. 2.
[18] See later p. 322.
[19] [2000] 1 All E.R. (Comm) 573 (at p. 633).
[20] (1958) 172 E.G. 637.
[21] See also *Gordon v. Selico Ltd* (1986) 278 E.G. 53.
[22] [2000] E.M.L.R 478, discussed later p. 319.

Co Ltd v. Payne[23] an aerial photograph with arrows appeared to show the boundaries of a property for sale by auction. The plaintiffs had relied on the photograph and did not actually see the land until after the sale. Arrows on the photograph in the particulars of sale appeared to show the extent of the property. One arrow wrongly included land not owned by the vendors. It was held that there was a misrepresentation of fact by the arrows and that this had induced the plaintiff to bid believing it to be included in the property. A misrepresentation can be made by a party saying that he or she has done something which they have not in fact done. In *Goldsmith v. Rodger*[24] the defendant was interested in selling his motor fishing vessel the *Atalanta* to the plaintiff. Both parties lived in London, and the plaintiff travelled to Wick in the North of Scotland to see the boat in question. He telephoned the defendant with a catalogue of faults including one saying that the boat had been put on the slip and he had found "rot and worm in the keel". This appeared to indicate that the plaintiff had examined the boat, which led to a lower price being obtained. The plaintiff had not examined the vessel, and saying he had done so when he had not, amounted to a misrepresentation. Donovan L.J. stated that this "was a misrepresentation, albeit innocent about an existing fact, and it induced the contract".

Statements which are not misrepresentations

18.5   A statement of belief or opinion is not a misrepresentation. In *Bisset v. Wilkinson*[25] a farmer at Avondale in the South Island of New Zealand told a person interested in purchasing the land that he believed "it would carry 2,000 sheep". The Judicial Committee of the Privy Council held that this was merely a statement of opinion honestly believed by the farmer. The land had not been used as a sheep farm before and all he had done was give his opinion. The claim for recission therefore failed. The person making the statement must genuinely hold the opinion. If he or she does not, then the statement may become one of fact and be actionable. In *Smith v. Land and House Property Corporation*[26] the plaintiff wished to sell his hotel at Walton-on-the-Naze. The advertisement stated that the property was let to "Mr Frederick Fleck (a most desirable tenant) at a rental of £400". In fact Mr Fleck had fallen behind with his rent and the plaintiff was in dispute with him over the matter. It was held that the vendors were not entitled to express the view that they did. They knew the opinion expressed was false. This amounted to an actionable misrepresentation. Bowen L.J. stated[27] "if the facts are not equally known to both sides, then a statement of opinion by the one who knows the facts best involves very often a statement of material fact, for he impliedly states that he knows facts which justify his opinion."

If the party has special skill and knowledge, or was the only one to be in the position to know the truth, his statements are more likely to be taken as statements of fact. The representee should be able to infer that the other party is using reasonable care in making the statement.[28] Persons whose business is selling goods and services and other professionals

---

[23]   (1994) 45 E.G. 156.
[24]   [1962] 2 Lloyd's Rep. 249.
[25]   [1927] A.C. 177.
[26]   (1885) 28 Ch. D. 7.
[27]   At p. 15.
[28]   See *Esso Petroleum Ltd v. Mardon* [1976] Q.B. 801.

are therefore less likely to fall back on the claim that their words were only opinion.[29] In *Cremdean Properties Ltd v. Nash*[30] it was held that it was not possible to avoid the Misrepresentation Act by a clause purporting to treat a statement as merely being opinion. On the other hand, if the person has no special skill or knowledge then their statements are less likely to be actionable. In *Economides v. Commercial Union Assurance Co plc*[31] in an insurance policy a student made a statement about the cost of replacements for the contents of a flat including valuables. His flat was burgled and the total cost of replacement was subsequently found to be far higher than the sum stated. The judge held that the plaintiff did not have objectively reasonable grounds for his statement of the value of the contents of his home. The Court of Appeal thought differently, stating that in relation to an insurance policy the insured was only under an obligation to be honest. If his statement, made in genuine belief and in good faith there was no implied representation that there were reasonable grounds for belief. The defendants were therefore unable to avoid their liability to make good his claim on the ground of misrepresentation.

Statements of future conduct or intention are not usually regarded as misrepresentation. However, if a person mis-states his real intention this can amount to a misrepresentation. In *Edgington v. Fitzmaurice*[32] a company prospectus invited persons to invest in developing the company for trading purposes. The directors really intended to use the money to pay off their debts. The Court of Appeal held that this was a misrepresentation. The defendants did not intend to do as they had said they would. Bowen L.J. made one of his most famous remarks that:

18.6

> "the state of a man's mind is as much a fact as the state of his digestion. It is true that it is very difficult to prove what the state of a man's mind at a particular time is, but if it can be ascertained it is as much a fact as anything else. A misrepresentation as to the state of a man's mind is, therefore a misstatement of fact."[33]

The famous judge took a robust view of human psychology in keeping with Victorian attitudes at that time.

Sales talk or advertising does not normally amount to misrepresentation. There are exceptions which prove the rule, for instance in *Carlill v. Carbolic Smoke Ball Company*.[34] In *Dimmock v. Hallett*[35] the vendor of some land, Bull Hassocks farm, described it as "fertile and improvable". It was actually swampy marshland next to the River Trent. It was held that they were words of "mere advertising flourish" by the auctioneer and had no legal effect. Advertisements can also contravene consumer protection legislation by being misleading or offensive and can incur criminal penalties.[36] A misstatement of law is not a misrepresentation, but a deliberate misstatement of the law may be actionable.[37]

---

[29] The particulars of property provided by estate agents nevertheless often contain the disclaimer that all statements are only opinion, not fact. This is not likely to succeed, being regarded as a form of exemption clause (see Chap. 17).
[30] (1977) 244 E.C. 547.
[31] [1997] 3 W.L.R. 1066.
[32] (1885) 29 Ch. D. 459.
[33] At p. 483.
[34] [1893] 2 Q.B. 163.
[35] (1866) LR 2 Ch. App. 21.
[36] Consumer Protection Act 1987 s. 20.
[37] *West London Commercial Bank v. Kitson* (1884) 13 Q.B.D. 360.

Similarly statements about the objectives and purposes of a document can be a misrepresentation such as that planning permission exists.[38] A statement of foreign law is
treated as a statement of fact (because it has to be proved in an English court).[39] Finally,
silence does not normally amount to misrepresentation, nor is there a general duty of
disclosure of information to the other contracting party. There are a number of important exceptions and qualifications to this rule, which we discuss elsewhere.[40]

An inducement to contract

18.7   The statement must be a real inducement to enter into the contract, though it need not
be the only reason for so doing. This is largely a question of fact which can be inferred
in most cases. The burden of proof is on the representee to show that a reasonable person
would have been induced to make the contract. However, it may be possible to show that
the person themselves was induced by the statement, even though a reasonable person
might not have been, and for them to succeed in their claim. In *Museprime Properties Ltd
v. Adhill Properties Ltd*[41] Scott J. stated that a representation was material "if it is something that induces the person to which it is made whether solely or in conjunction with
other inducements to contract on the terms on which he does contract." The Court supported the view that the question was first, whether a reasonable person would have been
induced, then the burden shifts to the representee to show he or she was induced to act
as they did. In *County Nat West Bank v. Barton*[42] Norritt L.J. stated that the concept of
an inducement was a wide one. The misrepresentation did not have to be the sole reason
for contracting, nor was it essential that it's effect should be to induce some positive
action. The abstention from doing something "bearing on the material interests of the
party concerned was enough". The requirement of inducement was further described by
Stevenson L.J. in *JEB Fasteners Ltd v. Marks Bloom and Co.*[43] as being satisfied if the
"misrepresentation plays a real and substantial part, though not by itself a decisive part,
in inducing a plaintiff to act, it is a cause of his loss and he relies on it, no matter how
strong or how many other matters which play their part in inducing him to act".

As these statements of law indicate, the concepts of inducement and materiality are
often merged into a single requirement. The terminology, as in other areas of contract
law, is often confusing and may overlap. Essentially, inducement and materiality relate to
the question of causation, in other words, the misrepresentation must have led to a
contract being formed. It need not however be the only ground for entering the agreement. The inter-relationship of factors was set out by Rix J. in *Avon Insurance v. Swire
Fraser*[44]:

> "The test of causation is inducement . . . the misrepresentation need not be the sole
> or decisive inducement as long as it materially contributed to the decision of the
> representee to enter into the contract . . . a material misrepresentation, *i.e.* one likely

---

[38] *Laurence v. Lexcourt Holdings* [1977] 1 W.L.R. 1128.
[39] *André et Cie SA v. Ets Michel Blanc and Fils* [1977] 2 Lloyd's Rep. 166.
[40] See Chap. 15.
[41] (1991) 61 P and CR 111 (at p. 125).
[42] *The Times,* July 29, 1999.
[43] [1983] 1 All E.R. 583 (at p. 589).
[44] [2000] 1 All E.R. Comm. (at pp. 578–579).

to influence a reasonable man, sets up a presumption or inference (of fact, not law) that the claimant has been induced, subject to rebuttal, the burden of which is on the defendant."[45]

Where there is no inducement to contract

If the words were immaterial to the plaintiff, they did not induce the contract and there is no misrepresentation. The words may have been immaterial to the representee, or his or her judgment to make the contract not influenced by the representation. This is also often linked with the question of reliance. Reliance and inducement are often treated as interchangeable. In *Smith v. Chadwick*[46] the plaintiff was unable to show either that the misrepresentation had induced a contract, or that he had relied upon it. Equally, if the representee is unaware of the misrepresentation at the time of contract, it cannot be said to have influenced their mind sufficiently to be an inducement. In *Horsfall v. Thomas*[47] the buyer could have discovered a defect had he looked for it, but he did not. The state of repair of the cannon being sold by the Mersey Steel and Iron Company had not influenced his judgment. The concealment of a defect in the weapon had no effect on his mind, nor had it influenced his judgment and therefore he had no claim for fraud. Bramwell B. stated[48]: "If the plug which it was said was put in to conceal the defect had never been there, his position would have been the same; for, as he did not examine the gun or form any opinion, as to whether it was sound, its condition did not affect him."[49]

18.8

On the other hand, a representee is not required to search for faults. The fact that the person has been given the opportunity to test does not mean that the representor is free from liability. In *Redgrave v. Hurd*[50] the plaintiff, a solicitor, had advertised in the *Law Times* for a partner, "an efficient lawyer and advocate of about 40" who would also purchase the plaintiffs "suburban residence". The plaintiff showed the defendant his account books but the defendant only glanced at them briefly. It turned out the legal practice had become almost worthless. Even though he had not examined the account books carefully when he could have done so, the defendant was entitled to rescind the contract on his counterclaim. The mere fact of having the opportunity to test or look at goods to see if the representation is true does not, therefore, automatically deprive the person of a claim for misrepresentation.[51] Nevertheless, if the person does investigate or test, then the right to rescind for the misrepresentation may be lost. The representee is relying on their own inspection rather than on the misrepresentation. A distinction is sometimes drawn between (a) a patent and (b) latent defects in the goods being sold. A reasonable inspection might reveal (a) but not (b). The right to rescind would not be lost for the latter. In *Attwood v. Small*[52] there had been statements made about the profits of a mine which was for sale. The plaintiffs got their own agents to examine the accounts. They were

---

[45] See also *Redgrave v. Hurd* (1881) 20 Ch. 1 (at p. 21), as explained by Lord Blackburn in *Smith v. Chadwick* (1884) 9 App. Cas. 187 (at p. 196).
[46] (1884) 9 App. Cas. 187.
[47] (1862) 1 H and C 90, 158 E.R. 813.
[48] At p. 824.
[49] This case can be said to be the high water mark of *caveat emptor* or "let the buyer beware".
[50] (1881) 20 Ch. 1.
[51] *Alliance and Leicester Building Society v. Edgestop* [1993] 1 W.L.R. 1462.
[52] (1838) 6 Cl. and Fin. 232, 7 E.R. 684.

unsuccessful in alleging fraud, having looked into the matter themselves and not relied on the misrepresentation alone. By contrast, in *S. Pearson and Sons Ltd v. Dublin Corporation*[53] it was held by the House of Lords that even if a representee carried out his or her own investigations, this would not deprive them of an action if the representations were fraudulent.

Reliance

18.9   The concept of misrepresentation is rooted upon reliance and as such is one of the best examples of reliance theory in contract law. If the representee relied on the statement, she or he may be able to have the contract set aside even if there were other factors which led him or her to make the contract. Reliance is a wider concept than inducement. In *JEB Fasteners Ltd v. Marks Bloom & Co*[54] the Court of Appeal held that there was no "true reliance". The representation had to be a "real and substantial, though not necessarily decisive" part in the inducement.[55] Sir Sebag Shaw made it clear that the question of misrepresentation was whether it in any "material degree" affected the judgment of whether or not to take over the other company. In *Atlantic Lines Ltd v. Hallam Ltd, The Lucy*,[56] Mustill J.[57] stated that the statement had a "material influence on conduct of the negotiations". Once a statement is shown to be an inducement, then a presumption of reliance may apply. In *County Nat West Bank Ltd v. Barton*[58] the Court held that if a false statement was likely to play a part in the decision of a reasonable person to enter into a contract, there was a rebuttable presumption that it did do so. The effect of the presumption was therefore to alter the burden of proof on the question of reliance. Reliance could also be established by demonstrating that the false statement induced the representee to persevere in a decision already reached. In *Barton* Morritt L.J. said that the first question was whether the representation was of such a nature as would be likely to induce a person into a contract. If so the presumption would apply that a reasonable person would rely upon it. In order to rebut the presumption, the representor could show that the other party (a) never knew of the statement until after they had entered into the contract, (b) discovered before they entered into the contract that the statement was false or (c) showed by words or clear conduct that the statement did not induce their decisions. Morritt L.J. thought it was "hard to imagine facts sufficient to rebut it which did not fall within any of these three categories". However, it would be wrong to say the presumption could only be rebutted in certain specified ways. The Court of Appeal held that there could be a representation in allowing a person to persevere with a decision already reached.

The question of materiality

18.10   This is a debatable requirement. Materiality may be seen as either a requirement in it's own right, or included in the categories of inducement or reliance. The misrepresentation does

---

[53] [1907] A.C. 351.
[54] [1983] 1 All E.R. 583.
[55] At p. 594.
[56] [1983] 1 Lloyd's Rep. 188.
[57] At p. 201.
[58] *The Times*, July 29, 1999.

not have to be material in the sense of equitable mistake, *i.e.* fundamental, or go to the root of the contract.[59] The representation must relate to a fact which would induce a reasonable person to enter into the agreement. It is possible for a contract to provide that a particular statement (or even all) are to be regarded as material.[60] Materiality was regarded as a key requirement of misrepresentation by the Court of Appeal in *Downs v. Chappell*[61] where Hobhouse L.J. described a representation as material "when its tendency, or its natural and probable result, is to induce the representee to act on the faith of it in the kind of way in which he is proved to have in fact acted. The test is objective." In *Avon Insurance plc v. Swire Fraser Ltd*[62] Rix J. explained that the test of causation under the Misrepresentation Act s. 2(1) was whether or not the misrepresentation was material to the transaction. Unlike mistake, there is no requirement that the misrepresentation be fundamental, or even of substantial importance, so long as it acts as an inducement. If however the representation relates to something insignificant or to a trivial question of fact, it will not be sufficient to be actionable. The requirement of materiality acts to exclude trifling or minor matters. This would provide too easy an escape route from a contract if every false statement of fact were ground for recission.

THE FOUR TYPES OF MISREPRESENTATION

The type of misrepresentation is determined by the state of mind of the person making the statement. Did the person intend to deceive the other party? Was he or she negligent or honest in their belief that the words were true? These are questions of intention, objectively determined in theory but with a high degree of subjectivity, *i.e.* intention to defraud requires a guilty mind. At common law there were only two varieties of misrepresentation: fraudulent and wholly innocent. Two further grounds for action were added in the 1960's. First, the action for negligent misstatement as a result of the House of Lord's judgment in *Hedley Byrne v. Joseph Heller and Partners*.[63] This gave an action in negligence for careless words even without a contract between the parties. *Hedley Byrne* was a landmark decision for the common law and has led to an entire new branch of tort claims. Secondly, the Misrepresentation Act 1967, s. 2(1) provided a new statutory action. This is now the main category of claims, with good reason, as we shall discuss.   **18.11**

Fraudulent misrepresentation

The essence of fraudulent misrepresentation is dishonesty and intention to deceive. Fraudulent misrepresentation requires a high standard of proof. Even in civil cases, fraud is a serious matter. The claim for fraud is an action in the tort of deceit. In *Derry v. Peek*[64] the directors of a company in Plymouth issued a prospectus which stated that by Act of Parliament the company had the right to use steam power. The tramway which they hoped to operate could be moved by animal power or, with the approval of the

---

[59] See Chap. 21.
[60] *e.g.* See contracts of insurance, discussed in Chap. 15.
[61] [1996] 3 All E.R. 351.
[62] [2000] 1 All E.R. (Comm) 573.
[63] [1964] A.C. 465.
[64] (1889) 14 App. Cas. 337.

Board of Trade, by steam power. The plaintiff purchased some shares as a result of the statement. Approval for steam power was not given. The House of Lords held that the directors were not guilty of fraud, as the statement was made honestly at the time. The directors believed it was true so there was no fraud. Lord Herschell stated that the requirements of the action for fraud were that a false representation had been made: (1) knowingly, (2) without belief in it's truth, or (3) recklessly or carelessly as to whether it be true or false. "To prevent a false statement being fraudulent, there must, I think, always be an honest belief in its truth."[65] The definition of fraud in *Derry v. Peek* is a narrow one.[65a] Fraud is not established lightly.

18.12   The old rule has stood the test of time and is still applied. In *Hughes v. Clewley "The Siben"*[66] the defendant placed an advertisement in a yachting magazine offering a discothèque in the Algarve for sale in part exchange for a quality sailing yacht. The plaintiff sold his yacht to the defendant, who also offered a villa, which was used for an escort business. The defendant was held liable for fraudulent misrepresentation. First, he had represented that he would be owner of the discothèque at the time of sale, when he knew he would not. This had induced the contract. Secondly, he had stated that the discothèque was making a profit of £1,500. He knew the profits were significantly less than this, so the statements were deliberate lies. The plaintiff was therefore entitled to damages for fraud. Rescission was refused, as a part of the agreement was the provision of girls for money as part of the escort services. Since there was an element of sexual immorality and this rendered the contract tainted with illegality, it was not right for the Court to order rescission.[67] Hobhouse L.J. in *Downs v. Chappell*[68] identified three elements in deceit. First, it is necessary to prove the representation was fraudulent, secondly, that it was material, and third, that it induced the plaintiff to act to their detriment. The "fiction of fraud" plays an important part in the meaning of the claim under the Misrepresentation Act 1967, s. 2(1), as we shall discuss shortly.

Negligent misrepresentation

18.13   Negligent misstatement is really an action in the tort of negligence. It can be brought against another contracting party or without any contract being formed if proximity exists. The person making the statement must be under a pre-existing duty of care, such as a professional person advising a client. Few cases in the twentieth century of the English common law have had such an impact as the House of Lord's judgment in *Hedley Byrne & Co Ltd v. Heller & Partners Ltd.*[69] The plaintiffs asked the defendants to make enquiries about the finances of a company called Easipower Ltd. The defendants were Easipower's bankers and they told Hedley Byrne that Easipower were in a satisfactory financial state. The plaintiffs took this to mean that Easipower was safe to do business with, and so made an advertising contract with them. When Easipower went into

---

[65]   At p. 374.
[65a]   Fraud for the purposes of the Insolvency Act 1986 is also confined to actual dishonesty as explained in *Derry v. Peek*, see *Molander v. Evans, The Times*, June 25, 2001.
[66]   [1996] 1 Lloyd's Rep. 35.
[67]   See Chap. 20.
[68]   [1997] 1 W.L.R. 426.
[69]   [1964] A.C. 465.

liquidation, the plaintiffs brought an action against the defendants claiming damages for negligent misstatement. The House of Lords held that negligent words could lead to liability in negligence at common law. This was a watershed in the common law. The defendants were not liable because their advice was tendered with an exemption of liability that it was given "without responsibility".[70] However, the principle was established that negligent misstatement was an actionable branch of the tort of negligence. A contract between the plaintiff and defendant is not necessary. The defendant makes a statement without reasonable belief in it's truth or falsehood. It does not require the plaintiff prove dishonesty. There has to be a "special relationship" between plaintiff and defendant. This normally only applies to persons who have a special skill, such as giving professional advice, in relation to the subject matter. It can arise if the person makes a voluntary assumption of responsibility, in other words, takes it upon themself to make the statements under a duty of care. The action for negligent misstatement in tort requires fault on the part of the defendant to be proved. Negligence is determined by a series of principles, each of which creates obstacles to liability for the defendant. The person alleging negligence has to show that a duty of care existed between themself and the defendant, that the latter's action fell below the standard of reasonable care expected of such a person and that the type of injury was reasonably foreseeable. The claimant has, therefore, a number of hurdles to overcome. *Hedley Byrne* has proved the progenitor of a fruitful source of tort claims.[70a] Where a contract exists, claimants tend to prefer the statutory action to which we now turn.

Action under the Misrepresentation Act 1967, section 2(1)

The 1967 Act introduced a statutory form of action based upon a "fiction of fraud". **18.14** This is now the most significant category of misrepresentation. The statutory action only applies if the parties have made a contract. The person making the statement has to prove that he or she actually believed, or had reasonable grounds to believe, what they said was true. The burden of proof is therefore reversed. This is of considerable advantage to claimants. The action under s. 2(1) is now the most popular form of redress for misrepresentation. In *Spice Girls v. Aprilla World Service*[71] the plaintiffs made a contract with the defendants, a motor cycle manufacturer, to promote their products. This included launching a special "Spice Girls Scooter" with a silhouette of the five Spice Girls on top. Shortly after the contract was signed Geri Halliwell, one of the five, left the group and the scooter promotions campaign turned into a "total marketing flop", costing the defendants millions of pounds in lost profits. The Spice Girls sued for unpaid royalties and motor cycles promised to them when the defendants refused to carry on with the sponsorship contract. The defendants counterclaimed for misrepresentation on the ground that they had been induced to enter the contract by photographic images of five members of the group and that this implied that the group would remain intact. Since one member of the group had already decided to leave, this amounted to actionable misrepresentation. Arden J. held that the

---

[70] See Chap. 16.
[70a] The 1990's witnessed a rash of major actions, particularly against financial institutions and large companies. See *Caparo Industries plc v. Dickman* [1990] 2 A.C. 605.
[71] [2000] E.M.L.R. 478.

pictures amounted to a misrepresentation that the group would remain as five girls. When this was no longer true the group were bound to correct this as failing to do so amounted to a misrepresentation. Under s. 2(1) the defendants had failed to discharge the burden of showing that they had reasonable grounds for believing that the representation in the form of the advertising images was true.[72]

Innocent misrepresentation

18.15   Innocent misrepresentation occurs when the state of mind of the representor is free from blame. The person told the truth as they saw it and had no opportunity to know of it's falsehood. At one time all non fraudulent misrepresentations were deemed innocent. Nowadays the expression "innocent" can only be applied if the representor is neither negligent nor covered by s. 2(1).[73]

Remedies for Misrepresentation

Damages

(1) Fraudulent misrepresentation

18.16   Damages for fraud are based on the tort action of deceit. The measure of damages is designed to place the injured party in the position they would have been in if the wrongdoing had not been committed, *i.e.* as if the statement had not been made. In other words, as if no transaction had been made between the parties. In contract law generally damages are to protect the expectation interest, *i.e.* what the party would have obtained if the contract had been performed.[74] In the tort of deceit, the defendant must pay for all the direct consequences of their wrongdoing. The person making the statement is liable for all the actual losses directly flowing from their statement, and damages are not limited to negligence rule based upon the reasonable foreseeability. The extended measure of damages was originally suggested by Lord Atkin in *Clark v. Urquhart*[75] where it was held that the measure of damages under s. 84 of the Companies (Consolidation) Act 1908 for untrue statements in a prospectus should be applied to a common law action for fraud. In *Doyle v. Olby (Ironmongers) Ltd*[76] it was firmly established that the principle of damages for deceit was the tortious and not the contractual measure. This had two important results. The plaintiff was to be put in the position as if the fraudulent misrepresentation had not been made, and he was entitled to all the actual losses flowing directly from the breach. This rule was applied in *East v. Maurer*[77] and was later confirmed in *William Sindall plc v. Cambridgeshire County Council*[78] and *Smith New*

---

[72] See also *Howard Marine and Dredging Co. Ltd v. A. Ogden and Sons (Excavations) Ltd* [1978] Q.B. 574.
[73] However, as a recent example of the use of the word in it's older meaning, see Rix J. in *Avon Insurance plc v. Shire Fraser Ltd* [2000] 1 All E.R. (Comm) 573.
[74] See Chap. 24.
[75] [1930] A.C. 28.
[76] [1969] 2 Q.B. 158.
[77] [1991] 2 All E.R. 733.
[78] [1994] 1 W.L.R. 1016.

Court Securities Ltd v. Citibank NA.[79] The latter is now the leading case on the quantification of damages for fraudulent misrepresentation. Lord Browne-Wilkinson summarised the rules as follows:

(a)   the defendant is liable for all the losses flowing directly from the transaction;

(b)   such damage need not be foreseeable;

(c)   it must however have been directly caused by the transaction;

(d)   the plaintiff could recover the full price paid, minus any benefits received by them as a result of the transaction;

(e)   the plaintiff was entitled to consequential losses caused by the transaction, *i.e.* losses which flowed from the breach; and

(f)   the plaintiff had to take reasonable steps to mitigate his loss once he discovered the fraud.

The fraud measure does not always lead to a greater recovery than that under con-   **18.17**
tractual principles. In *Downs v. Chappell*[80] it was held that where a plaintiff had been induced to enter into a transaction either by fraud or by negligent misrepresentation relating to the profitability of a business, he was entitled to his income and capital losses, up to the date when he discovered he had been misled and had an opportunity to avoid further losses. Normally profits are calculated under expectation principles in contract law.[81] In *Clef Aquitaine SARL v. Laporte Materials (Barrow) Ltd*[82] the claimant entered into a number of contracts in reliance on a fraudulent misrepresentation. The transactions turned out to be profitable but the claimant argued that other more profitable contracts would have been entered into but for the fraud. The Court of Appeal held that there was no need to show that the contracts entered into as a result of fraud were loss making but the claimant could argue that other more favourable transactions would have been entered into instead. The measure of damages in such a case being established by the reliance test comparing the claimant's position before the fraudulent statement and their position as a result of reliance upon it.

(2) Damages in the tort of negligence

In an action for negligent misstatement at common law, the measure of damages is based on the tort of negligence, where the rule is that the type of loss must be reasonably foreseeable. Damages in negligence are normally based on the reliance principle in order to put the injured party back into the position they were in prior to the wrongdoing.[83] In *Banque Bruxelles v. Eagle Star Insurance Co. Ltd*[84] the House of Lords held that the measure of damages for negligent misstatement at common law, even in a "no transaction" case, were the foreseeable consequences of having received negligently incorrect information and not all the foreseeable losses caused by entering the transaction.

---

[79] [1997] A.C. 254.
[80] [1996] 3 All E.R. 344.
[81] See later Chap. 24.
[82] [2000] 3 All E.R. 493.
[83] Discussed Chap. 24.
[84] [1997] A.C. 191.

(3) Damages under s. 2(1)

18.18   The correct measure of damages under s. 2(1) has been a source of long running debate. In *Royscott Trust Ltd. v. Rogerson*[85] Balcombe L.J. held that the correct measure of damages under s. 2(1) was that for fraudulent misrepresentation. This was because of the language of the section which talked about a "fiction of fraud". The crucial words in s. 2(1) "shall be so liable" were held to refer to fraud. This meant a finance company recovering all the losses flowing from a misrepresentation even if they had been unforeseeable. *Royscot Trust* is an important judgment, placing as it does a plaintiff who uses s. 2(1) in a superior position to that of a person claiming fraudulent or even negligent misrepresentation at common law. The result is that the measure of damages under s. 2(1) is now as good as fraud without having to prove deceit. Under the Act the burden of proof is reversed and placed upon the person making the statement. If a contract has been formed between the parties, a s. 2(1) claim is likely to be the best option from the claimant's point of view. The rule in *Royscot* is generous to plaintiffs. Defendants who may be merely negligent are now equated with intentional wrongdoers. In *Smith New Court Securities Ltd v. Citibank*[86] Lord Browne-Wilkinson appeared to have reservations about the correctness of the principle, and Lord Steyn expressly doubted equating a morally innocent person with one guilty of fraud. Section 2(1) was described with some justification as a "mighty weapon" by Rix J. in *Avon Insurance plc v. Swire Fraser Ltd.*[87] In this case the claimants issued proceedings under s. 2(1). On the issue of whether the nature of damages was tortious (and based on fraud) or contract, Rix J. held that the answer was clearly the fraud measure, as laid down in *Royscott Trust Ltd v. Rogerson.* The judge expressed his doubts as to the wisdom of the rule, indeed to the point of disapproval. The test for the measure of damages appeared to influence Rix J., in determining liability. The judge held that "where there was room for the exercise of judgement, a misrepresentation ought not to be too easily found". The claim under s. 2(1) was unsuccessful. The nature of damages under s. 2(1) can be criticised.[88] The irony of the present law is that liability under s. 2(1) is easier to establish than the more serious allegation of fraud. Section 2(1) includes those who are negligent but not fraudulent in their intent. The burden of proving fraud under *Derry v. Peek* is an onerous one, whereas we have seen that under s. 2(1) the burden shifts to the defendant to show that the representer believed, or had reasonable grounds for believing that the representation was true. In the circumstances, persons who might otherwise wish to argue for fraud may now be in a better position if they bring proceedings under s. 2(1) This does not seem to be a satisfactory state of the law.

(4) Damages in lieu of rescission under s. 2(2)

If a misrepresentation has been made non-fraudulently, the court may award damages in lieu of, *i.e.* instead of, rescission if it would be equitable to do so having regard to three factors. First, the nature of the misrepresentation, secondly, the loss that would be

---

[85] [1991] 3 All E.R. 294.
[86] [1997] A.C. 254.
[87] [2000] 1 All E.R. (Comm) 573.
[88] See Stewart-Smith and de Chassiron (2000) NLJ 865 who conclude: "It is hard to see the justification for visiting the same consequences on a fool as on a fraudster. *Royscot* is ripe for revision."

caused by it if the contract were upheld and thirdly, the loss that rescission would cause to the other party. There are two key questions to consider.

(a) The discretionary nature of s. 2(2)

The court has an equitable discretion to award damages instead of rescission under this subsection. Unlike damages at common law there is no right to such an award.[88a] Damages under s. 2(2) can be awarded without wrongdoing on the part of the defendant. A claimant will normally seek damages only if the primary remedy of rescission is unsatisfactory. If the right to rescission is lost or barred,[89] the orthodox view remains that damages are also unavailable and cannot be awarded. The claimant therefore has no remedy. A contrary view, that damages can be awarded even when the right to rescind had been lost, was expressed by Jacob J. in *Thomas Witter Ltd v. TBP Industries Ltd*.[90] The judge considered the section unclear and looked to the intention of Parliament. Jacob J. concluded that it was unlikely that Parliament intended that a representee should be left without any remedy so damages could be awarded even if rescission were not available. This view was affirmed by the Queen's Bench Division in *Zanzibar v. British Aerospace (Lancaster House) Ltd*,[91] in which the Court held that rescission and damages were to be regarded as alternative remedies. Where a right to rescission had been established, the Court had a power to declare that the contract remained in existence and award damages instead of rescission if it was equitable to do so. In the case in question, the right to rescind had been lost, but the judge considered that the remedy of damages was still available. In his opinion, the effect of s. 2(2) was to give the Court a power to award damages as an alternative to rescission whenever it was equitable to do so.

18.19

(b) The calculation of damages under s. 2(2)

The correct test for damages under s. 2(2) is still not clarified. There are three different views on the question. First, that the damages are "lower" than under s. 2(1). That is partly based on a reading of the section and also s. 2(3). Secondly, that a special measure applies under the section which is intended as compensation for the loss of the right to rescind. The third possibility is that damages should be limited to the old equitable remedy of indemnity.[92] The Court of Appeal discussed damages in lieu of rescission in *William Sindall plc v. Cambridgeshire County Council*.[93] Hoffman L.J. stated that there were three factors relevant to damages under s. 2(2) which had been laid out in the original Report which led to the Act.[94] These were the nature of the representation, the loss caused by the misrepresentation if the contract was upheld rather than rescinded and the loss to the non-fraudulent representor by rescission. The Law Revision Committee made it clear that s. 2(2) was enacted because it was thought that there might be hardship to the representor if they were deprived of the whole bargain because of a minor misrepresentation. In Hoffman L.J.'s view:

18.20

[88a] See Chaps 24 and 26.
[89] See pp. 324–326.
[90] [1994] T.L.R. 145.
[91] *The Times*, January 26, 2000.
[92] See *Adam v. Newbigging* (1888) L.R. 13 App. Cas 308; *Whittington v. Seal-Hayne* (1900) 82 L.T. 49.
[93] [1994] 1 W.L.R. 1016.
[94] 10th Report of the Law Reform Committee, 1962, Cmnd 1782.

(a) damages under s. 2(2) were to be assessed as losses caused by the misrepresentation if the contract was upheld, rather than from the making of the contract itself as under s. 2(1);

(b) damages under s. 2(2) should never exceed the sum which would have been awarded if the representation had been a warranty; and

(c) damages were likely to be less under s. 2(2) than under s. 2(1). This was clear from the reading of s. 2(3).[95]

The measure of damages is therefore likely to be different from that under s. 2(1). Evans L.J. in *Sindall* took the correct measure under s. 2(2) to be "the difference in value between what the plaintiff was misled into believing that he was acquiring and the value of what he in fact received".[96] This is actually closer to a contract measure of damages. Since damages are based upon equitable grounds, it may be that the courts are not constrained by any fixed common law rule. Nevertheless, this is an area where clarity is lacking where an authoritative ruling would be helpful.

Rescission

18.21 Contracts are voidable for misrepresentation. Rescission is the primary remedy for misrepresentation. This is a non judicial or self help remedy.[97] As such it is usually effective, immediate and avoids the cost of litigation. Rescission applies to all types of misrepresentation, even those which are innocent. The contract is rescinded at the option of the representee. If she chooses to continue with the contract she may do so, and the agreement will remain valid. Once the representee has made her decision to rescind or affirm, that is final. The decision must be communicated within a reasonable time to the other party. This is usually an express statement but could be by simply returning property to the other party. A person cannot rescind after they have done anything to affirm the contract with knowledge of the facts giving rise to the option to rescind. If it is impossible to find the other party, rescission may be possible by some other reasonable act.

In *Car and Universal Finance Co. Ltd v. Caldwell*[98], the defendant sold his Jaguar car to two men calling themselves Norris and Foster. Norris left a cheque which bounced. The car was sold to a third party. The fraudsters absconded. The defendant immediately informed the police and the Automobile Association about the fraudulent transaction. The Court of Appeal held that he had done all that he could and that this was enough. "In such circumstances an innocent party might evince his intention to disaffirm the contract by overt means falling short of communication or repossession". The defendant's actions were enough to amount to rescission. According to Lord Denning[99]: "In principle it seems to me that a seller can avoid a contract by an unequivocal act of election which demonstrates clearly that he elects to rescind it and to be no longer bound by it. It is sufficient if

---

[95] Section 2(3) provides that damages may be assessed against a person under subs. 2 whether or not he is liable under s. 2(1), but where he is so liable, any award under subs. 2 shall be taken into account in assessing liability under s. 2(1).

[96] At p. 1027.

[97] See Chap. 26.

[98] [1965] 1 Q.B. 525.

[99] At p. 531.

he asserts his intention to rescind "in the plainest and most open manner competent to him" Lord Denning was quoting from the speech of Lord Hatherley in *Reese River Silver Mining Company v. Smith*.[1] Under normal circumstances the person must communicate directly with the other party who is meanwhile entitled to treat the contract as continuing to exist until he or she has heard otherwise. An uncommunicated intention (according to Upjohn L.J. in *Caldwell*[2]) "by speaking to a third party or making a private notice, will be ineffective". Upjohn L.J. approved the basic principle that the act of rescission must "manifest that election by communicating with the other party his intention to rescind the transaction and claim no interest under it. The communication need not be formal provided it is a distinct and positive repudiation of the transaction".[3] The decision to rescind must be made within a reasonable time. Rescission is barred in the following circumstances.

(1) Counter restitution is impossible[4]

18.22

Restitution will not be awarded if the parties cannot be restored to their original position. In *Boyd and Forrest v. Glasgow and South Western Railway Company*[5] the work of laying a railway line had been completed two years before the action was commenced. "Restitution" said Lord Atkinson[6] was "absolutely impossible . . . the pursuers cannot take back what they gave, . . . the work was done, the parties cannot in any sense be restored, in relation to this contract, to the position they occupied before the contract was entered into". However, in the Australian case of *Vadusz v. Pioneer Concrete (SA) Pty Ltd*[7] it was held that even if counter restitution were not possible from the beginning, the contract might still be set aside in equity because the case was in fraud and equity would prevent a person enjoying the benefit of his deception.

(2) The representee has not acted within a reasonable time

A party must rescind the contract within a reasonable time. In *Leaf v. International Galleries*[8] the remedy of rescission was lost because five years had elapsed and this was regarded as too long a delay.

(3) Third parties have acquired rights in the subject matter of the contract

If a third party purchases goods in good faith and for value, the right to rescind may be lost. This is important in relation to cases of mistake.[9] The buyer must have title to pass goods on to a third party.

(4) Affirmation of the contract

18.23

Affirmation prevents a later recission of the contract. However a claimant must know of the facts giving him or her a right to rescind. In *Peyman v. Lanjani*[10] the Court of Appeal

---

[1] (1869) LR 4 H.L. 64 (at p. 74).
[2] At p. 554.
[3] At p. 554.
[4] The traditional Latin name for this rule *Restitutio in integrum*, is now better called "counter-restitution", see Millett L.J. in *Dunbar v. Nadeem* [1998] 3 All E.R. 376. See also Chap. 26.
[5] 1915 S.C. (H.L.) 20.
[6] At p. 28.
[7] (1895) 130 A.L.R. 570.
[8] [1950] 2 K.B. 86.
[9] See Chap. 6. However, see also *Shogun Finance Ltd v. Hudson* [2000] All E.R. (D) 306.
[10] [1985] Ch. 457.

held that in order to render the decision to rescind or affirm irrevocable, the party not only had to have knowledge of the facts giving rise to the election but of the right to elect itself. A person could not be treated as having elected to affirm unless he had "unequivocally demonstrated to the other party that he intended to proceed with it. Election was a "question of fact to be decided on the evidence". In the case in question, the plaintiff, an Iranian who spoke no English went into possession of the restaurant in James Street, London before he knew of the defect in the defendant's title. By the terms of the contract such conduct did not amount to irrevocable affirmation so he was entitled to rescind the contract. Affirmation can be inferred when a person keeps goods knowing they are defective or if the contract is still clearly subsisting. In *Long v. Lloyd*[11] the plaintiff drove a lorry from Hampton Court to Sevenoaks then to Rochester and back to Sevenoaks. By the time he returned to Sevenoaks he knew that the lorry had numerous faults as a result of which the vehicle was not capable of travelling at more than 40 miles per hour. On the following day, the plaintiff nevertheless sent the lorry to be driven by an employee to Middlesborough. Pearce L.J. held that by doing so the plaintiff had accepted the lorry "for better or for worse". This extinguished any right of rescission for misrepresentation after completion of the sale.

(5) Illegality in some circumstances

In *Hughes v. Clewley, The Siben (No. 2)*[12] it was held that rescission would not be allowed since part of the consideration had an immoral purpose. The effect of rescission would be to transfer a business being used for unlawful purposes from one party to the other. Clarke J. held that it would not be right for the Court to order rescission. This may now be regarded as another bar to rescission in addition to the four traditional headings.

MISREPRESENTATION OR NON-DISCLOURE BY AN AGENT OR EMPLOYEE

18.24 Liability under s. 2(1) can also apply when an agent makes a representation while acting within his or her authority on behalf of their principal. In *Gosling v. Anderson*[13] it was held that the principal could be liable at common law and under s. 2(1) for statements by the agent acting within the scope of his or her authority. In *Resolute Maritime Inc. v. Nippon Kaiji Kyoki* "The Skopas"[14] the plaintiff buyers of the vessel *Skopas* issued claims against the sellers and other persons involved in the sale of the vessel alleging misrepresentations as to the vessel's state of repair. They joined as defendants, the firm of brokers and the individual broker as defendants alleging breach of s. 2(1) of the 1967 Act. Mustill J. held that liability arising out of the Act rested on the principal, as contracting party, not on his agent. The brokers were held not liable. A principal is liable for the fraud of an agent under the rules of vicarious liability,[15] and they will also be liable if they expressly authorise an agent to make a statement which they know to

---

[11] [1958] 1 W.L.R. 753.
[12] [1996] 1 Lloyd's Rep. 35.
[13] (1972) 223 E.G. 1743.
[14] [1983] 1 W.L.R. 857.
[15] *Lloyd v. Grace, Smith and Co.* [1912] A.C. 716.

be false. Generally speaking, the state of mind of principal and agent are treated as one, so that misrepresentation by an agent will make a contract liable to be rescinded. In *Merritt v. Babb*[15a] it was held that an employee of a firm of valuers owed a personal duty of care to clients. Misrepresentation by an agent or employee can have other effects. For instance, if a shop assistant distorts or varies the written terms of a contract, his or her oral statements may be admissible as a term of the contract. This is an exception to the parol evidence rule.[16] It may also have an effect on the incorporation and extent of any exemption clauses contained in a written contract.[17]

Excluding Liability for Non-Fraudulent Misrepresentation

At common law it was not possible to exclude liability for a fraudulent misrepresenta-   **18.25**
tion.[18] This was void on public policy grounds. The Misrepresentation Act s. 3 covers exemptions for negligent misrepresentation and liability under s. 2(1). The section provides that if a contract term excludes or restricts liability for misrepresentation or any remedy, the term has no effect unless it satisfies the requirement of reasonableness.

The case law on exclusions of liability for misrepresentation subject to the reasonableness requirement was discussed earlier.[19] The issue of reasonableness was considered in *Walker v. Boyle*,[20] in which the National Conditions of Sale provided that "no error, misstatement or omission in any preliminary answer concerning the property shall annul the sale". The Court found the clause did not satisfy the reasonableness test. The fact that it had been used for many years in standard form, had been drafted by solicitors and that both parties had solicitors acting for them did not mean the clause met the statutory test. In *Toomey v. Eagle Star Insurance*[21] the Court held that a clause could exclude a party's right to rescind a contract for misrepresentation. This would however remain subject to a reasonableness test. If a misrepresentation is made by an agent then an exemption clause exempting the principal or limiting the agent's authority may fall outside s. 3.[22]

[15a] [2001] Lloyd's Rep. 468.
[16] See Chap. 12.
[17] See Chap. 16.
[18] *S. Pearson and Son Ltd v. Dublin Corporation* [1907] A.C. 351. See Chap. 16.
[19] See Chap 17. See also *Howard Marine and Dredging v. Ogden* [1978] 2 All E.R. 1134 and *Overbrooke Estates v. Glencombe Properties* [1974 1 W.L.R. 102, both cases under the Misrepresentation Act, s. 3.
[20] [1982] 1 All E.R. 634.
[21] [1995] 2 Lloyd's Rep. 88.
[22] *Overbrooke Estates v. Glencombe Properties Ltd* [1974] 3 All E.R. 511.

Chapter 19

ILLEGITIMATE PRESSURE

DURESS AT COMMON LAW

A contract cannot be made by means of violence or pressure such as threats of force or **19.1** economic blackmail.[1] The idea of a contract as a "meeting of minds" which developed in the nineteenth century led to the conclusion that if a person's willpower had been overcome by physical threats, there was no real agreement. The will theory of contract is no longer regarded as sound, so the rules against duress are now based upon another concept, that of illegitimate pressure. If pressure amounts to duress, a resulting contract will be voidable in the "absence of practical choice", *i.e.* the nature of the demands which were made, or the victim being placed in a situation in which he or she was given no realistic alternative.[2] The modern doctrine therefore concentrates on the conduct of the wrongdoer who exercises the duress whereas the old theory looked at the mind of the victim. The question becomes whether the pressure exercised was legitimate.[3] Duress was rarely pleaded in contract law until recent years. The rise of a new category, that of economic duress, has been an important development for contract law generally. Economic duress could become an important factor in determining the enforceability of promises. A promise intended to be binding and relied upon could become enforceable so long as it is not unconscionable or given under duress. Such a rule would provide an alternative to the requirement of consideration in every case.[4] Duress is an entirely procedural aspect of fairness. No question of substantive unfairness arises, unlike undue influence, which we also discuss later in this chapter.

The categories of duress

(1) Duress to the person

Originally duress involved violence, the threat of force against the person of the other **19.2** party or at least of some physical restraint. At common law therefore, duress had to be of a physical nature. In *Cumming v. Ince*[5] the threat of returning the plaintiff, Catherine

---

[1] The law goes back to *Whelpdale's case* (1604) 5 Co. Rep 119, 77 E.R. 239.
[2] See Lord Scarman in *Universe Tankships Inc of Manrovia v. International Transport Workers Federation "The Universe Sentinel"* [1983] A.C. 366.
[3] Smith, "Contracting under pressure: a theory of duress" (1997) 56 C.L.J. 343.
[4] See Chap. 8.
[5] (1847) 11 Q.B. 112; 116 E.R. 418.

Cumming, to a lunatic asylum was used to extract a deed from the plaintiff in favour of her two daughters. Mrs Cumming's consent had not truly been given to the agreement made at the Horns Tavern, Kennington which was unenforceable because of duress. The Court made it clear that:

> "If she was inducted to sign [the deeds] by fear of personal suffering brought upon her by confinement in a lunatic asylum by the act of the defendants, the resignation would appear to be brought about by a direct interference with her personal freedom. Is not this truly described as duress? And was the contract which resulted made with her free will?"[6]

Nowadays cases of duress to the person are quite rare. The leading authority is the Australian case of *Barton v. Armstrong*,[7] in which Armstrong, the Chairman of a company called "Landmark", threatened to kill Barton if he did not pay a large sum of money and purchase Armstrong's shares in the company. Barton sought a declaration[8] that the deed which he had exercised in favour of the defendant should be set aside for duress. The Court held that agreements procured by duress were not merely voidable but void. This view of the effect of duress is no longer good law however, duress merely rendering a contract voidable by one of the parties.[9] The Privy Council stated that the test for duress was whether the victim in such cases would have entered into the contract but for the threat.

(2) Duress to goods

19.3 At common law a contract was not normally invalidated by "duress of goods", *i.e.* threats to property rather than the person. So any agreement to pay for goods to be returned which had been wrongfully detained, or to prevent goods being illegally seized, was binding. The classic case is *Skeate v. Beale*.[10] The rule however was also that money which had already been paid to prevent seizure of the goods could be recovered.[11] Lord Denning described duress of goods in *Lloyd's Bank v. Bundy*[12] as:

> "A typical case is when a man in a strong bargaining position by being in possession of the goods of another by virtue of a legal right, such as by way of pawn or pledge or taken in distress. The owner is in a weak position because he is in urgent need of the goods. The stronger demands of the weaker more than is justly due: and he pays it in order to get the goods. Such a transaction is voidable. He can recover the excess".

Lord Denning cited *Astley v. Reynolds*[13] as authority. This appeared to contradict the earlier authorities which were themselves over subtle and confused. Duress of goods is

---

[6] At p. 421.
[7] [1976] A.C. 104.
[8] This remedy is discussed in Chap. 25.
[9] See later p. 333. But note contrary view by Lanham (1966) 29 M.L.R. 615.
[10] (1841) 11 Ad and E 983, 113 E.R. 688.
[11] *Maskell v. Horner* [1915] 3 K.B. 106 (discussed later p. 335); and *Astley v. Reynolds* (1731) 2 Str. 915, 93 E.R. 939.
[12] [1975] Q.B. 326 (at p. 337).
[13] (1731) 2 Stra. 915, 93 E.R. 939.

now included in the modern category of economic duress. In *Occidental Worldwide Investment Corp v. Skibs A/S Avanti, The Siboen and The Sibotre*[14] the Court reviewed the line of authority, of which *Skeate v. Beale* was the leading case, and the rule against duress to goods. Kerr J. stated[15] that he did not think that English law must always rule out such a claim. The judge's view has proved to be correct as English law now recognises a new and developing concept of economic duress.

(3) Economic duress

Economic duress arises from threats to a person's business, trade or economic interests. **19.4** The scope of economic duress was discussed in the House of Lords in *Universal Tankships of Monrovia v. International Transport Workers Federation "The Universe Sentinel"*[16] where by a majority of three to two their Lordships held that the money demanded by a trade union to cease "blacking" a vessel at Milford Haven was recoverable as it had been demanded by means of economic duress. The agreement was voidable as it had been procured by illegitimate pressure. The question is therefore what amounts to illegitimate pressure? In the '*Universe Sentinel*' the House of Lords held that it is the nature of the demand which is significant. The court should adopt a "combination of factors" approach to economic duress. This included (i) whether the pressure was legitimate (ii) the nature of the threats or pressure and (iii) the absence of practical choice. Threatening to do an unlawful act was *prima facie* illegitimate pressure from which economic duress could be inferred. A contract procured by such means would normally be voidable. On the other hand, threatening to bring a civil action is normally quite legitimate. This does not amount to economic duress, even if commercially threatening. It must not however fall within the tort of malicious prosecution. In *Metall und Rohstoff AG v. Donaldson Lufkin*[17] Slade L.J. expressed "great doubt" whether any general tort of maliciously instituting civil proceedings exists.

In *Kaufman v. Gerson*[18] there was a threatened prosecution of the plaintiff's husband for misappropriating money. The plaintiff was threatened that if she did not agree to reimburse the money taken out of her own assets, her husband would be prosecuted. The object of the agreement was therefore to "stifle a prosecution". To avoid dishonouring of "the good name of her family", the plaintiff agreed. It was held that this was duress and the contract set aside. This was illegitimate pressure even in the days when duress only applied to threats to the person. Sir Richard Collins M.R.[19] compared the situation with threatening a person with a pistol. Such an agreement would not be enforced. "What does it matter what particular form of coercion is used, so long as the will is coerced . . . It seems to me impossible to say that it is not coercion to threaten a wife with the dishonour of her husband and children".

A threat to breach a contract can be economic duress, but this is not an unswerving **19.5** rule. In *North Ocean Shipping Co. Ltd v. Hyundai Construction Co. Ltd "The Atlantic Baron"*[20] because the plaintiffs had affirmed the contract, their action failed. The Court

---

[14] [1976] 1 Lloyd's Rep. 293.
[15] At p. 335.
[16] [1983] 1 A.C. 366.
[17] [1989] 3 All E.R. 14 (at p. 51).
[18] [1904] 1 K.B. 591.
[19] At p. 597.
[20] [1979] Q.B. 705.

held that the duress had to be the main reason for breaching the contract, but did not have to be the only reason for agreeing to the other person's demands. In *B. and S. Contracts and Design Ltd. v. Victor Green Publications*[21] Kerr L.J. stated that a "... threat to break a contract unless money is paid by the other party can, but by no means always will, constitute duress. It appears from the authorities that it will only constitute duress if the consequences of a refusal would be serious and immediate so that there is no reasonable alternative open, such as by legal redress". Forced renegotiation of a contract can be economic duress if one party demands extra to complete or continue the contract.[22] This was discussed earlier in relation to consideration.[23] In *Atlas Express Ltd v. Kafco (Importers and Distributors) Ltd*[24] Tucker J. held that where a party to a contract was forced by the other to renegotiate to his disadvantage and had no alternative but accept the new terms offered his apparent consent to the new terms was vitiated by economic duress. The Court also held that there was no consideration for the new rate demanded. This adopts the older approach to such questions. Some of the rules on economic duress do in fact pre-date the development of the modern wider doctrine. In a very specialised area, namely salvage cases in Admiralty law, demands for extortionate payments which threaten that otherwise a party would not do the work of salvage of shipwrecked vessels have been set aside or not enforced.[25]

19.6   The most controversial category of economic duress is known as "lawful act" duress. This was discussed in *CTN Cash and Carry Ltd. v. Gallaher Ltd*[26] where a dispute over a stolen delivery of cigarettes led to a threat to withdraw credit. It was held that this did not amount to economic duress on the facts, but duress was not ruled out altogether in the case of persons threatening to do a lawful act. Steyn L.J. took the view[27] that "the fact that the defendants have used lawful means does not in itself remove the case from the scope of the doctrine of economic duress". However he also had misgivings about extending the doctrine too far. To take this action in a commercial context would be:

> "a radical one with far-reaching implications. It would introduce a substantial and undesirable element of uncertainty in the commercial bargaining process. Moreover, it will often enable bona fide settled accounts to be reopened when parties to commercial dealings fall out. The aim of our commercial law ought to be to encourage fair dealing between parties. But it is a mistake for the law to set its sights too highly when the critical enquiry is not whether the conduct is lawful but whether it is morally or socially unacceptable."[28]

Steyn L.J. did not entirely rule out the possibility of lawful act duress:

> "In this complex and changing branch of the law I deliberately refrain from saying 'never'. But as the law stands, I am satisfied that the defendants' conduct in this case did not amount to duress".

---

[21] [1994] I.C.R. 419.
[22] See Phang, "Whither Economic Duress?" (1990) 53 M.L.R. 107.
[23] See Chap. 8.
[24] [1989] 1 All E.R. 641.
[25] See *The Rialto* [1891] P. 175.
[26] [1994] 4 All E.R. 714.
[27] At pp. 718–719.
[28] At p. 719.

(4) The effect of duress

Duress makes a contract voidable, not void.[29] Innocent third parties are therefore less at   **19.7**
risk by any possible invalidity of the contract. There may also be a claim in restitution
law for money paid under a voidable contract. In *Maskell v. Horner*[30] the plaintiff was a
"dealer in produce" in Spitalfields Market. The owner of the market, the defendant,
demanded tolls for trading and if these were not forthcoming he would seize the trader's
goods. The plaintiff brought an action in restitution for the money paid. It was held that
he could not recover for mistake of fact or law simply because he did not wish to be
involved in litigation with the defendant. He could recover on the basis of duress, in that
he only paid to avoid seizure of his goods, and had not made the payments voluntarily.
The plaintiff succeeded in his action for "money had and received" to recover the
payments.[31]

UNDUE INFLUENCE IN EQUITY

Undue influence has it's roots embedded in Equity. It now also has an important part to   **19.8**
play in contract law. The language of undue influence is full of words from Equity such
as "notice", "constructive notice", "abuse of confidence" and "constructive fraud" (we
shall discuss these as we proceed). The equitable doctrine is wider than it's common law
counterpart, duress. It goes beyond threats or overt pressure and extends beyond procedural fairness. The court will look to see if there is "manifest disadvantage" to the influenced party in cases of "presumed" undue influence. If there is, the contract can be set
aside. This takes into account the substantial fairness of what was agreed.[32] A classic
example of the doctrine of undue influence is *Allcard v. Skinner*,[33] in which the plaintiff,
Miss Allcard, "desirous of devoting herself to good works" was introduced to a Miss
Skinner lady superior of a Protestant institution in Finsbury North London, known as
"The Sisters of the Poor". The plaintiff was 35 years old at the time, and unmarried.
When she joined the community she promised to observe their rules of poverty, chastity
and obedience. This meant giving up her possessions, nor was she allowed to seek advice
from anyone outside the community. In 1872 she inherited some stocks and shares which
she transferred to the defendant, and also made a will in the defendant's favour. Some
years after she left the order, Miss Allcard brought action to have the transactions set
aside for undue influence. The presumption of undue influence in her favour was not
rebutted on the facts, but Miss Allcard eventually lost her action because she had
affirmed the transaction.[34]

---

[29] Lord Scarman in *Universe Tankships v. ITF* [1983] 1 A.C. 366. The court rejected the view of the majority in
Barton v. Armstrong [1976] A.C. 104 that duress makes a contract void.
[30] [1915] 3 K.B. 106.
[31] On this action in restitution law, see Chap. 26.
[32] See Chap. 14.
[33] (1887) 36 Ch 145.
[34] See later p. 347.

The categories of undue influence

19.9   Undue influence can apply to contracts, deeds and also to gifts. Following the judgment of Cotton L.J. in *Allcard v. Skinner*[35] undue influence is divided into three categories:- (a) actual undue influence applies where there was real influence exercised by a dominant party over a vulnerable person which results in a concluded transaction, (b) presumed undue influence applies "where the relationship between the parties raises a presumption that the stronger party had influence over the weaker party which was exercised and which in the circumstances was undue. Presumed undue influence is further subdivided into: (i) recognised relationships where the presumption will apply *e.g.* solicitor and client, doctor and patient etc. and (ii) relationships not in fixed categories where influence can be presumed in certain circumstances. This is usually based upon a relationship of trust and confidence between the parties, *e.g.* husband and wife. The presumption of undue influence can be rebutted by demonstrating that the influenced party had independent advice, or was not unduly influenced.[36]

(1) Actual undue influence

19.10   The requirements of actual undue influence were set out by Slade L.J. in *BCCI v. Aboody*[37] being that: "(a) the other party to the transaction (or someone who induced the transaction for his own benefit) had the capacity to influence the complainant; (b) the influence was exercised; (c) its exercise was undue; and (d) its exercise brought about the transaction." Lord Scarman in *National Westminster Bank v. Morgan*[37a] adopted a dictum from a nineteenth century appeal from India, *Poosathurai v. Kannappa Chettiar*,[38] applying the codified Indian Contract Act 1872 s. 16(1) which defined undue influence as arising "where the relations existing between the parties are such that one of the parties is in a position to dominate the will of the other, and uses that position to obtain an unfair advantage over the other". In *Royal Bank v. Etridge (No. 2)*[39] Stewart-Smith L.J. stated the complainant had to "prove affirmatively" that she had entered into the "impugned transaction not of her own will but as a result of actual undue influence exercised against her".

The dominance must be such that a person is not in control of their own will, and that the influence brought about the contract. The influence exercised may be much more subtle than duress. Actual undue influence can be achieved by psychological means. Duress, as we have seen, is based upon threats. There is no need for any special relationship between the parties, who might even be strangers. Normally, however, the relationships between the parties will be close and personal. Unlike presumed undue influence, there is no need for "abuse of confidence". Although pressure is normally necessary it may be possible to claim actual undue influence without it. In *Bank of Montreal v. Stuart*[40] a wife was able to have a transaction set aside. She was a victim of actual undue influence even without pressure because she lacked a free will. Lord Macnaughton stated

---

[35]   (1887) 36 Ch. 145 at p. 171.
[36]   See later pp. 345–347.
[37]   [1990] 1 Q.B. 923 (at p. 967).
[37a] [1985] 2 W.L.R. 588 (at p. 599).
[38]   (1919) L.R. 47 Ind App. 1. Indian contract Act was a codification of nineteenth Century English Contract Law
[39]   [1998] 4 All E.R. 705 (at p. 711).
[40]   [1911] A.C. 120.

that: "She was ready to sign anything that the husband asked her to sign and do anything he asked her to do." Times change, and such a case is more likely to fall within the category of presumed undue influence to which we shall turn after first discussing an important aspect of the equitable doctrine.

The requirement of "manifest disadvantage"

A key requirement of presumed undue influence is that the transaction resulted in manifest disadvantage to the weaker party.   **19.11**

The need for a "manifest disadvantage" depends on the type of undue influence. It is not necessary in cases of actual undue influence but is a requirement of presumed undue influence. In *National Westminster Bank v. Morgan*[41] Lord Scarman had held that manifest disadvantage applied to both categories of undue influence. In *CIBC Mortgages v. Pitt*,[42] the House of Lords overturned this and held that manifest disadvantage is *not* required in order to show actual undue influence. The Law Lords made a distinction between the two categories. In *BCCI v. Aboody*[43] Slade L.J. stated that the question of manifest disadvantage was to be determined "in the circumstances subsisting at the time of the transaction". Both actual and presumed undue influence were discussed (and rejected) in *Dunbar Bank plc v. Nadeem*.[44] In order to invoke the doctrine the influence had to be "undue". Neither coercion, nor pressure, nor deliberate concealment was a necessary element in the case of actual undue influence according to Millet L.J. Although the husband had complete domination of the wife's will he had not taken unfair advantage of his position. The transaction as seen through his eyes, was obviously beneficial to his wife and was intended by him to be for her benefit. She was obtaining a beneficial interest in the house for the first time.[45] "Far from seeking to exploit the trust which she reposed in him for his own benefit, he was seeking to give her an interest because he was "getting on". The plaintiff also failed to establish a case of presumed undue influence. The question of manifest disadvantage was crucial to the outcome. There was no manifest disadvantage as the plaintiff had for the first time obtained a beneficial joint interest in the equity on the matrimonial home.

Is manifest disadvantage still necessary even in cases of presumed undue influence?

Since *CIBC Mortgages plc v. Pitt*, doubts have persisted as to whether the requirement   **19.12** of manifest disadvantage is necessary even in relation to cases of presumed undue influence. Lord Browne-Wilkinson in *Pitt* expressed the view that "the exact limits of the decision in *Morgan* may have to be considered in the future".[46] The courts have shown little inclination to follow this view until recently. In *Dunbar Bank v. Nadeem*[47] manifest disadvantage was the central issue in the Court of Appeal. The Court of Appeal took the requirement of manifest disadvantage at face value and applied it. The judge had found that this had been demonstrated by the wife because she had incurred some

---

[41] [1985] 1 All E.R. 821.
[42] [1993] 4 All E.R. 433.
[43] [1990] 1 Q.B. 923.
[44] [1998] 3 All E.R. 876.
[45] At p. 883.
[46] [1993] 4 All E.R. 433 (at p. 439).
[47] [1998] 3 All E.R. 876.

personal liability for her husband's debts, which amounted to £1,267 million, in return for a share of the property which was mortgaged to the defendant bank. The Court of Appeal disagreed. Manifest advantage was not made out. The Court of Appeal also took account of the bank's generous actions afterwards.

Manifest disadvantage is an example of substantive fairness rather than just a procedural requirement. In *Aboody* Slade L.J. in the Court of Appeal stated,[48] "I regard victimisation . . . and unfair advantage to be examples of the creation of a disadvantage and I would hold a disadvantage would be a manifest disadvantage if it would have been obvious as such to any independent and reasonable persons who considered the transaction at the time with knowledge of all the relevant facts." The requirement of "manifest" was said to mean "after a fine and close examination of the facts". In *Barclays Bank v. Coleman*[49] the Court of Appeal reaffirmed the status of manifest disadvantage in cases of presumed undue influence. Manifest disadvantage remained "for the time being" a requirement, indeed the disadvantage did not have to be large or even medium sized. This could be small, "provided that the disadvantage was clear, obvious and more than *de minimis*". In *Coleman* the charge over Miriam Coleman's home was subject to far greater financial risks than she was aware, and this was a clear and obvious disadvantage to her. In determining whether a transaction is manifestly disadvantageous the Court agreed that an objective view must be taken of it at the time the transaction was entered into.[50] Nourse L.J. stated: "We, like the judge, are bound to hold that manifest disadvantage is a necessary ingredient in a case of presumed undue influence. At the same time, the House of Lords have signalled that it may not continue to be a necessary ingredient indefinitely . . . There must be a disadvantage and it must be clear and obvious. But that does not mean that it must be large or even medium-sized. Provided it is clear and obvious and more than de minimis, the disadvantage may be small".

Absence of manifest disadvantage will prevent a claim of presumed undue influence if the complainant has received no independent advice prior to entering a transaction. In *Leggatt v. National Westminster Bank*[51] the re-arrangement of a mortgage in order to save a partnership business was held to be to the claimant wife's advantage. She failed therefore to rebut the presumption of undue influence. In *Royal Bank of Scotland v. Etridge (No. 2)* Lord Nicholls suggested that the label manifest disadvantage be discarded as giving rise to ambiguity.[52]

(2) Presumed undue influence

19.13 Undue influence may be presumed from two categories of relationship. First are "special relationships" to which the presumption will be applied, unless there is other evidence to the contrary. This is known as "class 2A" undue influence. The second group is more amorphous. The presumption depends on the circumstances of each case and requires proof that there was a relationship capable of involving undue influence. This is often to be found where there is trust and confidence arising out of a relationship, and a weaker party is influenced by the stronger in relying upon him for advice, help or security. This

---

[48] At p. 965.
[49] [2000] 1 All E.R. 385.
[50] At p. 400.
[51] [2001] 1 F.L.R. 563.
[52] *The Times*, October 17, 2001.

is characterised as "class 2B" relationships. The origin of this dichotomy is to be found in the Court of Appeal judgment in *BCCI v. Aboody*.[53] The difference between actual and presumed undue influence lies in the rule that in the latter there is the abuse of a relationship of trust and confidence. In *Royal Bank of Scotland v. Etridge (No. 2)*[54] Stuart-Smith L.J. stated that since the vice of the transaction lies in the abuse of trust "The transaction must result in some unfair advantage in the person to whom the trust is reposed . . . at the expense of the person who relies upon him". The equitable doctrine of undue influence extends to protect the "vulnerable from exploitation", according to Stuart-Smith L.J., "it is brought into play whenever one party has acted unconscionably in exploiting the power to direct the conduct of another".

(a)   Class 2A presumptions: Special relationships

In order to avail himself of the presumption, the claimant must belong to a particular category recognised by law. There is no definitive or exhaustive list but the main headings are by now well established by case law. Special relationships have been held to include: **19.14**

    (a)   solicitor and client[55];

    (b)   doctor and patient[56];

    (c)   parent and child[57];

    (d)   member of religious order and superior[58];

    (e)   persons engaged to be married[59]; and

    (f)   housekeeper and elderly employer.[60]

The category of class 2A presumptions does not include husband and wife.[61] The presumption will not apply, even though one of the special relationships exists, if it cannot have influenced the particular transaction. The presumption of undue influence can of course be rebutted.[62] In *Bullock v. Lloyds Bank Ltd*[63] the plaintiff, Hazel Bullock, aged 21 executed a deed of settlement with no advice except that of her father, Henry Macnaughton-Jones, and his solicitor, in favour of the defendant bank. The plaintiff's father was "financially embarrassed" at the time. The deed was set aside for presumed undue influence between father and daughter, even though the father in persuading the daughter to sign was not activated by any "selfish or self-seeking motive." The Court found that a settlement by a "young girl only just of age can only stand if executed under

---

[53] [1990] 1 Q.B. 953.
[54] [1998] 4 All E.R. 705 at 712.
[55] *Wright v. Carter* [1980] 1 Ch. 27.
[56] *Mitchell v. Homfray* (1881) 8 Q.B.D. 587.
[57] *Bainbridge v. Browne* (1891) 18 Ch. 188.
[58] *Allcard v. Skinner* (1887) 36 Ch. 145.
[59] *Re Lloyds Bank Ltd, Bomze and Lederman v. Bomze* [1931] 1 Ch. 289.
[60] *Re Craig (Decd.)* [1970] 2 All E.R. 390.
[61] *Barclays Bank v. O'Brien* [1994] 1 A.C. 180.
[62] See later pp. 345–347.
[63] [1955] Ch. 317.

the advice of a competent adviser".[64] Since the evidence established that the plaintiff's understanding of the nature and importance of the settlement was very imperfect and incomplete, the deed was set aside. The relationship of parent and child is a class 2A case if the parent is dominant, however if the child is dominant over an elderly or infirm parent or relative this is treated a class 2B case.

Although the relationship of husband and wife is no longer regarded as a special relationship for Class 2A purposes (nor are cohabitees), there is lingering authority for treating persons who are engaged as falling into this category. A number of the older cases may now be out of date. In *Re Lloyd's Bank Bomze v. Bomze*[65] Fanny Bomze (then Miss Lederman) was engaged to Mark Bomze, a doctor. After the engagement she agreed to hand over £4,000 as a gift to enable him to pay off a mortgage and to buy into a medical practice. The marriage proved unhappy. She sued for a return of the money because of undue influence. It was held that the agreement had to stand, though the presumption of undue influence applied to engaged persons. In *Wright v. Carter*[66] an action by the plaintiff Colonel Charles Ichabod Wright to have a gift from his solicitor set aside raised a presumption of undue influence in a fiduciary relationship like that of solicitor and client. This was a special relationship. There was no need to prove trust and confidence. The presumption would be rebutted if the solicitor could prove (i) the client was properly advised, (ii) that he had competent independent advice and (iii) that the price paid was a fair one.

Class 2B presumptions: "Trust and confidence"

19.15   The second category of presumption is based upon the particular relationship. There is no requirement of domination being exercised, merely that a relationship exists which contains the possibility of influence. The list does not depend upon any fiduciary relationship and new categories may be added as times change. Class 2B relationships involve the abuse of trust and confidence misplaced by a vulnerable person. This has been held to exist in relationships of:

(a)   husband and wife[67];

(b)   banker and client[68];

(c)   elderly farmer and neighbour upon whom he depended[69];

(d)   young musician and successful rock manager[70];

(e)   elderly great uncle and nephew[71];

(f)   other more distant family relations where there is a confidential relationship[72];

---

[64] At p. 326.
[65] [1931] 1 Ch. 289.
[66] [1903] 1 Ch. 27.
[67] *Barclays Bank v. O'Brien* [1994] 1 A.C. 180.
[68] *Lloyds Bank v. Bundy* [1975] Q.B. 326.
[69] *Goldsworthy v. Brickell* [1987] 1 Ch. 378.
[70] *O'Sullivan v. Management Agency and Music Ltd* [1985] 1 Q.B. 428.
[71] *Cheese v. Thomas* [1994] 1 W.L.R. 129.
[72] *Tate v. Williamson* (1866) L.R. 2 Ch. App. 55.

(g)   fellow members of a charitable committee[73] and;

(h)   employer and employee[74].

Class 2B presumptions may apply on the facts to any type of relationship. In *George Smith v. William Kay*[75] the House of Lords stated the main requirement of prescribed undue influence to be an "abuse of confidence". This requirement betrayed the doctrine's origins in the law of Equity. Lord Kingsdown[76] stated that: "The principle applies to every case where influence is acquired and abused, where confidence is reposed and betrayed". It also applied to situations where the law presumes "confidence put and influence exerted". The concept of "trust and confidence" offers a wide range of possibilities not limited to the traditional fiduciary relationships. Nevertheless, the doctrine is based largely upon well established categories often with overtones of a fiduciary element.

In *Tate v. Williamson*[77] an undergraduate at Oxford University ran up debts of nearly £1,000 to his college, and, when pressed to pay, turned to his family for help. He asked his Great Uncle who suggested the young man go to another relative (the Great Uncle's nephew) for help. This person suggested selling some freehold property owned by the student to himself for £7,000. The relative discovered that the property was worth £20,000 but did not tell the debt-ridden student who signed over the property to him. The young man had become addicted to alcohol at university and sadly died prematurely at the age of 24. In an action brought by his executors the House of Lords held that there was a fiduciary relationship which led to a presumption of undue influence, and that there had been a breach or abuse of confidence.[78] In *Tufton v. Sperni*[79] two members of a committee set up to promote a Moslem cultural centre in London were deemed to be within a relationship of trust and confidence with one another. This allowed the Court to set aside the sale of a house between the parties at an exorbitant price. Members of a religious order who do not stand in the position of superior and disciple as in *Allcard v. Skinner*[80] can be in a relationship where the class 2B presumption arises. In *Roche v. Sherrington*[81] two members of "*Opus Dei*", a Roman Catholic organisation, were held capable of attracting the presumption in relation to gifts made by one of the parties.

A good example of a class 2B case of trust and confidence is *Lloyds Bank Ltd v. Bundy*[82] in which an elderly farmer, "Old Herbert Bundy", was the owner of a farm in Wiltshire which was his home and only asset. Both the defendant and his son Michael had been customers of Lloyds Bank for many years. The defendant was influenced to execute a charge, which he later increased, over his farm guaranteeing his son's company's overdraft. When the son got into difficulties the plaintiff Bank sought

19.16

---

[73] *Tufton v. Sperni* [1952] 2 T.L.R. 516.
[74] *Credit Lyonnais Bank Nederland NV v. Burch* [1997] 1 All E.R. 144.
[75] (1859) 7 H.L.C. 750; 11 E.R. 299.
[76] At pp. 310–311.
[77] (1866) LR 2 Ch. App. 55.
[78] For a brief account of the factual background to this case, see Nash, "with friends like these. . ." (2000) N.L.J. 960.
[79] [1952] 2 T.L.R. 516.
[80] (1887) 36 Ch. 145 (see p. 335).
[81] [1982] 1 W.L.R. 599.
[82] [1975] Q.B. 326.

possession of the farm to recover the charge. The Court of Appeal held that a relationship of trust and confidence existed in the relationship of elderly parent and son. The
charge was set aside for undue influence. The father had received no independent advice.
Lord Denning set out a wider principle for setting contracts aside in this case, that of
inequality of bargaining power.[83] Tripartite relationships such as here between stranger
and influenced parties and third parties are discussed again later.[84]

The same two factors between elderly parents and child and a financial institution
lending money to the latter also led to a finding of undue influence (and to the suggestion of a widening criterion of inequality of bargaining power) in *Avon Finance Co. Ltd
v. Bridger*.[85] Lord Denning based his judgment in favour of "George Bridges, another
father let down by his son" on inequality of bargaining power, but both Brandon and
Brightman L.J.J. based their analysis on the relationship between the son and his elderly
parents, which raised a presumption of undue influence of which the building society
ought to have been aware. If trust and confidence exist in fact, there may in theory be no
relationship to which it might not apply. In *Goldsworthy v. Brickell*[86] the Court of Appeal
held it could apply to the relationship between an elderly farmer aged 85 and a neighbour who acted as a voluntary farm manager. This was a relationship in which one had
ceded a degree of trust and confidence so that the other person was in a position to exercise undue influence to enter the transaction. It was not necessary to show that the
person had assumed a dominating position however. The Court applied the test of
whether the transaction "manifestly and unfairly disadvantaged" the donor or grantor.
The presumption was raised if the transaction "was so improvident, that it could not be
reasonably accounted for on the grounds of friendship, relationship, charity or other
motives on which ordinary men acted".[87]

19.17 Actions alleging undue influence are increasingly common among the many varied
and stormy relationships in the music and entertainment industry between management
and their rock and popstar clients. In *Tolhurst v. Smith*,[88] there was a dispute between
Lawrence Tolhurst and other members of the rock bank "The Cure" and their recording company. The issue was whether a recording agreement been obtained by undue
influence. It was held that there was the possibility of undue influence in the relationship but Chadwick J. rejected the argument that the agreement had been procured as a
result of it's exercise. The test was whether there was "some feature which raises the
presumption that the influence – latent in the relationship – has been operative in
procuring the transaction." In *O'Sullivan v. Management Agency Ltd*[89] the plaintiff was
an entertainer, Gilbert O'Sullivan, who sued his management over their handling of his
business affairs. The Court of Appeal held that there was a fiduciary relationship which
raised a presumption of undue influence. Although there was no pressure on Gilbert
O'Sullivan to make the agreement "that does not matter[90] . . . "the onus was on those
asserting the validity of the agreements to know that they were the consequence of the

[83] Discussed Chap. 14.
[84] See pp. 343–347.
[85] [1985] 2 All E.R. 281.
[86] [1987] Ch. 378.
[87] These words were first used by Lindley L.J. in *Allcard v. Skinner* (1887) 36 Ch. 145
[88] [1994] 2 E.M.L.R. 508.
[89] [1985] Q.B. 428.
[90] According to Dunn L.J. at p. 463.

free exercise of Mr O'Sullivan's will in the light of full information regarding the trans-action. That has not been done. He had no independent advice about these matters at all". The agreement between the parties was therefore held to be voidable because of undue influence.

UNDUE INFLUENCE BY THIRD PARTIES

A number of the cases already discussed illustrate that an action for undue influence may   **19.18** also be brought against a contracting party who benefited as a result of influence by a third person. For instance, a bank or building society which obtained security for re-mortgaging of property jointly owned by a married couple may be sued by one of the spouses to have the charge set aside. If the wife was influenced to enter into the agree-ment by pressure from her husband, or indeed anyone by their domestic partner, then the charge on the property may be voidable against the bank because of undue influence.[91]

The requirements of an action claiming undue influence by a third party

The first step is to establish either actual or presumed undue influence by the principal   **19.19** debtor.[92] Until recently these were mostly based on pressure exercised by a husband for a share of his wife's equity a share of in the matrimonial home. The key question is whether the third party had notice of the potential undue influence. If the bank as cred-itor fails to take account of this notice, the charge may be set aside. There are two types of notice: (a) actual notice, which is a question of fact and (b) "constructive notice" *i.e.* the creditor should have known about the undue influence. This may arise from (i) the relationship between the principal debtor and the influenced party and (ii) the fact that the transaction is not beneficial to the contracting party. In the latter case the creditor should be "on inquiry" as to undue influence If the agreement is capable of benefiting both partners, there is no constructive notice as such, but the creditor must nevertheless take steps to avoid constructive notice, usually by informing the person to seek inde-pendent legal and financial advice.

The leading case is the House of Lord's judgment in *Barclays Bank plc v. O'Brien*,[93] a case involving misrepresentation which also gave guidance on the applicable principles of undue influence in such situations. Nicholas O'Brien obtained his wife's signature on a guarantee for an overdraft for his business using the matrimonial home in Slough, jointly owned with his wife Bridget, the defendant, as security. The husband misrepresented the amount of the security to her, saying it was only £60,000 when it was in fact £135,000. The business got into difficulties and the creditor Barclays Bank, brought action to enforce it's loan. The defendant argued that there had been undue influence and misrep-resentation and that the transaction should be set aside. The House of Lords held that if there had been undue influence by the husband then the creditor had to take reasonable steps that the agreement had been freely entered into without such influence. Otherwise

---

[91] *Williams and Glyn's Bank Ltd v. Boland* [1981] A.C. 487.
[92] *Dunbar Bank v. Nadeem* [1998] 3 All E.R. 876 (discussed earlier p. 335).
[93] [1994] 1 A.C. 180.

the bank was fixed with constructing notice of the wife's right to have the transaction set aside. Reasonable steps included a warning (at a meeting not attended by the husband) of the potential liability and the risks involved, and advising the wife to take independent legal advice.

19.20   The House of Lords stated *per curiam* that a creditor should be regarded as on inquiry when the transaction was not to the financial advantage of the wife and there was a substantial risk that the husband had obtained the wife's agreement by misrepresentation or undue influence. Lord Browne-Wilkinson rejected the idea that the husband was an agent for the bank in making the loan, or that there was a "special equity" in favour of wives in general. The House of Lords held that the Bank should have had constructive notice of the risk of undue influence. Mrs O'Brien, had been influenced and misled by her husband as to her liability and potential losses. She had not received proper independent advice as to the matter. The legal charge on her home was therefore voidable for undue influence exercised by the third party, namely her husband. A second possibility of holding the lending bank liable, though not applicable to the husband and wife example but in exceptional cases to other third party situations, would be that the influencing party acted as the agent of the bank in procuring the transaction. This is likely to be rare as the influencing party is in most cases ostensibly acting on his or her own behalf.

The burden of proof remains on the influenced party to prove that the creditor had constructive notice. In *Barclays Bank plc v. Boulter*[94] the plaintiff had to establish her case and the burden of proof rested on her. However the Court stated that it was easily discharged. Julie Boulter needed only to show that the bank knew that she was a wife living with her husband and that the transaction was not on it's face to her financial advantage. The burden was then on the bank to show that it took reasonable steps to satisfy itself that her consent was properly obtained. The Court stated that a rule requiring the burden of proof to be on the lending bank to show that it had no notice of undue influence would be very unreasonable.

19.21   The influenced person may also have an action against her legal advisers. In such triangular situations there is the possibility of negligence against an independent adviser, such as a solicitor, who failed to give proper advice and warning of the risks at the time. In *Kenyon Brown v. Desmond Banks and Co*,[95] Lance L.J. held that a solicitor was in breach of his duty of care if he failed to address the appropriateness of the loan and whether it was in the wife's best interests. A solicitor is not required to advise on the wisdom of the transaction however.[96] Solicitors may be held liable in negligence if they do not take proper steps. The principles applicable to determining whether a bank was able to rely on the fact that the wife had received legal advice before entering into a charge, in order to rebut the presumption of undue influence, were set out by the Court of Appeal in *Royal Bank of Scotland v. Etridge (No. 2)*.[97] We discuss this case shortly, and the rules relating to the duty of cove of solicitors later.[98]

---

[94] [1999] 1 W.L.R. 1919.
[95] (1999) 149 *The New Law Journal*, 1832.
[96] *Clark Boyce v. Mouat* [1994] 1 A.C. 428.
[97] [1998] 4 All E.R. 705.
[98] See p. 343 and pp. 346–347.

The aftermath of *Barclays Bank v. O'Brien*

Barclays Bank v. O'Brien has proved a fertile precedent. The proverbial floodgates of lit- **19.22**
igation have been opened. The courts have seemed reluctant to extend the principle too
far, indeed they now appear keen to limit it.[99] An interesting exception is *Credit Lyonnais
Bank Nederland v. Burch*[1] which extended the relationships covered by undue influence
beyond the family circle to employees. In *CIBC Mortgages plc v. Pitt*[2] the House of
Lords applied *Barclays Bank v. O'Brien* but concluded that the creditor had neither
actual notice nor was fixed with constructive notice of the third party's undue influence.
The principles laid out in *O'Brien* now apply not only for spouses but also cohabitees. In
Massey v. Midland Bank plc[3] the defendant and Mr Potts were lovers who shared a home.
She granted a charge to the plaintiffs induced by her partner's fraud, and also undue
influence. The charge was to her disadvantage but the Court of Appeal refused to set it
aside. The defendant had been advised by a solicitor (who was also her partner's solicitor) and the bank had taken sufficient steps believing she had been advised by professional solicitors. They were not required to go further and check the content of the
advice. A similar conclusion was reached in *Banco Exterior Internacional v. Mann*[4] in
which the Court of Appeal considered the bank were not required to go into detail about
the quality of the advice given by the solicitor. The bank were entitled to conclude that
this was of a reasonable professional standard.

   In *Royal Bank of Scotland v. Etridge (No. 2)*[5] the Court of Appeal dismissed eight
conjoined appeals by spouses against banks which had obtained possession orders over
matrimonial homes. The test was whether "at the time the value was given and in light
of all the information in the banks possession, including its knowledge of the state of the
account, the parties relationship and the availability of legal advice to the wife, there was
still a risk that the wife entered into the transaction as the result of her husband's undue
influence or misrepresentation". The House of Lords upheld a number of appeals in
Etridge (No. 2) depending upon the facts. The banks were not to proceed with such
transactions until the wife was properly advised. Lord Nicholls stated: "A bank is put on
inquiry whenever a wife stands as surety for her husband's debts. The bank must then
take steps to bring home to the wife the risks involved."

   This illustrates the volatile nature of the rules and judicial policy making in this area. **19.23**
Some of the appeals to the House of Lords were unsuccessful in *Etridge (No. 2)*, one of
which was that of Mrs Etridge herself.[6] Susan Etridge had signed a legal charge in favour
of the Royal Bank by a second mortgage on the property as security for overdraft facilities granted to her husband, Anthony, for business purposes. The husband defaulted
and the bank took action over their home, at Laverstoke in Hampshire. The wife claimed
undue influence in the transaction. The Court of Appeal held that there was a good case
for undue influence. The need for caution in overturning transactions for undue influence
was expressed by Lord Nicholls, who stated:

---

[99] *Leggatt v. National Westminster Bank* [2000] All E.R. 1458. However, see *Royal Bank of Scotland v. Etridge,
The Times*, October 17, 2001.
[1] [1997] 1 All E.R. 144.
[2] [1993] 4 All E.R. 433.
[3] [1995] 1 All E.R. 929.
[4] [1995] 1 All E.R. 936.
[5] *The Times*, October 17, 2001, reported in the Court of Appeal [1998] 4 All E.R. 706.
[6] [1997] 3 All E.R. 628.

"... it is plainly neither advisable nor practical that banks should be required to attempt to discover for themselves whether a wife's consent is being procured by the exercise of undue influence of her husband. This is not a step the banks should be expected to take. Nor, further, is it desirable or practical that banks should be expected to insist on confirmation from a solicitor that the solicitor has satisfied himself that the wife's consent has not been procured by undue influence ... [T]he circumstances in which banks are put on inquiry are extremely wide.. They embrace every case where a wife is entering into a suretyship transaction in respect of her husband's debts. Many, if not most, wives would be understandably outraged by having to respond to the sort of questioning which would be appropriate before a responsible solicitor could give such a confirmation. In any event, solicitors are not equipped to carry out such an exercise in any really worthwhile way, and they will usually lack the necessary materials. Moreover, the legal costs involved, which would inevitably fall on the husband who is seeking financial assistance from the bank, would be substantial. To require such an intrusive, inconclusive and expensive exercise in every case would be an altogether disproportionate response to the need to protect those cases, presumably a small minority, where a wife is being wronged.

The furthest a bank can be expected to go is to take reasonable steps to satisfy itself that the wife has had brought home to her, in a meaningful way, the practical implications of the proposed transaction. This does not wholly eliminate the risk of undue influence or misrepresentation. But it does mean that a wife enters into a transaction with her eyes open so far as the basic elements of the transaction are concerned."

Manifest disadvantage is still an issue in many of the earlier cases. In *Bank of Cyprus (London) Ltd v. Markou*[7], in which the judge held that in order to see if the transaction was manifestly disadvantageous for the purpose of presumed undue influence, the matter had to be viewed from the perspective of the parties to the transaction, not merely from the perspective of the creditor or debtor. The knowledge of the husband and wife was relevant to whether the agreement was a disadvantage to the wife. An independent person looking at the argument would have said to Mrs Markou "This is wholly disadvantageous to you. You should not do it". Even if the wife receives no independent advice, a transaction will not be set aside if it is not to her manifest disadvantage.[8]

19.24   The doctrine of undue influence also applies even if the instigator or beneficiary of the transaction was a third party other than the husband, as in the cases so far discussed. In *Naidoo v. Naidu*[9] the Court held that undue influence was not limited to cases where the transaction was in favour of, or had been instigated by, the person who stood to gain. The primary issue was the abuse of a position of trust. If the transaction was with someone in whose favour the husband wanted his wife, the complainant, to make the agreement, then undue influence was available. If the husband abused the relationship by instigating the agreement, any resulting transaction could be voidable. In *Naidoo* the

---

[7] [1999] 2 All E.R. 707.
[8] See also *Barclays Bank plc v. Coleman* [2000] 1 All E.R. 385, (see earlier p. 336).
[9] *The Times,* November 1, 2000.

husband had left his affairs in the hands of his solicitor, Bushell, who sold one of the husband's properties to his (Bushell's) wife, in spite of higher offers for the farm from other interested parties. The transaction was set aside even though Mrs Bushell did not appear to have notice of the undue influence, apart from the low price she paid for the farm and her husband's relationship with the plaintiff.

The category of relationships included as involving trust and confidence and the protection afforded to them was extended to employees in *Credit Lyonnais Bank Nederland v. Burch*,[10] a case which also illustrated the link between undue influence and unconscionability. The defendant, Helen Burch, began working for a Mr Peloci when she was eighteen. As well as being an employee, she also did baby sitting for him and visited his family at weekends. When his tour operating business got into financial straits he got the defendant to put her flat up as collateral security for his overdraft with the plaintiff bank. The company went into liquidation, whereupon the bank proceeded against the defendant to recover the security. The Court of Appeal held that the transaction was voidable for undue influence. The bank should have been put on inquiry by the fact that an employee with no financial interest in the company had created a charge on her home as security based on affection and keeping her goodwill with her employer. Nourse L.J. viewed the transaction as being not only disadvantageous but also unconscionable. The result was so damaging to her as to be "shocking to the conscience of the Court". The terms were to the manifest disadvantage of the defendant so the bank had constructive notice and had not taken reasonable steps, either by explaining the situation to her nor by suggesting that she obtain independent advice. The case shows the links between the two equitable doctrines of unconscionability and undue influence. Miss Burch had been advised by the bank to get independent advice but she did not do so. However the Court found that the arrangement was so risky to her financial well-being that even greater steps were required.

REBUTTING THE PRESUMPTION OF UNDUE INFLUENCE

The presumption of undue influence is rebuttable. The relevant question is whether the influenced party had a free choice. Even free choice may not be enough however. Independent advice is the vital factor in rebutting undue influence. Even if this was obtained, there may however be other reasons why the person entered into the transaction. The court must look at the litigation as a whole. The position regarding advice was set out in *Credit Lyonnaise Nederland v. Burch*[11] by Millett L.J. who stated that the presence of legal advice was not a "panacea". "The court will examine the advice which was actually given. It is not sufficient that the solicitor has satisfied himself that the complainant understands the legal effect of the transaction and intends to enter into it. That may be a protection against mistake or misrepresentation; it is no protection against undue influence". In *Naidoo v. Naidu*[12] the Court stated in order to rebut the presumption it had to be proved that the complainant entered into the transaction "as a result of the free exercise of an independent will". The "independent, qualified and fully informed

19.25

---

[10] [1997] 1 All E.R. 144.
[11] [1997] 1 All E.R. 144.
[12] *The Times*, November 1, 2000.

adviser" assumed an "onerous burden". Where the person advised had been subject to undue influence by another person, the adviser had to ensure not only that his client was free from improper influence but was able to reach an independent decision on her own and understood both the nature and effect of the transaction.

In *Banco Exterior Internacional SA v. Thomas*[13] the Court of Appeal considered the situation where advice had been given but not taken. Patricia Dempsey was a widow living alone in straitened circumstances. She agreed to a charge on her house of up to £75,000 in Ealing as security for borrowings to her "close personal friend" John Mulchay who would pay her a regular income in return. The bank advised Mrs Dempsey to get independent legal advice as to the nature and effect of the guarantee and legal charge. The bank did not know of her collateral arrangement with Mr Mulchay, nor did they enquire about her motive in altering the transaction. Mrs Dempsey's former solicitor who had been asked for the title deeds advised her strongly against the transaction and also telephoned the bank saying he regarded her plans as improvident. He later told the bank that despite his strong advice to the contrary, Patricia had decided to proceed. When Mulchay got into financial difficulties the bank sought to enforce the guarantee and legal charge against Mrs Dempsey. She died before the action was brought to trial so the action continued against her executors.

19.26   The Court of Appeal held that a bank was not required to inquire into the personal relationships between those with whom it had business dealings or as to their personal motives for wanting to help one another. The bank had no reason to do more than ensure that the parties knew what they were doing and wanted to do it. Mrs Dempsey received legal advice from an independent solicitor before signing as to the nature and effect of the transaction. It was not alleged that she had failed to understand. This was enough to rebut the presumption of undue influence. The bank was entitled to enforce it's security because the presumption of undue influence was rebutted. The Bank had done enough to avoid constructive notice. Mrs Dempsey had received independent advice before signing. She ought to have understood what she was doing, indeed she appeared to do so. The bank was not required to intrude too deeply into the nature of the relationship between Mrs Dempsey and Mr Mulchay, so there was no notice of undue influence to put them on inquiry.[14]

19.27   The position regarding the rebuttal of the presumption of undue influence in third party situations involving a solicitor was set out by the Court of Appeal in *Royal Bank of Scotland v. Etridge (No. 2)*.[15] There were nine rules in such cases:

(a)   when the wife acts through a solicitor the bank is ordinarily not put on inquiry and may rely on the solicitor to carry out his professional function of advice;

(b)   if the wife does not use a solicitor, her bank should urge her to seek independent legal advice;

(c)   any solicitor involved in the transaction, even if also acting for the lending bank, owes a duty of care to the wife;

---

[13] [1997] 1 W.L.R. 221.
[14] See also *Leggatt v. National Westminster Bank* [2000] All E.R. 1458 where the presumption of undue influence was rebutted by the transaction being to the wife's advantage.
[15] [1998] 4 All E.R. 705.

(d)   the bank does not acquire imputed notice, *i.e.* knowledge from what any solicitor to the transaction learns in his dealings with the wife;

(e)   the bank is not required to investigate or question the independence of any solicitor acting in this matter;

(f)   the bank is not required to question the sufficiency of the advice given;

(g)   nor importance attached to the fact that the solicitor has not provided the bank with full or adequate confirmation that he followed instructions;

(h)   any solicitor owes a duty of care to the wife but also to the lending bank, even if he is not acting for them; (even though the two parties have a conflicting interest there is a common interest in ensuring that the wife entered into the transaction with informed consent and free from the undue influence of her husband); and

(i)   the bank cannot rely on the solicitor acting competently or in accordance with the rules if it knows or ought to know that this is false. The net effect of these rules is to limit the potential liability of banks quite markedly after an era of claims ushered in by *O'Brien*. This is an area where the law can change quickly however.

REMEDIES FOR UNDUE INFLUENCE

A contract is voidable by the person influenced. Being an equitable doctrine, the **19.28** courts may also refuse to order specific performance or to grant rescission. Where counter-restitution is not possible the courts may also award fair compensation as a means of doing practical justice between the parties.[16] There is also the possibility of the equitable remedy of an account for profits.[17] The right to rescind may be lost. Relief in cases of undue influence is barred on grounds similar to misrepresentation.[18] This includes:

(a)   affirmation of the transaction after the influence has ceased;

(b)   inability to make counter restitution;

(c)   lapse of time or delay in taking action; or

(d)   third party rights would be affected.

Affirmation and lapse of time applied to the claim in *Allcard v. Skinner*.[19] The right to rescind was lost by affirmation and because of lapse of time. After making the will and handing over her wealth in 1872, Miss Allcard resigned from "The Sisters of the Poor"

---

[16]   *Mahoney v. Purnell* [1996] 3 All E.R. 61.
[17]   *O'Sullivan v. Management Agency and Music Ltd* [1985] 3 All E.R. 351.
[18]   See Chap. 18.
[19]   (1887) 36 Ch. 145.

in 1879. The plaintiff immediately revoked her will, but took no steps to pursue legal action to retrieve her property for six years. It was held that she had lost the right to have the transaction set aside for undue influence. She had "acquiesced" in the gifts and her action therefore failed.

Chapter 20

ILLEGALITY AND PUBLIC POLICY

THE ROLE OF PUBLIC POLICY

Public policy has traditionally had a part to play in determining that contracts which **20.1** infringe it's view of correct behaviour are rendered void or illegal at common law.[1] The concept of what is contrary to public policy, immoral, indecent or illegal has changed radically over the centuries and some of the case law in this area has become increasingly out of date. The Law Commission produced a Consultation Document in 1999 recommending a fundamental overhaul of this whole area.[2] The role of public policy in contract law is therefore ripe for review. Within this disparate collection of rules covering a wide spectrum of wrongful agreements, statutory illegality remains alive and relevant both in the formation and performance of contracts. Two important aspects of illegality remain the rules on restraint of trade, and in the complex interrelationship of contract law, restitution and property rules on the effect of illegal transactions. Restraint of trade is a highly developed and active part of commercial contract law and practice. We shall discuss this separately at the end of the chapter.

The meaning of illegality in contract law is wider than conduct which infringes the criminal law. A "contract" to have a person killed is obviously illegal and cannot be enforced, but illegality in contract law extends far beyond this, to include a wide range of activities for one reason or another "against public policy". Of course there are dangers in such a doctrine. Public policy as a ground for invalidating an agreement is a powerful weapon, which has to be kept on a tight rein. In *Richardson v. Mellish*[3] Burroughs J. described public policy as "a very unruly horse, and once you get astride it, you never know where it will carry you. It may lead you from the sound law. It is never argued at all but when other points fail". Other judges have taken a more robust sporting posture on public policy. In *Enderby Town FC Ltd v. The Football Association,*[4] Lord Denning replied that: "With a good man in the saddle, the unruly horse can be kept in control. It can jump over obstacles." Lord Denning was of course one of the most interventionist of judges and favoured greater use of the public policy argument. Public policy can also appear in different disguises in contract law. For instance, in the

---

[1] See generally Enonchong, *Illegal Transactions* LLP (1998).
[2] "Illegal Transactions: The Effect of Illegality on Contracts and Trusts", Law Commission Consultation Paper No. 154 (1999). See Buckley, "Illegal Transactions: Chaos or Discretion" (2000) 29 Legal Studies 155.
[3] (1824) 2 Bing 229, 130 E.R. 294 (at p. 303).
[4] [1971] Ch. 591 (at p. 606).

important question of the meaning of consideration,[5] the control of exemption clauses[6] and on the issue of intention to create legal relations.[7] The courts now tend to avoid getting too involved in public policy. In modern times it is usually said that policy is a matter for Parliament to debate and decide. The Law Commission in it's Consultation Paper suggests that public policy be restricted to what is current rather than of an historic dimension. The courts should judge whether a contractual provision is contrary to public policy in the light of policy at the present day. Contracts considered contrary to public policy in the past should no longer be regarded as subject to the illegality rules if the conduct in question is deemed acceptable by modern standards.[8] Illegality therefore raises the whole issue of the relationship between law and morality.[9]

Illegality can be raised by the court in the public interest

20.2   The public policy aspect of illegality is well illustrated by the courts' power to raise the question of illegality. Public policy is allowed to supersede the parties intentions. The question of illegality can be raised by the court and does not have to be pleaded by either of the parties themselves. The Court of Appeal has now expressed a strong statement of the courts' role in relation to illegality. In *Birkett v. Acorn Business Machines Ltd,*[10] the Court of Appeal said that it had an "overriding duty" not to enforce a contract tainted with illegality, in the public interest. Only when the court could eliminate any other possible answer with complete confidence should an unpleaded case of illegality be allowed to succeed. If a transaction was on it's face manifestly illegal, a court should refuse to enforce a contract whether or not either party alleged illegality. Even if the contract was not on it's face manifestly illegal, if there was persuasive and comprehensive evidence of illegality the court should refuse to enforce it even if the illegality had not been pleaded. The principle behind the court's intervention of its own motion was "to ensure that its process was not being abused by inviting it to enforce *sub silentio* a contract whose enforcement was contrary to public policy."[11]

The effect of illegality on contracts may be best described as a defence against enforcement of a contractual provision. This avoids the use of the words 'void' and 'unenforceable' which are both ambiguous in relation to the various effects of illegality. The Law Commission treats illegality as a defence to the right of a party to enforce a contract, or as a defence to a valid claim for damages for breach of contract.[12] Whether this defence operates or not depends upon the classification of the illegality and the parties' own role in wrongdoing. We return to the Law Commission's recommendations for reform in this area later.[13] Meanwhile we shall consider the categorisation of illegal contracts.

---

[5] See Chap. 7.
[6] See Chaps 16 and 17.
[7] See Chap. 11.
[8] Law Commission Consultation Paper (1999) "Illegal Transactions: The Effect of Illegality on Contracts and Trusts" Recommendation 9.6.
[9] See Devlin, *The Enforcement of Morals* (1965, Oxford), particularly Chap. 3 "Morals and the Law of Contract".
[10] [1999] 2 All E.R. (Comm) 429.
[11] The Court of Appeal cited as authority *Bank of India v. Trans Continental Commodity Merchants* [1983] 2 Lloyd Rep. 298, and in *Re Mahmoud and Ispahani* [1921] 2 K.B. 716.
[12] Law Commission, para 2.2
[13] See pp. 362–363.

ILLEGALITY BY STATUTE

If a statute or regulation declares certain types of activity against the law, this will affect **20.3** the performance of any contract involving the conduct in question. Legislation may make certain contracts illegal as formed,[14] either by (a) express prohibition or (b) making the activity involving the contract impliedly illegal. However, it may be that only the manner of the contract's performance is unlawful. There is therefore a distinction between a contract being illegal (a) as formed and (b) as performed. The function of the court is to interpret the statute in order to determine the effect of the regulations on a contract. This is usually based on the intention of Parliament. The courts may thus have to imply a prohibition, as statutes are often silent on the question of contractual illegality. In *Hughes v. Asset Managers plc*[15] the Court refused to hold a contract impliedly illegal and therefore unenforceable. Saville L.J. could find "nothing to indicate that this is what Parliament intended to do, when enacting this statute, nor anything to indicate any good reason or public need for such a result".

Contracts illegal as formed

(1) Express statutory prohibition

If the contract is expressly forbidden by law, it is unlawful and any attempted agreement **20.4** to contravene the Act will be void. It is relatively rare for a statute to spell out the effect on contracts.[16] Nevertheless, industry still has a lot of "red tape" with which to cope, and these can make certain terms or indeed the whole contract unlawful. In *Re Mahmoud & Ispahani*[17] the provision in question was the Seeds, Oils and Fats Order 1919 made under Defence of Realm Regulations which made dealing in linseed oil without a licence an offence. Since the contract was illegal by statute, "as formed" neither party could enforce it nor could either party use the illegality as a defence, even the innocent plaintiff, because the contract was prohibited by statute. Bankes L.J. stated that since the Order prohibited the making of the contract "it is open to a party, however shabby it may appear to be, to say that the legislature has prohibited this contract".[18] The Court would not lend it's aid to the enforcement of the contract. In his judgment Atkin L.J. rejected the idea of an estoppel in such cases where one party had been deceived, stating that it would "reduce the legislation to an absurdity".[19]

(2) Contracts impliedly illegal as formed[20]

A contract can also be impliedly illegal. This is far more common than the previous cat- **20.5** egory. The courts are often unwilling to reach this conclusion. In *St John Shipping Corp*

---

[14] In the 1990's there was public controversy over the issue of illegal sales of "Arms to Iraq" (Report of the Scott Inquiry into the Export of Defence Equipment, February 15, 1996).
[15] [1995] 3 All E.R. 669 (at p. 674).
[16] As an example, see the Financial Services Act 1986 s. 5.
[17] [1921] 2 K.B. 716.
[18] At p. 724.
[19] At p. 732.
[20] See Furmston, "The Analysis of Illegal Contracts" (1966) 16 University of Toronto LJ 267. This article sets out a clear taxology of illegal contracts in this amorphous area.

v. Joseph Rank Ltd[21] Devlin J. stated that "a court ought to be very slow to hold that a statute intends to interfere with the rights and remedies given by the ordinary law of contract". In *Phoenix General Insurance Co. of Greece SA v. Administratia Asigurarilor de Stat*[22] Kerr L.J. stated on the question of whether illegality was to be implied, "Whether or not the statute has this effect depends on considerations of public policy in the light of the mischief which the statute is designed to prevent, its language, scope and purpose, the consequences for the innocent party, and any other relevant considerations." Lord Wright in *Vita Food Products Inc v. Unus Shipping Company Ltd*[23] pointed out that each case had to be considered on it's merits. Public policy and implied illegality "may at times be better served by refusing to nullify a bargain save on serious and sufficient grounds".

Contracts which are illegal in their performance

20.6   A contract which is not illegal at it's inception may be performed in a way which renders it unlawful. In *St John Shipping Corporation v. Joseph Rank Ltd*[23a] a ship was in contravention of the "Plimsoll line" laws, *i.e.* the permissible limit of legal subversion of a vessel. Overloading a ship so that its load line is below water constitutes a potentially grave risk to the lives of the crew. The plaintiffs were prosecuted as a result and the defendants claimed that the plaintiffs had performed the charter of the vessel in an illegal manner. It was held that illegal performance in this case did not make the whole contract illegal. This Act was designed to protect sailors and prosecute offenders. It did not, however, render every contract for the carriage of goods by sea in contravention of the Act illegal. The Court of Appeal rejected the idea that the contract was illegal simply because the plaintiff had disregarded safety regulations. The defendants contract was therefore not tainted with unenforceable illegality.

Illegality in performance did not prevent payment under a contract in the Scots law case of *Dowling and Rutter v. Abacus Frozen Foods Ltd.*[24] The Court of Session held that where a contract for services was carried out by employing foreign asylum seekers without work permits, the supplier of the workers was still entitled to payment. Lord Wheatley held that illegal performance alone did not invalidate a contract. The court had to determine the nature and effect of the illegality.[25] Additionally, even if a person is party to an illegal arrangement, statutory employment rights may still be available. In *Leighton v. Michael*[26] the Employment Appeal Tribunal held that a person could bring a complaint of sex discrimination against an employer even if illegality tinged her contract of employment. Annabel Leighton was employed for seven years at a fish and chip shop in Ross-on-Wye without tax and national insurance being deducted from her wages, a fact about which she had complained to her employer. The performance of the work without paying tax was a fraud on the revenue. The EAT held that the claim for sex discrimination should stand: "There was nothing in the statute, or public policy, to

---

[21]   [1957] 1 Q.B. 267 (at p. 287).
[22]   [1987] 2 All E.R. 152 (at p. 176).
[23]   [1939] A.C. 277 at (p. 293).
[23a]   [1957] 1 Q.B. 267.
[24]   *The Times*, April, 26, 2000.
[25]   The leading English authority in the area of illegality of performance is *Archbolds (Freightage) Ltd. v. S. Spanglett Ltd* [1961] 1 Q.B. 374.
[26]   [1996] I.R.L.R. 67.

disqualify a person . . . from protection by reason of illegality in the fact of, or in the performance of the contract of employment if the claim is not founded upon, or seeking to enforce contractual obligations".

Similarly in *Hall v. Woolston Hall Leisure Ltd*[27] the Court of Appeal held that the claimant, Jill Hall, was entitled to pursue her claim for sex discrimination on the grounds of pregnancy even although she had connived with her employer in the performance of her contract of employment by accepting payment of wages without the deduction of tax and national insurance contributions. The general rule is that contracts which defraud the revenue are illegal and that neither party can enforce them.[28] However, if the parties are not equally blameworthy, for instance in a case of Social Security fraud by one partner in a relationship, the other party may be allowed to retain or acquire enforceable rights or property despite the illegality.[29]

Terms rendered void by statute

A particular type of term can also be rendered void by statute. A good example of this **20.7** is recent legislation to protect whistleblowers which treats 'gagging' or confidentiality clauses as void. The Public Interest Disclosure Act 1998 protects individuals who disclose information which is in the public good. They are given rights against victimisation and unfair dismissal.[30] The information given will usually be about criminality, dishonesty or breach of health and safety law in the workplace. The Act makes any provision which purports to preclude a worker from making a protected disclosure void. Confidentiality or gagging clauses have been commonplace in employment contracts in recent years. The Consumer Protection (Distance Selling) Regulations 2000 contain a provision[31] which prevents the parties contracting out of the Regulations in question.[32] Any term to which the Distance Selling Regulations apply is rendered void if inconsistent with provisions for the protection of consumers contained in the regulations.

CONTRACTS CONTRARY TO PUBLIC POLICY AT COMMON LAW

(a) Contract to commit a crime

A contract for the express purpose of committing a crime is illegal. Such an agreement **20.8** is not an enforceable contract. The expression "contract killer" is therefore an oxymoron. Agreement to commit less serious offences may also be void for public policy. In *Bigos v. Bousted*[33] the defendant, Richard Algernon Bousted, was in breach of currency exchange control regulations in force at that time in providing money to his daughter to stay in

---

[27] [2000] 4 All E.R. 787.
[28] *Alexander v. Rayson* [1936] 1 K.B. 169.
[29] *Tinsley v. Milligan* [1994] 1 A.C. 340, discussed later p. 362.
[30] Employment Rights Act 1996 (as amended) s. 43A-L. The 1998 Act added additional subsections to the 1996 Act.
[31] Reg. 25.
[32] See Chap. 4. Numerous terms are declared void by the Unfair Contracts Terms Act 1977 (see chap. 17).
[33] [1951] 1 All E.R. 92.

Rapallo on the Italian Riviera. He made a contract with the plaintiff, Mrs Bigos, that if she paid a sum of Italian money to his daughter he would give her the equivalent sum in England. The defendant also gave the plaintiff some share certificates by way of security. The deal broke down and the defendant brought action to recover his share certificates. The Court held the agreement was illegal as it was a criminal offence to breach the regulations. An agreement to commit an assault on another person is contrary to public policy. In *Allen v. Rescous*[34] the defendant agreed to pay the plaintiff a sum of money to beat another person "out of a close". The Court held that the "consideration and whole contract is illegal and void". A similar rule seems to apply to contracts to commit a civil wrong such as publishing libellous material.[35]

Contracts to procure corruption or benefiting from a crime

A contract for the purpose of soliciting or procuring corruption[36] or to allow a criminal or his estate to benefit from his crime is contrary to public policy.[37] This is an aspect of the rule preventing a person from benefiting from their own wrongdoing.[38] The application of the benefit rule is less clear cut in relation to more minor offences.[39] A contract to procure corruption in a foreign country is not necessarily illegal in England.[40]

Sexual immorality may invalidate a contract

20.9   Traditionally the courts would not enforce a contract which was regarded as sexually immoral. The law goes back to *Da Costa v. Jones*[41] in which Lord Mansfield held that a wager on the gender of a notorious French diplomat, the Chevalier D'Eon who dressed as a woman, was void as against public decency.[42] In *Pearce v. Brooks*,[43] the plaintiffs were coach-builders who brought an action against the defendant, a prostitute, for the cost of hiring a "brougham" (a type of carriage). The plaintiffs knew that she was a prostitute and that the carriage would be used for "immoral purposes" and as a result they failed to recover payment for the hire on the grounds of the immorality of the contract. Similarly in *Benyon v. Nettlefold*,[44] an annuity was granted to Caroline Nettlefold in return for "illicit future cohabitation", *i.e.* that she become the person's mistress. The agreement was held to be unenforceable. The law drew some subtle distinctions, however, so a contract to let premises to a prostitute for immoral purposes was illegal, but letting a room purely as her place of residence was not.[45] Most of the case law in this area now belongs to a bygone era.

---

[34] (1677) 2 Lev 174, 83 E.R. 505.
[35] *Clay v. Yates* (1856) 1 H and N 73.
[36] *Parkinson v. College of Ambulance Ltd & Harrison* [1925] 2 K.B. 1, discussed later p. 360.
[37] *Beresford v. Royal Insurance Co. Ltd* [1938] A.C. 586.
[38] This is also dealt with under the Forfeiture Act 1982.
[39] *Marles v. Philip Trant and Sons Ltd.* [1954] 1 Q.B.; also *St John Shipping Corp v. Joseph Rank Ltd* [1957] 1 Q.B. 267.
[40] *Westacre Investments Inc. v. Jugoimport* [1999] 3 All E.R. 864.
[41] (1778) Comp. 729, 98 E.R. 133.
[42] In the eighteenth century, wagering contracts were lawful, unlike today, see later pp. 357–358.
[43] (1866) LR 1 Exch 213.
[44] (1850) 3 Mas and G 94, 42 E.R. 196.
[45] *Appleton v. Campbell* (1826) 2 C & P 347, 172 E.R. 157.

Nevertheless in *Armhouse Lee Ltd v. Chappell*,[46] it was stated that "on any view of the law, public policy still precludes the enforcement of contracts for the promotion of an undoubtedly immoral purpose such as prostitution. *Pearce v. Brooks* remains good law".

The categorisation of what the law regards as immoral is now more restricted in light of **20.10** modern attitudes. In *Armhouse Lee Ltd v. Chappell*[47] publishers brought an action to recover payments for advertisements for telephone dating and sex lines which had been placed in one of their magazines. The defendant was, according to the Court, a "self proclaimed pornographer" who refused to pay and argued that the subject matter of the contract to advertise was immoral, and so could not be enforced. The Court of Appeal rejected this defence taking the view that there was no generally accepted moral code against the sex lines, which were in fact regulated by law. The Court also rejected a general public decency role in this area on the ground that it was not for individual judges to impose their own moral attitude on others. The Court of Appeal accepted that some aspects of the telephone sex lines might be unenforceable, for instance calls by a subscriber who dialled the line. However, the contract between the provider and an advertiser was not tainted by illegality. The advertisements had to be paid for and were not an illegal contract. The Court approved a statement of Sir Nicholas Browne-Wilkinson in *Stephens v. Avery*,[48] that "the court's function was to apply the law, not personal prejudice. Only in a case where there is still a generally accepted moral code can the court refuse to enforce rights in such a way as to offend that generally accepted code." The courts are still prepared to allow immorality to effect a remedy in contract law. The running of an escort business, which was in fact a front for prostitution leading to the payment of girls for sex, was held to be immoral in *Hughes v. Clewley, The Siben (No 2)*.[49] The action was brought to obtain rescission of a contract by which the plaintiff had agreed to swap his yacht, a De Loran car, and a sum of money for a villa and discothèque in the Algarve owned by the defendant. The plaintiff's claim for fraudulent and negligent misrepresentation succeeded but the fact that the villa was being used for immoral purposes meant that the court considered it would not be right to order rescission.[50]

Gambling transactions

At common law betting and wagering was not regarded as contrary to public policy.[51] **20.11** However, since the Gaming Act 1845 s. 15, gaming contracts are void for illegality. Money owed on such contracts cannot be recovered. This rule is nowadays seen as anachronistic and in need of reform.[52] In *O'Callaghan v. Coral Racing Ltd*,[53] an arbitration clause in a gaming contract, under which disagreements between bookmakers and their clients could

---

[46] *The Times*, August, 7, 1996.
[47] *The Times*, August, 7, 1996.
[48] [1988] 1 Ch. 449.
[49] [1996] 1 Lloyd's Rep. 35.
[50] Also discussed in Chap. 18.
[51] See Lord Mansfield in *Da Costa v. Jones* (earlier p. 356).
[52] This may be "on the cards". In December 1999, the Home Secretary Jack Straw announced a review of the gambling industry which could lead to legalisation. The *Daily Telegraph* December, 10 1999, commented that "Britain's antiquated gambling laws had been caught in a hideous time warp, dreamed up in an era when the state thought it knew best and betting was regarded in a similar light to sex shops and prostitution". See also *The Times*, June, 14, 2001 suggestions for reform.
[53] *The Times,* November 26, 1998.

be referred to a third party, was held to be part of a void agreement which could not survive independently. and so was unenforceable. Lotteries are rendered unlawful by the Lotteries and Amusements Act 1976 s. 1 which provides that "all lotteries which do not constitute gaming are unlawful" except as provided by the Act. It is an offence to tickets, sell or distribute tickets or advertise a lottery unless it is exempted. Lotteries connected with "exempted entertainments", *i.e.* sales of work, fêtes, bazaars, are not unlawful though offences can be committed in the manner in which they are conducted.[54]

The National Lottery is specifically exempted and made lawful by the National Lottery Act 1993 s. 2(1) which provides that "a lottery that forms part of the National Lottery shall not be unlawful".[55] Free lotteries are lawful if there is no requirement of payment or purchase in order to be eligible to win a prize, *e.g.* if the sign "no purchase necessary" is exhibited at the place of sale. In *Russell v. Fulling,*[56] the claimant sued for a sum of money due under an agreement to operate a scratchcard lottery under which the shopkeeper was supplied with scratchcards to give away at his discretion to customers or potential customers in his shop. The High Court held that this was an unlawful lottery and the agreement was unenforceable since the majority of cards distributed were limited to purchases, even though the scheme's rules expressly stated that no purchase was necessary for the cards to be distributed. The result was that any contract or loan made in connection with the scheme was an agreement with an illegal purpose and therefore unenforceable. Syndicates within the National Lottery would appear to be binding as they constitute an internal agreement between the ticket holders themselves, rather than with the organisers. In *Abrahams v. Trustee in Bankruptcy of Abrahams,*[57] Lindsay J. held that since Liselotte Abrahams had paid money into a lottery syndicate she had the right to have her winnings administered with the rules of the syndicate and was therefore entitled to her share.

Contracts which oust the jurisdiction of the courts

Contracts which oust the jurisdiction of the courts are contrary to public policy. This means excluding the courts from adjudication of any dispute of what the parties agree is a contract. Arbitration clauses do not fall under this heading, as they are enforceable as a dispute resolution process. There normally remains an appeal on point of law or misconduct by the arbitrators so the courts are not excluded from the procedure.[58] On the other hand, the parties may say that what they have agreed is not a legally binding contract. If that is the intention of the parties, the courts will be excluded from applying the rules of contract law.[59]

Miscellaneous examples of public policy

20.12   Other categories of illegality have existed for many years but are rarely applied in modern times. Among these are contracts prejudicial to the family. This includes a

---

[54] S. 3.
[55] Proof of purchase of a winning ticket may give a legal claim, see "Lost ticket, couple 'have a case' over £3m in prize" *Daily Telegraph,* April 24, 2001. Contrast the rule in relation to football pools (see Chap. 11).
[56] *The Times,* June 23, 1999.
[57] *The Times,* July 26, 1999.
[58] *Scott v. Avery* (1855) 5 H.L.C. 811. See Arbitration Act 1996, ss 67–71.
[59] Discussed earlier in Chap. 11.

contract to find a partner for another person, (*i.e.* "matchmaking"), which at common law is unenforceable.[60] The activities of dating agencies introducing potential friends or partners to one another are now governed by ordinary contractual principles and constitute legally binding arrangements.[61] Other categories of public policy lie largely dormant but could revive with a change of circumstances, *e.g.* the prohibition against trading with an enemy in time of war would become relevant if the United Kingdom were once again to be at war.[62] Even today however the old categories retain the potential to generate new case law. The practice of supporting litigants financially or obtaining a share of their winnings in court were both rendered unlawful in earlier times as champerty and maintenance. The Criminal Law Act 1967 de-criminalised both as offences but did not repeal the common law rule on champertous agreements being void in contract law. The position on solicitors charging on a 'no win, no fee' basis under s. 58 of the Courts and Legal Services Act 1990 has revolutionised the area of conditional fees.[63] Under Law Society rules solicitors may be entitled to up to 75% of the damages obtained. In spite of the situation now being subject to regulation, the question of illegality in solicitors arrangements and fee sharing is still the subject of litigation.[64]

THE DIFFERING EFFECTS OF ILLEGALITY OF CONTRACTS

The traditional view is that illegality makes the contract void or unenforceable by one of   **20.13**
the parties. If a contract is void from the beginning then there never was contract. In the case of illegality, however, the effect is not so straightforward. Illegality can affect the contract in a variety of ways. The contract may sometimes be enforced by an innocent party, or if the parties are not equally at fault or one party withdraws or repeats the transaction on time. Furthermore, property rights may be capable of being transferred under an illegal contract. Since the purported transaction is not strictly a contract, property concepts and restitutionary remedies have a part to play in this area of law. The courts have great flexibility in relation to the effect of illegality. The courts are also historically more prepared to intervene than in other areas of void contracts such as mistake at common law.[65]

Flexible approach to enforceability

An illegal contract may be unenforceable by (a) both parties or (b) only one of them, in   **20.14**
certain circumstances. If the whole contract is void for illegality in theory neither can sue upon it. However an innocent party may have a remedy, even if the agreement is tainted, depending on whether a party is (a) guilty, (b) innocent or (c) the parties are equally to

---

[60] *Hermann v. Charlesworth* [1905] 2 K.B. 123.
[61] See "£350 Payout for Missing Dates" *The Times,* August 4, 1999, a news item referring to a successful action by a disappointed client against a dating agency in Portsmouth County Court.
[62] See Chap. 22 on the effect of war on contracts.
[63] Conditional Fees Agreements Order 1995 (S.I. 1995 No. 1674).
[64] *Thai Trading v. Taylor* [1998] 3 All E.R. 65; *Mohamed v. Alaga* [1999] 3 All E.R. 699; *Awwad v. Gerachty & Co.* [2000] 1 All E.R. 608.
[65] See Chap. 21.

blame or *"in pari delicto"*. The basic principle, if both parties are equally guilty and the contract is illegal as formed, is that it cannot be enforced by either of them. If the illegality is only in the performance of the contract then the right to enforce the contract may continue. In *St John Shipping Corporation v. Joseph Rank Ltd*,[66] in spite of the overloading of the vessel, in breach of safety regulations, recovery of the freight charges was allowed. If the parties are not equally guilty (or indeed if one is innocent) then the courts take a more flexible attitude allowing the contract to be enforced or rights passed. This approach was described by Bingham L.J. in *Saunders v. Edwards*:[67]

> ". . . the courts have (as it seems to me) to steer a middle course between two unacceptable positions. On the one hand it is unacceptable that any court of law should aid or lend its authority to a party seeking to pursue an object or agreement which the law prohibits. On the other hand, it is unacceptable that the court should, on the first indication of unlawfulness affecting any aspect of a transaction draw up its skirts and refuse all assistance to the plaintiff, no matter how serious his loss or how disproportionate his loss to the unlawfulness of his conduct".

Bingham L.J. stressed the practical aspect of doing justice in each case: "the courts have tended to adopt a pragmatic approach to these problems, seeking where possible to see that genuine wrongs are righted so long as the court does not thereby promote or countenance a nefarious object or bargain which it is bound to condemn." Bingham LJ summarised the law into two general propositions: (i) "where the plaintiffs action in truth arises directly *ex turpi causa*, he is likely to fail" [*i.e.* from his own wrongdoing][68] however (ii) "where the plaintiff has suffered a genuine wrong to which allegedly unlawful conduct is incidental, he is likely to succeed".[69]

(1) Money paid under an illegal contract: the general rule

20.15   If both parties are equally guilty of the illegality, neither may enforce a remedy in restitution for money paid. In *Holman v. Johnson*[70] Lord Mansfield stated that "no court will lend its aid to a man who founds his cause of action upon an immoral or illegal act." The rule is illustrated by *Parkinson v. College of Ambulance Ltd and Harrison*,[71] in which the plaintiff, Colonel Parkinson, was approached to see if he was interested in obtaining a knighthood. He had an interview with Harrison, the Secretary of the College of Ambulance, and agreed to make substantial payments to the College. He received a letter from HRH Princess Christian who was president of the College thanking him for his donation. The aim of his benevolence, of course, was to obtain the knighthood which he did not in fact receive. It was held that the plaintiff could not recover his agreed contribution to the College in contract as according to Lush J. he was "precluded by the illegality of the contract from relying on it".[72]

---

[66] [1957] 1 Q.B. 267.
[67] [1987] 2 All E.R. 651 (at pp. 665–666).
[68] Citing *Alexander v. Rayson* [1936] 1 K.B. 169.
[69] Citing *Bowmakers Ltd v. Barnet Instruments Ltd* [1944] 2 All E.R. 579.
[70] (1775) 1 Cowp. 341; 98 E.R. 1120.
[71] [1925] 2 K.B. 1.
[72] At p. 16.

(2) Exceptions to the general rule against recovery of money or benefits

(a) The parties are not equally to blame: or, in pari delicto.[73]

If the parties are not equally to blame, recovery may be allowed of money paid under an   **20.16**
illegal contract. In *Kiriri Cotton Co. Ltd v. Dewani*,[74] the Privy Council held that a breach
of regulations by a landlord did not prevent recovery of a deposit by the tenant. In
Mohammed v. Alaga,[75] the defendants were a firm of solicitors bound by professional
rules. The plaintiff, however, was ignorant of the fact that there was any reason why the
defendant should not make the agreement with him. It was held that he was unable to
recover the shared fees received under the agreement, but he was allowed the restitutionary remedy of *quantum meruit* as remuneration of a reasonable sum for the services he
had rendered as the parties were not tainted to the same degree.[76]

(b) One party withdraws from the illegality on time: locus poeniteniae

If one party withdraws from the illegal transaction he may make recovery. The so-called
locus poeniteniae allows credit for repentance but this must be made (a) on time and (b)
on a voluntarily basis. Timeliness is a question to be determined in light of the proposed
illegality. In *Kearley v. Thomson*[77] performance of the illegal purpose had already begun
to be carried out and it was therefore too late to escape the consequence of unenforceability. On the other hand, in *Taylor v. Bowers,*[78] the court held that repudiation was possible at any time until the conclusion of the contractual performance.

(c) Oppression or deception

Money paid under an illegal transaction may also be recovered if a party was forced to   **20.17**
enter the illegal agreement. This is sometimes called "oppression" and is wider than
common law duress.[79] The rule also applies if the party was deceived into entering into
the contract as a result of (i) fraudulent misrepresentation or (ii) the money being paid
under a mistake. In *Oom v. Bruce*[80] an action on a policy of insurance of goods on board
a ship the *Elbe*. This had been made in St Petersberg in ignorance of the fact that hostilities had broken out between Britain and Russia on the Oct 17 1807, the day before the
vessel sailed. The vessel and it's contents were seized and confiscated. The Court held
that the contract in question was void because it was made after war had broken out and
the agent of the insured was entitled to the return of the premium which had been paid
under mistake of fact.

(3) Title to property may pass under an illegal contract

Property may be transferred under an illegal contract. A party may acquire title to property in goods or even land if a contract is carried out, even although the contract
remained unperformed, the illegality would have prevented it's enforcement. In *Singh v.*

---

[73] See Grodecki, "In pari delicto, potior est condictio defendtis" (1955) 71 L.Q.R. 254.
[74] [1960] A.C. 192.
[75] [1999] 3 All E.R. 699.
[76] See Chap. 26.
[77] (1890) 24 Q.B.D. 742.
[78] (1876) 1 Q.B.D. 291.
[79] See Chap. 19.
[80] (1810) 12 East 225; 104 E.R. 87.

Ali[81] the defendant sold a lorry to the plaintiff but registered the vehicle in his own name in order to defraud the authorities. The defendant later refused to return the lorry to the plaintiff. The Privy Council held that the plaintiff had a right to the vehicle notwithstanding the illegality as property had passed. This rule was applied again by the Court of Appeal in *Belvoir Finance Co Ltd v. Stapleton*[82] in which the plaintiff was able to recover three cars sold to him by the defendant under an illegal transaction even after the vehicles had been transferred to an innocent third party. The contract having been executed, title passed despite the fact that the contract would otherwise have been unenforceable for illegality.[83]

(4) A claim based upon an independent cause of action may succeed

20.18   In *Bowmaker Ltd v. Barnet Instruments Ltd*[84] the plaintiff let some machine tools to the defendant under a series of hire purchase arrangements, in breach of war time regulations. The defendant failed to make the required payments and later argued that the plaintiffs' were not entitled to have the tools returned because the contract was illegal. The plaintiffs claim in conversion succeeded. They did not have to base their claim on the illegal contract but instead could rely on their own proprietary right to the articles, which they were able to recover. The rule applied where a limited interest in property was created in property under a contract involving that illegality. A plaintiff could recover the property so long as they did not have to rely on the illegality to establish the proprietary right. This is sometimes called the "reliance" principle.[85] Reliance may not be sufficient if the conduct of the plaintiff has been reprehensible or extreme,[86] or if a statutory provision has as it's intention the total unenforceability of any contract in contravention.[87]

The point arose again in *Tinsley v. Milligan*[88] where Lord Browne-Wilkinson stated that the following propositions emerged from the judgment in *Bowmakers*. First, that property in chattels and land could pass under a contract which was illegal and which otherwise would have been unenforceable as a contract. Secondly, that a plaintiff could enforce property rights so acquired provided he or she does not need to rely on the illegal contract for any purpose other than the basis of his or her claim to a property right. Thirdly, that it was irrelevant that the illegality of the underlying agreement was either pleaded or used in evidence. If the plaintiff had acquired a legal title under the illegal contract, that was enough. In *Tinsley v. Milligan* the parties were friends living in a house which they had jointly purchased which was registered in the sole name of the plaintiff, Stella Tinsley, but on the understanding that the plaintiff and the defendant were joint beneficial owners of the house which they ran as a lodging house. The reason for the house being in the plaintiff's name alone was to enable the defendant, Kathleen Milligan, to make false claims for social security benefits, although the plaintiff had also made false claims. The defendant repented of the fraud and told the truth to the Department

---

[81] [1960] A.C. 167.
[82] [1971] 1 Q.B. 210.
[83] See Higgins, "The Transfer of Property under Illegal Transactions" (1962) 25 M.L.R. 149.
[84] [1945] K.B. 65.
[85] See Gooderson [1958] C.L.J. 199; Enonchong (1995) 111 L.Q.R. 135; Cook (1972) 35 M.L.R. 38.
[86] According to dictum of Parcq L.J. at p. 72 in *Bowmakers* [1945] K.B. 65.
[87] *Amar Singh v. Kulubya* [1964] A.C. 142.
[88] [1994] 1 A.C. 340.

of Social Security. When the parties quarrelled the plaintiff in whose name the house was vested moved out leaving the defendant in sole occupancy.

The House of Lords held that the defendant was entitled to her share of the property **20.19** notwithstanding the conspiracy to illegality. A person could claim an interest in property based on either a legal or equitable title, if she was not forced to plead or rely on the illegality. This applied even if the title relied upon was acquired in the course of an illegal transaction. In *Tinsley*, by showing she had contributed to the purchase of the house and that there was a common understanding between the parties that the property would be owned equally, the defendant had thereby established an equitable right. *Tinsley v. Milligan* extended the *Bowmakers* principle beyond legal title to include equitable interests. In *Tribe v. Tribe*[89] property was transferred to defeat creditors and the equitable presumption of advancement was defeated to allow recovery of the property as long as the illegal purpose had not been carried out. The illegality could be pleaded to rebut the presumption of advancement, *i.e.* that the transaction was a gift.

As we have discussed, even if a contract is unenforceable because of illegality, a plaintiff may be entitled to succeed on a separate action such as a collateral contract,[90] so long as this is untainted by any illegality. The tainting rule will prevent any other linked contracts being enforced.[91] A party might also bring a tort action[92] if this is unconnected with the illegality, or seek severance of the illegality, though this is often impermissible.[93]

(5) The "affront to public conscience" test

An affront to public conscience test has been applied to determine the extent to which a **20.20** remedy should be available where there is an illegal transaction. In *Tinsley v. Milligan* the House of Lords stated *per curiam* that a public conscience test had no place in determining the extent to which rights created by illegal transactions should be recognised. The test was first put forward by Hutchison J. in *Thackwell v. Barclays Bank plc*,[94] originally as a test for whether or not a contract should be deemed illegal or contrary to public policy. This later developed into a ground for allowing one of the parties to obtain some benefit or to recover under the contract if it would not be an affront to public conscience to allow them to do so, in other words, an overriding discretion for the courts to do justice in the individual case. This was applied in *Howard v. Shirlstar Container Transport*,[95] and in two earlier cases, *Saunders v. Edwards*[96] and *Euro-Diam v. Bathurst*.[97] In *Tinsley v. Milligan*[98] both Lord Goff and Lord Browne-Wilkinson criticised this development as being of doubtful authority in terms of precedent, and also as undesirable in principle. The affront to public conscience test appears to have come full circle with Lord Mansfield's famous words in *Holman v. Johnson*,[99] and as such has a long and distinguished pedigree. Given the comments of the House of Lords, however, it cannot be said

[89] [1995] 4 All E.R. 236.
[90] *Strongman Ltd (1945) v. Sincock* [1995] 2 K.B. 525.
[91] *Spector v. Ageda* [1973] Ch. 30.
[92] *Saunders v. Edwards* [1987] 1 W.L.R. 11–16.
[93] *Bennett v. Bennett* [1952] 1 K.B. 249.
[94] [1986] 1 All E.R. 676.
[95] [1990] 1 W.L.R. 1292.
[96] [1987] 2 All E.R. 651.
[97] [1990] Q.B. 1.
[98] [1994] 1 A.C. 340.
[99] See earlier p. 358.

to be established as sound law, and the test has now also been criticised by the Law Commission in its consultation paper to which we shortly turn.

(6) Illegality may effect other remedies

Illegality may be a factor preventing the use of an equitable or other remedy. In *Hughes v. Clewley The Siben*[1] which involved a sale of a discothèque in exchange for a luxury yacht and also a villa used for immoral sexual purposes; it was held that the Court would not order rescission for fraudulent misrepresentation because of this illegality.

Reforming the Law on Illegality

20.21   The law on illegal contracts has become outdated, complex and lacking in clear principle. There are now proposals to rationalise the rules in English law. Other common law jurisdictions have attempted law reform with mixed success. The New Zealand Illegal Contracts Act 1970[2] gave the courts in that country a discretion to award a choice of remedies if the court considered it just to do so. Although s. 6 of the New Zealand Act provides that illegality renders a contract void and of no effect and, apart from *bona fide* purchasers for value, no property may pass, the courts are given a wide equitable discretion under s. 7. This includes granting restitution of property, ordering compensation to be paid, varying the contract or validating the contract either in whole or in part. This wide discretion is in contrast to English law's reliance on either restitutionary or property principles to deal with the effects of void contracts.

The Law Commission and reforming illegal transactions

20.22   In 1999 the Law Commission commented that: "The rules relating to when illegality is a defence to the enforcement of contractual obligations are numerous and complex. It is difficult to extract the various principles applied by the courts and some of the principles are hard to reconcile."[3] This has led to recommendations for root and branch law reform. The Law Commission for England and Wales published it's views in a Consultation Paper, provisionally putting forward ideas which would radically change the treatment of illegal contracts. The core of the system put out to consultation would be a wide but structured discretion allowing the courts to deal with illegality. This would largely replace the present rules. Instead of being void for illegality, the plaintiff's claim would be allowed "unless the court decides that because of the involvement of illegality it would not be in the public interest to allow the claim".[4] Under this system many currently void contracts, even contracts to commit a crime would be valid, subject to the court's discretion (which would however be likely to be exercised). Illegality, under the proposed scheme would act as a defence, unless the court decided otherwise. A court would have a discretion to decide whether or not illegality should act as a defence to a

[1] [1996] 1 Lloyd's Rep. 35.
[2] See *Dawson* 1985 L.M.C.Q. 46.
[3] "Illegal Transactions: The Effect of Illegality on Contracts and Trusts", Consultation Paper No. 154 1999.
[4] Provisional recommendation 9(b).

claim for contractual enforcement whenever either (i) the formation, (ii) purpose or (iii) performance of the contract involved the commission of a legal wrong.

The remedy of reversal of unjust enrichment should apply to all contracts unenforceable for illegality. The proposed discretion would not apply where the consequences of the illegality is expressly declared by statute, nor should the equitable "clean hands" doctrine apply, *i.e.* where the parties are not in *pari delicto*, and one is entirely innocent of wrongdoing. A claim for breach of contract would be allowed unless the involvement of the illegality is such that it would not be in the public interest to allow the claim. A legislative provision should make clear public policy, is only to be judged as to contemporary public policy not as to the headings that existed in the past. The courts' discretion would not be unrestricted. The judges would be required to consider:

(a)   the seriousness of the illegality involved;

(b)   the knowledge and intention of the plaintiff;

(c)   whether denying relief would act as a deterrent;

(d)   whether denying relief would further the purpose of the rule which renders the contract illegal

(e)   and; whether denying relief is proportionate to the illegality involved.

The proposed changes would not extend to provisions in restraint of trade, nor where the law of frustration applies, to contracts void or voidable for other reasons, *e.g.* under the Unfair Terms in Consumer Contracts Regulations 1999, or for misrepresentation or undue influence.[5]

CONTRACTS IN RESTRAINT OF TRADE AT COMMON LAW

In this highly specialized area of commercial law we encounter our old common law **20.23** friend reasonableness, hand in hand with public policy.

If one party restricts his or her economic freedom by a contractual undertaking that they will not conduct trade or business or take employment within certain limits, this is *prima facie* void as contrary to public policy. The rules go back to an earlier era and show a stronger connection with freedom of enterprise. The doctrine of restraint of trade is aimed at preserving freedom of movement in the labour market, improving competition, controlling monopoly and ultimately avoiding unconscionability and unfairness. The common law of contract now only plays a very secondary role in this area; power which is subject to regulation by statute, public authorities and, increasingly, European Union competition law.[6] As such it has now left the confines of general contract law. The restraint of trade doctrine has links with both undue influence and unconscionability. All three are interlinked being concerned with the fairness of certain types of agreement. The basic purpose and rationale of each of these is different. In *Panayiotou v. Sony Music*

---

[5] For a discussion of these proposals, see Buckley, "Illegal transactions: chaos or discretion? (2000) 20 Legal Studies pp. 157–180.
[6] See Whish, "Competition Law" (with B. Sufrin) (4th ed, Butterworths, London, 2001).

Entertainment[7] (a contractual dispute between the singer, George Michael, and his recording company) in which both unconscionability and restraint of trade were argued, Parker J outlined the distinction: "The common law jurisdiction to declare a contract unenforceable as a restraint of trade, [is based upon] the public policy consideration . . . of free trade. The test to be applied, where the contract is one which attracts the doctrine of restraint of trade, is a test of reasonableness: the court does not have to be satisfied that the defendant has behaved in a morally reprehensible way." On the other hand: "In the case of the equitable jurisdiction to relieve against unfair and unconscionable bargains, the particular public policy consideration is that of preventing unfair advantage being taken of the weak and vulnerable."[8] The rules of restraint of trade are underpinned by principles of free trade, competition and freedom of contract, rather than individual fairness.

Applying the restraints of trade doctrine

20.24   The first issue is to determine whether the doctrine applies to the contract or term in question. If it does, the restraint is *prima facie* void at common law, *i.e.* there is a presumption of unenforceability. The restrictive term will only be upheld if it is (a) reasonable between the parties and (b) in the public interest. There are three elements to the reasonableness test between the parties. First, do the parties have legitimate interests to protect? Secondly, the time limit of the restraint in question and thirdly, the area covered by the restraint of trade. Reasonableness should be judged at the time the contract is made as between the parties. However, this may include in all the circumstances, *i.e.* to take account of events after the contract was formed, in considering the public interest. Certain restraints may also be said to be *prima facie* valid, *i.e.* unenforceable only if *unreasonable*. There are three stages in applying the restraint of trade doctrine.

(1) Stage one: does the restraint of trade doctrine apply?

This is the preliminary but necessary starting point. If the doctrine does not apply, the clause in question is valid if agreed between the parties. If the doctrine applies, the situation changes and the term becomes *prima facie* void and must therefore be shown to be reasonable. On the other hand, it is important to ascertain on which side of the line the agreement falls. In many commercial relationships, for instance employment, individuals agree to work exclusively with one company during the whole of their employment contract. This does not constitute a restraint of trade, albeit that the individual's right to work elsewhere during the time is removed. Many employers and contracts also allow employees to work elsewhere as independent contractors under conditions laid down by their employers.

20.25   New and different commercial devices arise in practice. The question has to be whether the doctrine attaches to the contract or otherwise. In *Servais Bouchard v. Prince's Hall Restaurant Ltd*,[9] the plaintiffs were a firm of wine growers and shippers from Beaune in Burgundy and the defendants owned a restaurant in Piccadilly. The plaintiffs sought

---

[7] [1994] E.M.L.R. (at p. 317).
[8] For a discussion of unconscionability and other fairness doctrines see Chap. 14.
[9] (1904) 20 T.L.R. 574.

damages and an injunction for breach of an agreement to take shares in the restaurant in return for the defendants taking all their supplies of red and white Burgundies and Chablis wine's from them in future. The contract was unlimited as to time. Jelf J. gave judgment for the plaintiffs and this was upheld on appeal. The Master of the Rolls, Sir Richard Collins held that the agreement did not come within the restraint of trade doctrine, so was not invalidated as contrary to public policy, but even if it did it was reasonable. The other two members of the Court agreed with this conclusion, though they also discussed the restraint of trade doctrine and the unlimited time period of the contract. The headings of restraint of trade are now well established although new categories such as exclusive retaining or distributorships can still be added by case law. Exclusive or "*solus*" agreements are now very much part of the modern economy and since the 1960s have become subject to the restraint of trade rules.[10]

The issue of whether the restraint of trade doctrine applied also arose in *Watson v.* **20.26** *Prager*[11] in which the plaintiff was a boxer, Michael Watson, and the defendant was his manager Michael Prager, also known as the boxing promoter, Micky Duff. The management agreement was made on standard terms drafted by the sports governing body by the British Boxing Board of Control. The defendant as manager had to negotiate terms to the boxer's benefit and both the plaintiff and his manager had to observe the Regulations of the BBBC. The manager was allowed under the terms of the agreement to promote boxing matches, including boxers whom they managed. The plaintiff claimed that this constituted an unreasonable restraint of trade. The central issue was whether the restraint of trade doctrine applied.

Scott J. held that when the regulations of a professional body were restrictive of the ability of sportsmen to earn their living, the doctrine of restraint of trade applied. By analogy, similar restrictions were to be found in the contract between the boxer and his manager which was also subject to the restraint doctrine. There was a conflict of interest when the manager was also the promoter of a boxing match, since the interest of the promoter of fights was clearly different from that of the manager who was there to act for the boxer. The terms of the agreement were therefore subject to the restraint of trade doctrine and unenforceable.

(2) Stage two: reasonableness between the parties

(9) The legitimate interests protected

If the person relying on the restrictive covenant can show that he or she has a legitimate **20.27** interest to protect, this goes some way to prove the term reasonable. One of the earliest cases in the modern law on restraint of trade is *Nordenfelt v. Maxim Nordenfelt Guns & Ammunition Co.*[12] The defendant owned a patent for manufacturing machine guns. When the defendant sold his business, the buyers protected themselves against him setting up a new company in competition with their own, by inserting two clauses preventing the defendant from making guns or engaging in any activity as a rival to their own business. The House of Lords held that such a covenant in restraint of trade was to be regarded

---

[10] See p. 368. The leading case is *ESSO Petroleum Co. Ltd v. Harper's Garage (Stourport) Ltd* [1968] A.C. 269 concerning a petrol station near Kidderminster being tied to a particular multi-national supplier.
[11] [1993] 1 E.M.L.R. 275.
[12] [1894] A.C. 535.

as *prima facie* void, but could be upheld if it was reasonable.[13] In *Nordenfelt* the House of Lords upheld the clause even though it was worldwide in it's application and extended for many years. The restraint was necessary to protect a legitimate interest of the purchasers of the business as the market for weapons of this kind was limited and the company had bought the business and with it the right to the recognition and goodwill of the defendant's reputation.

(b) The extent of the restraint: time and area.

20.28 The restrictive covenant must be reasonable both in period of time and geographical area. Each case is different and has to be determined on it's facts. The issue is largely based upon an economic criteria determined by the market for goods and services covered by the business activity involved. This could mean anything from a small town in the Cotswold to be entire world. In *Nordenfelt v. Maxim Nordenfeld Guns and Ammunition Ltd*[14] the market in machine guns was a global one, so a world wide restriction was reasonable. In *Mason v. Provident Clothing and Supply Co. Ltd*[15] by contrast a covenant on a person not to sell clothing or start up a similar business within 25 miles of Islington was held to be too wide. However, in *Attwood v. Lamont*[16] a restriction on a tailor and outfitter not to work within 10 miles of Kidderminster was held to be reasonable. Professional contracts such as those between a solicitor and law firm often contain a restriction on working for other firms within a specified radius.

(c) The consideration for the restraint

Many commercial restraints of trade are straightforward bilateral contracts in which the restrictive covenant is purchased for a price, and the resulting term is therefore a bargain from which both sides obtain a benefit. For instance, in setting up a 'tying' arrangement by which public houses are limited to selling the product of a single brewery, the landlord would normally be offered an incentive, such as discounts on price, re-furbishing or developing of the premises and other benefits. The brewery in return obtains security in retailing of it's own beers.[17] The public interest of greater choice is often badly affected by such agreements which are found in many sectors of retailing.[18]

(3) Stage three: Reasonableness in the public interest

20.29 Society as a whole has an interest in improving competition and freedom of choice. The wider economic good also has a role to play in policing such agreements. The guardians of this interest in the United Kingdom are the Office of Fair Trading, Competition Commission and the Department of Trade and Industry. The powers of the Commission are set out in the Competition Act 1998. The Act is divided into two parts. Chapter one deals with anti-competitive agreements, including price fixing and imposing resale prices.

---

[13] The Office of Fair Trading and the Competition Commission exercise important powers on behalf of the public and wider economic interest in this area, particularly under the Competition Act 1998.

[14] [1894] A.C. 535.

[15] [1913] A.C. 724.

[16] [1920] 3 K.B. 571.

[17] "Tied Public" houses are now no longer enforceable as being against the public interest by limiting consumer, choice.

[18] In *Cowage Ltd v. Crehan, The Daily Telegraph*, September 25, 2001 the ECJ held that breach of a beer-tie agreement under Art. 85 of the E.C. Treaty which distorted competition entitled a party to the agreement to a claim for damages.

Chapter two forbids those with a dominant market share from abusing the position. The Act allows the Office of Fair Trading and regulators such as Oftel powers to acquire information and impose fines on those who break the law. This can be for up to 10 per cent of total United Kingdom turnover for each year. Contracts which infringe the Act are unenforceable.[19] Competition law is nowadays a highly developed area of commercial practice increasingly influenced by the law of European union.

PARTICULAR REMEDIES FOR DEALING WITH RESTRAINT OF TRADE

The remedies for restraint of trade generally follow those for other types of contractual terms void for public policy but special considerations apply in this area notably because of the long term relational aspects of the interests protected.

Injunctions

The primary remedy in relation to restraint of trade is the use of the equitable remedy of an injunction to prevent the threatened breach of a restrictive covenant.[19a] If the clause is void and therefore unenforceable, the party subject to it is free to ignore the clause at any time.   **20.30**

Severance of the clause from the rest of the contract

It has been established since *Henry Pigot's* case[20] that an illegal term or even a part of a term may be severed from an agreement leaving the rest of the contract intact. In *Pickering v. Ilfracombe Railway Co.*,[21] Willes J. stated that the general rule was: "where you cannot sever the illegal, from the legal part of a covenant, the contract is altogether void; but where you can sever them, whether the illegality be created by statute and by common law, you may reject the bad part and retain the good". This is similar to the "blue pencil" rule striking out offending clauses while leaving the remainder of the contract standing and valid. In *Attwood v. Lamont*[22] it was held that the covenant was a single entity for the protection of the plaintiff's business, which could not be severed without altering the nature of the covenant. In *Marshall v. N. M. Financial Management Ltd*[23] the plaintiff, Anthony Marshall, was an exclusive agent for the defendant, a financial services company, paid by commission. He was only entitled to receive commission after he left the defendant's employment if he did not become an "Independent Intermediary or become employed or represent an Appointed Representative of any company directly or indirectly in competition with the company". The judge held that the unlawfulness could be severed. This left the plaintiff's claim for renewal of commission enforceable.

---

[19] Flynn, *Competition: Understanding the 1998 Act*, (1999, Palladian).
[19a] See Chap. 26.
[20] (1614) 11 Co. Rep. 27, 77 E.R. 1177.
[21] (1868) LR 3CP 235 (at p. 250).
[22] [1920] 3 K.B. 571.
[23] [1995] 4 All E.R. 785.

20.31   The principles on which severance is made were summarised in *Sadler v. Imperial Life Assurance Co of Canada Ltd.*[24] First, that the unenforceable provision is capable of being removed without the necessity of adding to or modifying the wording of what remains. This is the "blue pencil rule" (a necessary but not sufficient requirement of severance). Secondly, that the remaining terms remain supported by consideration. Thirdly, that the removal of the unenforceable provisions does not change the character of the contract so that it becomes something other than "the sort of contract the parties entered into". Finally, in *Marshall* (above) the judge, Jonathan Sumption QC, added that "the severance must be consistent with public policy".

[24] [1988] I.R.L.R. 388 (at p. 392).

Chapter 21

COMMON MISTAKE AND REMEDIES FOR MISTAKE AT COMMON LAW AND IN EQUITY

Introduction

The parties may make a contract under a misapprehension of facts at the time of contracting or as to some fundamental assumption prior to entering the agreement. If the factual basis proves non-existent or fundamentally lacking, the resulting agreement may be void for mistake. The error must be so basic as to rob the agreement of it's consideration. Mistake covers major unforeseen circumstances before a contract is formed. The related doctrine of frustration, with which we deal in the following chapter, applies to unexpected events after the contract has come into being. The effects of the two doctrines are dramatically different. Mistake renders a contract void from the beginning. Frustration, on the other hand, is a ground for discharging an agreement. The contract is valid up to and until the frustrating event, at which point it terminates automatically.[1]

21.1

There are two categories of mistake which are really different doctrines. In common mistake, both sides make the same misunderstanding over a fundamental aspect of the agreement. Offer and acceptance match but mistake robs the agreement of it's validity. In agreement mistake, the parties never reach agreement.[2] The rules of the two doctrines are different, although they can be seen as one in relation to their effect and remedies.

Like a number of other doctrines in English contract law, mistake is narrowly defined. Parties are expected to look out for themselves when they make an agreement. If they do not do so, the law will not step in to protect them. In *Clarion Ltd v. National Provident Institution*[3] Rimer J. stated that "it is ordinarily no part of equity's function to allow those who have made such [bad] bargains to escape from them".[4] Despite fusion of the two systems in 1873, the rules of common law and equity co-exist separately in relation to mistake. The common law takes a narrow view of common mistake because of the risk to third parties who acquire rights under a "void" agreement. Mistake at common law is hard to establish. Equity typically has a more liberal attitude both in its concept of mistake and in its effect. Equity remains the main remedy for

21.2

---

[1] See Chap. 22.
[2] See Chap. 6.
[3] [2000] 1 W.L.R. 1888.
[4] At p. 1906.

mistake in most cases, while the common law doctrine has proved sterile. Some have even doubted if there is a doctrine of mistake at common law, and others have suggested merger.[5] Other legal systems, meanwhile, have a more extensive law on mistake. The rules of error have developed more in European civil law and also their "hybrid" cousin, Scots law. Unfortunately, the English law of mistake has fossilised owing to a dearth of recent case law. There are calls for mistake to be reformed and updated. This is a slow process by case law, and private law reform is not a pressing issue for Parliament. We shall discuss this later.[6]

A preliminary question: Did the contract allocate the risk?

21.3   One of the primary functions of contract law is the allocation of risks. Dealing with commercial risks is a vital part of business planning and contracts provide one of the means for controlling the financial and legal ramifications of unexpected events. The rules of contractual mistake only apply if there is no express term in the agreement covering the matter. There must be no agreed term dealing with the risk. In *Associated Japanese Bank (International) Ltd v. Credit du Nord*,[7] Steyn J. stated:

> "Logically, before one can turn to the rules as to mistake, whether at common law or in equity, one must first determined whether the contract itself, by express or implied condition precedent or otherwise, provides who bears the risk of the

Flowchart F: Doctrines of Mistake in Contract Law

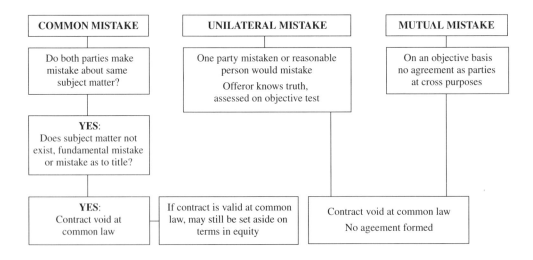

---

[5] See Phang, "Common Mistake in English law: the proposed merger of common law and equity" (1989) 9 Legal Studies 291.
[6] See pp. 383–385.
[7] [1989] 1 W.L.R. 255 (at p. 268).

relevant mistake. It is at this hurdle that many pleas of mistake will either fail or prove to have been unnecessary. Only if the contract is silent on the point is there scope for invoking mistake."

In *William Sindall plc v. Cambridgeshire County Council*[8] the Court of Appeal held that the contract had allocated the risk so it could neither be void for mistake, nor set aside for misrepresentation. A contract to purchase a piece of land at Netherhall School, in Cambridge was subject to various delays over obtaining planning permission. The land was to be used to build houses, however, it's value fell dramatically during the period of the late 1980s. The plaintiffs in the meantime found that there was a sewer running across the land. This would interfere with the plaintiff's plans to build the planned number of houses on the site. The plaintiff therefore sought to rescind the contract for misrepresentation or alternatively for contractual mistake. The judgment in favour of the plaintiff at first instance was overturned on appeal, there being neither mistake nor misrepresentation.[9] The Court of Appeal held that the parties had provided for the matter and this meant that neither the common law nor equitable rules on mistake applied. Similarly in *Kalsep Ltd v. X-Flow BV*,[10] Pumphrey J in the Chancery Division held that before either unilateral or common mistake could be considered in relation to a contract, the court had to determine whether the contract allocated the risk of mistake to one of the parties. In this case the contract had excluded matters which might have been considered under the doctrine of mistake.

COMMON MISTAKE AT COMMON LAW

Common mistake applies where there is an agreement between the parties but a shared misapprehension about a fundamental matter at the time the contract was formed renders the contract void at common law.[11] Common mistake developed in gradual stages as a doctrine.

The subject matter of the contract does not exist

This is also known as *res extincta*, literally "the thing is extinguished". If both parties are mistaken about the existence of goods which form the subject matter of a contract of sale at the time the contract is formed, the Sale of Goods Act 1979, s. 6. provides that such a contract is void.[12] The rule under the Act only applies to "specific" goods. It does not cover generic goods, *i.e.* of a type freely available from other sources. At common law, non existence of the subject matter can also be a ground for nullifying a contract

21.4

---

[8] [1994] 1 W.L.R. 1016.

[9] This case also contains an interesting discussion of misrepresentation (see Chap. 18).

[10] *The Times*, May 3, 2001.

[11] Tylor, "General Theory of Mistake in the Formation of Contract" (1948) 11 M.L.R. 257; Slade, "The Myth of Mistake in the English Law of Contract" (1954) 70 L.Q.R. 385.

[12] Section 6 reads: "Where there is a contract for the sale of specific goods, and the goods without the knowledge of the seller have perished at the time when the contract is made, the contract is void."

although the grounds for doing so must be exceptional.[13] The leading case is *Gustavus Couturier v. Hastie,*[14] in which the plaintiffs were merchants at Izmir who sold corn which both parties thought was then en route from Thessaloniki to London. Unknown to both parties, the corn had by that time deteriorated and been sold to a third party in North Africa. The House of Lords held that the buyers were not liable to pay for the corn. The reasoning of the case is not straightforward and there are different explanations for the judgment.[15] First, the subject matter having ceased to exist, the contract was void for common mistake. Secondly, Martin J. took the view that there was an implied condition precedent that the corn existed. If the corn did not exist then the contract was not binding. This approach is in line with traditional theory which puts the parties' intentions ahead of any judicial ground to intervene for mistake. The two views can be reconciled in the sense that the implied term test is sometimes seen as one of the tests underpinning common mistake.

21.5   The High Court of Australia rejected the view that *Couturier* was a mistake case in *McRae v. Commonwealth Disposals Commission.*[16] *Couturier* was seen as being based on the construction of the contract. The seller promised to deliver corn and did not do so. The buyer therefore was not liable to pay the price. This is an application of the traditional consideration approach to mistake. By orthodox principle, consideration rules out a developed category of mistake at common law. If, however, there is a total failure of the consideration, the buyer does not have to pay; he has a restitutionary claim if any part of the price has already been paid.[17] In spite of these doubts, it seems that non existence of subject matter is a secure ground for rendering a contract void for mistake at common law. In *MaCrae* the defendants asked for tenders for the purchase of an oil tanker lying on Journmaund Reef, approximately 100 miles north of Samarai. The vessel was said to contain oil. The partners, F. E. and Keith McRae, were salvage experts who bid for and were awarded the contract at a price of £285. The wreck was supposed to be off the coast of Queensland, however, no warranty was given as to"condition, description, quality of otherwise". The plaintiffs were unable to locate Journmaund Reef on a map supplied by the Commission, nor were they able to find where the wreck of the tanker was lying. The plaintiffs fitted out a salvage expedition and proceeded to the location but found no tanker. The High Court of Australia held that the defendants were liable for breach of contract having promised that there was an oil tanker at the locality in question. It was not a case of a contract nullified by mistake. Even if there were an element of mistake, the Commission could not rely on the mistake as it had been induced by themselves "recklessly and without any reasonable ground for asserting the existence of the oil tanker". The High Court of Australia held that the defendants had warranted that the ship existed. They took the view *Couturier* was based upon the construction of the contract and total failure of consideration. The correct approach in this limitation was to see if there was an implied condition precedent as to the existence of the subject matter. The Commission had taken no reasonable steps to ensure that the tanker existed. They took the risk and therefore had to bear the loss. In

---

[13] Note that a more liberal attitude towards mistake applies in equity (see p. 378).
[14] (1856) 5 H.L.C. 673, 10 E.R. 1065.
[15] See Atiyah, "*Couturier v. Hastie* and the Sale of Non-Existent Goods" (1957) 73 L.Q.R. 340.
[16] (1951) 84 C.L.R. 377.
[17] See Chap. 26.

McRae there was no implied condition precedent about the existence of the tanker which would have absolved the Commission.[18]

Fundamental mistake

The doctrine of common mistake also extends to mistakes which are fundamental to the   **21.6**
contract. The leading case is the House of Lord's judgment in *Bell v. Lever Brothers.*[19]
The defendants, Bell and Snelling, were chairman and vice-chairman of the plaintiff's company in West Africa. The plaintiffs agreed to pay large sums of money to the two men by way of severance payments at the end of their employment. It transpired that the two men could have been summarily dismissed from their positions because they were in breach of their contracts of employment, having been engaged in making personal gains on the market. The House of Lords held by a majority of three to two that the agreement to pay the money was not void for common mistake. A mistake as to a quality was not sufficient,[20] however, there was a category of mistake at common law which applied if a mistake were fundamental to the whole consideration. The mistake must be of the most serious nature and the contract radicaly and essentially different to that agreed. In *Bell* the mistake was held not to satisfy the test. This has led to doubts over the very existence of the doctrine at common law.[21]

Fundamental mistake was held to apply in *Sheikh Brothers Ltd v. Ochsner,*[22] in which a contract in Kenya to cut and process sisal was held to be void. The yield of the estate was never sufficient to meet the requirements of the contract and the Privy Council applied *Bell v. Lever Brothers* to hold the contract void subject to a fundamental mistake. The mistake was as to a matter of fact essential to the contract. The contract in question was governed by the Indian Contract Act 1872, a codified version of English contract law introduced in the days of the British Empire, s. 20 of which provided that: "where both parties to an agreement are under a mistake as to a matter of fact essential to the agreement, the agreement is void." This went further than the English common law at the time, (or perhaps even today). In *Griffiths v. Brymer,*[23] a contract to view the coronation procession of King Edward VII was held void for common mistake when made after the procession was cancelled due to the King having appendicitis.[24] In this case the contract was made after the decision to operate on the King had already been taken. It was therefore void for common mistake and money paid was recoverable in restitution as having been paid under a mistake of fact.

---

[18] On the qualification of damages in this case, see Chap. 24.
[19] [1932] A.C. 161.
[20] The merits of the argument in *Bell v. Lever Brothers* appear to be against the company, however, see comments by Steyn J. *in Associated Japanese Bank v. Credit Du Nord* [1989] 1 W.L.R. 255 (at p. 267). Because of a corporate merger, Lever Brothers were keen to terminate the two service agreements. Otherwise the holding seems contradictory. The common mistake of the parties in *Bell* seemed to go to the root of the contract.
[21] In *Solle v. Butcher* [1950] 1 K.B. 671 (at p. 691), Lord Denning took the view that *Bell v. Lever Brothers* was authority for there being no doctrine of common mistake at common law. This opinion is widely rejected. See *Cheshire* (1944) 60 L.Q.R. 175; *Stoljar* (1965) 28 M.L.R. 265.
[22] [1957] A.C. 136.
[23] (1903) 19 T.L.R. 434.
[24] The Coronation cases are largely about frustration, see Chap. 22.

21.7   Fundamental mistake can also be linked with a total failure of consideration. In *Strickland v. Sarah Turner*[25] the plaintiff purchased an annuity on the life of a man, Edward Lane of Sydney, New South Wales, who was already dead. It was held that the money had been paid without consideration and so was recoverable in restitution.[26] A rare recent example of common mistake succeeding for fundamental mistake is the Court of Appeal's judgment in *Nutt v. Read.*[27] In this case an assured shorthold tenancy granted by a mistake was held to be void and another agreement over the same subject matter voidable in equity. The plaintiffs, Anthony and Simonetta Nutt, had an agreement for the sale of *The Rest*, a caravan and it's pitch at a caravan site in Surrey. The parties to the contract were held to have made a common mistake that *The Rest* was a chattel which could be sold separately from it's pitch. There were two distinct agreements which were interlinked, the first being an agreement for the sale of the chalet which was void, and another agreement for the right to station the chalet on the land which could be subject to equitable mistake. The first agreement was void at common law. Chadwick L.J. found that the parties to that agreement thought that the chalet was capable of being sold separately from the land. This was held to be a mistake so fundamental that it led to a conclusion that the agreement was void and *Bell v. Lever Brothers* was applied. The second agreement relating to the shorthold tenancy was also based on a common mistake to both parties and was voidable in equity and could be rescinded.[28]

Mistake as to the quality of goods

21.8   A mistake about the quality of goods does not in general make a contract void at common law. Mistakes as to quality are simply too commonplace and offer too wide an opportunity to escape from a contract. It is only if a mistake makes the contract an essentially different thing than that bargained for that it renders a contract void. A distinction is traditionally drawn between a mistake as to (i) the substance of the contract, which may be capable of making the contract void and (ii) a mistake as to the quality or attributes of the thing contracted for, which can never make the contract void.[29] This idea was originally derived from Roman law. In *Associated Japanese Bank v. Credit du Nord*[30] Steyn J. expressed the view that it was "no longer useful to invoke the civilian distinction". As far as substance and attributes of the subject matter is concerned, Steyn J.[31] accepted that the "civilian distinction ... has played a role in the development of law" but the principle enunciated in *Bell v. Lever Brothers* is "markedly narrower in scope than the civilian doctrine". The distinction described is hard to maintain, though it does at least offer some minimal scope for mistakes as to quality. Substance or attributes is really a false dichotomy (or at best a very subtle one) since substance is largely an aspect of a collection of qualities. In *Bell v. Lever Brothers* Lord Atkin expressed the requirement for mistake as being "the existence of some quality which

---

[25] (1852) 7 Exch. 208, 155 E.R. 919.
[26] See later Chap. 26.
[27] *The Times*, December, 3 1999; (1999) 96 LSG 44.
[28] We discuss the equitable doctrine of mistake later pp. 378–381.
[29] See Tylor, "General Theory of Mistake in the Formation of Contract" (1948) 11 M.L.R. 257.
[30] [1989] 1 W.L.R. 255 (at p. 268).
[31] At p. 268.

makes the thing, without the quality, essentially different from the thing it was believed to be".[32]

The guiding principles of common mistake, including mistakes as to quality, were discussed by Steyn J. in *Associated Japanese Bank (International) Ltd v. Credit du Nord SA.*[33] The vital elements being that:

   (a)   the law ought to "uphold rather than destroy apparent contracts";

   (b)   common mistake like frustration was "designed to cope with the impact of unexpected and wholly exceptional circumstances on apparent contracts";

   (c)   the mistake must be "substantially shared by both parties and relate to facts as they existed at the time the contract was made"; and

   (d)   *Bell v. Lever Brothers* laid down the test of common mistake as being the subject matter of the contract must be rendered "essentially and radically different" from that which the parties believed to exist.

There was also a fifth guiding principle which was not discussed in *Bell v. Lever Brothers*, which concerned what is to happen if the person relying on the mistake had no reasonable grounds for his or her belief. In the view of Steyn J., the party relying on the mistake cannot be allowed to do so, "not because principles such as estoppel or negligence require it, but simply because policy and good sense dictate that the positive rules regarding common mistake should be so qualified . . . a recognition of this qualification is consistent with the approach in equity where fault on the part of the party adversely affected by the mistake will generally preclude the granting of equitable relief".[34]

In light of the foregoing, it is not surprising that mistakes as to quality are rarely successful at common law. In *Nicholson and Venn v. Smith-Marriott*[35] some table linen and napkins were sold as "bearing the crest of King Charles I" and with the statement that they had "belonged personally to the King". In fact they were of later origin and therefore of considerably less value. The sellers were held liable because the goods did not correspond with their contractual description and so there was a breach of implied condition under the Sale of Goods Act 1893, s. 13(1). Hallett J. took the view that there was also a mistake at common law.[36] The table cloths were in his opinion, "essentially different from the thing as it was believed to be . . . so the contract had been entered into under such a mutual mistake of fact as to vitiate the parties consent, free the parties from the contract and entitle them to recover the full purchase price".[37] The court relied on *Bell v. Lever Brothers*, but Hallett J. did admit (as to his holding of mistake) that it was "without undue confidence in the correctness of my judgment".

21.9

---

[32] At p. 218.

[33] At pp. 268–269.

[34] At p. 278.

[35] (1947) 177 L.J. 189. For another example of mistake as to quality, see the Michigan case of *Sherwood v. Walker* 33 N W 919 (1887).

[36] See the views of Lord Denning in *Solle v. Butcher* [1950] 1 K.B. (at p. 692) who disagreed. The contract was not in his opinion void from the beginning, *i.e.* at common law, but rather voidable in equity. (See later pp. 376–379.)

[37] At p. 192.

Mistake as to title: *Res Sua*

21.10   A mistake as to the vendor's title to land may render a contract void at common law. This may no longer be regarded as a separate category but rather subsumed within the categories already discussed. In the leading case *Cooper v. Phibbs,*[38] Sir Edward Crofton sold some land in County Sligo, to Joshua Cooper who shortly thereafter was declared a "lunatic". Part of the transaction was the lease of a salmon fishery. When Joshua died it was found that one of his heirs was already a tenant of the fishery and so Sir Edward Crofton had no title to grant. The House of Lords held that the transaction, having been made under a common mistake as to the plaintiff's title, should be set aside. This category of mistake, known as *res sua* is a very narrow doctrine. Lord Atkin in *Bell v. Lever Brothers* regarded this as equivalent to mistake for non existence of subject matter:

> "Corresponding to mistake as to the existence of the subject matter is mistake as to title, cases where, unknown to the parties, the buyer is already the owner of that which the seller purports to sell him. The parties intended to effectuate a transfer of ownership: such a transfer is impossible."[39]

21.11   Lord Denning considered *Cooper v. Phibbs,* a case of mistake in equity rather than at common law, in *Solle v. Butcher*[40] where he stated:

> "... the House of Lords in 1867 in the great case of *Cooper v. Phibbs,* affirmed the doctrine there acted on as correct ... The mistake there as to the title to the fishery did not render the tenancy agreement a nullity. If it had done, the contract would have been void at law from the beginning and equity would have had to follow the law. There would have been no contract to set aside and no terms to impose. The House of Lords, however, held that the mistake was only such as to make it voidable, or in Lord Westbury's words, "liable to be set aside" on such terms as the court thought fit to impose ... The principle so established. . . is in no way impaired by *Bell v. Lever Bros. Ltd* which was treated in the House of Lords as a case at law depending on whether the contract was a nullity or not. If it had been considered on equitable grounds, the result might have been different."[41]

For Lord Denning of course there was really only one doctrine of common mistake, namely the equitable one. We turn now to mistake in Equity.

COMMON MISTAKE IN EQUITY

21.12   Equity in general follows the law on mistake, but the nature of equity allows it a discretionary power to award or deny a remedy as the circumstances require. The test of

---

[38] (1867) L.R. 2, H.L. 149.
[39] [1932] A.C. 161 (at p. 218).
[40] [1950] 1 K.B. 671 (at pp. 693–694). Lord Denning cited the early case of *Lansdown v. Lansdown* (1730) 2 Jac and W 205, 37 E.R. 605.
[41] Lord Denning also claimed that the principle of *Cooper v. Phibbs* had been "fully restored" by *Norwich Union Fire Insurance Society Ltd v. Price* [1934] A.C. 455 (at p. 462–463).

mistake in equity is also less strict than the common law. A material or radically different mistake in equity may be sufficient to deny specific performance or order rescission or rectification or to set the contract aside "on terms". In three cases, Lord Denning set out his view on a wider doctrine of mistake in equity than exists at common law.[42] In one of these, *Magee v. Pennine Insurance Co Ltd*,[43] Lord Denning M.R. stated that equity had superseded the law in relation to mistake: "A common mistake, even on a most fundamental matter, does not make a contract void at law: but it makes it voidable in equity."

In *Solle v. Butcher*, Lord Denning set out the test for mistake in equity: "A contract is also liable in equity to be set aside if the parties were under a common misapprehension either as to facts or as to their relative and respective rights, provided that the misapprehension was fundamental and that the party seeking to set it aside was not himself at fault."[44] Law and equity had merged into a single doctrine, according to the Master of the Rolls. Lord Denning's views on the merger of law and equity are not universally shared.[45]

In *Associated Japanese Bank (International) Ltd v. Credit du Nord*[46] Steyn J. described   **21.13** Lord Denning's words as "representing his own view". Steyn J. was of the opinion that Denning's interpretation of *Bell v. Lever Brothers Ltd* did not do justice to the speeches of the majority. Common law and equity were not a single doctrine. Steyn J's view remains the better authority. In *Solle v. Butcher*[47] the parties were partners in a firm of estate agents who agreed to rent for five flats, unaware that rent control restrictions were in operation. The contract was held valid at common law. Both Buckhill L.J. and Lord Denning held that it should be set aside on terms for common mistake in equity. The test for mistake in equity was wider than that at common law, however, the party relying on the mistake must not be at fault.

The fault rule may not be restricted to equity. In *McRae v. Commonwealth Disposals Commission*[48] the High Court of Australia stated that a party cannot rely on mistake where it was "entertained by him without any reasonable ground" or "deliberately induced by him in the mind of the other party". In *Nutt v. Read*,[49] a case already mentioned, the equitable doctrine was applied to a second agreement relating to the right to station a chalet on a caravan site at Box Hill in Surrey which was held to be voidable in equity. Chadwick L.J. agreed with the judge that the parties were under a "common misapprehension" both as to the facts and their respective rights in relation to the pitch which did not include the chalet situated upon it. "There was no finding that [the plaintiffs] . . . were at fault in relation to that misapprehension. It reflected the advice which Mr Nutt had been given by his solicitors . . . in connection with his purchase of the chalet. The judge expressed the view that all parties were hopelessly at sea about the true effect in law of their proposed transaction." This was sufficient to constitute common mistake in equity.

---

[42] *Solle v. Butcher* [1950] 1 K.B. 671; *Frederick E. Rose (London) Ltd v. William H. Pim Junior & Co. Ltd* [1953] 2 All E.R. 739; *Magee v. Pennine Insurance Co. Ltd* [1969] 2 Q.B. 507. See also Goff J. in *Grist v. Bailey* [1967] Ch. 532.
[43] [1969] 2 Q.B. 507 (at p. 514).
[44] At p. 693.
[45] See Cartwright, "Solle v. Butcher and the Doctrine of Mistake in Contract" (1987) 103 L.Q.R. 594.
[46] [1989] 1 W.L.R. 255.
[47] [1950] 1 K.B. 671.
[48] (1951) 84 C.L.R. 377 (at p. 408).
[49] *The Times*, December 3, 1999.

21.14   The Court of Appeal's judgment in *Nutt v. Reid* therefore re-affirms that common law and equity still retain their own separate doctrine of mistake. Steyn J. in *Associated Japanese Bank v. Credit du Nord*[50] stated that:

> "A narrow doctrine of common law mistake (as annunciated in *Bell v. Lever Bros Ltd*), supplemented by the more flexible doctrine of mistake in equity (as developed in *Solle v. Butcher* and later cases), seems to me to be an entirely sensible and satisfactory state of the law . . . Where common law mistake has been pleaded, the court must first consider this plea. If the contract is held to be void, no question of mistake in equity arises. But, if the contract is held to be valid, a plea of mistake in equity may still have to be considered."

Evans L.J. in *William Sindall v. Cambridgeshire County Council*[51] also discussed the relationship between mistake at common law and in equity. The court found that the contract had allocated the risk, so there was no common mistake and his comments were therefore strictly speaking obiter. Evans L.J. assumed two distinct categories:

> "It must be assumed, I think, that there is a category of mistake which is 'fundamental' so as to permit the equitable remedy of rescission, which is wider than the kind of 'serious and radical' mistake which means that the agreement is void and of no effect in law . . . The difference may be that the common law rule is limited to mistakes with regard to the subject matter of the contract, whilst equity can have regard to a wider and perhaps unlimited category of 'fundamental' mistake."

21.15   Equity will not allow a party to escape from a bad bargain. The jurisdiction of equity does not extend to relieving a party from a contract on the ground of a mistake of fact when this was not about the subject matter or terms of the agreement but merely as to the commercial consequences and effect. This was confirmed by the Chancery Division in *Clarion Ltd v. National Provident Institution,*[52] in which the mistake did not relate to the subject matter but only to it's "potential for commercial exploitation". This was not a ground for relief in equity on the grounds of mistake. In *Clarion Ltd* an agreement for switching between units in different pension funds on the basis of historic rather than forward pricing was not void for mistake. Rimer J. held that the defendant's mistake was not as to subject matter but only as to the potential for commercial exploitation by the claimant. The agreement would not be set aside in equity merely because it was a bad bargain. According to the judge,[53] "it is ordinarily no part of equity's function to allow those who do make such [bad] bargains to escape from them". The Court held that mistake would only operate in equity as in the common law where the mistake related to the subject matter, the terms of the contract or as to identity. A mistake as to commercial wisdom or effect was not capable of relief in equity. A mistake as to the making of an agreement, *i.e.* as to it's terms or subject matter, would however be another matter.

---

[50] [1989] 1 W.L.R. 255 (at pp. 267–268).
[51] [1994] 1 W.L.R. 1016 (at p. 1042).
[52] [2000] 1 W.L.R. 1888.
[53] At p. 1906.

Rimer J. referred to Evans L.J.'s words in *William Sindall* as "at most a somewhat tentative obiter comment".

NON EST FACTUM: DOCUMENTS SIGNED BY MISTAKE

Non est factum is best described as a separate category of mistake. If a party signs a document, objective theory applies, and the party is deemed to have agreed to it's terms unless there has been misrepresentation, mistake or *non est factum*. The risk applies even if he or she has neither understood nor read the document in question.[54] The Latin phrase *non est factum* is translated as "it is not my deed" but means literally "nothing has been done". This is a defence to the enforcement of a contract. The rule developed in Elizabethan times when illiteracy was widespread. In *Thoroughgood's Case*[55] a deed was read out to such a person: "Goodman Thoroughgood you are a man unlearned and I will declare it unto you . . . that you do release to William Chicken all the arrearages [arrears] of rent that he doth owe you . . . and then you shall have your land again." It was held in the Court of Common Pleas that a deed executed by an illiterate person did not bind them if read falsely either by the grantee or by a stranger. Thoroughgood had never properly agreed to the document so it was not enforceable against him. There are also more modern illustrations. A bizarre example is *Lewis v. Clay,*[56] in which the plaintiff asked the defendant to "witness" a deed for him. He showed the defendant some papers, over which he held a piece of blotting-paper into which were cut a number of holes. The plaintiff told the defendant that the content of the document had to remain private. Naïvely, the defendant signed within the blank spaces. The papers were promissory notes made out to the plaintiff, for £11,000. It was held, somewhat surprisingly, that the defendant had not been negligent, so *non est factum* applied and he was freed from his obligation.

21.16

In modern times, cases applying the rule are rare indeed. (No pun intended.) For the plea of *non est factum* to succeed, there must be some radical difference between the document in question and what the person signing it believed it to be. At one time the rule was that the document had to be different in nature. A mere difference in content was not sufficient. This was designed to keep the rule within limits. The distinction proved to be untenable and was rejected in *Saunders v. Anglia Building Society*[57] where in a dispute over the sale of a house in Dagenham, Essex, the House of Lords laid out the parameters of the modern version of this ancient rule. In *Saunders* the Law Lords affirmed that *non est factum* is still alive and in so doing turned down the opportunity to abolish the defence altogether, as some had urged. On the facts, the defence of *non est factum* failed, because the difference between what Rose Gallie signed and what she believed she was signing was not great enough to establish the defence. Lord Reid noted that the doctrine had to be kept within limits if it was not to shake the confidence of those who habitually, and rightly, rely on signatures when there is no obvious reason to doubt their validity. According to Lord Wilberforce, the defence of *non est factum* was only available

21.17

[54] *L'Estrange v. Graucob* [1934] 2 K.B. 394.
[55] (1582) 2 Co Rep 9a, 76 E.R. 408 (at p. 409).
[56] (1897) 67 L.J. Q.B. 224.
[57] [1971] A.C. 1004. The case is known as *Gallie v. Lee* in the Court of Appeal [1969] 2 Ch. 17.

where "the transaction which the document purports to effect is essentially different in substance or in kind from the transaction intended". Lord Reid noted that the doctrine does not excuse a person from taking reasonable precautions.[58] "He must prove all the circumstances necessary to justify its being granted to him, and that necessarily involves his proving that he took all reasonable precautions in the circumstances." The defence is made out however, according to Lord Pearson,[59] if the signor is subjectively wrong in a "fundamental" or "radical" way about the document which need not be of a different type of transaction. The signor must not be careless and the burden of proof is on the person to show that they were not so.

21.18   The plea of *non est factum* is infrequently argued in modern times and rarely succeeds. It was applied in *Lloyds Bank plc v. Waterhouse*[60] where Purchas L.J. in the Court of Appeal laid down three requirements which a defendant had to establish:

(a)   he was under a disability (in *Waterhouse* this was illiteracy);

(b)   the document which he had signed was fundamentally different from the document he thought he was signing; and

(c)   he was not careless in that he had not failed to take proper precautions to ascertain the significance of the document he was signing.

Purchas LJ discussed the "substance and contents" distinction (which we have discussed above) and rejected it. "It is better to adopt the test which is supported by the authorities [prior to *Howatson v. Webb*] and is sound in principle. This is that the difference to support plea of *non est factum* must be in a particular which goes to the substance of the whole consideration or to the root of the matter."[61]

The Effect of Mistake

At common law

21.19   A contract is void at common law for mistake. If the contract is void, (a "void contract" was correctly described as a "meaningless expression" by Devlin J. in *Ingram v. Little*[62]), then title to goods cannot pass applying the rule *nemo dat quod habet* a party who has obtained goods cannot pass on a good title to a third party.[63] This explains the apparent reluctance of the courts to hold contracts void. Even so, if money has been paid or services rendered, there may be important remedies in restitution law which we consider later.[64] A void contract is, therefore, not without legal consequences.

---

[58]   At p. 1016.
[59]   At pp. 1035–1036.
[60]   [1993] 2 F.L.R. 97.
[61]   At p. 109. The earlier authority referred to is *Howatson v. Webb* [1908] 1 Ch. 1, which laid down the rule that the substance of the contract, not just its contents, had to be different. This is now overruled.
[62]   [1961] 1 Q.B. 31 at (p. 64).
[63]   See Chap. 6.
[64]   See Chap. 26.

In equity

If the contract is not void at law, equity may grant relief. This may take the form of either (i) refusing to order specific performance of the contract, (ii) setting the contract aside "on terms", *i.e.* rescinding the contract in whole or in part or (iii) ordering rectification of the contract if the terms of a written document do not correctly record the preceding agreement of the parties.

(1) Refusal of specific performance

A party may ask the court for an order for specific performance to compel the performance of the contract. This is an equitable remedy and therefore discretionary. It is not usually ordered in England if damages would be an adequate remedy.[65] If there has been a mistake which is sufficiently serious, the court can refuse to order specific performance (had it chosen to do so otherwise), thereby acknowledging the mistake. In *Grist v. Bailey*,[66] a common mistake case, Goff J. held the contract was not void at common law but was made under a "mutual fundamental misapprehension" for which the Court refused to grant specific performance. In the case of unilateral mistake, if one party contributes to the other's mistake, albeit innocently, he or she may be refused specific performance. In *Denny v. Hancock*,[67] specific performance was refused where the purchaser's mistake over the boundary of property being sold at auction had been caused by an innocent mistake on the vendor's part.

(2) Rescission or setting aside "on terms"

In equity a contract is valid until set aside by the court for mistake. In setting aside for mistake the court may impose such terms as it thinks just or equitable. This remedy was applied in *Torrance v. Bolton*,[68] in which a property being sold at auction at a hotel in Rugby was described in an advertisement as "absolute freehold". There were in fact no fewer than three mortgages on the property. The particulars had been read out in the auction room immediately prior to the sale. The plaintiff, Dr Torrance, was deaf and did not understand that he was buying an equity of redemption. The contract to purchase the farm at Clifton-on-Dunsmore, Warwickshire was rescinded. The advertisement was misleading and the onus was on the vendor to show otherwise. This was sufficiently serious to amount to equitable mistake. The contract was rescinded and his deposit returned.

21.20

Lord Denning in *Solle v. Butcher* made reference to *Torrance v. Bolton*:

"Whilst presupposing that a contract was good at law, or at any rate not void, the court of equity would often relieve a party from the consequences of his own mistake, so long as it could do so without injustice to third parties. The court, it was said, had power to set aside the contract whenever it was of opinion that it was unconscientious for the other party to avail himself of the legal advantage which he had obtained."[69]

[65] See Chap. 26.
[66] [1967] Ch. 532.
[67] (1870) LR 6 Ch. App 1.
[68] (1872) LR 8 Ch. App. 118.
[69] [1950] 1 K.B. 671 (at p. 692).

The test for Lord Denning of this equitable doctrine was that a contract will be set aside if the mistake of the one party has been induced by a "material misrepresentation of the other, even though it was not fraudulent or fundamental; or if one party, knowing that the other is mistaken about the terms of an offer, or the identity of the person by whom it is made, lets him remain under his delusion and concludes a contract on the mistaken terms instead of pointing out the mistake".[70] The right to rescind for mistake in equity may be lost by affirmation, lapse of time, counter restitution being impossible, or a third party acquiring the property for value.

(3) Rectification

21.21   If a document does not accurately record the true contract between the parties, *e.g.* whether a piece of land such as a hedgerow or lane was included in a sale of property, the writing may be subject to rectification in equity. The traditional view was that the writing had to be inaccurate as far as both parties intentions were concerned, not merely one of them, so a unilateral mistake by one was not enough.[71] However, in *A Roberts and Co Ltd v. Leicestershire County Council*[72] it was held that a party could have rectification if only one was mistaken but the other knew and took advantage of this. Also in the past it was necessary that there had to be a contract between the parties. In modern law a "continuing common intention" is sufficient.[73] In *Mace v. Rutland House Textiles Ltd*[74] common intention was all that was required for rectification, without any other outward expression of agreement and a sub-lease prepared by an agent retained by both parties (in this case a solicitor) could be rectified. The remedy for rectification is variable. The court may either alter the written document or make an order for specific performance of the rectified contract. It will not do so against a good faith purchaser without notice, nor if a party delays in seeking the remedy. The equitable doctrines of "laches" will bar rectification if the claimant waits too long. The equitable nature of rectification was described by Buckley L.J. in *Thomas Bates v. Wyndhams (Lingerie) Ltd.*[75] The defendant's conduct must be such as to make it inequitable that he or she should be allowed to object to the rectification of the document: "The graver the character of the conduct involved, no doubt the heavier the burden of proof may be . . . the conduct must be such as to effect the conscience of the party who has suppressed the fact that he has recognised the presence of a mistake".[76]

21.22   The document must fail to record both parties' intentions, so a unilateral mistake will generally not be sufficient. In *Riverlate Properties v. Paul*[77] it was held that unilateral mistake is not enough. However, if one party is mistaken and the other knows of the mistake and takes advantage of it then rectification may be allowed.[78] In *Thomas Bates & Son Ltd v. Wyndham's (Lingerie) Ltd*[79] Buckley L.J. set out the principles for allowing rectification on the ground of unilateral mistake as being:

---

[70] Significantly, Lord Denning would have found for the defendant in *Smith v. Hughes* on this basis and have held the agreement in *Cundy v. Lindsay* as voidable, not void. (See Chap. 6.)
[71] *Riverlate Properties Ltd v. Paul* [1975] Ch. 133.
[72] [1961] Ch. 555.
[73] *Joscelyne v. Nissen* [1970] 2 Q.B. 86.
[74] *The Times*, January 11, 2000.
[75] [1981] 1 W.L.R. 505.
[76] At p. 521.
[77] [1975] Ch. 133
[78] See *A. Roberts and Co. Ltd v. Leicestershire County Council* [1961] Ch. 55.
[79] [1981] 1 W.L.R. 505.

"First, that one party, A, erroneously believed that the document sought to be rectified contained a particular term or provision, or possibly did not contain a particular term or provision which, mistakenly, it did contain; second, that the other
party, B was aware of the omission or the inclusion and that it was due to a mistake
on the part of A; third, that B has omitted to draw the mistake to the notice of A.
And I think there must be a fourth element involved, namely that the mistake must
be the one calculated to benefit B."[80]

In *Collins v. Jones*[81] the Court held that rectification of a unilateral document would not
be granted if by doing so it would become something other than was intended at the
time. This would apply even if by doing so it would achieve a result more in keeping with
the general intention of the person drafting the document. It was in fact impossible to
do what the party had intended to do at the time and rectification would not be granted
to do something else at a later date.[82]

The standard of proof for rectification is the civil standard of balance of probabilities.   **21.23**
In order to establish the common intention of the parties, Brightman L.J. in *Thomas
Bates* stated: "[A]s the alleged common intention *ex hypothesi* contradicts the written
instrument, convincing proof is required in order to counteract the cogent evident of the
parties' intention displayed by the instrument itself."[83] When a document omits something and thereby becomes invalid it may be rectified to cure the fault. As with other
examples of the remedy, the courts will only do so if there is "clear and convincing evidence" of the matter omitted. In *Pappadakis v. Pappadakis,*[84] Park J. added that the equitable doctrine required a high degree of proof of two matters in particular. First, that
although the document said one thing the parties intended it so say another, and secondly, evidence of what the other thing was intended to be.

THE REFORM OF MISTAKE IN CONTRACT LAW

In 1966 the Law Revision Committee (a forerunner of the Law Commission) recommended that in the case of mistake as to the person, contracts should be merely voidable,
thereby protecting the right of innocent third parties.[85] No action was taken to implement this proposal. There are several options available for the reform of the contractual
doctrines of mistake. This is an area where clarification and reform would be welcome.

Merge common law and equity

The two doctrines may have already merged *de facto*.[86] The equitable doctrine would   **21.24**
become the rule and make contracts subject to the equitable principle voidable rather

---

[80] At pp. 515–516.
[81] *The Times*, February 3, 2000.
[82] See also *Commission for the New Towns v. Cooper (GB) Ltd* [1995] 2 All E.R. 929 (at p. 946).
[83] *Thomas Bates & Son Ltd v. Wyndham's (Lingerie) Ltd* [1981] 1 W.L.R. 505 (at p. 521).
[84] *The Times*, January 19, 2000.
[85] Twelfth Report of the Law Revision Committee, Cmnd. 2958 (1966), and see also Diamond (1966) 29
M.L.R. 413.
[86] See Phang, "Common Mistake in English law: the proposed merger of common law and equity" (1989) 9
Legal Studies 291.

than void. Lord Denning took the view that the equitable doctrine had already pre-vailed. The weight of authority still supports two separate doctrines at law and in equity.[87] In the Australian case of *Taylor v. Johnson*[88] the High Court of Australia sug-gested that a unilateral mistake by one party, if known to the other party, should only make the contract voidable and not void. The Court held that if there was a fundamen-tal mistake about which one party, the contract knew and deliberately concealed from the other party should be set aside in equity. The High Court of Australia described a merged doctrine thus:

> "A party who has entered into a written contract under a serious mistake about its contents in relation to a fundamental term will be entitled in equity to an order rescinding the contract if the other party is aware that circumstances exist which indicate that the first party is entering the contract under some serious mistake or misapprehension about either the content or subject matter of that term and delib-erately sets out to ensure that the first party does not become aware of the existence of his mistake or misapprehension."[89]

Such an approach would help to sort out the difficulties we discussed earlier, particularly in relation to mistaken identity.

Apportionment of the losses between the parties

21.25   A radical but sensible approach to the inherent problems of mistake might be to divide the losses between the parties. This could be done on an equitable basis. Devlin J. in *Ingram v. Little*[90] made the strongest argument for apportionment of losses between the parties by recognising the fine distinction between the categories of mistake:

> "The dividing line between voidness and voidability, between fundamental mistake and incidental deceit, is a very fine one . . . But here, contrary to its habit, the common law, instead of looking for a principle that is simple and just, rests on the-oretical distinctions. Why should the question whether the defendant should or should not pay the plaintiff damages for conversion depend upon voidness or void-ability, and upon inferences to be drawn from a conversation in which the defendant took no part? The true spirit of the common law is to override theoretical distinc-tions when they stand in the way of doing practical justice. For the doing of justice, the relevant question in this sort of case is not whether the contract was void or voidable, but which of the two innocent parties shall suffer for the fraud of a third. The plain answer is that the loss should be divided between them in such proportion as is just in all the circumstances. If it be pure misfortune, the loss should be borne equally; if the fault or imprudence of either party has caused or contributed to the loss, it should be borne by that party in the whole or in the greater part."

---

[87]   See earlier pp. 371–379.
[88]   [1982–83] 151 C.L.R. 422.
[89]   At pp. 432–433.
[90]   [1961] 1 Q.B. 31 (at p. 73).

As Lord Devlin points out it, apportionment operates in relation to frustration. Common mistake and frustration have much in common.[91] The Law Revision Committee in 1966 rejected apportionment because "it would introduce into a field of law where certainty and clarity are particularly important that uncertainty which inevitably follows the grant of a wide and virtually unrestrained judicial discretion. Such a discretion is not appropriate in cases involving the transfer of property".[92]

Statutory reform

As we have noted, in it's Twelfth Report (on Transfer of Title to Chattels) the Law Revision Committee recommended that in cases of mistaken identity a contract should be voidable not void. A voidable contract would be capable of being rescinded only by notice to the other contracting party.[93] Such a rule goes some way towards protecting third party rights. The proposal has not been acted upon. Root and branch reform of mistake now requires fresh legislation. There is precedent for such a change in other jurisdictions. Under the New Zealand Contractual Mistakes Act 1977,[94] the court has a wide equitable discretion "as it thinks just" under s. 7(3) to apply mistake in contracts. The court may (a) declare the contract void in whole or in part or for any particular purpose, (b) cancel the contract, (c) vary the contract or (d) grant relief by way of restitution or compensation. The Act swept away much of the common law and replaced it with a codified system. On the central question as to what constitutes mistake, the mistake must be (a) material to one party and known to the other, (b) a common mistake or (c) a mutual mistake which occurs when the parties were influenced in their respective judgments about making the contract by a different mistake about the same fact (or under the New Zealand Act including law). The Act gives relief if there has been mistake in any of these categories, but only if at the time of contract it resulted in a "substantially unequal exchange". The risk of the mistake causing this unequal exchange must not have been on the party seeking relief. Such a broad equitable discretion as under the New Zealand legislation would not be to everyone's liking in England as it diminishes certainty and security in agreements. However, statutory reform in England would allow contractual mistake to revive and develop. A new Contractual Mistakes Act could cut through the tangled undergrowth of accumulated case law and allow the choked and endangered plant of mistake to flower and grow in the light of day, supported by a new set of statutory remedies.

21.26

---

[91] See Chap. 22. There are, of course, even more important differences.
[92] Twelfth Law Revision Committee Report, para. 9.
[93] At para. 16.
[94] Dawson, "The New Zealand Contract Statutes" [1985] L.M.C.Q. 42 (at pp. 43–44, 48–51) and (1985) 11 N.Z.L.R. 282.

Chapter 22

FRUSTRATION OF CONTRACT

Introduction

If the nature of the obligation changes fundamentally after the contract was formed, the **22.1** contract may be discharged by frustration.[1] The doctrine is narrow in it's scope, and the change of circumstances must render the contract impossible, totally different or commercially pointless. A mere inconvenient change of circumstances or increase in cost is not sufficient. Nor is it enough if just one party's projected mode of performance is made impossible. The substance of the agreement itself must be undermined. If frustration applies, the contract is automatically brought to an end at the time of the event and neither party need bring action to terminate or rescind the agreement (unlike breach of contract). The contract is not void from the beginning (unlike mistake at common law), neither does it necessarily lead to restitution of money or benefits (unless there is a total failure of consideration). Frustration is governed by it's own statute, the Law Reform (Frustrated Contracts) Act 1943.[2] If the parties have provided for the event which occurs, there is no frustration. This illustrates one of the primary functions of contract law, which is the allocation of risks. Contracts are designed to cater for the parties' rights and liabilities when events or contingencies arise during the course of performance of the contract. Terms which deal with such eventualities are usually called *force majeure* clauses.

In general, the happening of unexpected events does not discharge a contract, since one of the parties has probably already taken the risk. If the change of circumstances is sufficiently fundamental, the contract can be frustrated, but the event in question must have been unforeseen.

Rain stopped play: The law in inaction

The context of frustration is illustrated by the example of a person who buys a ticket **22.2** for a cricket match or tennis tournament. There is no play or play is severely restricted because of rain. If no play takes place on the day due to rain, the contract lacks any substance and is fundamentally different to that agreed by the parties. A person does not spend £25 in order to watch rain falling on the suburbs of Edgbaston or

---

[1] See generally Treitel, *Frustration and Force Majeure* (1994, Sweet and Maxwell, London).
[2] The Act is not mandatory, the parties are free to exclude it: s. 2(3).

Wimbledon. If there is no express provision on the ticket dealing with weather conditions, the contract may be frustrated. Under s. 1(2) of the Law Reform (Frustrated Contracts) Act 1943, the ticket holder is entitled to their money back, subject to a right to retain expenses.[3] In restitution law it might also be argued that there has been a total failure of consideration.[4] However, another argument is equally compelling, the possibility, even likelihood, of rain interrupting or preventing play during an English summer being a foreseeable event. The ticket was purchased in the knowledge that cricket is a weather affected sport and the spectator therefore took the risk that no play would take place. The vital ingredient in most cases is the writing on the back of the ticket, or a notice prominently displayed at the venue. The ticket may state "no refunds" or "event is subject to weather conditions", in which case the risk is with the spectator. A sign outside a county cricket ground in the West Country states: "Play is not guaranteed, under no circumstances will money be refunded." This means you are not entitled to get your money back even if there is no play. More usually the contract contains a provision covering the eventuality. This will prevent frustration occurring. In England the test match ticket states that if less than 10 overs are bowled you can apply for a full refund. Between 10 and 25 overs and you get 50% of the ticket price. More than 25 overs and you cannot claim at all. The terms of the contract will govern the situation and there is no frustration.[5] The third possibility is that used in American baseball, called a "rain check". This gives you a chance to use the ticket on a future occasion when the game does take place.[6] By offering you an alternative performance, there is no frustration.

THE COMMON LAW BACKGROUND TO FRUSTRATION

The rule as to absolute contracts

22.3   Until the middle of the nineteenth century, English contract law knew no doctrine of frustration. Contractual promises still had to be performed even after a major change in circumstances. Parties would be liable in damages for failure to do so even if performance had become impossible. The leading authority on the rule as to absolute contracts is *Paradine v. Jane*.[7] The plaintiff sued his tenant, Jane, for the rent of a farm. The defendant argued that since the farm had been taken over by armed men fighting for Prince Rupert and the Royalist cause in the English Civil War, he had been unable to do any farming. This meant that he could not earn a profit, as he had been ejected from the land. The defendant's argument was that the rent should not be due because

---

[3] See later pp. 402–403.

[4] We discuss this later in Chap. 26.

[5] Test tickets are sold subject to "Booking Conditions" that "all tickets are purchased on the basis that play is not guaranteed and under no circumstances other than those printed on the tickets concerning adverse weather conditions can any money be refunded".

[6] At the Sussex County ground in Hove, the ticket states: "If, due to adverse weather conditions no play takes place, this ticket may be presented at Reception and the holder will be presented with a replacement for a future days cricket at a home venue."

[7] [1647] Aleyn 26, 82 ER 897. See Ibbetson, "Absolute Liability in Contract: The Antecedents of *Paradine v. Jayne*" [sic], in *Consensus and Idem: Essays in Honour of Guenther Treitel* (1996, Sweet and Maxwell, London), pp. 1–37.

the lease had been brought to an end. The Court held for the plaintiff. The defendant still had to pay the rent even after the extraordinary events which had taken place around him. If you agreed to do something, you were bound to carry this out, or pay damages, even if external forces prevented you from performing the contract. The rule applied "notwithstanding any accident by inevitable necessity". If a party wished to avoid the rigours of this rule, he was free to provide against it in the contract by avoiding the risk. This was to remain the harsh position in English law for the next 200 years.[8]

In *Budgett and Co v. Binnington and Co*[9] the rule of absolute contracts applied in a **22.4** more modern context, that of shipping law. Under a bill of lading, 10 days were allowed for unloading. If this did not take place on time, the defendants had to pay agreed damages called demurrage. A strike prevented the unloading of a cargo of barley from the *Fairfield* at Bristol during the period. It was held that the consignees had to pay. They had undertaken that the cargo would be unloaded during the time or they would be liable. This was an absolute risk on their part which they could have avoided by express provision of the contract. As the lay days had been fixed, the consignees were liable to pay demurrage. Lopes L.J. stated: "This is . . . an absolute contract on the part of the merchant to have the cargo unloaded within a specified time. In such a case the merchant takes the risk."[10] If the party wished to avoid the rule he should have done so by allocating the danger as an "excepted risk." Such terms are often still written into contracts, insurance contracts provide a good example. Consumers not infrequently discover this, to their cost.

Contracting to do the impossible

Can freedom of contract be taken so far as to allow a party to agree to do the impossi- **22.5** ble? It has been held that parties are free to agree terms, even one which is impossible.[11] The law will hold them bound by such a provision. The courts will normally be very reluctant to reach such a construction of the contract. The Court of Appeal did so in *Enrico SpA v. Philipp Brothers "The Epaphus"*.[12] The parties had agreed a sale of Indian white rice to be shipped to a "main Italian port to be declared on vessel passing through the Suez Canal". By agreement between the parties, this was changed to a "North Italian port", and the buyers declared Ravenna as the discharge port. The vessel was unable to enter Ravenna, being too large for the harbour, and it was then arranged that the vessel should go instead to Ancona.

The Court of Appeal (with Croom-Johnson L.J. dissenting) held that the parties to a contract were free to agree upon any terms which they considered appropriate, including a term requiring one of the parties to do the impossible. Sir John Donaldson, the Master of the Rolls, stated:

---

[8] The rule in *Paradine v. Jane* remained law for even longer. Since the obligation was to pay money which could never be said to be impossible, the actual holding retained it's validity until modern times in propert law. A lease could not be frustrated until *National Carriers Ltd v. Panalpina (Northern) Ltd* [1981] A.C. 675. Only then did *Paradine v. Jane* finally succumb to the doctrine of frustration.

[9] [1891] 1 Q.B. 35.

[10] At p. 41.

[11] For a contrary view, see Wade, "Impossibility of Performance" (1940) 56 L.Q.R. 522.

[12] [1987] 2 Lloyd's Rep. 215.

"So far as I am aware, there is no authority which is directly decisive of this problem. It is therefore necessary to go back to first principles. My starting point is that parties to any contract are free to agree upon any terms which they consider appropriate, including a term requiring one of the parties to do the impossible, although it would be highly unusual for parties knowingly so to agree. If they do so agree and if, as is inevitable, he fails to perform, he will be liable to damages. That said any Court will hesitate for a long time before holding that, as a matter of construction, the parties have contracted for the impossible, particularly in a commercial contract. Parties to such contracts can be expected to contemplate performance, not breach."[13]

The *Epaphus* case is unusual, of course. When impossibility occurs after the contract is formed for reasons beyond the parties' control, the contract is discharged by frustration, as we shall now discuss.

THE DEVELOPMENT OF FRUSTRATION

22.6   Frustration as a ground for discharging a contract developed gradually and in a piece-meal fashion. The rule was applied in stages to different situations. The modern idea of frustration as a general principle was stated many years ago by Lord Wright in *Denny Mott and Dickson Ltd v. James B Fraser*:

"A rule of this character obviously admits of almost indefinite exemplifications, as numerous and diverse as are the possibilities of a contract being interrupted by a vital change of circumstances . . . [T]he application of the general principle must depend on the circumstances of the particular case. No detailed absolute rules can be stated. A certain elasticity is essential."[14]

The categories of frustration are no longer closed. The House of Lords in *Pioneer Shipping Ltd v. BTP Tioxide Ltd "The Nema"*[15] discussed the issue of a strike in Canada frustrating a charterparty. The rule in the past had been that such an occurrence could not lead to frustration. However, Lord Roskill[16] saw it differently, stating that he could see:

". . . no reason in principle why a strike should not be capable of causing frustration of an adventure by delay. It cannot be right to divide causes of delay into classes and then say that one class can and another class cannot bring about frustration of an adventure. It is not the nature of the cause of delay which matters so much as the effect of that cause upon the performance of the obligations which the parties have assumed one towards the other".

The House of Lords held that, in principle, frustration could also apply to strikes. Nevertheless, the categories remain important, and not only from an historical perspective. In

---

[13]   At p. 218.
[14]   [1944] A.C. 265 (at p. 274).
[15]   [1982] A.C. 724.
[16]   At p. 754.

Bank Line Ltd v. Arthur Capel and Co., Lord Sumner stated that "ultimately the frustration of an adventure depends on the facts of each case".[17]

The main categories of frustrating events

Although the traditional headings may no longer be watertight, they do remain afloat **22.7** and account for the bulk of reported examples of the doctrine of frustration. There have been some famous events which have led to numerous cases on frustration. The most famous of these have been the cancellation of the coronation of King Edward VII, the closure of the Suez Canal in 1956 as a result of the invasion by Anglo-French forces, President Nixon's prohibition on the export of soya beans from the United States in 1973, and the lengthy Iran-Iraq war in the Gulf in the 1980s. In everyday working life, lengthy illness causing absence from work can lead to frustration of a contract of employment.

(1) The subject matter of the contract is destroyed

This was the first category of frustration to develop. In *Taylor v. Caldwell*[18] the plaintiffs **22.8** agreed to pay £400 for the use of the Surrey Gardens and Music Hall for a series of concerts and fêtes. Before the first concert, the Music Hall was completely burnt down without the fault of either party. Blackburn J. held the contract was frustrated. There was an implied condition that the parties would be excused if performance became impossible from the destruction of the Music Hall. The continued existence of the subject matter was the foundation of the contract. In order to pay lip service to freedom of contract, the theory underpinning frustration was that of an implied term. The parties must have intended that the subject matter of the contract should continue to exist. Lord Sands in *James Scott & Sons Ltd v. R and N Del Sel*[19] was sceptical about the idea of the implied term theory: "A tiger has escaped from a travelling menagerie. The milkgirl fails to deliver the milk. Possibly the milkman may be exonerated from any breach of contract but, even so, it would seem hardly reasonable to base that exoneration on the ground that "tiger days excepted" must be held as if written into the milk contract."[20] The theoretical basis for frustration has now moved on, as we discuss later.[21]

(2) Illness or incapacity of a contracting party

The illness of an employee which renders him or her unfit for work will frustrate a contract **22.9** of employment. In *Condor v. The Barron Knights Ltd*[22] the 16 year old drummer of the group became ill from overwork. Edward Condor could have worked four nights out of seven in his doctor's opinion but the Court held that the plaintiff's contract of employment had been frustrated in a commercial sense. It was regarded as impracticable to hire a replacement for three nights a week since this would involve double rehearsals of the group's musical and comedy numbers. The contract had terminated automatically and there was no wrongful dismissal in hiring a permanent replacement. The court will

[17] [1919] A.C. 435 (at p. 459).
[18] (1863) 3 B & S 826, 122 E.R. 309.
[19] 1922 S.C. 592 (at p. 597).
[20] Quoted by Lord Reid in *Davis Contractors Ltd v Fareham UDC* [1956] A.C. 696 (at p. 720).
[21] See pp. 402–403.
[22] [1966] 1 W.L.R. 87.

take into account the nature of the work, the illness itself and the importance of the task involved. In *The Egg Stores (Stamford Hill) Ltd v. Leibovici*[23] the Employment Appeal Tribunal laid down the guiding principles in cases of this sort. The nine key factors were:

(a) the length of the previous employment;

(b) how long the employment was expected to continue;

(c) the nature of the job;

(d) the nature, length and effect of the illness or disabling event;

(e) the need for the employer to have the work done, and the need for a replacement to do so;

(f) the risk of the employer against obligations of redundancy payments or unfair dismissal if they employed a replacement;

(g) whether wages continued to be paid;

(h) the acts and statements of the employer including dismissing or failure to dismiss the employee; and

(i) whether, in all the circumstances, a reasonable employer could have been expected to wait any longer.

Other misfortunes making it impossible to continue with a contract of employment can also lead to frustration. In *Morgan v. Manser*[24] a stand up comedian of the time, "Cheerful Charlie Chester", was called up for the armed forces. His future engagements were frustrated once he entered the army (where possibly he was less cheerful). In *Hare v. Murphy Brothers*[25] the plaintiff's job was frustrated when he was sentenced to 12 months in prison for unlawful wounding after a brawl unconnected with his work. His contract was frustrated by the length of his sentence and was brought automatically to an end. The imprisonment had been caused as a result of the plaintiff's own act, nevertheless, this was regarded as an external event because it was unconnected with his employment and did not constitute a breach of his contract. Of course, not every bout of illness frustrates an employment contract. Such a rule would be absurdly inflexible and leave every employee at risk of losing their job. Most professional contracts now include provisions for payment of salary over lengthy periods of incapacity or illness.

(3) The non-occurrence of an event

(a) The "Coronation" cases and frustration of purpose

22.10 The "coronation seat" cases are among the most famous in the whole of contract law. Altogether no fewer than twenty cases came before the courts (most of them reported) arising out of the cancellation of the coronation of King Edward VII which should have taken place on June 26, 1902. The King was diagnosed as suffering from appendicitis, requiring an operation on the morning of June 24. The litigation arose out of claims by

---

[23] [1976] I.R.L.R. 376.
[24] [1948] 1 K.B. 184.
[25] [1974] 3 All E.R. 940.

persons who had made arrangements to view certain events due to take place in conjunction with the coronation, notably a procession through the streets of London and a
naval regatta on the English Channel. The plaintiffs were mostly persons who had rented
rooms or bought tickets to see the parade or watch a review of the Royal Navy at sea as
part of the festivities. The two leading cases are *Krell v. Henry*[26] and *Herne Bay
Steamboat Company v. Hutton*[27.] Although the facts of the two cases appear similar, the
outcomes of the actions were not.

In *Krell v. Henry*[28] there was an agreement to hire rooms at 56A, Pall Mall, for two
days. The contract made with the defendant's agent, Cecil Bisgood, made no mention of
the procession.[29] When the events surrounding the coronation were cancelled, the issue
was whether the £25 paid in advance was recoverable, and also whether the balance of
£50 was payable. The contract to let the rooms was held to be frustrated by the cancellation of the coronation procession and the balance of £50 ceased to be payable. The contract was discharged and neither party forced to perform thereafter. The test was whether
the substance or foundation of the contract, in this case the commercial object, had been
destroyed by supervening events. Frustration was not limited to destruction or non-
existence of the subject matter. According to Vaughan Williams L.J., the test was to
ascertain "not necessarily from the terms of the contract, but if required, from the necessary inferences drawn from surrounding circumstances recognised by both contracting
parties; what is the substance of the contract?". The court should ask the question
whether "the contract needs for its foundation the assumption of the existence of a particular state of things. In such case, if the contract becomes impossible of performance
by reason of the non-existence of the state of things assumed by both contracting parties
as the foundation of the contract, there will be no breach of the contract thus limited."[30]
This was then sub-divided into three questions. First, what was the foundation of contract? Secondly, was the performance prevented? Thirdly, was the event which occurred
in the contemplation of the parties when the contract was made? If all these questions
were answered in the affirmative, the contract would be frustrated.

The other main coronation case is *Herne Bay Steamboat Co v. Hutton.*[31] On this occa-   **22.11**
sion the contract was not frustrated. The defendant hired a boat, *The Cynthia*, to take a
party of friends from Herne Bay in Kent for a cruise to see the British Naval Fleet which
was at anchor at Spithead. A naval regatta would also take place on the day in question
and this was to form part of the defendant's entertainment. The total price was £250, £50
of which was paid as a deposit. The naval review was cancelled on the morning that the
plaintiff informed the defendant that the *Cynthia* was ready to sail. The Court of Appeal
held there had been no frustration. There was more than one possible object for the
hiring of the boat. A cruise along the South Coast of England, including two days at sea,
was still possible and also part of the contract. The fact that one element was missing, in
this case the review, was not fatal to the continuation of the contract. The Court of
Appeal held that the hiring of the boat had two objectives. First, taking people to see the
naval review, and secondly, taking them round the fleet. The contract which would go

---

[26] [1903] 2 K.B. 740.
[27] [1903] 2 K.B. 683.
[28] [1903] 2 K.B. 740.
[29] Parol evidence admitted to prove the point (see Chap. 12).
[30] At p. 749.
[31] [1903] 2 K.B. 683.

ahead in these circumstances was not sufficiently different from that which had been planned to justify frustration. The purpose and foundation of the contract had not been destroyed. In *Krell v. Henry* the main object of the contract had become impossible. A distinction between the cases may lie in saying that *Krell* was a total failure of consideration whereas *Herne Bay Steamboat*[32] was not. This view supposed that frustration and failure of consideration were the same thing. Since the House of Lords judgment in *Fibrosa, Spolka Akeyjna v. Fairbairn Lawson,*[33] this view is no longer tenable.

(b) The "other" Coronation cases

22.12   There were a large number of Coronation cases which came before the courts in 1902, which can be grouped under three main headings. Strictly speaking, the payment of money remained possible in all cases, even where frustration applied.

   (i) Total failure of consideration: If the consideration for the contract totally fails, then money paid under the contract may be recoverable in restitution law.[34] In *Blakely v. Muller* and *Hobson v. Pattenden*[35] the plaintiffs had bought seats in temporary stands specially built in the Strand to view the procession of the newly crowned King. Their claim included restitution of money already paid. The contract was held to be frustrated, but the plaintiffs did not recover their advance payment because as the law stood in 1902, frustration left the parties where they were at the time of the event.[36] The claim for total failure of consideration therefore failed. The Court disapproved of Darling J. in *Krell v. Henry* at first instance who had allowed the recovery of the £25 pre-payment. The common law position at the time is illustrated by *Chandler v. Webster*[37] in which a room at 7 Pall Mall was rented, the price of £141 to be paid immediately. He paid £100 but before he paid the rest procession was cancelled. The Court of Appeal held that despite the cancellation, the plantiff was not entitled to the return of his £100 but had to pay the balance of £41 as this was money due before the impossibility of performance arose. These cases show that the effects of frustration and total failure of consideration were different at common law. The former has now been reformed by statute, the Law Reform (Frustrated Contracts) Act 1943, as we shall discuss later.[38] The Act now distinguishes "frustration" and provides it's own statutory framework.

22.13   **(ii) Alternative arrangements offered:** If the contract provides for alternative performance, there will be no frustration. In *Clark v. Lindsay*[39] there was a contract for the hire of a room overlooking the route of the Coronation procession which provided that, if the procession was postponed, the hirer should have the use of the room on any later day on which the procession did take place. By agreeing to a substituted performance, the contract remained valid. In *Victoria Seats Agency v. Paget*[40] an agency had let property from the defendant near Charing Cross to view the celebrations. The contract stated that the licence was "for the Coronation procession" on June 26 or such other day as the

---

[32] See McElroy and Williams, "The Coronation Cases" (1941) 4 M.L.R. 241 and 5 M.L.R. 1.
[33] [1943] A.C. 32. The House of Lords held that frustration and total failure of consideration were distinguishable.
[34] See Chap. 26.
[35] (1903) 19 T.L.R. 186 (both cases reported under the same citation).
[36] The position is now different, see later pp. 404–406.
[37] [1904] 1 K.B. 493.
[38] See pp. 402–404.
[39] (1903) 19 T.L.R. 202.
[40] (1903) 19 T.L.R. 16.

procession would pass the premises. The contract also contained the provision: "Should the said procession not pass these premises I agree to refund to you the money paid to me as soon as the official announcement is made that it will not pass." Wills J. held the money did not have to be refunded. A procession did take place on October 25.[41] There was debate over whether this really was the Coronation procession contemplated by the parties, but holding that it was, there was no liability to repay the £75. In *Fenton v. Victoria Seats Agency*[42] the booking of rooms was also subject to a provision that if the procession were postponed the money would be "credited to the same or similar accommodation when the processions do take place, and in the event of either or both processions being abandoned, the money paid will be returned, less 10 per cent". The plaintiff was offered similar accommodation on the later date but refused and sued for the recovery of the money paid. The Court held he must fail because the alternative of a postponed procession was available.

(c) Common mistake and frustration

Frustration is linked with common mistake in that the test for each is similar. The court looks for a fundamental change in the obligation agreed by the parties. In frustration, the change occurs after formation. In common mistake, it must exist beforehand. The effect of each doctrine is different. The contract automatically ceases to exist for frustration but is void *ab initio* for mistake.[43] In *Griffith v. Brymer*[44] Wright J. held that a contract was void for mistake where the plaintiff had entered into an oral agreement at 11.00 a.m. on June 24 for the hire of a room to view the coronation procession. The decision to operate on the King, which rendered the procession impossible, had been made at about 10 o'clock on that morning. The agreement was therefore made on a "misapprehension of facts" and the plaintiff was entitled to recover his £100 as the contract was void for mistake.

(4) Commercial inconvenience is not sufficient to frustrate

If the commercial purpose of the contract is defeated, the contract may be frustrated. **22.14** This is a step beyond the coronation cases, but it remains a category which is kept within narrow limits. Too liberal an approach to frustration could undermine a large number of contracts. In *Davis Contractors Ltd. v. Fareham UDC*[45] a building contract affected by shortages and rationing after the Second World War was not frustrated by delay and lack of materials to construct houses for a local authority. The cost had increased and the work took considerably longer, but the House of Lords held there was no frustration. Lord Radcliffe stated that "it is not hardship or inconvenience or material loss itself which calls the principle of frustration into play. There must be as well as such a change in the significance of the obligation that the thing undertaken would if performed, be a different thing from the contracted for".[45a] The House of Lords took a similar view in *Tsakiroglou and Co Ltd v. Noblee Thorl GmbH*,[46] in which

---

[41]   The Coronation actually took place on August 9, 1902 at Westminster Abbey.
[42]   (1903) 19 T.L.R. 16.
[43]   The two doctrines were discussed and compared (though neither was applied) in *Amalgamated Investment and Property Co. Ltd v. John Walker and Sons* [1977] 1 W.L.R. 164.
[44]   (1903) 19 T.L.R. 434.
[45]   [1956] A.C. 696.
[45a] At p. 729.
[46]   [1962] A.C. 93.

a ship was prevented from going though the Suez Canal because hostilities had led to it's closure. The vessel had to sail by a longer route round the Cape of Good Hope making the cost greater, and lengthening the duration of it's voyage. Nevertheless, the contract was not frustrated for these factors alone, as the main purpose of the contract remained possible.

(5) Government intervention in contracts in time of war[47]

Frustration of contract is most common in times of war. For instance, it may become illegal to trade with the enemy.[48] Export restrictions may be put in place, goods or personnel requisitioned or called up for military service, and ships or buildings destroyed by military action. A contract will be discharged if the war conditions impose upon the parties a contract fundamentally different from that which they made. In *Tatem Ltd v. Gamboa*[49] a ship was chartered to the Republican Government during the Spanish Civil War. The ship was seized by the opposing Nationalists, and the Government refused to pay for the period thereafter on the ground that the contract had been frustrated. Goddard J. held that the seizure had destroyed the foundation of the contract and Republican Government were not liable to pay the price. Similarly, in *Metropolitan Water Board v. Dick Kerr and Co Ltd*[50] a contract to construct a reservoir was frustrated by the Government ordering the contractors to cease work during the First World War. In more recent times, the Iran-Iraq war led to interference with many commercial contracts in the Gulf due to hostilities.[51]

(6) Exercise of statutory powers

22.15 If statutory powers such as compulsory purchase are exercised, this can frustrate a contract. In *Walton Harvey Ltd v. Walker and Homfrays Ltd*[52] the lessees of St Peter's Hotel in Manchester contracted to allow a firm of advertising agents to erect certain "electrically illuminated advertisements" on the roof of the hotel for seven years. The local authority compulsorily acquired the hotel during the period of the lease under powers which it was known to possess and likely to use. Manchester Corporation then closed and demolished the hotel. This meant that, not surprisingly, the signs could no longer be exhibited. The Court of Appeal held that there was no frustration when powers were exercised which the parties knew existed and were liable to use. This is an example of foreseeability preventing frustration of a contract which we discuss later.[53]

(7) Supervening illegality

A contract will be frustrated if it's performance becomes illegal. In *Atkinson v. Ritchie*,[54] during the Napoleonic Wars, a vessel was due to proceed to St Petersburg and load with a cargo of iron and then return to London. The master of the vessel, when he heard a rumour of war between Britain and Russia, sailed away with the cargo only half loaded

---

[47] See McNair, "Frustration of Contracts by War" (1940) 56 L.Q.R. 173.
[48] See Chap. 20.
[49] [1939] 1 K.B. 132.
[50] [1918] A.C. 119.
[51] Including the inaptly named *Good Luck* hit by an exocet missile while trading in a prohibited area during the war, see *Bank of Nova Scotia v. Hellenic Mutual* [1992] 1 A.C. 233.
[52] [1931] 1 Ch. 274.
[53] See p. 401.
[54] [1809] 10 East 530, 103 E.R. 877.

fearing a hostile embargo on British craft by the Russian Government (an event which did occur six weeks later). The jury found that although he had acted in good faith and on "reasonable and well grounded apprehension", his action amounted to breach of contract. In modern times supervening illegality is a good ground for the discharge of a contract by frustration.[55]

If a contract governed by English law becomes illegal in a foreign country, there will be no frustration unless performance must take place there. In *Bangladesh Export Import Co Ltd v. Sucden Kerry SA*[56] Millett L.J. stated: ". . . the mere fact that performance has become illegal under the law of a foreign country does not of itself amount to frustration of the contract unless the contract requires performance in that country".

(8) Inordinate delay

Slight interruptions do not affect a contract, but if delay is severe or long lasting this may lead to frustration. This is to be judged at the time when parties come to know of the event. The probability of the delay lasting at the time rather than the outcome in retrospect is decisive of the issue. In *Denny Mott and Dickson v. Fraser and Co.*[57] Lord Wright stated: "The position must be determined as at the date when the parties come to know of the prevention and probabilities of its length as there appeared at the date."[58] In *Court Line Ltd v. Dant and Russell Inc*[59] a vessel the *Court Errington* was chartered on a time charter "to be prosecuted with utmost dispatch" carrying a cargo of lumber and scrap iron. As the ship was sailing downstream on the Yangtze river, war broke out between China and Japan. The Chinese Army prevented the vessel continuing it's journey to Shanghai by placing a barrier on the river. The ship should have reached Shanghai by August 19 but remained stuck at the barricade at Wu-Hu, 750 miles from its destination. On August 21 the Master was ordered by the charterer's agent to discharge the Shanghai cargo at Wu-Hu. This was completed by September 3, 1937. It was not until December 9 that a Japanese flotilla finally broke the barrier at Wu-Hu allowing the vessel to complete it's voyage. The owners contended that the ship was therefore still on hire and the charges to be paid. It was held that the "the fair inference from the facts was that the delay was likely to be indefinite". The fact that the barrier was pulled down was irrelevant. It was the likelihood of the length of delay at the time the event occurred which mattered.

22.16

(9) Strikes and industrial action

Until fairly recent times, strikes and other industrial action were deemed never to frustrate a contract.[60] If the interruption due to a strike appears likely to cause indefinite delay then the contract may be frustrated. In *Cleeves Western Valleys Anthracite Collieries Ltd v. Owners of The Penelope*[61] a time charter between Cleeves Western

22.17

[55] See also *Denny Mott and Dickson v. James Fraser* [1944] A.C. 265. The two doctrines may, however, be regarded as distinct in some ways, see para. 22.20.
[56] [1995] 2 Lloyd's Rep. 1 (at pp. 5–6).
[57] [1944] A.C. 265.
[58] At p. 277.
[59] [1939] 3 All E.R. 314
[60] See now *Pioneer Shipping Ltd v. BTP Tioxide* [1982] A.C .724 for the view that a strike may frustrate a contract (discussed earlier para. 22.6).
[61] [1928] P. 180.

Valley Collieries and the owners of the Greek steamship *Penelope* was frustrated by a long running strike. The contract was for the export of coal for 12 months starting in March 1926 from South Wales to various Mediterranean ports. The vessel was contracted to be "expected ready to load[62] between May 20 and June 20". The General Strike began on May Day 1926 with the result that no coal was exported from any of named ports until the end of December. Lord Merrivale M.R. held that the provision in the contract dealing with strikes did not truly cover the seriousness of the event of the General Strike. This had prevented performance of the contract which was frustrated. If an event turned out to be far worse in it's consequences than the parties could ever have foreseen, or had provided against in the contract, then frustration could still result.

(10) Leases and sales of land

The House of Lords resolved a long running debate in *National Carriers Ltd v. Panalpina (Northern) Ltd*[63] holding that a lease could be frustrated.[64] Similar doubts have been expressed over whether a sale of land could ever be frustrated. Usually in sales of land risk passes as soon as the contract is made, and this normally prevents frustration. Land as an entity is regarded as incapable of being destroyed. However, the rule against frustration appears to be slipping. In other common law jurisdictions contracts for the sale of land have been held frustrated.[65]

WHEN FRUSTRATION WILL NOT APPLY

The frustration must not be self induced

22.18 The doctrine of frustration does not protect a party whose own breach of contract causes the frustrating event. Self induced events cannot frustrate a contract. If the breach is one of the factors leading to the frustration, the latter doctrine does not apply. In *J. Lauritzen AIS v. Wijsmuller BV "The Super Servant Two"*[66] there was a choice of drilling rig to be used in North Sea oil installation. By choosing one rig rather than the other there was breach of contract which ruled out frustration. Bingham L.J. stated that frustration had to arise from "some outside event", rather than due to the act or election of the party seeking to rely upon it.

The burden of proof is normally on the party arguing for frustration. If, however, the claim is that the frustration is self induced or caused by the other's own act or breach then it is for the party alleging that this is so to prove it.[67] Self induced frustration may arise when the contract can only be performed with the co-operation of the other. For

---

[62] This phrase in standard contract form was discussed in *Maredelanto Compania Naviera SA v. Bergbau–Handel GmbH "The Mihalis Angelos"* [1971] 1 Q.B. 164 where breach rather than frustration was the issue (see Chap. 13).

[63] [1981] A.C. 675. This finally laid to rest the holding in *Paradine v. Jane* (see earlier pp. 390–391).

[64] However, on the facts the contract was not frustrated in this case.

[65] In Canada see *Capital Quality Homes Ltd v. Colwyn Construction Ltd* (1975) 61 D.L.R. 385 (Ontario Court of Appeal).

[66] [1990] 1 Lloyd's Rep. 1.

[67] *Joseph Constantine v. Imperial Smelting* [1942] A.C. 154.

instance, a shipowner must provide a ship and the charterer a cargo. The failure of one to perform makes it impossible for the other to proceed.[68] This is a breach of contract, not frustration.[69] Often a party causes the event by their own act or choice. This most often arises in the context of a party having to make an election in performing the contract. The choice of one possibility renders the other contract impossible. In *Maritime National Fish Ltd v. Ocean Trawlers Ltd*[70] only three out of five licences applied for were granted to use a type of trawl for fishing. This meant that two vessels chartered could no longer be used for fishing. The Privy Council held that the failure of contract was due to the charterers' own election, rather than frustration.

If only one party's performance is affected, there is no frustration. The happening of the event must undermine the common assumption of both parties. In some cases (such as *Krell v. Henry*) the supervening event though, affecting only one party's performance usually prevents the common objective or commercial purpose of the contract being achieved. In this situation the supervening impossibility will frustrate the contract. However, if the event occurs and prevents performance in a way intended by one party alone, there will be no frustration. In *Blackburn Bobbin Co Ltd v. Allen (TW) and Sons Ltd*[71] an outbreak of war prevented the sale of some Finnish timber at Hull. The defendants were unable to deliver because of the hostilities which prevented the export of the wood. The plaintiffs did not know that the timber they were purchasing had not already been shipped to England. The contract was not frustrated as only the performance of one party was affected and they could have provided for this risk in the contract. The plaintiffs thought they were buying timber which was already in this country. If impossibility is caused as a result of the act or default of one of the parties, then the contract will be discharged by breach not frustration. The burden of proof is on the innocent party who has to show that the contract has been rendered impossible due to the conduct of the other party.[72]   **22.19**

Foreseeability prevents frustration

If the event was foreseeable then the parties are deemed to have taken that risk into account and there is no frustration. In *Krell v. Henry,*[73] Vaughan Williams L.J. stated that the test was whether the event was "anticipated" or not. Lord Denning thought otherwise in *Ocean Tramp Tankers Corporation v. V/O Sovfracht "The Eugenia"*[74] in which he stated: **22.20**

> "The only thing that is essential is that the parties should have made no provision for it in their contract. The only relevance of it being unforeseen is this: If the parties did not foresee anything of the kind happening, you can readily infer that they have made no provision for it: whereas, if they did foresee it, you would expect them to make provision for it."

---

[68] *Sociedad Financiera de Biens Raices SA v. Agrimpek Hungarian Trading Co. "The Aello"* [1961] A.C. 135.
[69] Though sometimes confusingly referred to as the "frustrating breach" (see *Maredelanto Compania Naviera SA v. Bergbau–Handel GmbH "The Mihalis Angelos"* [1971] Q.B.164 (see Chap. 13).
[70] [1935] A.C. 524.
[71] [1918] 2 K.B. 467.
[72] *Universal Cargo Carriers v. Citati* [1957] 2 Q.B. 401.
[73] [1903] K.B. 740 (at p. 752).
[74] [1964] 2 Q.B. 226 (at p. 239).

By contrast, in *WJ Tatem v. Gamboa*[75] Goddard J. held a contract was frustrated even though the seizure of the ship in the middle of hostilities during the Spanish Civil War was foreseeable. This appears to stand in the face of the authorities.

Force majeure and hardship clauses

22.21   Commercial contracts often include *force majeure* clauses, which make express provision for various events and, where they apply, rule out frustration on the ground that the parties have allocated the risk. There is an exception to this rule in the case of supervening illegality, where a contract will be frustrated even if the parties have provided against this in their contract.[76] This is largely based on public policy considerations. A *force majeure* clause applied to prevent frustration in *P.J. van der Zijden Wildhandel NV v. Tucker and Cross Ltd (No. 1)*,[77] in which a contract to sell frozen Chinese rabbits provided against the risk that the seller should fail to make shipment on time "by reason of war, flood, fire or storm, heavy snow or any other causes beyond their control". The effect of a *force majeure* clause and the question of whether frustration was self induced also arose in *Czarnikow Ltd v. Centrala Handlu Zagranicznego "Rolimpex"*.[78] In 1974, as a result of heavy rain, the Polish Minister of Foreign Trade and Shipping banned the export of sugar made from sugar beet owing to shortages of supply. This occurred despite the fact that in Lord Denning's opening words he said: "In Poland sugar beet is best grown on a large scale." The contract was on standard form containing a *force majeure* clause under which the sellers were not be liable if delivery were prevented or delayed by government intervention. The exporters were a nationalised organisation largely under state control in the communist system then operating in Poland. It was held that the defendants were entitled to rely upon *force majeure* as defined in r. 18(a) of the rules of the Refined Sugar Association on the ground that the shipment had been prevented by "Government intervention beyond the defendants' control". The exporters were held to be a distinct legal person from the Polish ministry, so the ban on exports was not self induced by one of the parties.

THE TEST OF FRUSTRATION

22.22   There has been a long debate over the theoretical basis for frustration.[79] Initially the implied term theory put forward by Blackburn J. in *Taylor v. Caldwell* held sway. A contract contained an implied condition subsequent[80] that if an event occurred the contract thereby ceased to exist. In applying the frustration doctrine to the contract, the courts were merely doing what the parties would have done if they had considered the matter. This theory retained the purity of the common law and freedom of contract without

---

[75] [1939] 1 K.B. 132.
[76] See *Ertel Bieber v. Rio Tinto* [1918] A.C. 260.
[77] [1975] 2 Lloyd's Rep. 240.
[78] [1977] 2 Lloyd's Rep. 201.
[79] See Trakman, "Frustration and Contracts and Legal Fictions" (1983) 46 M.L.R. 38; Phang "Linkages in Contract Law – Mistake Frustration and Implied Terms Reconsidered" (1996) 15 Trading Law pp. 481–489.
[80] See Chap. 13.

appearing to involve judicial intervention. The flaw in this argument was exposed by Lord Radcliffe in *Davis Contractors Ltd v. Fareham UDC*,[81] where he expressed difficulty with the implied term approach to something the parties neither expected nor were able to foresee. As an alternative, Lord Sumner in *Hirji Mulji v. Cheong Yue SS Co Ltd*[82] described frustration as "a device by which the rules as to absolute contracts are recognised with a special exception which justice demands". In *J Lauritzen A/S v. Wijsmuller BV "The Super Servant Two"*[83] Bingham L.J. stated that:

> "The object of the doctrine was to give effect to the demands of justice, to achieve a just and reasonable result, to do what is reasonable and fair as an expedient to escape from injustice where such would result from enforcement of a contract in its literal terms after a significant change of circumstances."

This approach does not meet with universal approval. In *Notcutt v. Universal Equipment Co. (London) Ltd* the Court of Appeal rejected a test of injustice alone as a ground of frustration.[84]

The third and most widely accepted test is that enunciated by Lord Radcliffe in **22.23** *Davis Contractors v. Fareham UDC*,[85] namely that "frustration occurs whenever without default of either party a contractual obligation has become incapable of being performed because the circumstances in which performance is called for would render it a thing radically different from that which was undertaken by the contract . . . it was now this that I promised to do". The "radical or fundamental change in the obligation" approach is now the main test for frustration. This merges with the construction test which requires the court to look at the contract before and after the event to construe the nature of the obligation and how far, in light of the changed circumstances, it would now be a radically different contractual obligation. A fourth view is that stated by Lord Haldane in *Tamplin SS Ltd v. Anglo Mexican Petroleum Co*[86] that frustration occurs when the foundation of the contract has been undermined by the unforeseen event. Frustration occurs when something happens which in character and extent is so sweeping that the foundation of what the parties had in contemplation has disappeared and the contract itself has thereby vanished.

The fifth and final judicial explanation is, like the implied term theory, in accordance with traditional common law orthodoxy. Frustration is merely another way of saying that there is a total failure of consideration. If a party gets no benefit because of an event beyond their control, the contract fails. Under this theory there is no need for a doctrine of frustration because unanticipated events can be resolved by other traditional means. This view had much to commend it but is untenable in light of the House of Lord's judgment in the *Fibrosa* case (see earlier) where the House of Lords held that frustration is not the same as total failure of consideration. Indeed, a great deal of benefit could have been provided to the other party prior to the unforeseen occurrence and frustration be held to apply. The two concepts must therefore now be said to differ.

---

[81] [1956] A.C. 696.
[82] [1926] A.C. 497 (at p. 510).
[83] [1990] 1 Lloyd's Rep. 1.
[84] [1986] 1 W.L.R. 641 (at pp. 646–647).
[85] [1956[A.C. 696 (at p. 729).
[86] [1916] A.C. 397 (at p. 406).

THE EFFECT OF FRUSTRATION

22.24 A contract is discharged automatically at the date of frustration and ceases to exist from that point onwards. Until the event occurs, the contract remains intact and valid. Frustration brings the contract to an end without either party having to elect to do so. In this respect it is different from breach of contract which depends on the election of one of the parties rescinding the agreement. The contract is terminated for the future only, not retrospectively. Unlike one vitiated by mistake, the contract is not void from the beginning. The contract comes to an end at the date of frustration. In the words of Lord Summer in *Hirji Mulii v. Cheong Yue Steamship Co,*[87] the occurrence of the frustrating event brings the contract to an end, "forthwith, without more and automatically". Even if the cause of the frustration disappears, once a contract is discharged for frustration, it cannot be revived even if performance becomes again possible.[87a] The common law rule was that the rights of the parties froze at the moment of frustration. This was stated as the "loss lies where it falls". This common law rule has now been altered by statute.

The effect of frustration is now subject to the Law Reform (Frustrated Contracts) Act 1943. The Act is not mandatory, so it's provisions may be excluded by the parties.[88] The parties may make their own terms to deal with frustrating events, and these will be given effect by the courts. As a result of the 1943 Act, some of the older case law is now obviously out of date. The Act itself has not been a great regenerator of new case law.

The Law Reform (Frustrated Contracts) Act 1943

22.25 The Act applies "where a contract governed by English law has become impossible of performance or been otherwise frustrated, and the parties thereto have for that reason been discharged from the further performance of the contract."[89] The Act equates but treats as separate (a) impossibility of performance[90] and (b) frustration. The main effect of the 1943 Act was to reverse the traditional common law rule that the "loss lies where it falls", in other words, that sums paid before the frustration were lost but those payable thereafter ceased to be payable. The Act replaces the common law with a restitutionary regime, in other words, one based upon preventing unjust enrichment.[91]

(1) Section 1(2)

22.26 This section deals with money paid or payable before or after a frustrating event. Sums paid are now recoverable under the Act, subject to the right of the party to whom the money was paid to retain a "just sum" as expenses if it is just and equitable for them to do so. Sums due to be paid after the event cease to be payable. The court has a discretion in the allowance of expenses. According to Goff J. at first instance in *BP Exploration v. Hunt,*[92] this discretion is limited in that a party cannot recover more than his or her

---

[87] [1926] A.C. 497 (at p. 509).
[87a] See *Shanning International Ltd v. Lloyds TSB Bank, The Times,* July 2, 2001, concerning the lifting of prohibition with trading with Iraq.
[88] S. 2(3).
[89] S. 1(1).
[90] See Wade, "The Principle of Impossibility in Contract" (1940) 56 L.Q.R. 519.
[91] Goff J. took a slightly different view in *BP v. Hunt* [1979] 1 W.L.R. 783 (see p. 403).
[92] [1979] 1 W.L.R. 783.

actual expenses at the date of frustration and the expenses cannot exceed the pre-payment. It is only possible to allow expenses when the contract contains a stipulation for pre-payment. If the contract does not require a pre-payment then the other party undertakes the expenses at his or her own risk. In *Gamerco SA v. ICM/Fair Warning Agency Ltd* [93] Garland J. stated that proof of expenditure would be required before these would be off-set against the advanced payment.

(2) Section 1(3)

This deals with "valuable benefits" conferred on either party prior to the frustration. **22.27** This means the provision of goods or services or benefits in kind other than money. For instance, in building a house which is damaged by fire during it's construction, the owner of the house might nevertheless be left with part of the work completed which they can put to use. The Act deals with valuable benefit in an equitable way by awarding a just sum for these benefits subject again to a claim for expenses and also to the circumstances giving rise to the frustrating event. The two subsections are regarded as operating alongside one another. A recovery cannot be made for the same expenses under both headings.

Goff J. in *BP Exploration Co (Libya) v. hunt (No. 2)* [94] considered the process of calculating a s. 1(3) award:

> "That benefit has to be identified, and valued, and such value forms the upper limit of the award. Secondly, the court may award to the plaintiff such sum, not greater than the value of such benefit, as it considers just having regard to all the circumstances of the case, including in particular the matters specified in s. 1(3)(a) and (b). In the case of an award under s.1(3) there are, therefore, two distinct stages: the identification and valuation of the benefit, and the award of the just sum. The amount to be awarded will be limited to the amount of that benefit."

It is an indication either of the Act's success or total nonentity that there have only been **22.28** two cases which have dealt with it's delphic provisions.[95] The first of these was *BP Exploration Co (Libya) v. Hunt* (No 2)[96] which went to the House of Lords on various grounds but which is notable for the lengthy judgment of Goff J. at first instance.[97] Not all of this eminent judge's views have met with universal approval. The case itself concerned the taking into state ownership of oil wells belonging to British Petroleum and a Texan billionaire, Nelson Bunker Hunt, by President Gaddafi of Libya. The expropriation of the British companies' interests come first and thereafter an agreement was made with the American company's whereby the latter would drill and explore for the oil in return for taking a share of the profits when the oil came on stream. Eventually the American company interests were nationalised so the agreement between the two oil companies was frustrated. According to Goff J. in *BP Exploration (Libya) v. Hunt*

---

[93] [1995] 1 W.L.R. 1226.
[94] [1979] 1 W.L.R. 783 (at p. 801).
[95] There are numerous commercial disputes over frustration and it's effects, but most of these are dealt with by arbitration, rather than in the courts.
[96] [1979] 1 W.L.R. 783.
[97] Especially at pp. 799–806.

(No. 2), the purpose of the 1943 Act was the prevention of unjust enrichment, rather than restitution. Both ss 1(2) and 1(3) were concerned with this principle, though they operated in different ways. The Act set out to achieve justice between the parties. It did not seek to apportion the losses between the parties, although this was it's effect. The calculation of the just sum was not an arithmetic calculation but rather a matter of judicial impression. The discretion of the Court was limited under s. 1(2).[98] The just sum could not be for more than any pre-payment. The worth of any valuable benefit should be calculated after the frustrating event has occurred. It was not the restitutionary principle, *i.e.* the value of the services provided, which counted but the end product of the services themselves, if any remained.

20.29   A second discussion of the Act is contained in the High Court judgment in *Gamerco SA v. ICM Fair Warning (Agency) Ltd*[99] The plaintiffs were a Spanish company who agreed to promote a "Guns 'n Roses" rock concert at the stadium home of the football club, Atletico Madrid. The stadium was deemed to be unsafe so a licence to hold the event was not obtained, and the authorities banned the use of the stadium. The plaintiffs sought to recover advance payments and the defendants counterclaimed for damages for breach of contract. Garland J. held that a term was to be implied that the plaintiff would use "all reasonable endeavours to obtain a permit"[1] but they were not obliged to ensure that it remained in force. The contract had been frustrated as the defendants could not perform the concert. The Court held that the plaintiffs were entitled to recover advance payments under s. 1(2) and no deduction was to be made for the defendants' expenses. The calculation of the "just sum" was the key issue. Garland J. could see "no indication in the Act, the authorities or the relevant literature that the court is obliged to incline towards either total retention or equal division". The Court's task was to "do justice in a situation which the parties had neither contemplated not provided for, and to mitigate the possible harshness of allowing all loss to lie where it has fallen".[2] Courts should look at the "broad nature" of discretion and do justice on the facts of the case. The words in the Act "if it considered it just to do so in all the circumstances of the case" conferred a wide discretion. The Court in *Gamerco* had two priorities: (a) to do justice in a situation which the parties had neither contemplated nor provided for and (b) to mitigate the harshness of allowing all loss to lie where it had fallen.

(3) Miscellaneous provisions

20.30   Severance is applied to contracts governed by the Act. A part of a contract may be frustrated while another part remains a valid contract. Section 2(4) permits severance of part of a contract for frustration purposes. There are in addition a limited number of contracts which fall outside the Act, such as insurance contracts, certain contracts for the sale of goods or for carriage of goods by sea, and some charter parties.[3] The Act binds the Crown in contracts to which it is a party.[4]

---

[98] Garland J. in *Gamerco v. Fair Warning* described the remarks of Goff J. on s. 1(2) in *BP v. Hunt* as *obiter dicta.*
[99] [1995] 1 W.L.R. 1226.
[1] See Chap. 5.
[2] At p. 1235.
[3] S. 2(5).
[4] S. 2(2).

Chapter 23

Discharge by Breach and Performance

Breach of Contract

Introduction

The starting point for breach of contract is the pre-existence of a contractual obligation. **23.1** The existence of such an obligation and whether it is truly contractual can be problematic on occasion. In *William Cory and Son Ltd v. London Corporation*[1] London Corporation, acting as the sanitation authority for the Port of London, made a contract with the claimants who were barge owners to remove waste and refuse from Lett's Wharf and carry it by barge to Hornchurch where it was to be dumped. In 1948 the Corporation, acting this time as port authority for the Port of London, introduced a new set of bye-laws governing the comings and goings of barges on the river Thames. These regulations were more onerous than the rules laid down at the time the contract was made, under an Act of 1936. By passing new and more stringent rules the claimants argued that this amounted to a repudiation of their contract with the Corporation by anticipatory breach.[2] The claimants had accepted this repudiation and rescinded the contract. Their argument was that there was an implied or express term in the contract that the Corporation would not introduce more onerous terms which would affect the performance of the work and if they did so that this would constitute a breach of contract. The passing of the new bye-laws in 1948 rendered the contract commercially impossible thereafter and it was not disputed by both parties that the contract was frustrated from that date. The question was whether the making of the bye-laws constituted a breach of contract?

The King's Bench Division held that the Corporation were under a statutory duty to make regulations for the disposal of waste in the area of the port. The term for which the claimants argued was *ultra vires* of the Corporation and therefore void for lack of capacity.[3] If a provision was *ultra vires* it did not bind the parties. There could therefore be no breach of contract. Lord Asquith agreed that most contracts contained an implied term that neither party would attempt to prevent nor disable the other from performing the contract, and that a party who did prevent the other performing was guilty of breach of contract. However, the Court went on to state that:

---

[1] [1951] 2 K.B. 476.
[2] See pp. 410–412.
[3] On capacity to contract, see Chap. 11.

"There can be no breach, if the term in question is illegal, contrary to public policy, or (in the case of a corporation) *ultra vires* the contracting party, or for some other reason waste paper, because in such a case there is no binding obligation, and only a binding obligation can be violated. *You cannot break a rope of sand* . . . I consider that such a term, whether implied or even express, could not be valid."[4][5]

23.2 For contract lawyers the salient point remains that there has to be an obligation before there can be breach. Breach of contract may occur in a variety of ways:

(a) by non performance or defective performance;

(b) by promising the truth of a statement that proves false;

(c) through breach of a condition or warranty or breach depriving the other party of the substantial benefit of the contract[6];

(d) by stating that you no longer intend to be bound by the contract after performance has started. This is called "anticipatory breach" or renunciation;

(e) by making it impossible to perform the contract by one's own action[7]; or

(f) when there is fundamental breach going to the rest of the contract.[8]

Proving lack of performance, defective performance or that a promise was breached is a question to be judged by a construction of the contract.

If impossibility is brought about by one party then this is a breach of contract, rather than frustration.[9] In *Omnium D'Enterprises v. Sutherland*[10] a shipowner made it impossible to perform a charterparty by selling the steamship *Robert Bruce*, "free from any charter arrangements", to another owner. Bankes L.J. stated that: "the defendant put it out of his power to perform his part of the contract".[11] This amounted to a repudiation of the contract for which he was liable in damages. As well as disabling oneself, a party may also be in breach if he or she prevents performance by the other party.[12] The courts may also imply a term that the parties must take the necessary steps to ensure the contract is performed.[13] It is also possible that the parties' conduct or words may *not* amount to an actionable breach of contract. The contract itself, or a rule of law, may provide that the party has an excuse for non-performance. In the former case, the contract may contain an exemption from liability for non-performance. This is to be viewed in light of

---

[4] At p. 484.

[5] The case raises a number of interesting issues on the relationship of public law and contract. See also Arrowsmith, "The Impact of Public Law on the Private Law of Contract" in Helson, *Exploring the Boundaries of Contract* 1996, Dartmouth Publishing, Aldershot).

[6] Chap. 13.

[7] *Omnium D'Enterprises v. Sutherland* [1919] 1 K.B. 618.

[8] This doctrine is linked to exemption clauses, see Chap. 16.

[9] The impossibility may be created either during the performance or before the performance is due to begin.

[10] [1919] 1 K.B. 618.

[11] At p. 621.

[12] *Ogdens Ltd v. Nelson* [1905] A.C. 109.

[13] *The Unique Mariner (No. 2)* [1979] 1 Lloyd's Rep. 37.

the law on exemption clauses.[14] The contract may provide that the event is not a breach. A party may have a contractual right to terminate, for instance by giving an employee his or her agreed period of notice. In *Bridge v. Campbell Discount Co. Ltd*[15] the issue was whether a consumer credit agreement had been breached or whether the hirer was merely exercising a right to terminate. This was a question of construction on an objective determination of the intention of the parties. The House of Lords in *Bridge* held the contract had been breached rather than lawfully brought to an end.

The effect of breach

The effect of breach depends primarily on the nature of the term.[16] A breach of warranty **23.3** gives a right to damages, but otherwise the contract continues. A breach of a promissory condition allows the innocent party the option of either (a) affirming the contract and keeping it alive or (b) rescinding, *i.e.* bringing his obligation to perform the contract to an end. A breach of a condition or intermediate term does not of itself terminate the contract. The contract continues until the injured party either affirms the contract or chooses to rescind it. The classically phrased description is that of Asquith L.J. in *Howard v. Pickford Tool Co.*[17]: "An unaccepted repudiation is a thing writ in water and of no value to anybody: it confers no legal rights of any sort or kind." In *Heyman v. Darwins Ltd*[18] Viscount Simon stated[19]: "repudiation by one party standing alone does not terminate the contract. It takes two to end it, by repudiation, on the one side, and acceptance of the repudiation, on the other." Until a party opts to rescind, the contract continues. Strictly speaking, it is wrong to say that breach of a condition terminates or even entitles the innocent party to terminate.[20] Rather the breach of promise allows the promisee to withhold performance of his or her own contractual obligations. In *Heyman v. Darwins Ltd* Lord Porter stated[21]:

"Strictly speaking, to say that on acceptance of the renunciation of a contract the contract is rescinded is incorrect. In such a case the injured party may accept the renunciation as a breach going to the root of the whole of the consideration. By that acceptance he is discharged from further performance and may bring an action for damages, but the contract itself is not rescinded."

As we have noted, the innocent party has a choice of either (a) refusing to accept the breach and carry on, *i.e.* affirm the contract or (b) rescind, the contract, *i.e.* withholding performance and refusing to perform until the other has done so, or is ready and willing

---

[14] See Chaps 16, 17.
[15] [1962] A.C. 600.
[16] See Chap. 13.
[17] [1951] 1 K.B. 417 (at p. 421).
[18] [1942] A.C. 356.
[19] At p. 361.
[20] The now abolished doctrine of fundamental breach, as interpreted by Lord Denning in *Harbutt's Plasticine v. Wayne Tank Pump Ltd* [1970] 1 Q.B. 447, made it a rule of law that a contract was discharged by a fundamental breach. This was overruled by the House of Lords in *Photo Production Ltd v. Securicor Transport Ltd* [1980] A.C. 827. (See Chap. 16.)
[21] At p. 399.

to perform. He or she may also refuse to accept further performance from the other party. This only arises if the breach is sufficient to justify option (b), *i.e.* a breach of condition or substantial breach of an innominate term. The innocent party may also sue for damages in addition to rescission. If the breach amounts merely to a breach of warranty then the injured party has a right to damages only and must continue to perform their obligations or be themself in breach. Under the Sale of Goods Act, a breach of condition which has been accepted by the other party may nevertheless be treated as an *ex post facto* warranty.

23.4   A party may either positively affirm the contract or otherwise take the necessary steps to constitute rescission. Doing or saying nothing can in exceptional circumstances amount to acceptance of repudiation.[22] Rescission involves informing the other party, or otherwise bringing it to their attention. Conduct which indicates an intention to rescind is sufficient. Once the contract is rescinded it cannot be later affirmed, nor once affirmed can it later be rescinded for the same breach. Under normal principles, a party to a contract cannot take advantage of their own breach. This would be to allow someone to profit from their own wrongdoing.[23] However, a party may occasionally take advantage of their own breach if their own construction of the contractual relationship is later preferred to that of the innocent party.[24] The essence of rescission is that when one party terminates the contract, he or she is no longer required to perform any future obligations. The contract is not void from the beginning. In *Johnson v. Agnew*,[25] Lord Wilberforce explained the situation:

> "[I]t is important to dissipate a fertile source of confusion and to make clear that although the vendor is sometimes referred to in the above situation as 'rescinding' the contract, this so-called 'rescission' is quite different from rescission *ab initio*, such as may arise for example in cases of mistake, fraud or lack of consent. In those cases, the contract is treated in law as never having come into existence . . . In the case of an accepted repudiatory breach the breach has come into existence but has been put an end to or discharged. Whatever contrary indications may be disinterred from old authorities, it is now quite clear, under the general law of contract, that acceptance of a repudiatory breach does not bring about '*rescission ab initio*'."[26]

THE DOCTRINE OF ANTICIPATORY BREACH OF CONTRACT

23.5   Anticipatory breach of contract occurs when a party states in advance of the date of performance that they do not intend to perform their side of the bargain. The rule of anticipatory breach was established in *Hochster v. De la Tour*[27] that the innocent party has a choice. A party not in breach may either (a) rescind the contract and sue for damages immediately or (b) refuse to accept the renunciation, carry on with the contract and wait for the date of performance. If they do so, the contract survives. Until the non

---

[22] We discuss this later at p. 415.
[23] However, see *Alghussien Establishment v. Eton College* [1988] 1 W.L.R. 587.
[24] See *Thornton v. Abbey National, The Times*, March 4, 1993.
[25] [1980] A.C. 367.
[26] At pp. 392–393.
[27] (1853) 2 El and Bl 678, 118 E.R. 922.

breaching party rescinds, the contract remains alive. The innocent party retains their right to perform and sue for damages when the date of performance finally arrives. On the other hand, if the party affirms, they must perform or be ready and able to perform the contract, otherwise they risk paying damages for any subsequent breach.[28] Furthermore, as we discuss shortly, if the contract is frustrated between the affirmation and the date of performance, the innocent party will lose their remedies for breach of contract.[29]

Anticipatory breach may also be constituted by making it impossible to perform the contract. In *Universal Cargo Carriers v. Citati*[30] the charterers agreed to nominate a berth, provide cargo and finish loading before a certain date. Three days prior to commencement of the contract, the defendant had done none of these things. It was held that the shipowner could treat this as an anticipatory breach of contract, since the charters were clearly not able to perform the contract on time. The case is also authority for the rule that if a party rescinds for a reason which turns out later to be wrong, or inadequate, their action may nevertheless be supported if there are at the time facts in existence which would provide justifiable grounds for rescission.

These rules are illustrated by the leading cases. The option of bringing the contract to **23.6** an end and suing for damages immediately applied in *Hochster v. De la Tour*[31] in which the parties had agreed that the plaintiff would act as a tour leader for travel in Europe beginning on June 1. The agreement was made in April, but in May the defendant told the plaintiff that his services were no longer required. The plaintiff started his action for breach of contract on May 22. The defendants argued that he should be required to wait until the date of performance which was the June 1 as there was no breach of contract until that date. It was held that the plaintiff could commence proceedings immediately for damages even although the date of performance had not yet arrived. The expression anticipatory breach is misleading. Breach only occurs on the date of performance normally. English law treats the renunciation itself as a breach.

The second option for the innocent party is to keep the contract alive, wait till the time of performance arrives and then sue for damages. If a party takes this course they run the risk that the contract may be discharged for another reason before the date when performance is due. In *Avery v. Bowden*[32] the defendants had chartered a ship to be loaded at the Black Sea port of Odessa. The ship proceeded to Odessa only to be told by the defendants that they had no cargo and the captain was advised to go away. The captain stayed however in the hope that the defendants would fulfil their contract. While this contractual dispute was going on the Crimean War broke out between Britain and Russia rendering the contract frustrated by the outbreak of hostilities.[33] The plaintiffs' action for damages therefore failed. If a party affirms a contract after an anticipatory breach by the other party, he or she still must continue with further performance of their own obligations under the contract. In *Fercometal SARL v. Mediterranean Shipping Co "The Simona"*[34] the House of Lords held that if the innocent party elects to continue

---

[28] *Fercometal SARL v. Mediterranean Shipping Company "The Simona"* [1988] 3 W.L.R 200.
[29] *Avery v. Bowden* (1855) 5 E and B 714.
[30] [1957] 2 Q.B. 401.
[31] (1853) 2 El and B1 678, 118 E.R. 922.
[32] (1855) 5 E and B 714.
[33] See Chap. 22.
[34] [1988] 2 All E.R. 742.

with the contract and then later breaches the contract, they may be liable in damages. They cannot claim the other's anticipatory breach as an excuse. Lord Ackner stated that there was no *via media*, or middle way, between affirming or rescinding the contract. The innocent party must still perform their own side of the contract. Once a contract has started, if a party refuses to continue performance, the other party is excused further performance of his own obligations and may sue for breach immediately.[34a]

The case of Clydebank litter bins: Do rights have to be exercised reasonably?

23.7   An extreme example of a party soldiering on with a contract in the face of the other party's renunciation is *White and Carter (Councils) Ltd v. McGregor*,[35] a judgment which has been the subject of much discussion over the years. This tends to be a case which divides opinion. For some it is perfectly logical and reasonable. For many others it may be the former but it is not the latter. The pursuers (*i.e.* plaintiffs in Scots law) were in the business of supplying litter bins to local authorities throughout the country. They were not paid for this service but could enter into contracts with traders who wished to advertise on the bins, and so earn a profit in this way. The defender owned a garage in Clydebank, near Glasgow. On June 26, 1957 he agreed to hire space on the bins for a three year period. Later, on the very same day, the defender wrote to say he had changed his mind about the contract and no longer wished to go ahead. The pursuers refused to accept this as a repudiation. Obviously they had done nothing to perform when they received the message, nevertheless they went ahead. They prepared advertising plates, stuck them on the bins and displayed them around the town of Clydebank for the next three years. In due course they brought an action for the contract price at the Sheriff Court in Dunbarton.

The House of Lords held by a majority that they were entitled to succeed. The basic principle was affirmed, that even in the face of such a clear expression of intention to renounce, the other party had a choice. If they opted to continue with the contract that was their right no matter how unreasonable. Lord Reid stated[36]:

> "The general rule cannot be in doubt . . . if one party to a contract repudiates it in the sense of making it clear to the other party that he refuses or will refuse to carry out his part of the contract, the other party, the innocent party has an option. He may accept that repudiation and sue for damages for breach of contract, whether or not the time for performance has come, or he may if he chooses disregard or refuse to accept it and then the contract remains in full effect."

The pursuers had never made an attempt to procure other advertising, thereby taking reasonable steps to mitigate their loss.[37] However, no such duty arose here. It was only after the contract was discharged for breach that the duty to mitigate came into play.

[34a]   *Court v. Ambergate Railway Co.* (1851) 17 Q.B. 127.
[35]   [1962] A.C. 413. See Rodger (1977) 93 L.Q.R. 168 on the facts and whether the appellants had "made no effort" to relet the space.
[36]   At p. 427.
[37]   See Chap. 25.

While the contract subsisted, the duty to mitigate did not apply. Furthermore, the claim in *White and Carter* was for an agreed sum, so the rule about mitigation, being a damages rule, did not apply. The case was unusual in that the pursuers were effectively able to perform their side of the bargain without any need for cooperation from the other side.

Lord Reid had an answer for those who might consider the outcome of this case unfair **23.8** or even absurd. In a classic dictum he stated that:

> "It might be, but never has been, the law that a person is only entitled to enforce his contractual rights in a reasonable way, and that a court will not support an attempt to enforce them in an unreasonable way. One reason why that is not the law is no doubt, because it was thought that it would create too much uncertainty to require the court to decide whether it was reasonable or equitable to allow a party to enforce his full rights under a contract."[38]

The main criticism of *White and Carter* is that it allows unwanted performance and that this is economically wasteful.[39] There were limitations on the rule applying according to Lord Reid, however the House of Lords. First, it was a peculiarity of the case that no cooperation was required. In the normal case by refusing to cooperate the other party can be forced to restrict any claim to damages. Secondly, if the party has no legitimate financial or other interest in performing the contract other than claiming damages, they ought not to be entitled to perform.

The courts have been reluctant to follow *White and Carter*. Lord Reid's two qualifications have been applied (albeit by lower courts) in other cases. In *Hounslow London Borough Council v. Twickenham Garden Developments Ltd*[40] the defendants were employed to do building work on the council's land. The contract provided that if the contractor failed to proceed diligently with the work, the architect could give notice of default and fourteen days later terminate the contract. The defendants refused to accept this and carried on with the work. Megarry J. noted the two dissenting speeches in *White and Carter* (Lords Morton and Keith) and noted their emphasis on the duty to mitigate. There should equally be no entitlement to insist on aggravating the damages. *White and Carter* was rejected because a "considerable degree" of active cooperation was requisite and because the work was being done on the property of the borough. The important point was noted that the ratio of *White and Carter* involved accepting the two limitations placed on it by Lord Reid, although no mention was made of these by the two other Law Lords in the majority (Lords Tucker and Hodson). Without Lord Reid there was no majority for the decision. As Megarry J. commented:"Under the doctrine of precedent I do not think that it can be said that a majority of a bare majority is itself the majority."[41]

In *Clea Shipping Corporation v. Bulk Oil International Ltd "The Alaskan Trader"*[42] **23.9** Lloyd J. held that as a principle of law the innocent party had an unfettered right to choose whether or not to accept a repudiation of a contract. However, the court could in "exceptional cases" in the exercise of it's general equitable jurisdiction refuse to allow

---

[38] At p. 430.
[39] See Goodhart (1962) 78 L.Q.R. 263; Nienabar (1962) 17 C.L.J. 213.
[40] [1971] Ch. 233.
[41] At p. 254.
[42] [1984] 1 All E.R. 129.

an innocent party to enforce their full contractual rights if they had "no legitimate interest" in doing so apart from making a claim for damages. The High Court judge who was bound by higher authorities in both the House of Lords and Court of Appeal stated that he was entitled to conclude that there was some fetter, even if it was only in extreme cases. It was safest to use the language of Lord Reid in *White and Carter* as adopted by a majority of the Court of Appeal in the *Puerto Buitrago* case (see below). The "legitimate interest" test is an important qualification on *White and Carter*, one which reduces the possibilities for opportunistically exploiting situations like those we have been discussing.

23.10   Subsequent cases have also put limits on the right to continue with the contract. In *Gator Shipping Corp. v. Transasiatic Oil SA "The Odenfeld"*[43] Kerr J. would not allow a party to carry on regardless when it was "wholly unreasonable", "unrealistic" or "untenable". However, Kerr J. also agreed that the general rule of the innocent party to an election should be maintained. In the earlier case *Attica Sea Carriers Corp. v. Ferrostaal Poseidon Bulk Reederei "The Puerto Buitrago"*,[44] however, Lord Denning would not apply the rule in *White and Carter*. This had no application in a case where the plaintiff ought "in all reason" to accept the repudiation and sue for damages, provided damages were an adequate remedy. The Court of Appeal held that it was wholly unacceptable for the owners to seek to hold the charterers to the charter rather than seek damages. Kerr J. in *The Odenfeld*[45] limited the Denning view (and those of the Court of Appeal) to the "extreme facts of the case" and rejected any notion that parties could be in general forced into accepting a repudiation, because otherwise the Court would be ordering specific performance. The consequences of such a proposition would be extremely serious, noted Kerr J., and no trace of such a doctrine existed in our shipping law. The judgment in *White and Carter* is not without support. In *Decro-Wall International SA v. Practitioners in Marketing*[46] the Court of Appeal applied the rule in *White and Carter* as laid down by the majority decision of the House of Lords. The Court held that the defendants were not obliged to accept the contract as an end as a result of the plaintiffs' repudiation and disavowed any wider reading of Lord Reid's qualification in *White and Carter*.

REPUDIATION OF THE CONTRACT

The nature of a repudiatory breach

23.11   The test for a repudiatory breach was stated by Lord Coleridge in *Freeth v. Burr*[47] as being "whether the acts or conduct of the one do or do not amount to an invitation of an intention to abandon and altogether to refuse performance of the contract". Repudiation of a contract is not something to be inferred lightly. In *Woodar Investment Development Ltd v. Wimpey Construction Ltd (UK)*[48] Lord Wilberforce stated: "Repudiation is a drastic conclusion which should only be held to arise in clear cases of a

---

[43] [1978] 2 Lloyd's Rep. 357 (at p. 373).
[44] [1976] 1 Lloyd's Rep. 250.
[45] At p. 373.
[46] [1971] 1 W.L.R. 361.
[47] (1873–74) L.R. 9 C.P. 208 (at p. 213).
[48] [1980] 1 W.L.R. 277 (at p. 283).

refusal, in a matter going to the root of the contract, to perform contractual obligations." The intention and state of mind of the allegedly repudiating party is the key element. This is to be judged from the point of view of a reasonable person in the innocent party's position. Breach does not depend on the good faith or otherwise of the guilty party's intention.[49] In *Vaswani v. Italian Motors (Sales and Service) Ltd*[50] in the Privy Council, Lord Woolf pointed out[51] that *bona fide* motives of the party responsible do not prevent the conduct being repudiatory. It is the words and conduct of the breaching party which count, not their own subjective intentions in the matter.

There are two contrasting cases on the repudiation question which illustrate the difficulty in this area. Both cases appear to reach somewhat surprising conclusions on the facts. In *Federal Commerce and Navigation Company Ltd v. Molena Alpha "The Nanfri, the Benfri and the Lorfri"*[52] shipowners issued instructions not to issue bills of lading (contractual documents necessary for the charterers to operate a vessel for the carriage of goods by sea) for trade in the Great Lakes and Canada. At the time the shipowners believed that they were exercising a legal right to do so. This turned out to be unjustified. The House of Lords held that their conduct amounted to a wrongful repudiation even though they had taken legal advice and there was an ongoing dispute between the parties. The charters were therefore entitled to the contract as discharged. Lord Wilberforce stated that it was "irrelevant that it was the owners' real interest to continue the charters rather than to put an end to them. If a party's conduct is such as to amount to a threaten repudiatory breach, his subjective desire to maintain the contract cannot prevent the other party from driving the consequences of his actions".[53] It is no excuse to say that a party's conduct was as a result of taking legal advice. Lord Denning in *Federal Commerce*, in the Court of Appeal,[54] said "I have yet to learn that a party who breaks a contract can excuse himself by saying that he did it on the advice of his lawyers: or that he was under an honest misapprehension". The courts have to take an objective view of the words and conduct of the party at the time, rather than viewed with the benefit of hindsight.

In *Woodar Investment v. Wimpey Construction*[55] there was a contract to sell land at Cobham in Surrey. The contract stated that the purchasers, a firm of builders, could rescind if before completion of the contract compulsory purchase procedures were in place over the land. The purchasers exercised their right to rescind the contract, believing they had the right to do so on the ground that compulsory purchase procedures over the land had begun. At the same time the price of land had fallen and the purchasers believed that the transaction would be unprofitable.[56]

The issue in the House of Lords was whether the purchasers' apparent conduct amounted to a repudiation of the contract as a whole, which the other party could accept and bring the contract to an end. The House of Lords held that it did not. Like *Federal Commerce* this appears a strange decision at first sight. The Law Lords, by a majority of

23.12

---

[49] For a discussion of good faith, see Chap. 14.
[50] [1996] 1 W.L.R. 270.
[51] At p. 276.
[52] [1979] A.C. 757.
[53] At p. 780.
[54] [1978] Q.B. 927 (at p. 979).
[55] [1980] 1 W.L.R. 277.
[56] This may be an example of "efficient breach" (discussed earlier Chap. 13).

three to two, held that in order to constitute a repudiation there had to be an intention to abandon the contract. The purchasers did not necessarily intend to abandon the contract by this act alone. The justification of this was given by Lord Wilberforce: "It would be a regrettable development on the law of contract to hold that a party who *bona fide* relies upon an express stipulation in a contract in order to rescind or terminate a contract should, by that fact alone, be treated as having repudiated his contractual obligations if he turns out to be mistaken as to his rights."[57] Lord Wilberforce[58] concluded that:

> "Wimpey manifested no intention to abandon, or refuse future performance of, or to repudiate the contract. And the issue being one of fact, citation of other decided cases on other facts is hardly necessary. I shall simply state that the proposition that a party who takes action relying simply on the terms of the contract and not manifesting by his conduct an ulterior intention to abandon it is not to be treated as repudiating it."

Lord Salmon was one of those who dissented. For him (and Lord Scarman), Wimpey's conduct amounted to a repudiation: "I do not understand how Wimpey's honest belief in a bad point of law can in any way avail them."

23.13   There have been a number of other cases which have grappled with the repudiation question. In *Nottingham Building Society v. Eurodynamics Systems*[59] there was a contract for computer software. The contract contained a term that the defendants would deliver up the software and other documentation at the end of their contract. They became unable to complete the contract without further funding, which the plaintiff building society refused to grant. The defendants invoiced the plaintiffs for services rendered and when the plaintiffs disputed the bill, the defendants treated this as a repudiation. This was in turn treated as a repudiation by the plaintiffs who demanded their software back. The issue was who "repudiated" first and whether the other was justified in accepting it.

23.14   The Court of Appeal held that in considering whether there had been a repudiation the whole conduct of the party had to be assessed objectively to see if there was (a) an intention to abandon and also (b) a refusal to perform the contract. The Court of Appeal drew most of it's authority from *Woodar Investment*. On the facts, there was nothing in the overt acts of the plaintiff Building Society to show an intention to abandon the contract. Their refusal to pay the invoices "could not even arguably be interpreted as manifesting such an intention". The test was objective so internal communications by the building society were held to be irrelevant. These were subjective and an objective observer in the defendant's position would not have seen them. Peter Gibson L.J. [60] approved of *Woodar*:

> "It is common ground that the judge applied the right test, taken as it was from the decision of the House of Lords in *Woodar Investment Developments Ltd. v. Wimpey Construction (UK) Ltd,*[61] that in considering whether there has been a repudiation

---

[57] At p. 281.
[58] At p. 282.
[59] [1995] F.S.R. 605.
[60] At pp. 611–612.
[61] [1980] 1 W.L.R. 277.

by one party, one looks at the whole conduct of that party to see whether that conduct indicates an intention to abandon and refuse performance of the contract."

The Court of Appeal held that if one looked at "the overt acts" of the plaintiffs in relation to the defendants, there had been no repudiation by the plaintiffs.

In *Toepfer International GmbH v. Itex Itagrani Export SA*[62] there was a contract to buy **23.15** Argentine "flint" maize, to be delivered to Buenos Aires. The contract incorporated the GAFTA 64 standard form terms and so disputes were to be resolved under arbitration and English law, as many international commercial contracts do in the modern world. The buyers sold maize to sub-buyers who nominated the same vessel, *The Danobar Tanabe* to carry a quantity of grain under another contract. The sellers claimed that the buyers were in repudiatory breach of contract by doing so, since they had evinced an intention not to perform their obligations by being unable to perform both contracts at the same time.

The Commercial Court held that the buyers actions did not amount to a repudiation. Saville J. rejected the idea that the sellers had disabled themselves and that this amounted to a repudiation. The sellers advanced the argument that where one party makes a contract, but has or undertakes inconsistent obligations under another engagement with a third party, they are to be treated in law as being unable to perform the contract. According to Saville J., this was not English law:

"What must be established (apart from the other requirements of repudiation) is quite simple: namely that on the balance of probabilities the party in question cannot perform his obligations. The fact that that party has entered into inconsistent obligations does not in itself necessarily establish such inability, unless those obligations are of such a nature or have such an effect that it can truly be said that the party in question has put it out of his power to perform his obligations."[63]

The mere fact that the sub-buyer had contracted to load other goods on the vessel did not in itself establish that the buyers could not perform. At most established that the buyers might not be able to perform.

Acceptance of repudiation by rescission

This is the other side of the issue just discussed. The innocent party accepts the repudi- **23.16** ation and therefore rescinds the contract and brings his or her own obligation to perform to an end.[63a] The general rule is that acceptance of a repudiation must be notified to the other party. This is similar to the rules in offer and acceptance. In *State Trading Corporation of India Ltd v. M. Golodetz Ltd*,[64] the notification requirement was reduced to the phrase "overtly evinced" an intention. Kerr L.J. held that doing nothing, or

---

[62] [1993] 1 Lloyd's Rep. 360.
[63] At p. 362.
[63a] In *Eastbourne Borough Council v. Foster*, *The Times*, August 17, 2001 it was held that even with the acceptance of a repudiation of a contract of employment, if the employer continued to provide work, a contractual relationship could be said to continue.
[64] [1989] 2 Lloyd's Rep. 277.

[handwritten marginalia: continue to accept delivery]

silence, was not enough because this could only be equivocal.[65] However, the point arose again in *Vitol SA v. Norelf Ltd "The Santa Clara"*.[66] The House of Lords held that in some circumstances a mere failure to perform one's contractual obligations was capable of amounting to acceptance of an anticipatory repudiation of a contract by the other party. This depended on the type of contract and the facts of the case. In *Santa Clara* it resulted from the seller's failure to tender contractual documents at the appropriate time. It was held that silence on the facts could amount to acceptance of the breach. The House of Lords reviewed the basic principles of acceptance of a repudiation. The acceptance did not have to be in any form or language, nor effected personally or even by agent. Silence could be acceptance in exceptional cases, just as it could in offer and acceptance. The test was whether the conduct or communication was "clear and unequivocal" in showing the other party that the contract was at an end.

Lord Steyn viewed the issue before the House as whether silence or non-performance of an obligation was *ever,* as a matter of law, capable of constituting acceptance of a repudiation. Lord Steyn's answer was that it could do so, depending upon the particular contractual relationship and the circumstances of the case, expressing the view that Kerr L.J.'s statement in *State Trading Corp of India Ltd v. M. Golodetz Ltd*[67] (that saying and doing nothing could not constitute an acceptance of a repudiation) "goes too far". Failure to perform was not always equivocal and could amount to acceptance of a repudiation. An omission to act, in Lord Steyn's words, "may be as pregnant with meaning as a positive declaration . . . [A] failure to perform may sometimes be given [a colour] by special circumstances and may only be explicable to a reasonable person in the position of the repudiating party as an election to accept the repudiation".[68]

Non acceptance of a breach by affirmation of the contract

23.17 The party not in breach may not wish to accept the repudiation. He or she may do so by affirming the contract. This is done by conduct or by notifying the other party that he or she intends to carry on with the agreement. Acts or words are normally required for affirmation, although this can be inferred from the circumstances. In *Yukong Line of Korea v. Rendsburg Investment Corporation of Liberia*[69] Moore-Bick J. stated that a court should not adopt an unduly technical approach to deciding whether the innocent party had affirmed a contract following a repudiation. The court should look for "very clear evidence" that the innocent party had chosen to go on with the contract notwithstanding the other's repudiation. The court should generally be slow to accept that the innocent party had committed themself irrevocably to continuing with the contract.

The judge set out the main principles surrounding this question.[70] The injured party had a choice but once the choice had been made and communicated to the other party

---

[65] On the analogous point of silence in offer and acceptance, see Chaps 2 and 4.
[66] [1996] A.C. 800.
[67] [1989] 2 Lloyd's Rep 277 (at p. 286).
[68] At pp. 811–812.
[69] [1996] 2 Lloyd's Rep. 604.
[70] At p. 608.

to the contract, it was irrevocable. However, the "injured party will not be treated as having elected to affirm the contract in the face of the renunciation unless it can be shown that he knew of the facts giving rise to his right to treat the contract as discharged and of his right to choose between affirming the contract and treating it as discharged". The judge stated that the choice had to be communicated in "clear terms" and unequivocal. A party should not be held bound "by a qualified or conditional decision". Election could be express or implied and would be implied "where the injured party acts in a way which is consistent only with a decision to keep the contract alive or where he exercises rights which would only be available to him if the contract had been affirmed". The court concluded that: "Election, though the subject of much learning and refinement, was in the end a doctrine based on simple considerations of common sense and equity." The danger posed by acceptance of repudiation, or indeed of rescission or affirmation, is that if the innocent party gets it wrong they leave themself open to a counterclaim by the other party of breach of contract. The counterclaim could be for a larger amount than the original breach. Business men and women and their advisers need to tread with caution in this area. In consumer sales, failure to reject goods once the buyer knows of actionable defects will lead to the conclusion that they have been accepted and the right to rescind thereafter will be lost.[70a]

DISCHARGE BY PERFORMANCE

Performance depends upon what was promised, taking into account express promises **23.18** and also any implied obligations. Many contractual duties are strict, *i.e.* they do not depend upon fault. The implied conditions under the Sale of Goods Act 1979[71] as to the description and quality of goods sold in the course of a business make the seller liable even if he or she were not to blame. So when a bottle of lemonade produced by a manufacturer is sold in a sealed container which the seller was not in a position to inspect, they will be liable if the contents was not reasonably fit to drink.[72] Often contractual obligations are based upon a requirement of reasonable skill and care, in other words, a duty of care in negligence. If performance falls short of the obligation promised, this will be a breach of contract. The contract may finally provide its own express requirements as to the standard of performance required. A contract is discharged on both sides when there is complete performance. The burden of proof is on the party who alleges breach. Breach and performance are therefore merely different sides of the same question. A party is not required to prove performance, although this may become an issue in due course. Performance has to match what was promised in the contract before the agreement is discharged, but, as we shall see, this rule is subject to important exceptions.

The "entire contracts" or obligations rule

If the contract provides for payment on completion, or for anything short of com- **23.19** plete performance, then it is entire. Entire contacts arise if complete performance is

---

[70a] Sale of Goods Act 1979, s. 35.
[71] SS 13–15.
[72] See *Daniels v. Tarbard and R White Ltd* [1938] 4 All E.R. 258. (See Chap. 13.)

made a condition precedent to the other party paying the price. If the contract is construed as "entire", a party is not entitled to payment until they have performed their part of the bargain in full. Partial performance is not sufficient. In *Bolton v. Mahadeva*[73] a builder failed to install a heating system properly. The work was inadequate and the builder did not respond to requests to finish the job and put it right. Since there never was a complete system installed that worked, he was not entitled to payment, even for the value of the work done. It should be noted that the law draws a distinction between (a) incomplete performance and (b) defective performance. The entire contracts rule applies to (a) but not to (b). If performance is only defective, a party may recover the price subject to a claim for damages against them for the defective performance.[74] This is a difficult distinction to maintain. The rule is that it is the "obligation", not the "contract", that has to be entire. In other words, particular obligations, rather than the contract as a whole, attract the doctrine. The conventional terminology is to continue to use the expression "entire contracts".

The rule in *Cutter v. Powell*[75]

23.20   The leading authority on entire contracts is *Cutter v. Powell*.[76] A seaman agreed to serve onboard a ship, the *Governor Parry*, sailing to Liverpool from Kingston Jamaica as second mate for thirty guineas (a large sum of money for the work in those days). "T. Cutter", the seaman concerned, sailed from Jamaica on August 2. The ship was due to arrive on October 9, but Cutter died at sea on September 20 before the ship had reached its destination. The plaintiff was T. Cutter's widow, who sued to recover a proportionate part of the sum due to him in wages on a *quantum meruit* (*i.e.* remuneration for the value of the work done).[77] It was held she could recover nothing. The contract was entire and the plaintiff's husband had to finish the voyage in order to recover his thirty guineas.[78] The entire contracts rule was regularly written into sailors' contracts in the eighteenth century by express stipulation and (to modern eyes) allowed the exploitation of the weaker party.

In *Appleby v. Dods*[79] a seaman agreed to work for monthly wages onboard a ship bound for the port of Madeira, the islands of the West Indies and to return to London. The contract specified that they would not be entitled to any wages until the arrival of the ship back in London. The ship sailed from Gravesend and traded at Dominica and later Kingston Jamaica but was lost at sea in the course of her passage home. The seamen claimed the share of their wages due before the ship went down. It was held that they could not do so; this was an entire contract and they were only entitled to be paid when the vessel returned safely to port. Lord Ellenborough C.J. thought the terms of the contract fair and reasonable. The Court could not give a *pro rata* of the wages because

---

[73] [1972] 1 W.L.R. 1009.
[74] *Bolton v. Mahadeva* [1972] 1 W.L.R. 1009.
[75] Williams, "Partial Performance of Entire Contracts" 57 L.Q.R. 373; Stoljar, "The Great Case of *Cutter v. Powell*" (1956) 34 Can. Bar Rev. 288.
[76] (1795) 6 Term Rep. 320; 101 E.R. 573.
[77] See Chap. 26.
[78] Apparently normal wages for seamen on voyages at that time were a monthly sum of £4 per month. Here a much larger fixed sum was to be paid for the eight week voyage across the Atlantic.
[79] (1807) 8 East 300; 103 E.R. 356.

this would be against the express contract of the parties. The existence of the contract prevented a non contractual restitutionary claim.[79a] The doctrine of frustration did not exist at this time. This would have discharged the contract brought to an end through neither party's default.[80]

The public policy underpinning such contracts is set out in the judgment of *Appleby v.* **23.21**
Dods. The terms for payment for sailors only on return to Britain reflected "the anxious policy of the legislature to enforce the return home of seamen in their ships from the West Indies". This may underlie the large sum offered to the plaintiffs husband in *Cutter v. Powell*.[81] *Jesse v. Roy*[82] was another seamens' case where wages were the issue. The seaman, Jonathan Arrowgate Jesse, agreed to sail on the *Royalist* to the South Seas and back to procure a cargo of sperm oil and return with it to London. He agreed to be paid in lieu of wages, a ninety-fifth share of the net proceeds of the cargo. The *Royalist* became unfit to sail and was condemned in Timor where she was sold and broken up in a local port. The crew and cargo were transferred but Jonathan Jesse died before he got home to London. His family were not entitled to his share of the cargo, but they were entitled to a *quantum meruit* for his services onboard the second vessel. Lord Lyndhurst held that since the vessel never did arrive in the port of London, the plaintiff was not entitled to recover under the contract. The contract with the *Royalist* having been discharged, his estate was entitled to a restitutionary claim thereafter.[83]

The "entire contract" rule was applied in *Forman & Co Proprietary Ltd v. The* **23.22**
Ship "Liddesdale",[84] a case which illustrates that complete and precise performance in conformity with the contract is required. The *Liddlesdale* ran aground off the coast of Australia and was damaged as a result. The plaintiffs were a firm of ship repairers in Melbourne who worked on the British steamer owned by Robert Mackill, from Glasgow. As a result of the damage to the ship's hull, a number of steel girders or plate frames which were buckled had to be replaced or straightened. When the work was done, iron was substituted for steel. According to the plaintiffs this altered the structure of the vessel to her advantage giving greater flexibility. The defendants contended that the substitution "caused a rigidity" in the framework which was a source of danger. Iron girders were not, however, what the contract required, and the plaintiffs' alteration of the material used was inconsistent with their obligation to restore the vessel to her original condition prior to the accident. The plaintiffs had agreed to do repairs on the vessel for a sum of money. The work was of good quality and improved the vessel, however, it was not the work agreed under the contract. The plaintiffs had used iron girders where the contract specified steel.

The Privy Council held that they had not done what the contract required so they could not recover. Neither could they recover for doing something else of equal worth. This might have made a claim for restitution under an implied contract possible if the original contract were discharged, but the defendants had never agreed to this. There could, therefore, be no alternative recovery under *quantum merit*.

[79a]   This important rule is discussed in Chap. 26.
[80]   See Chap. 22.
[81]   The holding of *Cutter v. Powell* (1795) 6 Term Rep. 320 would now be subject to the Merchant Shipping Term Act 1995. See para. 23.31.
[82]   (1834) 1 CM and R 316, 149 E.R. 1101.
[83]   See Chap. 26.
[84]   [1900] A.C. 190.

When work is destroyed before completion of the contract

23.23   *Appleby v. Myers*[85] is another example of the entire contracts rule but is also relevant to frustration.[86] The plaintiff, Appleby, had contracted to do work on the defendant's property for a fixed sum payable when the work was completed. He was to erect machinery and keep it in repair for two years before the defendants were obliged to pay anything. After some machinery had been erected, but before the contract was complete, a fire accidentally destroyed the building and the work done. In the Court of Exchequers Chamber, Blackburn J. held that the parties were excused further performance of the contract, *i.e.* it was frustrated. The plaintiff was not entitled to sue for that part of the work which he had done. On the principle of *Cutter v. Powell*[87] Blackburn J. held: "The plaintiffs having contracted to do an entire work for a specific sum, can recover nothing unless the work be done, or it can be shewn that it was the defendant's fault that the work was incomplete, or that there is something to justify the conclusion that the parties have entered into a fresh contract."[88]

The plaintiff could not claim the value of the materials built into the house. Normally these will become a part of the other's property and have to be paid for, even if destroyed before the contract was completed. However, by agreeing to be paid a lump sum on completion, this right had been lost.

23.24   In *Liddesdale*, discussed earlier, the plaintiff had worked new materials into the property of the other party. The work was not what was contracted for, but was of value to the owners of the ship. The vessel did have some new girders, which were overall to its advantage in improving its structure. In the case of a contract to work materials into property of another, the rule is that unless the contract specifies otherwise, payment can be demanded for what was done. In a non contractual case there can be a restitutionary claim so long as some work was agreed. Blackburn J. stated the general rule in *Appleby v. Myers*: "Bricks built into a wall become part of the house; thread stitched into a coat which is under repair or planks and nails and pitch worked into a ship under repair, become part of the cost or ship; and therefore, the bricklayer or trailer or shipwright is to be paid for the work and materials he has done and provided, although the whole work is not complete."[89] In *Appleby v. Myers*, however, because there was a contract with payment only on completion, nothing could be recovered.

Exceptions to the entire contracts rule

23.25   The entire obligations rule is ameliorated in a number of ways. There are a number of exceptions to the entire contracts rule. In practice, particularly in larger commercial contracts, the parties make provision for staged payments as the work progresses in order to give the contractors a reasonable cash flow as work proceeds. Small domestic building contracts are usually entire. The builder must complete the work before he is entitled to be paid and it is less usual for each section of the work to be apportioned. In major construction and building works "staging" of payments is the regular practice. The

---

[85] (1867) LR 2 CP 651.
[86] See Chap. 22.
[87] See also *Munroe v. Butt* (1858) 8 E1 and B1 738, 120 ER 275 and *Sinclair v. Bowles* (1829) 9 B & C 92, 109 E.R. 35, as further examples of the rule.
[88] At p. 661.
[89] At p. 661.

innocent party who has not received their complete performance may sue for breach of contract, however, damages will be reduced if the non breaching party has received a benefit from the work already done, albeit in an incomplete way.[90]

(1) Divisible and severable contracts.

A divisible contract is one which allows a party to demand performance without ren- **23.26**
dering complete performance themself, or one in which the promises are independent of one another. Whether the contract is entire or divisible depends on the construction of the contract, the parties' intention, commercial practice or rules of law. It may also be an inference drawn from the circumstances. The presumption is in favour of entirety. In the early *Case of an Hostler*[91] a contract to keep a horse was payable at six pence per day and night to a total of £20. The Court stated that the plaintiff was not required to bring an action for every six pence because the promise was "entire in itself". The tendency is for the court to construe contracts as divisible rather than entire. This is usually a fairer solution, allowing a party to recover for the parts or instalments delivered or services rendered. The other party can still bring a counter claim for damages against the party in default for breach of contract to balance this. Contracts can also have both entire and severable obligations within them. This is a matter of construction of the agreement.

(2) Completion of performance is prevented by the promisee

If performance is prevented by the other party, a restitutionary claim for a reasonable **23.27**
price for what had been done in *quantum meruit* may arise. Thus in *Planché v. Colbourn*[92] the plaintiff agreed to write a volume on the history of armour and costume in a series called *The Juvenile Library* and to be paid 100 guineas for doing so. He did considerable research and work on the manuscript before the publishers decided to discontinue the series. The argument by counsel for the defendants, that the contract was entire and payment was only required when the work was completed, was rejected by Tindal C.J. in the Court of Common Pleas. It was held that the plaintiff was entitled to a reasonable sum for his work and effort in preparation for the work, for which he recovered £50 in *quantum meruit* as a fair remuneration. The claim in restitution for *quantum meruit* was only available because the contract was discharged by breach. A non contractual *quantum meruit* could not co-exist alongside a contract action while the contract remained alive.[93]

(3) Acceptance of partial performance by the promisee

If the promisee accepts less than complete performance she has to pay a reasonable sum **23.28**
for what they have received. There must be a choice available to accept or reject the work. It is possible to recover in a quantum meruit claim if the promisee had a choice between accepting or rejecting the partial performance and chose to accept it. There will then be an implied promise to pay a reasonable sum for the partial performance. In *Sumpter v. Hedges* the plaintiff agreed to put up two houses and a stable for £565. He failed to finish the work. The defendant completed the work using materials left by the plaintiff on the site. The plaintiff claimed (a) the value of the work done before the abandonment

---

[90] *Sumpter v. Hedges* [1898] 1 Q.B. 673.
[91] (1605) Yelv. 66, 80 E.R. 47.
[92] (1831) 8 Bing 14, 172 E.R. 876.
[93] See Chap. 26.

and (b) the cost of the building materials used by the defendant. It was held he could recover the cost of the materials left because the plaintiff had a choice whether or not to use these, but he could not claim for the work done before abandonment as the plaintiff had no choice as to accepting the performance.

(4) The doctrine of substantial performance

23.29   In *Williams v. Roffey Bros and Nicholls (Contractors) Ltd*[94] the Court of Appeal held that the plaintiff carpenter had substantially completed work on eight of the flats concerned and, despite some defective and incomplete work for which deduction was made, he was entitled to the price for the work he had substantially completed. This constitutes a major exception to the entire contracts rule. If the promisor provides substantial, but not exact, performance then the promisee is not discharged of their obligation to pay. The classic authority on this is *Boone v. Eyre*.[95] The plaintiff sold a plantation in the West Indies, along with the slaves who worked there, for £500 plus an annuity of £160 for life. The defendant claimed that since the plaintiff was not the legal owner of the slaves at the time of sale, he did not have a good title to convey. Lord Mansfield held that where a covenant went only to a part of the consideration, a breach may be paid for in damages if the party had substantially performed the rest, for "if this plea were to be allowed, any one negro not being the property of the plaintiff would bar the action". If the defendant does less than expected of him, he remains liable to pay damages for his non performance. It is a question of construction whether entire or merely substantial performance will suffice, as a condition precedent of payment.

23.30   In *Hoenig v. Isaacs*[96] there was a contract to decorate and furnish a flat for £750 on terms of payment "net cash, as the work proceeds; and balance on completion". The defendant paid £400 but refused to pay the outstanding sum of £350 on the ground that the work was defective. A wardrobe needed replacing and a bookshelf was too short and would have to be re-made. The defendant claimed that this was an entire contract so the plaintiff could not recover the balance. The Court of Appeal agreed with the Official Referee that there had been substantial performance so the defendant was bound to pay, less the cost of remedying the defects. Lord Denning expressed the issue as being whether "entire performance was a condition precedent to payment? That depended on the true construction of the contract".[97][98]

On the other hand, in *Bolton v. Mahadeva*[99] the plaintiff agreed to install central heating for a lump sum of £560. The installation was defective, the cost of remedying the faults being £174. The Court of Appeal held that there was no substantial performance. According to Cain L.J.: "In considering whether was substantial performance I am of the opinion that it is relevant to take into account both the nature of the defects and the proportion between the cost of rectifying them and the contract price. It would be wrong to say that the contractor is only entitled to payment if the defects are too trifling as to

---

[94] [1991] 1 Q.B. 1. (See Chap. 8.)
[95] (1779) 126 E.R. 160.
[96] [1952] 2 All E.R. 176.
[97] At p. 180.
[98] See also *Dakin (H) and Co Ltd v. Lee* [1916] 1 K.B. 566.
[99] [1972] 2 All E.R. 1322.
[1] At p. 1325.

be covered by the *de minimis* rule."[1] The nature and amount of defects in this case were "far different" from those in *Dakin v. Lee* and *Hoenig v. Isaacs.*[2]

(5) Breach of warranty

If the promisor merely breaches a warranty, this is not a sufficient reason to withhold payment, even though it means that he or she has not precisely performed what they agreed to do. This is really just the other side of the question of substantial performance.   **23.31**

(6) The Apportionment Act 1870

Section 2 of the 1870 Act provides that rents, annuities (this includes salaries) and other periodic payments by way of income are considered to accrue from day to day. Most contracts of employment are now included in the provision. This will prevent the entire contracts rule operating in this context

(7) The Law Reform (Frustrated Contracts) Act 1943.

In many of the circumstances so far discussed, *e.g.* death of one of the parties or destruction of the subject matter, the contract in question would now be frustrated. If so, the 1943 Act is likely to apply allowing payment for valuable benefit obtained before the frustration occurred. A claim under the Act is different from one in restitution.[3]

(8) The Merchant Shipping Act 1995

The outcome of *Cutler v. Powell* would now be covered by different rules. Employment protection has superseded freedom of contract and the entire contracts rule in the case of employees. The Merchant Shipping Act 1995 provides for the payment of seamen's wages which must be paid unless subject to (a) mistake, (b) reasonable dispute as to liability, (c) act or default of person claiming the amount or (d) any other cause, not being the wrongful act or default of the persons liable to make the payment or their servants or agents.[4] Under s. 30, a seaman is entitled to their wages when discharged or at up to monthly intervals (s. 30(4)). If a vessel is wrecked or lost (as in *Appleby v. Dods*), the seaman is entitled to wages until that point and for every day that they are unemployed for up to two months thereafter.[5]

For and against the entire contracts rule: Would a Law Reform (Lump Sum Contracts) Act be a good idea?

The entire contracts rule may appear harsh to modern eyes in it's application, particularly the old seamen's wages. There are nevertheless justifications for the rule, some of which were set out in the Law Commission Report on Pecuniary Restitution on Breach of Contract.[6] First, that the rule encourages contractors to finish the work. In the words of Lord Campbell in *John Munroe v. Phelpes Butt*: "it holds men to their contracts".[7]   **23.32**

---

[2] See earlier p. 422.
[3] See Chap. 22.
[4] S. 35.
[5] S. 38.
[6] Law Comm (1983) No. 121, paras 2.24–2.36.
[7] (1858) 8 El and Bl 738, 120 E.R. 275 (at p. 280).

There was, he said, "neither hardship nor injustice in the rule with it's qualifications". Secondly, if work is incomplete it puts the client in a stronger bargaining position to insist on getting the job finished. This is particularly true in small building contracts, such as private householders, where it provides a strong bargaining position to withhold payment until the work is completed. Thirdly, according to the Law Commission, "the present law, whatever its defects, has the merit of being reasonably certain and therefore may have the desirable effect of discouraging litigation".[8]

The Law Commission also recognised countervailing arguments against the "entire contracts" rule. First, that the rule smacks of being a penalty for not finishing performance. Secondly, most commercial construction contracts for large amounts provide for payment in stages. This avoids the rule. However many do not, including most contracts between householders and jobbing builders. Many of these are for not insignificant sums. Thirdly, the extent to which the rule shifts the bargaining power of the parties may be exaggerated. The Law Commission proposed a new remedy as a result of its deliberations. A party who does not fulfil an entire contract should be entitled to be paid for the benefit they had conferred. This would only apply if there had been partial performance[9] and the parties should still be free to agree that there would be no payment before complete performance or even substantial performance.

23.33   The Report contains a draft Bill, the Law Reform (Lump Sum Contracts) Bill. The Law Commission Report also contains a short dissent by Brian Davenport Q.C. For him "unless you come back and finish the job, I shan't pay you a penny" remains a good legal position in building contracts. He thought the recommendations of the Law Commission contained more disadvantages than advantages. The present law was flexible and if law reform was required, the apportioning of loss under the Law Reform (Frustrated Contracts) Act 1943 was a better model. The effects of the draft Bill would largely only be noticed in the small claims courts. It seems this argument has held sway as nothing has been done to implement the Law Commission's Report in this area.

Tender of performance

23.34   Finally, tendering of performance may be treated as equivalent to performance. If a person offers to perform and this is refused by the other party, this may be treated as breach. In *Startup v. MacDonald*[10] the plaintiffs agreed to sell linseed oil to the defendant to be delivered by the end of March, 1838. Delivery was tendered at 8.30 in the evening, March 31. The defendant refused to accept the goods because of the lateness of the hour. It was argued that it was unreasonable to deliver at that time of the evening. The Court held that the delivery constituted a proper tender of performance which should have been accepted.[11] Even though this was a Saturday, this "left time enough for completing the delivery" before midnight and this should have been treated as performance.

---

[8] Para. 2.26.
[9] Para. 2.34.
[10] (1843) 6 M & G 593, 134 E.R. 1029.
[11] The offer by Antonio's friends to Shylock in Shakespeare's *Merchant of Venice* could have been used by Antonio as tender of performance. This should have concluded the matter and would have avoided much unpleasantness in the process. See Keeton, *Shakespeare's Legal and Political Background* (1967, Pitman, London), Chap. 9.

Chapter 24

THE GOVERNING PRINCIPLES OF DAMAGES FOR BREACH OF CONTRACT

INTRODUCTION

The main objective of damages for breach of contract is compensation for breach of **24.1** promise. The classic dictum is that of Parke B. in *Robinson v. Harman*,[1] who stated: "Where a party sustains a loss by reason of a breach of contract he is, so far as money can do it, to be placed in the same situation with respect to damages as if the contract had been performed." This is traditionally known as the expectation principle.

In *British Westinghouse Electric and Manufacturing Co Ltd v. Underground Electric Rlys Co of London Ltd*[2] Viscount Haldane L.C. stated the general principle thus: "[A]s far as possible, he who has proved a breach of a bargain to supply what he contracted to get is to be placed, as far as money can do it, in as good a situation as if the contract had been performed."[3] In the same passage Viscount Haldane also explained that the question of damage was a question of fact, and the only guidance which the law can give is to lay down general principles "which afford at times but scanty assistance in dealing with particular cases". In other words, each case depends upon its own circumstances.

The corollary of the principle in *Robinson v. Harman* is that a plaintiff must not be placed in a better position by the award of damages for the other party's breach than they would have been in if the contract had been performed. The onus of proving damages lies on the plaintiff. These are determined objectively rather than subjectively in contract law. Contract law largely protects economic interests and hence damages are to compensate for pecuniary losses rather than non-pecuniary losses such as pain and suffering. In negligence actions the rule is the reverse, since tort damages have historically compensated for personal injuries and other non-pecuniary losses brought about by a range of wrongdoing.

Like many ancient principles there has been significant changes in the law relating to **24.2** damages in recent years. As we shall see, there is now scope for the allowance of damages for mental suffering and disappointed enjoyment in certain types of contract.[4] These are, by their nature, subjective. Contract law also eschews other common law categories such

---

[1] (1848) 1 Exch. 850; 154 E.R. 363 (at p. 365).
[2] [1912] A.C. 673.
[3] At pp. 688–689.
[4] See Chap. 25.

as aggravated punitive or exemplary damages (to punish the wrongdoing). This leaves only two types of damages in contract law: (a) nominal, *i.e.* awarded to mark the finding that a legal wrong has been done to the plaintiff who has, however, failed to prove substantial loss and (b) compensation for breach. The latter is historically, and remains, the paramount purpose of damages for breach of contract. Later we shall discuss the green shoot of a new principle tentatively emerging in contract law, namely damages based on profit making by the defendant even if the plaintiff suffers no loss.[5]

The two traditional tests: Expectation and reliance

24.3   Since around 1800 the governing principle of contract damages has been the protection of expectations.[6] This is also called "loss of bargain" or loss of profit. A party is entitled to what they have lost as a result of the contract not being performed. Even if the contract is executory, *i.e.* unperformed on both sides, expectation damages are normally available. For instance, if Delia buys a second hand car from dealer Fred, then changes her mind the next day before the car has been delivered to her, she will still be liable in damages for breach of contract. Fred is entitled to claim lost profit on this "volume sale" even though he appears to have suffered no immediate loss.[7]

The fact that expectation damages are available in contract law leads some to argue that the rule is too generous. According to this view, it would be preferable if only "reliance damages", *i.e.* actual losses resulting from wasted expenditure were recoverable. This would put the plaintiff back to the position before the contract was formed. Reliance is the normal test in tort law. It could therefore be argued that this would lead to greater symmetry between the two main branches of the law of obligations if contract law, too, had a similar approach to compensation. Reliance damages are not the same as reliance theory. Promissory estoppel is an example of the latter.[8] You may support a theory of reliance in contract law and still favour the expectation principle as the test for damages, as we discuss shortly.

(1) The expectation interest[9]

24.4   By adopting the expectation principle, contract law stresses the importance of performance and underscores the point by making a rule that if the contract is not performed, the measure of damages will reflect the failure of the guilty party to do so. The expectation rule acts as an incentive to perform. Expectation as the rule was confirmed by the Court of Exchequer in *Robinson v. Harman*,[10] where the defendant granted the plaintiff a lease over property, a house in High St. Croydon, to which he did not have title. The

---

[5] The restitutionary principle is discussed later on p. 433, and in Chap. 26.
[6] *Shepherd v. Johnson* (1802) 2 East 211; 102 E.R. 349. An earlier example in the common law world is the South Carolina case *Davis v. Richardson* (1790) 1 Bay 105 (discussed in Horowitz, *The Transformation of American Law* (1977, Harvard University Press), p. 173.
[7] For further discussion of this point, see p. 444.
[8] See Chap. 9.
[9] The Americans may have been the first to adopt this rule in the South Carolina case of *Davis v. Richardson* 1 Bay 105 (SC 1790) but it was quickly adopted in England also in *Shepherd v. Johnson* (1802) 2 East 211; 102 ER 349 and *McArthur v. Seaforth* (1810) 2 Taunt 257; 127 ER 1076.
[10] (1848) 1 Ex. 850; 154 E.R. 363.

plaintiff recovered damages for his "loss of bargain" or expectation, not just his wasted expenditure (*i.e.* reliance losses). The plaintiff was entitled to recover damages for the loss sustained by the non-performance of the contract. Parke B. laid down the basic rule, "where a party sustains a loss by reason of a breach of contract he is, as far as money can do it, to be placed in the same situation with respect to damages as if the contract had been performed".

(2) The reliance interest

Reliance is based upon the principle of putting the plaintiff in the position they were in before the wrongdoing was committed. Reliance represents an alternative principle in contact law by compensating for losses already incurred and expenditure sustained. For this reason it is sometimes called "wasted expenditure". Reliance is generally less generous than the loss of profit measure, however, it may be seen as fairer in that it compensates for actual losses, not for future gains or loss of profit to the plaintiff. In their seminal article on reliance theory, Fuller and Purdue found some justification in the expectation principle.[11] First, it was easier to prove than reliance losses, and secondly, it provided an incentive to perform a contract. If the party contemplating a breach of contract knows that by failing to perform they will be liable for the full loss of profits, they are discouraged from breaking the agreement.

24.5

Reliance losses can attach to losses not only during the contractual performance but also made in contemplation of a contract. In *Lloyd v. Stanbury*[12] the defendant sold his farm to the plaintiff. The defendant intended to build a bungalow on a remaining piece of land and the plaintiff was to provide him with a caravan meantime. The defendant withdrew before contracts were exchanged. It was held that the plaintiff was entitled to his wasted expenditure already incurred.[13] Reliance damages also have an impact on contract law in relation to misrepresentation. The action for fraudulent misstatement and also under the Misrepresentation Act 1967 s. 2(1) is in the tort of deceit. In *Clef Aquitaine SARL v. Laporte Materials (Barrow) Ltd*[14] the claimant entered into a contract in reliance on a fraudulent misrepresentation. The Court assessed damages by comparing the claimant's position before the making of the fraudulent statement with that which resulted after reliance upon the words. The reliance principle also draws wider support outside of contract law. The Human Rights Act 1998 applies the principle of reliance deriving its authority from the European Convention of Human Rights. The claimant should be placed in the position he or she would have been in if there had not been a breach of their rights under the Convention.

---

[11] "The Reliance Interest in Contract Damages", (1936) Yale Law Journal 52.
[12] [1971] 2 All E.R. 267.
[13] See also *Anglia Television Ltd v. Reed* [1972] 1 Q.B. 60.
[14] [2000] 3 All E.R. 493.

The two potential newcomers: Performance and restitution

(1) The performance interest

24.6   The recognition of another basis for the assessment of compensation for breach of contract is the performance interest. This has been on the horizon of contract law for the last 20 years but achieved it's strongest endorsement in the speeches of Lord Millet and Lord Goff in *Panatown Ltd v. Alfred McAlpine Construction Ltd*.[15] The two Law Lords dissented from the majority view that a promisee had no right to substantial damages in the case in question where a building being built for a third party was defectively constructed.[16] Lord Millett based his dissent on a broad principle which seems likely to take it's place among the pantheon of guiding principles of contract damages in years to come. The performance interest allows loss to be calculated simply on the basis that a party suffers loss because he or she does not receive the bargain for which they had contracted.

   The origin of this test can be traced to the judgment of Oliver J. in *Radford v. DeFroberville*,[17] a case described by Lord Millett as "seminal".[18] Applying the ancient maxim *pacta sunt servanda, i.e.* promises are to be kept because of their inherent binding quality, the Court held that a party had a right to substantial damages simply from the breach of any undertaking given to them. Oliver J. stated:

> "If he [a contracting party] contracts for the supply of that which he thinks serves his interests, be they commercial, aesthetic or merely eccentric, then if that which is contracted for is not supplied by the other contracting party I do not see why, in principle, he should not be compensated by being provided with the cost of supplying it through someone else or in a different way, subject to the proviso, of course, that he is seeking compensation for a genuine loss and not merely using a technical breach to secure an uncovenanted profit."[19]

In *Panatown* Lord Millett described this as "the language of defeated expectation with substantial damages being awarded for the loss of the performance interest".[20]

24.7   Lord Millett stated that the seed planted by Oliver J. "has long been in germination but it has been watered and nurtured by favourable judicial and academic commentators in the meantime. I think it is time to give it the imprimatur of your Lordship's House". Lord Millett agreed with the view of Steyn L.J. in *Darlington BC v. Wilshire Northern Ltd*[21] that rather than being a radical step, or one which would open the proverbial floodgates, it was based on "orthodox contractual principles". Lord Millet would, however, "for the present", restrict the performance interest to building contracts and other contracts for the supply of work and materials where there had been defective or incomplete work or delay. However, the principle could equally be applied where the contracting party has a family or commercial relationship with a third party, as for instance in

---

[15] [2000] 4 All E.R. 97.
[16] The case is discussed in greater detail in Chap. 10.
[17] [1977] 1 W.L.R. 1262.
[18] [2000] 4 All E.R. (at p. 162).
[19] [1977] 1 W.L.R. (at p. 1270).
[20] At p. 163.
[21] [1995] 1 W.L.R. 68.

Jackson v. Horizon Holidays[22] or to cases such as *Ruxley Electronics v. Forsyth*,[23] where it was, in the view of Lord Millett, correctly applied to the facts of that unusual case (which we discuss later in this chapter). So far the performance principle of damages remains tentatively on the brink of acceptance by the courts. It remains to be fully endorsed throughout contract law, though it clearly has a strong backing in third party situations.[24] Time will tell as to the extent to which it flourishes and grows.

(2) A fourth alternative: A "restitutionary" principle for contract damages?

The fourth principle is the most controversial. Damages based upon the equitable **24.8** remedy of an account of profits has not yet developed as a general principle in contract law, and may never do so. A limited instance of restitutionary damages has, however, now been recognised by the House of Lords,[25] albeit in the specialised area of the Crown and breach of confidence. The restitutionary principle allows a claimant to recover profits made by the defendant as a result of his or her breach of contract even if the plaintiff suffered no apparent substantial loss. The object being disgorgement of profits by the wrongdoing of the other party, rather than compensating the plaintiff for their loss. Such a principle could have a profound effect on contract law. It would alter the balance between contract and restitution law,[26] and would also discourage cynical use of "efficient" breach", *i.e.* breaking a contract if doing so would be more profitable to the defendant.[27] At present, the right to breach a contract has merely to be balanced against the liability under "secondary" obligation to pay damages. If it is more profitable to break a contract than perform it, there is nothing to stop a party from doing so. A restitutionary principle would require the giving up of all or part of this profit if it was unjustly gained The courts have traditionally rejected this principle.[28] A principle of good faith could also limit freedom to act in a similar way.[29]

The orthodoxy of damages based on a plaintiff's loss rather than the defendant's profit **24.9** is illustrated by the Scots law case of *Teacher v. Calder*.[30] A contract entered into between Adam Teacher, a wine and spirit producer, and James Calder, a timber merchant, provided that Teacher would lend the defendant £15,000 for five years in return for a share of the timber merchant's profits. Calder was supposed to keep at least £15,000 of his own capital in the business. He breached this undertaking by reducing the amount he held in the company and using the money to invest in a profitable distillery business elsewhere instead. It was claimed that the pursuer's damages should take account of the defendant's profits.

Lord Davey[31] thought "the contention was a novelty unsupported either by authority or principle". Damages in contract law are limited to the losses sustained by the

---

[22] [1975] 1 W.L.R. 1468. (See Chap. 25.)
[23] [1996] 1 A.C. 344. (See later pp. 442–444.)
[24] The literature in this area is extensive and broadly supports the new principle. See Cook (1998) 13 J.C.L. 91; Wallace, "Third Party Damage: No Legal Black Hole" (1999) 115 L.Q.R. 394 and Treitel (1998) 114 L.Q.R. 527.
[25] See comments by Lord Woolf in the Court of Appeal in *Attorney-General v. Blake* [1998] 1 All E.R. 833, and the judgment of the House of Lords [2000] 3 W.L.R. 625. The case and the issue of restitutionary damages is discussed in Chap. 26.
[26] See Chap. 26.
[27] See Chap. 13.
[28] *Surrey County Council v. Bredero Homes* [1993] 1 W.L.R. 1361.
[29] See Chap. 14.
[30] [1899] A.C. 451 (HL).
[31] At p. 50.

defendant's breach of contract. So Teacher was not entitled to have his damages calculated on the basis of the profits earned by the diverted capital, only his own losses from the extra profits which might have been earned in the timber business had the diverted capital remained there. Having strayed into new potentially ground breaking territory in discussing future developments in contractual damages, we return to existing law and the central issues of compensation surrounding the classic expectation rule.

THE CHOICE BETWEEN THE EXPECTATION AND RELIANCE PRINCIPLES

24.10   The traditional position is that the claimant has a choice between the two principles but that it is for the court to determine the correct basis of assessment for compensation. The plaintiff may choose in most cases between claiming for his or her lost performance or wasted expenditure, but they cannot do both. The latter is of course normally included within the performance interest as expenses were part of the unfulfilled expectation of profit from the contract. In *Anglia Television Ltd v. Reed*[32] the defendant was an actor, Robert Reed, who agreed to play a part in a television play. He repudiated the contract with the defendants within a few days. The plaintiffs eventually abandoned the production. They claimed £2,750 as the reliance measure of wasted expenditure. The plaintiff had a choice between expectation or reliance. According to Lord Denning:[33]

> "It seems to me that a plaintiff in such a case as this has an election: he can either claim for loss of profits, or for his wasted expenditure. But he must elect between them. He cannot claim both. If he has not suffered any loss of profits – or if he cannot prove what his profits would have been – he can claim in the alternative the expenditure which has been thrown away, that is, wasted, by the breach."[34]

The plaintiffs were entitled to their total wasted expenditure, not only after the contract was concluded (a sum of £854), but also their pre-contractual expenses in preparation for the production, bringing the total up to £2750. The existence of a choice was also recognised in *Bem Dis A Turk Ticaret S/A v. International Agri Trade Co Ltd "The Selda"*.[35] Clarke J. accepted counsel's submission that "an innocent party has an unfettered right to frame its claim as one for wasted expenditure rather than loss of profits".[36] However, clear words were needed to limit or exclude a wasted expenditure claim. The buyers had not expressed their decision in clear enough terms. The claim for the wasted expenditure survived.

[32] [1972] 1 Q.B. 60.
[33] At pp. 63–64.
[34] The High Court of Australia in *Commonwealth of Australia v. Amann Aviation Pty* [1991] 174 C.L.R 64 has cast doubt on whether there really is such a choice at all (see later pp. 438–439).
[35] [1998] 1 Lloyd's Rep. 416.
[36] At p. 419.

The limitations on the plaintiff's choice

(1) The "bad bargain" rule

If a plaintiff makes a bad bargain, in other words, a contract which could never make a **24.11** profit, then he or she will only be entitled to nominal damages. To compensate on a reliance basis would mean that the injured party would then be placed in a better position as a result of the breach than they would have been in if the contract had been performed. In *C and P Haulage v. Middleton*[37] the plaintiff had a licence for premises in Watford for six months on a renewable basis. He spent his own money on fixtures and fittings knowing these could not be removed these when the licence expired. The Court held that the plaintiff could not recover for his expenditure and was entitled to nominal damages only. The expenditure on improving the unit would have been lost because the contract provided they could not be removed. He had made a bad bargain, so he was not entitled to his wasted expenditure instead.

It is usually stated that the burden of proof is on the defendant to prove a bad bargain. In *CCC Films (London) Ltd v. Impact Quadrant Films Ltd*[38] the plaintiffs obtained a licence to distribute and exhibit three films. The defendant's breach prevented the plaintiff carrying out the contract. The plaintiff was therefore not in a position to know if the venture would have made a profit. The defendant is entitled to wasted expenses in such cases. The burden of proof was reversed. It was for the defendant to show on the balance of probabilities that the expenditure would *not* have been recouped.[39]

The question of burden of proof arose again in *Dataliner Ltd v. Vehicle Builders and* **24.12** *Repairers Association*.[40] The Court held that the burden of proof depended on the effect of the breach. According to Henry L.J., the burden normally remained on the plaintiff to show on the balance of probabilities that he or she made a good bargain, and at least recovered their expenditure. However, if the defendants breach makes this impossible to prove, the burden shifts to the defendant (or party in breach) to show that the plaintiff would not have recovered the expenditure, even without the breach. In *Dataliner* the defendants had failed to organise a trade show at Wembley Conference centre properly and this meant that the event failed to attract sufficient customers. The plaintiffs had incurred considerable expenditure in making an appearance at the exhibition which they were able to recover on the reliance test.

(2) Expectation losses are "too speculative"

If the profits from performing the contract are "too speculative", the plaintiff has no **24.13** choice and he or she may only claim their reliance losses for wasted expenditure. Difficulty in quantifying the loss is not sufficient to establish the "too speculative" rule; it must be virtually impossible to assess the profits from the contract. In *McRae v. Commonwealth Disposals Commission*,[41] the High Court of Australia awarded the plaintiffs only their wasted expenditure in seeking recovery of a sunken tanker (which was

---

[37] [1983] 3 All E.R. 94.
[38] [1985] Q.B. 16.
[39] The postal rule was applied. The tapes in question were (it was claimed) posted but never arrived. The Court of Appeal held that there had been acceptance by post. (See Chap. 4.)
[40] *The Independent*, August 30, 1995.
[41] (1950) 84 C.L.R. 377.

never found).[42] The non-existence of the vessel made it impossible to quantify the value of what had been lost. Generally, the courts are reluctant to come to such a conclusion. Damages were considered too speculative in *Sapwell v. Bass*,[43] in which the plaintiff was a breeder of racehorses and the defendant the owner of a stallion who was paid £315 so that his stallion could "serve" the plaintiff's brood mares. The defendant sold the stallion to a third party in South America making it impossible to carry out the contract. The plaintiff claimed damages for the foals which he had lost, including the possibility he had lost a valuable prize winning animal. The Court held the damages were too contingent, *i.e.* it was impossible to quantify the compensation which the plaintiff was claiming, and he received only a nominal amount. Jelf J. was not prepared to make "a pure shot or guess on a matter as to which I have in my view no legal basis of assessment to guide me". The Court also based it's holding on the fact that the damages were too remote on the *Hadley v. Baxendale* principle.[44]

24.14   Difficulty in assessing damages is not a reason for refusing to do so. In *Australia v. Amann Aviation Pty Ltd*[45] the High Court of Australia stated "mere difficulty in estimating damages does not relieve a court from the responsibility of estimating them as best it can". The Court approved Menzies J. in another Australian case, *Jones v. Schiffman*,[46] who admitted that the "assessment of damages . . . does sometimes, of necessity involve what is guess work rather than estimation". In England there is support for this view. Devlin J. commented in *Biggin and Co. Ltd v. Permanite Ltd*[47] that if evidence is not available, the court must do "the best it can". The Court added that the uncertainty of the profits from the contract by reason of contingencies was not a ground for a court's refusal to assess damages. A plaintiff must, however, make a reasonable quantification of his or her loss in their claim. Failure to prove the measure under separate headings may result in only nominal damages being recovered.[48]

Loss of opportunity damages

24.15   The speculative loss rule does not apply to a claim for the loss of an opportunity which can be recoverable in damages if the lost chance is quantifiable in monetary terms. The leading case is *Chaplin v. Hicks*[49] in which the defendant was a former actor turned theatrical producer. Sir Edward Seymour Hicks advertised a competition in the *Daily Express* for young women to send photographs to the newspaper to be shortlisted by readers for a prize. The winner of the competition would be offered a part in one of the defendant's plays. Six thousand photographs were sent in, each woman paying one shilling to take part in the competition. The plaintiff, Eva Chaplin, came top in her area (the country had been divided into four areas) and should have been put forward in a final round of winners. She was not properly notified, however, and by the time she

---

[42] Discussed earlier Chap. 21.
[43] [1910] 2 K.B. 486.
[44] See Chap. 25.
[45] (1991) 66 A.L.J.R. 123.
[46] (1971) 124 C.L.R. 303 (at p. 308).
[47] [1951] 1 K.B. 422 (at p. 438).
[48] *White Arrow Express Ltd v. Lameys Distribution Ltd* [1995] 15 T. L.R. 69 (see later p. 441).
[49] [1911] 2 K.B. 786.

heard of the time and place it was too late and she missed out on the final selection. The plaintiff sued for the loss of the chance to win the competition.

The Court of Appeal held that she was entitled to damages for breach of contract. The mere fact that such damages were difficult to assess did not in itself mean that the plaintiff could not succeed. The Court found that the damages were not too remote and that exclusion from a limited class of competitors could amount to a compensable injury. The measure of damages, was for "the good sense of the jury" to decide.[50] Fletcher Moulton L.J. stated: "They [the jury] must of course give effect to the consideration that the plaintiff's chance is only one out of four and that they cannot tell whether she would have ultimately proved to be the winner. But having considered all this they may well think that it is of considerably pecuniary value to have got into so small a class, and they must assess the damages accordingly."[51]

The loss of a chance principle was applied in *Manubens v. Leon*[52] when the plaintiff **24.16** was awarded damages for the loss of the chance to earn tips in his employment as a hairdresser's assistant. The main issue as far as the tips were concerned was remoteness.[53] Lush J. considered the loss was not too remote. The loss of opportunity to be considered for a tendering process was also considered in *Blackpool and Fylde Aero Club v. Blackpool BC*.[54] Loss of a chance can also apply to making a successful claim in tort. This was considered in *Kitchen v. Royal Air Force Association,*[55] in which the plaintiff, Hilda Kitchen, was the widow of a person killed in an accident. The claim was against the RAF Association and a firm of solicitors who had failed to prosecute an action for damages under the Fatal Accidents Act. She succeeded in recovering for the loss of a chance. According to Parker L.J.[56]: "If the plaintiff can satisfy the Court that she would have had some prospect of success, then it would be for the court to evaluate those prospects, taking into consideration the difficulties that remained." The Court of Appeal agreed that the judge's award of £2,000 should stand.

Lord Reid in *Daines v. Taylor*[57] put forward a test of "substantial chance or probabil- **24.17** ity" in cases of lost opportunity. This meant that the loss was not too speculative:

> "The issue and the sole issue is whether that chance or probability was substantial. If it was it must be evaluated. If it was a mere possibility it must be ignored. Many different words could be and have been used to indicate the dividing line. I can think of none better than substantial on the one hand, or 'speculative' on the other. It must be left to the good sense of the tribunal to decide on broad lines, without regard to legal niceties, but on a consideration of all the facts in proper perspective."

In the Court of Appeal in *Hotson v. East Berkshire Health Authority*[58] Dillon L.J. stated that a loss of a chance was recoverable so long as it was not "minimal or, as it has been

[50] At p. 796.
[51] At pp. 796–797.
[52] [1919] 1 K.B. 208.
[53] See Chap. 25.
[54] [1990] 1 W.L.R. 1195, discussed in Chap. 3.
[55] [1958] 1 W.L.R. 563.
[56] At p. 576.
[57] [1974] A.C. 207 (at p. 212).
[58] [1987] A.C. 750 (at p. 763).

put, a mere speculative possibility". The distinction between loss of a chance and speculative loss was discussed in *Allied Maples Group Ltd v. Simmons and Simmons*[59] in which the plaintiff sued a firm of solicitors for negligence in failing to pursue a claim. The plaintiff would succeed only if the chance was "substantial" rather than "speculative". A substantial chance lay "somewhere between something that just qualifies as real or substantial on the one hand and near certainty on the other".

The idea of a choice between expectation or reliance may be misguided

24.18 The idea that the plaintiff has a clear election between either expectation or reliance damages has not gone unchallenged. The High Court of Australia in *Commonwealth of Australia v. Amann Aviation Pty Ltd*[60] awarded only damages for wasted expenditure to a company whose contract to conduct aerial coastal surveillance for three years was wrongfully terminated. The main issue was whether the plaintiffs would have recovered their expenditure and made a profit, and there were various questions over what that profit might have been.

The High Court of Australia stated *per curiam* that the expressions "expectation", "loss of profits", "reliance" and "wasted expenditure" were all simply "manifestations of the principle that a person who has sustained loss by reason of a breach of contract is to be put in the position as if the contract had been performed. This is based on a single guiding principle deriving from *Robinson v. Harman*".[61] If it is not possible for a plaintiff to demonstrate whether or to what extent the performance of the contract would have resulted in a profit, he or she can seek to recover expenses reasonably incurred, *i.e.* "reliance" or "wasted expenditure" damages. Furthermore, if a plaintiff would not have recovered their wasted expenditure even if the contract had been performed they are only entitled to what they would have been if the contract had been performed, *i.e.* nominal damages only as they suffered no substantial loss. The first of these is the "speculative loss" rule and the second is the bad bargain principle. There is therefore only one principal, namely expectation.

24.19 The High Court of Australia disapproved Lord Denning's dictum in *Anglia TV v. Reed*[62] that the plaintiff had a "choice" or election between principles. It was inappropriate to regard damages assessed by reference to wasted expenditure as damages claimed in the alternative to the expectation principle, or that the plaintiff should be seen as having an election. Mason C.J. and Dawson J.[63] stated that "we do not regard the language of *election* or the notion that *alternative* ways are open to a plaintiff in which to frame a claim for relief as in a discussion of the nature of damages for breach of contract". There were simply two manifestations of the principle laid down in *Robinson v. Harman*.[64] The real question was whether:

---

[59] [1995] 4 All E.R. 907.
[60] [1991] 174 C.L.R. 64; [1991] 66 A.L.J.R. 123.
[61] (1848) 1 Ex. 850 (at p. 855); 154 E.R. 363 (at p. 365).
[62] See para. 24.10.
[63] [1991] 174 C.L.R. 64 (at p. 85).
[64] Citing as authority the High Court of Australia in *TC Industrial Plants Pty Ltd v. Robert's Queensland Pty Ltd* [1963] 37 A.L.J.R. 289 (at p. 292).

"... the contract, if fully performed, would have been and could be shown to have been profitable (even if the actual amount of profit is not readily ascertainable). If this can be demonstrated, a plaintiff's expectation of a profit, objectively made out, will be protected by the award of damages. Otherwise, subject to it being demonstrated that a plaintiff would not even have recovered any or all of his or her reasonable expenses, a plaintiff's objectively determined expectation of recoupment of expenses incurred will be protected by the award of damages."

The High Court of Australia cited the English case of *Hayes v. James & Charles Dodd*   **24.20**
(A Firm)[65] in which Staughton L.J. stated that the different expressions were simply manifestations of "the central principle enunciated in *Robinson v. Harman* rather than discrete and truly alternative measures of damages which a party not in breach may elect to claim". In *Hayes* the Court of Appeal held that the judge was entitled to assess damages in the circumstances on the basis of comparing the plaintiffs' actual situation with the position they would have been in if they had never entered into the transaction at all (wasted expenditure), rather than the position they would have been in had the transaction been successful. These are sometimes called the "no transaction" and "successful transaction" methods respectively. The Court noted: "[I]ndeed it may be that the plaintiffs were ... entitled to elect between the 'no transaction' and 'successful transaction method', but I need not express any concluded view on that point." They were, according to Staughton L.J., "quite properly denied any sum for the profit which they would have made if they had operated their business successfully".[66]

Should estoppel damages fulfil expectations or reverse detrimental reliance?

Promissory estoppel does not give a cause of action in English contract law but acts only   **24.21**
as a defence.[67] Other forms of estoppel which can create a right to sue such as proprietary estoppel,[68] are strictly speaking not contract law. In the Australian case of *Walton's Stores (Interstate) v. Maher*[69] the High Court of Australia recognised that a promissory estoppel could create a cause of action.[70] Damages were awarded on a reliance measure. The remedy for estoppel being equitable in nature, no mandatory rule applies, and the court must retain a discretion. In *Giumelli v. Giumelli*,[71] another Australian case, the Court found an equitable estoppel.[72] There were two alternatives in remedies based upon either the reversal of a detrimental reliance or the fulfilment of the parties expectations. The latter was the *prima facie* remedy, but detrimental reliance could be allowed in some cases.[73] If promissory estoppel were to create a cause of action in England, should

[65] [1990] 2 All E.R. 815 (at p. 820).
[66] At p. 820.
[67] See Chap. 9.
[68] See Chap. 9.
[69] (1988) 164 C.L.R. 387.
[70] A good example of a reliance theory. (See also Chap. 1.)
[71] [1999] H.C.A. 10.
[72] There was no conclusive statement on whether in Australian law there was only one equitable principle of estoppel. (See Chap. 9.)
[73] See Wright (1999) C.L.J. 476.

damages be awarded on the expectation or reliance principle? The existing case law largely shows the reliance measure, since equity is required to do no more than the minimum to prevent injustice. This approach has it's supporters. The view that equitable estoppel, being an alternative to consideration, should follow the contract model and enforce expectations also has it's adherents.[74] The matter remains to be decided in the English courts for the time being. As a theoretical debate over the expanding role of equitable estoppel and damages, this goes to the heart of the nature of contract law.

APPLYING THE TESTS FOR COMPENSATION FOR BREACH OF CONTRACT

Difference in value

24.22   The difference in value test applies particularly to contracts for the sale of goods under the Sale of Goods Act 1979 ss 50, 51. The measure of damages for breach of condition for non acceptance or non delivery of goods is "the estimated loss, directly and naturally resulting, in the ordinary course of events", from the buyers or sellers the breach of contract. By subs. 3 (of both sections) the *prima facie* rule is that where there is an "available market" for the goods in question, damages will be the difference between "the contract price and the market or current price" at the time when the goods ought to have been accepted or delivered, if there was no time fixed at the time of the other party's refusal to do so. If there is no available market, the damages will be assessed on general principles.

The rule is that damages will be calculated on the difference in value between the contract price and the market price. The market price is relevant because this determines what the cost to the plaintiff would be if he or she had to buy the goods afresh in order to obtain their expectation or performance interest. The idea that goods should be re-saleable when purchased is linked to this principle. The older version of the Sale of Goods Act (until 1994) spoke of "merchantable quality" as an implied condition of quality, illustrating the connection between contract law and the market place. The difference in value rule applies this more directly, as the classic measurement of the expectation principle.

A good example of the rule in operation is *Barry v. Davies*,[75] in which the claimant bid £200 each for two pieces of machinery at an auction. He failed to obtain the items because the auctioneer withdrew them on the basis that the claimant's bid was unreasonably low. He recovered almost £27,600 in damages for his loss. This was based on his right to obtain two new machines at the market rate. The unusual fact in this case was that the machines in question were new which meant that the claimant's loss was calculated on the price of obtaining two new articles. Since the machines were sold new at a price of £14,000 each, the claimant was entitled to £28,000 minus the £400 he would have paid had he acquired them from the defendant auctioneer. This can either be seen as sound in principle or as permitting the claimant an unreasonable windfall.

---

[74] For an interesting debate expressing the opposite views, see Cooke, "Estoppel and the protection of expectations" (1997) 17 Legal Studies 258 and Robertson, "Reliance and Expectation in estoppel remedies" (1998) 18 Legal Studies 360.

[75] [2000] 1 W.L.R. 1962. (See Meisel, "What Price Auctions Without Reserve?" (2001) 64 M.L.R. 468.)

The connection between the difference in value rule and the market price fluctuating **24.23** during the course of the contract is illustrated by *Sally Wertheim v. Chicoutimi Pulp Co.*,[76] a Privy Council appeal from the Province of Quebec. The plaintiff, a merchant in Hamburg, bought wood pulp from the defendants who manufactured this produce at the town of Chicoutimi on the St Lawrence river.[77] The wood pulp was delivered several months late by which time it's market value had fallen. The plaintiff had meanwhile sold his right in the goods to a third party. Since the buyer had sold the goods before actual delivery, the price he received then had to be taken into account. In this case the market price at the due date was 70s but when the goods were delivered was only 42s 6d. The plaintiff claimed the difference of 27s. 6d. per ton. He had sold them at 65s. This meant he had only lost 5s. on his contract price, not his claim for 27s. 6d. If there is no available market, compensation is based on general principles. The correct measure of loss in such a case under the Sale of Goods Act 1979, s. 51(2) is therefore "the estimated loss directly and naturally resulting in the ordinary course of events" from the breach of contract.[78]

If the plaintiff elects to accept the goods, even if there has been a breach of implied **24.24** condition, the term is treated as a breach of warranty. This is governed by s. 53 which also applies to sales of defective goods. The measure of loss is the difference in value between the goods as delivered to the buyer and the value of the goods if the seller had fulfilled the contract. The difference in value rule can also apply to contracts for services. In *White Arrow Express Ltd v. Lamey Distribution Ltd*[79] the defendants offered a "de luxe" delivery service for mail order clients, rather than their ordinary service which they failed to deliver. It was held that the difference in value measure was appropriate but that the plaintiffs had failed to prove clearly what the difference in value amounted to under the relevant heads of loss, and so they recovered only nominal damages.

An everyday example of the situation where difference in value, rather than cost of cure, is the appropriate test arises in cases in which a surveyor negligently values a property which turns out to be in less good a condition than the purchaser has been led to expect. In *Watts v. Morrow*[80] the plaintiffs, Ian and Lesley Watts, bought a house for £177,000 then discovered it needed substantial repairs amounting to a cost of £33,000. The "difference in value" of the house at the time of sale if the survey had been properly conducted was only £15,000. The Court of Appeal agreed with the judge's decision to apply the latter sum. The difference in value was the appropriate measure. The plaintiffs did, however, recover a small sum for the "physical inconvenience" of having the builders present in their home.[81]

Cost of cure or reinstatement

The alternative rule of damages requires the defendant to pay the cost of putting things **24.25** right after a defective performance. The cost of cure or reinstatement measure is often

---

[76] [1911] A.C. 301.
[77] The obligation to deliver was qualified by "if possible" ("si possible") because of the frozen ice on the river for several months. The Privy Council held the defendants in breach and bound to deliver nevertheless.
[78] *Bence Graphics International Ltd v. Fasson UK Ltd* [1998] Q.B. 87, criticised by Treitel (1999) 113 L.Q.R. 188.
[79] (1995) 15 T.L.R. 69.
[80] [1991] 1 W.L.R. 1421.
[81] See Chap. 25.

applied to contracts for services. The claimant is entitled to the cost of having the work finished and does not have to accept the difference in value to their property caused by defective workmanship. Rather they may claim the cost of the work necessary to perform the contract according to it's proper specifications. The cost of cure or repairs is often more than the difference in value in building cases. In *East Ham Corporation v. Bernard Sunley and Sons*[82] the defendant builders attached Portland Stone panels to a Girls' School in East Ham, which became detached due to defective fixing by the contractors. They were later repaired by the local authority who brought an action to recover the cost. The House of Lords held that cost of cure was the appropriate measure of damages. Lord Cohen referred to three possible measures of damages in such cases: (a) the cost of reinstatement, (b) the difference in cost to the builders of the actual work done and work specified and (c) the diminution in value of the work due to the breach of contract. The Law Lords applied the first of these as the usual rule in cases of building contracts. The likelihood or otherwise of reinstating was a factor to be taken into account.

In *Tito v. Waddell (No. 2)*[83] the inhabitants of an island in the Pacific Ocean made an agreement with the defendant company who wished to mine for phosphates. The Mining Company promised that when they were finished they would plant fruit trees and restore the island to it's former state. The islanders claimed reinstatement of their island when the defendants breached their agreement. The Court held that the correct measure was the difference in value rather than cost of cure. The question of whether reinstatement would take place was relevant as most of the islanders were now scattered elsewhere across the other Pacific Islands. In *Radford v. De Frobeville*,[84] the Court stated two further principles relevant to an award of cost to cure damages: (a) the intention of the plaintiff to reinstate and (b) whether the intention to reinstate was reasonable in the circumstances. The Court took into account the fact that there is no supervision of what the plaintiff actually does with his or her award. In some cases the cost of reinstatement could amount to a large windfall to the plaintiff if they have no intention of using the money for that purpose. It is also relevant that the cost of rebuilding might be out of proportion to the loss of value involved. This was one of the factors in *Tito v. Waddell* that counted against the islanders. The leading authority on cost of cure damages against difference in value is the case to which we now turn.

"A contest of absurdities": *Ruxley Electronics v. Forsyth*[85]

24.26   In *Ruxley Electronics and Constructions Ltd v. Forsyth*[86] the plaintiff was a very tall man who made a contract with the defendants to build a swimming pool. The pool had to be 7 feet and 6 inches at the deep end. When the pool was completed it was found to be only 6 feet 9 inches but otherwise built to specifications. The plaintiff claimed his cost of cure measure of damages rather than the difference in value. The former would amount to damages of £21,000, just under three times the price of the pool; the difference in value test would result in the plaintiff recovering only a nominal award. At first instance, it was

---

[82] [1966] A.C. 406.
[83] [1977] Ch. 106.
[84] [1977] 1 W.C.R. 1262.
[85] See Coote "Contract Damages, Ruxley, and the Performance Interest" [1997] C.L.J. 537.
[86] [1995] 3 W.L.R. 118.

held that the pool as constructed was of satisfactory quality, there was no diminution in value for the average person, and the plaintiff's intention to rebuild (if indeed he intended to do so) was unreasonable. The plaintiff recovered no cost of cure award or difference in value damages but did receive an award of £2,500 for loss of amenity or enjoyment in using the pool, the so called "consumer surplus".[87] The Court of Appeal overturned the judgment and awarded him cost of cure, *i.e.* the full £21,000, but the House of Lords restored the judge's judgment. An award for the consumer surplus was all that was justified.[87a]

The House of Lords recognised that the case raised a difficult dilemma. Lord Mustill[88] described the two positions as a "contest of absurdities". On the one hand, as the builders had failed to carry out the specifications of the contract, they should not be entitled to get away without loss. On the other hand, the cost of putting the swimming pool right, involving having to rip up the work done and rebuilding it again, would be disproportionate. It was held that where the expenditure was out of all proportion to the benefit obtained, the appropriate measure of damages was not the cost of reinstatement but the diminution in the value of the work occasioned by the breach, even if that would only result in a nominal award. The plaintiff received a sum for loss of "amenity", *i.e.* his own personal use and pleasure of the swimming pool. The question of reasonableness was central to the case, in particular in relation to the proportionality between the breach of contract and the cost of putting it right. If this was too large in comparison to the loss suffered, it would not be considered. The reasonableness in the circumstances of the plaintiff's intention (indeed the eventual likelihood itself) to rebuild were also crucial factors. Lord Jauncey used the example of a house to be built with the lower courses of blue brick. Instead the builder uses yellow bricks. Should the whole house be pulled down and the blue bricks rebuilt with yellow? No, this would "clearly be unreasonable". The plaintiff's loss was "not the necessary cost of reconstruction of the house which was entirely accurate for its design purpose, but merely the lack of aesthetic pleasure which he might have derived from blue bricks". To allow the plaintiff in *Ruxley* the cost of rebuilding would mean he would have recovered "not compensation for loss but a very substantial gratuitous benefit. Something which damages are not intended to provide".[89]

As a result of *Ruxley*, it can now be said that in assessing cost of cure damages the court will take account of three factors: **24.27**

(a) the cost of reinstatement and whether it is disproportionate to the benefit obtained[90];

(b) whether it is reasonable to ask for reinstatement; and

(c) whether the intention of the plaintiff to rebuild was relevant to the question of reasonableness.

---

[87] See later Chap. 25.

[87a] The consumer surplus was described as "authoritatively established" in this case by Lord Steyn in *Farley v. Skinner, The Times*, October 15, 2001 (HL).

[88] At p. 128.

[89] At pp. 124–125.

[90] The fact that reinstatement would be disproportionate to the claimant's loss in relation to a tort claim for replacing a chattel was applied to the assessment of damages in *Southampton Container Terminals Ltd v. Hansa Schiffahrts GmbH, The Times*, June 13, 2001.

There was nothing to compel a plaintiff to use his damages in a particular way. We have already discussed earlier that both *Ruxley* and *Radford v. DeFroberville* may prove to be harbingers of a new principle in the assessment of contract damages, the performance interest.[90a]

Loss of profits

24.28   Loss of profit or loss of bargain are synonymous with the expectation principle. Normally a claimant will wish to claim his or her loss of profit as this will inevitably be greater than their expenses if they are not to be held to have a bad bargain. Loss of profit from "volume sales" of goods such as second hand cars largely depends on whether demand exceeds supply or vice versa. In *Thompson (WL) Ltd v. Robinson (Gunmakers) Ltd,*[91] supply of the type of gun exceeded demand so the plaintiff had "lost" the sale and was entitled to his profit. On the other hand, in *Charter v. Sullivan*[92] the dealer was able to sell as many cars as he could obtain for sale. The Court held his damages from the lost sale were not recoverable. In another case involving a car, Lord Denning in *Lazenby Garages v. Wright*[93] held that a second hand BMW was a unique article for which there was no available market. The sellers could recover only the actual loss sustained on the transaction and nothing more. The seller had later re-sold the car at a higher price, so had suffered no loss and recovered only nominal damages.

Damages under the Commercial Agents (Council Directive) Regulations 1993

24.29   Wholly different principles applicable to the calculation of damages now have to be applied by English contract lawyers as a result of the implementation in the United Kingdom of the Commercial Agents (Council Directive) Regulations 1993.[94] The Regulations include a provision dealing with the calculation of compensation for agents whose contracts have been terminated.[95] Damages are calculated using two methods which are set out in the directive. First, an indemnity, and secondly, a compensatory system. The 1993 Regulations allow both of these systems to be used.

    The directive is based upon civilian rules for the calculation of damages. The directive used German law in the case of the indemnity approach and French law in the assessment of compensation. The British courts have recognised this in *Moore v. Piretta PTA Ltd,*[96] adopting German law in the former, and *King v. T. Tunnock Ltd* in the latter.[97] However, in *Barrett McKenzie and Co. Ltd v. Escada (UK) Ltd*[97a] the High Court held that in English law compensation should take account of the particular factors of each case as is traditional in England, rather than follow a tariff system as in France which

---

[90a]   See pp. 428–429.
[91]   [1955] Ch. 177.
[92]   [1957] 2 Q.B. 117.
[93]   [1976] 1 W.L.R. 459.
[94]   Implementing the Commercial Agents Directive 86/653/EEC, OJ 1986 No (2/382/17).
[95]   Reg. 17(6),(7).
[96]   [1999] 1 All E.R. 174.
[97]   *The Times*, May 12, 2000.
[97a]   *The Times*, May 15, 2001.

would be a recipe for injustice. The European Court of Justice has held that the directive applies to contracts being performed in the United Kingdom, even although these might state that they were governed by another jurisdiction. In *Ingmar GB Ltd v. Eaton Leonard Technologies*[98] compensation under the Regulations for breach of an agency agreement made in England was held to be based on the directive even though there was a stipulation that the contract was governed by the law of California.

---

[98] [2001] All E.R. (EC) 57.

Chapter 25

THE BOUNDARIES OF COMPENSATION

Introduction

The law sets limits on the extent of a party's liability to pay for his or her wrongdoing in **25.1** breaching a contract. In drawing lines the law attempts to strike a balance in terms of justice and social policy between the contracting parties. There are a number of well established legal rules in this equation. A plaintiff cannot recover for losses which are "too remote" from the breach of contract. Some types of losses are also, as a matter of policy, not covered by contract law. Non-pecuniary losses, such as mental distress, are traditionally not recoverable as a head of contract damages which are largely for economic or financial losses. This is the opposite of the position in tort law where pure economic loss is traditionally not recoverable. The position in contract is now changing.

The loss must have been caused by the breach of contract. Once a breach of contract is established the plaintiff is expected to take reasonable steps to mitigate his or her loss. In some cases contributory negligence by the plaintiff will lead to a reduction in the award. The need for placing such restrictions on the liability of defendants was expressed by Lord Wright in *Liesbosch Dredger v. Edison SS*:

> "The law cannot take account of everything that follows a wrongful act; it regards some subsequent matters as outside the scope of its selection, because 'it were infinite for the law to judge the cause of causes', or consequences of consequences. In the varied web of affairs the law must abstract some consequences as relevant, not perhaps on grounds of pure logic, but simply for practical reasons."[1]

REMOTENESS

The rules on remoteness determine the existence of liability and thereafter the quantum **25.2** or measure of damages once liability is established. The defendant is only liable in damages for the consequence of their wrongdoing if both tests are satisfied. In tort law the test of reasonable foreseeability generally applies to negligence claims. Remoteness is therefore a major liability issue in tort.[2] In contract law the claimant merely has to show

---

[1] [1933] A.C. 449 (at p. 460).
[2] *Overseas Tankship (UK) Ltd v. Miller Steamship Co. Pty Ltd "The Wagon Mound" (No. 2)* [1967] A.C. 617.

that the contract has been breached in order to establish liability. Breach of contract is actionable *per se* and nominal damages must be awarded. The remoteness rules, then, determine the extent of the claimants award and the defendant's consequential liability to pay substantial damages.

The Gloucester miller's tale: *Hadley v. Baxendale*

25.3   The leading case on remoteness is *Hadley v. Baxendale*,[3] in which the plaintiffs were millers, owners of the City Steam-Mills, in the city of Gloucester. The mill was worked by a steam engine which ground corn into meal, flour and bran. The crank shaft of the steam engine became broken and needed repair, which prevented the mill from working. The miller ordered a new crank shaft from W. Joyce and Co., an engineering firm in Greenwich. The old crank shaft was required as a pattern in order to make a new one, and to be certain that it would fit precisely. The defendants carried on business as "common carriers" under the name "Pickford and Co." and the plaintiffs handed the old crank shaft over to them to be taken from Gloucester to Greenwich. The defendants delayed in re-delivering the new shaft by several days with the result that the entire mill was out of action for that period. The plaintiffs claimed £300 for "loss of profits they would otherwise have received". The defendants argued that all they had been told when the crankshaft was entrusted to them was that it was the broken shaft of a mill, and that the plaintiffs were the millers in question. They denied liability on the basis that they had no knowledge of the potential losses to the plaintiff.

The Court of Exchequer held that as they could not have been reasonably expected to know that the entire mill would be out of action if they delayed in returning the crankshaft, then they were not to be held liable for the resulting loss of profits to the plaintiffs. The loss caused by the delay in returning the crankshaft was too remote. The result was "the rule in *Hadley v. Baxendale*", one of the most famous in contract law. Anderson B. stated:

> "Where two parties have made a contract which one of them has broken the damages which the other party ought to receive in respect of such breach of contract should be such as may fairly and reasonably be considered either arising naturally *i.e.* according to the usual course of things, from such breach of contract itself, or such as may reasonably be supposed to have been in the contemplation of both parties at the time they made the contract, as the probably result of the breach of it."

25.4   Alderson B.'s famous test appears to break down into two rules. The plaintiff is entitled to recover for losses either (a) arising naturally from the breach, that is, according to the usual course of things or (b) such as may "reasonably be supposed to have been in the contemplation of *both* parties at the time they made the contract as the probable result of the breach". The latter is expressed as a "reasonable contemplation" test. This requires knowledge on the defendant's part. The knowledge could be actual or imputed at the time of the contract. The two rules may now be regarded as "the statement of a single

---

[3] (1854) 9 Exch. 341; 156 E.R. 145.

principle . . . [which] application may depend on the degree of relevant knowledge possessed by the defendant in a particular case".[4] The Australian High Court used an English authority for this view.[5]

It is clear that the rule as originally formulated had two limbs. The second limb has proved the most important. The head note of *Hadley v. Baxendale* has been a source of confusion. It says that the defendants' clerk "who attended at the office, was told that the mill has stopped, that the shaft must be delivered immediately, and that a special entry, if necessary, must be made to hasten its delivery". If this is accurate, the plaintiffs should not have succeeded on the second limb of "the rule" in the case, as they surely had sufficient knowledge. It has been suggested that the head note may in fact be wrong. (A salutary reminder to the readers of law reports.)

In the Court of Appeal in *Victoria Laundry (Windsor) v. Newman Industries*[6] Asquith L.J. laid out the guidelines of the modern remoteness rule in contract law. He spoke of the requirement of reasonable foreseeability but it is clear that contract law requires knowledge of the consequences of a breach. This is a narrower requirement than the more abstract but wider concept of reasonable foreseeability in tort. Asquith L.J. expressed the remoteness rule in everyday language. The test was whether the damage was "on the cards" or "likely to result". In a later case, *Koufos v. C. Czarnikou Ltd "The Heron II"*,[7] the House of Lords used the colloquialisms "a real danger, "a serious possibility" and "liable to result" as the test of remoteness in contract law.

The two rules (if such they are) in *Hadley v. Baxendale* deal with different losses. The **25.5** first concerns injury leading to loss "arising in the usual course of events". In other words, the losses will be such as flow from the normal business understandings of the parties. In *Monarch Steamship Co. Ltd v. Karlshamus Oljefabriker A/B*[8] the cost of sending a delayed cargo of soya beans from Glasgow to Sweden was recoverable. Under the first limb, a party will, for instance, be able to recover for fluctuations in the market price when the contract is breached.[9] In the *Heron II* the House of Lords held that shipowners should realise that commodity prices change on the market and that delay in transit of a cargo of sugar from Romania to Iraq would result in losses for which the plaintiff was entitled to compensation.

On the other hand, the second rule in *Hadley v. Baxendale* will prevent the recovery of exceptional losses or those not known to the other party at the time of contract. In *Victoria Laundry* there was no recovery for the loss of a valuable contract of which the defendant was unaware. In *Horne v. Midland Railway Co.*[10] the plaintiffs were shoe manufacturers who had an exceptionally lucrative contract to supply the French army during the Franco-Prussian wars of 1870. The defendants were late in delivering the goods. They were held not to be liable for the losses arising from the high price of the order, since they did not have notice of the value of sale. The defendants were, however, liable for the ordinary losses under a contract of this type. A minority of the Court would not

[4] Mason C.J. and Dawson J. in *Commonwealth of Australia v. Amann Aviation Pty Ltd* [1991] 174 C.L.R. 64 (at p. 92).
[5] Citing *Koufos v. C. Czarnikow Ltd* [1969] 1 A.C. (at p. 385).
[6] [1949] 2 K.B. 528.
[7] [1969] 1 A.C. 350.
[8] [1949] A.C. 196.
[9] *Fyffes Group Ltd v. Reefer Express Lines Pty Ltd* [1996] 2 Lloyd's Rep. 171.
[10] (1873) LR 8 CP 131.

have allowed recovery of exceptional losses in this case, even if known to the defendant, unless they had expressly agreed to be liable for them.

25.6　In *Satef-Huttenes v. Paloma Tercera Shipping Co., "The Pegase"*[11] Goff J. discussed the two "rules", the first applicable to recovery of damages arising naturally, and the second rule depending on the contemplation of the parties when the contract was made. According to Goff J., the principle in *Hadley v. Baxendale* had been "analysed and developed and it's application broadened in the twentieth century, in particular as a result of *Victoria Laundry v. Newman Industries*[12] and *The Heron II*".[13] *Hadley v. Baxendale* was no longer stated in terms of two rules but rather in terms of a "single principle",[14] which may depend on "the degree of relevant knowledge held by the defendant at the time of the contract in the particular case". The courts have not been required "to pigeon hole the cases under one or other of the so-called rules in *Hadley v. Baxendale* but rather to decide each case on the basis of the relevant knowledge of the defendant". There has also been a "loosening of the rule that knowledge of special circumstances is only relevant if communicated to the other party in such a way that they expressly or impliedly took the risk of loss flowing from such special circumstances". The test for this modern version of remoteness was stated by Goff J. in *The Pegase*[15] as being whether:

> ". . . the facts in question come to the defendant's knowledge in such circumstances that a reasonable person in the shoes of the defendant would, if he had considered the matter at the time of making the contract, have contemplated that, in the event of a breach by him, such facts were to be taken into account when considering his responsibility for loss suffered by the plaintiff as a result of such breach".

The answer to the question would vary from case to case. The nature of the facts in question and how far they are unusual should be considered, and "the extent to which such facts are likely to make fulfilment of the contract by the due date more critical, or to render the plaintiff's loss heavier in the event of non-fulfilment".

25.7　A party does not have to contemplate the breach of contract[16] in question, as performance rather than breach is anticipated and it is only the type of damage that must be contemplated, not the event in detail. In *Vacwell Engineering Co. Ltd v. BDH Chemicals Ltd*[17] a scientist dropped an ampoule of chemicals into a sink which caused an explosion killing both the scientist and a colleague and causing extensive damage to property. Rees J. stated[18] that: "the explosion and the type of damage being foreseeable it matters not in the law that the magnitude of the former and the extent of the latter were not". Remoteness in a modern context was discussed in *Balfour Beattie*

---

[11] [1981] 1 Lloyd's Rep. 175 (at p. 182).
[12] [1949] 2 K.B. 528.
[13] [1969] 1 A.C. 350.
[14] [1981] 1 Lloyd's Rep. (at p. 182).
[15] [1981] 1 Lloyd's Rep. (at p. 183).
[16] See *Banco de Portugal v. Waterlow and Sons Ltd* [1932] A.C. 452.
[17] [1971] 1 Q.B. 88.
[18] At p. 110.

Construction (Scotland) v. Scottish Power plc.[19] The pursuers were the main contractors building a section of a motorway near Edinburgh. They needed a continuous supply of electricity in order to keep their concrete production plant in operation. The defenders agreed to set up a temporary electricity supply to this plant. When this failed, a bridge under construction could not be completed and later had to be rebuilt. The pursuers claimed the cost of the rebuilding work.

The House of Lords held that the loss incurred was too remote. There was no evidence of knowledge that the concrete power process had to be continuous. The parties had to have reasonable knowledge of the other's business but not every technical fact, particularly of something as vast and complicated as major motorway construction. According to Lord Jauncey:

> "It must always be a question of circumstances what one contracting party is presumed to know about the business activities of the other . . . However when an activity involves complicated construction or manufacturing techniques I see no reason why B who supplies a commodity that A intends to use in the course of these techniques should be assumed . . . to be aware of the details of all the techniques undertaken by and the effect thereupon of any failure of or deficiency in that commodity."[20]

The general principle of remoteness was laid down by Lord Wright in *Karlshamns Oljefabriker (A/B) v. Monarch Steamship Co. Ltd*[21] that what "reasonable business men must have taken to have contemplated as the natural and probable result of the contract was broken. As reasonable businessmen each must be taken to understand the ordinary practices and exigencies of the other's trade or business".[22]

Remoteness in tort and contract law contrasted and compared

In tort there are two different rules on remoteness. In negligence the test is that of "reasonable foreseeability" of the injury sustained by the claimant. In fraud actions, the tort of deceit allows recovery for all "the direct consequences" of the wrongdoing. This means that essentially the only limiting rule is one of causation. The defendant must compensate the claimant for everything that flows directly from their wrongdoing. The fraud rule applies to fraudulent misrepresentation and also (because of the application of a "fiction of fraud") to s. 2(1) Misrepresentation Act 1967.[23] The remoteness rules in contract law and negligence are narrower by comparison. In *H. Parsons v. Uttley Ingham and Co. Ltd*[24] Lord Denning suggested that in cases of personal injury or damage to property, *i.e.* non-economic loss cases, where there was concurrent liability in either contract and tort.[24a] The test of remoteness ought to be the same in both,

25.8

---

[19] 1994 S.L.T. 807.
[20] At p. 810.
[21] [1949] A.C. 196.
[22] At p. 224.
[23] See Chap. 18.
[24] [1978] 1 All E.R. 525.
[24a] See Chap. 1.

namely that of "reasonable foreseeability". In the same case Lord Scarman suggested there might be no difference between reasonable contemplation in contract and reasonable foreseeability in tort. Neither of these views can be said to be orthodox. It is better, therefore, to regard the remoteness rules in contract and tort as different. The watershed case of *Hadley v. Baxendale*[24b] remains one of the most influential cases in the history of the law. There are many views as to its true meaning and significance, for instance, that of Grant Gilmore[25] who saw it as deliberate judicial policy to encourage the growth of contractual undertakings. Contract law's narrower view of remoteness has been discussed by Gilmore.

DAMAGES FOR MENTAL DISTRESS

The rule against recovery

25.9   Some types of damage are traditionally regarded as not recoverable in contract law. The rule until recently was that contract law does not provide protection against mental distress. This covered everything from disappointment to humiliation and psychiatric illness caused by the other party's breach of contract. Such losses were seen as too remote. Since breach of contract is assessed objectively, the manner of the breach was irrelevant and, likewise, the subjective consequences for the individual concerned.

The rejection of mental distress as a head of damages was commented upon by Staunton L.J. in *Hayes v. James and Charles Dodd*,[26] in which he stated that: "I would not view with enthusiasm the prospect that every shipowner in the Commercial Court, having successfully claimed for unpaid freight or demurrage, would be able to add a claim for mental distress suffered while he was waiting for his money."[27] This position against recovery for mental distress is liberalising in some areas of contract law. Once again, this is an area of contract law in a state of flux.

25.10   The leading authority for rejecting mental distress damages for breach of contract is traditionally cited as *Addis v. Gramophone Co. Ltd*[28] The plaintiff in this case was dismissed from his employment as a manager of a company in India, for alleged dishonesty. The manner in which his contract was terminated and the resulting social ostracism within the British community in Calcutta caused him mental pain and anguish. It was held that damages for injured feelings were not recoverable. The view which was extrapolated from the case was that damages for mental distress or for the manner of breach could never be recoverable in contract. Even at an early date, the widely drawn ratio of this case had its critics. In a later case, *Cox v. Phillips*,[29] Lawson J. took the view that damages for distress, vexation and consequent ill-health could be recovered for breach of a contract of employment if this might have been in the reasonable contemplation of the

---

[24b]   (1854) 9 Ex. 341.
[25]   See *The Death of Contract* (1974, Ohio State University Press, Columbus, Ohio), pp. 49–53 for an interesting discussion. Professor Gilmore believed general contract law (a construction of the nineteenth century judges) had now deceased.
[26]   [1990] 2 All E.R. 815.
[27]   At p. 823.
[28]   [1909] A.C. 488.
[29]   [1976] 1 W.L.R. 638.

parties. However, in *Bliss v. South East Thames Regional Health Authority*[30] the Court of Appeal stated that this was wrong. According to Dillon L.J.: "For my part, I do not think that that general approach is open to this court unless and until the House of Lords has reconsidered its decision in the *Addis* case."[31] The view taken in *Cox* went too far, said the Court of Appeal. This has proved to be correct until recently, but *Addis v. Gramophone Co.* has now come under increasing attack and appears likely to be overruled before long. In *Johnson v. Unisys Ltd*,[32] another wrongful dismissal action, this time by a computer consultant who had a nervous breakdown after an unfair dismissal, the Court of Appeal reiterated the traditional view that damages for dismissal in employment contracts did not include compensation for injured feelings. *Addis* was described as a "cornerstone" of the law, "repeatedly followed", according to Lord Woolf. The House of Lords judgment in *Malik v. BCCI*,[33] which we discuss later, was distinguished as applying to financial losses resulting from loss of commercial reputation by reason of the employer's breach an implied term of trust and confidence in a contract of employment. The implied term did not apply to the circumstances of the dismissal itself and whether this was summary, unfair or without proper notice. Damages for such "subjective" losses, *i.e.* personal pain and humiliation, were within the province of tort law, not contract.

The House of Lords dismissed the appeal of the employee in *Unisys Ltd* but cast new light on *Addis* and in their speeches the Law Lords made inroads into the rule against recovery for mental distress. The House of Lords stated in *Unisys* that it would be an improper use of the judicial function for the Court to construct a remedy for the unfair manner of dismissal when Parliament had already created a scheme of compensation for dismissed employees. This is known as "unfair dismissal" and in 2001 the upper financial limit for such claims was just over £50,000. Wrongful dismissal is an action at common law. The employee, Johnson, had already made a claim for damages for unfair dismissal. The House of Lords held that if wrongful dismissal was the only cause of action, in the circumstances of the case, nothing could be recovered for the manner of the dismissal, even if this caused mental distress. However, financial losses caused by breach of the implied term of trust and confidence were recoverable. Most importantly, in unfair dismissal claims an employment tribunal could award compensation as it considered "just and equitable". This could, in appropriate cases, include the type of humiliation, distress and loss of reputation in the community which was the basis of the unsuccessful claim by Mr Addis in 1909.   **25.11**

Lord Steyn agreed with the other Law Lords but added his own voice to the grounds of the judgment. Lord Steyn regarded the headnote of *Addis* as wrong if it stated that an employee could never obtain damages or loss of employment prospects through the harsh and humiliating manner of their dismissal. However, although sympathetic to the claimant's action, there were three obstacles in their Lordship's view which he failed to overcome. First, the existence of a statutory scheme for unfair dismissal which did not provide for damages for mental distress.[34] Secondly, the evidential problem of proving that the claimants psychiatric illness was caused by the   **25.12**

---

[30] [1987] I.C.R. 700.
[31] At p. 718.
[32] [1999] 1 All E.R. 854 (CA); March 23, 2001 (HL).
[33] [1999] A.C. 20. The case is also known as *Mahmud v. BCCI*, (see later para. 25.20).
[34] The claimant had already succeeded in his unfair dismissal claim to an employment tribunal and later brought his action at common law to recover damages for the emotional distress of his nervous breakdown.

manner of his dismissal. Thirdly, there was the problem of remoteness which on the facts looked insurmountable. The majority also departed from the traditional view of *Addis* that injured feelings could never be recoverable arising out of a dismissal but chose to follow *Malik* in that injury to employment reputation was recoverable in contract but not for the psychiatric injury alone, which would be a step too far.

25.13   The courts are slowly recognising stress and psychiatric distress as compensatable injuries in breaches of contract other than dismissal.[35] In *Gogay v. Hertfordshire County Council*[36] the judgment in *Johnson* was distinguished in allowing a residential care worker's claim for damages for psychiatric injury and distress from being suspended over a false allegation of abuse of a child in her care. The Court of Appeal held that the judge had been correct to award the claimant damages for psychiatric illness brought on by the employer's breach of contract in suspending her. According to Hale L.J., there is "a clear distinction between a recognised psychiatric illness on the one hand, and hurt, upset and injury to feelings on the other". The case was distinguishable from *Addis v Gramophone Co. Ltd*, in that the employee suffered psychiatric illness rather than hurt feelings. Further, the case was distinguishable from both *Addis* and *Johnson v Unisys* in that this was a suspension from employment rather than a dismissal.

The question of distress in employment contracts is a good illustration of a situation specifically concerned with a long term relationship. Lord Steyn recognised this in *Unisys* in which he stated:

> "It is no longer right to equate a contract of employment with commercial contracts. One possible way of describing a contract of employment in modern terms is as a relational contract. If (contrary to my view) the headnote of *Addis's* case correctly states the ratio . . . I would now be willing to depart from it. That is not a particularly bold step. Indeed in *Mahmud's* [*i.e. Malik's*] case the House took that step."[37a]

In *Waters v. Commissioner of Police of the Metropolis*[37] the House of Lords held that an employer who does nothing to prevent psychiatric harm to an officer who has made an allegation of sexual harassment and assault will be in breach of a duty of care in negligence. Lord Hutton stated that this duty applied not only in tort but also under the contract of employment for mental as well as the more traditional physical injuries.

When Damages for Mental Distress may be Recoverable: Disappointed Expectations

25.14   The basic rule against recovery has now been modified so that there can no longer be said to be a blanket rejection of damages for mental distress arising from a breach of contract. In *Bliss v. S. E. Thames Regional Health Authority*[38] Dillon L.J. described two large

---

[35] See *Walker v. Northumberland County Council* [1995] 1 C.R. 702. This landmark tort claim has opened the door to numerous claims for stress related illness caused by work.
[36] [2000] I.R.L.R. 703.
[37] [2000] I.R.L.R. 720.
[37a] At p. 871.
[38] [1985] I.C.R. 308.

categories of contract where damages of this type could be awarded: contracts to provide (a) peace of mind or pleasure and (b) freedom from distress. This view has now taken a firm hold and been extended by a growing body of case law. It can now be said that there are five identifiable areas of claims for non-pecuniary loss under this heading in contract law.

(1) Contracts to provide peace of mind, enjoyment or entertainment

The largest category of such actions relate to package holidays which have turned out **25.15** to be a disappointing experience.[39] The origin of this modern flood in travel litigation is the judgment of Lord Denning in *Jarvis v. Swans Tours Ltd*,[40] in which the plaintiff was a solicitor, who booked a holiday in Switzerland. This was described in detail by the defendants, a firm of travel agents, who promised the plaintiff that he would have a great time. The holiday proved a disaster. The Court of Appeal awarded him damages for his loss of enjoyment. Mental distress could be recoverable in contract if the object of the contract was to provide entertainment or enjoyment, and there was a breach of this undertaking by the defendants. Damages were awarded for the disappointment, distress, upset and frustration caused by the breach. Lord Denning made a comparison with the loss of an enjoyable summer's evening at the opera in the Sussex Downs:

> "A good illustration was given by Edmund Davies L.J. in the course of the argument. He put the case of a man who has taken a ticket for Glyndebourne. It is the only night on which he can get there. He hires a car to take him. The car does not turn up. His damages are not limited to the mere cost of the ticket. He is entitled to general damages for the disappointment he has suffered and the loss of the entertainment which he should have had."[41]

The emotional distress of upset wedding arrangements resulted in a successful claim in the Scots case of *Diesen v. Samson*.[42] The pursuer brought action against the defender who was a photographer. The defender had been booked to take pictures of the pursuer's wedding, but he failed to appear. The Sheriff's Court at Glasgow held that this was not primarily a commercial contract to which the rule in *Addis v. Gramophone Co.* applied. Instead it affected the pursuer's personal, social and family interests and damages could be awarded for her distress at having no photographs of her wedding. The Court stated that: "What both the parties obviously had in their contemplation was that the pursuer would be enabled to enjoy such pleasure in the years ahead. This had been permanently denied her by the defender's breach of contract and, in my opinion, it is a fitting case for the award of damages."[43]

  In a case from the Canadian province of Ontario, *Dunn v. Disc Jockey Unlimited Co.* **25.16** *Ltd*,[44] the bridegroom booked a disc jockey for his wedding reception. The defendant did not turn up and various guests had to take turns playing the music. There was loss of

---

[39] Holidaymakers' rights were increased by the Package Travel, Package Holidays and Package Tours Regulations 1992 (see Chap. 13).
[40] [1973] 1 All E.R. 71.
[41] At p. 74.
[42] 1971 S.L.T. 49.
[43] At p. 59.
[44] (1978) 87 D.L.R. 408. Typical of most consumer actions, this had its origin in the Small Claims Court.

"ambience and enjoyment" as a result. The plaintiff brought an action for breach of contract and damages for disappointment, irritation and "general nervous fatigue". The Court awarded as damages the reasonable cost that would have been insured to hire a replacement at short notice. This was effectively the "cost of cure" measure.[45] In *Jackson v. Horizon Holidays*[46] the plaintiff recovered damages not only for himself but also his wife and two children after a disappointing and troublesome holiday in Sri Lanka. The case was once almost effectively confined to its own facts, and the result was distinguished in *Woodar Investment v. Wimpey Construction (UK) Ltd.*[47] However, its holding is confirmed and strengthened by the Contracts (Rights of Third Parties) Act 1999 which allows third party beneficiaries, such as family members, to sue under a contract made between two others. Alternatively, the plaintiff could claim his loss included the disappointed expectation of others.

The recovery of loss under this heading illustrates the role of reasonable expectations in contract law. The expectation of a holiday contract is not mere travel or accommodation, but also enjoyment. Contract law, therefore, once again protects the expectation principle. The leading case of *Panatown Ltd v. Alfred McAlpine Construction Ltd*[48] recognises a wider "performance interest" in contract law which allows claimants such as the father in *Jackson* to succeed for breach of contractual performance to others.[49]

(2) Contracts to provide freedom from mental distress

25.17   If a contract is created for the avoidance of distress, then a failure to do so, which causes mental suffering in the process, can lead to recovery of damages in contract. In *Heywood v. Wellers*[50] the plaintiff, Sheila Heywood, was a single parent living in Penge who met a married man with whom she had an affair. Later they split up but he began pestering and stalking her. The plaintiff went to the defendants, a firm of solicitors, to seek an injunction against her former companion. The defendants negligently failed to do so with the result that the plaintiff had to suffer further molestation. It was held by the Court of Appeal that she could recover for the mental distress caused as this was a reasonably foreseeable consequence of the solicitors' breach of contract.

(3) Physical inconvenience as a result of breach of contract

25.18   If mental distress is caused by physical inconvenience, this can be compensated as an additional head of damage. In *Perry v. Sidney Phillips and Son*[51] the plaintiff bought a house relying on a survey prepared by the defendants. Their report stated that the house was in good order, but it was found to have a leaking roof as well as other faults, such as a bad odour. The Court of Appeal awarded damages for the physical inconvenience caused by having to live in the house while the builders were doing repairs as it was a foreseeable consequence of the breach. It is the physical inconvenience rather than mental upset that gives the right of action. However, damages for the mental element of discomfort were recoverable.

---

[45] See Chap. 24.
[46] [1975] 1 W.L.R. 1468.
[47] [1990] 1 W.L.R. 277.
[48] [2000] 4 All E.R. 97.
[49] See Chaps 10 and 24.
[50] [1976] Q.B. 446.
[51] [1982] 3 All E.R. 705.

In *Bailey v. Bullock*[52] the plaintiff recovered damages against his solicitor for failure to act to recover possession of a house which had been leased to a third party. As a result of the delay, the plaintiff was required to live in a small house with his parents-in-law. Damages for discomfort and inconvenience were awarded. Barry J. stated that there was "a very real difference between mere annoyance and injury to feelings on the one hand, and physical inconvenience on the other".[53]

Inconvenience suggests physical discomfort in addition to emotional distress. The Court in *Bailey* applied an earlier case, *Hobbs v. London and S.W. Railway Co.*,[54] which was based on breach of contract where damages were awarded for "serious physical inconvenience and discomfort". The categories of recoverable loss for mental distress were considered in *Farley v. Skinner*,[55] in which the claimant brought an action against a chartered surveyor who had failed to advise him that a house he intended to purchase in East Sussex was affected by aircraft noise at nearby Gatwick Airport. The Court of Appeal held that the contract was neither one to provide pleasure nor peace of mind, nor was the injury within the category of physical discomfort. The House of Lords reversed this holding stating that if it was a major object of the contract to provide pleasure, relaxation or peace of mind, damages for such losses were recoverable.[55a] The whole contract need not be for that purpose. The noise of aircraft landing and taking off was a "confounded nuisance", which might affect the purchasers' enjoyment of the property and be the "fuel for irritation and annoyance", but that alone did not give rise to a claim in damages for breach of contract.

(4) Loss of amenity: "The consumer surplus"

The idea of subjective losses being recoverable in contract for disappointed expectations now includes the notion of the "consumer surplus".[56] This takes account of: (a) the plaintiff's subjective valuation of the expected contractual performance, (b) more than the objective difference in value between what was promised and what was delivered or done and (c) an amount to compensate for the plaintiff's subjective requirements or personal preferences. In *Ruxley Electronics and Construction Ltd v. Forsyth*[57] the plaintiff obtained £2,800 for his own "subjective" losses associated with the defective swimming pool. This was a non-pecuniary loss for loss of enjoyment rather than the economic difference in value of what he received.

25.19

The consumer surplus was discussed in *Ruxley* by the House of Lords.[58] The plaintiff's special personal preferences or "predilections" may be relevant but are not a special category of damages in contract law. Lord Mustill[59] expressed surprise at the size of Forsyth's damages for "the loss of the provision of pleasurable amenity". Lord Mustill would have preferred to base the extra award on the loss of disappointed expectations. He based this on the Court's general power to award such a sum as a middle way between difference in value

---

[52] [1950] 2 All E.R. 1167.
[53] At p. 1170.
[54] (1875) LR 10 Q.B. 111.
[55] (2000) 73 Con. L.R. 70.
[55a] *The Times*, October 15, 2001.
[56] See Harris, Ogus and Phillips (1978) 95 L.Q.R. 581.
[57] [1996] 1 A.C. 344.
[58] See Lord Lloyd at p. 370.
[59] At p. 374.

and cost of cure.[60] *Ruxley* has been approved by the House of Lords in *Farley v. Skinner* (above). The courts are moving towards the recognition of a promisee's "performance interest" which would provide a principled ground for awarded damages for "consumer surplus" as in the *Ruxley* case.[61]

(5) Damages for injury to commercial reputation

25.20   This is an interesting new development in contractual damages. The House of Lords in *Malik v. Bank of Credit and Commerce International*[62] awarded damages for breach of an implied term of trust and confidence leading to a loss of employees' commercial reputation in the manner in which the Bank conducted its operations.[63] The breach of contract occurred during the performance of the contract, rather than in the termination of the employment as in *Addis*, which was distinguished. Strictly the losses were financial, for loss of reputation rather than mental distress. The stigma of association with a corrupt and dishonest business had handicapped them in obtaining other employment after they had been made redundant.

The House of Lords held that there was a mutual obligation on the parties to a contract of employment of trust and confidence between employer and employee. This is a good example of a relationship influencing the development of contract law.[64] In the relationship between the parties, the employer owed an implied obligation not to carry on a corrupt and dishonest business. If it was reasonably foreseeable that in doing so employees would suffer a handicap in their future employment prospects, then damages would be recoverable for the financial losses sustained. It made no difference that the employees had not heard of the conduct until after leaving their employment.

Lord Steyn pointed out two important qualifications on the right to recover damages in these circumstances. First, the implied obligation only applies where there is "no reasonable and proper cause" for the employers conduct, and even then only if the conduct is intended "to destroy or seriously damage the relationship of trust and confidence". Furthermore, "the limiting principles of causation, remoteness and mitigation present formidable practical obstacles to such claims succeeding".[65]

25.21   The existence of damages for stigma compensation has been recognised in later litigation.[66] The employees in *Bank of Credit* felt unable to disclose the criminal activities of their employers because of fear of dismissal. Their right to reveal wrongdoing is now recognised by the Public Interest Disclosure Act 1998.[67] There is now less justification of silence condoning malpractices in the workplace. The obligation of trust and confidence in employment contracts may also grow as the implications of the Human Rights Act 1998 begin to develop new rights in

---

[60] See Chap. 24.
[61] See comments by the House of Lords in *Panatown Ltd. v. Alfred McAlpine* [2000] 4 All E.R. 97, and also see Poole, "Damages for Breach of Contract – Compensation and Personal Preferences" 1996 M.L.R. 272.
[62] [1998] A.C. 20. This case is also known as *Mahmud v. BCCI.*
[63] See Enonchong, "Contract Damages for Injury to Reputation" [1996] M.L.R. 592 and Hedley [1997] C.L.J. 485. Reputation is not the same as mental distress from a wrongful dismissal. *Addis* was not overruled in its wider interpretation.
[64] See Chap. 1.
[65] At p. 53.
[66] *Bank of Credit and Commerce (in liq.) v. Ali* [2001] 2 W.L.R. 735.
[67] Enacted into the Employment Rights Act 1996 as amended s. 43A–L.

employment law. Indeed it has been suggested that the implied duty of trust and confidence recognised in *Malik* could lead to a general incorporation of European Convention rights into contracts of employment.[68]

CAUSATION

The plaintiff must prove on the balance of probabilities that the breach of contract **25.22** caused the loss in question. Causation in law is capable of several different meanings. In contract law, the rule is that the defendant's breach need not be the sole cause, but it must be an effective cause of the plaintiff's loss. If the cause of the loss is due to the intervening act of the plaintiff themself, they cannot recover under that heading.[69] In *Galoo Ltd v. Bright Grahame Murray*,[70] a case involving a negligence action, the Court of Appeal held that a breach of contract would result in damages only if it were "the dominant or effective cause of the plaintiffs loss" and not if it had merely given the opportunity for the loss to be sustained. In both contract and tort, where there was a breach of duty the question of whether the breach was (a) a cause or (b) merely the occasion of it was to be answered by courts applying common sense to the facts of each case.

The Court of Appeal referred to *Quinn v. Burch Bros (Builders) Ltd*[71] where the plaintiff was an independent subcontractor carrying out plastering and similar work. In breach of their contractual undertaking to supply equipment "reasonably necessary" for the work, the defendant failed to supply a step ladder. The plaintiff found a folded trestle, stood on it to do the work, slipped and broke his hand. The Court of Appeal held the cause of the plaintiff's injury was his own choice to use unsuitable equipment. The defendant's failure, *i.e.* breach of duty, was only the occasion for the accident, not its legal cause.

The test of causation is the effective sequence of events. In *Monarch Steamship Co. Ltd* **25.23** *v. Karlshamns Oljefabriker*[72] Lord Wright stated that:

> "Causation is a mental concept, generally based on inference or induction from uniformity of sequence as between two events that there is a central connection between them. This is the customary result of an education which begins with earliest experience: the burnt child dreads the fire . . . The common law is not concerned with philosophical speculation, but is only concerned with ordinary everyday life and thought and expressions."

Lord Porter[73] treated the test of causation in contract law as being whether some event was the "effective cause". An unlikely event would break the causal connection. However, if the intervening event is in fact reasonably foreseeable then this will not excuse the defendant for their breach of contract.

---

[68] Hepple, "Human Rights and Employment Law" in *Amicus Curiae* (1998), referred to in Palmer, "Human Rights: Implications for Labour Law" [2000] 59 C.L.J. 168.
[69] *Beoco v. Alfa Laval Co. Ltd* [1995] Q.B. 137.
[70] [1994] 1 W.L.R. 1360.
[71] [1965] 2 Q.B. 370.
[72] [1949] A.C. 196 (at p. 228).
[73] At p. 212.

MITIGATION OF LOSS

25.24   A plaintiff cannot recover losses which could have been avoided. He or she has to take reasonable steps (if these become available) to minimise the loss and also avoid unreasonable steps which would increase their damages. So when a football manager is dismissed by his Chairman and is then offered a lucrative contract with a football club elsewhere, he is expected to take it rather than play golf and wait for his expensive three year "roll-over" contract to accumulate more and more damages.[74] Nevertheless, in cases of wrongful dismissal the plaintiff is not compelled to take employment of a lower status.[75] The requirement of mitigation only arises when there has been breach of contract. Until the contract has been breached,, the rule does not apply. In the case of a non-accepted anticipatory breach (*i.e.* the contract has been affirmed until the date of performance) the duty to mitigate does not apply.[76]

In *Brace v. Calder*[77] the plaintiff received only nominal damages. He had been dismissed from his employment as manager of a business carried on by four partners. Two of the partners retired and the other two offered him his job back. The plaintiff refused to take up his offer, being resentful about his previous dismissal. The Court of Appeal held that he had failed to mitigate his loss by taking what would have been a reasonable opportunity to continue his employment. The onus is on the defendant to prove that the plaintiff ought to have mitigated the loss. If the steps taken succeed in avoiding the loss, then this is not recoverable even if more steps might have been required. Loss which is unsuccessfully avoided cannot be recovered. The plaintiff is only required to act reasonably and to take reasonable steps.[78] If the plaintiff takes what are regarded as reasonable steps and suffers further loss, or a loss which would not have occurred otherwise, as a result of attempting to mitigate, such loss is also recoverable.[79]

25.25   A classic example of the mitigation rule is to be found in *Payzu Ltd v. Saunders*[80] in relation to a contract for the purchase of a quantity of crêpe de chine silk from the defendant. Delivery was required over nine months, payment for each instalment to be made within one month of delivery less 22 per cent discount. The plaintiffs failed to pay for the first instalment and the defendants, believing that this meant they did not have the means to pay (which was wrong), refused to deliver any more silk, unless they received cash on delivery. The plaintiffs refused to accept this suggestion. The market price had meanwhile risen. The plaintiffs brought action against the defendants for non delivery claiming the difference between the contract and (by now greater) market price.

McCardie J. held the defendants were wrong to refuse delivery as the plaintiffs failure to pay did not amount to an intention to repudiate the whole contract. The plaintiffs should have mitigated their loss by accepting the defendant's offer. The Court awarded

---

[74] "Roll-over" contracts are a type of service agreement for highly paid executives which retain an unexpired period of years (usually one to three) at any point in time. The recipient is therefore guaranteed the full unexpired period of salary if he is dismissed by way of compensation.
[75] *Yetton v. Eastwoods Froy Ltd* [1967] 1 W.L.R. 104.
[76] *White and Carter (Councils) Ltd v. McGregor* [1962] A.C. 413. (See Chap. 23.)
[77] [1895] 2 Q.B. 253.
[78] *Banco de Portugal v. Waterlow* and *Payzu v. Saunders* [1932] A.C. 452.
[79] *Melachrino v. Nicholl and Knight* [1920] 1 K.B. 692.
[80] [1919] 2 K.B. 581.

damages based on what the plaintiffs would have lost had they attempted to mitigate. The Court of Appeal upheld the court at first instance. The question of what steps a plaintiff should take to mitigate the loss were a question of fact and not of law.

Although it is conventionally described as a duty to mitigate, there is in law no such **25.26** duty. The plaintiff can do as he or she wishes but they will be unable to recover under a particular head of damages if they have not acted reasonably. Reasonableness is a question of fact. In *Sotiros Shipping Inc. v. Shmeiet Solholt, "The Solholt"*[81] Sir John Donaldson M.R. stated that:

> "A plaintiff is under no duty to mitigate his loss, despite the habitual use by the lawyers of the phrase 'duty to mitigate'. He is completely free to act as he judges to be in his best interests. On the other hand, a defendant is not liable for all loss suffered by the plaintiff in consequence of his so acting. A defendant is only liable for such part of the plaintiff's loss as is properly to be regarded as caused by the defendants' breach of duty."[82]

The Court approved Viscount Haldane L.C. in *British Westinghouse Electric and Manufacturing Co. Ltd v. Underground Electric Railways Co. of London Ltd*,[83] where it was stated that failure to mitigate "debars [a party] from claiming any part of the damage which is due to his neglect to take such steps". In *British Westinghouse* turbines which were less efficient than that provided by the contract were replaced by turbines which were more effective and this resulted in a net saving over the period. The damages awarded to the plaintiffs were reduced by the savings which had resulted.

CONTRIBUTORY NEGLIGENCE BY THE PLAINTIFF

Contributory negligence applies in the tort of negligence to diminish the defendant's lia- **25.27** bility under the Law Reform (Contributory Negligence) Act 1945. The 1945 Act apportions the loss between the parties and reduces the damages in percentage terms to the extent that the plaintiff was also negligent. The 1945 Act is based on fault, which is defined as "negligence, breach of statutory duty or other act or omission which gives rise to liability in tort".[84] If an action is purely in contract, contributory negligence does not apply.[85] If, however, there is concurrent liability in contract and tort, so that the breach of contract is also a breach of duty of care in negligence, then the damages may be reduced for contributory negligence.[86]

The overlapping of a contractual implied term and a duty of care in negligence **25.28** allows the power of apportionment made under the 1945 Act to apply. In *UCB Bank v. Hepherd Winstanley and Pugh*,[87] a case involving the liability of a firm of solicitors,

---

[81] [1983] 1 Lloyds' Rep. 605.
[82] At p. 608.
[83] [1912] A.C. 673 (at p. 689).
[84] S. 1(1).
[85] *Barclays Bank plc v. Fairclough Building Ltd* [1995] 1 All E.R. 289.
[86] *Forsikingsaktieselskapet Vesta v. Butcher* [1988] 2 All E.R. 43.
[87] *The Times*, August 25, 1999.

the Court of Appeal allowed contributory negligence to be taken into account where liability in contract overlapped with liability in tort.[88] In *Alliance and Leicester Building Society v. Edgestop*,[89] it was held that contributory negligence was not available in an action for deceit.[90] However, in *Gran Gelato Ltd v. Richcliff Group Ltd*[91] it was held that it was available as a defence to a claim under the Misrepresentation Act, s. 2(1). Sir Donald Nicholls V.C. in the Chancery Division took the view that "liability under the 1967 Act is essentially founded on negligence . . . This being so it would be very odd if the defence of contributory negligence were not available to a claim under the Act".[92] Since liability under s. 2(1) is now based on fraud, this latter view may no longer hold good. In 1993 the Law Commission Report "Contributory Negligence as a Defence in Contract"[93] recommended that contributory negligence in contract should apply to reduce damages if the plaintiff was themself in breach of a contractual duty to take reasonable care or exercise reasonable skill, but not to contractual actions generally if there was no duty in tort. There has been no legislation to implement this proposal.

LIQUIDATED DAMAGES AND PENALTY CLAUSES

25.29   The parties are free to agree their own figure for damages in the event of breach. If the sum is a reasonable pre-estimate of loss for the breach or "liquidated" damages, it will be enforced by the court. However, if the sum is excessive, extortionate or otherwise unreasonable it will be regarded as a penalty or punishment for non performance of the contract and it will not be enforced by the courts. When a penalty has been struck out, the injured party is entitled to damages based on the ordinary principles of quantification. Paradoxically, if the sum is upheld as liquidated damages, this will be awarded even if the losses turn out to be far greater than they were bargained for at the outset.

The expression "penalty clause" is used commercially for agreed damages clauses in general, *i.e.* even those intended to be, and adjudged as, liquidated damages. They are particularly common in the construction industry to deal with late performance. If a sum of money contained in a contract is really a restriction on the damages payable for breach, then different rules apply. This will be treated as a limitation clause and the rules on exemption clauses will apply.[94]

An early example of a penalty clause is *Kemble v. Farren*[95] in which the defendant was engaged to appear at Covent Garden Theatre commencing in October 1828 for the sum of £3. 6s. 8d. (£3.30p) per night that he appeared, over four seasons. The contract contained a clause that either party in breach of any stipulation contained in the agreement should pay the other £1,000 by way of "liquidated and ascertained damages". The defendant refused to perform during the second season and the plaintiff who was the manager of Covent Garden Theatre brought action against him. It was held that the provision was

---

[88]   See also *Vesta v. Butcher* [1989] A.C. 852.
[89]   [1994] 2 All E.R. 38.
[90]   See also *Standard Chartered Bank v. Pakistan National Shipping Corp., The Times,* July 27, 2000.
[91]   [1992] 1 All E.R. 865.
[92]   At p. 875.
[93]   Law Com. (No. 279) 1993.
[94]   See Chaps 16 and 17.
[95]   (1829) 6 Bing 141; 130 E.R. 1234.

a penalty and unenforceable. Liquidated damages were not available if they covered various stipulations of various degrees of importance unless each were specified in the agreement. The plaintiff recovered £750 as his true loss.

The distinction between liquidated damages and penalties

Following earlier cases in the House of Lords, namely *Clydebank Engineering and* **25.30** *Shipping Co. Ltd v. Don Jose Ramos Yzquierdo y Castaneda*[96] and *Public Works Commissioners v. Hills*,[97] and the Privy Council in *Webster v. Bosanquet*,[98] the law was summarised by Lord Dunedin in *Dunlop Pneumatic Tyre Co. Ltd v. New Garage and Motor Co. Ltd*.[99] The test of liquidated damages was whether at the time the contract was made the sum agreed was a genuine pre-estimate of the loss which was likely to occur if the term was breached. The use of the words "penalty" or "liquidated damages" was not decisive and the court has to determine whether the payment stipulated was in truth a penalty or liquidated damages. The essence of a penalty was a payment of money to terrorise the other party into performing or as a punishment for failure to do so. The test for liquidated damages was whether it was a "genuine covenanted pre-estimate of damage".[1]

Whether a sum stipulated is a penalty or liquidated damages is a question of construction to be decided on the terms and circumstances of each case viewed at the time of making the contract, not at the time of breach.[2] Lord Dunedin suggested four additional tests, deriving from earlier case law, to assist in the construction of the clause.[2a] A clause will be held to be a penalty if:

    (a)   the sum "is extravagant and unconscionable . . . in comparison with the greatest loss that could conceivably be proved to have followed from the breach";

    (b)   "the breach consists only in not paying a sum of money, and the sum stipulated is a sum greater than the sum which ought to have been paid";

    (c)   presumably when "a single lump sum is made payable by way of compensation on the occurrence of one or more or all of several events, some of which may occasion serious and others but trifling damage".[3]

On the other hand, "it is no obstacle to a sum being a genuine pre-estimate of damage that the consequences of the breach are such as to make a precise pre-estimation almost an impossibility". According to Lord Dunedin, "on the contrary, that is just the situation when it is probable that pre-estimated damage was the true bargain between the parties".[4]

---

[96] [1905] A.C. 6.
[97] [1906] A.C. 368.
[98] [1912] A.C. 394.
[99] [1915] A.C. 79 (at pp. 86–87).
[1] See *Clydebank Engineering and Shipbuilding Co. Ltd v. Don José Ramos* [1905] A.C. 6.
[2] See *Public Works Commissioners v. Hills* [1906] A.C. 368.
[2a] At p. 101.
[3] See Lord Watson in *Lord Elphinstone v. Monkland Iron and Coal Co.* (1886) 11 App. Cas. 332.
[4] Quoting Lord Mersey in *Webster v. Bosanquet* [1912] A.C. (at p. 298).

25.31 The rules set out are still applied today. In *Duffen v. FRA BO SpA*[5] a commercial agency agreement was held to contain a clause which was a penalty. Otton L.J. applied the rules in *Dunlop* in holding that the sum in question was not graduated with the unexpired duration of what was left of the contract. It could not therefore be a genuine attempt to estimate losses in advance of breach of an obligation. Even if termination occurred in the final month of the contract, the sum was payable. This would result in a "substantial windfall" which would be "extravagant and unconscionable". The sum payable did not bear a reasonable relationship to the loss suffered, even if the agreement was terminated for trivial reasons. The Court of Appeal held the clause unenforceable. However, since this was a contract for a commercial agency and the agent could not rely on the clause, he could claim compensation by an alternative route through the Commercial Agents (Council Directive) Regulations 1993.[6]

25.32 There have been all manner of cases over the years on provisions in hire purchase or consumer credit contracts which proved to contain penalties. For instance, in *Ford Motor Company v. Armstrong*[7] the Court of Appeal would not enforce a clause requiring a dealer to pay £250 "agreed damages" for every breach of an agreement with a manufacturer, some of which could only ever cause trivial loss. Clear words of expression are required in relation to liquidated damages clauses. In *Bem Dis A Turk Ticaret v. International Agri Trade "The Selda"*,[8] Clarke J. stated that "whether parties to a contract are free to agree that an innocent party should not be entitled to recover damages to which he would otherwise be entitled at common law, they must do so in clear terms". The Unfair Terms in Consumer Contracts Regulations 1999 list as potentially unfair clauses which require a consumer to pay a disproportionately large sum by way of compensation if they breach their obligation.[9] This follows the common law rule, and the clause would be unenforceable.[10] The regulations apply only to consumer contracts.

The effect of being a penalty or liquidated damages

25.33 If a clause is liquidated damages, the plaintiff is entitled to recover the sum without proof of substantial loss irrespective of the actual loss. It will be enforced even if the actual loss turns out to be for a greater or lesser amount than the sum agreed. In *Cellulose Acetate Silk Co. Ltd v. Widnes Foundry (1925) Ltd*[11] a clause provided a £20 per week sum for late delivery after 18 weeks. The actual losses eventually amounted to over £5,000. The House of Lords held the sum was not a penalty, so the plaintiff could only recover the loss as calculated by the clause, which was £600. Equally, if the clause is deemed to be a penalty, it will be unenforceable.[12] The court will then apply the normal rules for quantifying damages. If the loss eventually turns out to be larger even than the penalty, the plaintiff will recover this greater sum.[13]

---

[5] *The Times*, June 15, 1998.
[6] Reg. 17(6)(S.I. 1993/3053). This was introduced as a result of a European Union Directive (discussed Chap. 24).
[7] (1915) 31 T.L.R. 267.
[8] [1998] 1 Lloyd's Rep. 416 (at p. 419).
[9] Schedule 1 "Grey list" (e).
[10] See Chap. 15.
[11] [1933] A.C. 20.
[12] *Jobson v. Johnson* [1989] 1 W.L.R. 1026.
[13] *Wall v. Rederi A Bet Luggude* [1915] 3 K.B. 66.

Liquidated or agreed damages clauses remain widespread and popular as a precaution against breach of contract in many types of business. They have economic advantages for the contracting parties in reducing transaction costs and avoiding later difficulties about qualifying losses. The parties can know their future liabilities and accordingly insure.[14]

When the penalty rules do not apply

The rules against penalties do not apply to a number of common contractual situations, **25.34** in particular to events other than breach. The sum payable must be for a breach of contract and not some other occurrence.[15] This can arise in hire purchase agreements, when the finance company claims the right to retake possession of the goods and forfeit any instalments paid. The hire purchase contract might claim for the loss of profit on the transaction because of wear and tear or depreciation of the goods hired. These provisions were often not a true measure of loss and therefore could be regarded as penalties.[16]

The requirement of there being a breach of contract is illustrated by *Alder v. Moore*,[17] in which the defendant was a footballer who received payment from an insurance company for an injury which the insurers believed had resulted in a disability which would be permanent. He agreed he would not play football as a professional footballer again, and that if he did so he would repay the sum involved. The defendant did in fact resume his career again (for Cambridge United) and the plaintiffs took legal action. The Court of Appeal held that the sum in question was for an event which was not a breach of contract, so the rules on penalties did not apply. Playing football again was not a breach of contract as the agreement did not preclude him from doing so, so the sum paid by the insurers had to be returned.

The law on penalties does not apply to provisions for the withholding of payments, or **25.35** accelerated payments. These are commonplace in the building industry. There is a right of "set off" at common law so that if portions of the work are not done satisfactorily, sums owed on completion do not have to be paid. Normally withheld or accelerated payments fall outside the penalty rule. However, the rules on penalties can apply when a party is allowed too extensive a power to withhold payment under the contract.

In *Gilbert-Ash v. Modern Engineering*[18] a contractor could withhold or suspend payments "if the subcontractor fails to comply with any of the conditions in this subcontract". This was held to be a penalty clause. Lord Reid[19] stated that: "Read literally this provision would entitle the contractor to withhold sums far in excess of any fair estimate of the value of his claims. That would simply be to impose a penalty for refusing to admit his claims . . . So as it stands this provision is unenforceable."

---

[14] See *Scott and Goetz* (1977) 77 Col L.R. 554.
[15] *Exports Credits Guarantee Department v. Universal Oil Products Co.* [1983] 1 W.L.R. 399.
[16] *Bridge v. Campbell Discount Co. Ltd* [1963] 1 QB 887 and *Financings Ltd v. Baldock* [1963] 2 Q.B. 104. The situation is now subject to the Consumer Credit Act 1974 ss 99, 100 with regard to agreements for less than £15,000.
[17] [1961] 2 Q.B. 57.
[18] [1974] A.C. 689.
[19] At p. 698.

PUTTING DAMAGES INTO PRACTICE: THE ANALYSIS OF A CLAIM

25.36   The following item appeared in the *Birmingham Evening Mail* on February 1, 1999:

> "Birmingham-based band Ocean Colour Scene have launched a £200,000 legal action against the organisers of a music festival. The group was booked to headline last summer's Phoenix Festival at Long Marston Airfield, near Stratford-upon-Avon. But just three weeks before the event, the promoters, MFO Events, pulled the plug on the festival because of poor ticket sales. A spokesman for Ocean Colour Scene said: 'We intend to sue for breach of contract.' London-based MFO Events, a subsidiary of the country's biggest festival organiser, Mean Fiddler, had hoped to sell 45,000 tickets for the four-day extravaganza last July. It was scrapped when fewer than 20,000 fans bought the £75 passes. Manager Chris Cradock said: 'Our whole summer touring schedule was based around the Phoenix date so when it was cancelled we were left in limbo yet the promoters didn't offer us a penny in compensation.' Neither Mean Fiddler nor MFO Events would comment on the row."

The question to ask is how the figure of £200,000 was calculated. How would one frame a claim for damages in these circumstances, or defend the claim under established principles? The starting point is that the claim for £200,000 is the band's appearance fee either as a fixed sum or perhaps as a percentage of the ticket sales.[20] The fee is not the measure of damages, rather it is only the starting point for the calculation of losses due to the promoter's cancellation of the festival. We should begin with two columns, listing the expectation losses (A) and, as an alternative (but not in addition to), the reliance losses or wasted expenditure (B). The expectation or profits lost could include the profits from merchandising, t-shirts, programmes and so on, if the claimants were receiving a share of the profits and also sales of compact disks and tapes at the event. The band might also claim any fees from television royalties if the festival was being recorded, and consequential sales of compact disks to the public who might have viewed the event on television, potentially including an overseas market. Of course if the merchandising had been franchised out then obviously the band cannot claim any loss of profit.

25.37   Turning to "wasted expenditure" this could include transportation and staging costs for the event the band has already incurred or for which they are under a legal obligation to pay. The costs of special rehearsals, equipment or effects might be claimed, even a fee to a famous songwriter to write a song for the event. All of these items could go into column B.

The expectation profits are likely to exceed the expenses in B. If the expenditure of the claimants would not have been recouped (they might, for instance, have been performing at a reduced fee for charity), then they had made a classic "bad bargain" and their damages would be reduced to a nominal figure. From the defendant promoter's side, he would argue that potential sales of merchandising at the festival were "too speculative" and the sales of tapes and compact discs at High Street shops as a result of television broadcast, too remote. The former is unlikely to succeed as an estimate of sales could surely be made using marketing knowledge. The remoteness test might assist the

---

[20] Depending upon whose side one was on, the agreement could specify "actual" or "projected" sales. The claimants would be wise to ask for the latter. The promoter then bears the risk of failure.

defendant as long term compact disk sales were not likely to be in the contemplation of the parties at the time of contract. Damages for loss of commercial reputation might apply in this situation (although *Malik* is strictly limited to employees rather than contracts for services). This would be likely to be a key concern of the performers who would be anxious to avoid the bad publicity.

The disappointed expectations of those fans who had purchased tickets could be   **25.38** added to their refunded price as the festival was certainly intended to be a contract for entertainment. Such damages tend to be based on the disappointing performance itself rather than at the fact of termination of the event and, therefore, loss of pleasure. It is unlikely that cancelled travel arrangements to and from the festival would be recoverable. This would be a matter for private travel insurance if individuals had chosen to arrange their own coverage.

The promoter might claim that the claimants' lack of attraction to the public caused the poor sales and that this amounted to contributory negligence. However, there is no concurrent liability in contract and tort here, so the 1945 Act does not apply. The promoter could argue more strongly that the concert only took place at the band's own risk. No guarantee of actually holding the event had been given until ticket sales were confirmed. Until that date, the agreement between the parties was provisional or subject to a condition precedent.[21] Finally, after the cancellation the band is expected to take reasonable steps to find other events and concerts. Failure to mitigate their loss could reduce the damages awarded. The fact that they might, at the time of signing the agreement, have gone elsewhere and made a greater profit doing other events is irrelevant. Freedom of contract applies to rule out such an argument. The contract made with the defendants was their own free choice. They are only entitled to losses caused as a result of breach by their contracting opposite party.

---

[21] See Chaps 5 and 13.

Chapter 26

EQUITABLE REMEDIES AND RESTITUTION IN THE FIELD OF CONTRACT LAW

SELF HELP REMEDIES

It is wrong to assume that parties must always have recourse to lawyers or courts for a **26.1** remedy in contract law. Non-judicial remedies are common throughout contracts. We have encountered self help in the widespread use of rescission[1] for misrepresentation, undue influence, the right to withhold performance in the event of a repudiatory breach of contract, and in liquidated damages. Self help remedies enable the parties to act on their own without requiring the prior approval of a court of law. This avoids the cost and inconvenience of commencing legal action to establish a claim. As such, nonjudicial remedies are usually quicker and more efficient for the parties, though their apparent ease and flexibility contain hidden dangers for non-lawyers, such as the possibility of acting rashly or without legal foundation. This leaves one party open to a counterclaim by the other party for breach of contract if the remedy is wrongly used.[2] Generally speaking, in commercial contracts lawyers are necessary to pursue remedies or defend actions for anything other than simple small claims.

EQUITABLE REMEDIES IN THE CONTEXT OF CONTRACT LAW

The division between common law and equity still applies in the field of remedies. The **26.2** existence of two different systems, damages at common law and non-monetary remedies in the Court of Chancery, goes back many centuries. The common law remedy of a claim for damages remains the primary remedy for enforcing a contractual right. Equitable remedies are largely to be found in the field of property law, where their importance is reflected in the textbooks.[3] Specific performance remains an important remedy in land law.

The division between the two systems is by no means watertight. For instance, damages can be awarded as an equitable remedy. This blurs the distinction between common law and equity. The principles governing such damages are considered later in

---

[1] See O'Sullivan, "Rescission as a Self-Help Remedy" (2000) 59 C.L.J. 509.
[2] See Chap. 23.
[3] See Hanbury and Martin, "Modern Equity" (1997, 15th ed., Sweet and Maxwell), pp. 693–815.

this chapter.[4] Equitable remedies are discretionary. In equity the court will look at a range of factors, including whether it is just to do so before ordering or denying a remedy. The common law remedy of damages for breach of contract, being actionable *per se*, is mandatory in it's application. Even if no loss is suffered, nominal damages will be awarded as a mark of wrongdoing.

(1) Specific performance

26.3   Specific performance is the main equitable remedy in contract law. This allows a court to order a party to perform a contract in accordance with its terms. It is most commonly found in land law to enforce contracts for the sale of property, less often found elsewhere, and generally speaking, not at all in contracts for personal services. Specific performance can also be used selectively in contractual relations, for instance the refusal of specific performance is an equitable remedy for dealing with mistake.[5] Specific performance is often used in circumstances where an award of damages would be inadequate to supplement the common law. Being an equitable remedy, an order of specific performance is at the court's discretion. It is not possible for the parties either to expressly state that they will agree to specific performance or to exclude it altogether. This would be to fetter the court's discretion to do justice.[6]

It is easier to state the rules against the awarding of specific performance than to identify the circumstances in which it will be granted. The defendant must have acted equitably, so it will not be available if they have not done so. It is only ordered when it will be fair to do so, must take account of the conduct of the parties and will not be ordered if performance is impossible. In *Ryan v. Mutual Tontine Westminster Chambers Association* it was held that specific performance would not be awarded if it would require constant supervision by the court.[7] This was rejected as a general principle by the House of Lords in *Shiloh Spinners Ltd v. Harding*,[8] where the view was expressed by Lord Wilberforce that: "The Court's role was to satisfy itself, *ex post facto*, that the covenanted work has been done, and it has ample machinery, through certificates, or by enquiry, to do precisely this."[9] We return to this issue again shortly in the *Argyll Stores* case.

26.4   Specific performance is not normally awarded in contracts for personal services, although this is qualified by exceptions. In *Posner v. Scott-Lewis*[10] a covenant to employ a resident porter was specifically enforced. Specific performance will not be granted if the contract is too uncertain to be enforced.[11] Two further reasons against ordering specific performance are that: (a) damages would be an inadequate remedy or (b) it would cause severe hardship to the defendant. In *Patel v. Ali*[12] the defendant sold her house then did nothing to allow the plaintiff possession. Four years elapsed and the plaintiff sought specific performance. The court refused to order this despite the delay because of the defendant's severe difficulties including illness, her husband's bankruptcy and her personal need

---

[4] See paras 26.11–26.17.
[5] See Chap. 21.
[6] *Quadrant Visual Communications v. Hutchison Telephone UK Ltd* [1993] B.C.L.C. 442.
[7] [1893] 1 Ch. 116.
[8] [1973] A.C. 691.
[9] At p. 724.
[10] [1987] Ch. 25.
[11] See *Tito v. Waddell (No. 2)* [1977] Ch. 106.
[12] [1984] Ch. 283.

for the practical support of her neighbours. On the other hand, specific performance may be granted if there is no other remedy available or it is the best alternative remedy.[13] In the case of a unique item, such as a work of art or antique, which would be impossible to duplicate, the court may order specific performance as the only way of fulfilling the desired expectation in the item. In *Nutbrown v. Thornton*[14] Eldon C.J. ordered the transfer of the stock of a farm seized by a landlord on the basis that "this contract is very singular" and "very peculiar in its circumstances". The remedy of specific performance is very flexible. It should be sufficiently elastic in its application to fit a range of circumstances depending on the justice of the case. In the words of Megarry V.C. in *Tito v. Waddell (No. 2)*,[15] "the Court will decree specific performance only if this will . . . do more perfect and complete justice than an award of damages". This, after all, was its original equitable ideal. Equity is, nevertheless, constrained by precedent.

The difficulty in supervising an order for specific performance in a modern commercial setting arose in *Co-operative Insurance Society Ltd v. Argyll Stores Holdings Ltd*.[16] The defendants, Argyll Stores, trading as Safeways, had covenanted to keep a store in the Hillsborough shopping centre in Sheffield open for a period of 17 years. The reason behind such lengthy agreements being the desire of landlords of shopping centres to "anchor" certain key stores to their retail premises. "Keep open" covenants were introduced to avoid premature closure by these "anchor tenants", in this case the defendants. In spite of their undertaking, Argyll Stores carried out a business review and decided to "up anchor" and leave. The issue was whether they could be compelled to remain by an order of specific performance, or whether the landlords were only entitled to damages and an attempt to re-let.   **26.5**

The House of Lords refused to compel the defendants to carry on a business against their will. The Law Lords drew a distinction between specific performance as a "one-off" to obtain a particular outcome, as in selling a house, and a complex and continuing commercial relationship over many years. The difficulties of supervising such an order increased as the years went by. The two main reasons for declining to make the order sought were: (a) the long tradition in this area, or "settled practice", of not doing so and (b) the difficulty of drawing the order with sufficient precision to avoid wasteful litigation regarding compliance. The defendant might suffer far greater losses having to comply with the order than the plaintiff from the contract being broken. Lord Hoffman noted that specific performance had traditionally been regarded in English law as an exceptional remedy. The power to decree specific performance was available to do justice when the common law remedy was inadequate. The most frequent reason given in the case law for declining to order someone to carry on a business was that it would require constant supervision by the court. This proved to be decisive in *Argyll Stores*. Lord Hoffman quoted Dixon J. in the Australian case of *Williamson (J.C.) Ltd v. Luke and Mulholland*: "Specific performance is inapplicable when the continuous supervision of the court is necessary in order to ensure the fulfilment of the contract."[17]

The outcome was different in a decision of the Scottish courts three years later. In   **26.6**

[13] As in *Beswick v. Beswick* [1968] A.C. 58. (See Chap. 10.)
[14] (1804) 10 Ves. Jun 160; 32 E.R. 805.
[15] (1977) Ch. 106 (at p. 322).
[16] [1997] 2 W.L.R. 898. (See Jones (1997) 56 C.L.J. 488.)
[17] (1931) 45 C.L.R. 282 (at pp. 297–298).

Highland and Universal Properties Ltd v. Safeway Properties Ltd,[18] the Inner House of the Court of Session adopted a different approach to long leases of commercial stores. The obligation in a lease to keep the store open throughout normal business hours could be enforced by a decree of specific implement, the Scots law equivalent of specific performance. However, the courts still had a discretion to deny the remedy in exceptional circumstances. The Scottish experience had been that defendants had not had the difficulties in carrying out specific implement, neither had it led to much expensive litigation, nor to the difficulties envisaged by the House of Lords in supervising the order and in taking up a lot of court time. The key question was whether the terms of the decree of specific implement could be made sufficiently precise, and if so, whether the breach of the contractual obligation had been deliberate and, therefore, justified such an order. For these reasons the Court of session in Edinburgh upheld a decision ordering Safeways to keep open their retail store.

(2) Injunctions

(a) The use of injunctions in contract law

26.7   There are three types of injunction, classified as either (a) prohibitory, (b) mandatory or (c) interim. The most common is the prohibitory injunction which orders the defendant to cease or desist from doing some action. It is also to be found in tort and family law. A mandatory injunction orders the defendant to do something or undo something he or she has agreed not to do. A third kind of injunction is a temporary holding measure. An interim (known until 1999 as an interlocutory) injunction is designed to prevent something occurring pending the outcome of litigation. In *American Cyanamid Co. v. Ethicon Ltd*[19] the House of Lords stated that the two main grounds for such an order were: (a) the balance of convenience to the parties and (b) if the plaintiff could show that there was a serious issue to be tried. The use of injunctions is creeping into contract law in the field of employment contracts but it's main role is in relation to preventing restraint of trade.[20]

(b) Specific performance and injunctions in employment contracts

26.8   The contract of employment is an area of law where equitable remedies such as specific performance and injunction are now increasingly used as a remedy. Until *Hill v. Parsons and Co. Ltd*[21] cast doubt on the matter, it was a firm rule that specific performance requiring an employer to continue to employ a person would not be ordered. Employment protection legislation takes a similar view. In cases of unfair dismissal, the employment tribunal may order reinstatement but if the employer refuses to do so, the tribunal will make an award of additional compensation rather than compel them to take back the employee.[22] In recent years there has been some liberalisation of the general rule against specific performance of employment contracts by the use of injunctions. In *Powell v. London Borough of Brent*[23] the Court of Appeal ordered an interlocutory injunction in favour of employees to prevent their dismissal because the employer should have had

---

[18] 2000 S.L.T. 414.
[19] [1975] A.C. 396.
[20] See Chap. 20.
[21] [1972] Ch. 305.
[22] Employment Rights Act 1996, s. 117(3).
[23] [1987] I.R.L.R. 466 (at p. 477).

sufficient confidence in the employee to have him back to work. Sufficiency of confidence was to be judged by reference to "the circumstances of the case, including the nature of the work, the people with whom the work must be done and the likely effect upon the employer and the employer's operations if the employer was required by the injunction to suffer the plaintiff to continue in the work".

Injunctions can sometimes be used to prevent "contract jumping", *i.e.* getting out of an unwanted relationship and into another contractual arrangement. The law goes back to *Lumley v. Wagner*[24] where the plaintiff was Benjamin Lumley, the owner of Her Majesty's Theatre in London, and the defendant was Johanna Wagner, a German singer, who agreed to sing at the plaintiff's theatre and for no other party in the meantime without his written authority. She was approached by the manager of the Covent Garden Opera House, Frederick Gye, to sing there and the plaintiff sought to prevent this by an injunction.[25] The Court ordered the injunction because the positive and negative undertakings in the contract could not be separated. They would not on principle order specific performance of the contract as a whole. The limitations placed on their judgment by the Court meant that an injunction would not be ordered in contracts for personal services if this would be tantamount to ordering specific performance. The Court would not use its power to compel the defendant to sing at the plaintiff's theatre, although in reality she was largely compelled to do so by the Court ordering her not to sing elsewhere.

The rule that an injunction can be awarded to prevent breach of a negative promise in   **26.9** a contract for personal services does create certain difficulties. An injunction will not be ordered if it is merely an indirect way of ordering specific performance by another means. Thus; if the court, in ordering an injunction, is in reality preventing the defendant from working at all, unless she continues to work for the plaintiff. In *Warner Brothers Pictures Inc. v. Nelson*[26] an injunction was granted which was preventing Miss Nelson, better known at the actress Bette Davis, from working for anyone other than Warner Brothers for the remainder of a three year contract. Branson J. did not consider this equivalent to ordering specific performance, as it was open to her to take up other employment doing other things. The courts are now reluctant to go this far.

The basis of the judgment in *Warner Brothers* was rejected by Stamp J. in *Page One Records Ltd v. Britton.*[27] The Court refused an injunction which would have prevented a pop group employing another agent. The effect of the injunction would be to have bound them to their existing agent. In *Warren v. Mendy*[28] the Court of Appeal followed the reasoning of *Page One Records*, rather than *Warner Brothers.* The plaintiff was a boxing manager, Frank Warren, who sought an interlocutory injunction in a tort action for inducing breach of contract. The defendant was another manager, Ambrose Mendy, in a dispute over the management of the boxer, Nigel Benn. The Court of Appeal refused to grant an interlocutory injunction as this would indirectly amount to ordering specific performance of the boxer's contract for three years. Although Nigel Benn could have

---

[24] (1852) 1 De G.M. & G. 604; 42 E.R. 687.
[25] The same facts led to the case of *Lumley v. Gye* (1853) 2 E and B 216 which became the main authority on the tort of inducing breach of contract. A statue of Frederick Gye still stands in the foyer of Covent Garden Opera House.
[26] [1937] 1 K.B. 209.
[27] [1967] 3 All E.R. 822.
[28] [1989] 3 All E.R. 103.

worked elsewhere and other than as a boxer, it was not realistic to expect him to do so. The courts are nowadays reluctant to grant injunctions in contracts for personal services unless the defendant has a reasonable prospect of earning his or her living by alternative means.[29]

26.10   An injunction to restrain an employee who has agreed to take up a new job for a rival until his or her contract of employment has expired, so called "garden leave", was discussed in *Provident Fund Group plc v. Hayward*.[30] The Court of Appeal repeated the principle that a court would not enforce a contract for personal services between employer and employee. Equally, it would not grant an injunction in very wide terms which prevented any employee from working for anyone else during the continuance of his or her service agreement if the effect of such an injunction would be to compel the employee to work for their present employer. An injunction in the period of notice was therefore available at the court's discretion. In *Provident Fund* it was not granted because the defendant did not have any relevant confidential information, nor was there any real prospect of serious or significant damage to the plaintiffs due to the defendant working for a rival.

The use of injunctions is greatly increased as a result of public authorities' power to regulate contracts and breaches of European consumer law. The Office of Fair Trading now has the power to issue injunctions against the continued use of unfair terms under the Unfair Terms in Consumer Contracts Regulations 1999. The Stop Now Orders (EC Directive) Regulations 2001 introduce a new regulatory system of injunctions for infringements of consumer law across the European Union.[31]

(3) Damages in equity

26.11   The Chancery Amendment Act 1858, s. 2 gave the Court of Chancery the power to award damages in lieu of specific performance. This remedy is still commonly known by it's historical name, that of Lord Cairns' Act, but is now contained in the Supreme Court Act 1981.[32] Section 50 of the Act provides that where the court entertains an application for an injunction or specific performance, it may award damages "in addition to, or in substitution for, an injunction or specific performance". Since the merger of common law and equity in the Judicature Act 1873, the Chancery Division could have awarded damages where a common law court would have been able to do so. Lord Cairns' Act took this a step further by allowing damages in equity where the remedy would *not* be available at common law. This could apply, for instance, in the case of a *quia timet* injunction to prevent a harm which not yet occurred, damages for future loss or where the right was entirely equitable. In *Marcic v. Thames Water Utilities Ltd*[32a] it was held that damages for a future infringement of a claimant's right did not contravene the Human Rights Act 1998.

The equitable remedy normally operates as an alternative to specific performance or an injunction. For instance, if the right to an injunction has been lost or an injunction would be oppressive.[33] However, the basis upon which damages are assessed under the

---

[29] For a discussion in relation to sports contracts, see McCutcheon, "Negative Enforcement of Employment Contracts in the Sports Industry" (1997) 17 Legal Studies 65.
[30] [1989] 3 All E.R. 298.
[31] Discussed Chap. 15.
[32] See Jolowicz, "Damages in Equity – a Study of Lord Cairns' Act" [1975] C.L.J. 224.
[32a] (2001) 151 N.L.J. 1180.
[33] *Wrotham Park Estate v. Parkside Homes* [1974] 1 W.L.R. 798.

Act has always been controversial. Sir Thomas Bingham stated in *Jaggard v. Sawyer* that "the authorities show that there were, not surprisingly differing approaches to the exercise of this new jurisdiction".[34] The traditional guidelines for awarding damages in lieu of an injunction were set out many years ago by Smith L.J. in *Shelfer v. City of London Electric Lighting Co.*[35] as being that:

    (a)   the injury to the plaintiff's legal rights was small;

    (b)   the injury was capable of being estimated in money;

    (c)   the injury could be adequately compensated by a small money payment; and

    (d)   it would be oppressive to the defendant to grant an injunction.

In *Leeds Industrial Cooperative Society Ltd v. Slack (No.1)*,[36] Viscount Finlay stated that:

> ". . . if damages are given in substitution for an injunction they must necessarily cover not only injury already sustained but also injury that would be inflicted in the future by the commission of the act threatened. If no injury has yet been sustained the damages will be solely in respect of the damage to be sustained in the future by injuries which the injunction, if granted, would have prevented."

There are three views as to the nature of damages under Lord Cairns' Act. First, that **26.12** they are based on similar principles to those awarded at common law. Secondly, that they are based upon a special equitable rule in relation to property rights, namely the price a property owner would pay for "relaxing", *i.e.* giving up, a covenant connected with his or her land. This is also known as "loss of opportunity to bargain" damages. Thirdly, they may be regarded as restitutionary in nature.[37] The leading statement of principle for many years was that of Lord Wilberforce in *Johnson v. Agnew*[38] who stated that on both the balance of authorities and on principle, damages under the Act should be assessed in the same way as common law damages. In both *Johnson v. Agnew* and an earlier case *Wroth v. Tyler*[39] there was a single, once and for all, breach of contract by the defendant. In two later cases, *Jaggard v. Sawyer*[40] and *Wrotham Park Estate Co. v. Parkside Homes Ltd*,[41] damages were awarded to compensate for future wrongs, a loss for which the common law of contract did not provide a remedy. This was "put in context" by Millett L.J. in *Jaggard*: "In my view Lord Wilberforce's statement that the measure of damages is the same whether damages are recoverable at common law or under the Act must be taken to be limited to the case where they are recoverable in respect of the same cause of action."[42]

---

[34] [1995] 1 W.L.R. 269 (at p. 277).
[35] [1895] 1 Ch. 287 (at p. 322–323).
[36] [1924] A.C. 851 (at p. 857).
[37] We discuss this principle later. See paras 26.35–26.41.
[38] [1980] A.C. 367 (at p. 400).
[39] [1974] Ch. 30.
[40] [1995] 1 W.L.R. 269.
[41] [1974] 1 W.L.R. 798.
[42] [1995] 1 W.L.R. 269 (at p. 281).

26.13   In *Wrotham Park* the defendants build houses in breach of a restrictive covenant in favour of adjacent property owned by the plaintiffs. Since the houses had already been built, the Court refused a mandatory injunction on the ground that this would be an "unpardonable waste of much needed houses". The question was how damages in lieu of an injunction were to be assessed. Brightman J. concluded that: "a just substitute for a mandatory injunction would be such a sum of money as might reasonably have been demanded by the plaintiffs . . . as a *quid pro quo* for relaxing the covenant".[43] In other words, the sum they would agree as compensation for giving up their proprietary right. The damages awarded were five percent of the reasonably anticipated profits of the first defendants. This amounted to a sum of £2,500 apportioned between the 14 owners of the houses. Such damages could either be regarded as restitutionary, *i.e.* to force the defendant to give up a profit, or compensatory. The sum awarded in *Wrotham Park* appeared to support both possibilities.

26.14   The Court of Appeal's later judgment in *Jaggard* discussed the nature of equitable damages. According to Sir Thomas Bingham, the 1858 Act allowed the Chancery Court to award damages instead of awarding an injunction to restrain unlawful future conduct. The latter must be taken to have been intended to compensate the plaintiff for future unlawful conduct. The parties were owners of houses on a small residential estate in Maiden Newton, Dorset. The defendants built a house on a plot of land adjoining their own. The only access to the new house was by a private road. The use of this road as a means of access was a breach of a restrictive covenant with the plaintiffs as well as a trespass to Mrs Jaggard's land. She only brought proceedings when the building of the new house was well advanced. Heather Jaggard brought her action claiming a raft of alternative remedies against the defendants. First, a declaration that the construction of an access road was in breach of a restrictive covenant and that a road was a private right of way, secondly, an injunction to prevent the defendants using the roadway, and thirdly, as an alternative, damages in lieu of injunction. The judge awarded the plaintiff £694 in lieu of injunction as being her share of what he valued as the price the defendants would have to pay to release them from the covenant and for a right of way.

26.15   The Court of Appeal made clear that in this case the measure of damages awarded was to compensate the plaintiff. The Court valued her right, not at a random price, but what reasonably might be demanded by the plaintiff for relaxing the covenant for the right of way. The Court of Appeal also suggested that the basis for the award in *Wrotham Park* was compensatory, not restitutionary. Millett L.J. stated:

> "Brightman J.'s approach was compensatory not restitutionary. He sought to measure the damages by reference to what the plaintiff had lost, not by reference to what the defendant had gained. He did not award the plaintiff the profit which the defendant had made by the breach, but the amount which he judged the plaintiff might have obtained as the price of giving its consent. The amount of the profit which the defendant expected to make was a relevant factor in that assessment, but that was all."[44]

---

[43] At p. 815.
[44] At p. 291.

The decision of the Court of Appeal in *Surrey County Council v. Bredero Homes*[45] was distinguished because in that case the plaintiffs had "deprived themselves of any bargaining position". The plaintiffs would be unable to obtain an injunction anyway, so the defendant being no longer at risk of an injunction had no reason to pay anything for release from the covenant. "If the plaintiff delays proceedings until it is no longer possible for him to obtain an injunction, he destroys his own bargaining position and devalues his right. The unavailability of the remedy of injunction at one and the same time deprives the court of jurisdiction to award damages under the Act and removes the basis for awarding substantial damages at common law."[46]

A similar approach was taken by the Court of Appeal in *Gafford v. Graham*[47] in which **26.16** a landowner failed to seek an injunction on time to prevent the building of an indoor riding school. Because of his delay and acquiescence, the Court was not prepared to grant a prohibitory or mandatory injunction. Instead the correct principle was to compensate him for the injury to his legal rights. The essential prerequisite, said Nourse L.J., was that it would be oppressive to the defendant and unfair to grant an injunction. The measure of damages was a sum which the plaintiff might reasonably have demanded to relax the restrictive covenant, in this case £25,000.

The judgment in *Jaggard* was also approved in *Attorney-General v. Blake* in the House of Lords[48] where Lord Nicholls analysed Lord Cairns' Act and the subsequent case law. The Act had allowed damages for future losses "but did not alter the measure to be employed in assessing damages".[49] Under the Act damages may include those "measured by reference to the benefits likely to be obtained in future by the defendant". As far as the principle of the Act is concerned, Lord Nicholls stated:

> "The measure of damages awarded in this type of case is often analysed as damages for loss of a bargaining opportunity or, which comes to the same, the price payable for the compulsory acquisition of a right. This analysis is correct. The court's refusal to grant an injunction means that in practice the defendant is thereby permitted to perpetuate the wrongful state of affairs he has brought about".[50]

Lord Hobhouse rejected the idea that the damages in *Wrotham Park* were restitu- **26.17** tionary, *i.e.* to give up an unjust profit. What the plaintiff had lost was the sum which he could have exacted from the defendant as the price of his consent to the development. This was equivalent to compensatory damages for breach. They did not involve any concept of restitution and to describe them as such was an error. In *Attorney General v. Blake* the House of Lords awarded damages for breach of contract by an alternative means, namely the equitable remedy of an account of profits. We discuss this controversial development later.[51]

[45] [1993] 1 W.L.R. 1361.
[46] Millett L.J. in *Jaggard v. Sawyer* [1995] 1 W.L.R. 269 (at p. 292).
[47] (1998) L.S.G. 36; [1998] N.P.C. 66.
[48] [2001] 1 A.C. 268.
[49] Citing *Johnson v. Agnew* [1980] A.C. 367.
[50] At p. 281.
[51] See pp. 483–488.

(4) Declaration of a right

26.18   A party may ask a court to declare that a contract or contractual rights exists, or alternatively that there is no contract. The courts have a power to declare that a right exists,
without having to order that it is enforced. The declaratory judgment is a useful and
wide-ranging possibility, more frequently invoked in public law. A declaration may
affect not only the parties to a contract but other third parties. As such it can have a
role as a type of class action. Thus in *Eastham v. Newcastle United Football Club*[52] a
footballer obtained a declaration which affected not only his contractual relationship
with the club to whom he was bound by contract, but also the rules of the Football
League as well. This remedy is welcomed by those who see a wider social and political
role for contract law.[53]

RESTITUTION IN THE FIELD OF CONTRACT LAW

26.19   Restitution and contract law have had a close relationship for many centuries. For much
of this time restitution was reduced to a minor role in the shadow of contract law. For
much of this time restitution law now exists as a third branch of the law of obligations,
along with contract and tort. The relationship between contract and restitutio is
presently at an interesting crossroads. In current legal theory, contract and restitution do
not overlap.[54] If a contractual remedy exists between the parties, a restitutionary remedy
will be available only if:

(a)   there never was a contract;

(b)   a contract was improperly formed, *i.e.* offer and acceptance failed to reach the
point of agreement;

(c)   there was a "total" failure of consideration[55];

(d)   the contract was discharged by breach; or

(e)   the contract was void.

If there is a contract, the restitutionary remedy is barred. Restitution in this area may
therefore be seen as: (a) an adjunct to the law of contract (what used to be called "quasi
contract") or (b) a subject in it's own right based on the principle of unjust enrichment.
In a contractual setting this will allow an injured party to recover money paid or claim
the value of benefits conferred for the services rendered at the other's request; this is
called a *quantum meruit*. The word restitution has been mentioned earlier in different
areas of the law, *e.g.* that of setting contracts aside for misrepresentation, duress or
undue influence. Rescission was barred for voidable contracts if it was impossible to
restore the parties to their original position, or, as it was called, rescission *restitutio in*

---

[52] [1964] Ch. 413.
[53] See Wightman, *Contract: a Critical Commentary* (1996, Pluto Press, London and Chicago). This is an interesting and stimulative account of a different view of contract law.
[54] For a proposed shift to allow some concurrent liability in contract and restitution, see Smith, "Concurrent
Liability in Contract and Unjust Enrichment: The Fundamental Breach Requirement" (1999) 115 L.Q.R. 245.
[55] Some would argue a "partial" failure is now sufficient, see later para. 26.24.

integrum. This principle is now more often expressed as counter restitution. If full restitution on both sides remains possible, the contract may be set aside.

The development of restitution: From quasi-contract to unjust enrichment

The roots of contract and restitution law turn out on examination to be from different **26.20** plants. Restitution or quasi- contract developed from the old writ of *indebtitatus assumpsit*, a series of individual instances which were grouped around contract but different from contractual actions themselves, for which the remedy was mainly the writ of *assumpsit*, dating from the time of *Slade's* case in 1602.[56] Like contract itself, quasi-contract only applied to a number of particular instances. In *Moses v. Macferlan*[57] Lord Mansfield tried to find a single principle behind these examples. It was that "the gist of this kind of action is that the defendant, upon the circumstances of the case, is obliged by the ties of natural justice and equity to refund the money". The great eighteenth century Chief Tushco was supportive of such wide notions of equity: "This kind of equitable action to recover back money which ought not in justice to be kept is very beneficial and therefore much encouraged."[58]

As contract law reached its apex in the nineteenth century, quasi-contract melted in **26.21** the heat of its sun. The true basis of restitutionary claims lay mainly on the periphery of contract law and property, based on the principle of an "implied contract". The two main actions in restitution were for money had and received, where money had been paid under a void contract, or where there had been a total failure of consideration, and the action known as *quantum meruit* for the value of services rendered for another's benefit, again where no contract existed. This was historically known as quasi-contract.

In the last 20 years, partly as a result of academic pressure, this area has been trans- **26.22** formed into an area now called restitution law.[59] This combines quasi-contract, property and the general principle of unjust enrichment. This achieved its leading statement in three judgments of the House of Lords in *Lipkin Gorman v. Karpnale Ltd,*[60] *Woolwich Building Society v. Inland Revenue Commissioners*[61] and *Westdeutsche Landesbank Girozentrale v. Islington Borough Council.*[62] In *Lipkin Gorman v. Karpnale Ltd*, a solicitor who was a heavy gambler stole money from client's accounts. He spent the money at the defendant's casino, the Playboy Club, in London. The plaintiffs were his law firm, who sued the casino for the recovery of the money claiming that it had been paid over to the defendants under a void contract governed by the Gaming Act 1845.[63] The House of Lords held that the plaintiff was entitled to recover the sums gambled minus the actual winnings paid. In *Weltdeutsche Landesbank v. Islington* Lord Goff stated that: "Claims in restitution are founded upon a principle of justice, being designed to prevent the unjust enrichment of the defendant." Unjust enrichment has now emerged into the light of day as a general principle. However, in the ambit of contract law, the applications of restitution remain wedded to particular situations.

---

[56] See Simpson, "A History of the Common Law of Contract" (1987, Clarendon Press, Oxford).
[57] (1760) 2 Burr 1005; 97 E.R. 676.
[58] See also Lord Mansfield's attempted reform of the doctrine of consideration (discussed Chap. 7).
[59] See Goff and Jones, *The Law of Restitution* (1993, 4th ed, Sweet & Maxwell).
[60] [1991] 2 A.C. 548.
[61] [1993] A.C. 70.
[62] [1996] A.C. 669.
[63] See Chap. 20.

The main categories of restitution in the context of contract law

(1) Total failure of consideration

26.23   If the consideration for a contract totally fails then there may be a claim in restitution for money paid. In *Rowland v. Divall*[64] an "Albert" motor car which had been bought turned out to be stolen. The seller had no title to the vehicle so it had to be returned. It was held that the plaintiff was entitled to full recovery of the purchase price, even though he had obtained some benefit by having the use of the car for five months. The use of the car was deemed to form no part of the consideration in a sale of ownership of a chattel.

The expression "failure of consideration" has to be handled with care in this area. It does not mean the consideration required to form a contract, rather that the performance of the contract failed completely. In *Stocznia Gdanska SA v. Latvian Shipping Co*[65] Lord Goff described this as "whether the promisor has performed any part of the contractual duties in respect of which the payment is due".

26.24   The requirement of "total" failure may now be redundant. The requirement that the failure had to be total has now been doubted by some restitution lawyers who regard partial failure as sufficient if counter restitution is still possible.[66] The rule allowing only total failure to count may already have changed. In the Privy Council in *Goss v. Chilcott*[67] on an appeal from New Zealand, Lord Goff stated[68] *obiter* that:

> "Since no part of the capital can be repaid, the failure of consideration for the capital sum would plainly have been total. But even if part of the capital sum had been repaid, the law would not hesitate to hold that the balance of the loan outstanding would be recoverable on the ground of failure of consideration; for at least in those cases in which apportionment can be carried out without difficulty, the law will allow partial recovery on this ground."

Lord Goff cited the Australian case of *David Securities Pty Ltd v. Commonwealth Bank of Australia*[69] as authority in which it was stated[70] that: "In cases where consideration can be apportioned or where counter restitution is relatively simple, insistence on total failure of consideration can be misleading or confusing." In *Rover International Ltd v. Cannon Film Ltd*[71] the Court of Appeal approached the question by looking at the benefit bargained for by the plaintiff, rather than what was received in fact and whether this was a total or partial failure. Kerr L.J.[72] stated: "The test is whether or not the party claiming total failure of consideration has in fact received any part of the benefit bargained for under the contract or purported contract."

---

[64] [1923] 2 K.B. 500.
[65] [1998] 1 Lloyd's Rep. 609 (at p. 619).
[66] See Birks, "Failure of Consideration" in Rose, *Consensus ad Idem: Essays in Honour of Guenter Treitel* (1996, Sweet and Maxwell, London).
[67] [1996] A.C. 788.
[68] At p. 798.
[69] (1992) 175 C.L.R. 353.
[70] At p. 383.
[71] [1989] 1 W.L.R. 912.
[72] At p. 923.

The courts are sometimes prepared to find a failure of consideration where it appears **26.25**
to be less than total by apportioning the consideration, *i.e.* finding independent promises, only one of which fails totally. Traditionally, the judges have been unwilling to do
this in most cases. In the Australian case *Baltic Shipping Co v. Dillon*[73] the plaintiff, Joan
Dillon, was injured when the vessel on which she was a passenger on a cruise in the
pacific, the *Mikhail Lermontov*, struck a rock and sank. She had already enjoyed nine
days out of a holiday of two weeks onboard the ship when the accident occurred. The
plaintiff obtained damages for breach of contract which included the refunding of the
fare and compensation for disappointments and distress.[74] Joan Dillon also claimed a
complete refund on the fare as a total failure of consideration. The High Court of
Australia held that she was not entitled to this. Total failure of consideration would only
succeed if accompanied by counter restitution of benefits bargained for and received by
the claimant. The failure was only partial as the plaintiff had already received nine days
performance of the contract.

The concept of what constitutes "total failure" also has to be considered in the light **26.26**
of *D O Ferguson Associates v. M. Sohl*,[75] in which the plaintiff employed the defendants
as building contractors to renovate shop premises in Kensal Green. The price agreed was
£32,194. After disputes between the parties, the builders walked off the site and did not
return. They had already been paid £26,738 for the work done up to this point. The
builders then brought an action for the balance of the price and the defendant counter
claimed for damages and repayment of an overpayment made by him. It is this latter
point which is of interest. The judge held that the plaintiff had repudiated the contract
which was discharged by the defendant's acceptance of the breach. He went ahead and
employed alternative contractors who finished the job for less than the contract price
with the plaintiff. Significantly, the judge found that the value of the work done by the
plaintiffs was only £22,065. The defendant had therefore overpaid by over £4,000. The
judge awarded the defendant restitution of the overpayment of £4,673 as being given for
work which had not been done. In other words, there was a total failure of consideration
of this part of the work. The defendant also received £1 nominal damages for the plaintiff's breach of contract.

The Court of Appeal agreed. The nominal damages to the defendant, because he had **26.27**
suffered no loss, did not prevent his claiming restitution for the overpayment. He was
entitled to be repaid the sum on the basis that the consideration for it had wholly
failed. According to Hirst L.J.: "for the £4,673 there was indeed a total failure of consideration because £4,673 was paid by the defendant for work that was never done at
all".[76] "It matters not" said Hirst L.J., "that at some stage or other that sum of money
formed part of a larger instalment". On this analysis, a number of apparent "partial"
failures could be divorced from the main contract and satisfy the total failure requirement. In the case itself, the Court of Appeal adhered to the traditional view that the
failure had to be total.[77]

The arguments for and against allowing a partial failure of consideration are finely **26.28**
balanced. First, the autonomy of contract law and the parties' allocation of risk would

[73] (1993) 176 C.L.R. 344.
[74] See Chap. 25.
[75] [1992] 62 Build. L.R. 95.
[76] At p. 101.
[77] We refer to this case again in para 26.34.

be challenged. Secondly, contract and restitution should operate in their own respective spheres. This was the argument that kept tort and contract law apart until this was emphatically changed by *Donoghue v. Stevenson*.[78] A requirement of the failure being total also prevents claims being too easily available. There might, for instance, be claims for restitution in situations where the plaintiff has merely made a bad bargain. Otherwise he or she would claim damages for their expectation loss which would be a greater sum than restitution of benefits.

The orthodox view remains that the failure of consideration has to be total. For contract lawyers, the total failure rule remains an important watershed between a breach of condition and the restitutionary option. One can detect in this argument the jockeying for position when two different systems exist side by side and ultimately compete for their own bit of turf. It is a situation often encountered in the common law throughout history.

(2) Failed agreement

26.29 A restitutionary remedy may be available in a wide variety of "failed" contracts.[79] If the plaintiff pays money under a purported contract which is never formed, turns out to be void or is unenforceable through defect of form, money paid may be recoverable. In *Rover International Ltd v. Cannon Film Sales Ltd (No. 3)*[80] there was a void contract because the plaintiffs' company had not been legally incorporated when the contract was made. Instalments had already been paid, for which the Court of Appeal allowed a restitutionary remedy. The proper basis was an "equitable restitution as between the parties regardless of what their respective positions would have been had the contract been valid".[80a] If a contract is not formed due to lack of agreement, such as failure of offer or uncertainty, there may be a restitutionary remedy available in some circumstances.[81] This category also includes contracts which are unenforceable because of lack of consideration.[82]

(3) Illegal contracts

26.30 Contracts which are illegal or void as contrary to public policy may support a restitutionary remedy where the parties are not in *pari delicto*.[83] In *Mohammed v. Alaga and Co.*[84] an agreement between a firm of solicitors and a non-solicitor party to share fees earned by the firm in return for the latter introducing clients to them was held to be illegal and unenforceable. The plaintiff non-solicitor was, however, allowed to bring a restitutional action on a *quantum meruit* in respect of the value of the professional services rendered by him, and therefore entitled to reasonable remuneration for what he had done for the other party. The solicitors were more to blame for the illegality as they should have known what they were doing was illegal.

---

[78] [1932] A.C. 562.
[79] See Rose, *Failure of Contracts, Contractual, Restitutionary and Proprietary Consequences* (1997, Hart Publishing, Oxford). This is largely based upon a paper delivered at the SPTL conference at Queen's College, Cambridge in September 1996.
[80] [1989] 3 All E.R. 423.
[80a] At p. 431.
[81] See Chap. 5.
[82] See Chap. 7.
[83] See Chap. 20.
[84] [1999] 3 All E.R. 699.

(4) Frustrated contracts

At one time it could have been argued that frustration and total failure of consideration were synonymous. Since *Fibrosa Spolka Akcyjna v. Fairbairn Lawson* this position is no longer tenable.[85] The Law Reform (Frustrated Contracts) Act 1943 effectively introduced a special but distinct restitutionary régime for frustrated contract.[86]

(5) *Quantum meruit*

Quantum meruit is translated from Latin as "as much as is deserved". Restitution law will **26.31** allow recovery of a reasonable price or remuneration for services rendered by the plaintiff to the defendant. The service rendered must be either requested or accepted by the defendant. A *quantum meruit* can arise on either (a) a contractual basis or (b) a restitutionary or quasi-contractual basis, *i.e.* where there is no contract at all. It is the latter that is most commonly thought of as *quantum meruit*. In other words, as a substitute for a contract. The two cases may be hard to distinguish. If a gardener knocks at my door and offers to landscape a garden on the basis that he will be paid but no price is agreed at the outset, then *quantum meruit* under either head may apply. This may be either to fix a price for the contract or to entitle my gardener to a reasonable charge for his labours.[87] There are two important contractual situations in which a *quantum meruit* may be claimed.

(a) Performance of the contract is prevented by the other party's breach

In *Planché v. Colbourn*[88] the plaintiff had agreed to write a book on costume and armour **26.32** for a series of books called "The Juvenile Library" which was to be published by the defendants. He collected together material and wrote a part of the book before the defendants abandoned the series and cancelled the book. The plaintiff claimed alternatively in breach of contract and in *quantum meruit*. The disappointed author recovered 50 guineas in *quantum meruit* as a reasonable remuneration for the work he had done. It was necessary that no contract existed, however, for the restitutionary action to succeed. Tindal C.J.[89] stated that: "When a special contract is in existence and open, the plaintiff cannot sue on a *quantum meruit*, and part of the question here therefore was whether the contract did exist or not." The Court found that the work had been finally abandoned and no new contract formed. In these circumstances it would be permissible for the plaintiff to recover "the fruit of his labour".

(b) Contract is discharged by breach

If a contract is discharged by acceptance of a repudiatory breach the claimant may **26.33** bring an action in restitution. In *De Bernardy v. Harding*[90] the defendant erected seating to watch the procession for the funeral of the Duke of Wellington, and made an agreement with the plaintiff, as his foreign agent, to advertise and sell seats abroad. The plaintiff was to be paid a commission calculated as a percentage of the tickets sold.

---

[85] [1943] A.C. 32.
[86] Discussed in Chap. 22.
[87] This is now in statutory form under the Supply of Goods and Services Act 1982, s. 15. (See Chap. 12.)
[88] (1831) 8 Bing 14; 131 E.R. 305.
[89] At p. 16.
[90] (1853) 8 Ex. 822; 155 E.R. 1586.

After incurring expenses but before any tickets were sold, the defendant told the plaintiff that he did not wish to go ahead with the agreement because he wished to sell the tickets himself. The plaintiff thereafter sent all applications for tickets to the defendant and after the funeral sent a bill for his expenses and also work done in furtherance of the ticket sales.

The Court of Exchequer held that he could sue in quasi-contract on a *quantum meruit*. The original contract had been terminated following breach. Alderson B. stated: "Where one party has absolutely refused to perform, or has rendered himself incapable of performing, his part of the contract, he puts it in the power of the other party either to sue for a breach of it, or to rescind the contract and sue on a *quantum meruit* for the work actually done".

26.34   In *D O Ferguson and Associates v. Sohl*,[91] the defendant received both a common law remedy of nominal damages and the restitutionary remedy of repayment. The reason for the latter was that the contract was discharged by breach. The Court saw no objection in allowing two separate causes of action. A restitutionary remedy may, in exceptional circumstances, be available even if the contract remains undischarged. In *Miles v. Wakefield Metropolitan District Council*[92] the House of Lords held that a worker on industrial action, in the form of a "go slow", could not claim his wages under his contract of employment because he was deliberately working in a manner designed to harm the employer. The plaintiffs were, however, entitled to be paid on a *quantum meruit* basis for the amount and value of the reduced work performed and accepted by the employers.[93]

Restitution or the equitable remedy of an account of profits as the basis for damages in contract law

(1) The traditional view of commercial relationships

26.35   A party is free to pursue his or her own self interest in contractual relations. If he or she breaks a contract in so doing, they will have to pay damages to the other party. "Efficient breach", *i.e.* breaking a contract because it is more profitable to do so rather than perform it, is permissible in English law.[94] In *Occidental Worldwide Investment Corp v. Skibs A/S Avanti, "The Siboen" and "The Sibotre"*,[95] shipowners withdrew their vessels in May 1973 when the market price for chartering vessels increased. The owners were able to make larger profits by chartering to others than by carrying on with their existing contract. Their breach of contract led to an additional profit of over $3 million dollars. The plaintiff claimed damages for this amount or an equitable remedy an account of profits. The Commercial Court held that even though there had been a wrongful repudiation the plaintiff was only able to claim for his own loss not the profits made elsewhere by the defendants.

The restricted use of specific performance in English law means that there is generally no question of forcing a party to perform their obligations, though this is common

---

[91] [1992] 62 Build L.R. 95 (see earlier para 26.26).
[92] [1987] A.C. 539.
[93] See Lord Brightman at p. 553 and Lord Templeman at p. 561.
[94] See Chap. 13.
[95] [1976] 1 Lloyd's Rep. 293.

in most European civil law systems. A rule requiring a party to give up his profits for breaching a contract would have a similar effect. In *Tito v. Waddell (No. 2)*[96] Sir Robert Megarry stated that: "It is fundamental to damages that they are to compensate the plaintiff for his loss or injury . . . The question is not one of making the defendant disgorge what he has saved by committing the wrong, but one of compensating the plaintiff."[97] The judge quoted an Irish case, *Murphy v. Wexford County Council*,[98] where O'Connor L.J. stated, "you are not to enrich the party aggrieved; you are not to impoverish him; you are, so far as money can, to leave him in the same position as before".

A much criticised but leading authority rejecting profit or gain based damages is **26.36** *Surrey County Council v. Bredero Homes Ltd*[99] in which a piece of land at Leatherhead was sold to the defendants, Bredero Homes, who wished to build homes on it. The sale was made subject to planning permission being obtained. The defendants breached their covenant with the two councils involved, Surrey and Mole Valley, by building on the land 77 houses rather than the 72 agreed. They did so by obtaining further planning permission after the sale in breach of contract and earned themselves increased profits in the process. The plaintiffs did not seek an injunction at the time, but later, after the houses had been sold, sued for damages to recover part of the profit made by the defendants in breaching their agreement.

The plaintiffs claimed that because the breach was deliberate and cynical, they should be entitled to recover damages and that the Court should be prepared to award damages where an injunction could have been granted to prevent the defendant gaining from their wrongdoing.[1] These arguments were rejected by the Court of Appeal. The plaintiffs were only entitled to nominal damages. Steyn L.J. gave the reasons for denying any restitutionary principle in his judgment[2]:

> "The introduction of restitutionary remedies to deprive cynical contract breakers of the fruits of their breaches of contract will lead to greater uncertainty in the assessment of damages. It is of paramount importance that the way in which disputes are likely to be resolved by the courts must be readily predictable. Given the premise that the aggrieved party has suffered no loss, is such a dramatic extension of restitutionary remedies justified in order to confer a windfall in each case on the aggrieved party? I think not. In any event such a widespread availability of restitutionary remedies will have a tendency to discourage economic activity in relevant situations. The recognition of the proposed extension will in my view not serve the public interest. It is sound policy to guard against extending the protection of the law of obligations too widely."

The argument for "gain based" or restitutionary damages therefore failed.[3] The judgment in *Surrey County Council* has now been reviewed by the House of Lords in *Attorney-General v. Blake*,[3a] to which we shall shortly turn.

---

[96] [1977] Ch. 106.
[97] At p. 332.
[98] [1921] 2 I.R. 230.
[99] [1993] 1 W.L.R. 1361.
[1] See earlier para 26.11–26.17.
[2] At p. 1370.
[3] See Burrows (1993) L.M.C.L.Q. 453; Birks (1993) 109 L.Q.R. 518; O'Dair [1993] R.L.R. 31; and Smith (1994) J.C.L. 164, on this much discussed topic.
[3a] [2000] 3 W.L.R. 625.

(2) Do profit based damages already exist in English law?

26.37 Damages were denied in *Surrey County Council* because the action was brought in breach of contract. There are, however, three situations where recovery could arguably have been allowed:

(a)   infringement of proprietary rights under statute;[4]

(b)   equitable damages, *i.e.* in lieu of an injunction under Lord Cairns' Act 1858[5]; and

(c)   in narrow circumstances, an action in tort.

These may be regarded as "restitutionary" damages though each is probably better regarded as depending on other principles. The nature of damages may also be based upon other considerations in specialised areas. Gain to the defendant, rather than just loss to a plaintiff, is relevant in breach of a contractual or fiduciary duty of confidence.[6]

An interesting case which may or may not be an example of restitutionary damages is *Penarth Dock Engineering Co. Ltd v. Pounds.*[7] The defendant purchased a floating pontoon in Penarth dock then, despite reminders and protests from the plaintiffs, left it there for over a year. The dockyard was closing down so no use would have been made of the space. The plaintiffs appeared to suffer no real loss and the defendants gained by saving the expense of charges they would have otherwise incurred. The plaintiffs brought action for (a) breach of contract in failing to remove the pontoon and (b) trespass to their yard by leaving an object (*i.e.* the pontoon which by then was owned by the defendant) on their land without permission.

Lord Denning (sitting as a judge on the Queen's Bench Division) held that the defendant was in breach of his obligation to remove the pontoon by August 1962. He had to pay a reasonable charge for doing so. Damages were not to be measured by what the plaintiff had lost, but by the benefit gained by leaving the pontoon and having free use of the berth in the docks. Damages were assessed at £32.25 per week, leading to a total of £1064.25 awarded to the plaintiff. These may have been restitutionary in character or it could be argued they were in part for the trespass claim, as "he had been trespasser".[8] Lord Denning based his award as being "not what the plaintiffs have lost, but what benefit the defendant obtained by having use of the berth".

(3) The debate over profit based damages

26.38 There is now an increasing literature on this topic.[9] The Law Commission has also discussed the question.[10] The Law Commission Report came to the conclusion that the law in this area should be left to development by the courts rather than by statute.[11]

---

[4]   For instance, for breach of copyright where profit based damages may be allowed.
[5]   See earlier para. 26.11–26.17.
[6]   *Peter Pan Manufacturing Corporation v. Corsets Silhouette Ltd* [1964] 1 W.L.R. 96.
[7]   [1963] 1 Lloyd's Rep. 359.
[8]   At p. 362.
[9]   Goodhart [1995] R.L.R. 3; Jones (1983) 99 L.Q.R. 443; Birks [1987] L.M.C.L.Q. 421; and O'Dair (1993) [1993] R.L.R. 31.
[10]   "Aggravated, Exemplary and Restitutionary Damages", Consultation Paper (No. 132), 1993.
[11]   "Aggravated, Exemplary and Restitutionary Damages", Law Commission Report (No. 247), December 1997.

There were four main reasons for the recommendation against a general restitutionary principle:

(a) it would be difficult to draw the distinction between "innocent" and "cynical" breaches of contracts, which were based on the parties' own commercial reasons. This would lead to greater uncertainty in the assessment of damages in commercial and consumer disputes;

(b) in seeking to obtain restitutionary damages, the plaintiffs would be avoiding the common law duty to mitigate their loss;[12]

(c) restitutionary damages are really a modernised version of specific performance but not all contracts are specifically enforceable; and

(d) there would be difficulties in attributing the profits made by the defendants as a direct result of the breach of contract.[12a]

(4) The acceptance of an account for profits in equity as a basis for damages for breach of contract

The question of a private law remedy of allowing profit based damages for breach of contract arose in *Attorney General v. Blake*.[13] [14] The action arose out of an attempt by the British Government to prevent the former Soviet spy, George Blake, who escaped from Wandsworth prison and lived for the rest of his life in Moscow, from profiting from the royalties of the sale of his memoirs. In the Court of Appeal, Lord Woolf M.R. repeated the basic rule that damages for breach of contract are compensatory, not restitutionary. The Government's action failed but there is *obiter dicta* on the need for some restitutionary principle for damages for breach of contract. Lord Woolf noted that "the exclusively compensatory basis of damages for breach of contract does not lack judicial critics and there are signs that the traditional view that the rule admits of no exceptions may not long survive".[15] The law was "seriously defective" if the Court was unable to award restitutionary damages for breach of contract. This would mean a plaintiff was deprived of any effective remedy for breach of contract.

Lord Woolf made reference to the American case of *Shepp v. US*[16] (a similar case to *Blake*) where the American Court awarded damages on the equitable basis of the remedial constructive trust on the proceeds of publication of a book without prior clearance. There were two situations, according to Lord Woolf, which would justify a restitutionary award of damages. Both were based on cases where compensatory damages would be inadequate. These were (a) "skimped performance", where a defendant fails to provide the full extent of the services he or she has contracted to provide and for which they have charged the plaintiff (an example of this is the Louisiana case of *City of New Orleans v. Firemans Charitable Association*[17]), and (b) where a defendant obtains a profit by doing

26.39

---

[12] See Chap. 25.
[12a] Para. 3.46.
[13] [1998] Ch. 439 (CA).
[14] See O'Sullivan [1998] C.L.J. 258; Hedley (1998) N.L.J. 723.
[15] At pp. 456–457.
[16] (1980) 444 U.S. 507.
[17] (1891) 9 So. 486.

the exact opposite of what he has contracted not to do. This was the situation in *Blake*. Having promised under the Official Secrets Act 1911 not to disclose information, Blake had deliberately profited by doing the very thing in question. The House of Lords over-turned the Court of Appeal and allowed the Government's action to recover the profits of £80,000 in royalties.[18]

26.40   In exceptional circumstances where the normal remedies of damages, or other equi-table remedies such as specific performance, were inadequate compensation for a breach of contract, a court could order an account for profits by the defendants. This means handing over some or all of the profits made in breach of contract. Such a remedy was limited "as justice requires". The Crown was entitled to all the royalties and pre-pay-ments made to Blake by his British publishers in breach of his confidentiality agreement as a member of the Secret Intelligence Service, even although the material contained in his autobiography, *No Other Choice*, had in fact ceased to be confidential. According to Lord Nicholls:[19]

> "[T]here seems to be no reason, in principle, why the court must in all circum-stances rule out an account of profits as a remedy for breach of contract. I prefer to avoid the unhappy expression 'restitutionary damages'. When, excep-tionally, a just response to a breach of contract so requires, the court should be able to grant the discretionary remedy of requiring a defendant to account to the plaintiff for the benefits he has received from his breach of contract. In the same way as a plaintiff's interest in performance of a contract may render it just and equitable for the court to make an order for specific performance or grant an injunction, so the plaintiff's interest in performance may make it just and equitable that the defendant should retain no benefit from is breach of contract."

Lord Nicholls added that:

> "I consider it would be only a modest step for the law to recognise openly that, exceptionally, an account of profits may be the most appropriate remedy for breach of contract. It is not as though this step would contradict some recognised princi-ple applied consistently throughout the law to the grant or withholding of the remedy of an account of profits. No such principle is discernable."

26.41   Although the House of Lords allowed damages to be calculated on a profit making basis in *Blake*, Lord Steyn placed four tentative conditions on the principle. These were not intended to inhibit the long term growth of this fledgling, but as a word of caution. First, that there must be a breach of a negative stipulation (in this case not to disclose official secrets). Secondly, that the contract breacher has obtained a profit by doing the precise opposite of what he promised not to do. Thirdly, that the plaintiff has a special interest greater than the financial one of having the contract performed, and finally, that specific performance or injunction would be an ineffective remedy. In *Blake* the secrets had already been disclosed. The restrictions on the principle suggest that *Blake* might prove

---

[18] [2001] 1 A.C. 268 (HL).
[19] At pp. 284–285.

to have been an exceptional case in unusual circumstances. It might, however, emerge as a harbinger of a new stream of case law heralding a new principle for the compensation of damages for breach of contract. The dangers of extending the principle to commercial cases was expressed by Lord Hobhouse in his dissenting judgment. The consequences would be "far reaching and disruptive". The basis for their Lordships' judgment was wrong in principle. It was "a remedy based upon proprietary principles when the necessary proprietary rights were absent. This principle should have no part to play in contract law". If, in spite of this warning, damages based upon the restitutionary idea develop for breach, contract law will have crossed a new threshold at the beginning of the twenty-first century. Whether this turns out to be beneficial must await the verdict of history, but it proves that contract law remains receptive to change.

INDEX

Acceptance,
   See also **Agreement; Offer**
   battle of the forms. *See* **Battle of the forms**
   communication,
      cancellation of contracts concluded
         away from business premises,
         4.17
      Distance Selling Regulations, 4.18
      distant means, 4.17
      e-commerce, 4.18, 4.20
      electronic commerce, 4.20
      general rule, 4.8
      instantaneous communications, 4.8
      means, 4.7
      normal office hours, 4.9
      outside of normal office hours, 4.10
      postal rule. *See* **Postal rule**
      privatised mail services, 4.17
      requirement, 4.7
      unnecessary, where, 4.21–4.25
   conduct, by, 4.4–4.6
   correspondence with offer, 4.1
   counter offers, 4.2, 4.3
   distant means, 4.17
   e-commerce, 4.18, 4.20
   fact of, 4.1
   flexibility, 5.4–5.6
   inertia selling, 4.25
   mechanism, 2.2
   mirror image test, 4.1
   objectivity,
      application, 2.13
      detached, 2.10
      promisee, 2.9
      promisor, 2.8
      subjectivity and, 2.12
   postal rule, 4.11
   postal rule. *See* **Postal rule**
   privatised mail services, 4.17
   relaxed view of, 5.4–5.6
   reply is counter offer, where, 4.2, 4.3
   revocation of previously posted acceptance,
      4.26, 4.27
   silence, 4.22–4.24
   silence, by, 2.7

Acceptance—*cont.*
   subjectivity, 2.11, 2.12
   third party rights, 10.16
   unnecessary to communicate, 4.21–4.25
      inertia selling, 4.25
      silence, 4.22–4.24
      unilateral contracts, 4.21
      unsolicited goods, 4.25
   unilateral contracts, 4.21
   unsolicited goods, 4.25
   words, by, 4.1
Account for profits, 26.39–26.41
Advertisements,
   offer, 3.6
Affirmation of contract,
   breach of contract, 23.17
   misrepresentation, 18.23
   repudiation, 23.17
Agency,
   third party rights, 10.26
Agents,
   commercial, 24.28
   misrepresentation, 18.24
Agreement,
   certainty, 5.11–5.14
   failure,
      no contract resulting, 5.18
   mistake,
      case law, 6.4–6.6
      categories of mistake, 6.2
      effect, 21.1
      fact, of, 6.17
      generally, 6.1
      identity, 6.11–6.16
      mutual mistake, 6.7, 6.8
      narrow doctrine, 6.2
      subjective mistake, 6.3, 6.18
      unilateral mistake, 6.9, 6.10, 6.17
   offer and acceptance. *See* **Acceptance; Offer**
Amenity, damages for loss of, 25.19
Apportionment Act 1870, 23.31
Arbitration,
   third party rights, 10.22
Assignment,
   third party rights, 10.28

Auction sales,
    offer, 3.7

Battle of the forms,
    agreement on essential points, 5.9
    first blow approaches, 5.8
    flexible approach, 5.8
    general rule, 5.7
    knock-out approach, 5.8
    last shot doctrine, 5.8
    loudest shot wins argument, 5.8
    new approach, 5.10
    usual terms by course of dealing, 5.9
Bilateral contracts, 2.3, 2.4
    revocation of offer, 3.12
Breach of contract,
    affirmation of contract, 23.17
    anticipatory breach,
        meaning, 23.5, 23.6
        reasonable exercise of rights,
            23.7–23.11
    damages. *See* **Damages**
    effect, 23.3, 23.4
    generally, 23.1, 23.2
    reasonable exercise of rights, 23.7–23.11
        repudiation. *See* Repudiation
Breach of warranty,
    performance, 23.31
Business practice,
    sources of contract law, 1.12

Capacity,
    companies, 11.7
    intoxicated persons, 11.7
    mentally incapacitated persons, 11.7
    minors, 11.6
    parol evidence rule, 12.8
Catalogues,
    offer, 3.6
Causation,
    damages, 25.22, 25.33
Caveat emptor, 7.10
Certainty,
    formation of contract, 5.11–5.14
Collateral contracts,
    parol evidence rule, 12.7
    third party rights, 10.27
Commercial business practice,
    sources of contract law, 1.12
Commercial contracts,
    time of performance, 13.19–13.23
Common mistake,
    See also **Mistake**
    common law, 21.4–21.9
    equity, 21.12–21.15
    frustration and, 22.13
    fundamental mistake, 21.6, 21.7
    generally, 21.1
    meaning, 21.1
    quality of goods, 21.8, 21.9

Common mistake—*cont.*
    res sua, 21.10, 21.11
    scope, 21.2
    subject matter of contract not existing, 21.4,
        21.5
    title, 21.10, 21.11
Communication,
    acceptance,
        cancellation of contracts concluded
            away from business premises,
            4.17
        Distance Selling Regulations, 4.18
        distant means, 4.17
        e-commerce, 4.18, 4.19
        electronic commerce, 4.20
        general rule, 4.8
        instantaneous communications, 4.8
        means, 4.7
        normal office hours, 4.9
        outside of normal office hours, 4.10
        postal rule. *See* Postal rule
        privatised mail services, 4.17
        requirement, 4.7
        unnecessary, where, 4.21–4.25
    Distance Selling Regulations, 4.18, 4.19
    postal rule. *See* **Postal rule**
Companies,
    capacity, 11.7
Compensation,
    boundaries, 25.1–25.38
    damages. *See* **Damages**
    remoteness. *See* **Remoteness**
Conditions,
    consideration distinguished, 7.18
    precedent, condition, 13.5, 13.6
    subsequent, condition, 13.7
Conduct,
    acceptance by, 4.4–4.6
    estoppel by, 9.17, 9.18
Consideration,
    additional payments, promises of, 8.4
    adequate, need not be, 7.9, 7.10
    arguments for and against, 8.27, 8.28
    bargain between parties, 7.7
    basic rules, 7.9–7.16
    benefit, detriment or forbearance, 7.5, 7.6
    causally related to promise, 7.13
    composition agreements between debtor and
        creditors, 8.18
    condition distinguished, 7.17
    deed, promises made by, 8.19
    economic duress, 8.9–8.13
    function of rules, 7.3
    gifts, 7.17
    gratuitous promises, 7.17
    judicial reasons for enforcing promises, 7.8
    lacking, where, 7.4
    lesser sum, taking, 8.14
    meaning, 7.5–7.8
    moral obligation, more than, 7.18, 7.19
    motive distinguished, 7.16
    move from promisee, must, 7.16

Consideration—*cont.*
    part payment by third payment, 8.17
    past, 7.14, 7.15
    performance of duty imposed by law or statute, 8.2
    Pinnel's Case, rule in, 8.15–8.17
    practical benefit or mutual advantage, 7.8
    pragmatic approach to meaning of, 8.6–8.9
    pre-existing contractual obligations, 8.2
    price given in return for promise, 7.7
    promise and, 7.1–7.3
    reform, 8.25, 8.26
    restraint of trade, 20.28
    Stilk v. Myrick, rule in, 8.2, 8.3
    sufficiency in law, 7.11, 7.12
    third party rights, 10.23
    total failure, 22.12, 26.23–26.28
    variation of contract,
        additional payments, promises of, 8.4, 8.5
        composition agreements between debtor and creditors, 8.18
        deed, promises made by, 8.19
        generally, 8.1
        lesser sum, taking, 8.14
        part payment by third payment, 8.17
        performance of duty imposed by law or statute, 8.2
        pragmatic approach to meaning of consideration, 8.6–8.9
        pre-existing contractual obligations, 8.2
        Stilk v. Myrick, rule in, 8.2, 8.3
        third parties, promises made to, 8.3
Construction of contracts, 12.12
Consumerism,
    growth, 1.14
    sources of contract law, 1.14
Contents of contract,
    admissibility of evidence, 11.2, 11.3
    construction of contracts, 12.12
    evidence, 11.2, 11.3
    factual matrix, 12.2, 12.3
    generally, 12.1
    interpretation. *See* **Interpretation of contracts**
    parol evidence rule, 12.4, 12.5
        application of rule, 12.11
        capacity, lack of, 12.8
        collateral contracts, 12.7
        condition precedent, 12.6
        customs, 12.8
        draftsmanship, 12.8, 12.9
        exceptions, 12.6–12.11
        partly written, partly oral, 12.6
        purpose of contract, showing, 12.8
        reform proposals, 12.10
        subject matter of contract, 12.7
        vitiating factors, 12.8
Contra proferentem, 16.19–16.21
Contract law,
    detrimental reliance, reversal of, 1.7
    developments in law, 1.4
    functions, 1.6–1.8

Contract law—*cont.*
    human negotiations, 1.1
    making contracts, 1.8
    modern commercial world, changing rules for, 1.2
    nature, 1.1–1.5
    objectives, 1.6–1.8
    obligations, law of, 1.5
    outline, 1.19
    practitioners approach to, 1.3
    reasonable expectations, fulfilment of, 1.6
    reform, 1.18
    role, 1.8
    scope, 1.1–1.5
    sources. *See* **Sources of contract law**
Contract law and, 26.9
Contributory negligence, 25.27–25.28
Convention, estoppel by, 9.17
Corruption,
    contracts procuring, 20.9
Counter offers, 4.2, 4.3
Course of dealings,
    battle of the forms, 5.9
    exemption clauses, 16.17, 16.18
Creditors,
    composition agreements, 8.18
Crime, contract to commit, 20.8
Customary rules,
    implied terms, 12.17–12.19
    parol evidence rule, 12.8
    sources of contract law, 1.11

Damages,
    amenity, loss of, 25.19
    analysis of claim, 25.36–25.68
    causation, 25.22, 25.33
    choice between expectation and reliance, 24.10, 24.18, 24.19
    Commercial Agents (Council Directive) Regulations 1993, 24.28
    consumer surplus, 25.19
    contributory negligence, 25.27–25.28
    cure, cost of, 24.24
    difference in value, 24.21–24.23
    equity, 26.11–26.17
    estoppel, 24.20
    expectation, 24.3, 24.4
        choice between expectation and reliance, 24.10, 24.18, 24.19
        speculative losses, 24.13, 24.14
    generally, 24.1, 24.2
    limitations on claimant' choice,
        bad bargain rule, 24.11, 24.12
        speculative expectation losses, 24.13, 24.14
    liquidated damages. *See* **Liquidated damages**
    loss of opportunity, 24.15, 24.16
    mental distress,
        amenity, loss of, 25.19
        basic rule, 25.14
        freedom from mental distress, contracts to provide, 25.17

Damages—*cont.*
  mental distress—*cont.*
    peace of mind, enjoyment or
      entertainment, contracts to provide,
      25.15, 25.16
    physical inconvenience as result of breach
      of contract, 25.18
    rule against recovery, 25.9–25.13
  mitigation of loss, 25.24–25.26
  non-pecuniary losses, 25.1
  objective, 24.1
  penalty clauses. *See* **Penalty clauses**
  performance, 24.6, 24.7
  profits, loss of, 24.27
  promissory estoppel, 24.20
  reinstatement, 24.24
  reliance, 24.3, 24.5
    choice between expectation and reliance,
      24.10, 24.18, 24.19
  remoteness. *See* **Remoteness**
  reputation, injury to commercial, 25.20, 25.21
  restitution, 24.8, 24.9, 26.35–26.38
  tests,
    Commercial Agents (Council Directive)
      Regulations 1993, 24.28
    cure, cost of, 24.24
    difference in value, 24.21–24.23
    profits, loss of, 24.27
    reinstatement, 24.24
    Ruxley Electronics v. Forsyth, 24.25, 24.26
  third party rights, 10.32
  traditional tests, 24.3
Death of parties,
  termination of offer, 3.15
Debtors,
  composition agreements, 8.18
Deeds,
  consideration, 8.19
  form of contract, 11.10
Defences,
  third party rights,
    promisor, 10.19
    third party, 10.20
Destruction of subject matter of contract, 22.8
Discharge of contract,
  agreement, 8.20
  performance,
    Apportionment Act 1870, 23.31
    arguments for and against entire contracts
      rule, 23.32, 23.33
    breach of warranty, 23.31
    Cutter v. Powell, 23.20–23.22
    destruction of work before completion of
      contract, 23.23, 23.24
    divisible and severable contracts, 23.26
    entire contracts or obligations rule, 23.19
    exceptions to entire contracts rule, 23.25
    general rule, 23.18
    Law Reform (Frustrated Contracts) Act
      1943, 23.30
    Merchant Shipping Act 1995, 23.30
    partial performance accepted, 23.28

Discharge of contract—*cont.*
  performance—*cont.*
    prevention of completion of performance
      by promisee, 23.27
    substantial performance, 23.29, 23.30
    tender of performance, 23.34
Disclosure,
  absence of general duty, 15.1–15.6
  fiduciary duties, 15.11, 15.12
  guarantees, 15.13
  non-disclosure, actionability of, 15.7–15.14
  required, when, 15.7–15.14
  scope of duty, 15.14
  statement becoming untrue after contract made,
    15.8
  uberrimae fidei, 15.9, 15.10
  utmost good faith, contracts of, 15.9, 15.10
Distance Selling Regulations, 4.18
Distant means,
  acceptance, 4.17
Duress,
  categories,
    economic duress, 19.4
    goods, duress to, 19.3
    lawful act duress, 19.6
    person, duress to the, 19.2
  common law, 19.1
  economic, 8.9–8.13, 19.4–19.6
  effect, 19.7
  goods, duress to, 19.3
  lawful act duress, 19.6
  person, duress to the, 19.2

E-commerce,
  acceptance, 4.18
Economic duress, 19.4–19.6
  See also **Duress**
  consideration, 8.9–8.13
  lawful act duress, 19.6
Effect,
  mistake, 21.19
Employees,
  misrepresentation, 18.24
Employment,
  injunctions, 26.8–26.10
  misrepresentation, 18.24
  remedies, 26.8–26.10
  specific performance, 26.8–26.10
Equitable estoppel,
  See also **Estoppel**
  conduct, estoppel by, 9.17, 9.18
  convention, estoppel by, 9.17
  generally, 9.15
  promissory. *See* Promissory estoppel
  proprietary estoppel, 9.15, 9.16
  representation, estoppel by, 9.17
  single doctrine, 9.19–9.21
Estoppel,
  conduct, by, 9.17, 9.18
  convention, by, 9.17
  damages, 24.20

Estoppel—*cont.*
   equitable. *See* **Equitable estoppel; Promissory
      estoppel**
   incomplete formation of contract, 5.18
   meaning, 9.2
   promissory. *See* **Promissory estoppel**
   proprietary, 9.15, 9.16
   representation, estoppel by, 9.17
European law,
   sources of contract law, 1.16
Evidence,
   admissibility, 11.2, 11.3
   contents of contract, 11.2, 11.3
Exclusion clauses. *See* **Exemption clauses**
Exemption clauses,
   See also **Unfair Contract Terms Act 1977**
   "by nature" clauses, 17.18
   common law, 16.4
   consistent course of dealings, 16.17, 16.18
   construction of clauses,
      contra proferentem, 16.19–16.21
      fraud, 16.23
      limitation clauses, 16.22
   contra proferentem, 16.19–16.21
   course of dealings, 16.17, 16.18
   defence to action for breach of contract,
      17.17
   fraud, 16.23
   fundamental breach, 16.24–16.27
   generally, 16.1
   incorporation,
      modern approach to restrictive or onerous
         terms, 16.6–16.9
      oral statements varying written terms,
         16.10
      signature, 16.5–16.10
   limitation clauses, 16.22
   meaning, 17.17–17.21
   notices, 16.13, 16.14
   onerous or unusual terms, special notice of,
      16.15, 16.16
   privity of contract, 16.28
   qualifying or modifying obligation, 17.17
   reasonable expectations test, 17.21
   reasonableness, 16.29
   signature, 16.5–16.10
   signs, 16.13, 16.14
   special notice of onerous or unusual terms,
      16.15, 16.16
   standard form contracts, 16.2, 16.3
   third party rights, 10.22, 16.28
   tickets, 16.11, 16.12
   unsigned contracts,
      notices, 16.13, 16.14
      signs, 16.13, 16.14
      tickets, 16.11, 16.12
Expectation, 1.6
   damages, 24.3, 24.4
      choice between expectation and reliance,
         24.10, 24.18, 24.19
      speculative losses, 24.13, 24.14

Fairness,
   categories, 14.3
   choice of concepts, 14.31
   common law,
      inequality of bargaining power, 14.8, 14.9
      reasonableness, 14.6, 14.7
      restraint of trade, 14.13
      special notice test, 14.12
      test of fairness, 14.10, 14.11
   consumer and commercial contracts,
      15.31–15.34
   disclosure. *See* **Disclosure**
   English law, in, 14.2
   equity,
      good faith. *See* **Good faith**
      unconscionability, 14.14–14.20
   generally, 14.1
   good faith. *See* **Good faith**
   reasonableness, 14.6, 14.7
   restraint of trade, 14.13
   Stop Now Orders, 15.30
   transformation debate, 14.4, 14.5
   unconscionability, 14.14–14.20
Family,
   intention to create legal relations, 11.3
Fiduciary duties, 15.11, 15.12
Force majeure, 22.1, 22.21
Form of contract,
   arguments for and against, 11.12
   deeds, 11.10
   general rule, 11.8
   Scotland, 11.12
   writing,
      consumer protection, 11.10, 11.11
      contracts required to be evidenced in
         writing, 11.9
      contracts required to be in, 11.9
Formation of contract,
   acceptance. *See* **Acceptance**
   agreement. *See* **Acceptance; Agreement; Offer**
   agreements to agree, 5.15
   bilateral contracts, 2.3, 2.4
   capacity. *See* **Capacity**
   certainty, 5.11–5.14
   consideration. *See* **Consideration**
   estoppel, 5.18
   form 11.8–11.12. *See also* **Form of contract**
   good faith negotiations, 5.16
   incompleteness,
      agreements to agree, 5.15
      estoppel, 5.18
      generally, 5.15
      good faith negotiations, 5.16
      lock in agreements, 5.15
      lock out agreements, 5.15
      no contract resulting, 5.18
      use all reasonable endeavours to procure
         third party contract, promise to, 5.17
      use best endeavours, promise to, 5.17
   intention to create legal relations. *See* **Intention
      to create legal relations**

Formation of contract—*cont.*
   lock in agreements, 5.15
   lock out agreements, 5.15
   objectivity,
      application, 2.13
      detached, 2.10
      humour, 2.13
      promisee, 2.9
      promisor, 2.8
      subjectivity and, 2.12
   requirements, 2.1
   subjectivity, 2.11, 2.12
   unilateral contracts, 2.3, 2.5, 2.6
   use best endeavours, promise to, 5.17
Fraud,
   exemption clauses, 16.23
   misrepresentation, 18.12, 18.16, 18.17
Frustration,
   See also **Mistake**
   absolute contracts, 22.3, 22.4
   categories of frustrating events,
      destruction of subject matter, 22.8
      generally, 22.7
      illness, 22.9
      incapacity, 22.9
      industrial action, 22.17
      inordinate delay, 22.16
      leases, 22.17
      non-occurence of event, 22.10–22.13
      sales of land, 22.17
      statutory powers, exercise of, 22.15
      strikes, 22.17
      supervening illegality, 22.15
      war, government intervention in times of,
         22.14
   commercial inconvenience, 22.14
   common law background,
      absolute contracts, 22.3, 22.4
      impossibility, 22.5
   common mistake and, 22.13
   "Coronation" cases, 22.10–22.13
   destruction of subject matter, 22.8
   development of law, 22.6
   effect,
      general rule, 22.24
      Law Reform (Frustrated Contracts) Act
         1943, 22.25–22.30
   force majeure, 22.1, 22.21
   generally, 22.1
   hardship clauses, 22.21
   illness, 22.9
   impossibility, 22.5
   incapacity, 22.9
   industrial action, 22.17
   inordinate delay, 22.16
   leases, 22.17
   non-occurence of event, 22.10–22.13
      alternative arrangements offered, 22.13
      common mistake and, 22.13
      "Coronation" cases, 22.10–22.13
      purpose, frustration of, 22.10–22.13
      total failure of consideration, 22.13

Frustration—*cont.*
   not applying, where,
      force majeure, 22.21
      foreseeability prevents frustration, 22.20
      hardship clauses, 22.21
      self-induced, frustration must not be,
         22.18, 22.19
   operation of law, 22.2
   purpose, frustration of, 22.10–22.13
   restitution, 26.30
   sales of land, 22.17
   self-induced, frustration must not be, 22.18,
      22.19
   statutory powers, exercise of, 22.15
   strikes, 22.17
   supervening illegality, 22.15
   test, 22.22, 22.23
   total failure of consideration, 22.13
   war, 22.14
Functions of contract,
   making contract, 1.8
   role, 1.8
Fundamental breach, 16.24–16.27

Gambling contracts, 20.11
Gifts,
   consideration, 7.17
Good faith,
   arguments for and against, 14.28–14.30
   definition, 14.22–14.26
   English law, 14.27
   generally, 14.21
   meaning, 14.22–14.26
   negotiations, 5.16
   terms of contract, 13.24
   uberrimae fidei, 15.9, 15.10
   utmost good faith, contracts of, 15.9, 15.10
Goods,
   duress to, 19.3
   mistaken quality, 21.8, 21.9
Gratuitous promises,
   consideration, 7.17
Guarantees, 15.13

Hadley v. Baxendale, 25.3–25.6
Hardship clauses, 22.21
Hire purchase,
   Unfair Contract Terms Act 1977, 17.9
Historical background 1.9. *See also* **Sources of**
   contract law

Identity,
   mistake, 6.11–6.16
Illegality,
   affront to public conscience test, 20.20
   crime, contract to commit, 20.8
   effect,
      affront to public conscience test, 20.20
      deception, 20.17

Illegality—*cont.*
   effect—*cont.*
      flexible approach, 20.14
      independent action, claims based on,
         20.18, 20.19
      other remedies, effect on, 20.20
      title to property not passing, 20.17
      traditional view, 20.13
   express statutory prohibition, 20.4
   formed, contracts illegal as,
      express statutory prohibition, 20.4
      impliedly illegal, 20.5
      performance, illegality in, 20.6
      void, terms rendered, 20.7
   gambling contracts, 20.11
   impliedly illegal, 20.5
   independent action, claims based on, 20.18,
      20.19
   money paid under illegal contract,
      exceptions to general rule, 20.16–20.17
      general rule, 20.15
      one party withdrawing from illegality, 20.16
      oppression, 20.17
      parties not equally to blame, 20.16
   ousting jurisdiction of courts, contracts, 20.11
   performance, illegality in, 20.6
   procuring corruption or benefitting from crime,
      contracts to, 20.9
   public interest, 20.2
   public policy, 20.1
      common law, 20.8–20.12
      crime, contract to commit, 20.8
      gambling contracts, 20.11
      miscellaneous categories, 20.12
      ousting jurisdiction of courts, contracts,
         20.11
      procuring corruption or benefitting from
         crime, contracts to, 20.9
      sexual immorality, 20.9, 20.10
   reform of law,
      generally, 20.21
      Law Commission, 20.22
   restitution, 26.30
   sexual immorality, 20.9, 20.10
   statutory, 20.3
   title to property not passing, 20.17
   void, terms rendered, 20.7
Illegitimate pressure,
   duress. *See* **Duress**
   restraint of trade. *See* **Restraint of trade**
   undue influence. *See* **Undue influence**
Illness,
   frustration, 22.9
Implied terms,
   business efficacy test, 12.25, 12.26, 12.30
   clarity test, 12.30
   compelling test, 12.30
   courts, implied by,
      BP Westernport criteria, 12.29
      business efficacy test, 12.25, 12.26, 12.30
      clarity test, 12.30
      compelling test, 12.30

Implied terms—*cont.*
   courts, implied by—*cont.*
      Liverpool City Council v. Irwin, 12.27,
         12.28
      Moorcock principle, 12.25
      necessity test, 12.25
      non-contradictory test, 12.30
      officious bystander tests, 12.25, 12.26
      reasonable and equitable test, 12.30
      reasonableness in all the circumstances,
         12.26
      test at common law, 12.24
   customary rules, 12.17–12.19
   fact, implied in, 12.16
   generally, 12.14, 12.15
   law, implied in, 12.16
   non-contradictory test, 12.30
   officious bystander tests, 12.25, 12.26
   reasonable and equitable test, 12.30
   reasonableness in all the circumstances,
      12.26
   sale of goods legislation, 12.20–12.23
   statute, implied by, 12.20–12.23
Impossibility,
   frustration, 22.5
Incapacity,
   frustration, 22.9
Industrial action,
   frustration, 22.17
Inertia selling,
   acceptance, 4.25
Injunctions,
   employment, 26.8–26.10
   restraint of trade, 20.30
Innocent misrepresentation, 18.15
Intention to create legal relations,
   family affairs, 11.3
   general rule, 11.1
   personal and social relationships, 11.4
   presumption, 11.2
   relevance to other areas of law, 11.5
Intermediate terms, 13.15
   definition, 13.16
   meaning, 13.16
   rule, as, 13.17, 13.18
International law, 1.17
Interpretation of contracts,
   generally, 12.12, 12.13
   implied terms. *See* **Implied terms**
   meaning, 12.12
   principles, 12.13
Intoxicated persons,
   capacity, 11.7
Invitations to treat, 3.2, 3.3

Judges,
   role in development of contract law, 1.10

Lapse of time,
   offer, 3.14

Leases,
  frustration, 22.17
Limitation clauses 16.22. *See also* **Exemption clauses**
Liquidated damages,
  effect of being, 25.33
  meaning, 25.29
  penalties distinguished, 25.30–25.32
Lock in agreements, 5.15
Lock out agreements, 5.15
Lock-in agreements, 5.15
Loss of opportunity damages, 24.15, 24.16

Mental distress,
  damages,
    amenity, loss of, 25.19
    basic rule, 25.14
    disappointed expectations, 25.14–25.19
    freedom from mental distress, contracts to
      provide, 25.17
    peace of mind, enjoyment or
      entertainment, contracts to provide,
      25.15, 25.16
    physical inconvenience as result of breach
      of contract, 25.18
    rule against recovery, 25.9–25.13
Mentally incapacitated persons,
  capacity, 11.7
Mere puffs, 2.5
Minors,
  capacity, 11.6
Mirror image test, 4.1
Misrepresentation,
  affirmation of contract, 18.23
  agents, 18.24
  employees, 18.24
  exclusion of liability for non-fraudulent
    misrepresentation, 18.25
  fraudulent, 18.12, 18.16, 18.17
  generally, 18.3
  inducement to contract, 18.7
  innocent, 18.15
  materiality, 18.10
  mistake contrasted, 6.10
  negligent, 18.13, 18.17–18.20
  no inducement to contract, 18.8
  reliance, 18.9
  remedies,
    fraudulent misrepresentation, 18.16, 18.17
    negligent misrepresentation, 18.17–18.20
    rescission, 18.21–18.23
  rescission,
    affirmation of contract, 18.23
    counter restitution impossible, 18.22
    general rule, 18.21
    representee not acting within reasonable
      time, 18.22
    third party acquiring rights, 18.23
  statement or other assertion of fact which is
    untrue, 18.4
  statements not being, 18.5, 18.6
  statutory, 18.14

Misrepresentation—*cont.*
  types,
    determining, 18.11
    fraudulent, 18.12
    innocent, 18.15
    negligent, 18.13
    statutory, 18.14
  unenforceable, 18.2
  void, 18.1
  voidable, 18.1
Mistake,
  See also **Frustration**
  agreement,
    case law, 6.4–6.6
    categories of mistake, 6.2, 6.7–6.18
    effect, 21.1
    fact, of, 6.17
    generally, 6.1
    identity, 6.11–6.16
    mutual mistake, 6.7, 6.8
    narrow doctrine, 6.2
    objective test, 6.3
    rules, 6.2
    subjective mistake, 6.3, 6.18
    unilateral mistake, 6.9, 6.10, 6.17
  allocation of risk, 21.3
  common. *See* **Common mistake**
  documents signed by mistake, 21.16–21.18
  effect, 21.1
    common law, 21.19
    equity, 21.19
    rectification, 21.21–21.23
    rescission, 21.20
    setting aside "on terms", 21.19
    specific performance, 21.19
  fundamental, 21.6, 21.7
  generally, 21.1
  identity, 6.11–6.16
  misrepresentation contrasted, 6.10
  mutual, 6.7, 6.8
  non est factum, 21.16–21.18
  rectification, 21.21–21.23
  reform of law,
    apportionment of losses between parties,
      21.25
    generally, 21.23
    merger of common law and equity,
      21.24
    statutory, 21.26
  rescission, 21.20
  risk allocation, 21.3
  scope, 21.2
  setting aside "on terms", 21.19
  unilateral, 6.9, 6.10, 6.17
Mitigation of loss, 25.24–25.26
Motive,
  consideration distinguished, 7.16
Mutual mistake, 6.7, 6.8

Negligent misrepresentation, 18.13, 18.17–18.20
***Non est factum*,** 21.16–21.18

Notices,
    exemption clauses, 16.13, 16.14
Novation,
    variation of contract, 8.22

Objectivity,
    application, 2.13
    detached, 2.10
    humour, 2.13
    promisee, 2.9
    promisor, 2.8
    subjectivity and, 2.12
Offer,
    See also **Acceptance**
    advertisements, 3.6
    auction sales, 3.7
    battle of the forms. *See* **Battle of the forms**
    catalogues, 3.6
    counter offers, 4.2, 4.3
    cross-offers, 5.1
    death of one of parties, 3.15
    definition, 3.1
    difficult cases, 5.1–5.3
    display of goods in shops/supermarkets, 3.4
    flexibility, 5.4–5.6
    importance, 3.2
    invitations to treat distinguished, 3.2, 3.3
    lapse of time, 3.14
    meaning, 3.1, 3.2
    mechanism, 2.2
    objectivity,
        application of, 2.13
        detached, 2.10
        humour, 2.13
        promisee, 2.9
        promisor, 2.8
        subjectivity and, 2.12
    other statements distinguished, 3.2
    postal rule, 3.12
    price, statements of, 3.5
    rejection, 3.15
    relaxed view of, 5.4–5.6
    revocation, 3.10
        bilateral contracts, 3.12
        communication, 3.12
        example, 3.11
        postal rule, 3.12
        promissory estoppel, 3.14
        unilateral contracts, 3.13
    silence, by, 2.7
    statement of performance, 5.5, 5.6
    statements of price, 3.5
    subjectivity, 2.11, 2.12
    tenders, 3.8
        overlooked, 3.9
    termination, 3.9
        See also **Revocation of offer**
        conditions, subject to, 3.14
        death of one of parties, 3.15
        lapse of time, 3.14
        rejection, 3.15

Offer—*cont.*
    working time, 5.2
Oral contracts, 12.1
Ousting jurisdiction of courts, contracts, 20.11
Outline of contract law, 1.19

Package holidays, 10.33, 13.3
Parol evidence rule, 12.4, 12.5
    application of rule, 12.11
    capacity, lack of, 12.8
    collateral contracts, 12.7
    condition precedent, 12.6
    customs, 12.8
    draftsmanship, 12.8, 12.9
    exceptions, 12.6–12.11
    partly written, partly oral, 12.6
    purpose of contract, showing, 12.8
    reform proposals, 12.10
    subject matter of contract, 12.7
    vitiating factors, 12.8
Past consideration, 7.14, 7.15
Penalty clauses,
    effect of being, 25.33
    liquidated damages distinguished,
        25.30–25.32
    meaning, 25.29
    when not applying, 25.34
Performance,
    Apportionment Act 1870, 23.31
    breach of warranty, 23.31
    damages, 24.6, 24.7
    discharge of contract,
        Apportionment Act 1870, 23.31
        arguments for and against entire contracts
            rule, 21.32, 21.33
        breach of warranty, 23.31
        Cutter v. Powell, 23.20–23.22
        destruction of work before completion of
            contract, 23.23, 23.24
        divisible and severable contracts, 23.26
        entire contracts or obligations rule, 23.19
        exceptions to entire contracts rule, 23.25
        general rule, 23.18
        Law Reform (Frustrated Contracts) Act
            1943, 23.30
        Merchant Shipping Act 1995, 23.30
        partial performance accepted, 23.28
        prevention of completion of performance
            by promisee, 23.27
        substantial performance, 23.29, 23.30
        tender of performance, 21.34
    substantial, 23.29.23.30
    tender of, 23.34
    time of, 13.19–13.23
Personal and social relationships,
    intention to create legal relations, 11.4
Pigot's Case, rule in, 8.21
Postal rule,
    application of rule, 4.14
    distant means, 4.17
    examples, 4.12, 4.13

Postal rule—*cont.*
limitations, 4.15, 4.16
meaning, 4.11
privatised mail services, 4.17
revocation of previously posted acceptance,
4.26, 4.27
third party rights, 4.16
Precedent, condition, 13.5, 13.6
Price,
consideration, 7.7
offers and statement of, 3.5
Privity of contract,
See also **Third party rights**
exemption clauses, 16.28
historical background, 10.2–10.4
package holidays, 10.33
reform of rule, 10.5–10.8
statutory exceptions to rule, 10.33
Procuring corruption or benefiting from crime,
contracts to, 20.9
Profits, loss of, 24.27
Promissory estoppel,
See also **Equitable estoppel**
background, 9.2
basic principles,
reliance by promisee, 9.8
unequivocal promise, 9.7
case law, 9.5, 9.6
cause of action not created, 9.9
common law jurisdictions, 9.13, 9.14
damages, 24.20
estoppel, meaning of, 9.2
existing contractual relationships, application
to, 9.11
generally, 9.1
High Trees case, 9.5
limitations of the doctrine,
cause of action not created, 9.9
equitable factor, 9.10
existing contractual relationships,
application to, 9.11
revival of original obligation, 9.12
reliance by promisee, 9.8
revival of original obligation, 9.12
revocation of offer, 3.14
unequivocal promise, 9.7
United States, 9.14
variation of contract, 8.22
waiver, 9.3, 9.4
Promissory terms, 13.8
See also **Intermediate terms**
fundamental to contract, 13.14
importance of term, 13.9, 13.10
intention of parties, 13.12
legal precedent, 13.13
one type of breach possible, 13.14
statute, term classified by, 13.11
trade usage, 13.13
Proprietary estoppel, 9.15, 9.16
Public interest,
illegality, 20.2
restraint of trade, 20.29

Public policy,
illegality, 20.1
common law, 20.8–20.12
crime, contract to commit, 20.8
gambling contracts, 20.11
miscellaneous categories, 20.12
ousting jurisdiction of courts, contracts,
20.11
procuring corruption or benefiting from
crime, contracts to, 20.9
sexual immorality, 20.9, 20.10

Quantum meruit, 26.31–26.34

Reasonable expectations, fulfilment of, 1.6
Reasonableness, 14.6, 14.7
restraint of trade,
between parties, 20.27, 20.28
public interest, 20.29
Rectification,
mistake, 21.21–21.23
Reform of contract law, 1.18
Reinstatement,
damages, 24.24
Rejection of offer, 3.15
Reliance,
damages, 24.3, 24.5
choice between expectation and reliance,
24.10
detrimental, reversal of, 1.7
misrepresentation, 18.9
reversal of detrimental, 1.7
theory, 1.7
Remedies,
account for profits, 26.39–26.41
damages. *See* **Damages; Liquidated damages**
declarations, 26.18
employment, 26.8–26.10
injunctions use in contract law, 26.7
main remedies, 26.2
misrepresentation,
fraudulent misrepresentation, 18.16, 18.17
negligent misrepresentation, 18.17–18.20
rescission, 18.21–18.23
rescission, 18.21–18.23
restitution. *See* Restitution
restraint of trade,
generally, 20.29
injunctions, 20.30
severance of clause, 20.30, 20.31
self help remedies. *See* **Self help remedies**
specific performance, 26.3–26.6
undue influence, 19.28
Remoteness,
basic rule, 25.2
Hadley v. Baxendale, 25.3–25.6
tort and contract law contrasted, 25.8
Representations,
See also Misrepresentation
estoppel by, 9.17
terms distinguished, 13.1–13.3

Repudiation,
    acceptance by rescission, 23.16
    affirmation of contract, 23.17
    nature of repudiatory breach, 23.11–23.15
    non-acceptance of breach by affirmation,
        23.17
Reputation, damages for injury to commercial, 25.20,
    25.21
Rescission,
    acceptance of repudiation by, 23.16
    misrepresentation, 18.21–18.23
        affirmation of contract, 18.23
        counter restitution impossible, 18.22
        general rule, 18.21
        representee not acting within reasonable
            time, 18.22
        third party acquiring rights, 18.23
    mistake, 21.20
    variation of contract, 8.22
Restitution,
    account for profits, 26.39–26.41
    contract law and, 26.9
    damages, 24.8, 24.9, 26.35–26.38
    development, 26.20
    failed contracts, 26.29
    frustration, 26.30
    illegality, 26.30
    quantum meruit, 26.31–26.34
    quasi-contract, 26.20
    terms of contract, 13.24
    total failure of consideration, 26.23–26.28
    unjust enrichment, 26.20–26.22
    void agreements, 26.29
Restraint of trade, 14.13
    application of doctrine, 20.24–20.29
    consideration, 20.28
    extent of restraint, 20.28
    general rule, 20.23
    injunctions, 20.30
    legitimate interests, 20.27
    public interest, 20.29
    reasonableness,
        between parties, 20.27, 20.28
        public interest, 20.29
    remedies,
        generally, 20.29
        injunctions, 20.30
        severance of clause, 20.30, 20.31
    severance of clause, 20.30, 20.31
Revocation of offer, 3.10
    bilateral contract, 3.12
    communication, 3.12, 3.13
    example, 3.11
    postal rule, 3.12
    promissory estoppel, 3.14
    unilateral contract, 3.13

Sale of goods legislation, 12.20–12.23
Sales of land,
    frustration, 22.17
Scope of contract. *See* **Contents of contract**

Scotland,
    form of contract, 11.12
Self help remedies, 26.1
Sexual immorality,
    illegality, 20.9, 20.10
Signs,
    exemption clauses, 16.13, 16.14
Silence,
    acceptance, 4.22–4.24
    offer and acceptance by, 2.7
Sources of contract law,
    business practice, 1.12
    commercial business practice, 1.12
    common law judges, role of, 1.10
    consumerism, 1.14
    customary rules, 1.11
    European law, 1.16
    historical background, 1.9
    international law, 1.17
    relational contracts, 1.12
    standard form contracts, 1.13
    Statute law, 1.15
    trade practices, 1.12
Specific performance, 26.3–26.6
    employment, 26.8–26.10
Standard form contracts,
    abuse, 1.13, 16.2, 16.3
    exemption clauses, 16.2, 16.3
    sources of contract law, 1.13
    use, 1.13, 16.2, 16.3
Statute, implied by, 12.20–12.23
Statute law,
    sources of contract law, 1.15
***Stilk v. Myrick*,** rule in, 8.2, 8.3
Stop Now Orders, 15.30
Strikes,
    frustration, 22.17
Subjectivity,
    objectivity and, 2.12
    offer and acceptance, 2.11, 2.12

Tenders,
    offer, 3.8
        overlooked tenders, 3.9
Termination,
    offer, 3.9
        See also **Revocation of offer**
        conditions, subject to, 3.14
        death of one of parties, 3.15
        rejection, 3.15
Terms of contract,
    condition precedent, 13.5, 13.6
    condition subsequent, 13.7
    contractual obligations, 13.4
    efficient breach, 13.24
    good faith, 13.24
    implied. *See* **Implied terms**
    innominate, 13.15
    intermediate terms, 13.15
    promissory. *See* **Promissory terms**
    representations distinguished, 13.1–13.3

Terms of contract—*cont.*
    restitution, 13.24
    time of performance, 13.19–13.23
Third party rights,
    See also **Privity of contract**
    acceptance, 10.16
    agency, 10.26
    agreement for own test, 10.18
    arbitration, 10.22
    assignment, 10.28
    collateral contracts, 10.27
    common law,
        detriment rule, 10.24
        pre-existing exceptions, 10.25
    consideration, 10.23
    contract not covered by Act, 10.21
    court's discretion, 10.18
    crystallisation, 10.16–10.18
    damages, 10.32
    defences,
        promisor, 10.19
        third party, 10.20
    detriment rule, 10.24
    enforceable benefit,
        benefit conferred, 10.14
        express provision, 10.11
        intention of parties, 10.13
        limitation son enforceability of benefit
            conferred, 10.15
        purporting to confer benefit, 10.12
        who may benefit, 10.11
    enforcement by promisee, 10.20
    enforcement of contract by promisee,
        10.28–10.32
    exceptions, 10.21
    exemption clauses, 10.22, 16.28
    fact, reliance in, 10.17
    generally, 10.1
    joint promises, 10.27
    legislation, 10.9, 10.10
    postal rule, 4.16
    reasonable expectation of reliance, 10.17
    ruling out need for consent to variation, 10.18
    securing, 10.16–10.18
    tort, action in, 10.25
    trustee of promise, 10.26
    variation of contract, 8.22
Tickets,
    exemption clauses, 16.11, 16.12
Time of performance,
    commercial contracts, 13.19–13.23
Title,
    common mistake, 21.10, 21.11
    illegality, 20.17
Tort,
    third party, action by, 10.25
Total failure of consideration, 22.12, 26.23–26.28
Trade practices,
    sources of contract law, 1.12

Uberrimae fidei, 15.9, 15.10

Unconscionability, 14.14–14.20
Undue influence,
    actual undue influence, 19.10–19.12
        manifest disadvantage, 19.11
    categories,
        actual undue influence, 19.10–19.12
        general rule, 19.9
        presumed undue influence, 19.13–19.17
    equity, 19.8
    manifest disadvantage,
        actual undue influence, 19.11
        presumed undue influence, 19.12
    origins, 19.8
    presumed undue influence, 19.13–19.17
        Class 2A presumptions, 19.14
        Class 2B presumptions, 19.15–19.17
        classes, 19.13
        manifest disadvantage, 19.12
        rebutting presumption, 19.25–19.27
        special relationships, 19.14
        trust and confidence, 19.15–19.17
    rebutting presumption, 19.25–19.27
    remedies, 19.28
    roots, 19.8
    special relationships, 19.14
    third parties, by,
        aftermath of *Barclays Bank v. O'Brien,*
            19.22–19.24
        general rule, 19.18
        requirements of action, 19.19–19.21
    trust and confidence, 19.15–19.17
Unfair Contract Terms Act 1977,
    arbitration clauses, 17.10
    background, 17.1–17.3
    business liability, 17.5, 17.11
    but for test, 17.19
    contracts not covered, 17.6, 17.7
    contracts under which goods pass, 17.9
    contractual liability, 17.8
    core obligations, 17.6
    dealing as consumer, 17.12, 17.13
    definitions, 17.10
    effect of breach, clauses dealing with, 17.9
    exemption clauses, 17.18
    freedom from control, 17.5
    guarantees, 17.9
    hire purchase, 17.9
    indemnity clauses, 17.9
    interpretation,
        business liability, 17.11
        dealing as consumer, 17.12, 17.16
        private sales, 17.14
        written standard terms of business, 17.15,
            17.16
    nature of breach or obligation, 17.6
    negligence liability, 17.8
    obligations covered, 17.5
    private sales, 17.14
    purpose of clause, 17.20
    reasonable expectations test, 17.21
    reasonableness,
        commercial contracts, 17.26–17.31

Unfair Contract Terms Act 1977—*cont.*
    reasonableness—*conts.*
        consumer contracts, 17.34
        generally, 17.22
        judicial interpretation, 17.25
        "no refunds", 17.35
        residual issues, 17.32, 17.33
        Schedule 2 guidelines, 17.24
        section 11, 17.23
        statutory guidance, 17.22
        test, 17.4
    sale of goods, contracts for, 17.9
    scope,
        business liability, 17.5
        contracts not covered, 17.6, 17.7
        core obligations, 17.6
        nature of breach or obligation, 17.6
        obligations covered, 17.5
    secondary contract, avoiding Act by, 17.10
    varieties of, 17.1
    voidness, 17.3
**Unfair Terms in Consumer Contracts Regulations
    1999,**
    core exceptions, 15.17, 15.18
    excepted contracts, 15.27
    generally, 15.15
    meaning of fairness, 15.20–15.27
    non-individually negotiated terms, 15.17
    Office of Fair trading, role of, 15.28, 15.29
    parties, 15.16
    plain intelligible language, 15.19
Unilateral contracts, 2.3, 2.5, 2.6
    acceptance, 4.21
    revocation of offer, 3.13
United States,
    promissory estoppel, 9.14
Unjust enrichment, 26.20–26.22
Unsolicited goods,
    acceptance, 4.25
Utmost good faith, contracts of, 15.9, 15.10

Variation of contract,
    agreement, discharge by, 8.20
    consideration,
        additional payments, promises of, 8.4, 8.5,
            8.6
        composition agreements between debtor
            and creditors, 8.18
        deed, promises made by, 8.19
        generally, 8.1
        lesser sum, taking, 8.14
        part payment by third payment, 8.17
        performance of duty imposed by law or
            statute, 8.2
        pragmatic approach to meaning of
            consideration, 8.6–8.9
        pre-existing contractual obligations, 8.2
        Stilk v. Myrick, rule in, 8.2, 8.3
        third parties, promises made to, 8.3
    novation, 8.22
    Pigot's Case, rule in, 8.21
    promissory estoppel, 8.22
    provision in contract for, 8.21
    reform, 8.25, 8.26
    relationship between rules, 8.24
    rescission, 8.22
    third party rights, 8.22
    waiver, 8.22

Waiver,
    promissory estoppel, 9.3, 9.4
    variation of contract, 8.22
War,
    frustration, 22.14
Working time, 5.2
Writing requirement,
    consumer protection, 11.10
    contracts required to be in writing, 11.9
    evidenced in writing, contracts required to be,
        11.9